BRIEF EDITION

P9-CRO-676

Parameters of Power

Canada's Political Institutions

Faron Ellis
Lethbridge College

Heather MacIvor
University of Windsor

THOMSON

NELSON

Australia   Canada   Mexico   Singapore   Spain   United Kingdom   United States

THOMSON
—✳—
NELSON

Parameters of Power:
Canada's Political Institutions,
Brief Edition

by Faron Ellis and Heather MacIvor

Associate Vice President:
Editorial Director:
Evelyn Veitch

Editor-in-Chief, Higher Education:
Anne Williams

Acquisitions Editor:
Bram Sepers

Senior Marketing Manager:
Lenore Taylor-Atkins

Developmental Editor:
Linda Sparks

**Photo Researcher and Permissions
Coordinator:**
Indu Ghuman

**Senior Content
Production Manager:**
Tammy Scherer

Production Service:
ICC Macmillan Inc.

Copy Editor:
Susan Fitzgerald

Proofreader:
Joan E. Templeton

Indexer:
Kathy Sychra

Production Coordinator:
Ferial Suleman

Design Director:
Ken Phipps

Interior Design:
Suzanne Peden

Cover Design:
Glenn Toddun

Cover Image:
Darwin Wiggett/First Light

Compositor:
ICC Macmillan Inc.

Printer:
Thomson/West

**Library and Archives Canada
Cataloguing in Publication Data**

Ellis, Faron, 1962-
Parameters of power : Canada's
political institutions / Faron Ellis,
Heather MacIvor. — Brief ed.

Fourth ed. written by Heather
MacIvor. Includes bibliographical
references and index.

ISBN-13: 978-0-17-610373-6

ISBN-10: 0-17-610373-2

1. Canada—Politics and
government—Textbooks.
I. MacIvor, Heather, 1964-
II. MacIvor, Heather, 1964- .
Parameters of power.
III. Title.

JL65.E45 2007   320.971
C2007-900109-2

BRIEF CONTENTS

CONTENTS

CHAPTER 4: PARTIES AND PARTY SYSTEMS   123

CHAPTER 5: ELECTIONS AND VOTING   171

CHAPTER 6: THE POLITICAL EXECUTIVE AND PARLIAMENTARY DEMOCRACY   219

CHAPTER 7: THE PERMANENT EXECUTIVE AND ADMINISTRATIVE STATE   269

CHAPTER 8: ADMINISTRATION OF JUSTICE: THE COURTS AND THE CHARTER   305

FIGURES

POLITICAL BIOGRAPHIES

CANADIAN POLITICAL CHRONOLOGIES

CANADA BY THE NUMBERS

PREFACE
Faron Ellis

The brief edition of *Parameters of Power* attempts to provide a straightforward introduction to Canada's political institutions, without sacrificing the detail necessary to launch research projects and the weighty discussions that lead to a deeper understanding of politics in "the true north strong and free." For the most part, *Parameters* focuses on how Canadian politics is currently structured by the existing institutions, leaving discussion of proposed reforms for the classroom and research projects. Its *touchstone features,* such as the political biographies, chronologies, figures, and statistical data, are designed to be as exhaustive as those found in comprehensive Canadian government textbooks, sometimes more so.

Parameters is based on the premise that students need a comprehensive understanding of how existing political institutions are designed, and how they currently work in practice, before they begin to entertain proposals for reform. Although political scientists love to explore the possibility of new institutional arrangements, sometimes based in part on those that exist in other countries, introductory students often find our penchant for critique and improvement distracting, making it difficult for them to discern *what is* from arguments about what *should be.* This book attempts to avoid that dilemma by providing college and university students, politically engaged citizens, and in some cases advanced high-school students, with a compact and readable rendition of the current institutional framework that structures Canadian government.

Instructors will find within these pages the foundation upon which to build comprehensive lectures. They will also find ample, up-to-date touchstone material that can be used to highlight the major features of Canada's political institutions. These also provide a good launching pad for research papers and other course assignments. Every attempt has been made to systematically organize the mass of complex material that is Canadian politics into a coherent package, making it understandable for students who often have little or no background in the subject matter.

Students will find a concise, to-the-point discussion of how Canada's political institutions are structured and how they operate. They will be introduced to the primary source documents that help in determining the relationships between institutions, and between citizens and their governments. Particular emphasis is placed on the *master institution*: the Constitution Acts of 1867 and 1982, including the *Charter of Rights and Freedoms*, and how they impact on our daily lives.

Overall, students and instructors will find an approach to Canadian political institutions that credits their successes while examining their limitations. Despite the contemporary emphasis on crisis and the breakdown of political institutions in much of the world, Canada's political institutions continue to achieve their primary purpose: to balance the competing demands of providing order and unity while at the same time enhancing freedom and diversity. While no set of political institutions is perfect, including those in Canada, it is worth keeping in mind that citizens of this country enjoy more freedom and prosperity than do the vast majority of the world's populations. Much of this is due in no small measure to the relatively smooth functioning of the institutions that have been established by one of the oldest continuously operating constitutions on the planet. For students of Canadian politics at all levels, that alone makes our political institutions exciting, and certainly worth getting to know better.

STRUCTURE

The structure of the book is traditional in the sense that it lets the institutions themselves dictate its order and emphasis. That is to say, for the most part, *Parameters* uses the Canadian Constitution as its structural guide.

Chapter One provides an introduction to the subject matter by first briefly describing each of the topics in the following chapters, before entertaining a discussion of Canadian political culture and its important regional subcultures.

Chapter Two provides a comprehensive outline of the Canadian Constitution. Included is a description of how Canada's political institutions were first established by the British North America Act, 1867, and how they were modified by the Constitution Act, 1982, nonentrenched constitutional law, judicial interpretation, and conventions. It concludes with a brief history of constitutional development in Canada.

Chapter Three focuses on the development of federalism in Canada, including the important aspects of fiscal federalism and other intergovernmental arrangements.

Chapter Four introduces students to Canadian political parties and the four distinct party systems that have developed in Canada since Confederation. The placement of this material, early in the book, is designed to ensure that students and their professors are all on the same page when they banter about the names of sometimes long-departed, or sometimes relatively new, politicians and political parties.

Chapter Five discusses the Canadian electoral system and voting behaviour. It appears next for some of the same reasons cited for the previous chapter's placement, as well as its utility in setting up the following chapter dealing with the national Parliament. Chapter Five concludes with a brief discussion of Canada's most recent federal elections and, more importantly, provides the data that illustrate both the vote switching tendencies of Canadian and the detailed results of recent elections.

Chapter Six examines the political executive and parliamentary democracy in Canada by focusing on their relationship with the legislative process.

Chapter Seven examines the permanent executive and administrative state with specific emphasis on the federal budget, the country's overall fiscal situation, and the public service.

Chapter Eight explores the administration of justice, the courts, and how the Charter of Rights and Freedoms has changed the relationship between the judiciary and the other political institutions, as well as between citizens and the state.

Chapter Nine deals with nongovernmental actors, including the important roles played by the media and interest groups.

Chapter Ten provides a brief summary of where we have been and some guidance for Canadians in their lives as active citizens.

I sincerely hope that students and professors of Canadian government find this book as interesting to read as they find it useful for learning. Ultimately, I hope it will inspire students to become lifelong learners about their system of government. That means continuing on with a daily examination of politics, institutions, your own political behaviour, and that of your fellow citizens. It also means paying attention to politics in the media, exercising your right to vote, and otherwise reflecting on how politics affects you every day of your life.

FEATURES

Within each chapter of *Parameters,* students and professors will find a consistently themed series of touchstone features that illustrate with considerable detail important aspects of the institutions being discussed. The touchstone features are based on the logic that, if a picture is worth a thousand words, then a good table is worth a million. The touchstone features are organized into four categories:

- *Political Biographies,* primarily of prime ministers, but also of the current leaders of Canada's federal political parties, the chief justice of the Supreme Court, and the governor general.
- *Canadian Political Chronologies* that list and provide some description of the history of major institutional developments, occupants of important offices, or demographic and territorial changes.
- *Canada by the Numbers* features that consist largely of tabular data detailing sections of the Constitution, election results, fiscal information, seats in the legislative chambers, and other important statistical data.
- Other *figures* and graphics such as maps and schematics illustrating important features of the Canadian political system.

Each chapter of the book also includes some more conventional learning aids to assist students in mastering the material. These include

- *Learning Objectives* at the beginning of each chapter that alert students to what their professors will be expecting them to know once they have read the material.
- *Discussion Questions* at the end of each chapter to help students reflect on what they have read and to stimulate further learning. They can also be used as pretests for exams in that if you can correctly and insightfully answer the *Discussion Questions*, you will be on your way to doing well on your midterm and final examinations.
- A brief selection of *Suggested Readings* is included at the end of each chapter. These can be used to provide students with a head start on their research assignments and by students wanting further information and analysis of the topics covered in the chapter.
- Guidance for choosing Websites is provided at the end of each chapter. Although the content on most websites changes rapidly, and in some cases entire sites go missing altogether, enduring and credible sites such as those created and maintained by postsecondary education institutions and government agencies have been listed as a starting point for students' on-line research.
- One comprehensive *Glossary of Key Terms* is provided at the end of the book so that students wishing to look up a term do not have to search through subglossaries at the end of each chapter.

SUPPLEMENTS TO THE BOOK

TEXT WEBSITE. This website is intended to enhance the teaching and learning experience for instructors and students. Browse our extensive and helpful resources at http://www.parametersbrief.nelson.com.

INSTRUCTOR'S MANUAL. This comprehensive guide is organized to provide chapter outlines, overviews, and instructional tips. Available only as a downloadable supplement on the text website.

TEST BANK. This resource includes a variety of questions (multiple choice, short-answer, and essay questions) from which to construct tests and exams. Available only from your Thomson Nelson sales representative.

ACKNOWLEDGMENTS

I wish to thank the team at Nelson, particularly Chris Carson, Linda Sparks, and Bram Sepers. Special acknowledgment goes to Susan Fitzgerald, Joan E. Templeton, and Antima Gupta for their expertise and sound advice throughout the editing and production process. I am also grateful to the anonymous reviewers for their comments and suggestions about the proposed plan for this first brief edition.

I am indebted in many ways to the original authors of *Parameters*: Keith Archer, Roger Gibbins, Rainer Knopff, and Leslie Pal, all of whom provided me with excellent instruction, guidance, inspiration, and even a few trips to Flames games while I completed my B.A. and Ph.D. in the Department of Political Science at the University of Calgary. Heather MacIvor's revisions to their fine work also deserve recognition. Although this book deviates substantially from all of the previous editions of *Parameters,* it would not have been written without access to that foundational material.

My students at Lethbridge College deserve recognition for their inspiration and advice, primarily about what they are looking for in an introduction to Canadian government. Although most of them were not aware of it, they participated in the laboratory where many of the features and ideas in this text were first tested and later refined. Their insights have helped to make this book as straightforward and user-friendly as possible. Special recognition is owed to my fall 2006 Canadian government students who provided a final classroom test of the draft product. I would be remiss without recognizing my friend and colleague Marda Schindeler whose clear-headedness and direct approach to teaching political science is both refreshing and an inspiration. Her efforts have impacted many aspects of my academic life, and, as a result, this book.

My deepest gratitude goes to Leanne Wehlage-Ellis who provided loving support, inspiration, and advice (as well as postponed a number of important activities during the long, hot summer of 2006 when much of the writing took place). I dedicate this volume to Leanne, for her role as patriot, active citizen, and keen student of Canadian politics, and as representative of all the Canadians who take an interest in gaining a deeper understanding of their political institutions.

INTRODUCTION: INSTITUTIONS, POLITICS, AND POLITICAL CULTURE

POLITICAL INSTITUTIONS AND SOCIETY

Institutions in Daily Life

Because it happens so frequently, it shouldn't come as a surprise. Yet political scientists are often taken aback when they encounter students who, innocently enough, ask the question, "Why should I take a class in Canadian politics; governments don't affect me?" If the mild-mannered professor contains his emotions long enough to provide a strictly formal response, it typically goes something like this: "Political institutions impact on virtually all aspects of your life, whether you know it or not. Understanding how that comes about, and what it means, will serve you well for the rest of your life. Now, let's take a look at that course outline."

Working Canadians feel the effects of governments every month when they receive their paycheques. If they are paying attention, they will notice that the federal government has taken about a quarter of their hard-earned money in the form of income tax, another 4 or 5 percent for the Canada Pension Plan, and another couple of percent for Employment Insurance premiums. Then the province gets involved by claiming 10 to 15 percent of their pay. Eventually, the municipality gets in on the act, and by the end of the year, Canadians pay an average of 46.7 percent of their incomes to one level of government or another.[1]

Most students have yet to experience the full impact of governments on their incomes. But you still experience their effects every day when you attend a publicly funded college or university, apply for student loans, take some mode of transportation to get to class, and purchase textbooks, pizza, coffee, or beer. Tuition, transit fees, auto insurance premiums, and sales taxes applied to virtually all of your other purchases are all determined, directly or indirectly, by governments. Beyond that, governments have a say in deciding which television stations you watch, which companies are allowed to sell you phone service, under what conditions you will be allowed to drive a car, and what type of health care is available to you and your family. These are but a few of the many ways in which Canadians experience the effects of political institutions. In essence, Canadians "live politics daily." Every decision that leads to a tax, a regulation, or the legal availability of a service is made by people working within Canada's political institutions. The most visible of these are our federal and provincial politicians toiling away within the institutions of Parliament and the provincial legislatures. However, politicians are only the tip of the institutional iceberg. Government institutions are filled with tens of thousands of public service employees, civil servants, judges, police officers, social workers, and many others who implement the decisions made by our politicians.

Each of these government actors, including politicians, operates within a set of rules and norms of behaviour established by the particular institutions within which they work. When they obey the rules and excel at doing their jobs within the institutional culture of their workplaces, they tend to succeed and make governments work. When they stray from the institutional norms, they tend to make government less effective and less legitimate in the minds of Canadians. When they stray too far, they sometimes get fired or sent to jail. It should be remembered, however, that even though the misdeeds of government officials tend to make the news more often than do stories about government officials doing their jobs, the overwhelming majority of government actors are hard-working, dedicated, and honest individuals who help to make Canada one of the wealthiest and most just countries in the world.

This does not mean politics is uncontroversial. It is not. Nor does it mean that every government institution always operates properly, without major screw-ups. Mistakes are made, injustices are committed, and sometimes governments just make silly, or downright stupid, decisions. Be that as it may, to understand whether or not a policy decision is the best decision that could have been made under the circumstances, citizens need first to understand the institutions within which decisions are made. They need to know how institutions condition behaviour, and how they structure and limit the choices available to political actors. Canadians need to understand how institutions function and how they interact with other institutions, and with the political culture of the country, if they are going to seriously evaluate the impact of politics on their daily lives. Taking a course in Canadian government and politics is the first step on that journey of discovery. We think you will enjoy it. We know you will be a better citizen after you have successfully completed it.

■ The Approach of this Book

This book is about Canada's political institutions and their relationship to the society that they govern. The institutions that make up the Canadian state contain unique sets of rules, roles, authority structures, myths, symbols, and rituals. Most of the time, we obey rules because it is appropriate to do so, and because we believe that the state has the legitimacy to set and enforce them. When rules are broken, the state has the power to punish offenders. The ways in which we perceive government authority are shaped by the ways in which that authority is exercised. When political leaders or other agents of the state fail to live up to our expectations, or when they abuse their authority by violating the rules, the institutions within which they operate can lose some of their legitimacy. Even when our institutions work properly, their ability to solve problems may be constrained by outside forces or challenged by a shift in public perceptions and expectations of what governments should or should not be doing. When that happens, their legitimacy may also suffer. If a loss of legitimacy is great enough, and if it persists for long enough, the entire institutional structure may be weakened.

Nonpolitical institutions such as families, churches, or minor hockey leagues will suffer the same fate if they fail to meet the needs and expectations of their members. However, one important difference between political and nonpolitical institutions must be understood: although some people can live very productive and happy lives as functioning members of society without many nonpolitical institutions, nobody can live in a society without government. As the political philosopher Aristotle made clear, "Man is a political animal."[2] The only way to live apolitically, if it is possible at all, is to completely remove oneself from all contact with other people, something few of us would ever desire or attempt. As Thomas Hobbes, another important political philosopher, observed, life without politics would be "solitary, poor, nasty, brutish, and short."[3] At least part of what both of these philosophers meant is that politics, and political institutions, are necessary elements of civil society. Indeed, without political institutions, civilization is impossible.

This book will examine Canadian political institutions by focusing on their main purposes and functions. For our purposes, politics will be defined as the process of making and enforcing public policy decisions that affect all or part of a given population. An institution whose main function is to make or enforce public policy will be considered to be a political institution. For example, the House of Commons and the Senate enact laws that are proposed by the prime minister and Cabinet; therefore, these are all important political institutions. Once enacted, laws are applied and enforced by members of the civil service, the police, and the judiciary. These are also political institutions. The authority and power of most political institutions is broadly defined by the Canadian Constitution. Therefore—yes, you guessed it—the Constitution is a political institution. In fact, so important is the Constitution that we will define it as the "master institution," primarily because it sets the foundational rules that determine which political institutions will exist and how they will interact with other institutions.

At the beginning of the twenty-first century, Canada's national political institutions confront a host of challenges. But this is not new. History teaches us that the governments of all nations, empires, and cities throughout the ages have faced challenges. One can reasonably argue that confronting challenges and trying to solve problems is what political institutions are established to do. Although today's challenges sometimes seem irresolvable, and it may appear that our governing institutions are not equipped to effectively deal with the problems of our age, governments are in no danger of becoming extinct. Institutions can and do adapt to changing environments. The history of Canada's political institutions is a story of continuous adaptation, mostly successful, to changing conditions. After all, since Confederation in 1867, Canada has expanded from four to ten provinces (see Figure 1.1), experienced a couple of rebellions in the West and at least as many secessionist crises in Quebec, participated in two world wars, managed economic recessions and depressions, and in the process evolved into one of the most diverse and free countries in the world. There is no reason to suppose that today's problems and challenges will cause the Canadian state to disappear any time soon. And even if a secessionist crisis or some other catastrophic political event should cause the Canadian state to cease to exist, citizens of the former country would establish or adopt other political institutions of governance. After all, it is in their nature to do so.

The premise of this book is that political institutions and the societies that they serve constantly redefine themselves and each other. Neither exists in a vacuum, and neither is static or unchanging. As citizens' political attitudes and values change, partly in response to the performance of their governing institutions, so do the criteria by which they judge that performance. Later on in this chapter we will examine some of the most important aspects of Canada's political culture. It will inform our discussion as we proceed through the remaining chapters, but this is primarily a book about institutions. We will begin our formal discussion of Canada's political institutions in Chapter 2 with an examination of the master institution: the Canadian Constitution. Chapter 3 will review one of the most important aspects of Canadian institutional configuration: how the structure of Canadian government is federally divided between our national and provincial governments. Chapter 4 will be devoted to our most visible political institutions: our national political parties, their leaders, and the Canadian party system. Chapter 5 will examine how the leaders and their respective parties compete for power within the rules established by the Canadian electoral system. Once elected, political actors take their places within our legislative institutions, some becoming members of the political executive, the subject matter for Chapter 6. Chapter 7 will review how politicians are guided by the advice they receive from civil servants and then rely on them to implement public policy once decisions are made. Chapter 8 will examine the crucial role of the courts in interpreting the Constitution, particularly the Charter of Rights and Freedoms. Chapter 9 will examine the mass media and other nongovernmental organizations that play important roles in association with our political institutions. Chapter 10 concludes

FIGURE 1.1 Canada and Its Provinces

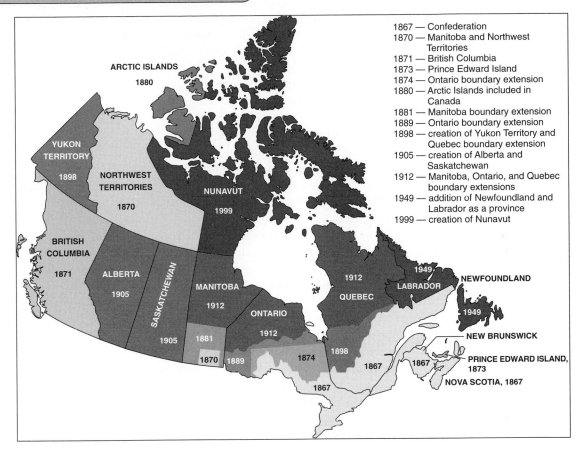

1867 — Confederation
1870 — Manitoba and Northwest Territories
1871 — British Columbia
1873 — Prince Edward Island
1874 — Ontario boundary extension
1880 — Arctic Islands included in Canada
1881 — Manitoba boundary extension
1889 — Ontario boundary extension
1898 — creation of Yukon Territory and Quebec boundary extension
1905 — creation of Alberta and Saskatchewan
1912 — Manitoba, Ontario, and Quebec boundary extensions
1949 — addition of Newfoundland and Labrador as a province
1999 — creation of Nunavut

our discussion with a review of where we have been and some guidance for citizens who will be interacting with Canadian political institutions for the rest of their lives.

CANADA'S POLITICAL INSTITUTIONS

The Constitution

Canada's Constitution truly is the country's master institution, and is comprised of much more than the written constitutional law found in the original British North America Act (BNA Act), 1867 (now known as the Constitution Act, 1867) and the Constitution Act, 1982. (Abridged versions of both appear in the Appendix to this book. Full versions appear on the Nelson Web pages.) To understand the Canadian Constitution in its entirety, one must be aware of the nonentrenched constitutional law that establishes many other institutions and sets the rules for putting the Constitution into practice. We must also be aware of the important judicial decisions that are made by the courts when sorting out disagreements about how the Constitution will be applied and what the various institutions will or will not be allowed to do. Furthermore, a series of constitutional conventions—long-standing practices and procedures—have developed into an unwritten part of the Constitution. Understanding each of these is important for coming to grips with how Canada's master institution impacts on politics and daily life in this country.

Although it is the supreme law of Canada, the Constitution cannot be enforced in the same way as other laws. Its power to constrain political actors depends largely on its legitimacy. Where the text of the Constitution conflicts with deeply held political values, it often ceases to operate altogether. For example, the British Crown is technically the source of all executive power in the Canadian state. Therefore, at least when considering the "letter of constitutional law," the Crown's chief representative in Canada, the governor general, could fire the prime minister and seize dictatorial power tomorrow. While such a coup would be technically legal under the provisions of the BNA Act, 1867, it would also be a gross violation of the democratic principles that sustain Canada's representative institutions. These principles underpin a convention that suggests only a prime minister and a Cabinet that enjoy the confidence of the House of Commons may exercise executive power. So direct rule by the governor general, despite being formally legal, would not be constitutional. If it were attempted, other political institutions would almost certainly intervene in support of the existing conventions, which are in turn supported by the most deeply held principles within the political culture.

While a constitution is intended to last for decades, even centuries, its meaning must evolve to keep pace with changing political attitudes. This evolution usually occurs without formally amending the written legal text. As new constitutional conventions develop, they gradually acquire the moral force to alter how political leaders exercise power. Also, judges interpret the Constitution in new ways that recognize and confirm the shifting standards of political legitimacy. But it would be an overstatement to suggest that the Constitution is constantly in flux. Certain core principles remain intact, although their meaning and their relative influence change as the political culture evolves. Federalism provides an important example of this evolutionary nature of a "living constitution."

Federalism

Canada is a federation, as are the United States, Germany, Australia, and many other states. Britain and France, the first European powers to colonize North America, are unitary states. In a federal state—also called a federation—the power to make binding decisions for the population is divided between two levels of government. The national (or federal) government is responsible for matters of national concern, such as defence, foreign affairs, and national economic matters like trade, the money supply, and interest rates. The regional (state or provincial) governments take care of local or regional needs. Each level of government has its own sources of tax revenue, and neither can invade the jurisdiction of the other without express consent. The regional governments are not subordinate to the national government. Their separate existence and powers are guaranteed by a written constitution that cannot be amended without their agreement. The courts resolve conflicts between the two orders of government.

In contrast, unitary states have only one senior government. The national government may establish local or regional agencies to assist in the delivery of services and the implementation of laws, but these agencies have no independent constitutional status of their own and may be abolished at any time. They exist solely to carry out the orders of the central government in the national capital.

In addition to these two ideal types, there is a third category of state: the quasi-federation. In quasi-federal states, the regional governments have their own separate constitutional status, distinct from that of the central government. But the regional governments are subordinate to the national government in that their independence is not complete. Their powers may be curtailed by the national government if they exercise those powers in a way that conflicts with national priorities.

Given that both of Canada's founding European nations were unitary states, but several distinct colonies existed at the time of Confederation, including at least one distinct ethnic and language group (the French) residing within the larger English political culture, it is not surprising that one of the most contentious issues during the Confederation debates was whether the new country should have a unitary or a federal structure. The advocates of federalism prevailed, although they had to accept some quasi-federal elements that were intended to make the national government more important than the provincial governments. The national government was given virtually all of the important powers of the time, including the residual powers not specifically granted to either the national or provincial governments, and the power to veto or delay provincial laws. The national government was also given unlimited taxation powers while the taxing powers of the provinces were limited. These elements of the written Constitution were clearly designed to ensure that the provinces were placed in a subordinate position and that their independence would be limited, even when they were acting within their own areas of jurisdiction.

Although the Fathers of Confederation built quasi-federalism into the written Constitution, the courts interpreted matters quite differently. During the first half-century of Confederation, judicial interpretation was largely responsible for balancing the powers between the national and provincial governments, making Canadian federalism much more classical in practice than a cursory review of its written Constitution would lead us to believe. When the political culture began to support the establishment of a welfare state, the balance of power shifted further to the provinces, not because they gained anything new in the written Constitution, but because the powers they were already assigned over health, education, and social services became some of the most important and costly areas of government activity. But as most of us are well aware, the national government was not left without the ability to regain some of its lost authority. Ottawa found other methods—in particular, the transfer of huge sums of money to the provinces—to intervene in areas of provincial policy-making and keep the federal government relevant.

Federalism illustrates the mutual influence of political institutions and the societies that they serve. Canadian federalism exists, in large measure, because the four founding provinces contained ethnically and geographically diverse populations. Neither Quebec francophones nor the distant Maritime colonies would accept a unitary state. They demanded a significant degree of self-government within the larger dominion. Over time, the provincial governments themselves began to shape the political attitudes of their populations. As they wrestled with Ottawa over scarce resources—principally tax revenues and policy-making powers—they created new political symbols to increase their legitimacy vis-à-vis the federal government. Thus, even though the electorates of the English-speaking provinces are socio-demographically rather similar, their provincial governments have helped redefine them as distinct political communities that can best be served by more autonomous provincial states.

Political Parties

Undoubtedly, the most visible and recognizable face of Canadian politics belongs to the political parties and their leaders who seek to form federal and provincial governments. Canadian political parties began as private organizations that typically represented a certain subculture, ideology, or national vision within one or more of the various political subcultures of the country. However, like all enduring political institutions, they evolved with the times as changes in the political culture, and in the dynamics of institutional interaction, dictated. At times, they initiated or significantly accelerated institutional and cultural developments. Today, although Canadian parties are still private organizations that control their own constitutions and exclusive memberships, they are much more stringently regulated and publicly financed than ever before.

Given the vast geographic, ethnic, linguistic, and cultural plurality of Canada, it is no accident that the most successful of Canada's political parties—indeed the only two to have ever governed the country, the Conservatives and the Liberals—have managed to bridge at least several of these important cleavages. Canada's first prime minister, Sir John A. Macdonald, was the first to successfully establish a functioning parliamentary coalition and build it into a formal political party. The Liberals, beginning with Canada's first French-Catholic prime minister, Wilfrid Laurier, and continuing with Canada's longest serving prime minister, William Lyon Mackenzie King, dominated party politics for much of the twentieth century.

Both of these national parties have tended to be based less on consistent ideologies and more on the immediate issues of importance to the residents of Canada's two central provinces, Ontario and Quebec, because they constitute a majority of Canadian voters. As a result, the regional political cultures of Canada have spawned a series of protest parties dedicated to representing the interests of regional, primarily Western, voters. The Progressives of the 1920s, the Depression-era Cooperative Commonwealth Federation (CCF) and Social Credit, the New Democratic Party (NDP), and more recently Reform and the Bloc Québécois, have each participated in shattering the political status quo by challenging both the operation and the effects of Canada's governing institutions.

So important has been the emergence of these parties that, when combined with changes in the political culture, communications technology, and the regional economies of the country, their entrance and exit from the scene tends to demarcate four distinct party systems in Canadian history.

■ The Electoral System and the Canadian Voter

Although the party system has seen tremendous change since Confederation, the same cannot be said for the electoral system. Some changes have been made with respect to such important issues as electoral advertising and financing, as well as the necessary addition of seats in the national Parliament to accommodate the addition of new provinces and populations. But beyond that, Canadians use pretty much the same system for electing members to the House of Commons and their provincial legislatures as they did when the country was founded.

Canada's national single-member plurality electoral system divides the country up into 308 roughly equal-by-population electoral districts (representation by population). These districts are known as constituencies or ridings, and each is allocated one representative to the House of Commons, who is commonly referred to as a member of Parliament or MP. Who that representative will be is determined in a winner-take-all election by voters living within the riding. In essence, when Canada holds a general national election, it actually holds 308 individual elections for 308 different House of Commons seats. Once the votes are counted, the leader of the political party that has won the most seats is asked by the governor general to become prime minister and form a government Cabinet. Members of other political parties form the opposition.

One of the many results of the Canadian electoral system is that it tends to over-reward parties with regional concentrations of votes. As such, Canadian party politics often appears even more regionally divided than is the country itself. Identification of one party with a particular region can alter the perceptions of voters within that region, and the perceptions of voters in other regions. The often-tumultuous entrance and exit of regional parties, along with the constantly shifting policy positions of the national parties, has conditioned Canadian voters' identifications with the parties. It has also impacted on their voting patterns.

Canadian voters tend to have only weak and flexible partisan attachments to their federal parties. Canadians are also know as vote switchers, moving in large numbers away from or toward one or another party at any given election. When these patterns of voting behaviour combine with the emergence of new parties or of charismatic new leaders of existing parties, as they did in the 1921, 1958, and 1993 federal elections, they have been known to produce tectonic shifts in the partisan political landscape. But even in nonmonumental elections, Canadian voters tend to exhibit a high level of vote switching between parties.

■ Parliament and the Political Executive

Canada's parliamentary system is modelled after the British Westminster system. It unites the legislative and executive powers in the Cabinet in Parliament, rather than separating them into independent bodies like in the American congressional system. Legislative power is formally exercised by two Houses of Parliament. This bicameral legislature contains a lower house, known as the House of Commons, and an upper house, known as the Senate. The political executive is comprised of the prime minister and the Cabinet, who perform the political functions of the Crown. The Crown's representative in Canada is the governor general.

The prime minister occupies the position at the top of the political executive because he or she leads the party with the most seats in the House of Commons. The Cabinet ministers must be drawn from the governing caucus, made up of MPs, and to a lesser extent senators, from the leading party, who were elected to represent particular constituencies in Parliament.

Canada also practises what is known as responsible government. This convention requires a Cabinet that loses the confidence of the Commons to resign as the government. In effect, the governor general delegates the powers of the Crown to the prime minister, and those powers must be relinquished when the legislative branch withdraws its support. Theoretically, the Commons uses its power to remove the Cabinet, thereby keeping the political executive accountable to the electorate. In practice, especially in majority government situations where a single party holds more than half the seats in the Commons, the government need not fear a loss of confidence. Strong norms of party discipline protect a majority Cabinet against defeat by the opposition parties. As a result, the House of Commons cannot really hold the executive to account. This changes dramatically in situations of minority government such as the recent Liberal minority led by Paul Martin (2004–2006) or the Conservative minority led by Stephen Harper that Canadians elected in 2006.

Both Houses of the federal Parliament have changed substantially over the years: the Senate primarily because of what it does not do, and the House of Commons primarily because of how it goes about doing what it does. The Senate, which is appointed by the prime minister, has almost as much formal power in the legislative process as the elected House of Commons. But senators rarely exercise that power to its fullest extent because they are not elected by the people and therefore lack the democratic legitimacy required by contemporary politicians. The House of Commons conducts its legislative business in much the same way as Westminster parliaments have done for centuries. But it too has adapted to changing times. Party discipline, which was relatively weak at the time of Confederation, has become the dominant ethos of the institution, making the political executive—in particular the Prime Minister's Office—even more powerful. At the same time, the number of MPs has increased and their regional distribution has changed dramatically since 1867. The Cabinet proposes almost all the bills that are eventually passed into law, and all legislation must be passed by both Houses of Parliament and signed by the Crown's representative.

Jean Chrétien's nearly 40-year career in the federal Parliament stretched from the early 1960s into the new millennium. He served in the Cabinets of two prime ministers, including acting as Trudeau's minister responsible for patriation in the early 1980s, prior to winning three consecutive majority governments as Liberal leader. Although his accomplishments were many, moving the federal government's finances from deficits to surpluses ranks among the most important. (© JIM YOUNG/Reuters/Corbis)

Born: 1934, Shawinigan, Quebec

Education: B.A. (St. Joseph Seminary, Trois-Rivières, 1955), LL.L. (Laval University, 1958)

Profession: Lawyer (called to the Quebec Bar in 1958)

1962–1963 Director, Bar of Trois-Rivières

Political Career:

MP
1963–1968 St-Maurice-Laflèche, Quebec
1968–1986 St-Maurice, Quebec
1990–1993 Beauséjour, New Brunswick
1993–2003 St-Maurice, Quebec

Leader
1990–2003 Liberal Party

Prime Minister
1993–2003

Other Ministries
1967–1968 Minister without Portfolio
1968 National Revenue
1968–1974 Indian Affairs and Northern Development
1974–1976 President of the Treasury Board
1976–1977 Industry, Trade and Commerce
1977–1979 Finance
1980–1982 Justice and Attorney General of Canada, Minister of State (Social Development), and Minister responsible for constitutional negotiations
1982–1984 Energy, Mines and Resources
1984 Deputy Prime Minister and Secretary of State for External Affairs

Political Career Highlights
1968–1972 Creation of ten national parks
1969 White Paper on Indian policy
1972 Berger Commission
1982 Patriation including Canadian Charter of Rights and Freedoms
1990–1993 Leader of the Opposition
1993 Elected prime minister with majority
1995 Quebec Sovereignty Referendum
1997 Reelected prime minister with majority
1998 First federal surplus since the 1960s
2000 Reelected prime minister with majority
2000 Clarity Act

Source: *First Among Equals: The Prime Minister in Canadian Life and Politics* (Ottawa: Library and Archives Canada), available on-line at www.collectionscanada.ca/primeministers/

The Permanent Executive

Similar to Canadian society and politics, Canada's permanent executive is, in its own way, diverse, vast, and complex. At the federal level, the public service is divided into dozens of ministries within which hundreds of departments, bureaus, and commissions exist to deliver federal programs and services and otherwise enforce public policy. Their responsibilities range from keeping the peace at home and in foreign lands—as with the military, Royal Canadian Mounted Police (RCMP), and the Canadian Security and Intelligence Service (CSIS)—to administering the employment insurance system, low-income benefits, and disability claims, all accomplished within the Ministry of Human Resources and Social Development. Provincial, territorial, municipal, and Indian reserve governments also administer a vast array of programs within their respective public services.

Important central agencies within the federal permanent executive include the Privy Council Office (PCO), the Prime Minister's Office (PMO), the Department of Finance, the Treasury Board Secretariat, and all the line departments that are more commonly known as ministries and are responsible for policy and programs in a particular field. Together they help the political executive develop and establish public policy, deliver federal government programs and services, and enforce regulations.

In total, the federal government expects to spend over $227 billion in its 2006–2007 budget year. Although more than 25 percent of this amount is transferred to the provinces and territories (about $60 billion), and a further 15 percent or so (about $35 billion) is spent on interest payments to service the federal debt, total federal government spending accounts for approximately 16 percent of Canada's entire economic activity as measured by Gross Domestic Product (GDP).

After decades of budgetary deficits—whereby the federal government collected less in revenue than it spent on programs and services, requiring it to borrow billions of dollars each year and accumulating almost $600 billion in debt— in the last decade federal government finances have undergone a remarkable transformation, placing Canada in an enviable fiscal situation compared to most countries in the world. In fact, the federal government now collects considerably more revenue than it spends on programs and services, leading to larger-than-expected budgetary surpluses and an overall reduction in the federal debt. Given the impact federal financing has on the public policy decisions of all federal agencies, this subject area will be a major focus of our discussion of the permanent executive.

The Administration of Justice

Canada's judiciary operates independently of the legislature and executive. But it too impacts upon and is impacted by the changing political environment. The judiciary is called upon to apply the laws and public policies established by the other branches of government, which are constantly changing. It imposes penalties for violations of laws and passes judgement on disputes that arise between citizens and their governments, between governments, and between citizens. In fact, one of the first things we will notice about the development of Canadian federalism is how it was fundamentally transformed and shaped by judicial review.

The judicial power is allocated to a hierarchical set of courts, most of them at the provincial level. At the top of this hierarchy is the Supreme Court of Canada, which since 1949 has been the final court of appeal and the ultimate authority on constitutional issues. The political influence of the Supreme Court grew significantly after 1982 when the Canadian Charter of Rights and Freedoms was proclaimed law. Its role in arbitrating between the rights of citizens and the legitimate roles and responsibilities of governments will be the primary focus of our discussion of the courts in Canada.

Nongovernmental Actors: The Media and Interest Groups

Any introduction to Canada's political institutions would not be complete without some discussion of nongovernmental actors. Most important among these are the news media. For the most part, Canada's news media consist of private companies that employ journalists who subscribe to a code of professional ethics. In their efforts to report the basic facts and events of political life in Canada, journalists face a wide variety of constraints on their ability to provide comprehensive political reporting. Competition within an increasingly internationalized, 24/7 news cycle combines with demands for more and more visually sensational images to produce what many critics claim is an increasingly shallow account of public life and public policy. Although these constraints are most intense within the television news business, print, radio, and even Internet news media are not immune to their effects.

The choices made by the news media about how and in what manner they cover Canadian politics have profound impacts on both citizens and political institutions. But the causal arrows go both ways. Citizens' tastes about the content and form of the political news they want to consume impact on the choices made by the media that provide the news. Similarly, politicians develop complex communications and governing strategies that are significantly influenced by how they believe their policies will be presented to voters by the news media. In fact, few politicians succeed for very long without becoming effective at using the news media to their advantage—for positively communicating policy and their approaches to government, while always striving to effectively deal with criticism.

Although undoubtedly the most important method for political communication between government actors and citizens, the news media are not the only important set of nongovernmental organizations in Canada. Numerous interest and pressure groups exist as another means for citizens to channel their demands upwards into the political process. Many of these organizations make use of the mass media to attempt to influence public policy, but many also engage in other tactics such as lobbying and presenting their arguments before parliamentary committees and the courts. Some of their activities—especially lobbying—are increasingly regulated by governments, but most are not. In their attempts to represent the increasingly complex demands of a diverse citizenry, some of whom choose to engage in this much more active form of political participation, most nongovernmental organizations remain private organizations that carry out their activities with little state interference.

Canada's political and nongovernmental institutions operate within and have an impact on the changing dynamics of the political culture of the country. Their activities are constrained by the limits of what Canadians accept as the parameters of legitimate political behaviour. At times, such institutions may be on the leading edge of defining new trends and limits. At other times, they may lag behind developments, causing their legitimacy to suffer until they either adapt to the new environment, or decline into irrelevancy.

POLITICAL CULTURE AND CANADA'S POLITICAL INSTITUTIONS

Political institutions are frequently challenged to adapt and evolve by changes in the domestic political culture, which are in turn influenced by the more broadly based cultural and technological changes within Western civilization. Although grounded by several fundamental principles, Canada's political culture is more diverse than it was 100 or even 50 years ago, and long-standing subcultures such as Québécois nationalism and Western regional alienation have been mobilized into new forms of political activity. At times, consensus about the form and functions of Canadian political institutions appears to be shrinking. And while most Canadians are fairly satisfied with the political system, their attitudes toward certain elements of it have lately become more negative. The decline in legitimacy, which can be traced in large measure to a failure of political institutions to quickly adapt to changing political values, raises questions about the continued viability of the institutions established in 1867. Moreover, subculture mobilization, notably Québécois nationalism, has sparked debate about the continued existence of our national political system.

As will be revealed throughout the chapters of this book, in the larger context, little of this is new. Canadian political institutions have faced challenges to their authority and legitimacy since Confederation. In fact, it can be argued that challenges to pre-Confederation institutions led to the creation of Canada. Dissent, including challenges to governmental authority, is an inherent component of the political culture. A general discussion of the sources of Canadian political culture, including the primary subcultures and ideologies that help explain both its origins and its development, will allow us to consider the limits political culture imposes on political authority and action. It will also go a long way toward expanding our understanding of the limits to which political institutions exist in a dynamic interchange with the Canadian political culture.

Political Culture

To understand a country's political culture, a distinction should be made between the broader culture of a specific society and its particularly political elements. The culture of a given population is made up of a unique mix of values, attitudes, and rituals. It is shaped by history, economy, religion, geography, demography, and immigration patterns, among other things. Different customs evolve in different societies in response to universal human needs, such as the securing of the necessities of life and socializing children. Cultures are also impacted by local conditions like climate, the availability and abundance of natural resources, and neighbouring societies. Within that broad culture, certain values, attitudes, and rituals are explicitly political; others are indirectly related to politics.

At the risk of oversimplifying, the *political* aspects of a given culture relate to power, authority, and the making and enforcement of rules for the entire community. Every human community needs to establish some legitimate authority, however informal or dispersed, to settle disputes and make collective decisions that bind all of its members. But we must be careful not to take the distinction between political and nonpolitical values and attitudes too far. A full understanding of the political culture of a society must be interpreted in the context of the broader culture that determines the basic attitudes about human nature embodied within that particular society. These include attitudes about the legitimate exercising of authority, the "natural" hierarchies that divide the government from the governed, and the major doctrines that sanctify authority.

The Liberal, Democratic, Pluralist Foundation of Canadian Political Culture

At its base, the Canadian political culture is liberal, democratic, and pluralist. It is founded on the principles of the rule of law, and grounded in a spirit of individual equality. It is no accident that these principles are enshrined in the first 15 sections of the Canadian Charter of Rights and Freedoms.

- *Liberal* implies liberty or freedom. Despite the myriad of government regulations, laws, and taxes that restrict Canadians' behaviour and actions, Canada was founded as, and remains, one of the world's most free societies. Canadians are free to make their own choices, within limits, as to how and where they live their lives, what jobs they work at, and what they do with their disposable income. They are free to criticize their governments and other important social institutions and to participate openly in a political process that allows them to challenge government decisions with which they may disagree.

- *Democratic* implies free and open competition for government, including decision-making processes that involve contests between conflicting ideas and approaches. Decisions are typically made by way of votes, either by the people's representatives, or, more infrequently, directly by the people themselves. Once a decision has been made, so long as it has been arrived at democratically, it must be considered legitimate, even by those on the losing side of the debate.

- *Pluralist* implies that Canadians are free to openly, voluntarily, and exclusively associate with others, in groups and organizations, without unreasonable state or government interference. Most importantly, so long as groups are not engaged in illegal behaviour, the state remains neutral as to which voluntary associations individuals chose to make.

- The *rule of law* implies that when the state does take action against citizens, its actions will not be arbitrary, and its procedures will be fair and known in advance. It also implies that government officials are not immune from these standards, that all are equal before and under the law, and that no one, including agents of the state, is above the law.
- *Equality* implies that the state will treat all citizens equally and will not systematically discriminate against individuals based on personal characteristics beyond their control.

Within these broad, foundational principles exists a Canadian population that is unusually diverse, comprising dozens of ethnic groups, two official language groups, many distinct socioeconomic classes, and several distinct regions. This does not mean, however, that Canada is divided into an infinite number of politically salient (i.e., influential) subcultures. As we will see, a social cleavage does not automatically shape political behaviour. Before a distinct group within the electorate can become an influential subculture, it must be mobilized by political leaders. In Canada, the two most salient subcultures are Quebec nationalism and Western regional alienation. Each has a distinct political perspective which inspires discontent with the current political system and demands for reform.

Quebec Nationalism and the Quiet Revolution

As we will see throughout this text, French Quebeckers have a strong attachment to their political community that dates back to at least the eighteenth century. The passive, inward-looking nationalism that emerged after the British conquest of New France was mobilized by the Quiet Revolution of the 1960s into a more aggressive campaign for greater provincial powers and revenues. The myths and symbols of Quebec nationalism have been used effectively to strengthen the attachment of francophones to the sovereigntist project.

Quebec nationalists range from hard-core sovereigntists, whose primary goal is to separate from Canada and establish an independent Quebec state, to "soft" nationalists who want to remain in Canada under certain conditions. Those conditions include greater autonomy for the provincial government and the constitutional recognition of Quebec as a "distinct society." At its core, there are at least three central themes in the mythology of Quebec nationalism: recognition of the "French fact" in Canada; the compact between French and English as the foundation for the country; and the sanctity of Quebec's right to self-determination.[4]

Most Quebec nationalists perceive the province of Quebec to be the homeland of the French "nation" and culture in North America. It is a distinct society within Canada, meriting special status within Confederation. Consequently, the provincial government has a special responsibility to protect and promote that distinct society, and it requires special powers to carry out that responsibility. If it cannot achieve and exercise those powers within the framework of Canadian federalism, it must become an independent state.

They also perceive Confederation to be the product of a compact between two founding nations: the French and the English. (There is little room in this mythology for the Aboriginal peoples of Canada or for other ethnic minorities.) It follows that Quebec is not, and never will be, one province among ten. It has the right to negotiate constitutional change directly with the federal government, on a nation-to-nation basis. It also claims a veto over any proposed amendment to the Confederation compact that does not meet Quebec's needs. In other words, even if the federal government and the other nine provinces agreed to a change in the Constitution, Quebec should have the right to block that change.

And finally, national Canadian political institutions cannot thwart the democratic will of Quebeckers. That will is sovereign, and it trumps all other constitutional values, including federalism or the rights of minorities within Quebec.

For the most part, the Supreme Court and the federal government reject the last two of these claims, while the other provinces refuse to accept the idea that Quebec deserves special status. The clash between the two-nations and equal-provinces visions of Canada is yet to be resolved, despite repeated efforts by political leaders.

The decisive event bringing Quebec nationalism to the forefront of Canadian politics was the Quiet Revolution, which fundamentally transformed Quebec politics in the early 1960s. Prior to that, the Quebec government espoused a minimalist, laissez-faire approach to the economy and allowed the Catholic Church to dominate the realms of education and social welfare. In this deeply conservative vision, Quebec francophones were a Catholic, agrarian people for whom modern commercial capitalism was a foreign activity better left to English-speaking Protestants. By 1960, this ideology was no longer an accurate description of reality: since the beginning of the century, Quebeckers had been leaving their farms in droves and integrating into modern urban, industrial society. The problem was that they had been integrated as workers into enterprises largely controlled and managed by the English community and using English as the language of work, a development that threatened the long-term persistence of French as the primary language in Quebec.

Responding to this reality, the Liberal government of Jean Lesage abandoned the antistatism of its predecessors. It determined that if the French language and culture were to survive in Quebec, the government would have to intervene in the economy to ensure that it was controlled and operated to a much greater extent by francophones. Commerce was no longer to be disdained as a foreign activity but to be embraced as a form of secular salvation and, wherever possible, to be conducted in French. By the same token, education and other social services had to be wrested from the Church and directed more explicitly to giving French Quebeckers the skills they needed to take control of economic enterprises rather than just supply their labour.

In its newfound interventionism, especially in economic matters, the Quebec government often wanted to go further than the other provinces in occupying realms of public policy activity that had been filled by the federal government. Ottawa, from the perspective of the new Quebec nationalism, could not be trusted to exercise its powers in a manner congenial to Quebec. Given that parliamentary

POLITICAL BIOGRAPHY 1.2 Brian Mulroney

In the 1984 federal election, Brian Mulroney won a record 211 seats, bringing a large number of Westerners and Quebeckers into the same government and Cabinet for the first time in a generation. He kept the coalition together in the 1988 election largely based on the issue of the Canada–U.S. Free Trade Agreement, but the coalition broke down after both the Meech Lake and Charlottetown attempts at constitutional reform failed to meet the approval of the various regional political cultures in Canada. (© Christopher J. Morris/CORBIS)

Born: 1939, Baie-Comeau, Quebec

Education: B.A. Political Science
   (St. Francis Xavier University, 1959),
   LL.L. (Laval University, 1964)

Profession: Lawyer (called to the Quebec
   Bar in 1965)

1974–1975 Member, Cliche Commission
1976–1977 Vice-President, Iron Ore
   Company
1977–1983 President, Iron Ore Company

Political Career:
MP
1983–1984 Central Nova, Nova Scotia
1984–1988 Manicouagan, Quebec
1988–1993 Charlevoix, Quebec

Leader
1983–1993 Progressive Conservative Party

Prime Minister
1984–1993

Political Career Highlights
1983–1984 Leader of the Opposition
1984 Elected prime minister with majority
1987 Constitutional Accord (Meech Lake)
1988 Canadian Multiculturalism Act
1988 Reelected prime minister with majority
1989 Canada–U.S. Free Trade Agreement
1990 Canada's Green Plan for a Healthy
   Environment
1991 Canadian participation in the Gulf
   War
1991 Goods and Services Tax
1992 North American Free Trade
   Agreement
1992 Constitutional Accord (Charlottetown
   Agreement)
1993 Nunavut Settlement Agreement

Source: *First Among Equals: The Prime Minister in Canadian Life and Politics* (Ottawa: Library and Archives Canada), available on-line at www.collectionscanada.ca/primeministers/

institutions are designed to be highly responsive to the majority, Ottawa would naturally follow the wishes of the English majority outside Quebec. The Quiet Revolution, in short, led to the demand for a transfer of powers from Ottawa to Quebec City, a demand that has dominated Quebec politics and shaped the national institutional landscape ever since.

Western Regional Alienation

The term "Western alienation" is something of a misnomer. Nonetheless, it will serve as convenient shorthand to describe this subculture that combines regional alienation, faith in the democratic wisdom of "the people," and a preference for strong and equal provincial governments. It emerged in opposition to the traditional political parties that implemented the National Policy of economic and territorial development in Canada. This subculture is entrepreneurial and highly distrustful of Central Canadian business, labour, and political elites. Its proponents tend to distrust national political institutions like the Canadian Parliament because they are dominated by members from Central Canada. Given that adherents to Western regional alienation tend to view the government in Ottawa as the source of the region's problems, they also tend to view *all* governments with some skepticism. Therefore, each of the political movements that have emerged from this subculture has incorporated some form of populism into its program: myths, symbols, and rhetoric that pit "the people" (however defined) against some outside, oppressive "enemies of the people." Initially, enemies included "Eastern capitalists" and their agents within the banks, the Canadian Pacific Railway, and the federal government. More recent targets include special interests and their agents within the national political and media establishments.

Western regional alienation shares many characteristics with Quebec nationalism. Most importantly, they both tend toward supporting more powers for their respective provincial governments in opposition to federal government powers. But they often differ significantly in their approaches to Confederation. Alienated Westerners, for the most part, have not advocated secession. Rather, they have mobilized their grievances into a series of federal and provincial political parties that have been guided by one prevailing ethos: to reform Canadian political institutions in a manner that will end the quasi-colonial status of the West within Confederation.

To that end, Western regional alienation has had its most dramatic impact on Canadian political institutions by way of the party system. Beginning at the start of the twentieth century, and continuing until the new millennium, Westerners have created a series of new political parties that have fundamentally altered the established patterns of politics in Canada. The agrarian protest movement of the early twentieth century spawned the provincial United Farmers parties. Realizing that their grievances, and therefore their ability to redress them, lay more with the federal government than with the provinces, Westerners brought their brand of political entrepreneurialism to Ottawa in the form of the Progressives (1921), the Cooperative Commonwealth Federation (CCF) and Social Credit (both in 1935), and the Reform Party (1993). In each case, Westerners argued that they would rather attempt to reform existing Canadian political institutions than separate from them, making alienated Westerners natural allies with "soft" Quebec nationalists, and often bitter enemies of Quebec sovereigntists.

Francophone Quebeckers have constituted a distinct group within Canada, with a common sense of political and social purpose, since at least 1759. In that sense, the

Quebec nationalist subculture is nothing new. But it acquired a new form in the 1960s, as a new generation of political leaders strove to modernize the provincial economy and to promote the status of francophones within their own "homeland" (hence the slogan of the Quiet Revolution, "*maîtres chez nous*," which means "masters in our own house"). As successive Quebec governments battled Ottawa to secure the necessary resources, some nationalists concluded that the only way to ensure the survival of the distinct society was to separate from Canada altogether. The Western regional alienation subculture has only rarely acquired a separatist tinge;[5] its primary concern has been the decentralization of power within the federation, coupled with reforms to national institutions that would give the four westernmost provinces—not to mention "the common sense of the common people"—greater influence in the central government.

Importantly for our inquiry into Canada's political institutions, it must be understood that the mobilization of these subcultures has been greatly assisted by the very institutions that they seek to change. Quebec nationalists have used the resources of the provincial government to promote sovereignty, while Western populists have repeatedly used the electoral system and the House of Commons as a forum for expressing their grievances.

It must also be understood that the emphasis on these two subcultures does not imply that other groups within the electorate (such as women, Aboriginal Canadians, or those living in Ontario, the Atlantic region, or the North) are unimportant. The point is that these other groups have not been mobilized effectively, or—in the case of Aboriginal Canadians—that their relatively recent mobilization has not yet had a major impact on our national institutions.

■ Ideology

Canadian politics is often portrayed as an ideology-free zone. Many critics of our national parties bemoan the apparent lack of rigorous intellectual discourse in our political life. While it is true that by most conventional measures Canadians appear to be unconcerned with abstract ideological principles, it is nevertheless important to identify and understand the major political ideologies in Canada. Ideologies do impact institutions, at a minimum by setting the parameters within which parties, legislators, and other political actors frame debates about public policy.

Political ideologies are concerned with power, human nature, and the proper relationship between the citizen and the state. But ideology differs from political culture in at least two ways.[6] First, an ideology is narrower and more distinct. Political culture refers to the overall distribution of political values within a population, whereas an ideology may be confined to a particular group. Note, however, that there are no purely ideological subcultures in Canada, as there are in other democracies (e.g., the working-class subcultures of Western Europe); political mobilization in this country appears to require a degree of regional concentration, which explains why we refer to "*Quebec* nationalists" and "alienated *Westerners*." Also, ideologies are explicit and often abstract systems of ideas, whereas political culture is less well defined. For example, a self-identified socialist may be fully conscious of his or her political beliefs, and may perceive them as a coherent outlook on the world. But most Canadians devote little attention to their political ideas, and do not seem to be troubled by contradictions among them. While the descriptions of the main tenants of Canadian ideologies that follow are necessarily incomplete, they are intended to provide a thumbnail sketch of the contending world-views that animate our political debate.

Right Wing versus Left Wing

Observers of Canadian politics will often use the terms "right wing" and "left wing" when describing political actors and the various aspects of public policy. Because these terms originated several centuries ago with the development of European legislatures, their meanings and applications are more nuanced at the beginning of the twenty-first century. Nevertheless, if we stick to the public policy domain of government involvement in the economic affairs of citizens, we can arrive at a general characterization of each (see Figure 1.2).

For the most part, left wingers tend to support more government intervention in the economy. Favourite policies include progressive income taxation whereby the rich pay a higher percentage of their incomes to the government than do the poor, support for higher business and corporate taxes, regulation of market forces, and a more general attempt to equalize the distribution of wealth. They tend to support more money for social welfare programs and social services more generally. If promoting material equality means restricting some freedoms, left wingers tend to accept this as a necessary consequence of engineering greater economic equality amongst individuals and groups. Generally speaking, left wingers tend to support larger governments and more intervention than do their political opponents.

Right wingers, on the other hand, tend toward supporting smaller governments and less intervention in the economic lives of citizens. They prefer lower taxes, smaller and less generous social programs, and less government regulation of the economy. If material inequality is the result, it is considered a natural outcome of free markets and open competition amongst individuals.

FIGURE 1.2 The Conventional Placement of Canadian Political Parties on the Right-Left Ideological Spectrum

NDP	Bloc Québécois	Liberal	PC	Conservative	Alliance	Reform

LEFT WING   CENTRE   RIGHT WING

(larger government,   (smaller government,
higher taxes,   lower taxes,
more generous   less generous
social programs . . .)   social programs . . .)

When noneconomic public policy comes into play, the distinctions between left and right become much more problematic. Some right wingers support state intervention in the personal lives of citizens to protect the "most vulnerable members of society" (i.e., children and the unborn) as well as the traditional values of Canadian society (i.e., family, community, and religion). That is, they are not opposed to using the power of the state to intervene in the private lives of citizens, restricting their choices to engage in certain noneconomic activities. Many on the left share this perspective, inasmuch as they too are not opposed to using the power of the state to protect the most vulnerable, although the left's list of who constitutes the "vulnerable" may be very different from that of the right.

Conservatism

Classical conservatives tend to believe that the needs of the organic community take priority over those of the individual, where the two conflict. Community, hierarchy, order, and tradition are at least as important as freedom, equality, and individual rights. Conservatives believe that power should rest with those who are best able to exercise it wisely—that hierarchy and inequality are natural and inevitable. Conservatives advocate a strong government to maintain law and order, because human nature is flawed. Often associated with the right, classical conservatism in Canada is also known as "Toryism." Its more contemporary variant—neoconservatism, often called neoliberalism—tends to advocate the market capitalism favoured by the right. Social conservatism, while sharing the right's support of free markets and less economically interventionist governments, tends to also favour the use of state power to preserve traditional moral values within society. Canadian conservatives are most likely to be found in the Conservative Party, the old Reform and Alliance Parties, and sometimes in the Liberal Party. They are rarely found in the NDP.

Liberalism

Classical liberals believe that individual rights and freedoms—based on the capacity for reason inherent in every human being—must be respected by those in power. Liberals defend private property, free markets, freedom of expression, and most other individual liberties. They tend to believe that society advances most when open competition between ideas and policies exists. They have little interest in protecting the traditional values of a society, believing that those values will survive in open competition with more progressive values if they are of any real importance. Liberals place a premium on liberty and are generally opposed to state intervention in citizens' lives if that intervention goes too far in restricting individual choice and action. They prefer small governments with restricted powers, in order to maximize individual liberty. They emphasize equality of opportunity, not equality of condition. For the most part, classical liberals would fall on the right of the left-right ideological continuum. Today, however, liberals are divided over the role of the state. "Business liberals" retain the traditional preference for small government and free markets, while "welfare liberals" believe that the state should provide income security and intervene in the market to promote economic justice.[7] Liberals can be found in the Canadian Liberal Party, the Conservative Party, and sometimes in the NDP.

Socialism and Social Democracy

Like conservatives, socialists believe that the public good must take priority over individual liberties, where the two conflict. But socialists seek equality of condition, in particular equality of economic condition, not just equal opportunity to compete in a free market, as preferred by liberals. They advocate extensive state involvement in the ownership and management of the economy to ensure that everyone benefits from the wealth of society. Social democrats are socialist reformers, who make a point of emphasizing the fact that they are not revolutionaries. That is, while they often seek radical change, they do so by pursuing power through elections. For the most part, socialists are usually found amongst the left wing of the Liberal Party and in the NDP. Socialists are rare in the Conservative Party, and were almost completely absent in Reform, but they did have some policy commonalities with "Red Tories" in the old Progressive Conservative Party. Many Bloc Québécois supporters tend toward socialist or social democratic ideologies.

Nationalism

Nationalists believe that "a people"—a group distinguished from its neighbours by language, ethnicity, religion, history, or some other criterion—has the right to govern itself directly. They tend to value a sense of pride in one's political community over other priorities. Nationalists can be either right wing or left wing, but given that they often promote the use of state intervention to protect "national characteristics" such as language and culture, they tend to have more in common with the overt social engineering aspirations of the left. As mentioned earlier, Quebec nationalism ranges from separatism to demands for a rebalancing of the federal system. In both cases, however, it should be noted that virtually all Quebec nationalists support state intervention in the private choices of citizens when it comes to protecting and promoting Quebec's distinctive culture, no matter how it is defined. The Bloc Québécois is made up exclusively of Quebec nationalists, but they can also be found in the Liberal Party and in the old Progressive Conservative Party. It remains to be seen how the new Conservative Party will accommodate Quebec nationalists.

Populism

Populists tend to believe that "the people" are best qualified to make decisions for themselves, instead of trusting political and economic elites to make decisions on their behalf. They are most often hostile toward existing authorities, which are perceived as unaccountable and corrupt. Populists are usually strong proponents of direct democracy. Some populists inject explicit moral or religious elements into their political programs and can be either left wing or right wing. Early in the twentieth century, most populists tended to be left wing advocates of increased government support for disadvantaged individuals and groups, especially beleaguered Canadian farmers. More recently they have tended to focus on the problems associated with an elitist political process that favours special interests at the expense of the mass of "common people." Some types of populists could be found in most Canadian parties at one time or another, but they were instrumental in founding the early prairie protest parties and more recently the Reform Party. At present, the political salience of populism appears to be waning as the new Conservative Party abandons the populist rhetoric and policies of the Reform and Canadian Alliance parties in favour of a more muted expression of neoconservatism.

Feminism

Feminists believe that the most important political division is that between the sexes, and that men and women should have equal opportunities in all spheres of life. Feminists seek to identify and change power structures that oppress women, such as gender stereotyping in the media, the "old boys' network" in party politics, and the "pink-collar ghetto" in the legislative and executive branches of government. Feminism is not a single unified body of ideas. For example, there are liberal, radical, and socialist feminists. Be that as it may, feminists are much more likely to be found in the NDP, and to a lesser extent in the Liberal Party, than in the Conservative Party. Because of their shared emphasis on equal rights, gender-based social justice, and the use of state action to ensure these goals, feminists are most often found on the left of the ideological continuum, and frequently on the far left.

Libertarianism

One other ideology is starting to make its presence felt in Canada. Libertarians are essentially classical liberals who believe that Canadian liberalism has gone astray. They tend to view contemporary liberalism within the Liberal Party as having much more in common with socialism than with classical liberalism. For the most, libertarians tend to side with neoconservatives when it comes to economic freedom, but believe that the often-too-close association of "neocons" with social conservatives, or "socons," makes conservatism vulnerable to the same state suppression of individual liberties as socialism, albeit often for different purposes and ends. Libertarians are not anarchists in that they believe a state is necessary, but they oppose its use for implementing grand social experiments. Libertarians tend to distrust the social engineering of the left as much as they oppose the moral engineering of the right.

Each of these ideologies plays a role in Canadian politics. Although this book is more concerned with the impact of political culture on institutions, we cannot overlook the connection between ideologies and institutions. Despite the fact that ideologies do not play as obvious a role in Canadian politics as they do in other Western democracies, it would be foolish to discount them completely in an analysis of our political institutions.

SOURCES OF CANADIAN POLITICAL CULTURE

Canada has never had a single political culture. Long before Confederation, French and British communities coexisted with the traditions of the various Aboriginal peoples. The legitimacy of the political institutions established in 1867 varied among the distinct linguistic and regional groups in the population, whose numbers multiplied with the settlement of the West and the industrialization of Central Canada. Territory quickly became an important political variable as provincial governments used the federal division of powers to deliberately mobilize regional political cultures in their struggles with Ottawa. Furthermore, the developing Canadian economy produced its own social cleavages, both between socioeconomic classes and among the various regions of the country. Understanding the sources of this diverse pattern of political orientations is important for understanding the impact of political culture on Canada's governing institutions. Two variables stand out: history and sociodemographics.

■ Historical Influences on Canadian Political Culture

The pattern of political orientations within a given country is decisively shaped by its history. The most influential accounts of the impact of Canadian history on our political culture are Louis Hartz's "fragment theory" and Seymour Martin Lipset's "formative events" approach. The application of these perspectives to the understanding of Canadian political history has led to a rich analytical tradition, including an attempt to understand the impact of the historical patterns of immigration on political culture.

The Fragment Theory

For proponents of the fragment theory approach, the political cultures of new nations founded by Europeans—Canada, the United States, Australia, New Zealand, and South Africa—were determined by their unique patterns of European settlement.[8] The colonists who left Britain, Ireland, and France brought their political attitudes with them. Ideologies that dominated the political attitudes in the mother country at the time of departure also made the trip to the new lands. But the immigrants did not bring the whole of European history with them. Rather, they brought the prevailing ideological "fragment" and used it as a basis for building political institutions. The fragment was preserved as the dominant ideology in the new society, but it was also cut off from its past, giving it little impetus for change and leaving the fragment frozen in the new political culture. Cut off from the dialectic of European ideological development, a society founded primarily by enlightenment liberals, for example, would likely freeze into place a predominately liberal political culture. Removed from the ideological development that saw feudalism give way to Toryism, which preceded conservatism, liberalism would have no opportunity to develop into socialism.

As applied to Canada, the *habitants* of New France were intensely conservative. They established institutions based on the quasi-feudal ideas of early modern France, accepted the quasi-feudal structure of the colonial economy, and looked to the Catholic Church for instruction and assistance. The English, Scottish, and Irish settlers, like those in the 13 colonies to the south, were more liberal in their outlook. After France ceded its colony to Britain in 1763, the two cultures—French conservatives and English-speaking liberals—clashed repeatedly. The *habitants* turned inward, determined to survive as a French Catholic community under the British Crown. The liberal English political culture dominated outside of Quebec.

After almost 250 years, fragment theorists argue, Canada's political culture is still shaped by the original European fragments. Quebeckers are more collectivist and state oriented, demonstrating an organic link to their quasi-feudal pasts. They are more deferential to their leaders, and more averse to risk. Conversely, English Canadians are more concerned with individual freedom and less tolerant of state interference in their lives. The fragment theory does not seek to explain every nuance of political culture. In fact, it emphasizes ideology as opposed to more broadly based political culture. Instead, it portrays the culture of the first European settlers as a blueprint for the foundational aspects of a political culture that will, of course, continue to develop over time.

In an influential analysis of the differences between Canadian and American socialist movements, Gad Horowitz argues that the political cultures of English Canada and its southern neighbour are less similar than they first appear.[9] Although both cultures are essentially liberal, Canadian liberalism is less "pure." It is influenced by both conservatism (which Horowitz calls "Toryism") and socialism, two collectivist ideologies that moderate the radical individualism of the classical liberal world-view. The "Tory touch," which was present well before Confederation, opened the door to the socialist ideas introduced by British immigrants in the twentieth century. Because Canada's political culture is not monopolized by a single liberal ideology, unlike American political culture, there is more room for legitimate opposing viewpoints. Critics of the Horowitz thesis argue that too much is made of Canada's Tory touch and that a more important rival to liberalism in English Canada was American-inspired republicanism—with its emphasis on the values of popular (i.e., elected) government, rooted in the will of the people. Each argument has some merit and the debate has made a substantial contribution to the historical analysis of Canadian politics.[10]

Immigration

Whether one subscribes to the fragment theory or not, it is difficult to ignore the impact that continuous waves of immigration have had on regional subcultures (see Canada by the Numbers 1.1). Each region has been disproportionately populated by different European fragments in varying numbers at different times in Canadian history: English, Scottish, and Irish in the Atlantic region, Ontario, and British Columbia; French in Quebec; and Americans, British, and other Europeans on the Prairies. Newer subcultures have developed over the past 50 years, as immigration patterns have changed. In effect, Canada's political culture is continuing to absorb new fragments all the time.

CANADA BY THE NUMBERS 1.1 Population Increases: Births and Immigration, Deaths and Emigration 1851–2001

CENSUS YEARS	TOTAL CANADIAN POPULATION (MILLIONS)	TOTAL POPULATION GROWTH (MILLIONS)	PERCENT INCREASE IN POPULATION	BIRTHS (MILLIONS)	IMMIGRATION (MILLIONS)	DEATHS (MILLIONS)	EMIGRATION (MILLIONS)
1851–1861	3.2	0.8	—	1.3	0.4	0.7	0.2
1861–1871	3.7	0.5	14.2	1.4	0.3	0.8	0.4
1871–1881	4.3	0.6	17.2	1.5	0.4	0.8	0.4
1881–1891	4.8	0.5	11.7	1.5	0.7	0.9	0.8
1891–1901	5.4	0.5	11.1	1.5	0.3	0.9	0.4
1901–1911	7.2	1.8	34.2	1.9	1.6	0.9	0.7
1911–1921	8.8	1.6	21.9	2.3	1.4	1.1	1.1
1921–1931	10.4	1.6	18.1	2.4	1.2	1.1	1.0
1931–1941	11.5	1.1	10.9	2.3	0.1	1.1	0.2
1941–1951	13.6	2.1	18.6	3.2	0.5	1.2	0.4
1951–1961	18.2	4.6	33.6	4.5	1.5	1.3	0.5
1961–1971	21.6	3.3	18.3	4.1	1.4	1.5	0.7
1971–1981	24.8	2.9	13.3	3.6	1.8	1.7	0.6
1981–1991	28.0	3.2	12.9	3.8	1.8	1.8	0.5
1991–2001	31.0	3.0	10.7	3.6	2.3	2.1	0.7

Note: Data in this table are derived from Statistics Canada data available on-line at www40.statcan.ca/l01/cst01/demo03.htm?-sdi=immigration. All secondary interpretations and calculations are the responsibility of the authors. (Adapted from Statistics Canada, Census of Population, 2001)

Most immigrant subcultures arriving after the basic foundations of Canada's political institutions have had, however, much less opportunity to impact the established institutional norms and practices. For the most part, new immigrant communities, while remaining attached to many of their more specific cultural values, tend to adopt the prevailing liberal, democratic, and pluralist values of the dominant political culture. This does not mean that these subcultures are unimportant, only that their importance tends to be conditional upon them being associated with or mobilized into a more salient regional subculture.

Formative Events

According to Seymour Martin Lipset, national political cultures are shaped by shared historical experiences. He attributes the "conservative" and "deferential" culture of English Canada to a single cataclysmic event: the American Revolution of 1776–1783.[11]

More specifically, Lipset argues that because Canadians refused to participate in the uprising against the British Crown, and because English Canada absorbed thousands of Loyalist refugees from the new American republic, our political culture is indelibly marked with the conservative and elitist values of eighteenth-century Britain. These values were embodied in Canadian political institutions, which not only preserved but also reinforced them. Subsequent "formative events," particularly the orderly development of the West (in contrast to the lawlessness of the American frontier), reinforced the relatively meek Canadian attitude toward authority figures.

Lipset's argument is based on shaky evidence, much of which is contradicted by empirical research. It also rests on the erroneous assumption that formative events affect every person and every group in the same way. In reality, most of Canada's formative events are perceived quite differently by various subcultures. It nevertheless alerts us to the impact that ongoing formative events can have on political culture. Subsequent milestones in Canadian history—such as Confederation itself, the National Policy of 1879, and the death of the Meech Lake Accord in 1990, just to mention a few—at times bitterly divided Canada's subcultures and created new myths and symbols of power, domination, and rejection. The National Policy was designed to counter the flow of trade across the Canada–U.S. border by creating a national market for the products manufactured in Ontario and Quebec; its effect was to turn Atlantic Canada toward dependency and Western Canada into a captive internal colony, stunting the economies of both peripheral regions and fuelling regional resentments. The defeat of the Meech Lake Accord was viewed as another slap in the face by Quebec nationalists, but as a victory for the forgotten common people by Western populists.

Whereas American history has usually been interpreted in a unifying way (with obvious exceptions, such as slavery and the Civil War), Canadian history has left a legacy of division and mistrust that repeatedly flares up into public debate about the very legitimacy of our political system. Riel, both world wars, and our more recent debates about institutional reform serve as but a few further examples. In this respect, it is legitimate to argue that formative events—especially those that shape a nation's political institutions—do leave indelible imprints on its political culture. Such events can further unite populations that already share basic political values, but they can also drive wedges between existing subcultures and create new cleavages.

■ Sociodemographic Influences on Canadian Political Culture

The diversity of Canada makes for singling out some sociodemographic variables as more important than others, a formidable challenge. Nevertheless, where political institutions and political culture are concerned, the task becomes much simpler because of one overriding factor: regionalism. Where significant clusters of one or more important sociodemographic characteristics are geographically concentrated, they have the potential to be mobilized into forces that can importantly condition the political culture and political institutions.

Political Geography

There is little doubt that political geography has shaped the national political culture and can help to explain the existence of regional political cultures. The sheer size and diversity of Canada clearly contribute to the sense of difference across the regions. As each province has developed, from the first European settlement to the present day, different landscapes, weather, and natural resources combined with different technologies and different public policies to produce a number of distinct regional economies. These, in turn, helped in creating distinct patterns of political values across the regions. This is not to suggest that geography determines culture; such one-sided explanations rarely offer any genuine insight. It means, instead, that the unique terrain and climate in each part of the country shape the social and political values of those who live there, thus creating the conditions for their mobilization into a formal subculture.[12]

While objective factors such as immigration patterns and geography help to explain the strength of Canadian regionalism, they do not tell the whole story. Regionalism is a subjective phenomenon, a social and psychological attachment to a particular place. Citizens with a strong sense of regional identification and commitment are more likely to vote on the basis of regional interests and to resent perceived mistreatment of their region by the national or provincial government, than are citizens more concerned with other aspects of their identities (e.g., gender, class, or language).

Despite recent changes in political culture—including the rise of nonterritorial cleavages—regionalism remains unusually influential in Canada's national politics. Cross-national comparisons between Canada and other industrialized democracies reveal the relative weakness of social class and church attendance as determinants of voting choice. Canadians are significantly more influenced by territorial cleavages—primarily region or province of residence—than are Western Europeans.[13] This may be due, in part, to the incentives set by our national institutions. In particular, the Canadian electoral system reflects the view that MPs represent territory, not ideology, and, as we will explore later, exaggerates regional differences among the various party caucuses in the House of Commons.

Federalism also importantly impacts on regional, or more specifically provincial, political cultures. Identifying with the partisan history of a province or region, or an entrenched regional position on constitutional matters—especially when that history or position differs significantly from those of other regions—reinforces regional and provincial attachments. It is no secret that one of the most tried and tested approaches to garnering votes, come election time, is for provincial politicians to pick a fight with Ottawa on behalf of the oppressed people of *their* province. And provincial politicians are not alone in exploiting—and therefore reinforcing—regional sentiments. Many federal politicians have been known to pit one region against another when they thought it served their electoral advantage, further reinforcing the us-versus-them aspects of Canadian regional political cultures.

Demography

The most obvious demographic influence on Canadian politics is the presence of a large francophone minority. Almost one-quarter (22.7 percent) of the population claim French as their mother tongue. Anglophones account for 59 percent, and allophones make up 17.6 percent. A majority of francophones live in Quebec, although there are significant francophone populations in New Brunswick and Ontario. While the language cleavage has always been a central issue in Canadian politics, its implications have become more serious since the Quiet Revolution mobilized a large component of Quebec nationalism into the sovereignty movement. Fears about the future of French in Canada help to fuel the campaign for a separate Quebec. Otherwise, the language cleavages appear to have little impact on political values; francophone and anglophone Canadians hold similar views on most political and social issues, although the former are slightly more permissive on moral issues.[14]

Aboriginal Canadians, who accounted for 3.3 percent of the population in the 2001 census, also seek to reform Canada's political institutions. The distribution of the Aboriginal population varies widely among the provinces and territories: from around only 1 percent of the Prince Edward Island and Quebec populations to more than 13 percent in Manitoba and Saskatchewan, and 83 percent in Nunavut.[15] The intensity of Aboriginal demands for institutional and economic autonomy also varies, but overall, Status Indians, Métis, and Inuit have become important players in debates over Canada's political future. Recent demands for enhanced political and legal status—ranging from an Aboriginal chamber of Parliament to the constitutional recognition of Aboriginal communities as "a third order of government" with significant sovereignty over their own affairs—pose significant challenges to our existing institutions.

Language and ancestry are only two of the demographic variables that can impact on political culture, but their important differences help to illustrate the more general proposition about the importance of regional concentration. One variable, francophone Quebec, is territorially concentrated, and has had a substantial impact on the choice of political institutions in Canada and on their development over time. The other, Aboriginal ancestry, is much more dispersed in the various parts of the country, has only recently exerted an influence on the larger political culture, and still has not had as significant an impact on Canada's institutional development as have other, more regionally defined subcultures.

Generally speaking, then, it would be impossible to gain a full understanding of Canadian political institutions without making some effort to understand the impact political culture has on the founding and continued development of those institutions. As has been discussed, it is also important to understand that causality is a two-way street. That is, not only does political culture impact on institutions, institutions impact on political culture, and both impact on the behaviour of political actors.

HOW INSTITUTIONS SHAPE POLITICAL BEHAVIOUR

Institutions shape individual behaviour and attitudes in at least three important ways. They set incentives for those who operate within them. They exploit symbols to legitimize the authority structures on which they are based. And they impose structured roles and rituals on actors inside and outside them. We will examine each of these aspects of institutional influence on individual and group behaviour.

▨ Incentives

Institutions create incentives for political actors: they require or encourage particular types of behaviour, and discourage or punish others. The effectiveness of these incentives depends on two factors: their congruence with the preexisting beliefs and motivations of the participants, and the clarity with which they are expressed. For example, a politician who intends to make a career out of getting elected has a stronger incentive to follow the rules and norms of behaviour established by the electoral and party systems than does a citizen who intends only to make a specific point by promoting a single issue over the course of a short campaign period.

One of the most important criteria for evaluating a political institution is its success in channelling the ambition of individual politicians to serve the public good. Failure to do so can result in corruption, self-seeking behaviour, and the disregard of the public good. While personal ambition is the product of individual psychology and is often condemned by those who fear its effects in political life, personal ambition should more properly be regarded as a crucial resource for democracy. An effective political institution will transform private goals into public good by creating incentives for ambitious politicians to serve the common interest. If an aspiring party leader, for example, can win a leadership contest by deceit and manipulation, he may well be motivated to engage in campaign tactics that undermine the health of his party. But if such behaviour is likely to be exposed and condemned, with fatal consequences for his campaign, the risks of dishonesty will typically be too great and tend to deter that sort of behaviour.

Every institution provides a structure of opportunities for those who are motivated to succeed within it. Similarly, political institutions set incentives—both formal and informal—for ambitious political actors. When a political institution channels ambition in ways that conflict with the political values of some citizens, the result can be a loss of legitimacy. For example, the authority of the Canadian Cabinet rests on the continued support of a majority of the members of the House of Commons. Consequently, the prime minister—as the leader of the largest party in the Commons—has a powerful incentive to ensure that his or her MPs remain loyal. That loyalty is secured through party discipline and a system of rewards, threats, and punishments that reinforce the team spirit already present among parliamentarians elected to represent the same party. A government MP who votes against a budget, or some other key piece of legislation, knows that he or she will provoke the displeasure of the prime minister and jeopardize that MP's own future political career. So the incentive structure for ambitious back-bench MPs (those who are not members of the Cabinet) within the government caucus is very clear: if you hope to rise to a Cabinet position, you must vote in favour of your party's proposed legislation. As we will see later, party discipline is often perceived by Canadian voters to be a barrier to a more genuine form of political representation. Nonetheless, as long as the relationship between our executive and legislative institutions remains unchanged, party discipline will continue to shape the behaviour of our members of Parliament.

Furthermore, political institutions structure the behaviour of all citizens, not just politicians. For example, it is sometimes argued that institutions which encourage rational, deliberative debate among citizens promote the development of civic virtues. By allowing nonpoliticians to acquire the habits of justice and community participation, as Aristotle might have put it, these institutions strengthen the commitment to democracy among the electorate. Institutions that create disincentives for public participation, on the other hand, may weaken citizenship and erode the foundations of democratic legitimacy. Critics of Canadian representative democracy often argue that the political parties, Parliament, and Cabinet government exclude the people from the decision-making process. These critics believe that the introduction of more direct-democracy provisions, particularly initiatives, referenda, and recall, would give citizens an incentive to become better informed about politics and strengthen their faith in our national institutions.

Symbolism

Political institutions both embody and create legitimating symbols. They help simplify a world of overwhelming complexity, reducing it to predictable routines and a set of shared meanings. These include the primary myths, symbols, and rituals that underpin the political system of a given state. There are a number of important points to make about political myths and symbols.

First, "myth" is not synonymous with "lie" or "deception." To be effective, any myth—political or otherwise—must have some basis in fact. Otherwise, the gap between myth and reality eventually becomes too great, and the myth loses its power to inspire political action or to legitimize political authority. For example, we may call Quebec nationalism a myth, because it is a powerful narrative of oppression combined with resentment against the anglophone majority in Canada (not to mention the anglophone minority in Quebec, which held a disproportionate share of economic power until fairly recently). Nonetheless, it is indisputably true that the francophone percentage of Canada's population is shrinking and that there are cultural differences between francophone Quebeckers and other Canadians, which might lead one to conclude that they cannot coexist within the same country. Similarly, Western alienation from Central Canada is a powerful myth that affects the ways in which many residents of the four westernmost provinces interpret political events. When former Prime Minister Chrétien made a speech in Edmonton in August 2001, in which he called upon Albertans to share the wealth from their oil and gas revenues with the rest of Canada, he inadvertently triggered an explosion of anger and fear about the federal government's intentions toward that province, and consequently, the entire region. That intense regional sensitivity and antagonism toward the federal government can be puzzling to non-Westerners, who may not be aware of the historical reasons for it.

Second, political myths and symbols are not static. They evolve over time, as social and economic circumstances change. It is also the nature of political myths to be based on a highly selective use of facts. Some facts and issues are given a great deal of attention by political actors and citizens alike, while others are selectively ignored.

Third, each political institution embodies its own set of myths and symbols, which are not always compatible with those of other institutions. The decisions of the House of Commons are legitimated, in part, by the symbols of the national political community such as the Crown, the prime minister, and a general election in which all Canadian citizens had the opportunity to participate. On the other hand, decisions taken collectively by the first ministers can be legitimated only by the symbols of federalism and provincial rights, which conflict with the idea of a single national interest. As we have seen, federalism necessarily creates a set of conflicting myths and symbols. These undermine the sense of a unified political community, which Aristotle, for one, considered to be an essential part of a good constitution.

Finally, we should bear in mind that political myths and symbols rarely carry the same meaning for all members of the community. There are always competing myths and symbols. Even a universal myth, such as the value of voting in a representative democracy, means different things to different people.

■ Structured Roles for Political Actors

The rules, rituals, and norms embodied in institutions tell us how to behave in varying situations. Without them, most human interactions would be chaotic and meaningless. When you go to vote in a federal election, or to church, or to a pub, you know what sort of behaviour is expected of you in your role as elector, worshipper, or lounge lizard. You probably (hopefully) behave quite differently in your roles as citizen, parishioner, or social animal. Each role imposes particular constraints on your actions, and each entails a set of rules that make your behaviour fairly predictable. Some of the roles are imposed without your consent, while others are negotiated with the people to whom you relate. The same is true for politicians, who (in all likelihood) behave rather differently with their friends and family than with voters. Often without realizing it, we expect politicians to perform according to a certain script to which we have become accustomed.

Political institutions provide the scripts for the actors who work within them. They define appropriate and inappropriate conduct for political behaviour and establish sanctions for inappropriate activities. Each political role is defined differently by its corresponding institution. For example, we expect the leader of a political party to defend his or her partisan position fiercely and to attack the ideas put forward by the other parties. But we would be appalled if the chief justice of the Supreme Court—whose role requires her to be as objective as possible—did the same. We expect the minister of finance to announce the details of the annual federal budget in the House of Commons, not in a bar in downtown Calgary or in a church in rural Nova Scotia. Some of these roles are defined in the written Constitution; others are informal and unwritten, and breaches are enforceable only in the political realm. As noted earlier, for example, the governor general has the right under the BNA Act to remove the prime minister and exercise executive authority directly. Governors general do not take advantage of this right, because the role of the Crown's representative has been greatly restricted by the growth of the democratic conventions in Canadian society.

Throughout this text we will pay particularly close attention to the various incentives, symbols, and structured roles within the Canadian political system as they are prescribed by the country's governing institutions.

CONCLUSION

The central theme of this book is that institutions shape political behaviour and values, and vice versa. As institutions evolve in response to changing social and cultural conditions, so do the incentives that these institutions create for the people involved with them. The challenge is to ensure that our political system adapts in positive ways, and that it continues to impose incentives that produce constructive behaviour among our politicians.

In formal terms, Canada's political institutions have changed relatively little since Confederation. The three branches of government are much as they were in the late nineteenth century, with the notable exception of the executive branch; its size and activities have expanded beyond anything that the Fathers of Confederation could have imagined. The constitutional division of powers between the federal and provincial governments, which was reasonably well suited to the conditions of 1867, is also intact. In practice, however, the division of policy-making duties between the two levels has mutated considerably over the decades. With the notable exception of the Constitution Act, 1982, Canadians have usually relied on nonconstitutional ways to change the rules of the political game.

Such ad hoc adaptations may no longer be adequate. The environment in which our political institutions operate has been transformed since 1867, and our institutions have not always kept pace. The population of Canada is larger and more diverse than ever. Its political attitudes and expectations—shaped by historical events and the mobilization of regional subcultures—are no longer compatible with many of the myths and symbols embodied in our institutions. Canadians again face a choice: try reforming our institutions (either through constitutional or nonconstitutional means) or make our existing politics and government work better. In either case, we will need a better-informed and more engaged public. It is hoped that this book will make a modest contribution toward achieving that goal.

DISCUSSION QUESTIONS

1. What is a political institution? List some of its defining characteristics. How might it differ from some other type of institution, such as a family or a private corporation?

2. How do political institutions shape the behaviour and attitudes of the individuals who participate in them? Give at least two original examples.

3. What are the principal features of Canada's political culture? How did they evolve?

4. What is Quebec nationalism and what is the likelihood of it continuing to be a factor in Canadian politics of the twenty-first century?

5. What is Western regional alienation and what is the likelihood of it continuing to be a factor in Canadian politics of the twenty-first century?

6. What are the primary characteristics of right wingers and left wingers, and where can you find examples of each?

7. What are the most important ideologies in Canada? Which, if any, do you subscribe to? Why?

8. Do you agree with the argument that political institutions shape the character of the people they govern? Why or why not?

SUGGESTED READINGS

Books and Articles

Aristotle, *The Politics* and *The Nicomachean Ethics,* various editions and translations.

David V. J. Bell, *The Roots of Disunity: A Study of Canadian Political Culture,* rev. edition (Toronto: Oxford University Press, 1992).

Harold D. Clarke, Allan Kornberg, and Peter Wearing, *A Polity on the Edge: Canada and the Politics of Fragmentation* (Peterborough, ON: Broadview Press, 2000).

D. C. Creighton, *Canada's First Century* (Toronto: Macmillan, 1970).

Robert A. Dahl, *A Preface to Democratic Theory* (Chicago: University of Chicago Press, 1956).

Anthony Downs, *An Economic Theory of Democracy* (New York: Harper, 1957).

David Elton and Roger Gibbins, "Western Alienation and Political Culture," in Richard Schultz, Orest M. Kruhlak, and John C. Terry, eds., *The Canadian Political Process* (Toronto: Holt, Rinehart and Winston of Canada, Ltd., 1979), 82–97.

C. E. S. Franks, *The Myths and Symbols of the Constitutional Debate in Canada* (Kingston, ON: Queen's University Institute of Intergovernmental Relations, 1993).

Roger Gibbins, *Regionalism: Territorial Politics in Canada and the United States* (Toronto: Butterworths, 1982).

Louis Hartz, *The Founding of New Societies* (New York: Harcourt, Brace, and World, 1964).

Gad Horowitz, "Conservatism, Liberalism and Socialism in Canada: An Interpretation" in Hugh G. Thorburn, ed., *Party Politics in Canada,* 5th edition (Scarborough, ON: Prentice-Hall Canada Inc., 1985), 41–59.

Seymour M. Lipset, *Revolution and Counterrevolution: Change and Persistence in Social Structures* (New York: Basic Books Inc., 1968).

John Meisel, Guy Rocher, and Arthur Silver, eds., *As I Recall/Si je me souviens bien: Historical Perspectives* (Montreal: Institute for Research on Public Policy, 1999).

John Stuart Mill, *On Liberty and Other Essays,* edited by John Gray (Oxford: Oxford University Press, 1991).

W. L. Morton, *The Kingdom of Canada* (Toronto: University of Toronto Press, 1970).

John Porter, *The Vertical Mosaic* (Toronto: University of Toronto Press, 1965).

Richard Simeon and David J. Elkins, "Regional Political Cultures in Canada," *Canadian Journal of Political Science* VII:3, September 1974, 397–437.

Nelson Wiseman, "The Pattern of Prairie Politics," in Hugh G. Thorburn, ed., *Party Politics in Canada,* 7th edition (Scarborough, ON: Prentice-Hall Canada, 1996).

Websites

The best places to start your Web search for any of the topics introduced in this chapter are the Nelson Web pages associated with this book and Canadian politics more generally. They can be located at www.parametersbrief.nelson.com and www.polisci.nelson.com.

NOTES

1. See Niels Veldhuis and Michael Walker, *Tax Facts 14* (Vancouver: The Fraser Institute, 2006).

2. Aristotle, *The Politics,* edited and translated by Ernest Barker (London: Oxford University Press, 1981).

3. Thomas Hobbes, *Leviathan* (Markham, ON: Penguin Books, 1968).

4. A good expression of Quebec nationalism can be found in the Quebec Government's 1995 Bill 1 and the Quebec National Assembly's 2003 unanimous resolution declaring Quebec a "nation." Each can be located on the Nelson Canadian political science Web pages at http://polisci.nelson.com/quebec.html.

5. See Faron Ellis, "An Angry, Wounded Province Flirts With Secession," in *Lougheed and the War with Ottawa, 1971–1984, Alberta in the 20th Century,* Vol. 11 (Edmonton: CanMedia Inc., 2003), 260–269.

6. See David V. J. Bell, *The Roots of Disunity: A Study of Canadian Political Culture,* rev. edition (Toronto: Oxford University Press, 1992).

7. See Colin Campbell and William Christian, *Parties, Leaders, and Ideologies in Canada* (Toronto: McGraw-Hill Ryerson, 1996).

8. Louis Hartz, "The Fragmentation of European Culture and Ideology," in Louis Hartz, ed., *The Founding of New Societies* (New York: Harcourt Brace, 1964).

9. Gad Horowitz, "Conservatism, Liberalism, and Socialism in Canada: An Interpretation," in *Canadian Labour in Politics* (Toronto: University of Toronto Press, 1968).

10. For a debate about the long-term prospects for Canadian conservatives that is based in part on the Hartz-Horowitz thesis, see Nelson Wiseman, "Going Nowhere: Conservatism and the Conservative Party," 57–69, and Faron Ellis, "Twenty-First Century Conservatives Can Succeed," 70–82, in Mark Charlton and Paul Barker, eds., *Crosscurrents: Contemporary Political Issues,* 5th edition (Toronto: Nelson, 2006).

11. See, for example, S. M. Lipset, *Revolution and Counterrevolution: Change and Persistence in Social Structures,* rev. edition (New Brunswick, NJ: Transaction Books, 1988 [1970]).

12. See Munroe Eagles, "Political Geography and the Study of Regionalism," in Lisa Young and Keith Archer, eds., *Regionalism and Party Politics in Canada.*

13. Russell J. Dalton, "Political Cleavages, Issues, and Electoral Change," in Lawrence LeDuc, Richard G. Niemi, and Pippa Norris, eds., *Comparing Democracies: Elections and Voting in Global Perspective* (Thousand Oaks, CA: Sage, 1996), Table 3.1, 325.

14. Neil Nevitte, *The Decline of Deference: Canadian Value Change in Cross-National Perspective* (Peterborough, ON: Broadview Press, 1996).

15. Statistics Canada, "Aboriginal Identity Population, 2001 Counts, for Canada, Provinces and Territories," accessed at www.statcan.gc.ca.

2 THE CONSTITUTION AS MASTER INSTITUTION

- *identify* and *explain* the major components of the Canadian Constitution
- *identify* and *explain* the various aspects of the British North America Act, 1867, and the Constitution Act, 1982, including the federal division of powers, the Charter of Rights and Freedoms, and the amending formula
- *identify* and *explain* the historical development of the Canadian Constitution

INTRODUCTION

A country's constitution is the master institution which sets the institutional ground rules for government and politics. It establishes other political institutions and determines their relationships with each other and with the people. It is the supreme law of the country. The British North America Act (BNA Act), 1867, Canada's founding Constitution, was primarily a set of rules outlining the relationship between governments and other institutions. By establishing a constitution "similar in Principle to that of the United Kingdom," the BNA Act generally left it to Parliament, the provincial governments, and the courts to determine how these relationships would apply to the governing of Canadian society within the context of the British common-law tradition. Since the adoption of the Constitution Act, 1982, with its entrenched Charter of Rights and Freedoms, Canadian citizens now have much more say in how these relationships are applied and how far governments can go in exercising their authority over the population.

After an introductory discussion of the general principles of constitutional law, this chapter will proceed with a basic description of the most important elements of the Canadian Constitution and the institutions it establishes. Each of these institutions will be explored in greater detail in the chapters that follow. The chapter concludes with a discussion of the most important developments in Canadian constitutional history. The Canadian Constitution is not a single document. Rather, the supreme law of the land includes several written documents, a series of written laws and judicial rulings, and a number of unwritten rules of political conduct. Getting to know these general categories is an important start to understanding Canada's master institution.

The *written* Constitution includes

- entrenched constitutional laws
- nonentrenched laws
- common law (judicial rulings and interpretations)

The *unwritten* Constitution is made up of

- constitutional conventions that guide the behaviour of politicians and voters

This body of constitutional law governs three primary relationships in Canadian politics and society:

- the balance among the various branches of government (i.e., legislature, executive, and judiciary),
- the division of powers and responsibilities among the national (federal) government and the provincial governments, and
- the relationship between the state and the people.

ENTRENCHED CONSTITUTIONAL LAW

The written Constitution overrides all other laws and is binding on all political actors, including citizens. Unlike ordinary statute laws, which are designed to change as new policies are proposed and new governments elected, constitutional laws are designed to remain in force for decades, or even centuries, and are therefore intentionally designed to be difficult to change or amend. Entrenched laws are contained in the written Constitution. The two principal documents are the 1867 and 1982 Constitution Acts (see the Appendix). The Constitution Act, 1867 (or BNA Act) established the new Dominion of Canada. It defined the powers of the national political institutions and divided jurisdiction over policy-making between the federal and provincial governments. However, it said very little about the relationship between citizens and the state. Individual rights were omitted and their protection was tacitly left to Parliament and the British common law (in Quebec, the civil law). The Constitution Act, 1982, defined individual and group rights by entrenching a Charter of Rights and Freedoms into the written Constitution. It also provided a formal amending formula for the first time.

■ The Constitution Act, 1867 — British North America Act

The British North America Act represents the founding constitutional document for Canada. It is divided into 11 parts containing a total of 147 sections and 6 schedules. Important among these are Parts III and IV, which establish executive and legislative powers, and Part VI, which defines the federal division of powers between the national government in Ottawa and the provincial governments.

The Union and the Crown

The preamble to the BNA Act, 1867, expresses the desire of the three confederating colonies—Canada, Nova Scotia, and New Brunswick—"to be federally united into One Dominion under the Crown of the United Kingdom of Great Britain and Ireland." After dispensing with some preliminary references to the Crown in Part I, the BNA Act addresses the initial structure of the Union in Part II. After dividing the colony of Canada into the two provinces of Ontario and Quebec, all the colonial territorial boundaries were kept in place. Provisions were also made for an inaugural Census of the Population and for decennial censuses thereafter.

Executive Powers

The preamble to the BNA Act also states that the new Constitution will be "similar in Principle to that of the United Kingdom," thereby establishing British-style parliamentary institutions, including the principle of parliamentary supremacy, or sovereignty, whereby parliaments are within their rights to enact laws in all areas of citizens' lives and all aspects of society, without being subject to the authority of another subconstitutional institution. Part III invests executive power with the Crown's representative in Canada, the governor general, who is also commander-in-chief of the military. The powers of the Crown are limited, however, in that the governor general shall act only "by and with the Advice of the Queen's Privy Council for Canada." That is to say, although the Crown is the formal head of state for Canada, its powers are constitutionally limited in that it will make decisions only when directed to do so by its political advisors. By constitutional convention, the prime minister and Cabinet, neither of which are referred to by formal title in the BNA Act, provide that advice. Part III also establishes Ottawa as the capital of Canada. Executive power and its relationship to legislative powers will be discussed in greater detail in Chapter 6.

Legislative Powers

Part IV establishes legislative power by creating one bicameral Parliament for Canada consisting of the Crown, an upper house, and a lower house. The Senate is discussed first, including the number of members it will have, the division of members into four equal regions (and the provincial subdivisions thereafter), the qualifications for membership and appointment, length of term in office, and a series of operational procedures. The composition and authority of the House of Commons is addressed next. The number of Commons members (MPs) is established by dividing the country into a series of electoral districts which contain roughly equal populations (representation by population), with each electing one representative. The roles and method of selecting a Speaker are outlined, as are some procedural rules and provisions for adjusting the number of MPs. Importantly, the Commons is granted superiority over the Senate with respect to the raising and spending of tax revenue, as will be discussed further in Chapter 6.

Provincial Constitutions

Provincial constitutions are established in Part V, including provisions for a lieutenant governor and an executive and legislative branch for each province, and some rules for membership in and election to the legislative assemblies. The final section of Part V states that many of the constitutional provisions set out for the Parliament of Canada, such as provisions relating to tax bills, money votes, and assent to bills, shall also apply to the provinces. We can extend that point further by saying that most of the formal political processes that are used at the national level are replicated, with some variation, in the provinces. Noteworthy differences include the lack of an upper house in any of the provinces and experiments with different electoral and referenda systems in some provinces. But for the most part, the principles and procedures used at the national level are also used in the provinces.

Federalism

All Canadian know a great deal more about the federal division of powers than they give themselves credit for. Our knowledge stems primarily from the fact that we "live federalism" on a daily basis, even if we don't use the terms found in Sections 91 and 92 of the BNA Act to describe our activities. Canadians instinctively know that the national government is responsible for coinage, currency, interest rates, and the money supply, because we know that we use Canadian "loonies," not Ontario or Newfoundland "bucks." Most of us understand that the Bank of Canada sets one interest rate, which determines how much our mortgages and credit card debts cost us. We understand that there is no Bank of Saskatchewan or Bank of Quebec establishing different interest rates for the various provinces. We know that we have a Canadian military, not an Alberta military, and that we send parcels through Canada Post, not Manitoba Post. We know that our driver's licences are issued by the provinces and that we can legally drink beer in Alberta and Quebec when we turn 18, but have to wait until we are 19 to legally "tip a few" in Ontario or British Columbia. Although the jurisdictional divisions are blurred by such things as shared-cost programs in health and education, issues that will be explained in the next chapter, reflecting on which order of government is regulating or otherwise impacting your day-to-day activities is one of the best ways to remember the federal division of powers.

Part VI of the BNA Act defines the division of powers between the national and provincial governments. In establishing a federal system of government for Canada, the framers of the Canadian Constitution intended the national (federal) government to dominate, with the provinces being assigned independent but subordinate powers.

Section 91 of the BNA Act enumerates the powers of the national Parliament and entrusts it to make laws for the "peace, order and good government" (POGG) of Canada in all matters not exclusively assigned to the provinces. This provision effectively gives to Ottawa what are known as the "residual powers." As their name implies, residual powers include any areas of jurisdiction that are not otherwise accounted for in the specified distribution of powers.

Section 91 continues by listing 29 specific federal government powers which include virtually all of the powers considered to be important for economic management in 1867. These include a general economic residual power over trade and commerce, as well as the authority to raise money by any mode or system of taxation and to borrow money on the public credit. They include authority over navigation and shipping, currency, banking, bills of exchange and promissory notes, interest, legal tender, bankruptcy and insolvency, patents of invention and discovery, and copyrights. The federal government is given power over the postal service, the census, statistics, and weights and measures. Other important areas of federal jurisdiction include Indians and land reserved for Indians, making the structure and governance of Indian reserves a matter to be determined by the federal Parliament and thus leaving Indian reserves with little independent constitutional status of their own (outside of the treaty rights that were recognized in 1982). The national Parliament is also given exclusive authority over criminal law and the authority to establish penitentiaries. Power over unemployment insurance was added to the list of federal powers in 1940, while authority over old age pensions was added in 1964.

Section 91 closes with a "deeming clause" designed to ensure that none of the federal government's enumerated powers could later be deemed to be subordinate to the provincial powers listed in Section 92. Furthermore, the federal government is given powers of reservation and disallowance of provincial legislation. Reservation is the process of having the lieutenant governor of a particular province, who is a federal government appointee, declare that provincial legislation will not take effect unless approved by the national government. Disallowance simply means that the federal government has the power to disallow a piece of provincial legislation, even if it falls within enumerated provincial jurisdiction.

One further important federal power with centralizing implications, the so-called spending power, is not mentioned anywhere in the Constitution, but has been implied from a number of explicit provisions. This power is related to the unequal division of financial resources between the two orders of government. By allowing Ottawa to spend its excess revenues on programs outside its areas of jurisdiction, the spending power is the basis of the well-established practice of "fiscal federalism," including the system of equalization grants through which Ottawa redistributes wealth from the richer "have" provinces (currently only Alberta and Ontario) to the eight poorer "have-not" provinces. The spending power also allows Ottawa to establish shared-cost programs, which provide part of the funding for provincial programs. These programs may come with strings attached, requiring provinces to adapt their programs to standards set by Ottawa. Such conditional grants permit Ottawa to influence policy-making in areas of exclusive provincial jurisdiction such as health and education.

When combined, the provisions of Section 91 establish a constitutional framework designed to centralize power in the national Parliament. This was certainly Macdonald's view, in that he understood the national Parliament to be similarly sovereign over the provinces as was the imperial Parliament still sovereign over

CANADA BY THE NUMBERS 2.1 Federal Division of Powers: Constitution Act, 1867, and Constitution Act, 1982

FEDERAL POWERS SECTION 91	PROVINCIAL POWERS SECTION 92	SECTION 92A	SECTION 93	CONCURRENT POWERS SECTION 95
peace, order, and good government	matters of local or private nature	nonrenewable natural resources, forestry and electrical energy rights	education	agriculture and immigration
trade and commerce	property and civil rights			
unlimited taxation	direct taxation			
military	health care			
money, currency, interest, banks, legal tender	welfare and social services			
bankruptcy, patents, copyrights	management and sale of public lands			
Indians and reserves	municipal institutions			
criminal law and penitentiaries	administration of justice, including federal justice			
marriage and divorce	solemnization of marriage			
unemployment insurance	saloon, tavern and other licences (including driver's licences)			
postal service, census, statistics, weights and measures	local works and undertakings			
shipping, navigation, sea coasts				
residual powers				

Canada. Yet if Canada were to be a federation with some division of sovereignty, the provinces would need to be given at least a limited amount of authority.[1]

Section 92 of the BNA Act establishes provincial areas of jurisdiction. These powers are restricted to what in 1867 were thought to be matters of a "merely local or private nature." Included are hospitals, charities, what we would today call social services and welfare, alcohol licensing, and the establishment of provincial prisons. The provinces are also given authority over the establishment of municipal institutions, making the boundaries and governmental structures of our municipalities a matter to be determined solely by the provincial governments and leaving local governments with no independent constitutional status of their own. The provinces also have authority over the management and sale of public land, including the timber on public lands. Section 92 intends to severely restrict the provinces' revenue-generating capacities by limiting their taxation powers to the imposition of direct taxes only. Although the interpretation of what constitutes a direct tax has been expanded over the years, as has the use of direct taxes such as the income tax, this clause was initially designed to ensure, among other things, that the provinces would be dependent on the federal government for subsidies, and would therefore require de facto federal government approval of any grand provincial initiatives.

Clearly, authority over property and civil rights is the most important area of jurisdiction granted to the provinces. But in 1867, it was assumed that property and civil rights would include aspects of citizens' lives that were for the most part private, and therefore would not attract much government attention. It was further assumed that authority over property and civil rights, in and of itself, would not significantly detract from the BNA Act's centralizing tendencies. However, as we shall see in Chapter 3, once the courts began settling jurisdictional disputes, they tended to place a much greater importance on this provincial power than did the original framers.

Other intentionally centralizing features of the BNA Act also creep into Section 92. Although this section deals with areas of exclusive provincial jurisdiction, it includes a declaratory power that gives Ottawa control over a number of "local works" that would normally fall under provincial authority. For example, any local works that extend beyond the provincial boundary, or connect one province to another or to a foreign territory are made federal jurisdiction. So too are any works that the federal government declares to be for the "general advantage" of the country or for the advantage of two or more provinces, even if those works are wholly situated within a particular province. Similarly, although the provinces are given exclusive jurisdiction over education in Section 93, if provinces infringe on denominational rights, affected groups may appeal to the federal government, which is authorized to step in and enact remedial legislation.

Two policy areas, agriculture and immigration, are explicitly assigned as concurrent jurisdictions in Section 95, meaning both orders of government are allowed to legislate in these areas. In situations where provincial and federal legislation conflict, the principle of federal paramountcy dictates that Ottawa's legislation will prevail. The historical development of this aspect of the Canadian Constitution will be discussed further in Chapter 3.

The Judiciary

Centralism is also reflected in the organization of the judicial system as set out in Part VII of the BNA Act. Whereas many federal systems divide judicial power so as to give each order of government its own courts, to interpret and apply its own laws, Canada's judicial structure is much more integrated. The judges of the most important provincial courts hear cases under both federal and provincial laws. Furthermore, the same final Court of Appeal ultimately resolves interpretive disputes arising under both sets of law: the Judicial Committee of the Privy Council (JCPC) until 1949, and the Supreme Court of Canada since then. The federal government appoints judges to the highest provincial Courts of Appeal as well as all federal courts, including Supreme Court justices. Parliament is also responsible for establishing the salaries, allowances, and pensions for all judges over which it has power of appointment. The role of the courts in interpreting the Constitution will be discussed in more detail in Chapter 3. The larger roles played by the courts in settling disputes between citizens, and between citizens and their governments, will be explored in more detail in Chapter 8.

Centralization and Parliamentary Sovereignty

The original allocation of responsibilities between the two sovereign orders of government in Canada suggests a level of centralization that allows us to legitimately question whether Canada was really intended to be a federal system at all, at least if we define federalism as divided sovereignty between two orders of government, each deriving its powers from a constitution rather than from another government, and neither of which is therefore subordinate to the other. In 1867 federalism was still very much a contested principle and the BNA Act reflects considerable indecision and ambiguity about how dedicated the new country would be to establishing a truly federal system.

Over time, however, federalism established itself as a central constitutional principle. Furthermore, as the historical review in Chapter 3 will demonstrate, Canadian federalism developed from a very centralized model to one of the world's most decentralized. Initially, judicial interpretation of the BNA Act served to narrow the scope of many federal powers while expanding provincial authority. Then, as provincial institutions became more established, Ottawa's powers of reservation and disallowance and the declaratory power fell into disuse. Finally, the dramatic expansion in the scope of government activities in the second half of the twentieth century occurred almost exclusively in areas of provincial jurisdiction such as health, education, and social services, thereby increasing the importance of provincial powers in relation to the powers of Parliament.

On the surface, federalism appears to clash with the British principle of parliamentary supremacy, so much so that many early detractors questioned how, if two constitutionally sovereign orders of parliamentary government exist, either one can be truly supreme? Although federalism placed some limits on parliamentary supremacy, it did not completely displace the principle. In fact, federalism itself places no substantive limits on what governments, at some level, may do. Until 1982, it was largely true that the two orders of government in Canada, taken together, were supreme in the sense that there were few substantive areas of citizens' lives in which one or the other, or both in combination, could not enact legislation. In short, the BNA Act had effected a more or less exhaustive distribution of the powers of government between Ottawa and the provinces. What could not legally be done by one order of government could legally be done by the other. The combined parliaments of Canada remained largely supreme, even if neither order by itself was fully sovereign.

All of this changed in 1982.

■ The Constitution Act, 1982

The Constitution Act, 1982, was the result of a series of political and legal events that led to Canada's Constitution being patriated, or brought home, from the United Kingdom. It contains seven parts, the most significant of which are the Canadian Charter of Right and Freedoms contained in Part I, Rights of the Aboriginal Peoples of Canada in Part II, equalization in Part III, and the amending formula in Part V (see the Appendix). By adopting the Constitution Act, 1982, Canada formally ended its constitutional association with the United Kingdom, inasmuch as the governments of Canada now have the opportunity to change the Constitution on their own, without those changes having to be enacted by the Parliament at Westminster. By entrenching a Charter into the written Constitution, the Constitution Act, 1982, also fundamentally changed the relationship between the Canadian people and their governments. No longer would Canadian governments be supreme to write legislation, at will, in all areas of Canadians' lives. For the first time, citizens could challenge legislation in the courts based on the argument that *no* government could legislate in a particular manner. Although citizen rights are not absolute, and can be reasonably limited by governments, the Charter fundamentally changed the dynamics of Canadian politics and the relationship between citizens and their governments.

The Charter of Rights and Freedoms

The Charter consists of the first 34 sections of the Constitution Act, 1982, and is divided into 12 categories of rights and freedoms and their application to the political and legal institutions. The Charter's short preamble acknowledges only the "supremacy of God" and the "rule of law" as Canada's founding principles. It then lists certain individual and group rights and freedoms that cannot be unreasonably restricted by any level of government in Canada.

The Charter begins by stating that Canadians are guaranteed certain rights and freedoms that no government can violate, but also that rights and freedoms are not absolute. In fact, Section 1 states that Canadian's rights and freedoms are subject to "reasonable limits" if the limits can be "demonstrably justified in a free and democratic society." This has been interpreted to mean that a two-stage process of reasoning is required to determine what constitutes a Charter violation. First, a court must determine whether a law infringes a Charter right; if so, the court must then consider whether the contravention can nonetheless be justified as a reasonable limit. For example, Canadians enjoy the right to free expression. If this were to be taken absolutely, any restrictions on speech would violate a citizen's right to free expression. However, the enacting of laws that restrict citizens' ability to advocate hate or violence against identifiable groups is determined to be a reasonable limit on the right to free expression. On the other hand, life imprisonment as punishment for writing a critical letter to the editor about your MP would likely not pass such a two-stage, reasonable limits test.

Section 2 of the Charter enumerates Canadians' fundamental freedoms. These cover many of what we would consider to be the *liberal* elements of the Canadian political culture and include freedom of conscience and religion and freedom of thought,

CANADA BY THE NUMBERS 2.2 Charter of Rights and Freedoms

CATEGORY	SECTION	ITEMS
Guarantee of Rights and Freedoms	1	reasonable limits as can be justified in free and democratic society
Fundamental Freedoms	2	conscience, religion, thought, belief, opinion, expression, press, peaceful assembly, and association
Democratic Rights	3–5	right to vote, five-year maximum duration of legislative bodies
Mobility Rights	6	right to enter, remain in, and leave Canada, move to other province
Legal Rights	7–14	life, liberty, and security of person, no unreasonable search and seizure, no arbitrary detention, habeas corpus, fair and timely trials, no cruel and unusual treatment or punishment
Equality Rights	15	individual and group equality without discrimination based on race, national or ethnic origin, colour, religion, sex, age, or mental or physical disability
Official Languages of Canada	16–22	English and French rights in Parliament, federal institutions, and New Brunswick
Minority Language Education Rights	23	right to have children educated in language of parents
Enforcement	24	apply to courts for remedy when rights infringed
General	25–31	recognition of Aboriginal rights, gender equality, and other rights
Application	32–33	applies to all governments, notwithstanding clause
Citation	34	Canadian Charter of Rights and Freedoms

belief, opinion, and expression, including freedom of the press and other media. Also included are several key *pluralist* elements including freedom of peaceful assembly and freedom of association.

Sections 3 to 5 enshrine Canadians' democratic rights. Note that in Section 3, voting rights are intentionally reserved for citizens and are restricted to the right to vote for members of the House of Commons and of provincial legislatures, but not for the Canadian Senate, municipal governments, or Aboriginal governments. Section 4 limits the maximum duration of any House of Commons or provincial legislature to no more than five years. This is an important clause in that it ensures Canadians will get the chance to reaffirm or remove from office their governments on a regular basis. As will be discussed below, it is also very important because it ensures a democratic check on governments that choose to use the Section 33 notwithstanding clause to enact laws they know will violate citizens' rights.

Section 6 of the Charter guarantees citizens' mobility rights such as the right to enter, remain in, or leave the country. It also ensures that citizens and permanent residents can move from province to province and gain a livelihood in their province of choice. Provinces can, however, enact laws that require reasonable residency requirements as qualification for receiving publicly provided social services and laws that favour existing residents of a province if the rate of employment in that province is below the Canadian average.

Sections 7 through 14 enshrine Canadians' legal rights. Many of these rights have been part of the British common-law system of jurisprudence for generations, with some dating back to Magna Carta. Included in the list are the rights to life, liberty, and security of the person, although these rights may be deprived if they are done so in accordance with the principles of fundamental justice. Canadians have the right to be secure against unreasonable search and seizure, to not be arbitrarily detained, upon arrest to be informed of the reasons and to retain legal council, and the right of habeas corpus. Canadians have the right to be informed without unreasonable delay of the specific offence for which they are being held or charged, to be tried within a reasonable time, to be presumed innocent until proven guilty, and to have a trial by jury, among others. Canadians also have the right to not be subjected to any cruel and unusual treatment or punishment.

Section 15 of the Charter guarantees individual and group equality rights. Section 15 (1) states that all individuals enjoy equal rights "before and under the law," including equal "protection and benefit" of the law without discrimination. It goes further to enumerate a list of specific individual characteristics upon which governments cannot discriminate when making laws. These include race, national or ethnic origin, colour, religion, sex, age, and mental or physical disability. But the language used in Section 15 indicates that this is not an exhaustive list. By using the terminology "and, in particular," rather than "exclusively," prior to the list of prohibited characteristics, the Charter allows for new items to be added. Recent additions have included sexual orientation and marital status. Because this subsection is substantiated by the Section 26 assurances that the enumeration of specific rights does not deny the existence of other rights, courts enjoy considerable interpretative latitude in adding new categories to the list of prohibited grounds for discrimination. Section 15 (2) extends equality protection to groups, and specifically exempts affirmative action programs aimed at ameliorating conditions of disadvantage from being challenged on the basis that they may violate the individual equality rights enumerated in subsection 1. Judicial interpretation of the Charter, including the tension between individual and group rights, will be discussed further in Chapter 8.

Sections 16 through 22 of the Charter protect Canadians' official language rights. They formalize English and French as the official languages of Canada and of the province of New Brunswick, making it Canada's only officially bilingual province. Canadians are entitled to use either of the two official languages in all institutions of Parliament, the government of Canada, and the federal courts.

Section 23 specifically enumerates minority language educational rights, including the right to have children receive public education in their parents' language, in areas where the numbers of minority French or English students warrant.

Section 24 deals with enforcement and allows anyone whose rights or freedoms may have been infringed or denied to apply to the courts to obtain remedy. It empowers the courts to determine remedy based on what it considers appropriate and just under the specific circumstances of the case. It also empowers the courts to exclude any evidence obtained in a manner that violates rights and freedoms, if admission of that evidence would bring the administration of justice into disrepute.

Sections 25 through 31 enumerate some important general features of the Charter including a guarantee that the Charter does not abrogate existing or future Aboriginal treaties and land-claim agreements, including rights and freedoms recognized by the Royal Proclamation of 1763; that enumerated Charter rights cannot be construed as denying the existence of other rights and freedoms; and that Charter interpretation will be consistent with the preservation and enhancement of Canada's multicultural heritage.

Sections 32 and 33 determine the application of the Charter and include the much-debated Section 33 notwithstanding clause. Section 32 states that the Charter applies to the governments of Canada, not to citizens and organizations acting in private matters. It also includes a three-year delayed application of Section 15 equality rights, which allowed governments time to revisit existing legislation that may have violated these newly enumerated rights.

The Section 33 notwithstanding clause was included to address the Charter's shift away from the British principle of parliamentary supremacy and toward the American principle of entrenched constitutional law. Prior to the Charter, Canadian governments were constrained mainly by the jurisdictional limits imposed by the federal division of power. Governments now, however, face substantive constraints on their freedom to write legislation even within their respective areas of exclusive jurisdiction. At the time the Charter was adopted, many of the provinces saw it as an unwarranted intrusion on their traditional jurisdictional sovereignty, and opposed it as a nationalizing and centralizing invention of a hostile federal government. All of the provinces except Quebec eventually agreed to accept a Charter, but only if it included an escape hatch of sorts. The result was the Section 33 notwithstanding clause, and although it grew out of provincial resistance to the Charter, both the provinces and the federal government can use its provisions.

Section 33 allows governments to enact legislation notwithstanding the fact that it will violate a Charter right or freedom. However, Section 33 only allows governments to violate some rights, but not others. It allows governments to make laws that violate any Section 2 fundamental freedoms, any Section 7 through 14 legal rights, and any Section 15 equality rights. The suspension of these rights is temporary in that any legislation that relies on the notwithstanding clause to override rights or freedoms must be renewed every five years. This is an important provision when we consider which rights *cannot* be suspended under Section 33. Notice that the Section 3 through 5 democratic rights, Section 6 mobility rights, and Section 16 through 23 language rights are not included and therefore cannot be overridden by using the notwithstanding clause. Most important among these is the prohibition against overriding democratic rights. When the five-year renewal provisions of Section 33 are combined with the Section 4 democratic right limiting governments to a maximum five-year term in office, Canadians are assured of having at least one opportunity to pass judgment on a government that overrides their rights before that government has the opportunity to reenact the legislation. In effect, Section 33 allows governments to claw back some of their sovereignty, but assures that Canadian voters will make the final determination about whether or not they agree with the suspension of their Charter rights.

Rights of Aboriginal Peoples and Equalization

Part II of the Constitution Act, 1982, enshrines existing Aboriginal and treaty rights, including those of Indian, Inuit, and Métis peoples. Part III deals with equalization and regional disparities by committing the federal and provincial governments to promoting equal opportunities for well-being, to economic development to reduce disparity, and to providing essential public services of reasonable quality. In addition, Part III requires the federal government to provide equalization payments to provincial governments so that they have sufficient revenues to provide reasonably comparable levels of public services at reasonably comparable levels of taxation. Part IV dealt with constitutional conferences to address Aboriginal issues but has since been repealed.

Amending Formula

Entrenched constitutions are enduring, foundational documents, establishing institutions which are intended to last for generations, if not centuries. Written constitutions are therefore intentionally designed to be difficult to change and typically can be altered only by special procedures. The BNA Act, 1867, adhered to these principles by not containing a comprehensive amending formula. Although it was the foundational master institution for the country of Canada, it was ordinary British legislation, passed by the Parliament at Westminster. Therefore, until 1982, only the British Parliament had the formal power to amend it. Canadian politicians of the late twentieth century changed all that when they devised and agreed on a comprehensive set of amending procedures, which are spelled out in Part V of the Constitution Act, 1982.

Sections 38 through 40 set out the general amending formula. Section 38 states that, unless otherwise specified, amendments to the Canadian Constitution must be ratified by resolutions of both houses of the federal Parliament and the legislatures of at least two-thirds of the provinces (currently, seven out of ten) together containing at least 50 percent of the population. The Section 38 rule is known as the seven-fifty rule. Formally, this means that the federal government is the only government with veto power. Although no single province can veto a constitutional amendment, any four provinces together can stop an amendment even if it is supported by the other six provinces and the federal government. Other combinations of provinces can also scuttle amendments supported by the majority of provinces and Ottawa. For example, because Ontario and Quebec have a combined population of greater than 50 percent of the total, those two provinces together have a combined veto, as does the combination of British Columbia, Alberta, and Ontario. Furthermore, if a province objects to an amendment, it may formally reject it, ensuring that the amendment will not apply to that province.

Section 39 subjects the seven-fifty rule to a three-year time limit in that once the first legislature approves the amendment, the seven-fifty rule must be satisfied within three years or the amendment dies unratified. Finally, an amendment that transfers powers over education or culture to the federal Parliament must be accompanied by an offer of financial compensation to any province that rejects it. A special list of matters subject to the general amending formula is given in Section 42.

Section 41 lists the subjects that can be amended only with the unanimous approval of all the provincial legislatures and the federal Parliament. The unanimity rule applies to the powers of the Crown, the composition of the Supreme Court, the two official languages, and the amending formula itself. In other words, changing the rules of how to change the Constitution requires the agreement of all of Canada's constitutionally recognized governments.

Section 43 permits a constitutional amendment affecting one or more provinces, but not all of them, with the consent of the provincial legislature(s) concerned and the federal Parliament.

Sections 44 and 45 give the federal and provincial governments the right to amend their own constitutions. Section 46 allows a legislature that has already ratified a proposed amendment to rescind its consent before the amendment takes effect. Finally, Section 47 limits the power of the Senate to a suspensory veto. In other words, the upper house of the federal Parliament can delay a constitutional amendment but cannot defeat it outright.

The Canadian people are noticeably absent from any mention in the amending processes and procedures. There exists no provision for referenda or other means of direct ratification by voters. Despite the inclusion of the Charter of Rights and Freedoms, and despite subsequent statutory provisions by some governments to give citizens some say in ratifying constitutional changes, the 1982 Constitution resembles the original 1867 document in that both are very much agreements between governments.

NONENTRENCHED CONSTITUTIONAL LAW

Canada's Constitution is not exhausted by its entrenched documents. Important parts are found in some laws that are considered to have semiconstitutional status, even though they are not formally entrenched. This body of law consists of statutes that regulate and apply the entrenched constitutional provisions, often by creating important state institutions of government. Examples include: the Supreme Court Act; the Canadian Bill of Rights; the Canada Elections Act; the Indian Act; and, more recently, the Constitutional Veto Act and the Clarity Act.

▪ The Supreme Court Act

The Supreme Court of Canada, obviously an important institution of the Canadian state, is not entrenched in the same manner as are the House of Commons or Senate. Instead,

Section 101 of the BNA Act enabled Parliament to "provide for the Constitution, Maintenance, and Organization of a General Court of Appeal for Canada." The Supreme Court was created in 1875 when Parliament passed ordinary legislation called the Supreme Court Act. Even still, for another 74 years the court remained subject to the overriding authority of the British high court, the Judicial Committee of the Privy Council (JCPC). As merely an intermediate appeal court between 1875 and 1949, the Supreme Court was not central to Canada's constitutional structure, thus not qualifying the Supreme Court Act as piece of constitutional legislation. After 1949, however, when the Supreme Court of Canada became the final court of appeal, the constitutional status of this institution was no longer in doubt. The Supreme Court Act, though an ordinary piece of legislation, subject to amendment or repeal through the normal legislative process, has since 1949 clearly become an important part of Canada's Constitution.

With the advent of the Charter in 1982, the Supreme Court's role as authoritative interpreter of the Constitution was dramatically expanded and its constitutional importance reaffirmed. Furthermore, Sections 41 (d) and 42 (d) of the Constitution Act, 1982, might be understood to confer entrenched status on the Supreme Court. Section 41 (d) subjects the "composition of the Supreme Court" to the unanimity provisions of the amending formula, while Section 42 (d) implies that other aspects of the Supreme Court are covered by the Section 38 seven-fifty formula. If the Supreme Court cannot be changed without resort to one of the amending formulas, it can be argued that the court now enjoys entrenched status. Yet the Supreme Court Act is not included in the schedule that lists the acts and orders that, together with the Constitution Act, 1982, compose the "Constitution of Canada." This somewhat ambiguous status means that much debate exists about whether or not the Supreme Court Act enjoys entrenched constitutional status. The consensus of interpretation seems to suggest that the court was not, in fact, entrenched in 1982, which means that the Supreme Court Act, an ordinary statute, is the document that continues to establish a central component of our constitutional structure.

Electoral Law

Electoral law and the electoral system itself enjoy similar quasi-constitutional status. Although no entrenched constitutional law explicitly prescribes how and in what form Canadian elections shall exist, the written Constitution does require elections for some federal and provincial institutions. Section 37 of the BNA Act states that there shall be elections for members of the House of Commons. Various sections of Part V of the BNA Act call for elections to provincial legislatures. Likewise, Section 3 of the Charter enshrines citizens' rights to elect members to those institutions. But while the entrenched Constitution enshrines democratic principles, it for the most part leaves the continually evolving implementation details up to governments. Parliament has therefore passed legislation such as the Canada Elections Act, the Electoral Boundaries Readjustment Act, and the regular amendments and adjust-ments to each, in order to establish the rules, procedures, and institutions that allow the entrenched constitutional law to be applied. How the electoral law is applied and its important effects on the establishment of party and electoral systems in Canada will be discussed further in Chapters 4 and 5, respectively.

The Bill of Rights

Another piece of nonentrenched constitutional legislation is the Canadian Bill of Rights, which was enacted by Parliament as ordinary legislation in 1960 and which, unlike the Charter, applies only to federal legislation. The Bill of Rights collects and expresses a number of common-law rights and freedoms that, although originating with the unwritten British Constitution, had been assumed to be part of the Canadian Constitution, given its mandated similarity "in principle" to the U.K. Constitution. This bill has remained in force even after the adoption of the Charter, although it is not often invoked in areas where the Charter substantially duplicates its provisions. The overlap between the Bill of Rights and the Charter is not complete, however, given that the former contains protections not found in the latter, such as property rights. Courts still occasionally use the extra provisions of the Bill of Rights when deciding civil liberties cases. The Supreme Court, Charter, and Bill of Rights will be discussed further in Chapter 8.

The Indian Act

When Section 91 (24) of the BNA Act entrenched authority over "Indians and Land Reserved for Indians" as an area of federal government responsibility, legislation was required to consolidate pre-Confederation Aboriginal laws and establish how the national government would exercise its Crown prerogatives in this area of its sovereign jurisdiction. The Canadian Parliament passed the Indian Act in 1876, and, although it has been subject to frequent legislative amendments, its basic features remained in place until 1985. At that time Parliament passed Bill C-31, legislation designed to bring the Indian Act into compliance with the Charter. Those amendments were designed to remove discrimination, restore status and membership rights, and expand Indian band control over membership and community life.

Constitutional Veto Act and Clarity Act

In the aftermath of the 1995 Quebec sovereignty referendum, which nearly thrust Canada into a secession crisis, the federal government decided to "lend" Quebec its veto over future constitutional changes that fall under the Section 38 seven-fifty amending formula. Parliament passed the Constitutional Veto Act in 1996, which states that federal government consent will not be granted to a constitutional change unless Quebec also agrees. To avoid the perception of special treatment for Quebec, Ottawa will similarly veto amendments not approved by any one of four other "regions": British Columbia, Ontario, the prairie West, and Atlantic Canada. Given that consent of the latter two regions is signified by the approval of two provinces with 50 percent of the region's population, Alberta, with a population exceeding half of the prairie total, also enjoys a lent veto. By giving four provinces veto power they do not enjoy as a matter of formal constitutional law, the Constitutional Veto Act, an ordinary piece of legislation, radically transforms the constitutionally entrenched amending formula. As such, this legislation clearly falls within the category of nonentrenched constitutional law.

When the Supreme Court ruled in the 1998 *Secession* reference that Quebec had no right to unilaterally secede from Canada, it went further by stating that any legal separation would require a negotiated constitutional amendment. But the court also ruled that if a province held a referendum based on a "clear" question, that produced a "clear" result in favour of secession, the rest of Canada had a constitutional obligation to negotiate the terms of secession with that province. The federal government responded in 2000 by passing the Clarity Act. It is designed to determine how, and under what circumstances, the federal government would negotiate with a province that had decided to separate from Canada. It gives the House of Commons the power to determine whether a provincial referendum question on secession is sufficiently clear about the province becoming an independent state, and whether the question provides a clear expression of the will of the population. It further specifies that the federal government would not accept a referendum question that focuses merely on negotiations, without expressly asking whether the province should cease to be part of the country. The federal government would also not accept as legitimate a question that obscured the secession question with statements about other possible economic or political arrangements. The Clarity Act states that the federal government would not enter into negotiations if the majority vote in favour of secession was too small or did not represent the entire electorate, although it does not specify exactly what is considered to be a "clear majority." Nevertheless, if a clear majority on a clear question were evident, the Clarity Act mandates the federal government to fulfill the Supreme Court's instructions to negotiate. It lists the subjects to be negotiated, including the borders of the province, the division of assets and liabilities, the rights and claims of Aboriginal peoples, and the protection of minority rights.

Each of the nonentrenched constitutional laws discussed here is a piece of ordinary federal legislation that may be amended or repealed by a simple majority of both Houses of Parliament. However, their subject matter is clearly within the constitutional realm in that they spell out the details of the general rules for those who operate our political system. Each is also subject to judicial interpretation and, as we saw with the Clarity Act, may be designed based on guidance from the courts.

JUDICIAL DECISIONS

The third element of written constitutional law is the common law, also called case law. This is the sum total of judicial interpretations of the Constitution. Entrenched constitutional law defines institutional power and duties in broad terms, which remain in force for many years. Because the people entrusted with writing constitutions cannot be expected to anticipate the future, they deliberately use vague and general language to cover all possible circumstances. And although the Canadian

Constitution is more specific than are many countries' constitutions, the precise meanings of many of its provisions are still left to judges, who must apply them to each unique situation. The process of authoritative constitutional interpretation is called judicial review.

The doctrine of judicial review is an American invention, based on an 1803 U.S. Supreme Court ruling that legitimized the courts' power to strike down laws that violate the Constitution.[2] The claim that a court can overrule an elected legislature is alien to the British tradition of parliamentary supremacy, which gives the legislative branch the final word on public policy. But in a federation that divides legislative power between two orders of government, some mechanism to settle disputes becomes a requirement of the system. Not coincidentally, before the proclamation of the Canadian Charter of Rights and Freedoms in 1982, judicial review in Canada was largely confined to sorting out division of powers disputes. Some of the most important cases will be discussed in Chapter 3. Since 1982, however, the courts have had the power to declare null and void any federal and provincial laws that infringe protected rights and freedoms. We will discuss judicial review of the Charter more fully later in this chapter as well as in Chapters 3 and 8.

CONSTITUTIONAL CONVENTIONS

We have seen that while entrenched constitutional law is supreme, it is most often written in broad terms, to permit its application over time and in changing circumstances. We have also seen that statute law is enacted to create institutions established by the Constitution and that the courts are called upon to make interpretive decisions of both statute law and the written Constitution. But this still does not provide a complete picture of the entire Canadian Constitution. Constitutional conventions, the unwritten elements of constitutional law, exist as another source of flexibility, to allow the Constitution to develop and change over time without the need for formal amendments.

Constitutional conventions are unwritten rules for political conduct based on custom and precedent. While a constitution must be stable and durable, it cannot be so rigid as to allow for no change or development. It must allow the political system that it establishes to have the ability to adapt to unforeseen circumstances. Over time, parts of a written constitution may fall into disuse. Others, which may have been appropriate when they were written, lose their moral force as the political culture changes. New conventions evolve and are added to the unwritten rules of political behaviour, even though they may directly contradict the entrenched constitutional law. While the courts cannot enforce conventions, they may be called upon to determine whether a particular convention exists and to provide guidance as to how it should be applied by governments. Conventions are unusually powerful in Canadian politics and, as the following examples indicate, change how our political system works to such an extent that it often bears little resemblance to what is written in the actual text of the Constitution acts.

Constitutional Monarchy

As it is written, the BNA Act gives the Crown, acting through the governor general, virtually unlimited executive power. Furthermore, the BNA Act states that the House of Commons meets only when the Crown desires, that it considers financial legislation which the Crown recommends, and that it can be dissolved and forced into an election whenever the Crown wants.[3] If one did not know how the system actually works, it would appear as though Canada were a dictatorship, ruled almost absolutely by an appointee of a distant monarch, and that the people and their representatives had little control.

The reality, of course, is very different. Canada is a constitutional monarchy in which the executive powers of the Crown are exercised by the prime minister and Cabinet. While, as a matter of law, they merely advise the Crown, in practice the governor general always defers to this political executive. Any attempt by a governor general to exercise executive power without the consent of Cabinet, and the House of Commons, would be an outrageous violation of democratic norms and constitutional conventions, even though it would be technically legal under the terms of the Constitution. The practices of democratic, responsible government in Canada, however, are inherited from the United Kingdom and, although not specified in the text of the BNA Act, they are enshrined in the preamble statement that Canada shall have "a Constitution similar in Principle to that of the United Kingdom." On that seemingly innocuous phrase rests not only the principle of constitutional monarchy, but also the entire structure of responsible government. This convention is so strongly embedded in the political culture that any governor general that tried to exercise the full range of the Crown's legal powers would likely succeed only in having those powers abolished and the conventions fully entrenched in the written Constitution.

Responsible Government

This prominent feature of the British or "Westminster" model of parliamentary government assures the integration of legislative and executive powers. Since the Cabinet, which exercises the Crown's executive powers, is drawn from the legislature, the political executive is in fact part of the legislature. It is, in a sense, the executive committee of the legislature. Furthermore, another important constitutional convention assures that any particular Cabinet continues to exercise the Crown's powers only so long as it retains the support, or "confidence," of a majority in the House of Commons.

By convention, a Cabinet that loses the confidence of the House of Commons must resign, and usually a new election is called. The leader of the party that wins the most seats in that election is then, by convention, called upon to form a new government. Any defeated Cabinet that refused to resign after a loss of confidence, or refused to step aside after an election loss, would be understood to be engaged in an act of revolution against the fundamental constitutional rules, even though it would not be violating the entrenched, written procedures. But what constitutes a loss of confidence is not always clear or agreed upon. Certainly when a government loses a vote designed as a motion of nonconfidence, or a vote on its budget or on other major legislation that it declares a matter of confidence, everyone typically agrees that the government must resign. At other times, the matter is not as clear.

For example, in 1968, Prime Minister Lester Pearson's Liberal government lost a vote because neither Pearson, who had announced his resignation and was on holidays, nor a number of Liberal MPs, who where campaigning for the Liberal leadership, were in the House to support the minority government. Pearson argued that the vote was more a mistake than a matter of confidence and the next day called for a formal vote of confidence, which his government won. The Progressive Conservatives acquiesced and a constitutional crisis was averted. Two months later, the new Liberal leader Pierre Trudeau called an election in which he won a majority. In other cases, there is no ambiguity. When Joe Clark's Progressive Conservative minority government lost a vote on its 1979 budget, everyone, including the prime minister, agreed it was a matter of confidence, thus triggering the 1980 election in which the Conservatives were defeated. More recently, when Paul Martin's minority Liberal government lost a formal opposition motion of nonconfidence late in 2005, after having refused to consider previous, less formal opposition motions as matters of confidence, the 2006 election was called and the Liberals were removed from office.

◼ Convention of Nonuse

Conventions often serve to ensure that anachronistic legal rules are operated in a manner consistent with current constitutional principles. Examples include the powers of reservation and disallowance affecting the relations between Britain and Canada and between Ottawa and the provinces, which fell into disuse over time as both international and domestic imperialism became unacceptable. Other centralizing features of the BNA Act, such as remedial legislation and the declaratory power, have suffered a similar fate. The convention of "nonuse" that has come to govern these powers reflects the changing practices of federalism and the expectations of provincial autonomy contained within Canada's regional political cultures. Other examples include senators' use of their formal powers to defeat House of Commons legislation. Although the Constitution provides the Senate with that power, citizens' expectations that the Senate will defer to the will of the democratically elected House of Commons are so engrained within the political culture that any attempt by senators to fully exercise their formal constitutional powers would likely be met by overwhelming support for the Senate's reform or outright abolishment. Although most conventions take time to get established and become accepted practice, they can be changed, almost immediately, if the political will exists to do so. Critics of the confidence convention cite the heightened levels of discipline it imposes on MPs as one of its disadvantages. Recently, all of Canada's major federal political parties have in one way or another supported some move toward allowing more free votes on matters that need not constitute confidence in the government. With this type of multiparty support, a determined prime minister could very quickly change how this convention is applied, as was done in the British Parliament in the 1980s.

Also, new conventions can emerge very quickly. After more than twenty years of constitutional wrangling by Canada's political elites, Canadians demanded that their governments grant them a final say on whether the country would adopt the Charlottetown Accord. By forcing their governments to grant them a ratification role that is not specified in the amending formula, the Canadian people may have instituted a new and powerful convention requiring citizen approval of any large-scale constitutional changes.

In summary, the Canadian Constitution consists of much more than the written documents known as the BNA Act and the Constitution Act, 1982. Although together these documents represent the core of constitutional law in Canada by prescribing the structure of the governing institutions, establishing the federal division of powers, and enshrining Canadians' fundamental rights and freedoms, by their natures they leave many aspects of constitutional law and practice undefined and allowed to evolve over time. Nonentrenched statute laws establish institutions, procedures, and mechanisms that put the Constitution into practice. The courts play an important role in interpreting and applying the Constitution to specific cases, while conventions, although not legally binding, often supersede the entrenched constitutional law in importance and practice. These are the major components of the Canadian Constitution and together they comprise the master institution of Canadian politics.

HISTORY OF CONSTITUTIONAL CHANGE IN CANADA

It is common to identify the birth of Canada as 1867, the year of Confederation. Constitutionally, however, this is somewhat misleading. The BNA Act of 1867 was certainly a constitutional watershed, but it was far from the beginning of Canada's constitutional development. Three colonies—Canada, Nova Scotia, and New Brunswick—joined together in 1867 to become the new Dominion of Canada (the colony of Canada was divided into the provinces of Ontario and Quebec as part of the Confederation agreement). Each of the formerly separate colonies, however, had a long constitutional history before 1867, and much of that history contributed to our current constitutional structure. The BNA Act, then, was far from a wholly new departure. It built on and incorporated many principles that were established in the pre-Confederation period. As new territories and provinces were added to the federation and functioning state institutions were established at the national and provincial levels, the Constitution evolved with the political culture. First, JCPC interpretation of the federal division of powers provided a much more decentralized application of the BNA Act than had been envisioned by its authors. Then, inspired primarily by the challenges brought about by Québécois nationalism and Western regionalism, Canada's political elites embarked on an extended period of repeated attempts at making wholesale changes to the entrenched constitutional law. Beginning in the early 1970s, Canadians witnessed four major attempts at rewriting the BNA Act (only one of which succeeded), two secession referenda in the province

THE CONSTITUTION AS MASTER INSTITUTION

1670	Royal Charter of the Hudson's Bay Company	Grants Company of Adventurers exclusive control of 4 million square km of land in Hudson's Bay drainage basin
1759–1760	Conquest	British defeat French on Plains of Abraham outside Quebec City and Montreal surrenders the following year
1763	Royal Proclamation	Provides for royal colonial government in colony of Quebec
1774	Quebec Act	Enshrines protection for French language, laws, and culture in British North America
1775–1783	American Revolution	Succeeds in creating a 13-state country independent from Britain on the North American continent
1785–1800	Loyalist influx	Thousands of United Empire Loyalists flee the newly created U.S.A. and settle in Nova Scotia and the western parts of Quebec
1791	Constitution Act	Breaks Quebec into two new colonies of Upper and Lower Canada
1836–1837	Rebellions	Demands for responsible government lead to violence in the Canadas and to Lord Durham's recommended solutions
1840	Act of Union	Reunites Upper and Lower Canada into the colony of Canada with two administrative divisions of Canada East and Canada West
1847–1848	Responsible government	Lord Grey grants legislative control of the executive
1860–65	U.S. Civil War	Temporarily stalls U.S. westward and northward territorial acquisitions and provides example of problems with a decentralized federation
1865–1867	Confederation debates	Canadians convince two Maritime colonies to join them in federal union with provisions for others to also join
1867	BNA Act	Establishes federal Constitution for new country with laws and institutions similar in principle to those of the United Kingdom
1868	Rupert's Land Act	Transfers Hudson's Bay territory to Canada
1869–1870	Riel and Manitoba Rebellion	Louis Riel leads Métis rebellion, establishing a provisional government in Manitoba
1871	BNA Act	Clarifies federal government's right to create new provinces
1875	Supreme Court Act	Creates a general but not final court of appeal
1885	Riel Saskatchewan Rebellion	Riel returns to lead Métis and Indian rebellion in Saskatchewan; Riel is captured, tried, and executed
1914–1918	WWI — POGG	Federal government temporarily suspends division of powers and assumes most constitutional authority by way of emergency powers clause

1926	Balfour Declaration	Recognizes colonial independence for self-governing British colonies
1929	*Persons* case	JCPC recognizes women as legal persons after Parliament and Canadian Supreme Court refuse
1930	Constitution Act — Western resources	Prairie provinces achieve full provincial status when natural resource rights for Alberta, Saskatchewan, and Manitoba are relinquished by the federal government
1931	Statute of Westminster	Formally recognizes Canadian independence in foreign affairs
1939–1945	WWII — POGG	Federal government temporarily suspends division of powers and assumes most constitutional authority by way of emergency powers clause
1946	Canadian Citizenship Act	First official legal designation of Canadian citizenship distinct from British citizenship
1949	Supreme Court	Supreme Court of Canada replaces the JCPC as the final court of appeal
1960	Bill of Rights	Federal government legislation protects many traditionally held common-law rights and freedoms
1970	FLQ — War Measures Act	Federal government imposes peacetime martial law by invoking the War Measures Act in response to FLQ terrorist activities in Quebec
1971	Victoria Charter	Proposed overhaul of the BNA Act, with amending formula, fails after being rejected by Quebec
1980	Quebec Referendum	Parti Québécois government loses first sovereignty association referendum by vote of 60% *no* to 40% *yes*
1982	Constitution Act — Charter	Patriates Constitution with inclusion of amending formula and Charter of Rights and Freedoms
1987–1990	Meech Lake Accord	Quebec round of constitutional reforms attempts to entrench Quebec's five minimum demands, but fails to meet requirements of amending formula
1992	Charlottetown Referendum	Canada round of constitutional reforms fails when it is rejected by voters in referendum, 54% *no* to 46% *yes*
1995	Quebec Referendum	Parti Québécois narrowly loses second sovereignty referendum by vote of 51% *no* to 49% *yes*
1996	Constitutional Veto Act	Federal government enacts legislation lending its constitutional veto to five regions
2000	Clarity Act	Identifies how and under what circumstances federal government will negotiate secession with provinces

of Quebec (neither of which succeeded), and one national referendum that brought this period of megaconstitutional politics to an end (if only temporarily).

Pre-Confederation Constitutional Development (1763–1867)

Reviewing the pre-Confederation constitutional history of the British North American colonies is important for understanding how the BNA Act was constructed. Although representative institutions existed first in the colony of Nova Scotia, developments in the united colony of Canada were particularly important. The BNA Act was this colony's fifth Constitution, not its first, and many of the provisions found in the original Constitution for the country of Canada can trace their development to this colony's struggles to deal with cultural and linguistic duality, while at the same time establishing representative institutions and responsible government.

The Royal Proclamation of 1763

The first British constitution for the former colony of New France was the Royal Proclamation, 1763, and the attendant instructions given to the colony's first governor. Although the Royal Proclamation was issued shortly after the 1763 Treaty of Paris formally ended the Seven Years' War between France and Britain, New France had in fact been under British military rule since Wolfe's defeat of Montcalm on the Plains of Abraham in 1759 and Montreal's capitulation in 1760. The Royal Proclamation replaced this temporary military administration with the first civilian constitution for the new British colony of Quebec.

While British settlers in the New World considered representative institutions their birthright, British imperial authorities thought it would be premature to force these "foreign" institutions on the French Catholic population of Quebec. Thus, although the Royal Proclamation promised representative institutions at some point in the future, it was assumed this would have to wait—at least until such time as British settlement and pubic policy had achieved the assimilation of the French population. In place of representative institutions, the Royal Proclamation conferred authority on an appointed governor who would be advised by an executive council from which Catholics were excluded.

The Quebec Act of 1774

By the 1770s, large-scale English settlement in the colony of Quebec had not yet occurred and seemed unlikely to materialize in the near future. In addition, the growing restiveness of the American colonies made it prudent to secure the loyalty of Quebeckers by abandoning assimilation as a constitutional strategy. To that end, the Quebec Act secured the "French fact" in Canada. Along with allowing the French language to survive in North America, it strengthened the protection of religious freedoms for Catholics, and guaranteed the future use of French civil law to govern private relationships, although British law would apply in criminal matters. It also allowed a quasi-feudal system of landholding to continue, although not indefinitely.

The Quebec Act did not, however, grant representative institutions. The imperial authorities concluded that the highly traditional, hierarchical French society they were protecting neither needed nor wanted representative democracy. Undoubtedly, the clergy and seigneurs, two important elements of colonial Quebec society that the authorities were trying to placate, were not well disposed to that level of democratic reform. Hence, the implementation of representative government was again put off until after the American Revolution dramatically changed the colony of Quebec.

The Constitution Act of 1791

Once the American Revolutionary War ended, a large number of United Empire Loyalists, having supported the losing side, fled the new republic for refuge in British territory. Although they were colonists, the Loyalists had long been accustomed to having representative institutions deal with their local affairs. They added their voices to Quebec's existing English inhabitants in demanding an elected assembly. By 1791, Britain was prepared to accede to their demands but the problem of linguistic and cultural heterogeneity influenced its institutional calculations. It was assumed that representative institutions could not effectively serve a community that was so thoroughly divided along cultural and linguistic lines because it opened up the possibility of one group tyrannizing the other. The dilemma made the establishment of a single representative assembly for the entire colony impossible.

A solution was found, however, in the general geographic distribution of the populations of the two cultures. Given that most of the English population, largely Loyalist settlers, was concentrated in the western part of the colony, and the French population remained largely in the eastern part of the Saint Lawrence Valley, dividing the colony in two seemed to provide a logical solution. Representative institutions could be established without abandoning the policy of accommodating the French. Both of the new colonies, English Upper Canada to the west of the Ottawa River and French Lower Canada to the east, could be given their own assemblies.

The Constitution Act, 1791, established a two-chambered, or bicameral, legislature for each. But the British imperial authorities continued to appoint the executive in the form of a governor for each colony who may or may not respect the wishes of the people's representatives. Furthermore, the governor could not be removed from office by the legislature. In other words, although representative institutions were put in place, responsible government would have to wait for further constitutional developments.

The 1840 Act of Union

By the early nineteenth century, responsible government had been firmly established in Britain but, for a number of reasons, the imperial government was still resisting the establishment of this institution in the colonies. The relationship between the mother country and the colony was at the heart of the recalcitrance. Because a colony by definition is not completely self-governing, it must, to some degree, be subject to imperial control. A colony that achieves full self-government ceases by that very fact to be a

THE CONSTITUTION AS MASTER INSTITUTION

POLITICAL BIOGRAPHY 2.1 John A. Macdonald

Sir John Alexander Macdonald was instrumental in creating Canada, including how the BNA Act was structured, in the territorial expansion to the Pacific, and in establishing the country's political and economic institutions. His picture adorns the Canadian $10 bill. (Pittaway & Jarvis/ Library and Archives Canada /C-000686)

Born: 1815, Glasgow, Scotland (emigrated to Canada in 1820)

Died: 1891, Ottawa

Education: Midland District Grammar School and John Cruickshank School, Kingston (Upper Canada)

Profession: Lawyer (called to the Bar of Upper Canada in 1836), Businessman

Political Career:

MP
1867–1878, 1887–1891 elected MP for Kingston, Ontario
1878–1882 elected MP for Victoria, British Columbia
1882–1887 elected MP for Carleton, Ontario

Leader
1867–1891 Conservative Party

Prime Minister
1867–1873, 1878–1891

Other Ministries
1856–1862 Joint Premier, Province of Canada
1847–1867 Various ministries, Province of Canada
1867–1873 Justice and Attorney General, Canada
1878–1883 Interior, Canada
1878–1887 Superintendant General of Indian Affairs, Canada
1889–1891 Railways and Canals, Canada

Political Career Highlights
1864–1865 Coleader, Great Coalition
1867 Father of Confederation, British North America Act
1867 Elected prime minister with a majority
1869 Purchase of Rupert's Land
1870 Red River Rebellion
1870 Manitoba enters Confederation as province
1871–1885 Building of Canadian Pacific Railway
1871 British Columbia enters Confederation as province
1873 Prince Edward Island enters Confederation as province
1873 North-West Mounted Police created
1873 Pacific Scandal brings down government
1873–1878 Leader of the Opposition
1878 Elected prime minister with a majority
1879 National Policy, including renewal of Canadian Pacific Railway (CPR) initiative, establishment of an industrial economy through tariff protection from U.S.

colony. And a colony whose government becomes completely responsible to its own locally elected assembly is self-governing. In any conflict between imperial and local priorities, a governor who is obliged to heed the advice of a Cabinet enjoying the confidence of the majority in the assembly is left with little choice but to defer to the assembly rather than to the imperial authority. Thus, as long as imperial control was considered important, responsible government was resisted. Further complications included colonial sources of income from Crown lands, duties, licences, and fines, which remained under the control of the executive rather than the legislature.

The inevitable result was conflict between the elected assemblies, which were entitled to discuss public policy but had little power to implement their wishes, and the executive, which exercised real power. The executive consisted of the imperially appointed governor and a council of advisors typically selected from the social and economic elite. Representatives of opposing social strata tended to dominate the assemblies. In Upper Canada the ruling elite was known as the Family Compact. In Lower Canada it was called the Château Clique. The predictable tension between the branches of government thus came to reflect, and was embittered by, social conflict between different segments of society. In Lower Canada the clash was intensified by the fact that the ruling elite was largely English, while the French majority controlled the assembly. The situation resulted in a classic example of competing interests lining up behind different institutions within the overall constitutional structure and struggling to make their respective institutions dominant.

By the 1830s, the constitutional conflicts in both Canadas instigated loud demands for responsible government, culminating in the rebellions of 1837–1838. In response, Britain appointed Lord Durham as governor for all of British North America except Newfoundland, mandating him with assessing the causes of the constitutional ills and preparing a solution. When Durham discovered "two nations warring in the bosom of a single state," he proposed a twofold solution. He recommended responsible government for all the colonies, but proposed the reunification of the two Canadas. He believed that competition for the executive within a united legislature would lead to cross-national coalitions, moderating conflict between the two cultural groups and preparing the colony for what Durham considered to be the ultimate solution: assimilation of the French into the more vigorous and enterprising English culture.[4]

Durham's union proposal was implemented almost immediately by the 1840 Act of Union, which reunited the two Canadas but continued to divide them administratively into Canada East and Canada West. Each was given equal representation in a single elected assembly even though the population of predominantly French-speaking Canada East (717 000) was much larger than that of predominantly English-speaking Canada West (432 000). To prevent the French population from dominating, a provision known as the double majority principle required majority approval from both of the administration divisions to pass most legislation. The official language of legislative debate was English, but French was recognized as early as 1842. Although Durham also recommended responsible government, it was not implemented until Lord Grey fulfilled the commitment in 1847–1848.

Responsible government only intensified the political dysfunctionality of an increasingly unworkable governing situation. Cultural and economic divisions that were once manageable became the focal point for bitter debates which frequently brought down governments and left the legislature deadlocked. Cooperation and accommodation were rare in a legislative structure that saw 18 different ministries come and go over the mere quarter-century of the Constitution's duration. The untenable political stalemate eventually led to the proposal by the Macdonald–Cartier–Brown Great Coalition to create a larger federal union with the Maritime colonies.

In 1864, the Nova Scotia assembly was leading a Maritime unity movement and had scheduled a meeting at Charlottetown to discuss proposals. Macdonald, having secured an invitation for a Canadian delegation, immediately persuaded the conference to abandon discussion of a Maritime union in favour of debate on the Canadian unity proposals. Meeting again a month later in Quebec City, delegates agreed to the basis for Confederation in what became know as the Quebec Resolutions. Once the legislatures of Nova Scotia, New Brunswick, and Canada adopted the resolutions, delegates met in London with the British government to draft the proposals into the legislation we know as the British North America Act of 1867.

▪ Post-Confederation Constitutional Developments (1867–1982)

Almost as soon as Confederation took root, its rules for the conduct of government came under challenge. Some provinces, particularly Ontario and Quebec, claimed that the division of powers in Sections 91 and 92 of the BNA Act imposed too many restrictions on their revenues and policies. As more provinces joined the federation, their divergent perspectives on government and society produced more calls for reform. Beginning with the first Premiers' Conference in 1886, provincial governments demanded formal amendments to the Constitution. Without an amending formula, the degree of provincial consent required quickly emerged as a stumbling block that would remain until the 1982 patriation agreement entrenched a formal amending process.

The British North America Act, 1867

Unanswered questions about the required amount of provincial consent did not prevent some formal amendments to the BNA Act from being made. Almost immediately after Confederation, the BNA Act was amended to clarify the federal government's right to establish new provinces and to alter the boundaries of existing provinces, with the agreement of the affected provinces. Other examples include the 1940 agreement to transfer responsibility for unemployment insurance to the federal government, with the resulting amendment enshrined as clause (2a) of Section 91. The federal government was also granted control over old age pensions via amendments passed in 1951 and 1964, which now appear as clause 94A. In all cases where the division of powers was amended, the federal government secured the unanimous agreement of the provinces before proceeding to the British Parliament, all the while refusing to formally acknowledge that unanimity was required.[5] Although altering the text of the BNA Act was hardly a routine procedure, it was clearly achievable.

But most of the adjustments to our system of government, particularly the relationships among the senior governments, have occurred without formally amending the Constitution. Many began as incremental, short-term solutions to immediate practical problems, and then persisted for decades by the force of institutional and political inertia.[6] They include the federal spending power in provincial jurisdictions, executive federalism, and the complex structure of intergovernmental relations, all of which are discussed in Chapter 3.

Undoubtedly, the most significant changes to the federal system of government in Canada came about not because the BNA Act was amended, but because of how the JCPC interpreted it. The British high court took a very different view of the division of powers than did Macdonald. When asked to pass judgment on whether an area of government activity was properly a matter of federal government jurisdiction, possibly under its powers over trade and commerce, POGG, reservation, or disallowance, or whether the activity was properly a matter of provincial jurisdiction, possibly under their powers of property and civil rights, the JCPC was much more likely to rule in favour of provincial jurisdiction. In fact, it dramatically rebalanced the federation away from its quasi-federal centralization toward a more classical federation of equal orders of government. The JCPC was also instrumental in changing how Canadian governments approached the legal status of half the Canadian population. In the famous *Persons* case of 1929, the JCPC overruled both Parliament and Supreme Court of Canada by declaring that women were legally persons and as such qualified for legal protection under the law. Much more will be discussed about the JCPC's decisions and the other developments in Canadian federalism in Chapter 3.

The Statute of Westminster

Even though this piece of British legislation explicitly states that it does not alter the BNA Act, it did have important implications for federal government powers. Following the 1926 Balfour Declaration's acknowledgement that the self-governing members of the British Commonwealth, including Canada, were autonomous and not subordinate to the United Kingdom, the British Parliament passed the *Statute of Westminster*. It removed the last of British imperial authority over the Dominions. The statute ensured that the U.K. could no longer make ordinary laws for any of the former colonies, unless asked to do so, nor could the U.K. nullify laws made by these countries. Furthermore, the British Parliament would no longer act for these countries in international affaires. From that point on, Canada would manage its own foreign affairs, and have the power to independently enter into international treaties, including declaring war and peace.

Victoria Charter

By the early 1970s, the mobilization of Quebec nationalism into an aggressive separatist movement challenged the entire constitutional system of government in Canada. Shortly after the radical Front de Libération du Québec (FLQ) separatists had been suppressed via the imposition of martial law, the federal government convened a constitutional conference in Victoria in an attempt to address Quebec's legitimate constitutional concerns. The resulting Victoria Charter contained many of the rights and freedoms now found in the Charter, including official language rights. It also included provisions to allow for the provinces to participate in Supreme Court appointments, and guarantees that three justices from Quebec would be assigned to the court.

Most importantly, the Victoria Charter would have patriated the BNA Act and included an amending formula. While every province would not be granted a veto over major constitutional change, as had been suggested by the failed Fulton–Favreau formula of 1965, both Ontario and Quebec were granted vetoes by virtue of their populations. Major constitutional changes affecting all provinces would also require at least two Western provinces which together had 50 percent of the total population, and at least two Atlantic provinces.

The Victoria Charter failed to get adopted as constitutional law when Quebec premier Robert Bourassa, who had initially agreed on the proposal while meeting in Victoria, later refused to ratify it. His decision was based in part on the federal government's refusal to provide financial compensation for provinces that opted out of amendments transferring powers to Ottawa. It was also based on the strong opposition that the Victoria Charter encountered in Quebec because of the view that the province did not receive full recognition of its demands.

Patriation

René Lévesque's 1976 Parti Québécois (PQ) election victory brought to power Quebec's first separatist government. It also provoked intense concern outside the province and inspired dozens of proposals for institutional reform. In 1978, Prime Minister Pierre Trudeau introduced Bill C-60 as another attempt at a constitutional renewal solution. The bill contained a charter, an amending formula, and important reforms to some national political institutions. One of the proposals was the replacement of the Senate with a House of the Provinces, which would comprise delegations from the provincial governments. The bill encountered fierce opposition, including a constitutional challenge in the courts, and it died when the House of Commons was dissolved for the 1979 election. When Joe Clark's Progressive Conservatives formed a minority government, Trudeau announced his retirement from politics and the constitutional issue was placed on the back burner. But the Clark government was short-lived, lasting only nine months after it lost the confidence of the House upon defeat of its first budget. Trudeau shelved his retirement plans and led the Liberals to a majority victory in the 1980 election, just three months prior to the Parti Québécois government holding its sovereignty association referendum. Trudeau campaigned vigorously on behalf of the No forces, promising to renew the federation by way of constitutional change that would accommodate the new realities of Québécois nationalism. When Quebeckers voted 60 percent against secession, the stage was set for another round of formal constitutional negotiations.

The Constitution Act, 1982

Trudeau's vague promises to Quebeckers led many to believe that he had promised to devolve powers to the provinces. Indeed, when federal and provincial officials met to set the agenda for constitutional discussions, the reallocation of powers was included as a priority item. Trudeau had also previously proposed reforms to the Senate and the Supreme Court, an entrenched Charter of Rights, and an amending formula based on the regions. But the political situation had changed dramatically since he made those particular commitments. By the time the First Ministers' Conference (FMC) convened in September 1980, Trudeau had been reelected with a majority, the PQ government had lost the referendum, and the separatists were facing a tough election battle within a year. Trudeau revoked the concessions he had made to the provinces in Bill C-60, and reimposed his preferred centralist view of Confederation.[7] Many Quebeckers felt that Trudeau had broken his promise of constitutional renewal. That sense of betrayal, coupled with the renewed conflict between Quebec nationalism and the equal-provinces vision of Confederation being promoted by Western premiers, particularly Alberta, doomed the September 1980 FMC to failure.

Shortly thereafter, Trudeau decided to proceed with his constitutional project unilaterally. That is, he would proceed without the consent of any of the provinces. He argued that unanimous provincial consent was not legally required, even when altering the division of powers. Because it was not entrenched, the principle of unanimous provincial consent lacked the status of constitutional law. If it existed at all, the unanimity rule was a constitutional convention, and conventions were unenforceable. Legally, according to this view, Ottawa was entitled to unilaterally transmit requests for amendment to Britain, and that is precisely what it proposed to do. The federal package would not address all the matters that had been on the constitutional agenda, only those that Trudeau considered essential: patriation; the Victoria Charter amending formula, plus the option of a national referendum to override the provincial governments; and the entrenchment of a Charter of Rights. The referendum proposal was the clearest indication of Trudeau's strategy to undermine the premiers' opposition by going over their heads directly to the Canadian electorate. Although two provinces, Ontario and New Brunswick, supported Ottawa's initiative, the other eight, led by Alberta and Quebec, mounted vigorous opposition.

The so-called "Gang of Eight" provinces challenged Ottawa's unilateralism in the courts. They argued that (1) the convention of provincial consent existed and (2) it was legally binding. The dissident premiers signed an accord on April 16, 1981, setting out their counterproposals to the Trudeau package. They demanded, among other things, an amending formula based on provinces and not on regions. They insisted that any future changes to the division of powers require the consent of at least seven provincial legislatures representing at least 50 percent of the national population (the seven-fifty rule). They also wanted assurances that up to three provinces could opt out of amendments, making them not applicable within those provincial borders. This "Alberta formula" was eventually adopted as the 1982 amending formula and reflected the "governments' constitution," in contrast to the "citizens' constitution" found in Trudeau's Charter and referendum proposal. Having lost the sovereignty association referendum, Lévesque's PQ government felt compelled to participate in the process, but as the price of its signature to the accord it demanded full financial compensation for any province that opted out of amendments transferring provincial powers to Ottawa. The Gang of Eight also proposed a very limited Charter of Rights, whose weak guarantees echoed the 1960 Bill of Rights.

Under pressure from opposition parties in the House of Commons, Trudeau agreed to postpone any unilateral action pending a court ruling on its legality. Three of the dissenting provinces—Quebec, Manitoba, and Newfoundland—had solicited reference opinions from their own Courts of Appeal, all of which declared Trudeau's unilateral approach to be unconstitutional. The federal government appealed these rulings to the Supreme Court. The central issue in what became known as the Patriation Reference was, in the absence of a written amending formula: what were the constitutional conventions governing constitutional amendments? Specifically, did a constitutional convention exist that required either unanimous or substantial provincial consent to an amendment altering the division of powers between Ottawa and the provinces? In September 1981 the Supreme Court ruled that while Ottawa was legally entitled to proceed unilaterally, its package would be unconstitutional in political terms unless it received "substantial" provincial consent. The majority of the justices ruled that while such an amendment would be constitutional in law—without an amending formula, there were no written rules to be broken—it would violate an important constitutional convention. This ruling essentially upheld the decisions of the three provincial Courts of Appeal by providing an extended discussion of constitutional conventions, including the statement that "the main purpose of constitutional conventions is to ensure that the legal framework of the Constitution will be operated in accordance with the prevailing constitutional values or principles of the period." Substantial provincial consent constituted one of those principles.

The Supreme Court's ruling sent the 11 senior governments back to the constitutional bargaining table. In November 1981, most of them succeeded in hammering out a package that became the basis of the Constitution Act, 1982. Both sides made considerable compromises, beginning with a series of tradeoffs over the issues of parliamentary supremacy and entrenched rights. Parliamentary supremacy implies that governments shall be reasonably unfettered when making laws so long as they stay within their own areas of jurisdiction. Entrenched rights place constraints on governments, even when they are acting within their legitimate areas of jurisdiction. They also give the Supreme Court the power to enforce rights by striking down laws that violate those rights. The provinces reluctantly accepted the Charter in exchange for the Section 33 notwithstanding clause power to override some of its provisions. The premiers hoped to use this concession to parliamentary supremacy as a means to protect their jurisdictions against the Charter's nationalizing standards. The federal government reluctantly accepted Section 33 in order to get agreement on the Charter, correctly believing that as Charter rights became more fully ensconced in the Canadian political culture, public identification with those rights would make it difficult for provinces to frequently use the notwithstanding clause override. By accepting a stronger version of the Charter than it would have preferred, the Gang of Eight also achieved agreement on its preferred amending formula, minus Quebec's key demand of compensation for opting out in most cases.

Although Trudeau's referendum proposal was scrapped, it played a crucial role in the November 1981 negotiations. When the first ministers reached a deadlock, Trudeau suggested that it be broken by submitting the two contending packages to a national vote. Lévesque endorsed that suggestion, thus alienating the other seven dissenting premiers and destroying the Gang of Eight's unity. With the common front shattered, the other seven premiers were free to make a deal with Ottawa. The dealmaker was Ottawa's decision to accept both the notwithstanding clause and the seven-fifty amending formula. The Western provinces also secured a new Section 92A that guaranteed the provinces a new measure of control over the exploitation of their nonrenewable natural resources, something that had particular appeal to Alberta premier Peter Lougheed whose government was engaged in a bitter constitutional battle with the federal government over Trudeau's National Energy Program. In what became known in Quebec as the "night of long knives," the federal government and all the provinces except Quebec hammered out a deal in an overnight negotiating session to which the Quebec delegation had not been invited. They presented the deal to a clearly unnerved Lévesque prior to the next morning's resumption of discussions. Even though the outraged Quebec government refused to accept the deal, in November 1981 the federal government and nine provinces signed an accord that led to the 1982 patriation of the Canadian Constitution with an entrenched Charter and amending formula.

The sovereigntist Quebec government refused to recognize the deal. Lévesque reasoned that the package neglected his province's decentralizing demands while implementing Trudeau's centralizing agenda. His government appealed to the Supreme Court to strike down the Constitution Act, 1982, based on the argument that to proclaim an amendment without Quebec's consent would violate two constitutional conventions. The first was the convention of unanimous provincial consent to amendments that altered the division of powers. In its 1982 Quebec Veto Reference, the court upheld its previous reference case ruling that no unanimity convention existed. The second was the convention based on Quebec nationalists' claim that Confederation was a deal between two founding nations, English and French. Because Quebec is the homeland of the French nation in Canada, nationalists in that province claim the right to veto any proposed change to national institutions. The Supreme Court justices also dismissed this argument, ruling that there was no historical evidence to support the alleged convention of Quebec's special status. As such, Quebec's claim to a unilateral veto was declared to be unfounded in both law and convention.

Despite Quebec's continued opposition, the federal government asked Britain to enact the deal, resulting in the new Constitution Act coming into force on April 17, 1982. Although patriation represented the triumph of Trudeau's vision of Canada—a strong central government representing a national community of equal citizens—it did not end megaconstitutional political debate. The Quebec nationalist myth of two nations, which had provoked recurring constitutional crises since 1960, was not reflected in the 1982 reforms, and therefore remained an unresolved irritant. Indeed, given that both the Charter and the new amending formula constitute a forceful denial of the two-nations theory, Quebec governments have continued to deny the legitimacy of the 1982 Constitution Act and to demand further constitutional changes to protect the province's distinct society. Similarly, while the Charter was a nationalizing response to Western regionalism, it did not address a key Western demand of devolving more powers to the provincial governments. The continuing strength of both Quebec nationalism and Western regionalism would provoke subsequent rounds of megaconstitutional negotiations.

Post-Patriation Attempts at Constitutional Reform

Bringing Quebec back into the Constitution would not be an easy process. Although the Quebec government has never formally approved the Constitution Act, 1982, its provisions apply as fully in that province as they do in the rest of Canada. Short of declaring that the Constitution would not apply in Quebec, a move tantamount to a unilateral declaration of independence, future Quebec governments would have to either live with the new Constitution or be prepared to agitate for further constitutional negotiations to satisfy Quebec's demands. In doing so they would discover that most Canadians outside of Quebec were generally content with the new Constitution and were looking forward to life without ongoing constitutional strife.

Ten days after the Supreme Court of Canada rejected Quebec's claim to a veto over the November 1981 deal, Quebec's National Assembly passed a resolution setting out the conditions for its acceptance of the new Constitution. To get Quebec onside, a new agreement would have to recognize the fundamental equality of two founding Canadian peoples. Furthermore, it would have to recognize that Quebec, by virtue of its language, culture, and institutions, forms a distinct society, with all the attributes of a distinct national community, within the Canadian federal system. Additionally, the amending formula would have to either maintain Quebec's right of veto or entitle Quebec to not be subject to amendments that diminish its powers. It would also have to ensure that Quebec's demand for reasonable and obligatory compensation be met. This resolution established Quebec's bargaining position for future negotiations, and succeeded in achieving its goals, at least inasmuch as both the Meech Lake and Charlottetown Accords would have given the Quebec government what it wanted. Unfortunately for Quebec, the two-nations vision had little appeal outside Quebec, where the equal-provinces vision dominated public perceptions of federalism. The distinct-society clause appeared in direct competition to the idea of a federation of equal provinces. In this respect, as in others, the constitutional aspirations of Quebec nationalism were directly opposed to those of the other nine provinces. This contradiction proved fatal to both accords.

The Quebec Round and the Meech Lake Accord

After the separatist Parti Québécois government was defeated in December 1985, the Liberal government of Premier Robert Bourassa set out five minimum conditions under which Quebec would agree to sign the Constitution Act, 1982. The five demands were as follows:
- constitutional recognition of Quebec's distinct society
- restoration of Quebec's constitutional veto
- greater control over immigration
- a role in selecting future senators and Supreme Court justices from the province (together with the entrenchment of the Supreme Court)
- restrictions on the federal spending power in areas of provincial jurisdiction

With relatively little acrimony, and after negotiations within which Progressive Conservative Prime Minister Brian Mulroney conceded not only to Quebec's demands, but also to many of the Western provinces' decentralization proposals, the Meech Lake Constitutional Accord was signed by the federal government and all 10 provinces. Although Meech Lake was designed to meet Quebec's five minimum demands, the accord was also shaped by the principle of provincial equality. Quebec's demands, apart from the distinct-society clause, were granted to all the other provinces on an equal basis. Thus, Quebec's demand for a say in Supreme Court appointments became a general right of provinces to submit lists of potential Supreme Court appointees, from which Ottawa would select the winning candidate. Similarly, Quebec's desire for a constitutional role in immigration policy became the right of all provincial governments to negotiate constitutionally entrenched agreements "relating to immigration." Quebec's proposal to restrict federal spending power gave rise to a general provincial right to opt out of national shared-cost programs with reasonable compensation from Ottawa. Finally, Quebec's demand for a veto over future constitutional amendments resulted in a proposal to expand the list of subjects that could be amended only with unanimous provincial consent, thus effectively extending a veto to every province. This strategy not only respected the equality of the provinces, it also ensured the other premiers' agreement with Quebec's demands because it guaranteed that every player won (with the possible exception of the federal government).

THE CONSTITUTION AS MASTER INSTITUTION

Had the accord been entrenched, it would have demonstrably, possibly radically, further decentralized powers from Ottawa to all of the provinces. But the Meech Lake Accord was left unratified when it failed to meet the requirements of the new amending formula. The reasons for its failure rest with the process by which it came into being and the reaction to that process by a citizenry that was increasingly less deferential to politicians, within an increasingly participatory Canadian political culture. Essentially, Meech was an attempt by proponents of the old governments' constitution approach to regain some of the ground they had lost in 1982. It reflected the governments' constitution not only in its content but also in the way it was formulated and presented to the public.[8] Politicians seemingly assumed that the 1982 amending procedures would be implemented in the old way. A deal would be negotiated by the first ministers, who would use their majority government powers to swiftly pass enabling legislation through their respective legislatures. Thus, the accord was worked out behind closed doors, by a small number of political elites, and presented to the public as an unalterable fait accompli. Problems with this approach arose almost immediately when some of the premiers who had signed the accord were removed from power before they could pass enabling legislation. Some of the politicians who replaced the departing premiers objected to some of the accord's main provisions. Several had campaigned on those objections and were under considerable public pressure to live up to their election promises after winning government.

Had all the original consenting governments been able to quickly pass enabling legislation, Meech Lake would have succeeded and become part of the Canadian Constitution. When that did not happen, the amending formula provisions that had been adopted in 1982 became central to the process. As we have seen, under Section 41 of the Constitution Act, 1982, certain elements of the Constitution can be amended only with the unanimous consent of the federal and provincial governments. Others fall under the Section 38 general formula requiring the consent of only Ottawa and seven provinces representing 50 percent of the Canadian population. The amendments contained in the Meech Lake Accord fell into both categories. For example, entrenching the right to opt out of shared-cost programs with financial compensation required meeting only the Section 38 seven-fifty formula. However, changing the amending formula to meet Quebec's demand for a veto and granting that same provision to all the provinces, thereby extending the unanimity provisions, required unanimous consent. Instead of dividing the accord into two packages corresponding to the two different amending formulas, it was presented as a "seamless web" that had to be passed as a whole or not at all. This meant simultaneously meeting the requirements of the unanimity and seven-fifty amending formulas. This may not have been as big a problem as it turned out to be had there been no deadline. However, it must be remembered that the general amending formula includes a three-year deadline for ratification. Having to meet both the general and the unanimity provisions meant that the accord had to be ratified by all 10 provincial legislatures and the federal Parliament within three years of the Quebec government passing its enabling legislation on June 23, 1987. Thus, opponents of Meech could sink the entire package by persuading even a single province to not ratify it before midnight, June 23, 1990.

The ratification process was delayed by legislative hearings in some provinces, and, while that was going on, the premiers of New Brunswick and Manitoba lost power before their legislatures had ratified the accord. A third, Newfoundland's Brian Peckford, passed the accord through his legislature before losing an election. However, the new premier, Liberal leader Clyde Wells, followed through on his election commitment to rescind Newfoundland's approval. These developments gave citizens' groups and politicians opposed to Meech the time they needed to mobilize public opinion against the accord. Although Meech was eventually ratified in New Brunswick after the adoption of a "parallel accord," it failed to pass in Newfoundland and Manitoba. After an intense, eleventh-hour marathon session of first ministers' negotiations, an amended Meech Lake Accord was presented to the recalcitrant provincial legislatures. In Manitoba, despite all the party leaders agreeing to suspend the normal legislative procedures to enable passage of the accord in the few hours that remained before the June 23 deadline, Aboriginal discontent with the Meech process sealed the accord's fate. Suspension of the normal legislative procedures requires unanimous consent of all members of a legislature. Elijah Harper, a prominent Aboriginal member of the Manitoba legislature, reflected Aboriginal peoples' discontent by repeatedly refusing to consent to expedite the procedures, leaving no time to ratify the accord before the deadline. Because the accord did not gain approval in Manitoba, Newfoundland's Wells refused to submit it to a final vote in the legislature of that province, and Meech Lake failed because it could not meet the twin requirements of the Canadian amending formulas.

The Canada Round and the Charlottetown Accord

When Meech died, the Quebec government refused to participate in any future constitutional negotiations as one province among ten equals. Instead, the province would pursue a two-nations strategy. Quebec would wait until the rest of Canada came up with its own constitutional proposal, and would then negotiate on a nation-to-nation basis. In the meantime, Quebec would undertake its own public consultations on the Constitution and develop its own positions. Given that all of Canada's politicians had learned some hard lessons about citizen unrest concerning the closed-door, elitist processes used to secure both the 1982 patriation agreement and Meech Lake, all of them would consult widely with Canadians when attempting to achieve a new agreement. Although most of the hard bargaining went on behind closed doors, the federal minister for Constitutional Affairs, former Prime Minister Joe Clark, worked diligently to keep the media and public informed. The first ministers were also joined at the negotiating table by teams from the territories and four national Aboriginal organizations. The resulting two-track consultation and negotiating processes—one track in Quebec and another in the rest of Canada (ROC)—began in the fall of 1990 and culminated with the announcement of the Charlottetown Accord in August 1992.

The Quebec track featured two sets of public consultation on future constitutional options: the constitutional committee of the provincial Liberal Party, chaired by Jean Allaire, and the Bélanger–Campeau Commission. The latter was a broad-based task force with members from all parties in the Quebec National Assembly as well as from the private sector. The Allaire Committee was more highly nationalistic and decentralist than the Bélanger–Campeau Commission, but both bodies proceeded on classic Quebec nationalist assumptions.

For its part, the federal government established the Citizens Forum on Canada's Future, chaired by Keith Spicer, and a joint constitutional amendment committee of the Senate and House of Commons, chaired by Gérald Beaudoin and Jim Edwards. The Spicer Commission found considerable discontent with the political process, particularly the secretive and unaccountable backroom deals of first ministers. The Beaudoin–Edwards Committee, which recommended that any future constitutional deal be submitted to the public in a referendum, shared concerns about the legitimacy of the recent constitutional processes. The Spicer Report also found that most Canadians outside Quebec preferred a strong central government, much to the dismay of both Quebec nationalists and many Western regionalists.

Matters were brought to a head in May 1991 when, in response to the Bélanger–Campeau recommendations, the Quebec legislature passed a law requiring a provincial referendum on either sovereignty or a new constitutional deal no later than October 28, 1992. The federal government responded in the fall of 1991 by releasing a new set of constitutional proposals it called "Shaping Canada's Future Together." While the federal proposals were primarily a response to Quebec's ultimatum, the fallout from Meech Lake determined much of their substance. Political leaders in the ROC sought to avoid the perception of a reform package determined almost exclusively by Quebec's concerns, emanating from private negotiations of first ministers and presented for legislative approval as a seamless and unalterable web. The outcome of the Canada round would have to reflect both the citizens' constitution and the governments' constitution, while satisfying populist demands for direct democracy and the equal-provinces vision that resonated so strongly outside of Quebec. Much in the package, particularly the Senate reform provisions, ultimately contradicted the Quebec nationalist agenda, even though the entire exercise had originated as a way to satisfy Quebec. Predictably, it failed to do so. Nevertheless, despite his reservations about the offer, Quebec premier Bourassa agreed to sign what became the Charlottetown Accord.

The Charlottetown Accord was a wide-ranging and complex set of proposed constitutional reforms that would have led to sweeping changes in the Canadian federal state. Its highlights include the following:

- a "Canada clause" expressing fundamental Canadian values intended to guide the courts in their interpretation of other parts of the formal Constitution, including both the federal division of powers and the Charter
- substantial reform of Parliament including an enlarged House of Commons (with at least 25 percent of its seats reserved in perpetuity for Quebec) and a smaller, elected Senate based on equal representation of the provinces
- a series of reforms relating to Aboriginal peoples, including constitutional recognition of an inherent right of self-government, recognition of Aboriginal governments as one of Canada's "three orders of government," and enhanced participation of Aboriginals in the central institutions of government

- some decentralization, including controls on the federal government's spending power, Ottawa's withdrawal from six areas of exclusive provincial jurisdiction, and provincial opting out of shared-cost programs, with compensation
- constitutional entrenchment of regular First Ministers' Conferences
- a constitutional commitment to respecting Canada's "social and economic union"
- a tightening of the constitutional amending procedures by subjecting more areas to the unanimity requirement
- a host of matters that would need legal interpretation to determine what they meant, as well as others that would be dealt with at the newly constitutionally enshrined First Ministers' Conferences

Despite the desire to be more inclusive of the citizenry and its developing culture of participation, the actual process of amendment would remain in the hands of politicians. This time, however, ratification would first be subject to being approved by voters in a national referendum. Because there is no provision for a referendum in the 1982 amending formula, results from the Charlottetown referendum would not be constitutionally binding, but they would certainly carry substantial political weight.

Given that Quebec was already committed to holding a referendum on sovereignty in October 1992, the provincial government simply changed the question. Instead of asking Quebeckers to approve sovereignty, they asked them to accept the Charlottetown Accord. In the post-Meech Lake populist fallout, British Columbia and Alberta had also committed themselves to consulting their populations through referenda. Ottawa had also passed legislation enabling a national referendum. The prospect of having three provinces' citizens receive a direct-democracy say on the fate of the accord, without other Canadians having a similar opportunity, was something the federal government could not abide. As such, the Mulroney government decided to hold a referendum in the ROC while Quebec arranged a separate referendum under its law. Both were held on October 26, 1992, and may have established a new constitutional convention requiring similar ratification for other megaconstitutional initiatives, should any occur. After a spirited national debate during the Charlottetown referendum campaign, one that saw the emerging influence of two new federal political parties achieve national stature by campaigning against the accord (the Western-based populist Reform Party and the separatist Bloc Québécois), the Charlottetown Accord was rejected by a majority of voters nationally, and in a majority of the provinces. All of the Western provinces rejected the accord, as did Nova Scotia and, significantly, Quebec. There were many reasons for voters' rejection of Charlottetown, but the bottom line was that too many Canadians, especially those who were searching for an end to protracted national unity squabbles over the Constitution, did not view Charlottetown as a final resolution. Rather, its many unresolved provisions and entrenchment of First Ministers' Conferences appeared to only further institutionalize constitutional bickering. When considering the specific provisions of how the accord would change the federation, outside Quebec it was perceived as giving Quebec too much while the concessions to the ROC, particularly the West, were seen as too weak. Within Quebec it was perceived as not giving that province enough, but as providing the West with too much. In short, the conflict between the two-nations vision of Canada and the equal-provinces principle was unresolved, and possibly remains irresolvable.

CONCLUSION

The Canadian Constitution is a complex mix of entrenched constitutional law, enabling statute law, judicial interpretation, and convention. Although the Constitution was only infrequently amended between 1867 and 1982, it continued to develop and adapt to changes in the political culture through minor amendments, the establishment of constitutional conventions, and judicial interpretation. The Constitution's main written provisions are contained in the British North America Act, 1867, and the Constitution Act, 1982. The former establishes a federal state and parliamentary government. The later includes an entrenched Charter of Rights and Freedoms that represents a direct challenge to the principles of parliamentary sovereignty. Since 1982, the Canadian Constitution also includes an amending formula that proved to be a major obstacle to implementing further megaconstitutional packages during the Meech Lake and Charlottetown processes. Nevertheless, the Canadian Constitution has demonstrated itself to be an amazingly adaptable master institution for a country that has undergone dramatic changes in its structure, politics, and political culture since first being established almost a century and a half ago.

DISCUSSION QUESTIONS

1. Were the original, centralizing intentions of the BNA Act more appropriate for Canada than the decentralizing aspects of later constitutional development? Why?
2. Is it better to try to have most of the important constitutional provisions written into the constitution or is convention a better way to approach constitutional development?
3. How much latitude should the courts be given in expanding the definition of rights in Canada?
4. Would it ever be possible to have another round of megaconstitutional reforms adopted in Canada? Is it likely?
5. Can the Canadian Constitution ever fully resolve the tension between the two-nations myth and the doctrine of provincial equality?
6. Should the provinces have more power? Should the federal government?

SUGGESTED READINGS

Books and Articles

Herman Bakvis and Grace Skogstad, eds., *Canadian Federalism: Performance, Effectiveness, and Legitimacy* (Toronto: Oxford University Press, 2002).

Keith Banting and Richard Simeon, *And No One Cheered: Federalism, Democracy and The Constitution Act* (Toronto: Methuen, 1983).

Alan C. Cairnes, *Disruptions: Constitutional Struggles, from the Charter to Meech Lake*, edited by Douglas E. Williams (Toronto: McClelland and Stewart Inc. 1991).

Roger Gibbins, editor with Howard Palmer, Brian Rusted, and David Taras, *Meech Lake and Canada, Perspectives from the West* (Edmonton: Academic Printing and Publishing, 1989).

James Ross Hurley, *Amending Canada's Constitution: History, Processes, Problems and Prospects* (Ottawa: Minister of Supply and Services Canada, 1996).

J. Peter Meekison, Hamish Telford, and Harvey Lazar, eds., *Reconsidering the Institutions of Canadian Federalism* (Montreal and Kingston: Institute of Intergovernmental Relations/McGill–Queen's University Press, 2004).

Peter H. Russell, *Constitutional Odyssey: Can Canadians Become a Sovereign People?*, 2nd edition (Toronto: University of Toronto Press, 1993).

Robert A. Young, *The Struggle for Quebec: From Referendum to Referendum?* (Montreal and Kingston: McGill–Queen's University Press, 1999).

Websites

The Nelson political Web pages, specifically those associated with the topics in this text, are a very good place to start your search for information on the Canadian Constitution. The federal government site and all of the provincial governments' sites have documents, histories, and in many cases interactive lessons about the Canadian Constitution and its application in and adaptation by each of the provinces.

A variety of college, university, and research institutes also provide valuable primary documents and useful summaries of the constitutional development in Canada.

NOTES

1. See Robert C. Vipond, "1787 and 1867: The Federal Principle and Canadian Confederation Reconsidered," *Canadian Journal of Political Science,* 22 (1989).
2. See *Marbury v. Madison,* 5 U.S. 137 (1803); available on-line at www.findlaw.com.
3. R. MacGregor Dawson, *The Government of Canada,* 5th edition, rev'd Norman Ward (Toronto: University of Toronto Press, 1970).
4. See Janet Ajzenstat, *The Political Thought of Lord Durham* (Kingston and Montreal: McGill-Queen's University Press, 1988).
5. James Ross Hurley, *Amending Canada's Constitution: History, Processes, Problems and Prospects* (Ottawa: Minister of Supply and Services Canada, 1996), 19–20.

6. See Jennifer Smith, "Informal Constitutional Development: Change by Other Means," in Herman Bakvis and Grace Skogstad, eds., *Canadian Federalism: Performance, Effectiveness, and Legitimacy* (Toronto: Oxford University Press, 2002),

7. See Roy Romanow, John Whyte, and Howard Leeson, *Canada Notwithstanding: The Making of the Constitution 1976–1982* (Toronto: Carswell/Methuen, 1984), 60–61

8. Alan C. Cairns, "Citizens (Outsiders) and Governments (Insiders) in Constitution-Making: The Case of Meech Lake," in Alan C. Cairns, *Disruptions: Constitutional Struggles, from the Charter to Meech Lake,* edited by Douglas E. Williams (Toronto: McClelland and Stewart, 1991).

3 CANADIAN FEDERALISM

LEARNING OBJECTIVES

- *identify* the concepts of independence and hierarchy as they are enshrined in the British North America Act, 1867
- *identify* the concepts of interdependence and parity as they developed in Canadian federalism
- *identify* the political culture that is the basis for Canadian federalism
- *identify* and *account for* the development of classical federalism in Canada by way of judicial review
- *explain* the factors that brought about and encourage fiscal federalism in Canada

INTRODUCTION

Federalism is a foundational element of the Canadian state. It intrudes into most aspects of Canadian political life and shapes a broad array of public policies. In fact, few aspects of political life in Canada are immune to the impact of federalism. However, despite federalism's pervasiveness, it is not necessarily well understood as a principle or in its application to political practices and institutions. This is partly because federalism is a dynamic aspect of Canadian politics rather than a fixed set of constitutional rules and institutional manifestations. Canada's federal features have changed dramatically over time, and not entirely in a consistent direction. It is important, therefore, to consider federalism in evolutionary terms, to understand its core principles, and to realize how deeply embedded it is in contemporary debates—not only about constitutional parameters, but also about the minutiae of public policy.

We will continue to define federalism as a system of divided sovereignty between two orders of government, each of which owes its powers to a constitution rather than to the other order of government, and neither of which is therefore subordinate to the other. As a federation, Canada has a formal constitutional division of powers in which fields of jurisdiction are prescribed to each order of government, within which it is supreme. The constitutional division of powers takes the form of a written contract between the national and provincial governments. Neither party can unilaterally alter this contract. Disputes arising over interpretation of this contract are referred to a neutral arbitrator, the Supreme Court of Canada.

All of the above formalities become somewhat blurry when we move from the conceptual terrain to political reality. The federal government's spending power, for example, introduces a good deal of fluidity into the constitutional division of powers, and opinions differ as to the Supreme Court's neutrality when it is asked to adjudicate disputes over the division of powers. But the principles are important, no matter how contested they may be or how imperfect might be their application.

Political scientists commonly treat federalism as the middle concept in a tripartite classification, the two poles being the unitary state and confederalism (see Figure 3.1). According to this usage, despite Canada being referred to as a confederation, it is actually a federation. A true confederation, in the modern sense, is a league of fully sovereign states that join together only for limited purposes, such as foreign policy, defence, or a common currency. A central authority administers these shared matters, but this authority does not govern individuals directly; its "citizens" are component states or polities, which retain full sovereignty over their "national" citizens. Having created the central authority, the component polities may also withdraw from it or disband it altogether. In sum, the central authority depends for its very existence on the states that created and sustain it. A unitary state, the other pole of the classification, is the mirror image of a confederation. Although there is usually some degree of devolution of governmental power to local authorities in a unitary state, typically to municipal or regional governments, sovereignty is invested in the central government. In a unitary state, local and regional governments are the creatures of, and can be reorganized or disbanded by, the central government. To summarize, in a confederation, the central government is a creature of the constituent governments; in a unitary state this relationship is reversed.

Unlike both confederal systems and unitary states, which have a single locus of sovereignty either at the centre or in the units, federalism is a system of divided sovereignty. Each order of government governs the same citizens, but for different purposes within defined areas of jurisdiction. Yet the expression of divided sovereignty found in the division of powers is only the beginning of the story. Federal systems of government also provide for the representation of subnational communities within the national governing institutions and, moreover, include a vast network of intergovernmental institutions through which the national, provincial, and territorial governments exchange influence and manage complex interdependencies.

Federalism is predicated on a respect for diversity. It assumes that a people choose federal institutions because they are attempting to accommodate the cultural

FIGURE 3.1 Canada and the Unitary, Federal, and Confederal Schematic

UNITARY	Quasi-Federal Centralized	FEDERAL Classical	Decentralized	CONFEDERAL
sovereignty at centre		divided sovereignty		sovereignty with units
Canada 1914–1918 (WWI) and 1939–1945 (WWII)	Canada 1867 ▶	Canada 1880 ▶ Canada 1920 ▶	Canada 2000	

differences that exist in an already federated society. As we will see, however, federalism itself may shape that society as much as be shaped by it. Federations establish governments that excel in protecting, nourishing, and promoting even greater political diversity in an already divided society.[1] But federalism does not simply divide a polity; rather, it promotes unity in the face of diversity because federal systems of government are designed to protect diversity while attempting to achieve unity. The resulting tension is an intrinsic feature of federal states, one that is managed but never resolved. As the following discussion will illustrate, the Canadian federal state has swung from one priority to the other, moving from a very centralized form of federalism to one of the world's most decentralized as it has striven to maintain the delicate balance between unity and diversity.[2]

CANADIAN FEDERALISM

It may be difficult to imagine Canada as having anything other than a federal system of divided sovereignty. But in 1867, modern federalism was still a new and rather ill-understood American invention. Canada was only the third modern state to adopt a federal system (after the United States and Switzerland), and the first to combine federalism with parliamentary institutions. There were no precedents from which to learn, and many Canadians in the late 1860s were unsure that it was the right decision. The recently concluded American Civil War was blamed largely on the instability that resulted from the U.S.A.'s federal division of powers, causing the concept to be viewed with considerable suspicion. Nevertheless, given that neither Quebec nor the Maritime colonies would have ever agreed to dissolve themselves into a unitary state, dividing sovereignty between two orders of government was a necessary, if not desirable, requirement of unity. Thus, the BNA Act, 1867, embodied the logic of federalism only hesitantly and ambiguously. Indeed, based on a literal reading of its provisions, the BNA Act could be characterized as quasi-federal at best.[3]

■ Quasi-Federalism in the BNA Act

Although the Confederation agreement exhibited important features of federalism, the emergence of a fully federal constitution remained in doubt for some time. On the one hand, the BNA Act established the provinces and gave them areas of exclusive jurisdiction. On the other hand, the Constitution contained provisions reflecting the views of such influential founders as John A. Macdonald, who did not believe the provinces amounted to much. He saw the new Constitution as an instrument for building a great new nation on the northern half of the North American continent, extending from the Atlantic to the Pacific and expressing its identity and purpose primarily through its national government. Federalism and provincial powers were a necessary concession to the existing local sentiment, but to Macdonald, their powers were relatively unimportant in the larger scheme of things. Ottawa had been given all the powers important to building a vibrant modern state, especially the economic and residual powers. As the new nation became more established, Macdonald believed that the provinces would fade even further into insignificance.

Others believed that the provinces would eventually establish themselves as legitimate and important orders of government that would play meaningful roles in a truly federal state. Both sides knew that although the initial rules of the divided sovereignty game were spelled out quite clearly in the BNA Act, with the federal government receiving the lion's share of the important powers, convention and nonentrenched written laws would be important when it came to the actual operation of Canadian federalism. Simply put, the existence of entrenched constitutional law was no guarantee against conflict, ambiguity, or the continual adaptation of political institutions to changing conditions.

To some extent, it can be argued that divided sovereignty was not represented at all in the 1867 BNA Act. The presence of such centralizing devices as reservation and disallowance implied that the provinces were not sovereign, even in their spheres of apparently exclusive jurisdiction. Yet despite these indications of centralism, it is difficult to ignore completely the fact that the Constitution granted some exclusive powers to the provinces. Put another way, the 1867 BNA Act was at odds with itself in the matter of federalism, providing constitutional resources for the proponents of both unitary centralism and a much more decentralized, divided sovereignty. How this tension would resolve itself, whether Macdonald's vision or that of his opponents would carry the day, is a question that would take some time to answer.

Independence and Hierarchy

The federation established in 1867 was characterized by two key institutional qualities: mutual independence (as opposed to interdependence) between the two levels of government, and hierarchy (as opposed to parity).[4]

Mutual independence refers to the fact that, with a few exceptions, notably the concurrent powers over agriculture and immigration found in Section 95,[5] the national and provincial governments were expected to operate independently of each other. That is, powers were divided into "watertight compartments" and each order of government had its own defined policy fields, over which it exercised sovereign legislative, executive, and administrative authority. Each had its own access to revenue by way of specified taxation powers, and although the provinces were intentionally limited in their taxing abilities, it was thought that they would have adequate resources to fulfill their limited mandates. If they had to come begging to the federal government for money to launch more ambitious plans, this seemed only appropriate given the provinces' subordinate status.

Hierarchy was implemented by the provisions that made the federal government paramount when the two levels of government conflicted with each other in the management of their exclusive policy fields. Ottawa possessed the power to delay or veto provincial laws, and the residual power to legislate in fields not explicitly controlled by the provinces. A clear hierarchy was established in which the federal government was expected to prevail over the provinces. Without a strong central government, it was feared, the new Dominion of Canada could not build a strong national economy. In the worst-case scenario, the federation might collapse completely.

Independence, reflected in the division of policy fields and fiscal powers into watertight compartments, was consistent with the classical model of federalism. Federal government paramountcy was not. Over time, the hierarchical elements in the Constitution would fall into disuse because the political cost of exercising them was too high. So too would independence, as the federal spending power led to many "national" programs, funded partially by Ottawa, but in areas of provincial jurisdiction. Therefore, even though Canada did not begin with a fully federal constitution, it nevertheless developed a federal system of government. But when combined with the growing number of provinces and the unforeseen effect of the division of powers, federalism itself doomed both the watertight compartments and federal paramountcy over the long term.

The erosion of independence and hierarchy is partially explained by the character of Canada's federal institutions. First, federalism creates institutional incentives for the actors who operate within them. The establishment of provincial governments creates a focus for local political grievances and ambitions. In effect, ambitious provincial politicians have an incentive to get the best deal from the federal government, in order to prove their worth to the voters. Over time, the provinces have learned that ganging up on Ottawa is more effective than going it alone; one premier cannot credibly claim to be the equal of the prime minister, whereas 10 premiers (or 9, if Quebec refuses to participate) have a better chance of asserting parity within Confederation.

Second, the numerical balance between Ottawa and the provinces has changed dramatically since 1867. Between 1873 and 1949, six new provinces were added to the original four, each with its own local needs and conditions (see Canadian Political Chronology 3.1). As the number of provinces grew, Ottawa's dominance at the bargaining table shrank.

Third, the division of jurisdictions in the BNA Act—which initially favoured the central government—has now tipped the balance of power toward the provinces. By the end of the twentieth century, federal powers over defence and railways were far

DATE	PROVINCE OR TERRITORY	DESCRIPTION	ENABLING ACT OR PROVISION
1867	Ontario, Quebec, New Brunswick, Nova Scotia	Three British colonies unite under a federal Constitution, creating four provinces by dividing the colony of Canada in two	British North America Act, 1867
1870	Rupert's Land, North-Western Territory	Admission of Rupert's Land and the North-Western Territory, to be named North-West Territories	British order-in-council
1870	Manitoba	Formation of province of Manitoba from new North-West Territories, with federal government maintaining control of land and most resources	Manitoba Act, 1870
1871	British Columbia	Admission of British Columbia as a province with its current provincial boundaries	British order-in-council pursuant to Constitution Act, 1871
1873	Prince Edward Island	Admission of Prince Edward Island as province	British order-in-council pursuant to Constitution Act, 1871
1880	Arctic islands	Admission of "all British Territories" and possessions in North America, and adjacent islands, except for Newfoundland and Labrador	British order-in-council pursuant to Constitution Act, 1871
1881	Manitoba	Extension of the boundaries of Manitoba	Manitoba Boundaries Extension Act, 1881
1888	Ontario	Extension of Ontario boundary to include District of Keewatin areas north and west of Lake Superior-Hudson Bay watershed, because JCPC ruled in an 1884 decision that the province of Ontario, not Manitoba, had a legitimate claim to the territory	Ontario Boundary Act, 1888
1898	Yukon	Formation of the Yukon Territory from the North-West Territories	Yukon Territory Act, 1898
1905	Alberta	Formation of province of Alberta from North-West Territories, with federal government maintaining control of land and most resources	Alberta Act, 1905, pursuant to Constitution Act, 1871

DATE	PROVINCE OR TERRITORY	DESCRIPTION	ENABLING ACT OR PROVISION
1905	Saskatchewan	Formation of province of Saskatchewan from North-West Territories, with federal government maintaining control of land and most resources	Saskatchewan Act, 1905, pursuant to Constitution Act, 1871
1912	Manitoba, Ontario, Quebec	Extension of Manitoba and Ontario to their present boundaries; extension of Quebec boundaries to include Ungava district	Ontario, Quebec and Manitoba Boundaries Extension Acts, 1912
1949	Newfoundland	Admission of the British colony of Newfoundland and Labrador with boundaries as per JCPC ruling of 1927	Newfoundland Act, 1949
1999	Nunavut	Creation of new territory of Nunavut out of the eastern Arctic areas of the Northwest Territories	Constitution Act 1999, Nunavut

less important than they had been in 1867, while most Canadians considered the provincial realms of health care, education, and social services to be among the highest political priorities.

Political Cultural Basis of Federalism

Political culture has an important influence on Canadian federalism, especially the most politically salient subcultures of Quebec nationalism and Western regionalism, each of which has exerted increasing pressure on Canadian federalism over the past half-century or so. But regionalism has always existed in Canada, including in the Maritime (now "Atlantic") provinces, whose citizens and politicians were among the earliest critics of the hierarchical principles enshrined in the BNA Act. In many cases they were critics of Confederation itself. When joined by Quebec decentralists and led by Ontario Reformers, they made up a powerful provincial rights movement that presented an immediate challenge to the hierarchical principles of the BNA Act.

Provincial Rights Movement

Provincial rights advocates argued that the federal principle of divided sovereignty entailed two equal orders of government, neither of which owed its existence to the other. Both were created by the Constitution and neither should consider itself supreme. These advocates engaged in a vigorous politics of interpretation, both in and out of the courtrooms, to establish their vision of federalism as the dominant reading of the BNA Act. Their project had three main dimensions. First, they had to overcome Macdonald's view that the relationship between Ottawa and the provinces was like that between Canada and Britain, one of imperial-colonial subordination. Although it would be 60 years after the BNA Act was implemented that Canada became fully independent from Britain with the passing of the Statute of Westminster, and some would argue that the process was not fully completed until the 1982 patriation agreement, provincial rights advocates had much quicker success in establishing mutual independence, and they would do so largely by working within the confines of the BNA Act.

Advocates of provincial rights had to establish that provincial jurisdiction was truly exclusive, meaning that the federal government did not have concurrent jurisdiction to enact paramount legislation in areas of provincial responsibility. In other words, they had to establish a jurisdictional division of watertight compartments. Additionally, they had to ensure that the provinces' compartments were significant enough to create a reasonable balance of power between the two orders of government. In essence, they had to establish as the norm a more classical, or balanced, federalism. Although much of what the early provincial rights advocates achieved was done by convincing the courts to reinterpret the BNA Act in their favour, a matter to be discussed in the next section, the movement could not have been sustained over the long term unless it resonated within and, to a certain extent, furthered the development of two distinct regional political subcultures: Quebec nationalism and Western regional alienation.

Quebec Nationalism

As discussed more extensively in Chapter 1 and other places throughout this text, Quebec nationalism has placed considerable demands not only on federalism in Canada, but on the entire concept of Canada. Quebec's demand for more provincial authority arises, in large measure, from the "compact theory" of Confederation which views Confederation as a deal between two founding nations, the French and the English. As understood by Quebec nationalists, Quebec is the primary home of the French nation in North America. Therefore, the Quebec government is that French nation's chief institutional expression. The rest of Canada is the home of an English Canadian nation, which constitutes a majority in the federal Parliament, and as such naturally and perpetually controls the federal government. In short, Ottawa is primarily the government of English Canada, just as Quebec is the true government of the French nation. As was discussed previously, this two-nations myth implies that Quebec is not a province like the others; it requires special status and powers to protect its founding nation status, and it has the right to negotiate changes to the federation one-on-one with the federal government. This perspective, with its attendant symbols of French humiliation at the hands of the English, drives Quebec's demands for independence and parity within the federal system, as well as demands for national sovereignty and outright independence from Canada.

The two-nations mythology also underlies Quebec's recurring demand for constitutional recognition as a distinct society. Yet in many ways, Canada's Constitution already recognizes Quebec's distinctiveness. Britain's Quebec Act of 1774 granted the former French colonists the right to practise the Roman Catholic faith and to use French civil law (as opposed to English common law) in settling their private disputes. The BNA Act perpetuated these rights, and Canadian federalism itself represents a major concession to Quebec in that, had it not been for the cultural uniqueness of that province, much more pressure would have been applied during the Confederation debates to make Canada a unitary state. Be that as it may, successive Quebec governments have argued that the BNA Act protections are insufficient, and have used the two-founding-nations argument to demand more autonomy for the province of Quebec and its government. When that occurs, as it recently did with the Meech Lake round of constitutional negotiations (1987–1990), other provinces are often quick to follow suit, as they did with the Charlottetown round (1992).

Clearly, the Quebec nationalist subculture has an ongoing, enduring, and important influence on the development of Canadian federalism. This is the case as much for the powers that the Quebec government enjoys within the federation and continually attempts to enhance, as it is for the reaction it engenders. Inevitably, the other provinces will attempt to force the federation to concede most powers granted to Quebec to all provinces.

Western Regional Alienation

Throughout the twentieth century, Western regionalism has been a particularly potent political force that has been mobilized by different groups striving to address subcultural grievances. When large numbers of immigrants arrived on the Canadian prairies in the late 1800s and early twentieth century, they began agitating for provincehood, only to be stalled by the CPR and the federal government. Once provinces were established in Alberta and Saskatchewan in 1905, full provincial rights over resources were withheld for 25 years, as they had been previously when Manitoba was created. Most Prairie residents again blamed the federal government and its agents—the banks, the CPR, "eastern industrialists," and the various provisions of the National Policy—for demanding that Westerners pay a premium for a national economic strategy designed to benefit the Central economy more than the Western periphery.

Agrarian protest against the federation ensued and spawned the provincial United Farmers parties as well as multiple federal party efforts that are described in the next chapter. Agrarian protest also pitted the Alberta government against the federal government when the provincial Social Credit government of Premier William Aberhart openly challenged the BNA Act's division of powers, particularly with respect to federal powers over banking, debt, interest, and bankruptcy. During the first two terms of the Alberta Social Credit government, the federal government used its power of reservation and disallowance six times. The courts—including the Supreme Courts of Canada and Alberta, as well as the JCPC—declared another dozen or so Alberta acts outside of provincial jurisdiction. Despite its more general penchant for siding with the provinces in Canadian federalism disputes, in 1943 even the JCPC had to acknowledge that the Alberta Debt Adjustment Act "as a whole constitutes a serious and substantial invasion of the exclusive legislative powers of the Parliament of Canada."[6] But open defiance of the Constitution only seemed to enhance the Alberta government in the eyes of its electorate, further reinforcing the regional political culture of alienation and protest by "proving" that the Constitution was rigged against the province.

Since 1960, Western regionalism has been mobilized as a political resource for a new form of province building, a technique inspired by the Quiet Revolution governments in Quebec, but quickly seized upon by Western premiers, particularly those of Alberta and British Columbia. As provincial governments mobilized regional grievances, provincial challenges to central power grew, and the legitimacy of the federal government diminished. The battles between the federal and provincial governments eventually culminated in the 1980–1982 constitutional negotiations—and battles—that produced the Constitution Act, 1982.

Western Canadians have long complained that the source of their grievances originates with Central Canadian dominance of the House of Commons. As will be discussed in greater detail in later chapters, seats in the House of Commons are distributed among the provinces in rough proportion to their shares of the national population. Together, Ontario and Quebec account for approximately three-fifths of the House seats (181 of 308, or 59 percent), while the four Western provinces claim less than one-third (92 of 308 seats, or 29 percent). With the Atlantic provinces accounting for a further 10 percent or so, it is not only mathematically possible for a party to form a majority government with almost no Western seats, as the Liberals did in 1980, but some provinces, particularly Alberta, frequently have very little or no representation within the governing parliamentary caucus. Even when the Western provinces have seats in government, such as during the 1984–1993 Mulroney governments, their numerical disadvantage is reinforced by the conventions of party discipline and Cabinet solidarity. These ensure that Western MPs cannot openly address regional issues for fear of threatening their party's electoral chances in Ontario and Quebec. The general rule in Canadian electoral politics, then, is that any party seeking to form a majority government must cater to the interests of Central Canada.

From the Western perspective, matters tend to get even worse when the threat of Quebec separatism dominates the national political agenda as it did during the last quarter of the twentieth century. At the same time the West was emerging as a new, culturally self-confident, economic power, Quebec, a province viewed as being in decline by many Westerners, was threatening to break up the country and was therefore receiving more than its fair share of attention and resources from the national government. Again, many Westerners believed that their region was expected to pay an extraordinary cost to keep Quebec satisfied. When combined with their lack of representation within the Liberal governments of the period, Westerners again felt not only shut out of the corridors of power, but exploited by their national political institutions.

Western discontent with the federal system exploded in the 1970s as the resource-based economic interests of Alberta, and to a lesser extent Saskatchewan and British Columbia, clashed head-on with those of industrial Ontario and Quebec. When the Organization of Petroleum Exporting Countries (OPEC) caused the world price of oil to increase dramatically, the Alberta economy and those of its two closest neighbours grew tremendously while Central Canada stagnated. Ongoing tension between Ottawa and Alberta erupted in a new national-unity crisis when the Trudeau government introduced its National Energy Program (NEP) in the fall of 1980. The NEP was designed to control the increase in Canadian oil prices, keeping them well below the world price, and to provide greater oil-generated tax revenues for the federal government, thereby stemming the westward flow of economic power. But it went much further. The NEP aimed to Canadianize ownership of the oil industry, to shift exploration from provincial lands, primarily in Alberta, to "Canada lands" in the North and offshore. Albertans viewed the NEP as a direct attack on their prosperity by a hostile federal government. The Alberta government, backed by the Quebec government, among others, viewed it as an attack on provincial jurisdiction over natural resources.

Alberta premier Peter Lougheed responded by declaring the federal energy plan to be a direct attack on Alberta's constitutional rights. As a result, the premier announced that the province would be cutting back oil shipments to the rest of the country by 15 percent and would challenge many of the NEP's provisions in court. Although Alberta and the federal government reached an energy-pricing and revenue-sharing agreement the following year and world oil prices collapsed, making a shambles of both the NEP and the Alberta-Ottawa energy accord, the "energy wars" and Ottawa's NEP led to an extra $79 billion being transferred from Alberta to Ottawa.[7] The national-unity and constitutional questions inspired by the fight over energy policy led to the Alberta government's insistence, and the federal government's acceptance, of inserting the enhanced Section 92 (a) guarantees of provincial jurisdiction over nonrenewable natural resources into the 1982 constitution patriation agreement.

More importantly, the NEP brought Western resentment of Canada's political institutions to a head. The NEP was implemented by a national Liberal government that held only two seats in Western Canada, none west of Manitoba, but that nonetheless commanded a solid parliamentary majority. Thus, even to Western Canadians outside Alberta, the NEP demonstrated a serious flaw in federal institutions.

In 1984, Western Canadians again voted massively for the Progressive Conservatives. This time, however, they ended up on the winning side. They hoped that a federal Cabinet with a large Western contingent would be more sensitive to regional concerns. That hope ended in 1986, when the Mulroney government awarded a major contract for the maintenance of Canada's CF-18 aircraft to a Montreal firm, despite the fact that a cheaper and technically superior bid had been submitted by a Winnipeg firm. For many Westerners, this event brought into even sharper focus the flaw in Canada's parliamentary regime: even when the West was solidly represented on the government benches, Ontario and Quebec would always carry greater weight in a chamber based on representation by population. More damningly, it was now evident to many that Western members of a governing party would be unable to do anything about it.

So powerful was the Western discontent with the CF-18 contract, and a series of other Central Canadian-appeasing initiatives by the Mulroney Conservatives, that it galvanized support for the formation of a new political party. The Reform Party entered national politics under the slogan "The West Wants In." One of the many institutional reforms proposed by the Western-based party over the 15 or so years of its existence was the reestablishment of a more clear independence between federal and provincial jurisdictional responsibilities, not by rewriting the Constitution, but by having the federal government extricate itself from areas of provincial jurisdiction that already existed in the division of powers. Prime Minister Stephen Harper's new Conservative government has also advocated this approach. In a sense, both have supported a move back to the more classical federalism that was in place in the early part of the twentieth century and was brought about largely by way of judicial interpretation of the BNA Act.

Interstate and Intrastate Approaches by Quebec Nationalists and Western Regionalists

The Quebec nationalist agenda for institutional reform overlaps with the Western regionalist agenda in one key respect: both want to carve out the broadest possible sphere of fiscal and legislative autonomy for provincial governments. However, the two agendas contradict each other in an equally fundamental way: whereas Quebec nationalists claim special status for their province, Westerners—like most "English" Canadians—are more likely to subscribe to the notion of Canada being composed of 10 equal provinces. Whereas Quebec's constitutional agenda is driven by nationalism, that of the Western provinces is fuelled by regional alienation and populist rejection of our representative democratic structures. Nonetheless, both subcultures agree on one central point: Canada's national political institutions do not adequately serve regional interests.

Although the two subcultures agree on one possible solution to the problem—shifting more powers from Ottawa to the provinces—they disagree over the other: how to reform our national institutions in order to enhance their capacity to express and accommodate regional interests. Political scientists refer to the two competing approaches—parity and reform to national institutions—as interstate federalism and intrastate federalism, respectively.

- Interstate federalism attempts to resolve regional conflict through negotiations between heads of government meeting at First Ministers' Conferences. Provincial premiers are not just the heads of provincial governments; they are national political figures in their own right and the designated spokespersons for regional interests in federal politics. Claims to provincial parity are the logical accompaniment to interstate bargaining.
- Intrastate federalism attempts to resolve regional conflicts by reflecting regionalism within the institutions of the central government, primarily the upper house of Parliament. Under this approach, regional electorates would choose their national representatives—in Canada's case, senators—bypassing their premiers and allowing their regional concerns a voice in the national Parliament.

In general, Quebec nationalists favour interstate federalism. It is analogous to the intergovernmental negotiations among national leaders, which fits the two-nations vision of Confederation. Western regionalists have tended to focus on intrastate solutions, which would enhance the representation of the smaller provinces within the national political system.

Whatever form Canada's federal system may take in the future, its current legitimacy is clearly linked to the strength of regionalism in various parts of the country. A 2002 survey asked Canadians whether their national, provincial, or local government gave them "the most for their money."[8] Respondents in Atlantic Canada were the most likely to name the national government (36.6 percent), whereas those in Quebec and Alberta disagreed. Some 22 percent of Quebec respondents thought they received the best value from the federal government (almost exactly the same percentage as Ontario), while only 7.8 percent of Albertans felt the same way. Conversely, Albertans were by far the most likely to identify the provincial government as the best value provider (44.4 percent), compared to 35.7 percent in Quebec and 29 percent across the entire country. It is probably fair to conclude that these findings reflect more than simple regional sentiment. The high score for the national government in the Atlantic provinces is a logical result of that region's dependence on federal transfers and equalization, whereas Alberta's resource wealth makes it a net contributor to the fiscal system.[9] Even so, other findings reveal a consistent regional pattern of opinion toward the various levels of government. Quebeckers and residents of the two westernmost provinces reported feeling less "trust and confidence" in the federal government than did those in the Atlantic region, in the Prairies east of Alberta, and in Ontario.[10] These findings suggest that Quebec nationalism and Western alienation undermine public support for the national government in three very influential provinces, and partially explain why the governments of each of those provinces made referenda preparations prior to the national vote on the Charlottetown Accord.

■ Classical Federalism through Judicial Review

Perhaps because the BNA Act enshrined the principles of independence and hierarchy, the Fathers of Confederation did not foresee the need for an entrenched mechanism to settle disputes between governments. They had assumed that although both levels of government would likely legislate in overlapping areas of citizens' lives, federal paramountcy would ensure that Ottawa's legislation prevailed. When provinces strayed too far outside what the federal government considered to be their areas of jurisdiction, federally constituted courts would side with Ottawa by striking down provincial legislation. As a last resort, the federal government could reserve or disallow provincial legislation. What the founders seem not to have anticipated, however, was a generally one-sided judicial interpretation of the division of powers, in favour of the provinces.

By the time the Supreme Court of Canada was established in 1875, Ottawa was already uneasy about some provincial legislation. Rather than employ the politically contentious reservation and disallowance procedures, the federal government decided to create a national court to referee intergovernmental disagreements. The Supreme Court Act included a reference provision under which the federal government could leave the constitutionality of provincial laws to be determined by this "independent" body. If the purpose of the new court was to preserve federal paramountcy, it failed— not because of its own decisions, but because its rulings could be appealed to the JCPC in London. For its part, the JCPC disapproved of the quasi-federal elements in the BNA Act and did its best to put the provinces on a more equal footing. Its decisions had a dramatic impact on the federation, moving it from an extremely centralized form of

Sir Wilfrid Laurier was prime minister during the period of classical federalism at the dawn of the twentieth century, when Canada experienced massive immigration, the completion of the National Policy, and the addition of Alberta and Saskatchewan as provinces. Laurier lost two elections (1891 and 1911) campaigning in support of free trade with the U.S.A. Between those two elections he won four consecutive majority governments and served for 15 consecutive years as prime minister. His portrait adorns the Canadian $5 bill. (William James Topley / Library and Archives Canada / C-001971)

Born: 1841, St. Lin, Canada East

Died: 1919, Ottawa

Education: B.C.L. (McGill University, 1864)

Profession: Lawyer (called to the Bar of Canada East in 1864)
1866–1867 Editor of *Le Défricheur*
1869–1878 Ensign, Arthabaskaville Infantry

Political Career:

MLA
1871–1874 Quebec

MP
1874–1877 Drummond-Arthabaska, Quebec
1877–1919 Quebec East, Quebec

Leader
1887–1919 Liberal Party

Prime Minister
1896–1911

Other Ministries
1877–1878 Inland Revenue
1896–1911 President of the Privy Council

Political Career Highlights
1887–1896: Leader of the Opposition
1896 Elected prime minister with a majority
1896 Adoption of the regulations on the Manitoba Schools Question
1898 Creation of Yukon Territory
1899–1902 Canadian participation in the South African War
1900 Reelected prime minister with a majority
1900 Formation of Department of Labour
1903 Alaska Boundary Dispute
1903 Construction of a second transcontinental railway
1904 Reelected prime minister with a majority
1905 Creation of provinces of Saskatchewan and Alberta
1908 Reelected prime minister with a majority
1909 Formation of Department of External Affairs
1910 Naval Service Bill
1911–1919 Leader of the Opposition

Source: *First Among Equals, The Prime Minister in Canadian Life and Politics* (Ottawa: Library and Archives Canada), available on-line at www.collectionscanada.ca/primeministers/

federalism to a more classic form with a more equal balance of powers between the two orders of government. It should be remembered that the JCPC achieved this without changing the written provisions of Sections 91 and 92.

The Judicial Committee of the Privy Council's Watertight Compartments

Until 1949, when appeals to London were abolished, Britain's JCPC was the final court of appeal for Canada. The court was established in 1833 to hear appeals to the Crown against the decisions of colonial governments.[11] Under the 1865 Colonial Laws Validity Act, an "imperial statute" could override a law passed by colonial parliaments when the two conflicted. The JCPC, as the highest court in the Empire, had the ultimate responsibility for determining whether or not Canadian laws conflicted with British laws, the most important of which was the BNA Act. The JCPC had the authority to overturn constitutional rulings of the Canadian Supreme Court, as well as the right to hear constitutional appeals directly from provincial courts. In fact, the Supreme Court was bypassed altogether in about half of the JCPC's cases dealing with the BNA Act.[12] This fact alone demonstrates just how much judicial review of the Canadian Constitution, especially in these crucial early years, was primarily a British operation.

While the JCPC's impact on Canadian federalism is still a matter for heated debate, one point is clear: it sought to diminish Ottawa's paramountcy and to establish more "watertight compartments" of jurisdictional authority between the two orders of government. Beginning with the 1881 case of *Citizens Insurance Co. v. Parsons*, the JCPC began a process whereby it expanded the provincial power over property and civil rights while restricting the federal government's powers over "Peace, Order and Good Government" (POGG) and trade and commerce. Parsons raised the question of whether an Ontario law regulating the terms of insurance contracts could be sustained as provincial legislation under the power over property and civil rights, or whether it more appropriately belonged within the scope of the federal trade and commerce powers. Here was a clear example of a law that could plausibly be understood as falling under either of the two overlapping powers. The JCPC concluded that this type of ambiguity and overlap was unacceptable and sided with provincial powers, as it did in 15 of 18 division of powers cases between 1880 and 1896. For the most part, the JCPC subscribed to an understanding of federalism in which sovereignty is divided into exclusive areas of jurisdiction. As such, it strived to carve watertight compartments out of the general and overlapping language of the division of powers. But it went further.

As discussed in the previous chapter, in 1867 the Fathers of Confederation had deliberately subordinated the provincial governments to the national government. The POGG clause gave Ottawa a broad residual power to legislate on all matters not expressly reserved to the provinces. The JCPC effectively reversed this relationship, interpreting Section 92 (13), "Property and Civil Rights in the Province," as a residual-powers clause and restricting the application of the POGG clause to temporary national emergencies, such as war or pestilence. The JCPC went as far as to boast that it had transformed the Canadian Constitution by making the provinces equal in authority to the federal government.[13]

The assault on the POGG clause began in 1896, with the *Local Prohibition* case. The JCPC ruled that the POGG residual power was strictly limited to matters that were "unquestionably" of national importance. The clause certainly did not empower Ottawa to ride roughshod over any and all areas of jurisdiction that were exclusively assigned to provinces. To do so would destroy the autonomy of the provinces, making a sham of the federal principle. The POGG residual power was narrowed further in the 1922 *Board of Commerce* reference. The court declared that in a serious national emergency, the POGG clause might temporarily authorize the federal government to regulate property and civil rights. In all other circumstances, however, property and civil rights matters must be left exclusively to the provinces. In the 1925 *Snider* case, the lords repeated that only a severe national emergency could trigger the use of the residual powers. When the Great Depression combined with a serious Prairie drought to throw millions of Canadians out of work and create near-famine conditions in Western Canada, the Bennett government brought in New Deal legislation to address the crisis. In 1937 the JCPC declared most of the New Deal laws outside of federal jurisdiction, or *ultra vires*, on the grounds that they dealt with property and civil rights. It dismissed the argument that the unemployment rates, as high as 30 percent, amounted to a national crisis severe enough to invoke the POGG clause.

Even when the federal government's powers were strengthened, the victories often proved temporary at best. In two 1932 rulings—the *Aeronautics* reference and the *Radio* reference—the JCPC ruled in favour of the central government. Both cases involved the federal government's power to implement international treaties. Did Ottawa, by virtue of signing a treaty with other sovereign states, acquire the capacity to legislate in areas of provincial jurisdiction in order to carry out its responsibilities under that treaty? In the *Aeronautics* reference, the JCPC ruled in favour of a more centralist interpretation of the BNA Act, citing the need for uniformity of legislation in areas of common concern to all the provinces. In the *Radio* reference, the court again agreed that the federal government must have the power to implement treaties. But by 1937, in the *Labour Conventions* case, the court reversed the 1932 rulings, stripping Ottawa of the power to enforce international treaties in fields of provincial jurisdiction. The court returned to its pro-province approach by distinguishing between treaty making and treaty implementation, arguing that the former was an executive power and the latter a legislative responsibility. Therefore, while the national executive had the right to negotiate and sign foreign treaties, it did not have unlimited power to enact them into law. This ruling remains in effect, forcing Ottawa to carefully consider provincial powers when crafting international treaties.

Although the impact of the JCPC's constitutional interpretations has attracted considerable criticism, its decisions have defenders. Alan Cairns has argued that "the provincial bias of the Privy Council was generally harmonious with Canadian developments," and that the JCPC's popularity with Quebec governments—which generally favoured provincial autonomy—may well have saved Canada from breaking up.[14] Contrary to the complaints of centralist lawyers that the committee had reduced the federal government to an empty shell, in practice, the federal government was far from helpless in the face of JCPC decisions. After the committee struck down the Employment and Social Insurance Act in 1937, the BNA Act was amended in 1940 to insert "Unemployment Insurance" into Section 91. So while the JCPC did not solely determine the evolution of Canadian federalism, it did set many of the rules under which the provincial and federal governments competed for power and resources.

Centralist Challenges

During the period of JCPC rebalancing, Canada, like the rest of the Western world, had to deal with the tremendous upheavals of two world wars and an unprecedented economic depression. Each of these global events triggered a challenge to the federal principle of divided sovereignty.

At the outbreak of World War I in 1914, the federal Parliament quickly enacted the War Measures Act. This act gave the federal Cabinet wide-ranging emergency powers, which the government used aggressively, even in areas normally within provincial jurisdiction. In effect, federalism came to a complete, albeit temporary end. Federalism was essentially suspended as Canada went through a formative, nation-building experience. Although Canada entered the war automatically as a British colony, there is no question that the war helped forge the sense of national identity on which full Canadian independence would be built. The impact of the war on Canada was massive. Canadian casualties were greater in absolute terms, not just relative terms, than American casualties. Even the 1917 conscription crisis, which highlighted major divisions between the English and French communities in Canada, was a nation-building event, at least inasmuch as it domesticated the wartime experience, giving it added political dimensions unique to Canada. More importantly, a Canadian nationalism developed at exactly the same time as did an assertive and powerful federal government.

Although the impact of the war on Canada's national identity would be long lasting, its effect on federalism was not. Once the war was over, the JCPC went back on the attack against the federal trade and commerce power, reducing it to a power that was subordinate to all others. While this interpretation did not last, the court left the trade and commerce power severely weakened. Thus, while the First World War interrupted constitutional decentralization, it clearly did not defeat it.

The next centralist challenge occurred during the Great Depression, but as we have seen, it had an even more muted impact on federalism. When the Bennett Conservatives got around to responding to the crisis, they did so by attempting to imitate U.S. president Franklin Delano Roosevelt's New Deal economic and social welfare legislation. But the Canadian efforts came late in the government's mandate. When the Conservatives were defeated in the 1935 election by William Lyon Mackenzie King's Liberals, King refused to implement the plan. Rather, he referred the legislation to the JCPC, which struck down most of its provisions. In refusing to consider the Depression a crisis sufficient enough to warrant calling it an emergency, the JCPC did not consider the federal government's POGG powers to be in play.

CANADIAN FEDERALISM

Without an emergency, the JCPC advised that this type of economic and social welfare proposal would fall under provincial property and civil rights powers rather than under federal jurisdiction over trade and commerce. King responded by appointing the Rowell–Sirois royal commission, which will be discussed below. So while the Depression presented another centralist challenge to the JCPC's understanding of a balanced, classical federalism model, it had no immediate impact on changing the court's interpretations or the practice of federalism in Canada.

When World War II started, not only did Canada have to make its own decision about entering the war (it quickly decided to actively engage in supporting the Allied powers), it again invoked the emergency powers contained in the War Measures Act. It also considered the emergency to include post war reconstruction. As such, until the mid-1950s it extended some of its control over areas normally considered to be within provincial jurisdiction. Furthermore, at this time, unlike during World War I, the federal government sought and received unanimous support from the provinces to change the Constitution to give Ottawa power over unemployment insurance (1940) and to give it concurrent powers over pensions (1951). Even more importantly, in 1949 the federal government decided that the JCPC would no longer make the final decisions about Canadian federalism, or any other matters.

The Supreme Court of Canada

Appeals to the JCPC were abolished in 1949, and the Supreme Court became the final arbiter in Canadian constitutional disputes. The Canadian court was still bound by the JCPC's rulings (*stare decisis*), but over time, a court made up of judges appointed by the prime minister tended to look more favourably on federal powers than did the British judges of the JCPC.

In 1952, when asked to rule which order of government had authority over aeronautics, the Supreme Court relied on the JCPC's "national concern" doctrine to uphold the federal government's authority, even though the case involved a property use dispute between neighbours concerning a Manitoba landing strip. The national concern approach was reinforced in 1967, when the court determined that control over offshore minerals is not expressly included in the BNA Act, thereby awarding it to the federal government under its residual powers. By 1988, the court was determining that the national government is within its authority to provide solutions to problems, if it can be established that resolutions to national problems are not obtainable through provincial cooperation. This applies to both new matters that were not anticipated in 1867 and to matters that may have been local at the time of Confederation, but have since become clearly national in scope, even in the absence of an emergency. This federal power is qualified, however, in that there must be serious potential consequences of provincial inability to address the problem. In summary, for the most part the Supreme Court no longer interprets provincial authority over property and civil rights as an implicit residual-power clause capable of trumping Parliament's right to legislate in matters affecting the country as a whole.

Instead, some observers argue, the Supreme Court has turned Section 91 (27)—the federal government's power to make criminal law for the entire country—into an effective residual-powers clause for Ottawa. In policy fields ranging from environmental protection to tobacco advertising, the court has recognized the federal Parliament's exclusive right to make laws that define criminal offences. Again, the federal power is tempered in that Parliament cannot use the criminal-law power to "invade areas of exclusively provincial legislative competence." As the court ruled in the *Firearms* reference case, Ottawa must have a very good reason for creating new criminal offences in policy fields that would otherwise be exclusively or concurrently provincial. The court has also reasserted federal paramountcy over interprovincial trade, with the qualification that Ottawa's encroachment on provincial jurisdiction must be part of a broad regulatory scheme that the provinces could not accomplish on their own.

Overall, it is safe to say that the Canadian Supreme Court has rejected the JCPC's subordination of the federal trade and commerce power to the provincial property and civil rights power, leading us to conclude that the Supreme Court is more sympathetic to the national government than was the British court. But the change has not been as extreme as provincial-rights advocates had feared. A 1979 study concluded that the justices had "favoured the provincial interest at least as often as they favoured the federal interest."[15] This conclusion appears to remain valid today. However, instead of dividing powers into federal and provincial watertight compartments, the Canadian court has often expanded the scope of shared powers. For example, by relying on the criminal-law power as the basis for a federal role in environmental regulation or firearms registration, the court has expanded a federal power that requires provincial administration. That is, while Ottawa writes the statutes, the provinces administer, enforce, and prosecute. In effect, the court has not deliberately expanded federal powers at the expense of the provinces, or vice versa; rather, it has expanded the power of government generally and opened up new areas of overlap within which the two levels of government must cooperate. And it is here that the provinces still hold considerable political resources to overcome the effects of judicial review. Provincial losses at the Supreme Court have often been followed by wins in subsequent political bargaining with Ottawa.

Thus, the establishment of the Supreme Court as Canada's final arena for constitutional appeal set the stage for an even more important role for the court to play in defining the evolutionary course of Canadian federalism. And indeed the court continues to play an important role, as the previous chapters have shown and future chapters will further illustrate. However, its role has to a certain extent been overshadowed by the larger dynamics of intergovernmental cooperation and conflict, leaving recent developments in Canadian federalism to be defined primarily by political agreement rather than by judicial interpretation.

■ Cooperative and Collaborative Federalism

Over the years, Canadian federalism has continually adapted to changing conditions. At various times, the balance of power between Ottawa and the provinces has shifted back and forth. The period from 1945 to the mid-1970s was characterized by intergovernmental agreements often called "cooperative federalism." Since the 1980s, it has been replaced by "collaborative federalism." In both periods, however, Ottawa transferred billions of dollars to the provinces to pay for programs in areas of provincial jurisdiction, resulting in a high degree of fiscal interdependence. The key difference between the two terms revolves around the degree to which Ottawa could set priorities in provincial areas of responsibility. Clearly, the cooperative period involved strong federal government leadership. The collaborative period saw greater equality between the orders of government. The differences typically turned on the question of how many conditions Ottawa put on its grants to the provinces, otherwise known as the "federal spending power."

The division of taxing powers and spending responsibilities that was established between the two levels of government in the BNA Act was clearly a product of late-nineteenth-century thinking. Few politicians of that time could imagine the scope and complexity of government activity that would be involved in building the modern Canadian welfare state. Although the federal government began to transfer money to the provinces almost immediately after Confederation, it tended to help pay for programs, such as agriculture and immigration, over which both governments had jurisdiction. Ottawa's propensity to help out grew during the first half of the twentieth century, as its capacity to raise revenues outstripped that of the provinces, which faced the soaring costs of providing social programs. Over time, Ottawa's spending was expanded into exclusively provincial jurisdictions—most notably health care, postsecondary education, and social welfare.

The federal spending power has no clear basis in the Constitution. Indeed, Quebec governments have long argued that it violates the division of powers, inasmuch as Ottawa imposes conditions on fiscal transfers to the provinces and thus, in effect, legislates in provincial policy fields. When Ottawa unilaterally slashed its transfer payments for health care and other social programs in the mid-1990s, as it struggled to eliminate the federal deficit, outraged provincial governments banded together and demanded greater independence in their exclusive jurisdictions. By the beginning of the twenty-first century, however, the "deficit wars" have given way to the "surplus wars." Having regained the financial wherewithal to use its spending power for national purposes, Ottawa has again begun to impose new conditions on fiscal transfers. For their part, the provinces, still stinging from the "downloading" of the federal deficit, insist on retaining their new autonomy over social spending.[16] Consequently, our governments are involved in a tug of war: the federal government is trying to reassert a measure of paramountcy over the politically sensitive field of social policy, while the provinces are collectively asserting their right to set "national" standards in their own fields of jurisdiction. So, although interdependence is now firmly established, the two senior orders of government are still battling over the shape and form of what has become known as fiscal federalism.

The economic disparities among Canada's governments and regions have always affected the balance of powers in Canada's federal system. The hierarchical federation established in 1867 depended on continual economic growth, which would allow the federal government to carry out its nation-building program. That program was seriously threatened by the recessions of the 1870s and 1880s, as was the legitimacy of the new national government among citizens who had never fully accepted the loss of their colonial independence. As the fiscal resources of the federal government shrank, so did its paramountcy over the provinces. Back in 1887, the first Premiers' Conference demanded more money from Ottawa to meet the provinces' constitutional responsibilities. When observing the most recent premiers' meetings, it would appear as though little has changed. But much *has* changed as the fiscal relationships between the national government and the provinces evolved to meet the changing circumstances of Canadian society, as well as the changing dynamics of intergovernmental relations.

Over the past century, the degree to which the national government can assert paramountcy in provincial jurisdictions has been largely determined by its ability to generate revenue at a given time. When Ottawa reaps sufficient revenues from taxation and distributes them among the provincial governments via cash transfers, it can set priorities in provincial policy fields, making the federal government the dominant partner in Confederation. When its revenues shrink—because taxing power shifts to the provinces, because of economic recession, or because of high interest payments on the public debt—so do its cash transfers to the provinces and, consequently, its power to intervene in provincial areas of jurisdiction. In short, the federal spending power, and Ottawa's ability to determine priorities in provincial policy fields, varies with the amount of money that Ottawa can actually spend.

Collectively, the financial relationships between the federal and provincial governments are called "fiscal federalism." The word *fiscal* refers to public finance. While fiscal federalism is hardly the sexiest topic in political science, it does have a direct and significant impact on the lives of Canadians. It impacts on everything from tuition fees paid by postsecondary students to the access Canadians have to health care and the amount of money welfare recipients receive. So while fiscal federalism may appear dull, its effects on the day-to-day lives of Canadians are anything but.

Early Fiscal Federalism

The 1867 Constitution gave the provincial governments jurisdiction over education, health care, and social welfare. At the time, these were not particularly important or costly areas of public policy. Private and religious charities delivered social services, especially in Quebec, and governments spent relatively little to fill the gap. Ottawa was responsible for the big-ticket items of the late nineteenth century: railways, defence, and other nation-building programs associated with the National Policy. It only made sense to have the central government take the lion's share of tax revenues. However, the BNA Act provided for an unconditional transfer of money to the provinces, at a rate of 80 cents per capita, in compensation for the taxing powers that the provinces had ceded to Ottawa. Almost immediately, the Atlantic provinces began to press for more generous unconditional grants from Ottawa. These early block grants were the precursors of the current equalization program discussed below. Yet despite the reality of national transfers to the provinces, every effort was made during this early period to preserve the watertight compartments in Sections 91 and 92.

During the first 50 years of Confederation, the fiscal imbalance between the two levels of government became acute. The unconditional federal transfers to the provinces continued and were gradually enriched. By 1912, the first conditional grants were introduced, but the sum total of transfer payments still proved inadequate when the Great Depression of 1929–1939 put enormous demands on provincial social services. At the same time, provincial revenues were gutted and the provinces demanded a dramatic increase in financial assistance from Ottawa. But the Depression had also reduced Ottawa's revenue-generating capacity. The fiscal crisis of the 1930s prompted the federal government to appoint a royal commission to recommend improvements. The Rowell–Sirois Commission, named after its chairmen, issued its report in 1940 while Canada was fully engaged in World War II. Two of its key recommendations were (1) to centralize taxing powers in Ottawa, in order to prevent federal-provincial tax competition, and (2) to make the ad hoc system of unconditional fiscal transfers permanent.[17] The commission was strongly opposed to conditional grants, mostly for practical reasons. It argued that joint administration of social programs would provoke intergovernmental conflict and destroy the watertight compartments that were still perceived as the bulwarks of federalism.[18]

The combination of World War II and the Rowell–Sirois Report brought significant and lasting changes to the fiscal relationship between the two senior levels of government. Under the 1940 tax-rental agreement, the provinces gave Ottawa complete control over personal and corporate income tax. The cost of participating in a global conflict was staggering, as was the centralization of policy-making power required to mount a national war effort. The consolidation of taxing powers in Ottawa may have begun as an emergency measure, but it persisted until 1957, with the consent of all the provinces except Quebec.

After peace was restored in 1945, the federal government turned its attention to a new goal: the management of the national economy through Keynesian fiscal and monetary policies. Following the teaching of John Maynard Keynes, a British economist, the Keynesian model of government was designed to prevent future economic crises like the Great Depression. It prescribed strong central control over employment, inflation, and public spending. When the private business cycle turned downward, the government would step in, possibly through deficit financing, and stimulate the economy to keep it from falling into depression. Once the business cycle turned upward, the government would step back, run surpluses to pay down its debt, and let the private sector expand and create wealth. At the same time as it was adopting Keynesian monetary and fiscal policy, the federal government was planning for an unprecedented expansion in the size and activities of the public sector. A "welfare state" would be developed to provide income security and health care to every Canadian who needed help. Postsecondary education would grow rapidly, as Canada's young people prepared for life in the new, information-based economy. Together, the Keynesian approach to government and the growth of the welfare state gave the federal government a reason to maintain its wartime control over tax revenues.

Creation of the welfare state prompted a massive expansion in the scope of the federal spending power. Although public health insurance and other social programs were largely federal initiatives, because the 1867 Constitution had assigned these as areas of provincial responsibility, the provinces delivered most of the programs and services. Consequently, the federal government became heavily involved in financing programs in provincial areas of jurisdiction. In order to maintain its control of income tax, while at the same time ensuring that the 10 provincial governments carried out its wishes, the federal government developed the complex modern system of fiscal federalism. It collected income taxes from every Canadian—except those in Quebec, which has long collected its own income tax—and distributed part of the proceeds to the provincial governments on the condition that their programs met the criteria set by Ottawa.

In effect, the federal government used its spending power to determine provincial programs, spending priorities, and standards. By attaching conditions to the receipt of federal funding, Ottawa was able to legislate indirectly in provincial fields of jurisdiction. Given that provincial jurisdiction is sovereign, there is nothing Ottawa can do constitutionally to force the provinces to play by its rules. All provinces are within their constitutional rights to refuse to participate in Ottawa's "national" social program adventures. However, the federal government has considerable leverage in that it can refuse to grant its proportion of program revenue to a recalcitrant province, hence the importance of provincial "opting out with compensation" demands during constitutional negotiations.

The Evolution of Fiscal Federalism: 1945–2005

Fiscal federalism evolved to address two major imbalances in the revenues of Canada's 11 senior governments: a revenue-generating imbalance between Ottawa and the provincial governments, and an imbalance among the 10 provinces. It should be noted at the outset that considerable disagreement exists on how severe these imbalances are. The federal government has long argued that the provinces are not as hard done by as many premiers would have Canadians believe. According to the federal government, in the 2005–2006 budget year, Ottawa had access to just over $200 billion in revenue, about 55 percent of all government revenue in Canada. That same year, the provinces had access to just over $160 billion, including municipal property tax revenue, or about 45 percent of total government revenue. These numbers certainly put the federal government in a position to transfer money to the provinces in support of their program spending, which it does. When the $42 billion Ottawa transferred to the provinces is included, the various proportions of total government revenue are reversed, with the provinces now having access to over $200 billion (or 55 percent) and the federal government's share reduced to less than $160 billion (or about 45 percent).[19]

Premiers tend to respond with an acknowledgement of the revenue situation, but justifiably point out that they are responsible for delivering the country's most expensive social programs like health care, education, and social services. It is here, they argue, that a fiscal imbalance still exists, especially with respect to the growing costs of the federal government's vision of universal health care. Given that each order of government has some valid arguments, the debate over revenue sharing continues. We shall deal with how the governments are currently sharing revenue by addressing the imbalance between the provinces first, then moving on to the alleged imbalance between the federal government and the provinces.

It is more obvious that an imbalance between the provinces does indeed exist. When considering this imbalance, it is important to remember that Canada's have provinces—currently only Ontario and Alberta—have a greater capacity to raise revenue than do the have-not provinces (see Canada by the Numbers 3.1). Without subsidies from Ottawa, the have-not provincial governments would not be able to provide services comparable to those available in the wealthier parts of the country. In an effort to ensure this does not happen, the federal government tops up the revenue of the have-nots through a system of equalization.

The importance of the equalization program, established in 1957, was recognized when it was entrenched into the 1982 Constitution. Its purpose is to ensure that all of Canada's provincial governments have adequate revenues to provide reasonably comparable levels of public services, at reasonably comparable levels of taxation. In simple terms, the federal government gives all the provinces a fixed percentage of the income tax collected in their "territory" in order to pay for provincial programs. The have-not provinces receive an additional transfer to top up these tax revenues, which are calculated on a per capita basis.

The current equalization formula, which is again being renegotiated by the 11 senior governments, brings the total per capita revenues for each have-not province almost up to the average per capita revenues of the five middle-income provinces. This makes Quebec the perennial big winner in total dollars, almost $4.8 billion in 2005–2006, but the Atlantic provinces receive the most in per capita terms (see Canada by the Numbers 3.1). In 2005–2006, equalization payments ranged from almost $2000 per capita for Prince Edward Island to less than $83 per person for Saskatchewan. Of course this means that the overall impact of equalization on provincial revenue varies significantly across the country. In 2004–2005 it ranged from none for Ontario and Alberta, to just under 10 percent of the Quebec government's total revenue, to over 20 percent of the Atlantic provinces' revenue. It is important to understand that equalization does not promote federal paramountcy or imply that the federal government has invaded areas of provincial responsibilities because there are no federal government conditions attached to equalization money. That is, provincial governments can spend equalization dollars at their discretion, in any areas they decide are priorities.

CANADA BY THE NUMBERS 3.1 Equalization Entitlements 2005–06

	PEI	NB	NL	NS	MB	QC	BC	SK	TOTAL
($ millions)	277	1348	861	1344	1601	4798	590	82	10 900
($ per capita)	1996	1793	1668	1432	1359	632	139	83	—

Source: Department of Finance Canada, Transfer Payments to the Provinces, available at www.fin.gc.ca/fedprov/eqpe.html, accessed June 2006. Reproduced with the permission of the Minister of Finance, 2006.

CANADA BY THE NUMBERS 3.2 Total Equalization Entitlements 1982–83 to 2006–07

YEAR	N.L.	P.E.I.	N.S.	N.B.	QUE.	MAN.	SASK.	B.C.	CANADA
(millions of dollars)									
1982–83	464	118	574	488	2782	439	—	—	4865
1983–84	539	125	605	517	2977	466	—	—	5229
1984–85	578	129	620	540	3074	480	—	—	5422
1985–86	653	134	596	604	2728	427	—	—	5143
1986–87	678	138	620	643	2942	471	285	—	5775
1987–88	807	163	734	724	3151	727	299	—	6605
1988–89	839	177	835	771	3393	795	457	—	7267
1989–90	895	192	885	884	3355	958	639	—	7808
1990–91	919	194	949	868	3627	914	531	—	8002
1991–92	874	186	850	967	3464	853	479	—	7673
1992–93	886	168	908	870	3589	872	490	—	7784
1993–94	900	175	889	835	3878	901	486	—	8063
1994–95	958	192	1065	927	3965	1085	413	—	8607
1995–96	932	192	1137	876	4307	1051	264	—	8759
1996–97	1030	208	1182	1019	4169	1126	224	—	8959
1997–98	1093	238	1302	1112	4745	1053	196	—	9738
1998–99	1068	238	1221	1112	4394	1092	477	—	9602
1999–00	1169	255	1290	1183	5280	1219	379	125	10 900
2000–01	1112	269	1404	1260	5380	1314	208	—	10 948
2001–02	1055	256	1315	1202	4679	1362	200	240	10 310
2002–03	875	235	1122	1143	4004	1303	106	71	8859
2003–04	766	232	1130	1142	3764	1336	—	320	8690
2004–05[1]	762	277	1313	1326	4155	1607	652	682	10 774
2005–06	861	277	1344	1348	4798	1601	82	590	10 900
2006–07[2]	687	291	1386	1451	5539	1709	13	459	11 535

[1]Entitlements for 2004–05 exclude $150 million in additional Equalization related to the 2004 renewal.

[2]Figures for 2006–07 are as proposed in Budget 2006 and include one-time adjustments.

Source: Department of Finance Canada, available at www.fin.gc.ca/budget06/pdf/fp2006e.pdf. Reproduced with the permission of the Minister of Finance, 2006.

Shared-cost programs address the alleged imbalance between Ottawa's greater revenue-generating capacity and the provinces greater spending responsibilities. During the heyday of cooperative federalism in the 1950s, the principal form of cost-sharing was the conditional or matching grant. Ottawa offered money to the provinces to offset the costs of new programs in health care, postsecondary education, and social welfare. For every dollar spent on these programs, Ottawa would reimburse the provinces 50 cents. Put another way, for every dollar a province spent, the federal government would give them an additional dollar to spend. But the grants were conditional in that the provincial program had to meet criteria set by the federal government. As noted earlier, this meant that the federal spending power was used to legislate indirectly in provincial jurisdiction.

As the provinces spent lavishly on new hospitals, universities, and social-assistance programs, they committed Ottawa to ever larger reimbursements. While the direct transfer of federal cash gave the national government effective paramountcy, at least in the broad sense of setting policy priorities, it made controlling the federal budget virtually impossible. A substantial portion of Ottawa's spending decisions were being made elsewhere, that is, in the provincial capitals. Accountability was also an issue, because the federal Parliament—which is constitutionally responsible for monitoring and approving the spending plans of the executive branch—had no role in fiscal federalism.

By the 1970s, the federal government was losing its economic preeminence in the federal system. The provinces had gained enormous power and policy-making capacity as their government bureaucracies and corresponding program spending grew. At the same time, the Keynesian approach to government was discredited by a prolonged economic slump that began with the 1973 OPEC oil price shock. Meanwhile, the federal government faced new and growing constraints on its spending power. After almost three decades of annual budget surpluses, it consistently incurred deficits after 1974. Over time, as the total federal debt mounted and annual interest payments on that debt grew, Ottawa lost its ability to launch new spending initiatives. It also could no longer afford to cover half of what the provinces were spending on existing programs. Combined, these two factors reduced the federal government's ability to strongly influence the pattern of provincial program development.

In response to this fiscal crisis, the federal government gradually reduced its cash transfers to the provinces. In the process, it relinquished much of its control over provincial policy-making. The transition from cooperative to collaborative federalism began in 1977, when Ottawa negotiated the Established Programs Financing (EPF) framework with the provinces. Cash grants for health care and postsecondary education were replaced, at least in part, by "tax points." Instead of collecting income taxes and then sending the money to the provinces, as under the extended wartime tax-rental agreement, the federal government agreed to let the provinces collect their own income taxes and decide how to spend the revenues.

By reducing its direct cash transfers, the federal government hoped to regain control over its own expenditures (which would no longer be determined by provincial priorities), and to shift more financial responsibility for programs to the provinces. To the extent that tax points replaced direct transfers, EPF was a program of block funding, not conditional funding. By reducing its cash subsidies, the federal government effectively gave up its control over programs in areas of provincial jurisdiction.

The other major cost-sharing program was the Canada Assistance Plan (CAP), which was established in 1966 to provide conditional grants to the provinces for their social-assistance programs, with Ottawa contributing 50 cents for every dollar of eligible provincial welfare expenditures. Again, as the federal purse strings tightened, CAP became a serious obstacle to federal budget management (see Canada by the Numbers 3.3). In 1990, at the same time that Ottawa froze the cash portion of its EPF transfers, it set a 5 percent "cap on CAP" for the wealthiest provinces. In other words, Alberta, British Columbia, and Ontario would no longer receive an automatic reimbursement of 50 percent of their welfare costs. Rather, the federal contribution would increase CAP payments by a maximum of 5 percent a year, regardless of provincial spending. The cap on CAP took effect at the start of a serious recession, which hit Ontario particularly hard and placed unusual demands on its welfare system. As the CAP transfer shrank and the cost of social assistance rose, the federal contribution to welfare costs in Ontario fell to only 25 percent.[20]

The trend from conditional to block funding continued into the 1990s. Successive federal governments were forced by fiscal constraints to reduce the cash portion of shared-cost programs and rely more heavily on tax points. The 1995 Canada Health and Social Transfer (CHST), which replaced EPF and CAP, was the culmination of this trend. The changes reflected the federal government's attempt at completing the move away from shared-cost financing of provincial programs towards block funding for all of Ottawa's commitments. These developments were motivated not by the desire to erode federal paramountcy, but by the urgent need to rescue the Canadian economy from impending disaster.

There are at least three important elements of the CHST worth noting. First, it must be understood that the CHST was a block grant and the only conditions attached to the funding were associated with health care and residency. Provinces had to adhere to the five principles of the Canada Health Act—public administration, comprehensiveness, universality, portability, and accessibility. They were also prohibited from denying social assistance because of provincial residency requirements. If a province violated either of these conditions, it risked a federal "claw back" of funds. However, Ottawa gave up any right to dictate the types of programs that the provinces could deliver in these fields.

Second, each province was free to allocate the CHST among the three components (health care, postsecondary education, and social welfare) as it saw fit. In practice, given the strong public support for the health-care system, this meant that postsecondary education and welfare were left relatively unprotected. When the federal government introduced the CHST, it predicted that the provinces would spend 43 percent of the total transfer on health care. By 2004, the federal estimate had risen to 62 percent, suggesting that the concerns of postsecondary institutions and social-welfare advocates were justified. Moreover, the CHST monies went into general provincial revenues, not directly into social programs. If they so chose, provinces could spend their CHST dollars on other policy priorities.

CANADA BY THE NUMBERS 3.3 Health and Social Federal Transfers to the Provinces 1982–83 to 2006–07

YEAR	N.L.	P.E.I.	N.B.	N.S.	QUE.	ONT.	MAN.	SASK.	ALTA.	B.C.	Y.T.	N.W.T.	NUN.	CANADA
(millions of dollars)														
1982–83	351	80	514	459	4449	5141	621	616	1478	1877	14	33	—	15 633
1983–84	385	85	563	498	4924	5684	688	678	1606	2089	14	37	—	17 252
1984–85	405	91	607	537	5272	6139	747	729	1702	2256	16	40	—	18 541
1985–86	432	98	654	580	5640	6669	806	781	1848	2401	18	43	—	19 971
1986–87	459	104	697	615	5925	7197	863	825	1996	2483	19	47	—	21 231
1987–88	481	110	736	645	6150	7824	924	857	2099	2650	20	52	—	22 548
1988–89	502	116	785	676	6444	8479	972	889	2225	2846	22	55	—	24 011
1989–90	535	124	837	710	6820	9237	1030	920	2369	3003	24	60	—	25 669
1990–91	549	128	868	732	7087	9485	1057	910	2432	3126	26	64	—	26 463
1991–92	564	129	894	756	7414	9849	1080	908	2492	3240	29	69	—	27 424
1992–93	591	132	923	766	7731	10 085	1128	936	2556	3349	32	71	—	28 300
1993–94	608	135	946	760	7967	10 320	1133	969	2583	3461	34	75	—	28 991
1994–95	623	135	953	760	8048	10 537	1131	985	2519	3574	33	79	—	29 377
1995–96	623	138	964	769	8136	10 740	1151	1003	2577	3673	34	81	—	29 889
1996–97	561	124	866	691	7311	9 651	1035	902	2313	3343	30	73	—	26 900
1997–98	513	118	820	652	6936	9 314	979	855	2257	3293	30	70	—	25 839
1998–99	517	122	845	671	7099	9 751	1010	885	2401	3440	30	70	—	26 841
1999–00	545	136	934	746	7467	11 246	1128	1004	2856	3941	31	42	29	30 105
2000–01	560	142	976	782	7835	12 033	1193	1044	3069	4175	32	47	31	31 918
2001–02	580	152	1035	832	8205	13 177	1277	1111	3387	4526	33	45	31	34 392
2002–03	581	153	1044	838	8316	13 498	1291	1114	3477	4597	34	46	32	35 022
2003–04	636	168	1148	921	9182	15 009	1423	1221	3869	5092	37	52	36	38 794
2004–05	698	186	1265	1014	10 172	16 713	1577	1342	4315	5663	42	58	40	43 085
2005–06	768	206	1396	1120	11 304	18 648	1753	1481	4839	6325	46	64	45	47 993
2006–07	752	202	1372	1100	11 157	18 503	1728	1449	4805	6277	45	64	44	47 499

Note: Total may not add due to rounding. Includes cash and tax transfers provided under Established Programs Financing and the Canada Assistance Plan up to 1995–96; the Canada Health and Social Transfer (CHST) up to 2003–04; the Health Reform Transfer (2003–04 and 2004–05); the 2003 CHST cash supplement and 2004 CHST cash supplement for health based on notional drawdown schedules; and the Canada Health Transfer and the Canada Social Transfer for 2004–05 and beyond.

Source: Department of Finance Canada, Transfer Payments to the Provinces, available at www.fin.gc.ca/budget06/pdf/fp2006e.pdf, accessed June 2006. Reproduced with the permission of the Minister of Finance, 2006.

Third, the amount transferred under the CHST was substantially smaller than the total of the two programs it replaced. Without consulting the provinces, the federal government cut its transfers by one-third over the first two years of the CHST.[21] Under the initial CHST formula, the cash portion of the transfer would have shrunk relative to the value of the tax points. Within a year, Ottawa had recognized the implications of this trend for its ability to impose national standards, and announced that cash transfers would not fall below a certain percentage of the total CHST package.

The political fallout from the CHST was enormous. Provinces wondered why they should have to follow national standards in their own fields of jurisdiction, especially those imposed by a federal government that had slashed its cash transfers. Ottawa provided a response in its 1999 budget. By that time, two things had changed: (1) Ottawa's fiscal position had improved dramatically, and (2) health care had become the dominant issue in Canadian politics. Prime Minister Martin announced immediate and substantial increases in cash transfers under the CHST—all of which would be targeted to health care. This marked the beginning of Ottawa's efforts to reassert itself in provincial policy fields, as it was the first time since 1977 that the federal government had earmarked funds expressly for health care.

For the next several years, the 11 senior governments wrangled over health-care funding, with the provincial governments claiming that federal cash transfers amounted to only 15 cents for every dollar of health-care spending. By February 2003, the first ministers concluded the Accord on Health Care Renewal, and Ottawa created a new Health Reform Transfer targeted at primary health care. The accord also revamped the CHST by dividing it in two: the Canada Health Transfer (CHT), accounting for 62 percent of the former total CHST payment, and the Canada Social Transfer (CST), worth the remaining 38 percent. The purpose of dividing the CHST was twofold; to give Ottawa the public recognition for supporting health care it believed was its due, and to satisfy the provinces' demands for flexibility in allocating funds among other social programs according to their respective priorities.[22]

In its March 2004 budget, which included further health-care funding increases, the federal government claimed that its share of total health-care funding topped $34 billion a year, or about 40 percent of all public spending on health care in Canada.[23] As usual, the provinces begged to differ. At the July 2004 meeting of the Council of the Federation, the premiers argued that the new federal funding was insufficient.

Prime Minister Stephen Harper's new Conservative government, although in power for only six months at the time this is being written, has further increased health-care spending and is engaged in ongoing discussions with the provinces over the state of Canada's fiscal federalism (see Canada by the Numbers 3.4). The conflicts over money and control may be abated somewhat by two factors: (1) given the amazing turnaround in federal government finances over the past decade, as will be discussed in more detail in later chapters, the federal government has more money to spend on programs than it has had in decades, or possibly has ever had; and (2) the Harper government has campaigned on a promise of interfering less in provincial areas of jurisdiction. Nevertheless, given that Ottawa and the provinces cannot even agree on the size of their respective contributions to such programs as health

CANADA BY THE NUMBERS 3.4 Total Federal Transfers to the Provinces 2006–07

YEAR	N.L.	P.E.I.	N.B.	N.S.	QUE.	ONT.	MAN.	SASK.	ALTA.	B.C.	Y.T.	N.W.T.	NUN.	CANADA
(millions of dollars)														
Health and Social	771	208	1128	1407	11 439	18 970	1772	1486	4926	6435	47	65	45	48 699
Equalization	686	291	1451	1386	5539	0	1709	13	0	459	506	739	827	13 608
Total	1359	471	2446	2668	16 450	18 970	3329	1486	4926	6707	552	805	872	61 041
Per Capita	2639	3400	3249	2840	2154	1498	2814	1498	1498	1561	17 793	18 448	29 001	1877

Totals may not add due to rounding. The health and social transfer figures in this table are subject to revision through the regular CHST/CHT/CST estimation process. In 2004, the Canada Health and Social Transfer (CHST) was restructured and two separate transfers were created, the CHT and the CST. The CHST/CHT/CST cash amounts include notional annual allocations under the 2003 CHST Supplement and the 2004 CHST Supplement for Health. The Health Reform Transfer was integrated into the CHT in 2005-06, as agreed by First Ministers in September 2004. The figure for Equalization in 2004-05 does not include the special payment of $150 million legislated as part of Budget 2004. Equalization associated with the CHST/CHT/CST tax transfer is included in both CHST/CHT/CST (under "Tax") and Equalization figures. Totals have been adjusted to avoid double counting.

Source: Department of Finance Canada, Transfer Payments to the Provinces, available at www.fin.gc.ca/fedprov/eqpe.html, accessed June 2006. Reproduced with the permission of the Minister of Finance, 2006.

care, let alone the proper use of the federal spending power or its enforcement, it would be premature to declare the wrangling over fiscal federalism to be a thing of the past. Indeed, one overriding feature of fiscal federalism remains unchanged. Decisions are still being made by political consensus, as opposed to formal voting rules, because Canadian governments refuse to yield even a modicum of their individual sovereignty to some neutral enforcement body. Compared to other federal states, these aspects of Canada's intergovernmental relations mechanisms are rather undeveloped and arguably very ineffective.

INTERGOVERNMENTAL RELATIONS IN CANADA

No More Watertight Compartments

If the fiscal imbalance between the two levels of government has had a marked impact on the evolution of Canadian federalism, so too has the practical overlap between the powers listed in Sections 91–95 of the Constitution. The scope of modern government was unimaginable to the Fathers of Confederation. Today the federal and provincial governments are active in many fields that are not explicitly assigned by the Constitution to either order of government. Matters such as consumer protection, multiculturalism, and environmental protection do not fall easily into watertight compartments. As a result, governments must work together to develop and implement policies in virtually every field of activity.

Historically, the key intergovernmental relationships (IGRs) have been (1) those between the national government and one or more provincial governments and (2) those among the provinces themselves. Relations in the former category are now labelled "FPT," for "federal, provincial, and territorial"; the shorthand for the latter two is "PT." In legal and constitutional terms, the three territories do not enjoy the status of provinces; they are created and controlled by the federal government. Nonetheless, the leaders of their governments are now included in most meetings of the first ministers, and they have been full participants in the Annual Premiers' Conference (now the Council of the Federation) since 1991. For the most part, when we refer to premiers, we are including leaders of the territorial governments.

Generally speaking, Canadian intergovernmental relations are managed by the executive branch of government. Members of the political and permanent executives meet regularly to share information, hammer out agreements, and try to resolve disputes. These activities are collectively called "executive federalism." The formal relations among the executives of Canada's senior governments occur at three distinct levels:

1. *Peak:* First ministers' meetings (the leaders of some or all various governments), the Council of the Federation, and bilateral meetings between two or more government leaders.
2. *Ministerial:* Some or all of the various cabinet ministers responsible for a particular policy field: for example, the Canadian Council of Ministers of the Environment or the Council of Ministers of Education.
3. *Official:* The public servants who make and enforce policy in a specific field: for example, the Deputy Ministers' Committee, which supports the work of the Canadian Council of Ministers of the Environment.

Peak Institutions

The peak institution at the FPT level is the First Ministers' Conference (FMC).[24] The first official FMC was the 1906 Dominion-Provincial Conference on fiscal relations; the second was held in 1918 and the third in 1927. The FMC did not become a regular event until after the fiscal crisis of the Great Depression, which prompted the Rowell–Sirois Commission to recommend frequent "Dominion-Provincial Conferences," with a permanent secretariat to coordinate IGRs. When the welfare state began to take shape after World War II, FMCs became annual events (see Canadian Political Chronology 3.2). While their official purpose was to discuss fiscal relations, and especially the creation of national shared-cost programs in provincial policy fields, they quickly became the most prominent arena for federal-provincial combat. By the 1960s, the Quiet Revolution in Quebec had sparked a more aggressive attitude on the part of several premiers. The agenda now included oil and gas pricing, constitutional amendments, and provincial demands for more powers and greater autonomy from Ottawa.

Despite the increasingly hostile dynamic, the first ministers met 21 times between 1971 and 1983. The Canadian Intergovernmental Conference Secretariat (CICS) was created in 1973 to provide logistical support for FMCs and other intergovernmental

CANADIAN POLITICAL CHRONOLOGY 3.2   First Ministers' Conferences (FMCs) 1906–2005

PRIME MINISTER	NUMBER OF FMCs	YEARS	SUBJECTS
Wilfrid Laurier	1	1906	financial subsidies to the provinces
Robert Borden	1	1918	soldier and land settlement, transfer of natural resources
William Lyon Mackenzie King	5	1927 1935 1941 1945 1946	constitutional, financial, social and economic subjects; recommendations of Rowell–Sirois Commission; post war reconstruction; welfare-state programs
Louis St. Laurent	6	1950 (3) 1955 (2) 1956	constitutional amendments, fiscal arrangements, welfare-state programs
John Diefenbaker	4	1957 1960 (2) 1961	hospital insurance, fiscal arrangements, provincial sales taxes
Lester Pearson	9	1963 (2) 1964 (3) 1965 1966 1967 1968	Canada Pension Plan, fiscal arrangements, welfare-state programs including postsecondary education and student loans, recommendations of Royal Commission on Bilingualism and Biculturalism, constitutional amendments
Pierre Trudeau	23	1969 (3) 1970 (3) 1971 (3) 1973 1974 1975 1976 (2) 1978 (3) 1979 1980 1981 1982 1983 1984	Constitution (Victoria Charter, patriation), economy, fiscal arrangements, unemployment, natural resources, Native issues
Joe Clark	1	1979	energy policies

PRIME MINISTER	NUMBER OF FMCs	YEARS	SUBJECTS
Brian Mulroney	14	1985 (3)	economy, Native issues, Constitution
		1986	(Meech Lake and Charlottetown),
		1987 (3)	fiscal arrangements
		1989	
		1990	
		1991	
		1992 (4)	
Jean Chrétien	7	1993	economy, fiscal arrangements, Constitution
		1994	(required by section 49), health care,
		1996	social programs
		1997	
		1999	
		2000	
		2003	
Paul Martin	2	2004	health care, Native issues
		2005	

Source: Canadian Intergovernmental Conference Secretariat, www.scics.gc.ca/pubs/fmp_e.pdf

meetings. Its limited mandate left the responsibility for agenda-setting, compliance, and policy development to the individual governments, and there was no genuinely intergovernmental mechanism for dispute resolution and enforcement. During this period, some premiers aggressively challenged the legitimacy of the federal government, and claimed an equal right to speak for Canadians, causing Prime Minister Trudeau to come to loathe FMCs. His successor, Brian Mulroney, promised Canadians a new era of intergovernmental harmony and cooperation. He chaired several FMCs on social and economic issues, Aboriginal concerns, and constitutional reform. However, the failure of the Meech Lake and Charlottetown agreements ultimately poisoned the relationship between Ottawa and the provinces. Consequently, little was accomplished at the other FMCs.

Under the Chrétien government (1993–2003), formal gatherings of government leaders were infrequent. Prime Minister Chrétien chaired only seven FMCs. Unlike the highly charged and media-driven events of the 1970s and 1980s, these were private and relatively low-key meetings. None was devoted to constitutional change. As such, they tended to produce agreements and accords that were, at best, morally binding on the governments. For the most part, Chrétien preferred to discuss matters of shared concern in less public and formal settings. There are no written records of these deliberations, but it is reasonable to assume that the participants found it somewhat easier to reach an understanding in the absence of television cameras and entourages anxious to score political points.

Prime Minister Paul Martin, like Mulroney before him, came to office promising a new era of intergovernmental collaboration, but few provincial governments had forgotten that Martin was the architect of the now notorious 1995 federal budget. His short time in office produced little innovation in IRGs beyond the federal government promising to spend more money on health care and Aboriginal issues, as well as a promise to negotiate a new agreement on equalization payments. When talks failed to produce a new, comprehensive equalization deal, the prime minister eventually signed separate accords with the premiers of Newfoundland and Nova Scotia. These, as has been the pattern in Canadian federal politics, immediately produced calls for similar deals from other premiers.

Concerning the FMC as an institution, it has no more legal or constitutional status than it had in 1906. For the most part, it lacks all of the formal characteristics of an institution, including the constitutional authority to bind governments, an established set of rules and procedures, or a permanent organizational structure. Rather, it is an ongoing, ad hoc response to the most immediate political concerns on the part of its participants, the prime minister, and the premiers.

Until 2003, the peak institution at the provincial level was the Annual Premiers' Conference (APC). Starting with its inception in 1960, APC meetings were held to discuss issues of common importance. They were chaired, on a rotating basis, by each of the provinces in turn. The APC lacked a permanent secretariat or staff, relying instead on whatever resources the host government for each year could provide. The turnover of premiers and territorial leaders varied: sometimes there was considerable continuity from one year to the next, while other annual meetings turned into get-acquainted sessions for new members. As a result, the institutional memory of the APC was unreliable and it could not pursue goals that required more than a year or two to accomplish.

More recently, at the initiation of the Quebec government, the new Council of the Federation was established to create a formal and stable structure that can exercise effective "leadership on national issues of importance to provinces and territories."[25] The council meets at least twice a year and receives and considers reports from provincial ministerial and official committees. A steering committee, made up of deputy ministers responsible for intergovernmental relations, and a permanent secretariat carry out the work of the council between the twice-yearly meetings of the government leaders. In principle, they are responsible for monitoring progress on the strategic goals set by the council and for helping to identify shared priorities for future interprovincial collaboration. Because the Council of the Federation is so new, judgment has not yet been rendered on its utility. But clearly, its success as an institution will be based at least partially on the ability of the premiers to turn it into something more than a mechanism for providing a common front to demand more money out of Ottawa.

In addition to these national peak institutions, the Council of Atlantic Premiers and the Western Premiers' Conference meet at least once a year. These regional PT groups have established working relationships with their counterparts in neighbouring U.S. states, such as the Western Governors' Association and the New England Governors. Since the 9/11 terrorist attacks, the primary focus of the annual cross-border meetings has been trade and border security, although the premiers and governors also deal with economic development, environmental policy, and energy issues.

Ministerial and Official Councils

FMCs and other peak institutions of executive federalism receive considerable media coverage. However, most of the actual work is accomplished at the ministerial and official levels. The FPT and PT ministers responsible for particular policy sectors meet regularly, as do their deputy ministers and other senior civil servants. Some of these are national councils, others are regional forums. In 2005, the CICS reported 48 FPT and PT ministerial meetings, compared to 49 meetings of officials. These numbers are consistent with the yearly averages since 1974.[26] Interestingly, there is a growing trend for provincial and territorial ministers and officials to meet without their federal counterparts, ostensibly to coordinate work on purely provincial matters. In reality, these gatherings tend to mirror PT peak meetings in that they often seem to be less concerned with interprovincial issues and more focused on forging a common front against Ottawa.

In addition to the formal intergovernmental meetings just described, there are countless informal contacts between ministers and officials. Most of these arise in the day-to-day business of administering policy in shared jurisdictions. Some involve specialists in intergovernmental relations; others involve policy experts looking for best practices and other useful advice, or members of the various intergovernmental committees that do the heavy lifting for the political executives. As the number of FPT and PT councils and forums has grown in recent years, so has the volume of intergovernmental agreements (numbering somewhere between 1500 and 2000 in 2003).[27]

Federalism and "Glocalization"

In the coming years, relations between the federal and provincial governments will be further complicated by the participation of two additional levels of government: supranational and municipal. It is often argued that globalization has shifted policymaking and enforcement authority upward to supranational agencies, and downward to local bodies (hence the new buzzword *glocalization*[28]). However, any potential transfer of power to Canadian cities should not be overstated. As much as Canadians cities have changed over the past century, their functions remain focused on local infrastructure and local public service delivery. Their constitutional status as "creatures of the provinces" also provides a stumbling block to their recognition as equal to the other orders of government. The Martin government put cities at the centre of its policy agenda, and the Harper government has acknowledged their important role in Canada. However, at least one previous prime minister attempted a similar move into what is constitutionally a provincial area of responsibility, with little success. In the 1970s, the Trudeau government decided to dabble in urban affairs by establishing a department responsible for cities. It accomplished little and was finally disbanded in the early 1980s.

Still, the sheer size and complexity of Canada's major cities provide their advocates with considerable ammunition to argue for more influence within the federation. Given that the metropolitan populations of Canada's largest cities (Toronto, Montreal, Vancouver, Calgary, Ottawa, and Edmonton) are all approaching or have already exceeded the one-million mark—meaning they will all soon service populations larger than six Canadian provinces—it makes some intuitive sense to include them in negotiations that involve PT leaders. Be that as it may, municipalities' lack of independent constitutional status means that any increased authority for them will have to be negotiated with the senior governments.

In the meantime, Canada's largest cities are at the mercy of their provincial masters, as evidenced by how the cities were forced to bear the brunt of federal and provincial downloading in the 1990s. Essentially, when the federal government cut transfers to the provinces in order to get its fiscal house in order, the provinces did the same to municipalities, for similar reasons. Since then, Canadian cities have struggled to maintain their existing infrastructure of roads, waterworks, and public transit, while expanding populations demand new facilities. The implications of the fiscal crisis in municipal governance are profound. Most Canadians (almost 80 percent in 2001) live in cities or towns.[29] They need safe housing and streets, clean drinking water, and adequate policing. In response, both the Martin and Harper governments committed themselves to tax breaks for cities. The direct transfer of money from the federal government to municipalities is considerably more problematic. Although provincial governments have accepted federal participation in specific urban projects like inner-city redevelopment and upgrading the facilities surrounding ports, they are less fond of proposals for long-term federal funding of municipal activities. Provincial governments argue that if Ottawa wants to give money to cities, it should do so by increasing transfers to the provinces, which in turn will determine what are the municipal priorities are within their respective jurisdictions. Future federal efforts to subsidize cash-strapped cities will likely only complicate the already acrimonious aspects of fiscal federalism.

At the supranational level, the North American Free Trade Agreement (NAFTA) and other binding international treaties may alter the balance of power between the provinces and the federal government. Before the 1980s, international trade agreements usually focused on tariff barriers to the import of foreign goods. Under Section 91 of the BNA Act, the federal government has jurisdiction over tariffs and other import policies. The global push toward open markets has forced states to reduce or eliminate tariffs. Recent rounds of trade negotiations, whether at the World Trade Organization (WTO) or within particular regions—such as the European Union (EU) or North America (NAFTA)—have focused on nontariff barriers to trade, many of which fall under provincial jurisdiction. Recall that the JCPC ruled that the federal government has the power to make binding treaties, but lacks the power to implement them in fields assigned to the provinces. Consequently, the new emphasis on reducing nontariff barriers has forced the federal government to seek provincial cooperation in the negotiation and implementation of trade deals with other countries. Although the premiers do not enjoy formal standing with the WTO, or most other international bodies, the division of jurisdictions in the BNA Act gives them considerable capacity to frustrate the implementation of trade treaties that impact on their policy fields, as most do.

At its first meeting in July 2004, the Council of the Federation unanimously demanded full provincial participation in Canada's international activities that impact on their jurisdictional responsibilities. This demand makes some sense, given the increasing emphasis in global trade talks on culture, education, and other provincial jurisdictions. Ottawa, unsurprisingly, does not see it this way. It generally denies provincial governments their own seats at the bargaining table, preferring instead to consult with the provinces on national priorities and implementation mechanisms. Even when there are no binding international agreements at stake, the federal government appears determined to conduct international affairs on its own, although Quebec has recently been given some status at meetings involving culture and education.

Whatever the long-term impact of international treaties such as Kyoto and NAFTA on provincial jurisdictions, one broader point is clear; the territorial logic of federalism is in direct conflict with the nonterritorial logic of globalization. Whereas provincial jurisdiction is territorially bound, NAFTA and other trade treaties transcend (indeed, tend to erode) political and geographic borders. As the nation-state yields more of its sovereignty to supranational organizations, it also surrenders some of its authority to individuals and the private sector.

CONCLUSION

At Confederation, Canada's federal system was characterized by independence and the paramountcy of the national government. Initially through judicial interpretation, and then because of the creation of a welfare state, a more balanced and interdependent federation resulted. At the beginning of the twenty-first century, the Canadian federation is a highly interdependent system in which the provinces and territories claim equality with Ottawa. Put another way, Canada has moved from being one of the world's most centralized federations to one of its most decentralized. Clearly, Canadian provinces enjoy much more autonomy than do most subnational governments in other federal systems.

The two regional subcultures of Quebecois nationalism and Western regional alienation will likely be the main drivers of continued evolution of the federation over the next century. Nevertheless, given the financial entanglement between all of Canada's governments, and their continuing disagreements about how much Ottawa contributes to programs and what is a just form of equalization, it is likely that interdependence is going to be a feature of Canadian federalism for some time to come. Ottawa will continue to seek ways of demonstrating that it is a relevant government for all Canadians, while the provincial governments will jealously guard the parity that they have achieved over the previous 140 years of federal evolution in Canada.

DISCUSSION QUESTIONS

1. How was Canadian federalism intended to be structured, according to the BNA Act, 1867?
2. How does federalism differ from unitary government and confederalism? Which of the three best describes Canada? Why?
3. How have the rulings of the JCPC and the Supreme Court of Canada affected the balance of power between the federal and provincial governments? How great has been their impact?
4. How has Canada's system of fiscal federalism changed since the 1970s? What is the historical significance of the CHST?
5. Will the federation change because of a new emphasis on local and/or international priorities? If so, how? If not, why not?
6. Briefly explain the meanings of "interdependence" and "parity" in the context of Canadian federalism.

SUGGESTED READINGS

Books and Articles

Herman Bakvis and Grace Skogstad, eds., *Canadian Federalism: Performance, Effectiveness, and Legitimacy* (Toronto: Oxford University Press, 2002).

David Cameron and Richard Simeon, "Intergovernmental Relations in Canada: The Emergence of Collaborative Federalism," *Publius: The Journal of Federalism,* 32:2 (Spring 2002).

Alain-G. Gagnon and Hugh Segal, eds., *The Canadian Social Union without Quebec: Eight Critical Analyses* (Montreal: Institute for Research in Public Policy, 2000).

Roger Gibbins, *Regionalism: Territorial Politics in Canada and the United States* (Toronto: Butterworths, 1982).

James Ross Hurley, *Amending Canada's Constitution: History, Processes, Problems and Prospects* (Ottawa: Minister of Supply and Services Canada, 1996).

Harvey Lazar, ed., *Toward a New Mission Statement for Canadian Fiscal Federalism* (Montreal and Kingston: McGill–Queen's University Press/Queen's University School of Policy Studies, 2000).

J. Peter Meekison, Hamish Telford, and Harvey Lazar, eds., *Reconsidering the Institutions of Canadian Federalism* (Montreal and Kingston: Institute of Intergovernmental Relations/McGill–Queen's University Press, 2004).

François Rocher and Miriam Smith, eds., *New Trends in Canadian Federalism,* 2nd edition (Peterborough, ON: Broadview Press, 2003).

John T. Saywell, *The Lawmakers: Judicial Power and the Shaping of Canadian Federalism* (Toronto: University of Toronto Press/Osgoode Society for Canadian Legal History, 2002).

Websites

The Canadian Intergovernmental Conference Secretariat, an agency of the federal government, maintains a website (www.scics.gc.ca) listing all major intergovernmental meetings that took place in recent years. There are links to major documents (statements or agreements) produced by or at these meetings. This website is an excellent resource on fiscal and executive federalism.

The federal Department of Finance provides a wealth of information about the fiscal relations between the federal and provincial/territorial governments. Go to www.fin.gc.ca and click on the "Transfer Payments to Provinces" icon. You can also access these pages from the website of the Intergovernmental Affairs Secretariat within the federal Privy Council Office; go to www.pco-bcp.gc.ca and click on "Other PCO Sites: Intergovernmental Affairs."

For a different perspective on IGRs, check out some of the provincial sites. Alberta's Department of International and Intergovernmental Relations (www.iir.gov. ab.ca) is an excellent source of information. Most provincial IGR sites are less informative, although the British Columbia site provides useful links to other governments (www.bced.gov.bc.ca/departments/igr/). See also the Ontario site (www.mia.gov. on.ca) and the Quebec site (www.mce.gouv.qc.ca).

NOTES

1. See for example Alan C. Cairns, "The Government and Societies of Canadian Federalism," *Canadian Journal of Political Science*, 10 (1977).

2. See Ronald L. Watts, *Comparing Federal Systems*, 2nd edition (Montreal and Kingston: Institute of Intergovernmental Relations/McGill–Queen's University Press, 1999).

3. See K. C. Wheare, *Federal Government*, 4th edition (London: Oxford University Press, 1963).

4. These dichotomies are taken from J. Peter Meekison, Hamish Telford, and Harvey Lazar, "The Institutions of Executive Federalism: Myths and Realities," in J. Peter Meekison, Hamish Telford, and Harvey Lazar, eds., *Reconsidering the Institutions of Canadian Federalism* (Montreal and Kingston: Institute of Intergovernmental Relations/ McGill–Queen's University Press, 2004), 4.

5. Other concurrent powers were less explicit: Sections 91 and 92 awarded legislative powers over criminal law and marriage to Ottawa, while the administration of those laws was left to the provinces.

6. See David K. Elton, "Alberta and the Federal Government in Historical Perspective, 1905-1977," in Calro Calderola, ed., *Society and Politics in Alberta: Research Papers* (Toronto: Methuen Publications, 1979).

7. See Robert Mansell, Ron Schlenker, and John Anderson, *Energy, Fiscal Balances and National Sharing* (Calgary: Institute for Sustainable Energy, Environment and Economy, University of Calgary, 2005).

8. Richard L. Cole, John Kincaid, and Andrew Parkin, "Public Opinion on Federalism in the United States and Canada in 2002: The Aftermath of Terrorism," *Publius: The Journal of Federalism,* 32:4 (Fall 2002), Table 3, 129.

9. See Mansell et al. for a compilation of the total and per capita net federal fiscal balances of Canada's provinces and territories.

10. Cole and Kincaid, "Opinion on Federalism," 142

11. Donald V. Smiley, *The Federal Condition in Canada* (Toronto: McGraw-Hill Ryerson, 1987).

12. Peter H. Russell, Rainer Knopff, and Ted Morton, "Introduction," in Peter H. Russell, Rainer Knopff, and Ted Morton, eds., *Federalism and the Charter* (Ottawa: Carleton University Press, 1989), 6.

13. Viscount Haldane, "The Work for the Empire of the Judicial Committee of the Privy Council," *Cambridge Law Journal,* 1 (1923), 150; quoted in Alan C. Cairns, "The Judicial Committee and Its Critics," in Douglas E. Williams, ed., *Constitution, Government, and Society in Canada: Selected Essays by Alan C. Cairns* (Toronto: McClelland and Stewart, 1988), 90.

14. Cairns, "The Judicial Committee and Its Critics," 61–63.

15. Peter W. Hogg, "Is the Supreme Court of Canada Biased in Constitutional Cases?," *Canadian Bar Review,* 57 (1979).

16. The three territories have separate fiscal relationships with Ottawa, which will not be discussed here. For information on Territorial Formula Financing, which makes up the large majority of public revenues in the three territories, go to www.fin.gc.ca and click on "Transfer Payments to Provinces."

17. Canada, *Report of the Royal Commission on Dominion-Provincial Relations,* volume 1, abridged by Donald V. Smiley (Ottawa: Carleton University Press, 1963 [1940]), 210–14.

18. *Report of the Royal Commission on Dominion-Provincial Relations,* 210–14.

19. See the federal government's *2006 Budget: Focusing on Priorities—Recent Evolution of Fiscal Balance in Canada,* available on-line at www.fin.gc.ca/budget06/fp/fpa2e.htm.

20. See Paul A. R. Hobson and France St-Hilaire, "The Evolution of Federal-Provincial Fiscal Arrangements: Putting Humpty Together Again," in Harvey Lazar, ed., *The State of the Federation 1999–2000: Toward a New Mission Statement for Canadian Fiscal Federalism* (Montreal and Kingston: Institute for Intergovernmental Relations/McGill–Queen's University Press, 2000).

21. Alain-G. Gagnon and Hugh Segal, "Introduction," in Alain-G. Gagnon and Hugh Segal, eds., *The Canadian Social Union without Quebec: Eight Critical Analyses* (Montreal: Institute for Research in Public Policy, 2000).

22. See Canada, Department of Finance, "Backgrounder: Canada Health Transfer," March 2004; and "Federal/Provincial/Territorial Fiscal Relations in Transition: A Report to Canada's Western Premiers from the Finance Ministers of British Columbia, Alberta, Saskatchewan, Manitoba, Yukon, Northwest Territories and Nunavut," June 2003, 6; available on-line at www.scics.gc.ca.

23. Canada, Department of Finance, "Federal Support for Health Care: The Facts," March 2004; available on-line at www.fin.gc.ca/facts/fshc6_e.html.

24. After the failure of the intergovernmental bargaining over the Meech Lake and Charlottetown Accords, these events were renamed First Ministers' Meetings, or FMMs, perhaps to lower public expectations by presenting a more relaxed image.

25. "Council of the Federation: Founding Agreement," December 5, 2003; accessed on-line at www.scics.gc.ca.

26. The data for 2003 are available on the Canadian Intergovernmental Conference Secretariat website (go to www.scisc.gc.ca and click on "Conference Information"); the historical data are from Julie M. Simmons, "Securing the Threads of Co-operation in the Tapestry of Intergovernmental Relations: Does the Institutionalization of Ministerial Conferences Matter?," in Meekison, Telford, and Lazar, eds., 285–311, Table 1, 289.

27. Johanne Poirier, "Intergovernmental Agreements in Canada: At the Crossroads Between Law and Politics," in Meekison, Telford, and Lazar, eds., 427

28. Thomas J. Courchene, "Glocalization: The Regional/International Interface," *Canadian Journal of Regional Science,* 18:1 (Spring 1995)

29. Data retrieved on-line at geodepot.statcan.ca/Diss/Highlights/

4 PARTIES AND PARTY SYSTEMS

LEARNING OBJECTIVES

- *identify* and *explain* the development of the major parties in Canada
- *identify* and *explain* what political parties are, including how they are organized, financed, and regulated
- *identify* and *explain* the four distinct Canadian federal party systems, including the historical development and important features of each

INTRODUCTION

Political parties are at the heart of Canadian politics. They are the most visible and identifiable elements of our political system and, in one way or another, are integral to all other aspects of government. Parties are voluntary organizations that have members and leaders. They recruit candidates for elected office, one of whom becomes prime minister, while others serve as cabinet ministers and parliamentarians. Directly or indirectly, parties establish public policies that determine everything from how much tax we pay on our textbooks, iPods, and clothes, to whether or not we go to war and what kind of health, education, and social services are available in our communities.

As in other countries, Canadian parties operate within a party system. The concept of party systems, at least in Western democracies, refers to the relationship between the various parties as they compete for votes and seats within a given political culture. At the most basic level, party systems are often classified by the structure of party competition. That is, the classification system rests on how many parties regularly win enough votes to gain representation within the legislative assembly. Accordingly, competitive party systems can be classified as

- *one-party dominant systems*, in which many parties compete for votes but only one regularly gets enough support to form a government
- classic *two-party systems*, in which many parties may compete, but two parties dominate, each alternately having an opportunity to govern when the electorate decides the party in power needs to be replaced
- *multiparty systems*, in which a few larger parties compete with a number of smaller parties, each winning at least some share of the legislative seats

Generally speaking, the national Canadian party system has never been one-party dominant, although we came close during the 1940s and 50s when the Liberals ran off a string of five consecutive majority victories. Some conditions of one-party dominance can be found in provincial politics, particularly in Alberta. For the most part, the national party system has oscillated between variants of classic two-party competition and multiparty competition. Using R. Kenneth Carty's historical model of Canadian party systems as our launching point, we can identify four distinct periods of Canadian party system competition[1] (see Canadian Political Chronology 4.2).

- First party system (1867–1917), in which classic two-party competition between the Conservative and Liberals was the norm
- Second party system (1921–1962), in which multiparty competition existed between the dominant Liberals, a weakened Conservative party, and a host of minor, mostly Western, protest parties
- Third party system (1963–1988), in which two-plus or two-and-one-half party competition existed between the Liberals and Conservatives, and a third party, the New Democratic Party (NDP), which never competed for power, but also never withered and died as tends to be the fate of minor Canadian parties
- Fourth party system (1993–present), in which multiparty competition again appears to be the norm

The four party-systems model will inform the analysis throughout this chapter, so understanding the dates covered by the four periods and the number of parties competing will be necessary prior to us filling in the details about which political actors occupied what roles. We will begin with a brief introductory discussion of each of the contemporary parliamentary parties, followed by a description of how the parties operate as legal entities while attempting to represent various aspects of a dynamic political culture. The chapter will conclude by returning to a more formal historical analysis of the development of the Canadian party systems.

CANADA'S NATIONAL POLITICAL PARTIES

Only two political parties have ever governed Canada: the Conservatives and the Liberals (see Canada by the Numbers 4.2). They are often referred to as the "traditional parties." The Conservatives were the first, and the most recent, to hold power, while the Liberals have governed the most—60 percent of Canada's 140-year existence. Each has had its values grounded in Canada's predominantly liberal political culture. But each has also been importantly conditioned by other influences, including competition from new parties as they gained entry into the party system by representing interests not accommodated by the established parties.

After the post-Confederation consolidation of the two traditional parties during the first party system, the most significant new parties, often called "third parties," were established by Prairie voters as protests to the Central Canadian dominance of the traditional parties. The Progressives (1921 election), Social Credit (1935 election), and Cooperative Commonwealth Federation (CCF) (1935 election) smashed their way into the system, destroying the cozy two-party arrangement and forcing the traditional parties to accommodate the emerging diversity of interests in a rapidly changing country.

The Liberals responded better to the new dynamics than did the Conservatives. Hence, the Liberals governed for all but five years of the second party system. But when the Progressive Conservatives rebuilt their competitiveness in the West (1958 election), the protest parties faded from the scene, leaving the remnants of one, the CCF, to found the NDP, and the other, Social Credit, to disappear from the national scene after lingering temporarily as the Quebec-based Ralliement des créditistes.

The thirty-year period of relatively stable two-plus party competition during the third party system was again shattered by a protest from the West, but this time with help from Québécois nationalists. When both the Bloc Québécois (BQ) and Reform (1993 election) entered the system, they helped the Liberals return to power by reducing the governing Progressive Conservatives, as well as the NDP, to minor-party status in Parliament. But in just over a decade, both parties, particularly the Conservatives, have rebuilt their national organizations and much of their credibility with voters.

◼ The Conservatives

Canada's oldest political party has undergone many transformations in its history, most recently by reconfiguring itself as a merger between the Progressive Conservative Party and the Reform–Alliance Party.

Ideologically, it began as a classical conservative, Tory, pro-Confederation party willing to use state management of the economy and society to build a new nation. For most of its history, the Conservative Party has maintained strong Canadian nationalist beliefs and, at times, has been openly anti-American in its election campaigning. More recently, however, the party has adopted a more neoconservative or "centre-right" perspective by supporting free markets and trade. It has become more suspicious of state intervention in the economy and much less anti-American in its rhetoric and policy positioning.

Thirteen of the Conservatives' 24 leaders have become Canadian prime minister. The party's founder, John A. Macdonald, served longer than any other Conservative prime minister. Macdonald won six majority governments (four in a row beginning in 1878) and governed for a total of 19 years. Only four other Conservative leaders ever won majorities (see Canada by the Numbers 4.2). Robert Borden served for 9 years, winning a majority as Conservative leader in 1911, and another as leader of the World War I Union government in 1917. R. B. Bennett won one majority in 1930 and served as prime minister for 5 years during the Great Depression. John Diefenbaker won three elections; two were minorities that bookended his only majority victory in 1958. Brian Mulroney served for 9 years beginning in 1984 and was the first Conservative leader since Macdonald to put together back-to-back majority wins.

The origins of the Conservative Party predate Confederation itself. Macdonald brought together a coalition of pro-Confederation Tories, Liberal–Conservatives, and Québécois Blues in the colonial legislature of the United Province of Canada. They expanded that coalition to include like-minded Maritimers during the Confederation debates, English-speaking business interests in Montreal, and Grand Trunk railway interests.

Under Macdonald, the Conservatives designed the Canadian state, its initial economic structure, and its territorial expansion. Most of this was accomplished through a series of policies known as the National Policy. Key among its many measures were expanding the young nation to the Pacific through the purchase of Rupert's Land and the enticement of British Columbia to join the federation on the promise of building the transcontinental Canadian Pacific Railway. Macdonald also built a protective tariff wall around Canada in a successful effort to industrialize the Central Canadian economy. Immigration policies recruited large numbers of new-comers into the industrial heartland and the emerging agriculture-based Prairie hinterland.

Throughout his long reign, Macdonald's support was based largely on a compact between English Ontario voters and French Quebeckers. Over time, and especially after the hanging of Louis Riel, Conservative support in Quebec dropped off signifi-cantly. In fact, so dismal were Conservative prospects in Quebec that in only 3 of the 33 elections since 1891 have the Conservatives won more seats than any other party (1958, 1984, and 1988).

When Macdonald died immediately following the 1891 election, the party drifted, appointing four different leaders in four years. The Conservatives were defeated in the 1896 election and began their first extended period in Opposition. Quebeckers remained wary of the party, as did an increasingly large number of Western voters who began questioning the National Policy and the high costs Prairie farmers were expected to pay in maintaining the economic and transportation infrastructures.

When Borden became prime minister in 1911, he did so largely because of strong support from Ontario, with that province alone providing him with over half of his total seats (73 of 134). After winning the 1917 election as leader of the largely English, pro-conscription Union Government, the Conservatives' prospects in Quebec continued to diminish. Furthermore, the nationalizing effects of World War I in English Canada could not forestall the growing unrest against the Conservatives on the Canadian Prairies. When combined with dismal electoral prospects in Quebec, Prairie voters' rejection of the Conservatives led to a second long period in Opposition for

CP PHOTO (Tom Hanson)

Born: 1959, Toronto, Ontario

Education: B.A. and M.A. Economics
(University of Calgary, 1985 and 1991)

Profession: Economist, president of
National Citizens Coalition

Political Career Highlights
1981 PC executive assistant
1987 Chief policy officer for Reform Party
1989 Legislative assistant to Deborah Grey,
Reform's first MP
1993 Elected MP for Calgary West
2002 Elected leader of Canadian Alliance
2002, 2004, and 2006 Elected MP for
Calgary South West
2004 Elected leader of Conservative Party
of Canada
2006 Elected prime minister of Canada
with a minority

Source: *First Among Equals, The Prime Minister in Canadian Life and Politics* (Ottawa: Library and Archives Canada),
available on-line at www.collectionscanada.ca/primeministers/

the "party of Confederation." Calgarian R. B. Bennett secured the Conservatives their only majority victory (1930) in the ten elections between 1921 and 1957. The party attempted to solve its problems on the Prairies by recruiting to their leadership Manitoba Progressive John Bracken, who led the Conservatives into the 1945 election. They also changed their name to the Progressive Conservatives (PC). But most of the old Progressive vote had already been won over by Social Credit in Alberta, the CCF in Saskatchewan and Manitoba, and the Liberals elsewhere, leaving Bracken and his successor, George Drew, destined to be Opposition leaders only.

Even when John Diefenbaker brought the Progressive Conservatives back to power with a minority victory in 1957, he did so without substantial support from Quebec and the three most westerly provinces, including his home province of Saskatchewan. In 1958, Diefenbaker brought Westerners and Quebeckers into the fold, securing a landslide majority and devastating the Prairie protest parties in the process. However, his leadership style created divisions within the party and the PCs' support outside of the West proved ephemeral.

Leadership divisions plagued the Conservatives until Diefenbaker resigned and former Nova Scotia premier and "Red Tory" Robert Stanfield was elected PC leader in 1967. Despite Stanfield's attempts to move the party closer to the centre of the ideological spectrum, he lost three successive elections to Pierre Trudeau's Liberals.

Albertan Joe Clark assumed the PC leadership in 1976. Based largely on strong support from the West, and despite winning only 2 of Quebec's 75 seats, Clark led the PCs to a minority victory in 1979, a fascinating election in which the PCs (36 percent) won less of the popular vote than the Liberals (40 percent), but still managed to win more seats. His government was short-lived, however, and after losing the 1980 election, Clark faced a leadership revolt of his own, eventually losing the party leadership to Brian Mulroney in 1983.

Mulroney built a successful winning coalition for the PCs by adding Québécois nationalists to the strong Western base. In 1984 he led the PCs to a landslide majority victory that rivalled Diefenbaker's 1958 sweep. Under his government, the PCs reversed their historical opposition to free trade and implemented their most important policy initiative since Macdonald: the Canada–U.S. Free Trade Agreement. The free trade issue dominated the 1988 election and helped Mulroney keep his fragile electoral coalition together, despite cracks beginning to appear on the Western front.

Frustrated with the Mulroney government's fixation with Quebec, and with its dismal fiscal record of large deficits and increasing taxes, many Westerners joined ranks with the new Reform Party after the 1988 election. When the proposed Meech Lake and Charlottetown constitutional solutions to the Quebec problem failed, and Québécois nationalists began deserting the PCs for the Bloc Québécois, Mulroney's PC coalition broke down and his successor, Canada's first female prime minister, Kim Campbell, was left to face voters' wrath.

No Canadian party had ever been defeated as soundly as were the 1993 Campbell PCs. The party was reduced from holding a 169-seat majority to only 2 seats, last among the five parties that gained representation in the House. For the next three elections the PCs would square off against not only the again dominant Liberals, but also former members of its once governing coalition: Reform–Alliance in the West and the BQ in Quebec. One of the surviving PC MPs from the 1993 election, Jean Charest, assumed the PC leadership, but after tentatively rebuilding some support for the party in the 1997 election, he abandoned federal politics to become provincial Liberal leader in Quebec. Former prime minister Clark returned as leader, but the PCs lost both votes and seats in the 2000 election. Nova Scotia MP Peter MacKay was elected leader in 2003, and, despite promising not to entertain merger talks with the Canadian Reform Conservative Alliance (CA or Alliance), he quickly negotiated a deal with its leader, Stephen Harper. The deal saw the weaker PCs merge with the Western-based Alliance to form the new Conservative Party of Canada.

Harper won the first merged Conservative Party leadership contest and succeeded in reducing the Liberals to a minority government in the 2004 election. Despite coming from the Reform–Alliance segment of the new coalition, Harper has transformed the new party into a more moderate, centre-right conservative party than was Reform, and in doing so, won a minority victory in the 2006 election, bringing the party back to power for the first time in 12 years.

■ The Liberals

The Liberal Party of Canada became known as Canada's "natural governing" party after holding office for two-thirds of the entire twentieth century and occupying the position as Canada's most pragmatic federal political party (see Canada by the Numbers 4.2). They have also demonstrated superior ability to quickly adjust to Canada's evolving political culture and corresponding competition from new parties.

For the most part, the Liberals have attempted to occupy the centre of the ideological spectrum by adjusting with the times. The party's ideological origins are found in classical British liberalism, including support for individual rights, economic liberties, a less interventionist government, and free markets and trade. However, once in power, the party quickly compromised its ideological rigour by successfully adopting the National Policy agenda, completing its last stages, and adopting a more business-friendly liberalism.[2] During their long reign in power for most of the second party system, Liberal pragmatism reached its height. At the start of the third party system, they continued to change with the times by embracing welfare liberalism and presiding over the establishment of the Canadian welfare state. After a period of ideological drift under Pierre Trudeau's leadership, which saw the Liberals become much more economically interventionist and more anti-American than they typically had been in the past, the Liberals returned to a more familiar form of business liberalism under Jean Chrétien's leadership.

All but 1 of the Liberals' 11 leaders became Canadian prime minister. In fact, only 2 never won elections: Edward Blake in the 1880s and John Turner in the 1980s. Most won multiple majorities: Alexander Mackenzie (one majority), Wilfrid Laurier (four consecutive majorities), William Lyon Mackenzie King (four majorities and two minorities), Louis St. Laurent (two majorities), Pierre Trudeau (three majorities and one minority), and Jean Chrétien (three consecutive majorities). Two others, Lester Pearson (two minorities) and Paul Martin (one minority), were less successful but nevertheless led their parties to at least one election victory.

Like those of the Conservative Party, the origins of the Liberal Party of Canada are found in the colonial legislature of the United Province of Canada. The party included among its ranks those opposed to Macdonald's Confederation plans and his close association with urban business interests. The rural Clear Grits of Canada West and the anticlerical Rouges of Canada East formed a loose coalition in opposition to Macdonald. Their post-Confederation successors took power from the Conservatives under Mackenzie's leadership when the Macdonald government became embroiled in the patronage issues surrounding the Pacific Scandal. But their time in government did not last long and it fell to Laurier to build a party that could successfully compete with the Conservatives.

After losing the 1891 election on a platform that supported free trade with the Americans, Laurier adopted policies that resembled those of the Conservative Party he was seeking to replace. He made peace with big business and railway interests, as well as with the Catholic Church in Quebec. After winning the 1896 election, he continued implementing the main provisions of the National Policy, including encouraging a

POLITICAL BIOGRAPHY 4.2 Liberal Party Leader Stéphane Dion

CP PHOTO(Ian Barrett)

Born: 1955, Quebec City, Quebec

Education: B.A. and M.A. Political Science (Université Laval, 1977 and 1979), Ph.D. Political Sociology (Institut d'études politiques de Paris, 1986)

Profession: Political Science professor Université de Montréal

Political Career:
1996 Elected MP for Saint-Laurent/ Cartierville in by-election
1996–2003 Intergovernmental Affairs Minister
1997, 2000, 2004, 2006 re-elected MP for Saint-Laurent/Cartierville
2000 Clarity Act
2001–2003 Minister responsible for Official Languages
2004–2006 Environment Minister
2006 Elected Liberal party leader and leader of the official Opposition

Source: Parliament of Canada biography available at www.stephanedion.parl.gc.ca/biography.asp?lang=en

large influx of immigrants which contributed to Canada's population growth leading the Western world at the turn of the twentieth century. Laurier's most important contribution to Liberal Party success lay in his ability to bring Quebec voters into the Liberal fold, a voting base that would help sustain the Liberals for the better part of the next century. His success in the West was much more limited. In supporting the National Policy-based notion of Canada as an economic empire of the Saint Lawrence Valley, Laurier demonstrated to Westerners that both of the traditional parties were destined to treat the West as an internal colony. Their response would be to form parties of their own that would compete directly with the two Central Canadian parties.

It was during the second party system, characterized by the Western protest parties, that the Liberals best demonstrated their penchant for pragmatism. When the Progressives brought the cozy two-party system to a crashing end in the 1921 election, King deftly recruited many of their parliamentary leaders into his governing coalition as he embarked on a regional brokerage strategy that would add substantial Western support to his Central Canadian and Maritime bases. King's pragmatism is likely best illustrated by his skilful handling of the divisive conscription issue during World War II and the 1942 referendum on the issue. His position of "conscription if necessary, but not necessarily conscription" demonstrated his pragmatic approach to the issue and generally appeased both pro-conscription English-speaking Canadians and anticonscription Quebeckers.

When Canadian socialism appeared to be making headway during the third party system, the Liberals became the champions of the welfare state, building on programs such as universal family allowance (1945) and old age security (1951), and introducing new shared-cost programs like medicare (1966). Despite never winning a majority government, Pearson's tenure as leader and prime minister is often credited with allowing the Liberals to legitimately define themselves as the defenders of the welfare state.

The late-1960s and early-1970s were tumultuous for Canada. At the same time Canada celebrated its centennial with Expo '67 festivities in Montreal, the FLQ crisis was about to explode onto the national political scene. When the economic crisis of the 1970s descended on Canadians, the Trudeau Liberals were increasingly preoccupied with national unity. Given the Quebec secession crisis, their focus may have been well motivated. It certainly instigated Trudeau's greatest contribution to Canadian politics: the patriation agreement that resulted in the Constitution Act, 1982, and the adoption of the Charter of Rights and Freedoms. The result, however, was that economic matters took a back seat to national unity. Despite a prolonged, continual increase in taxes, the party presided over the beginning of a two-decade period of federal government deficits. Yet, in spite of their economic record, for the most part, the Liberals kept winning elections—based primarily on winning almost all of Quebec's seats at the same time they were almost completely shut out from winning Western seats.

When Turner succeeded Trudeau, the party was handed the most severe electoral defeat in its history. Canadian voters humbled the Liberals, reducing them from a majority government of 147 seats after the 1980 election to just 40 seats after the 1984 vote. Despite considerable dissention within in his parliamentary caucus, Turner remained leader and fought the 1988 election by reversing the Liberals' historical position on the issue of free trade with the Americans. The gambit worked in that, although he lost the election, he succeeded in rebuilding the party's support base (83 seats) and preparing the ground for the next leader.

Jean Chrétien led the party back to power in 1993 after its longest period in Opposition since the Borden governments. The Chrétien government's greatest legacy was clearly found in its completion of the fiscal reforms that had begun with the previous Progressive Conservative government. Under the guidance of his finance minister, Paul Martin Jr., the Chrétien Liberals balanced the federal government budget and began to slowly pay down some of the accumulated debt. Facing an opposition that was divided amongst four competing parties, the Chrétien Liberals won three consecutive majority governments. But they did so based on a new pattern of support, one not seen before in Canadian party history. For the first time, the Liberals won majority governments without winning the majority of Quebec seats. In all three elections, Ontario MPs made up more than half, and sometimes nearly two-thirds (1997), of the total number of Liberals elected.

After a protracted internal power struggle, Chrétien reluctantly surrendered the leadership to Martin, just in time to witness the conservative parties end their vote splitting and the BQ rebuild its support base. Although Martin managed to keep the Liberals in power by winning a minority victory in 2004, fallout from the party's misdeeds associated with the federal sponsorship program contributed to its defeat in 2006. Although the party remains strong in Ontario and the Maritimes, it will be up to the new Liberal leader, Stéphane Dion, to develop a strategy to rebuild the party's support base in Quebec and make inroads with the increasingly important Western electorate.

The New Democratic Party

Canada's New Democratic Party (NDP) was founded in 1961 as a response to Diefenbaker's near annihilation of the Western protest parties in 1958 (see Canada by the Numbers 4.2). A series of discussions between the remaining elements of the Prairie-based Cooperative Commonwealth Federation (CCF) and organized labour, primarily the Canadian Labour Congress (CLC), led to the decommissioning of the CCF and the establishment of the new party. The NDP would dedicate itself to representing the demands of farmers, labour, and urban professionals. It would organize itself around a democratic socialist platform and appeal for votes based on its mantra of "defender of the working Canadian" against exploitation by big business, and capitalism more generally.

The NDP's commitment to socialism must be qualified within the context of Canada's predominantly liberal political culture. When compared to many European socialist parties, the NDP's social democratic platform appears less doctrinaire and much less ideologically extreme. Nevertheless, within the context of Canadian parties, the NDP is Canada's most ideologically grounded party. It is much more likely to advocate for government intervention in the economy than are either the Liberals or the Conservatives. Over the nearly half-century of its existence, it has consistently supported greater governmental regulation of the private economy and higher taxes for big business, corporations more generally, and wealthy individuals. It is a staunch supporter of more generous social-welfare programs, a state monopoly on health-care delivery, interventionist environmental policies, and an overall lessening of American influence in the Canadian economy and culture.

Former Saskatchewan premier Tommy Douglas was the first leader of the NDP, having previously brought the CCF to power in his home province, where he spearheaded the drive for a socialized national health-care program. Under Douglas, the NDP built its support on part of the old CCF base in the West—primarily in British Columbia and Manitoba, as Saskatchewan voters stuck with Diefenbaker during his tenure as PC leader. Alberta and Quebec have largely shunned the NDP for most of its existence, as had Maritime voters until the most recent elections. Under Douglas the NDP added modest Ontario support to its Western base. The party's ability to solidify the organized-labour vote, however, has been an ongoing challenge for the party.

CP PHOTO (Richard Lam)

Born: 1950, Hudson, Quebec

Education: B.A. Political Science (McGill University, 1970), M.A. and Ph.D. Political Science (York University, 1971 and 1983)

Profession: Political science professor, Ryerson Polytechnic

Political Career Highlights

1982, 1985, 1988, 1997, and 2000 Toronto city councillor

1984–1988 and 1994–1997 Member of Metro Toronto Council

1991 Lost election to become mayor of Toronto

2001 President of Canadian Federation of Municipalities

2003 Elected NDP leader

2004 and 2006 Elected MP for Toronto–Danforth

Ontario MP and former CCF stalwart David Lewis became leader in 1971 and succeeded in bringing the NDP closer to power than it had ever been before or has been since. The party captured 31 seats in the 1972 election and propped up Trudeau's minority government in exchange for the government adopting some NDP policies on natural resources and Crown corporations. Ed Broadbent succeeded Lewis and led the NDP to its most successful election showing. In 1988 the NDP won 43 seats, a high mark for the party. However, even as it was achieving its zenith nationally, the party lost ground in Ontario in 1988 and generally went into decline elsewhere after that.

The NDP was the first party to elect a female leader when Yukon MP Audrey McLaughlin was selected in 1989. But the party was decimated in the 1993 election (winning only 9 seats), which led to another leadership change. Nova Scotian Alexa McDonough was elected leader and helped rebuild some of the party's support in the 1997 election, most notably in the Maritimes, a new area of support for the NDP. But the party struggled with ideological issues during her term as leader and lost ground again in the 2000 election.

Toronto city councillor Jack Layton became leader in 2003 and has rebuilt NDP support back to levels similar to those it achieved in the 1970s and 1980s. He has campaigned primarily on a moderate left-of-centre platform, adopting a somewhat less ideologically socialist agenda in an effort at dispelling the party's image as less fiscally responsible than either of the traditional parties. Although the NDP remains weak in Quebec and is struggling in its former heartland of the Prairies, it does appear to be making inroads with urban voters in both Ontario and British Columbia, and has played an active role in the recent minority parliaments.

■ The Bloc Québécois

Quebeckers' anger over the rejection of the Meech Lake Accord instigated the creation of the separatist Bloc Québécois (BQ or Bloc). Under the leadership of former Mulroney cabinet minister Lucien Bouchard, a parliamentary party was created out of eight Quebec MPs, six former PCs and two ex-Liberals, who broke with their parties in the spring of 1990. The Bloc contests only Quebec seats for the federal Parliament and typically relies on the provincial Parti Québécois (PQ) for its extra-parliamentary organization during national elections.

The overall purpose of the Bloc is not to represent a distinct ideological dimension within the Canadian electorate. Rather, its goals are to represent Québécois nationalists in the federal Parliament and to assist the PQ in future sovereignty referenda. As such, it tends to support government initiatives that it determines to be in Quebec's interests and will further its goal of an independent Quebec nation. That being said, the Bloc tends toward the social democratic side of the ideological spectrum when voting on most social and economic policy proposals.

As founder, Bouchard served as inaugural Bloc leader, helping the young party raise its profile by campaigning effectively for the No side in the 1992 Charlottetown Accord referendum. He then led the party to 54 seats in the 1993 election, besting Reform by 2 seats and landing the Bloc the title of Canada's official Opposition (see Canada by the Numbers 4.2). Shortly after the nearly successful 1995 Quebec sovereignty referendum, Bouchard left Ottawa to become Parti Québécois leader and Quebec premier. Michel Gauthier succeeded him as Bloc leader but lacked Bouchard's charisma and stepped down after less than a year on the job. He was replaced by BQ MP Gilles Duceppe who had been the party's first elected member after winning a 1990 by-election.

Despite a poor 1997 campaign effort, the party retained most of its seats during that election. It did, however lose 10 MPs and the mantle of official Opposition. Support dropped further in the 2000 election and it appeared that a resurgent Liberal Party would eventually displace the Bloc in Quebec. However, the party's fortunes rebounded when the sponsorship program scandal began to dominate Quebec voters' attention. In his third campaign as BQ leader, Duceppe led the party to its best results yet, again winning 54 seats and more firmly establishing it as the dominant federal party in Quebec. Although the Bloc is now faced with a resurgent Conservative Party in Quebec, unless the Conservatives can more fully overcome the historical voting patterns of Quebeckers, the Bloc Québécois is likely to benefit from "federalist" vote splitting between the two traditional parties for some time to come.

Born: 1947, Montreal, Quebec

Education: B.A. Political Science (Collège Mont-Saint-Louis)

Profession: Union negotiator for Confederation of National Trade Unions

Political Career Highlights

1990 Won by-election for Laurier–Ste. Marie, becoming the first MP to be elected as Bloc Québécois candidate

1993, 1997, 2000, 2004, and 2006 Reelected MP for Laurier–Ste. Marie

1997 Elected Bloc Québécois leader and became leader of the official Opposition

1997, 2000, 2004, and 2006 Led Bloc Québécois in federal elections

CP PHOTO (Andrew Vaughan)

Reform and the Canadian Alliance

The Reform Party of Canada was founded in 1987, less than two years into the Mulroney government's first mandate, by Westerners who were already sensing that the new PC government would not live up to their expectations. Westerners' grievances were many, and most voters in that region expected quick redress after what they perceived to be years of hostile federal Liberal government treatment of their issues and concerns. When Central Canadian concerns more generally, and Quebec issues in particular, again dominated the national government's agenda, many Westerners revived an argument as old as Macdonald's National Policy and declared that neither of the two traditional parties were capable of, or interested in, making Western concerns their focus.

Under the slogan "The West Wants In," Reform was founded as a populist, non-separatist, exclusively Western party that would contest federal seats only in the West and North.[3] Just one year after its founding, the party contested the 1988 election. It received considerable interest from Alberta voters, winning 15 percent of the vote in that province, but garnered less than 3 percent of the vote nationally and won no seats. In response, the party decided to reconstitute itself as a national party (1991) that would contest elections in all of Canada, although initially it would not focus on attempting to win Quebec ridings. Ideologically, the party added fiscal conservatism and some social conservatism to its populism, and was generally considered to be distinctly on the right of the Canadian ideological spectrum. Its populism, however, allowed key MPs to frequently voice their opinions on a number of hot-button social issues in the name of representing their constituents' interests. The resulting publicity created an impression in the minds of many Canadian voters that the party was much more right wing and socially conservative than were either its membership or voting base. There is little doubt, however, that Reform carved out an electoral niche for itself on the ideological right. It opposed much of the existing welfare-state arrangements, supported free markets and trade, and was opposed to most of the Quebec-centred constitutional agenda. As such, it tended to elect MPs primarily in constituencies where these sentiments represented significant plurality or majority opinion.

Under its only leader, Preston Manning, son of former long-time Alberta premier, Ernest Manning, Reform broke into the established party system by winning a 1989 Alberta by-election shortly after the 1988 general election. It followed up in the fall of the same year with a victory in the inaugural Alberta Senate election. Prime Minister Mulroney eventually appointed Reform's candidate, Stan Waters, to the upper house. To this day, Waters is credited as being Canada's only elected senator. Reform successfully campaigned on the No side in the 1992 Charlottetown Accord referendum and made its major breakthrough into Parliament a year later. Reform won 52 seats in the 1993 election, primarily in Alberta and British Columbia, but including other Prairie seats and 1 Ontario victory. Despite narrowly losing the title of official Opposition to the Bloc, Reform established itself as the dominant federal party in the West and helped ensure that the once dominant PCs were largely eradicated from the Western electoral map.

Reform's parliamentary debut met with mixed results as the party struggled to accommodate the seemingly contradictory demands of maintaining its populism and acting as a cohesive parliamentary party. In spite of a massive organizational effort east of the Manitoba–Ontario provincial boundary, and a superb campaign effort that included a go-for-broke strategy, the party failed to make a breakthrough in Central Canada during the 1997 election. Although it increased its national seat total to 60 and supplanted the BQ as official Opposition, it lost its only Ontario seat and failed to make significant inroads in ridings outside the West (see Canada by the Numbers 4.2).

After the perceived failure of the 1997 election, Manning decided that a new political vehicle would be required to advance his cause of realigning federal party politics. After an elaborate and contentious series of consultations with party members that he called the United Alternative (UA) from 1998 to 2000, Manning convinced Reformers to abandon their Western vehicle for a new party called the Canadian Reform Conservative Alliance (CA or Alliance). Although the UA attracted some interest from provincial PC MLAs, the federal PCs wanted nothing to do with Manning's invitation to join the new party, making it appear to be little more than a rebranding of Reform. Manning also failed to convince Alliance members that he should be leader of the new party. In the first CA leadership contest (2000), Manning was rejected in favour of former Alberta PC cabinet minister Stockwell Day. Sensing opportunity, Prime Minister Chrétien called an election before the Alliance could get its organization in order and define an image for itself in voters' minds. In a campaign that was fraught with mistakes and a leader clearly not yet ready for the rigours of a national campaign, the CA nonetheless made progress. Although it did little to alter the vote splitting that was arguably providing the Liberals with easy electoral victories, especially in Ontario, the Alliance won more seats in the 2000 election (66), and more votes (25 percent) than Reform had ever won, including 2 new Ontario seats. But Day had little time to savour the small victory or begin to establish his leadership credentials. He immediately faced a rebellion from within his own caucus. Made up largely of disgruntled Manning supporters, 8 of the rebellious MPs would break away from the CA and form their own parliamentary caucus. They would become known as the Democratic Representative Caucus (DRC) and would eventually form a parliamentary working association with the 12-member PC caucus.

Facing mounting challenges to his leadership, Day asked the Alliance executive to hold a leadership contest. He again ran as a candidate but was defeated by former Reform MP Harper. Despite campaigning as the contender least likely to entertain a merger between the CA and PC parties, Harper almost immediately broached the topic with PC leader Joe Clark. Upon being rejected, Harper moved to heal the divisions within his own party, convincing the DRC to disband and bringing most of its members back into the CA caucus. More importantly, he set about to impose some discipline on that caucus, keeping its often raucous behaviour out of the media spotlight as he rebuilt the fractured organization.

Once Peter MacKay replaced Clark as PC leader, Harper pursued merger negotiations with much more vigour. Facing the prospect of a Paul Martin-led Liberal landslide, and under considerable pressure from within his own party and the Canadian business community, MacKay relented and merger talks pursued in earnest. Harper and MacKay worked out a deal that led to the 2003 union of the CA and PC parties into the new Conservative Party of Canada (CPC). The new party was founded primarily on terms similar to those found in the old PC Party constitution, including its leadership selection process and the adoption of the Conservative brand. The Alliance contributed its greater organizational muscle to the new entity, including its superior network of well-funded constituency organizations, its much more stable financial position, and its much larger parliamentary caucus.

More importantly, the CA contributed the senior leadership team when Harper decisively won the inaugural leadership contest which MacKay declined to enter. Again sensing opportunity, the Liberals called the 2004 election before the Conservatives could hold a policy convention and establish much credibility with voters. Despite winning fewer votes than the total its two founding entities won in the 2000 general election, the new Conservatives won substantially more seats and established a base from which to expand. They achieved a measure of that expansion by winning a minority government in the 2006 election.

WHAT IS A POLITICAL PARTY?

A *political party* is an organization of members who work together to achieve one or more common goals. If we break down this definition into its component parts, we gain a clearer understanding of what parties are, what they do, and why they do it:

- *An organization* implies that parties are more or less stable institutions with their own formal constitutions and bylaws and their own informal rules of behaviour. They typically have two distinct levels: national (the parliamentary party, central office, and party executive) and local (the constituency associations).

- *Members* implies exclusivity and reflects the fact that only a small fraction of Canadians become formal members of political parties; only about 2 percent[4] of the total population are members at any one time. About 16 percent of Canadians will hold a party membership at some point in their lives. In general, party members are not demographically representative of the population. They are more likely to be white, male, middle-aged, prosperous, and more highly educated than the average Canadian voter.[5] They also tend to be better informed about politics than most people and hold stronger views about public policies and political principles. To survive and prosper, each party organization must provide incentives to attract and retain members and to engage them actively in its operations.

- *Working together* indicates that parties are social organizations that bring people together to coordinate their efforts in pursuit of common goals.

- *Achieving one or more common goals*—most importantly, winning votes and maintaining their organizational health—are purposes pursued by all parties. Beyond this generalization, the goals of parties vary widely.

In Canada we typically categorize parties into two general types. For *brokerage* or *cadre* parties, such as the Liberals, PCs, and the new Conservative Party, the primary goal is to exercise power by winning enough parliamentary seats to form a government. These parties tend to be dominated by their leaders and caucuses. Their memberships are small, especially between elections, and they used to rely on corporations for much of their revenue. *Missionary* or *ideological* parties, whose chances of forming a government are more remote, may focus instead on promoting their distinct principles and policy priorities. Reform began as a missionary party with a mandate to voice Western protest and populism. By initially limiting its electoral efforts to only one region of the country, it acknowledged that it would not form a government. The NDP has promoted a social democratic ideological approach to government. In doing so, it has never captured enough support to form a national government, although it has held power in four provinces at various times. These parties are often more internally democratic, placing the ultimate authority over policy in the hands of their members, who are proportionally more numerous and more continuously active than those in brokerage or cadre parties. They tend to provide a larger share of party revenue than do members of brokerage or cadre parties.

■ Party Structures in Canada

The structural elements of Canada's major national parties are broadly similar, importantly conditioned by other institutions such as the electoral system, and include three organizational components: the extraparliamentary organization, the parliamentary party, and the party's central office.

The bedrock of the extraparliamentary organization is the constituency association, which is run by a local executive. It is responsible for recruiting and nominating candidates for office, raising funds, and recruiting volunteers and members. Other important elements of the extraparliamentary organization are the leader, who is elected by the members and has important fundraising, campaign, and policy functions; the national executive, which attends to party business between conventions; and the biennial national convention, formally the highest authority in the party, which passes policy resolutions and elects the national executive.

The parliamentary party includes the leader, who either determines the government's agenda while serving as prime minister, or, when in opposition, leads his or her party's charge against the government. It also includes the parliamentary caucus, which staffs other leadership roles such as House Leader, whip, and caucus chair. Other important elements of the parliamentary party are the leader's office and parliamentary staffs, who communicate with the constituency associations, organize events, and coordinate various political activities.

The party's central office includes a national headquarters, run by a national director and a small permanent staff that expands dramatically during election campaigns. It provides the day-to-day administration for the party, keeping track of and communicating with members, raising funds, and organizing conventions and other major events. The central office also includes an official agent who is responsible for recording all financial transactions, disclosing them to Elections Canada, and keeping the party in compliance with the Canada Elections Act.

Party structures evolve in response to incentives set by the institutions within which they operate. In Canada, the primary incentives are as follows:

- Canada's parliamentary institutions reward parties capable of electing large numbers of MPs and organizing them into stable, cohesive caucuses. The incentive to obtain or stay in power usually produces a powerful sense of unity and team spirit within a parliamentary party.

- Within the government caucus, the cabinet system concentrates power in the hands of the prime minister (and to a lesser extent Opposition leaders), providing the leader of the governing party with unparalleled authority. Other factors that reinforce the authority of leaders include the regulatory requirements of the electoral laws, the news media's focus on individual personalities, and the influence of party leaders on voting behaviour.

- Canada's electoral system determines the structure of our extraparliamentary parties and affects the size of the parliamentary wings. It divides the country into 308 separate constituencies, each of which elects one MP to the House of Commons. Consequently, our extraparliamentary parties are divided into as many as 308 local organizations, one for each constituency in which they wish to run candidates. A strong tradition of localism is reinforced by the structure imposed by the electoral system.

- Finally, the Canada Elections Act regulates party financing and sets other requirements for parties that wish to obtain the benefits flowing from registration with Elections Canada. Most recently, Bill C-24, An Act to Amend the Canada Elections Act and the Income Tax Act (Political Financing), brought the most significant changes in the legal regime for national political parties since 1974. The details are discussed later in the "Finance" section of this chapter.

The working relationship among the various party elements is complex. Despite a hierarchical organizational structure, with leaders at the top and members somewhere around the bottom, in practice the different elements of the party structure enjoy considerable autonomy. The power to make binding decisions is shared among groups and individuals operating at all levels of the organization. In Canada, this means that the elements at the centre of the party—the leader, the party caucus, and the national headquarters—make decisions for the party as a whole, while the local constituency associations implement those decisions with some degree of flexibility.

This is known as the franchise model of party organization. It combines a national "brand name," advertising strategy, and "product line" (policy and leadership) with local "product delivery" (candidate nomination and campaigning) attuned to the regional market.[6] In practice, this means that constituency associations choose the party's candidates for the House of Commons and provide the necessary services to secure their election. All candidates are expected to use the party logo on their campaign signs and literature, and to sell the party platform (with some limited leeway to appeal to purely local sentiment). In return, they benefit from the expertise of the headquarters staff, well-researched policies, and—ideally—a popular national leader. Although some parties allow their leaders to attempt to assert their authority in local party affairs—the clearest example is the power of the Liberal leader to appoint candidates, over the heads (and sometimes the objections) of the activists in those particular ridings—the portrayal of Canadian parties as franchise systems is an apt model for understanding Canadian parties.

Functions of Canadian Parties

Candidate Selection

Parties monopolize the selection of candidates for elected office, making it rare for anyone to be elected to the House of Commons without having first gained the nomination of a political party. Given that most of the 308 constituency elections pit as many as a half-dozen candidates from the various parties against each other and only one gets elected, securing a party nomination is no guarantee of victory. It is, however, in most cases a necessary first step.

Although the new electoral laws (Bill C-24) subject nomination contests to state regulation for the first time, Canada's major political parties have traditionally given their constituency associations a good deal of autonomy in selecting candidates. Still, the majority of party nomination contests—approximately two-thirds—have only one candidate and are therefore won by acclamation. Sitting MPs enjoy an especially easy road to renomination; almost 90 percent of them are unopposed. As a consequence, relatively few members typically attend nomination meetings.[7] Although the constituency association has the right to select the candidate, the Canada Elections Act requires the leader to endorse all candidates, thereby providing leaders with the power to veto selections made by the local party organization.

Leadership Selection

For the first half-century following Confederation, the parliamentary caucus chose the party leader (see Canadian Political Chronology 4.1). The shift to leadership conventions began early in the twentieth century, partly because the major parties wished to appear more democratic. A leadership convention is a gathering of delegates—individuals who are chosen by ordinary members to represent the local membership and make decisions on their behalf. The delegates gather at the convention, meet the candidates, listen to speeches, and make their choices. The first national convention was held by the Liberals in 1919 and was won by Mackenzie King. The Conservative Party followed suit and at its 1927 convention selected R. B. Bennett as leader. The CCF–NDP has held leadership conventions since its founding in 1933.[8]

Early conventions (from 1919 to 1958) were small, elite dominated, and rarely competitive. Beginning in 1967, leadership conventions were transformed into huge events with as many as a dozen candidates and thousands of delegates. As the number of constituency delegates mushroomed, the means by which they were chosen became increasingly controversial. Organizers for the various leadership candidates would invade each constituency, sign up as many "instant members" as they could, and bus many of them to the delegate selection meeting to vote for their candidate's slate of delegates. These tactics often led to bitterly divisive trench warfare at the constituency level, which tended to tarnish the entire process as the news media focused on abuses such as the mass recruitment of recent immigrants, minors, and the homeless.[9]

Since 1985, some Canadian parties have experimented with one member, one vote (OMOV) systems of leader selection. In an OMOV system, every party member can vote directly for the leadership candidate of his or her choice. These tentative steps towards adopting a new system have been driven by the desire of some parties to become more democratic and to open their processes up to more members. Advances in communication technology—e.g., telephone systems linked to computer databases—have made it possible for party members to vote from their homes or a local polling station instead of having to incur the costs of travelling long distances to cast ballots at a convention.

In 1998, the federal PCs held a leadership contest in which all party members cast paper ballots in their constituencies for their choice. But instead of awarding the

LIBERAL	CONSERVATIVE	PROGRESSIVE	CCF/NDP	SOCIAL CREDIT	RALLIEMENT CRÉDITISTE	REFORM/ ALLIANCE	BLOC QUÉBÉCOIS
			First Party System *1867–1917*				
Alexander Mackenzie *1873–1880*	*Conservative* John Macdonald *1867–1891*						
Edward Blake *1880–1887*	John Abbott *1891–1892*						
Wilfrid Laurier *1887–1919*	John Thompson *1892–1894*						
	Mackenzie Bowell *1894–1896*						
	Charles Tupper *1896–1900*						
	Robert Borden *1901–1920*						
			Second Party System *1921–1962*				
William Lyon Mackenzie King *1919–1948*	Arthur Meighen *1920–1926*	Thomas Crerar *1920–1922*					
	Hugh Guthrie *1926–1927*	Robert Forke *1922–1926*					
	Richard Bennett *1927–1938*						
	Robert Manion *1938–1940*		*CCF* J. S. Woodsworth *1932–1942*	John Horne Blackmore *1935–1944*			
	Richard Hanson *1940–1943*		M. J. Coldwell *1942–1960*	Solon Earl Low *1944–1961*			
	Progressive Conservative Gordon Graydon *1943–1945*		Hazen Ague *1960–1961*				
	John Bracken *1945–1948*						
Louis St. Laurent *1948–1958*	George Drew *1948–1956*						

LIBERAL	CONSERVATIVE	PROGRESSIVE	CCF/NDP	SOCIAL CREDIT	RALLIEMENT CRÉDITISTE	REFORM/ALLIANCE	BLOC QUÉBÉCOIS
Lester Pearson 1958–1968	John Diefenbaker 1956–1967						
			Third Party System 1963–1988				
			NDP				
Pierre Trudeau 1968–1984	Robert Stanfield 1967–1976		Tommy Douglas 1961–1971	Robert Thompson 1961–1967	Réal Caouette 1963–1971		
	Joe Clark 1976–1983		David Lewis 1971–1975	Réal Caouette 1971–1976			
John Turner 1984–1990	Brian Mulroney 1983–1993		Ed Broadbent 1975–1989	André-Gilles Fortin 1976–1977			
				Fabien Roy 1979–1980			
			Fourth Party System 1993–present				
Jean Chrétien 1990–2003	Kim Campbell 1993		Audrey McLaughlin 1989–1995			*Reform* Preston Manning 1987–2000	Lucien Bouchard 1991–1996
	Jean Charest 1993–1998		Alexa McDonough 1995–2003				Michel Gauthier 1996–1997
						Canadian Alliance Stockwell Day 2000–2002	
	Joe Clark 1998–2003					Stephen Harper 2002–2004	
Paul Martin 2003–2006	Peter MacKay 2003						
Stéphane Dion 2006–	*Conservative* Stephen Harper 2004–		Jack Layton 2003–				Gilles Duceppe 1997–

leadership to the candidate with the largest number of votes across the country, the party assigned 100 points to each constituency. These points were distributed among the leadership candidates in proportion to their share of the vote in that riding and the points from all 301 constituencies were totalled to determine the winner. The Canadian Alliance elected its first leader in 2000 and took the OMOV rule more literally. All party members voted in their constituencies (or by telephone in some rural ridings) and the candidate receiving the majority of the total votes, wherever those votes were cast, became leader. Because the first ballot did not produce a majority for any candidate, a runoff vote was held two weeks later. Stockwell Day won convincingly over former Reform leader Preston Manning. The party used a similar OMOV system for its March 2002 leadership contest, although voting was conducted by mail-in ballot. Stephen Harper beat Day and two other candidates by winning a majority of votes on the first ballot. When the PCs and Alliance merged in 2003, they opted for the PC method of leadership selection. Former Alliance leader Harper beat his two opponents on the first ballot, with 55.5 percent of the points (16 149 out of 30 800).[10]

The BQ also uses OMOV to elect its leaders, as does the NDP. The latter was more reluctant to abandon conventions altogether, largely because OMOV conflicted with the institutional arrangement between the party and its affiliated unions—it is impossible to guarantee a specific percentage of the vote to a particular group when all members are empowered to cast ballots. Consequently, the NDP used a hybrid system in 1995. All party members were allowed to vote in primaries for the leader of their choice; the last-place finisher was dropped from the convention ballot, and the delegates were expected to reflect the primary results in their own decision-making. At the convention, however, delegates ignored the membership at large. Former MP Lorne Nystrom, who had won the primaries, placed third (and last) on the first ballot at the convention. Former Nova Scotia NDP leader Alexa McDonough, who had run a fairly distant third in the primaries, ended up winning the leadership after first-place finisher Svend Robinson pulled out before a second ballot could be held. The federal NDP subsequently decided to follow several of its provincial wings, adopting a straight OMOV system for its next leadership contest. Toronto municipal councillor Jack Layton won the 2003 contest by a convincing margin over long-time MP Bill Blaikie.

The federal Liberals continue to use a hybrid system. When members gather at local meetings to elect delegates to a leadership convention, they cast a separate ballot for the leadership candidate of their choice. The delegate spots from each riding are allocated among the candidates in rough proportion to their shares of the local vote. The PCs, who were disappointed with the lacklustre media coverage of their 1998 contest, adopted the same system for their June 2003 leadership vote. The Liberals' refusal to abandon the leadership convention altogether reminds us that the old system of party leadership selection does provide parties with important benefits. Conventions provide an opportunity for activists from across the country to network with one another and rub elbows with party leaders and notables, strengthening the national party organization and helping to bridge gaps between partisans in different regions.

New leadership-selection provisions were contained in Bill C-24 and were put into practice for the first time during the 2006 Liberal leadership contest.[11] All candidates seeking the leadership of a registered party are required to make their campaign finances public. By requiring weekly disclosure during the last month of a leadership contest, the law gives party members or delegates some insight into possible conflicts of interest and other potential problems before they make their final choice.

■ Regulation and Financing of Canadian Parties

The relationship between parties and the state is complicated. On the one hand, parties are voluntary, private organizations of citizens. This implies that they should be subject to little, if any, state regulation. On the other hand, because parties perform functions that are essential to the operation of the political system, they are also public institutions. This perspective suggests that parties should be both funded and regulated by the state. The tension between the public and private characters of parties has become more acute in recent years as the public has grown increasingly suspicious of political ethics. Until recently, Canadian parties were subject to relatively little regulation compared to those in other Western democracies. Since the 1970s, however, their internal operations have been subject to increasing legal scrutiny.[12] The growing recognition of parties as public entities has expanded both their regulatory burden and the financial support they receive from the state.

Registration

To some extent, Elections Canada treats all registered parties equally. The chief electoral officer maintains a *Registry of Parties* for the purpose of administering the act. Only registered parties are eligible for state monetary benefits, and each must meet the same criteria for registration including nomination of at least one candidate at each general election; submission of an annual fiscal report; and filing of an application for registration that includes the signatures of 250 party members, an official party name and logo, and the names of the party's leader and three other officers.

With the enacting of Bill C-24, the era of parties as private clubs is definitely over. For the first time, the internal operations of national parties are subject to state regulation and penalties for violations. The key provisions of the law include requirements that constituency associations ("electoral district associations," or EDAs) register with Elections Canada or forfeit the opportunity to receive or spend funds. Nomination contests, which used to be governed by the parties, are subject to new regulations. Anyone who wishes to seek the nomination of a registered party must appoint a financial agent. Those who raise or spend $1000 or more are required to file a report with Elections Canada after the nomination meeting. Spending limits designed to ensure that the wealthy do not squeeze out less affluent contenders have been imposed on nomination contestants. Leadership contests are also subject to new regulation.

Parties must inform Elections Canada as soon as a leadership race begins. All leadership candidates must register with the agency, and each must begin to report any campaign donations and expenditures as soon as the chief electoral officer and the party leader certify candidacy registration. The candidate's official agent is required to file a financial report in each of the four weeks immediately preceding the leadership vote and to submit a complete report within six months after the race ends. Note, however, that the law does not impose spending limits on leadership contests. The establishment and enforcement of such limits is still left to the discretion of the party itself.

Finance

Money is the "mother's milk" of politics. Election campaigns in the television age are hugely expensive, running into millions of dollars for the major national parties. Maintaining a national organization between elections is also a costly undertaking. In order to survive, major national parties must raise substantial amounts of money every year. Until the Election Expenses Act took effect in 1974, reliable information on parties' financial affairs was difficult to find. That law, however, required every registered party to disclose its annual revenues and expenditures, and to file a separate report after each election campaign. It also imposed limits on campaign spending and guaranteed public subsidies for party activity.

The Bill C-24 amendments to the 1974 act have further altered the finance regime. For the first time, the law limits contributions to the parties and their candidates. Corporations and unions, once the most significant sources of funding for some parties, are now severely restricted in their capacity to donate both money and gifts in kind. Contributions to national parties from corporations, trade unions, and other associations are banned, although small contributions (approximately $1000 annually) can be made to local constituencies, candidates, and nomination contestants. Individual citizens are also limited to contributing a maximum of approximately $5000 annually.

To make up the shortfall in donations, Bill C-24 introduced a new system of annual, tax-supported public allowances for registered parties (see Canada by the Numbers 4.1). Each party that received at least 2 percent of the national vote in the previous election is entitled to approximately $1.75 annually for every vote it won. The new regime also increases the proportion of campaign expenses that is reimbursed to most parties (50 percent of national party campaign expenses) and their candidates (60 percent for those receiving at least 10 percent of the vote). The Elections Act also regulates how much the parties and candidates can spend during an election, broadcast time allocations, and third party spending (see Chapter 5). The end result is that in Canada, electoral activity is now primarily funded by the public sector, and not by private interests and individual contributors.

The Harper government's Accountability Act, introduced in the spring of 2006, proposes to tighten restrictions further on political donations to parties and candidates. Specifically, there will be a complete ban on donations by corporations and unions, including in-kind donations. The maximum limit for individual contributions to registered political parties will be lowered from $5000 to $1000, as will the limits for donations to electoral candidates, nomination contestants, and riding associations. The limits are cumulative in that they are the maximum amounts any individual can give to all candidates, contestants, and riding associations across Canada. The act will also put a $1000 limit on individual contributions to party leadership candidates, prohibit cash donations of more than $20, and lower the contribution amounts after which tax receipts must be issued from $25 to $20.[13]

The parties' recent financial returns reveal how dramatically the new funding regime has changed the way they are financed. In 2003, prior to Bill C-24, the Bloc

CANADA BY THE NUMBERS 4.1 Pre- and Post-Reform Registered Party Financial Transactions Returns

2003	ALLIANCE			LIBERAL			NDP			BLOC			PC		
	$ IN MILLIONS	# OF CONT.	$ PER CONT.	$ IN MILLIONS	# OF CONT.	$ PER CONT.	$ IN MILLIONS	# OF CONT.	$ PER CONT.	$ IN MILLIONS	# OF CONT.	$ PER CONT.	$ IN MILLIONS	# OF CONT.	$ PER CONT.
Business	1.3	799	1651	10.8	3461	3125	0.1	166	662	0.07	67	1003	1.2	1493	744
Individuals	5.4	81 153	66	6.2	17 871	347	4.8	32 836	146	0.4	5146	86	3.2	16 419	192
Unions	0	0	0	0.1	34	3292	5.2	239	22	0.02	12	1692	0	0	0
Other	1.6	364		7.0	351		0.06			0.5			0.02		
2003 Totals	8.3			24.1			10.1			1.0			4.3		

2004	CONSERVATIVE			LIBERAL			NDP			BLOC			GREEN		
Contributions	10.9	68 382	160	5.2	17 429	271	5.2	30 097	173	0.9	8775	98	0.4	3606	97
Allowances	7.9			9.1			2.9			2.7			0.5		
2004 Totals	18.8			14.4			8.1			3.6			0.9		

2005															
Contributions	18.2	166 976	107	9.0	36 060	221	5.2	52 272	98	0.8	11 373	65	0.4	5366	77
Allowances	7.3			9.1			3.9			3.1			1.1		
2005 Totals	25.5			18.1			9.0			3.8			1.5		

2004: BQ had $33 372 — Conservatives had $39 240, Greens had $0, Liberals had $498 173, NDP had $100 transferred from registered associations, candidates, leadership contestants, and nomination contestants.

2005: BQ had $37 565, Conservatives had $340 202, Greens had $29 234, Liberals had $1 079 998, NDP had $15 320 transferred from registered associations, candidates, leadership contestants, and nomination contestants.

In 2003, as the Liberals moved from the leadership of Chrétien to that of Paul Martin, they raised a hefty $24 million. Some $10 million of that came from the corporate sector.

The same year the Canadian Alliance and the Progressive Conservatives, the two ancestors of the current Conservative Party of Canada, took in a combined $12.6 million. Roughly $2.4 million of that came from business.

2003—Alliance $1 416 314 from 239 EDAs
2003—Liberals $6 617 930 from 261 EDAs
2003—Bloc Quebecois $476 035 from 43 EDAs
2003—Green Party collected a total of $234 518: $170 968 from 951 individual contributors, $63 300 from 5 businesses, and $250 from 1 unincorporated organization.

Source: Data compiled and used to create the above table were taken from the Web site of Elections Canada: www.elections.ca. They are used with the permission of the chief electoral officer but extrapolations and analysis rest with the authors.

Québécois received most of its money from individuals, over half of its total, with most of the remainder coming from its electoral district associations (EDAs), which are also largely funded by individuals. Canada's two conservative parties, the Alliance (65 percent from individuals and almost another one-fifth from EDAs) and the Progressive Conservatives (nearly three-quarters from individuals) relied much more heavily on donations from individual Canadians than did the Liberals (about one-quarter from individuals and a similar amount from EDAs). The Liberals received the lion's share of donations from corporations, almost 45 percent of their total, whereas the NDP received over half its funding from unions. The Liberals' total take of $24.1 million in 2003 was more than all of the other parties combined. The NDP's $10.1 million ranked it second, with the CA third ($8.3 million). The PCs ($4.3 million) collected only about half what the CA managed, while the BQ raised only about $1 million.

By 2004, the first year under the new regime and an election year, the new Conservative Party ($18.9 million) generated almost one-third more revenue than did the Liberals ($14.4 million). Without union contributions, the NDP lost ground ($8.1 million) while the BQ more than tripled its take to $3.6 million. One minor party also greatly benefited, as the Green Party almost quadrupled its total revenue to $900 000 from under one-quarter million in 2003. Beneath the surface, the numbers tell an even more troubling tale for the Liberals. The Conservatives found about four times as many individuals (68 382) willing to contribute to their organization than did the Liberals (17 429). Although their average contribution was smaller, the Conservatives raised more than twice as much from individuals as did their major competitors. The pattern repeated itself again in 2005, and the overall discrepancy between the two major parties' overall financing will be accelerated once the allowances are adjusted for the 2006 election outcome.

WHAT IS A PARTY SYSTEM?

There are many definitions of *party system*. Some experts include every official party, while others restrict their focus to the parties in Parliament. For the sake of brevity, this chapter takes the latter approach and we have restricted the discussion of Canada's party system to the five parties that have won seats in the House of Commons since 1993. We therefore define the Canadian party system as follows: *The sum total of the parties represented in the House of Commons at a given time.* This does not mean that the smaller parties are irrelevant. But collectively, the 11 smallest parties received only 5.5 percent of the vote in the 2006 federal election, with the Green Party accounting for most of that (4.5 percent). None of the minor parties, including the Greens, was able to win a seat. The four parties that did win seats captured a combined total of 94.5 percent of the votes. Each gained enough House representation to meet the 12-seat threshold required to obtain official party status in Parliament.

However party systems are defined, one core idea remains constant: in democratic states with two or more parties, no party operates in isolation. Each affects and is affected by their opponents within the system. Parties compete with each other for money, votes, and other scarce resources. When one party in a system adapts to a change in the competitive environment, the others have to make choices about whether or not to follow suit. In the electoral context, a strategic choice by one party often provokes a response from rival parties and may even inspire the creation of one or more new parties. On the other hand, if one party is too dominant, two or more smaller parties may merge in order to provide a more effective challenge. The many dynamics of these relationships combine to form a party system that operates within, and is impacted by, the larger political culture.

■ From Where Do Political Parties Come?

Political parties do not simply appear on the political scene, as if from nowhere. They arise at particular points in time in response to a variety of opportunities and constraints, with the purpose of achieving particular representational or governing objectives. The three major theories of party development emphasize social cleavages, mobilization, and institutional explanations.[14] Given that most of this book focuses on institutions, we will limit ourselves here to the social cleavages and mobilization theories.

Social Cleavages: Political Culture and Class

Societal approaches to the development of the party system emphasize the role played by changes in the economy, social relations, and the political culture of a particular society. From this perspective, a party system is largely determined by and reflective of social relations and the collective attitudes of individuals. To understand the development of a particular party system, one must examine the evolution of the underlying social relations. By implication, a party system would change only if the underlying social forces also changed. Although there are many variants of the social approach to party development, two have been particularly popular in Canada: the political culture model and the class politics model. As we saw in Chapter 1, the political culture of a given country is the overall pattern of political orientations within its population. Canada does not have a single political culture, but rather a set of subcultures, including Quebec nationalism and Western alienation. The political culture model suggests that the number and ideological diversity of parties in a given party system reflect the different subcultures found in the electorate.

When we talk about social divisions, and their effect on voting behaviour, we refer to them as cleavages. In general, social cleavages are based on long-term demographic characteristics such as religion, region, and class. However, new ideological cleavages such as environmentalism and populism are emerging in Western societies. As we will see in Chapter 5, the mere presence of a particular cleavage does not automatically affect the party system. To understand why some subcultures shape the national party system and others do not, we need to consider two other important factors: the institutional incentives and constraints that affect the creation of political parties, and the organizational strategies that are required to transform a societal cleavage into a viable political vehicle. In other words, political parties cannot survive unless they mobilize substantial support—both electoral and financial—from within the subculture(s) they are attempting to represent.

Mobilization

Politicians are strategic actors. They are active agents with considerable power to define the salient political issues and to mobilize voters behind their prescribed solutions. That power has its limits, however, and politicians must choose carefully which strategies they employ in attempting to appeal to new elements within the electorate or in solidifying an existing base.

A political entrepreneur is an individual who identifies an unmet need in the political marketplace. In Canada, the most entrepreneurial frequently establish new parties to fill those needs. But they never start from scratch. They identify an existing or latent subculture and attempt to mobilize its members by appealing to their unexpressed political values. To create a new party, a political entrepreneur requires a preexisting base in the electorate, among one or more groups of voters whose political needs are not met by existing parties. They also need the opportunity to exploit dissatisfaction with the existing party system, as well as the resources—money, volunteers, media attention—to establish and market a new alternative.

But the mobilization of targeted groups of voters is not solely the responsibility of entrepreneurs seeking to create new parties. The leaders of existing parties also make strategic choices when they decide which subcultures they wish to attract, and which to strategically avoid. In so doing, they can reshape voting patterns that might otherwise remain intact. The most basic choice is whether to retain and reinforce the party's existing base or to risk alienating that base by reaching out to subcultures that have not previously been included in the party's electoral coalition. Either option carries risks and opportunities.

Maintaining the traditional base is typically the safest strategy in the short term. But if that base shrinks, or if its ties to the party weaken, the party may fade away over the long term. The troubled relationship between the NDP and organized labour illustrates this point. Even in the heyday of the union movement, the NDP failed to capture a plurality of the labour vote. In the 1990s, relations between the party and its key labour supporters became tense and sometimes antagonistic. Furthermore, unions must now abide by the new contribution rules in Bill C-24, which limit the amount of money and volunteer labour they can donate. Partly in response, NDP leader Jack Layton has deliberately targeted environmentalist voters to expand his party's base. Given the performance of the Green Party in the last two elections, it is not yet clear whether those appeals will have much effect.

Trying to bring new subcultures into the existing electoral coalition is also risky. It can pay off handsomely in the short term, but it has the potential to erode a party's traditional base in the long term. The collapse of the federal Progressive Conservative Party in 1993 provides a classic example. When he became party leader in 1983, Brian Mulroney promised to win power by appealing to voters in Quebec. In order to do so, he had to find a way to bridge the ideological and regional chasm between Western populists—a core element of the party since the days of John Diefenbaker—and Quebec nationalists. The PCs won a smashing victory in 1984, taking every seat in Alberta as well as a majority of Quebec's francophone ridings. But the PC's connection with Québécois voters was fleeting, and in exchange for the dubious prize of temporary Quebec nationalist support, the Tories ended up sacrificing their Western base and the conservative principles that had sustained their members in Ontario and the Atlantic region. In 1993, Quebec PC voters shifted en masse to the Bloc Québécois while Westerners flocked to Reform, destroying two key components of the PC base.

Compared to the leaders of established parties, political entrepreneurs have more freedom to concentrate on one particular subculture and to mobilize it in the most effective way: by refusing to compromise the needs and goals of that specific group of voters. From this perspective, the five-party system that emerged in 1993 represents not a transformation of Canadian politics, but simply the latest reflection of a stable pattern of subcultures within the electorate. The subcultures themselves are not new; the novelty lies in their successful mobilization into separate party organizations by entrepreneurial political leaders.

Preston Manning seized the opportunity to create Reform based on the Western populist subculture, while Lucien Bouchard exploited the unfilled political market for a Québécois nationalist party by creating the Bloc. Manning's initiative demonstrated the pitfalls of beginning as a regional party prior to expanding nationally. Once branded as a Western party, Manning could never make a significant breakthrough into vote-rich Central Canada. The Bloc experiment illustrates a different dilemma. Given its single defining purpose—to get Quebec out of the country—it is intentionally designed to remain confined within the borders of one province, thereby never competing for power. Its electoral fortunes are therefore particularly dependent on the relative levels of support for Quebec sovereignty and the relative strength of its competitors in that single province, two factors not under its control. A different type of political entrepreneurship is evident in the decision by Canadian Alliance leader Stephen Harper and PC leader Peter MacKay to merge their two parties into one entity. Their intent was to bring two of the subcultures in the Mulroney coalition—conservatives and Western populists—back together and it certainly demonstrates greater potential to provide a governing party than either of the more overtly regional strategies pursued by Reform or the Bloc.

In summary, party systems are shaped by several long-term factors, among which social cleavages, mobilization strategies, and institutions are the most important. As society changes, parties and their leaders are continually presented with new opportunities and challenges. Parties must adjust their mobilization strategies or risk being left behind by competitors who more quickly adapt to the changing dynamics within the party system as it interacts with the institutions and society at large. To understand the continuity and change in Canada's national party system, we must consider all these variables and remember that parties are also often the agents of change within the institutions and society.

CANADIAN POLITICAL CHRONOLOGY 4.2 Canada's Federal Party Systems

First Party System (1867–1917)

Classic Two-Party Competition
Conservative (Liberal-Conservative)
Liberal

Dominant Politics—patronage (state-building)
Focus—constituency
Type of Parties—parliamentary caucus
Leadership—caucus choice—proven parliamentarians
Finance—civil service and private capital
Media—party newspapers

Transition
Civil Service
Farmers

Second Party System (1921–1962)

Multi-Party Competition
Liberal
Conservative (Progressive Conservative)
Progressive
Social Credit
Cooperative Commonwealth Federation

Dominant Politics—regional brokerage (nation-building)
Focus—region
Type of Parties—ministerialist
Leadership—managed conventions—known politicians
Finance—kickbacks and corporations
Media—independent press/radio—P.R. consultants

Transition
Diefenbaker
Protest Parties

Third Party System (1963–1988)

Two-plus (2 ½) Party Competition
Liberal
Progressive Conservative
New Democratic Party
Ralliement Créditiste

Dominant Politics—electronic (agenda-building)
Focus—nation
Type of Parties—personal
Leadership—open conventions—outsiders
Finance—public funding—mass appeals—corporations and unions
Media—independent press/radio/TV—pollsters

Transition
Regionalism
BQ/Reform

Fourth Party System (1993–)

Multi-Party Competition
Liberal
Conservative
Bloc Québécois
Reform (Canadian Alliance)
Progressive Conservative
New Democratic Party

Dominant Politics—region
Focus—fiscal and democratic accountability
Leadership—open—OMOV
Finance—public
Media—independent press/radio/TV/internet

Conservative

Liberal

Progressives

Social Credit

Progressive Conservative

CCF

New Democratic Party

Ralliement Créditiste

Bloc Québécois

Reform   CA

Conservative

1867 1872 1874 1878 1882 1887 1891 1896 1900 1904 1908 1911 1917 1921 1925 1926 1930 1935 1940 1945 1949 1953 1957 1958 1962 1963 1965 1968 1972 1974 1979 1980 1984 1988 1993 1997 2000 2004 2006

Macdonald Mackenzie ----Macdonald---- ---------Laurier--------- ----Borden---- Union ----King---- Bennett ----King---- --St. Laurent---- Diefenbaker Pearson ----Trudeau---- Clark Trudeau Mulroney ----Clark Trudeau Mulroney---- ----Chrétien---- Martin Harper

Con. Maj. / Lib. Min. / Con. Maj. / Con. Maj. / Con. Maj. / Con. Maj. / Con. Maj. / Lib. Maj. / Lib. Maj. / Lib. Maj. / Lib. Maj. / Con. Maj. / Union Maj. / Lib. Min. / Lib. Min. / Lib. Maj. / Con. Maj. / Lib. Maj. / Lib. Maj. / Lib. Maj. / Lib. Maj. / Lib. Maj. / Con. Min. / Con. Maj. / Con. Min. / Lib. Min. / Lib. Maj. / Lib. Maj. / Lib. Min. / Lib. Min. / Con. Min. / Con. Maj. / Con. Maj. / Lib. Maj. / Lib. Maj. / Lib. Min. / Lib. Min. / Con. Min.

Note: The general categorizations of the four party systems has been taken from R. Kenneth Carty, "Three Canadian Party Systems: An Interpretation of the Development of National Politics," in George Perlin, ed., *Party Democracy in Canada: The Politics of National Party Conventions* (Toronto: Prentice-Hall Canada Inc., 1988), 15–30. The dates signifying the beginning and end of the various systems correspond to election years and have been altered somewhat from Carty's original model. Most importantly, the dates for the second system include all of the "transition" elections at the end of that system before it passed into the third system.

152 CHAPTER 4

NEL

HISTORY OF THE CANADIAN PARTY SYSTEMS

Carty and his colleagues[15] have provided a broad account of party systems in Canada incorporating the following variables:

- the dominant type of politics practised
- relationships among the various networks within each party (the caucus, the leader and his or her entourage, and the local members in the constituencies)
- impact of changes in other national institutions upon the party system
- number of parties inside and outside Parliament
- methods of choosing party leaders
- relationships between national parties and particular subcultures (regional, linguistic, economic, and ideological)
- sources and regulation of party finance
- technologies of mass communication.

As these variables change over time, so does the party system. By situating the party system within its broader political context, Carty determines that at certain times, the changes in Canadian party politics were so dramatic that rather than think of one continuous, evolving party system since Confederation, we must consider Canada to have had four distinct party systems (see Canadian Political Chronology 4.2). This approach allows us to develop a richer and more useful understanding of Canadian party politics. We can now more fully explore the model introduced at the start of this chapter by adding the above variables and situating each of the four party systems in its historical context.

- First party system (1867–1917): classic two-party competition; patronage politics focused on state-building; the leaders of the two caucus parties were chosen by the parliamentary caucus; activity was focused locally on the electoral constituencies, with little competition from outside of Parliament; private, unregulated parties were financed primarily by the civil service and private capital; communication with voters was done almost exclusively through party newspapers run by partisan editors.
- Second party system (1921–1962): multiparty competition; regional brokerage politics focused on nation-building; ministerialist parties with powerful regional ministers emerged, focused on representing the various regions of the country, and had to adapt to many challenges from new parties originating outside of Parliament; leaders began to be chosen by managed conventions with known politicians; private, unregulated parties were financed largely through kickbacks from corporations; communication was achieved by way of an independent press that was complimented by radio, the addition of public-relations consultants, and during the 1957 to 1962 transition period, by television.
- Third party system (1963–1988): two-and-one-half party competition; electronic politics focused on issue agenda-building; personalized parties emphasized leaders who were chosen at open, competitive conventions; the established parties faced little competition from outside Parliament; regulated parties were

funded through mass public appeals and increasingly supported by pubic money; television communication superseded print and radio and was complimented by the addition of public-opinion pollsters.

While most Canadian scholars agree with Carty's analysis of the first three party systems, there is considerable debate about the fourth party system. While it is difficult to assess the long-term importance of current political events or the ways in which today's trends will develop in the future, for the moment let us assume that the third party system ended in 1988 and that the fourth system began to take shape in 1993. On that basis, if we apply Carty's variables we find the following:

- Fourth party system (1993–present): multiparty competition; electronic politics focus on targeted constituencies of voters, often in a particular region; personalized parties emphasize leaders who are chosen through open, competitive processes that may or may not involve a convention; all of the parties face increasing competition from newcomers created from both within and outside of Parliament; parties are fully regulated and increasingly publicly funded, with mass appeals to individuals as the only source of private revenue; television communication still dominates but is increasingly supplemented by Internet and other personalized communications technologies.

There have also been three periods of transition between the party systems: 1917–1921, 1957–1962, and 1988–1993. The transitional periods are marked by flux, uncertainty, electoral volatility, and typically dramatic disruptions in the established voting patterns that often lead to the emergence or elimination of minor parties.

First System: 1867–1917

Canadian politics at the time of Confederation were the product of British colonial rule. Although legislatures had existed in Upper and Lower Canada since 1791, there was no incentive for their members to form disciplined caucuses until after responsible government had been granted in the 1840s. In the Parliament of the United Province of Canada, building a legislative majority meant bridging the linguistic, cultural, and religious divide that separated French-speaking Catholics in Canada East (Quebec) from English-speaking Protestants in Canada West (Ontario). In the pre-Confederation period, relatively weak coalitions of conservative English-speaking representatives joined with their conservative French-speaking counterparts under the Liberal–Conservative label. They were opposed by an equally fragile alliance of Liberal anglophones and francophones. Divisions among the various subcultures frequently brought down governments over linguistic, cultural, and religious issues as the loose alliances among parliamentarians shifted.

The Confederation agreement was in part designed to resolve these problems by establishing a federal system that relegated language and cultural issues to the provinces. But the French–English cleavage remained a powerful force in national politics. To form a majority government, a party had to win seats inside and outside

Quebec. At the same time, the prime minister had to unite MPs from both language groups into a functioning caucus. Before 1878, the incentives for party discipline that accompany "a Constitution similar in Principle to that of the United Kingdom" were undermined by the persistent localism of Canada's political culture. The situation required strong leadership, and in the 1880s and 1890s, parliamentary caucuses became increasingly cohesive and leader dominated. Preoccupied with bridging the gaps among MPs from the various regional, religious, and linguistic subcultures, leaders rarely risked creating more divisions by staking out clear ideological doctrines. Both the Conservative and Liberal parties hugged the centre of the political spectrum during the first party system, focusing on establishing the state institutions and building the country by implementing the major provisions of the National Policy.

Macdonald and his Conservatives were the first to succeed at building a cohesive party organization and dominated the first three decades of Confederation. Laurier was the first Liberal leader to make a serious effort at organizing his Opposition coalition into a party that could consistently compete for power. Both parties also minimized divisions by keeping power in the hands of their parliamentary caucuses. As classic examples of cadre parties, the Liberals and Conservatives were slow to develop extraparliamentary organizations. For example, in the first 50 years after Confederation, the Liberal Party held only one national convention. The Conservatives held none. Both parties limited political debate to the parliamentary forum and wooed supporters through the widespread use of patronage.

The first party system was also characterized by dominant leaders; secretive, and sometimes corrupt, party finance; and a partisan press. Because the two parties were so ideologically similar, the personalities and rhetoric of their leaders became the main focus of electoral competition. The leader was not just the living symbol of his party; he was also its chief fundraiser, which added significantly to his workload, especially when the leader was also serving as prime minister. Leaders sought party funds from industrialists and financiers who in turn sought out government contracts as state and economic institutions were established. When Macdonald's begging letters to the head of the Grand Trunk Railroad provoked the 1873 Pacific Scandal, eventually bringing down his Conservative government, some tentative efforts were made to clean up party patronage and fundraising. These had little effect until after World War I.

Managing the press in a diverse, decentralized, and often locally parochial system was difficult. The task was, however, made somewhat easier by the open partisanship of most newspapers, many of which were established by the parties themselves or by very close friends of the parties. Over time, Macdonald knew that he could count on sympathetic treatment from Conservative papers and that Liberal papers would savagely attack him. Laurier understood that he would enjoy the unqualified endorsement of Liberal editors and would have to endear harsh criticism from Conservative papers.

After a rather tumultuous start, the party system became more stable, was representative of the major cleavages within Canadian society at the time, and, for the most part, served the young country well as its politicians established functioning state institutions, a national economic structure, and sea-to-sea territorial expansion.

■ Second System: 1921–1962

During the first two decades of the twentieth century, Canadian society underwent important changes that placed considerable strain on the party system. The continual movement toward urbanization and industrialization in the Central provinces, the rapid agrarian settlement of the Prairie provinces, and the continued support by both political parties of the National Policy—which was correctly perceived as favouring the industrializing centre at the expense of the agrarian periphery—led many in the out-lying regions to question the degree to which their interests could ever be adequately represented by either established party. While the settlement of the Prairies was initiated by the Conservatives and facilitated by massive immigration under Laurier's Liberals, neither the Liberals nor the Conservatives fully mobilized this expanding pool of voters. After World War I, the stage was set for an expansion of the party system as a direct result of the emergence of a new subculture: Western populism.

The tensions within the party system were heightened during the conscription crisis of World War I (1914–1918). The conscription issue blurred the distinction between the two political parties and confused political allegiances by forcing the creation of the Union government. It also inflamed French–English tensions and reinforced the attachment of the Quebec nationalist subculture to the Liberal Party. In 1917 the Liberals won 62 of the 65 seats in Quebec. In 1921, they won all 65 and would continue to win the vast majority of federal seats in that province until the 1958 election signalled that the end of the second party system was in sight.

A significant institutional change also affected party development during this era. The Civil Service Commission Act, 1918, placed the authority for recruitment of the civil service squarely in the hands of a nonpartisan agency. This important change not only led to the creation of a professional civil service, it also eliminated the parties' access to their most important patronage device and a major source of funding. As the number of cleavages in the electorate continued to multiply—with the addition and growth of new provinces, further immigration, the enfranchisement of women, and the rise of Québécois nationalism—it fell upon the parties to weave the growing diversity of interests into a national political community. From local patronage machines, Canadian parties had to transform themselves into regional brokers. Competition from political entrepreneurs, particularly in the West, hastened the transformation. As the populists adequately demonstrated to their traditional party foes, legions of voters were ready to be recruited into extraparliamentary organizations that were capable of delivering votes come election time.

The Liberals and Conservatives adopted regional brokerage strategies based on the premise that conflict could best be mediated within the extraparliamentary parties, rather than between competing parties inside Parliament. One key element in that strategy was the development of ministerialism, a system in which individual cabinet ministers represented particular regional, cultural, or economic groups within the party decision-making process. At the same time, the ministers were required to explain and communicate those decisions to the members of their designated constituencies. Regional interests would be brokered into the system through the party in power by way of powerful regional lieutenants within the Cabinet, or within the caucus in the case of the party in Opposition. The Liberals were without question the better brokers of competing interests, at least if the measure of success is electoral victories. The Liberals won seven of the nine elections held from 1921 to 1953 and governed for 31 of 36 years.[16] Only two men led them throughout this period: Mackenzie King and Louis St. Laurent, both of whom were noted conciliators.

The electoral record of the period also illustrates the limitations inherent in the regional brokerage model. Groups that perceived the Liberal and Conservative parties as either unwilling or unable to effectively represent their interests had an incentive to establish "third" parties to speak on their behalf. Highly mobilized subcultures that were concentrated in a particular region—notably, Western populists—were the most electorally successful. Others, attempting to represent latent subcultures scattered across the country (the working-class voters courted by left wing parties) met with less success, but nevertheless also emerged during the second party system.

The two-party competition of the first system was shattered in the 1921 election when a collection of Progressives elected 65 MPs—14 more than the Conservatives. The Progressives won all but a handful of Prairie seats and almost one-third of the Ontario seats (most in northern or rural Ontario). As the second-place party in the House of Commons, the Progressives were entitled to form the official Opposition. However, the Progressive caucus was dominated by an unwieldy group of populist members who were hostile to the existing system of disciplined party combat, arguing it placed inordinate power in the hands of party leaders. Thus, instead of using their Western regional base as a platform from which to challenge the Central Canadian orientation of the major parties, the Progressives refused the mantle of official Opposition, rejected most conventional approaches to party solidarity, propped up the minority Liberal government, and failed to congeal as an effective parliamentary force. Progressive leader T. A. Crerar was even co-opted into the government ministry. This cooperation with the governing party cost the Progressives much of their populist support over the next decade, and the party disappeared as a parliamentary presence by the 1935 election.

Despite their inability—or unwillingness—to congeal into an effective parliamentary party, the Progressives succeeded in inaugurating a new era of regionally based third parties, including a new party of the left. By the late 1920s, there had emerged in Parliament a loose association of labour MPs with some of the more radical Progressive MPs. They were known as the Ginger Group, for the spice they added to parliamentary debate. At the instigation of the Ginger Group and the League for Social Reconstruction—a university-based group of socialists modelled on the British Fabian Society—a meeting of the Western Labour Conference in 1932 voted to create a new socialist political party. The party held its founding convention in Regina the next year, calling itself the Cooperative Commonwealth Federation—Farmer, Labour, Socialist. As its subtitle suggested, the CCF tried to appeal to a regionally based farmer constituency, particularly in the West, the working class of the industrial Centre, and intellectual socialists. The farmer-labour alliance within the CCF was an uneasy one. The tendency of farmer votes to be tightly clustered geographically and of labour votes to be more dispersed resulted in the CCF's winning more contests in rural Western constituencies than in urban constituencies. Thus the parliamentary wing of the CCF had a distinctly Western-farmer character, which made it more difficult for the party to appeal to the urban working class. Divisions within the union movement regarding both its organizational structure and its approach to political action compounded the problems and further limited the electoral reach of the CCF amongst one of its most important targeted group of voters.

Whereas some forms of regional discontent found voice in the leftist CCF, others were more at home in the populist Social Credit Party. Following the political ideas of British engineer Major Clifford Douglas, articulated by fundamentalist minister and radio preacher William ("Bible Bill") Aberhart, Social Credit emerged during the 1935 election, in the middle of the Great Depression, as an important voice for Western farmers. Social Credit's electoral support came almost exclusively from Alberta, and from 1935 to 1957 it captured all but a handful of the Commons seats from that province. The party collapsed in 1958 when most of its voters switched to the Conservative Party, led by the fiery Westerner John Diefenbaker.

At the beginning of the second party system in 1921, leadership conventions were becoming the preferred method for choosing party leaders. This development reflected another important change: the establishment of extraparliamentary wings by all the major parties. National party offices, staffed by permanent employees, began to appear. As the caucus lost the power to choose the leader and the representational functions of government backbenchers shifted to regional ministers, power within party structures became more decentralized. Successive fundraising scandals convinced party leaders to delegate their fundraising chores to party "bagmen." These individuals, many of them senators, met privately with corporate and individual donors to solicit funds for the new party organization and for the new demands of national campaigns.

Meanwhile, the partisan press had disappeared, primarily a victim of the marketplace, as advertisers demanded mass exposure and did not want their products associated with the blatant partisanship of the first party system. The public was also demanding more independent news coverage and less partisan editorial analysis. Competition from the new medium of radio compounded the need for both independence and exploring broader advertising markets beyond narrow groups of partisans.

The second party system began to be transformed into the third system with the 1957 election, which brought the Conservatives to power for the first time since 1935. Although Conservative leader John Diefenbaker managed to win only a minority, the period of unchallenged Liberal dominance had been interrupted. In the 1958 election, Diefenbaker returned a massive PC majority, nearly wiping out the CCF and Social Credit, prompting the former to found the NDP. At the same time, the Liberals spent their time in Opposition rebuilding their organization from the ground up. By the time the second transitional period ended in 1963, Canada's national party system and the environment in which it operated had changed dramatically.

Third System: 1963–1988

Party development in this third system was influenced by profound social and cultural changes. Canadian society was far more urbanized and industrialized in the 1960s and 1970s than it had ever been, making Canada's regions less socially and economically differentiated. There was also a shift of economic power westward. The economic centre of the country moved from Montreal to Toronto, and as Western economic clout grew, from Winnipeg to Vancouver and Calgary. The electoral realignment brought about by Diefenbaker integrated Westerners once again into one of the two major parties. Thereafter, the representation of third parties in Parliament gradually declined until only the NDP remained.

Parties that thrived in the third party system were forced to adapt themselves to electronic politics and a new emphasis on political leadership. By 1963, most Canadians had access to television news. Party leaders now had to appeal to a broader spectrum of the electorate and sell the party's platform and principles in both official languages. All three parties sought to overcome subcultural cleavages instead of brokering among competing interests. They attempted to use television, and other new technologies, to define political issues beyond the regions. The increasing availability and sophistication of public-opinion polling enabled the leaders to bypass traditional sources of information by directly measuring the attitudes and preferences of Canadian voters. Once-powerful regional ministers were relegated to the background as it was no longer necessary to have regional spokesmen represent the views of a specific section of the country. Such information could now be obtained more systematically, and more accurately, through scientific public-opinion polling.

The institutional environment for political parties also changed in important ways during the third party system. The shift to cooperative and then to executive federalism increased the prominence of provincial premiers in national politics, which further reduced the brokerage role of the national parties and effectively ended the ministerialist approach to regional representation in the federal government. But regionalism remained a central theme of public discussion, and no amount of nationalistic rhetoric could change the regional reality of partisan politics. Despite their attempts to appeal to the national electorate, the three parliamentary parties were often very regionally fragmented. For most of this period, the electoral system gave the Liberal Party a disproportionate share of Quebec seats and shut out both the Conservatives and the NDP in that province. Likewise, the Conservatives (and to a lesser extent the NDP) were strong in the West, where the Liberals were very weak. Only Mulroney can be credited with putting together an electoral coalition that included strong representation from each of Canada's regions and provinces.

A second major institutional change was the fundamental shift in the registration and financing of political parties brought about by the 1974 Election Expenses Act. As noted earlier, the act established public financing of parties through a variety of measures including a system of tax credits for political donations, as well as partial, public reimbursement of campaign expenses for the parties and their candidates. It created a more open and accountable funding system in which parties were required to publicly declare their revenue and expenditures. Finally, it set limits on the amount of money parties and candidates could spend in election campaigns and on the amount of television exposure parties could purchase. The net effect of these changes was a substantial improvement in the financial stability of each of the major parties (albeit with significant fluctuations, depending on the party's electoral performance) and a consequent expansion in their national headquarters. Parties responded to the new institutional environment by developing direct-mail campaigns and appealing for funds beyond their small memberships.

As party organizations became stronger, more stable, and more financially secure, they were increasingly dominated by the party leader and his entourage, who were increasingly reliant on professional consultants to craft their campaigns. When the costs of campaigning soared, local party members in the constituencies felt increasingly neglected. Parties tried to create new incentives for their members, including a vast increase in constituency-delegate positions at leadership conventions, but throughout the third party system many Canadians who wanted to participate in politics began to drift away from the parties, often toward pressure groups. Changing political values and intractable economic problems combined with the parties' penchant for issue agenda brokerage to undermine the credibility of party politics and open the door for antiparty appeals. As we will see in the next chapter, issue agenda brokerage is the process of using campaign professionals (pollsters and ad executives) to find out what immediate cluster of issues can be cobbled together into a winning platform. The process results in parties that do not have stable platforms from one election to the next and often make campaign promises in the short term that they have no intention or ability to implement in the longer term. To overcome this perceptual problem, platforms became increasingly vague and content free. Over time, these practices eroded the major parties' ties to the electorate, while alienating potential party members who sought more meaningful politics. By the late 1980s, the stage was set for another transformation leading to a new, fourth party system.

■ Fourth System: 1993–Present

Brian Mulroney's strategic decision to draw the Quebec nationalist subculture into the Conservative electoral coalition ultimately led to the collapse of the party. Often outraged, and certainly feeling betrayed, much of the Western populist subculture defected to the Reform Party after 1988, while the establishment of the Bloc Québécois in 1990 provided a political home for many Quebec nationalists. Although the 1988 election produced little overall change from the previous election in 1984, the results of the 1992 Charlottetown Accord revealed deep voter frustration with the three old-line parties. The two unsuccessful rounds of constitutional negotiation symbolized for many Canadians that their politicians were out of touch with the average voter's interests, alienating many not only from the parties, but from the political process more generally.

The breakdown of the Mulroney coalition into the regional entities of Reform and the Bloc are the most visible elements of the fourth party system. The Reform–Alliance parties increased their share of the vote and their seat totals in each of the four elections they contested from 1988 to 2000. They did so, however, by garnering a larger and larger share of the Western vote and seats. Despite repeated attempts to break through into Ontario—indeed, the entire premise for the Alliance rebranding—they repeatedly failed to crack the Liberal stranglehold on seats in that province.

So tight was the Liberal grip on Ontario seats that the party lost only 6 of the 305 electoral contests in that province during the three general elections from 1993 to 2000. Each produced a Liberal majority government that was dependent on Ontario for over half its representation. In 1997, Ontario voters delivered almost two-thirds of the Liberal majority. And the most recent election results indicate that, after making some gradual progress in winning back their traditional support base in Quebec, the Liberals are again heading in the wrong direction in that province, leaving Ontario, and particularly the city of Toronto, as the bedrock of Liberal support and party activity.

Despite demonstrating many of the characteristics of a party in decline during the 1997 and 2000 elections, the Bloc remains a prominent electoral fact in Quebec federal politics. With the Bloc returning to the 50-plus seat levels in the past two elections, and the Conservatives demonstrating some unanticipated momentum with Quebec voters, that province may well witness some of the most competitive multi-party contests in the country over the next few electoral cycles.

The NDP has also gradually rebuilt its electoral credibility, again garnering support consistent with its 1970s and 1980s levels. It represents a greater threat to the Liberals than to the Conservatives given that NDP support tends to be found more in areas of Liberal strength, such as Canada's big cities, than in areas where the Conservatives are the major competition. Although its parliamentary caucus is still disproportionately Western, primarily British Columbian, the NDP has begun the process of adding pockets of Ontario support, while maintaining some modest Atlantic representation.

The merger of the Alliance and PC parties into the new CPC represents the most significant development in the fourth party system—at least since the advent of Reform and the Bloc. Despite making significant inroads into Ontario, and more recently and modestly into Quebec, the Conservative minority victory of 2006 returned a government that for the first time in Canadian history contained a majority of its members from the Western provinces. Thus, although the regional fragmentation of all the parties appears to have lessened slightly after the 2006 election, it remains an important reality.

Parties in the fourth system have made modifications in their approaches to campaigning, with election platforms regaining some of their former prominence. Beginning with Reform's Blue Book of policy declarations in the early 1990s—which

YEAR	TOTAL SEATS	CON/PC/CPC			LPC			PROG/SC/REF/CA		
		# SEATS	% VOTE	% SEATS	# SEATS	% VOTE	% SEATS	# SEATS	% VOTE	% SEATS
First Party System		*Con*								
1867	180	**100**	34.5	(55.6)	62	23.1	(34.4)			
1872	200	**102**	39.8	(51.0)	97	36.4	(48.5)			
1874	206	68	31.3	(33.0)	**134**	41.5	(65.0)			
1878	206	**137**	42.3	(66.5)	64	34.0	(31.1)			
1882	211	**135**	40.8	(64.0)	75	32.2	(35.5)			
1887	215	**127**	49.4	(59.1)	86	45.3	(40.8)			
1891	215	**121**	50.7	(56.3)	91	45.9	(42.3)			
1896	213	86	48.2	(40.2)	**118**	41.6	(55.4)			
1900	213	80	47.2	(37.6)	**129**	50.8	(60.6)			
1904	214	75	46.4	(35.0)	**137**	50.9	(64.0)			
1908	221	86	46.7	(38.9)	**133**	49.3	(60.2)			
1911	221	**135**	49.9	(61.1)	85	45.8	(38.5)			
1917	235	**153**	56.9	(65.1)	82	39.2	(34.9)			
Second Party System								*Prog*		
1921	235	50	30.4	(21.3)	**116**	41.2	(49.4)	65	24.8	(27.7)
1925	245	116	46.7	(47.3)	**101**	40.7	(41.2)	24	8.8	(9.8)
1926	245	91	45.4	(37.1)	**125**	45.5	(51.0)	23	6.2	(9.4)
1930	245	**135**	48.2	(55.1)	90	44.0	(36.7)	12	3.3	(4.9)
								SC		
1935	245	40	30.1	(16.3)	**174**	46.0	(71.0)	17	4.1	(6.9)
1940	245	40	30.6	(16.3)	**181**	54.5	(73.9)	10	2.6	(4.1)
		PC								
1945	245	67	27.9	(27.3)	**126**	41.6	(51.4)	13	4.1	(5.3)
1949	262	41	29.7	(15.6)	**190**	49.2	(72.5)	10	3.6	(3.8)
1953	265	51	31.0	(19.2)	**170**	48.8	(64.2)	15	5.4	(5.7)
1957	265	**112**	39.0	(42.3)	105	41.2	(39.6)	19	6.6	(7.2)
1958	265	**208**	53.7	(78.5)	49	33.8	(18.5)	0	2.6	(0.0)
1962	265	**116**	37.2	(43.8)	100	37.3	(37.7)	30	11.6	(11.3)
Third Party System										
1963	265	95	32.7	(35.8)	**129**	41.7	(48.7)	24	11.9	(9.1)
1965	265	98	32.7	(37.0)	**131**	40.2	(49.4)	5	3.7	(1.9)
1968	264	72	31.7	(27.3)	**155**	45.6	(58.7)	0	0.9	(0.0)
1972	264	107	35.0	(40.5)	**109**	38.4	(41.3)	15	7.6	(5.7)
1974	264	95	35.7	(36.0)	**141**	43.2	(53.4)	11	5.1	(4.2)
1979	282	**136**	35.9	(48.2)	114	40.1	(40.4)	6	4.6	(2.1)
1980	282	103	32.5	(36.5)	**147**	44.3	(52.1)	0	1.7	(0.0)
1984	282	**211**	50.0	(74.8)	40	28.0	(14.2)	0	0.1	(0.0)
								Ref		
1988	295	**169**	43.0	(57.3)	83	31.9	(28.1)	0	2.0	(0.0)
Fourth Party System										
1993	295	2	16.0	(0.7)	**177**	41.3	(60.0)	52	18.7	(17.6)
1997	301	20	18.8	(6.6)	**155**	38.5	(51.5)	60	19.4	(19.9)
								CA		
2000	301	12	12.2	(4.0)	**172**	40.8	(57.1)	66	25.5	(21.9)
		Con								
2004	308	99	29.6	(32.1)	**135**	36.7	(43.8)			
2006	308	**124**	36.3	(40.3)	103	30.2	(33.4)			

CCF/NDP			BP/CRED/BQ			OTHER	
# SEATS	% VOTE	% SEATS	# SEATS	% VOTE	% SEATS	# SEATS	% VOTE
						18	42.4
						1	23.8
						4	27.2
						5	23.6
						1	27.0
						2	5.3
						3	3.4
						9	10.2
						4	2.1
						2	2.8
						2	4.0
						1	4.3
						0	3.9
						4	3.6
						4	3.8
						6	2.9
						8	4.5
	CCF						
7	9.3	(2.9)				7	10.5
8	8.4	(3.3)				6	3.9
				BP			
28	15.6	(11.4)	2	3.3	(0.8)	9	7.5
13	13.4	(5.0)				8	4.1
23	11.3	(8.7)				6	3.5
25	10.7	(9.4)				4	2.5
8	9.5	(3.0)				0	0.4
	NDP						
19	13.6	(7.2)				0	0.3
17	13.4	(6.4)				0	0.3
				Cred			
21	17.9	(7.9)	9	4.7	(3.4)	1	0.8
22	17.0	(8.3)	14	4.4	(5.3)	1	0.4
31	17.8	(11.7)				2	1.2
16	15.4	(6.1)				1	0.6
26	17.9	(9.2)				0	1.7
32	19.8	(11.3)				0	1.7
30	18.8	(10.6)				1	3.1
43	20.4	(14.6)				0	2.7
				BQ			
9	6.9	(3.1)	54	13.5	(18.3)	1	3.6
21	11.0	(7.0)	44	10.7	(14.6)	1	1.6
13	8.5	(4.3)	38	10.7	(12.6)	0	2.3
19	15.7	(6.2)	54	12.4	(17.5)	1	5.6
29	17.5	(9.4)	51	10.5	(16.6)	1	5.5

(cont'd)

(CANADA BY THE NUMBERS 4.2 *cont'd*)

In this table, the seat total of the party that formed the government is shown in boldface. For each party, the first number is the total number of seats for the party; the percentage of national vote is in the second column; the percentage of total House seats won by the party is shown in parentheses.

Key to Party Names:

LPC = Liberal Party of Canada

Con/PC/CPC = Conservative (1867–1941), Progressive Conservative Party of Canada (1942–2003) and Conservative Party of Canada (2004–   )

CCF/NDP = Cooperative Commonwealth Federation (1933–1961) and New Democratic Party of Canada (1961–   )

BP/Cred/BQ = Bloc Populaire Canadien (1945), Ralliement créditiste (1965–1968), and Bloc Québécois (1993–   )

Prog/SC/Ref/CA = Progressives (1921–1935), Social Credit (1935–1984), Reform Party of Canada (1987–2000), and Canadian Alliance (2000–2003)

1867 — Conservative includes 29 Liberal–Conservative seats (11.1% vote).
    Liberal includes 1 Independent Liberal seat (0.4% vote).
    Other includes 18 Anti-Confederation seats (7.9% vote) and 33.8% vote for candidates with unknown affiliation.

1872 — Conservative includes 36 Liberal–Conservative seats (12.9% vote), 2 Independent Conservative seats (0.7% vote), and 1 Conservative Labour seat (0.45% vote).
    Liberal includes 2 Independent Liberal seats (1.64% vote).
    Other includes 1 Independent seat (1.64% vote) and 22.2% vote for candidates with unknown affiliation.

1874 — Conservative includes 26 Liberal–Conservative seats (12.4% vote) and 3 Independent Conservative seats (0.7% vote).
    Liberal includes 5 Independent Liberal seats (2% vote).
    Other includes 4 Independent seats (3.2% vote) and 24% vote for candidates with unknown affiliation.

1878 — Conservative includes 49 Liberal–Conservative seats (15.8% vote), 2 Independent Conservative seats (0.2% vote), and 1 Nationalist Conservative seat (0.1% vote).
    Liberal includes 1 Independent Liberal seat (1% vote).
    Other includes 5 Independent seats (2.7% vote) and 20.9% vote for candidates with unknown affiliation.

1882 — Conservative includes 39 Liberal–Conservative seats (12.6% vote), 1 Nationalist Conservative seat (0.2% vote), and 1 Independent Conservative seat (0.2% vote).
    Liberal includes 2 Independent Liberals seats (1.1% vote).
    Other includes 1 Independent seat (1.6% vote) and 25.4% vote for candidates with unknown affiliation.

1887 — Conservative includes 26 Liberal–Conservative seats (7.3% vote), 3 Independent Conservative seats (1.6% vote), and 2 Nationalist Conservative seats (0.5% vote).
    Liberal includes 6 Independent Liberal seats (2.16% vote).
    Other includes 1 Independent seat (1.2% vote), 1 Nationalist seat (0.7% vote), and 3.3% vote for candidates with unknown affiliation.

1891 — Conservative includes 20 Liberal–Conservative seats (5.6% vote), 3 Independent Conservative seats (1.9% vote), and 1 Nationalist Conservative seat (0.2% vote).
    Liberal includes 1 Independent Liberal seat (0.7% vote).
    Other includes 2 Independent seats (0.8% vote), 1 Nationalist seat (acclamation), and 2.2% vote for candidates with unknown affiliation.

1896 — Conservative includes 15 Liberal–Conservative seats (3.8% vote).
    Liberal includes 1 Independent Liberal seat (0.2% vote).
    Other includes 4 Nationalist seats (1.5% vote), 2 Patron of Industry seats (3.9% vote), 2 McCarthyite seats (1.3% vote), and 1 Independent seat (1.4% vote).

1900 — Conservative includes 10 Liberal–Conservative seats (2.9% vote) and 1 Independent Conservative seat (1.4% vote).
    Liberal includes 1 Independent Liberal seat (0.5% vote).
    Other includes 3 Independent seats (1.4% vote) and 1 Independent Labour seat (0.4% vote).

1904 — Conservative includes 5 Liberal–Conservative seats (1.54% vote) and 1 Independent Conservative seat (0.5% vote).
    Other includes 1 Independent seat (1.45% vote).

1908 — Conservative includes 3 Liberal–Conservative seats (1.3% vote) and 1 Independent Conservative seat (0.5% vote).
    Other includes 1 Independent seat (1.5% vote) and 1 Labour seat (0.9% vote).

1911 — Conservative includes 3 Independent Conservative seats (1% vote) and 1 Liberal–Conservative seat (0.5% vote).
　　　　Other includes 1 Labour seat (0.9% vote).
1917 — Conservative includes all Union Government seats and votes.
　　　　Liberal includes all Opposition seats and votes.
1921 — Conservative includes 1 Independent Conservative seat (0.4% vote).
　　　　Progressive includes 3 Labour seats (2.7% vote), 2 United Farmers of Alberta seats (0.7% vote), 1 United Farmer of Ontario seat (0.1% vote), and 1 Independent Progressive seat (0.1% vote).
　　　　Other includes 4 Independent seats (3% of vote).
1925 — Conservative includes 1 Independent Conservative seat (0.5% vote).
　　　　Liberal includes 1 Independent Liberal seat (1% vote).
　　　　Progressive includes 2 United Farmers of Alberta seats (0.3% vote).
　　　　Other includes 2 Labour seats (1.8% vote) and 2 Independent seats (0.5% vote).
1926 — Conservative includes 1 Independent Conservative seat (0.3% vote).
　　　　Liberal includes 8 Liberal–Progressive seats (1.9% vote) and 1 Independent Liberal seat (0.6% vote).
　　　　Progressive includes 11 United Farmers of Alberta seats (2% vote) and 1 United Farmers of Ontario seat (0.2% vote).
　　　　Other includes 4 Labour seats (1.7% vote) and 2 independent seats (0.8% vote).
1930 — Conservative includes 1 Progressive Conservative seat (0.4% vote).
　　　　Progressive includes 9 United Farmers of Alberta seats (1.5% vote).
　　　　Other includes 3 Liberal–Progressive seats (1.2% vote), 2 Labour seats (0.7% vote), 2 Independent seats (0.6% vote), and 1 Independent Labour seat (0.4% vote).
1935 — Conservative includes 1 Independent Conservative seat (0.02% vote).
　　　　Liberal includes 1 Independent Liberal seat (1.23% vote).
　　　　Other includes 1 Reconstructionist seat (8.7% vote), 1 Independent seat (0.4% vote), 1 United Farmers of Ontario–Labour seat (0.4% vote), and 4 Liberal–Progressive seats (0.7% vote).
1940 — Conservative includes 36 National Government seats (29.2% vote), 3 Conservative seats (1.2% vote) and 1 Independent Conservative seat (0.2% vote).
　　　　Liberal includes 2 Independent Liberal seats (3.2% vote).
　　　　Social Credit includes 3 New Democracy seats (1.6% vote).
1945 — Liberal includes 8 Independent Liberal seats (1.8% vote).
　　　　Progressive Conservative includes 1 Independent Progressive Conservative seat (0.3% vote).
1953 — Liberal includes 1 Liberal–Labour seat (0.2% vote).
1957 — Liberal includes 1 Liberal–Labour seat (0.16% vote)
1958 — Liberal includes 1 Liberal–Labour seat (0.16% vote).
1962 — Liberal includes 1 Liberal–Labour seat (0.2% vote).
1963 — Liberal includes 1 Liberal–Labour seat (0.21% vote).
1965 — Conservative includes 1 Independent Progressive Conservative seat (0.17% vote).
1968 — Liberal includes 1 Liberal–Labour seat (0.12%).
2000 — Other includes 0.8% Green Party.
2004 — Other includes 4.3% Green Party.
2006 — Other includes 4.5% Green Party.

Source: *History of Federal Ridings since 1867—Parliament of Canada*, available at www.parl.gc.ca
Elections Canada: Past Elections, available at www.elections.ca/
Appendix A from Hugh G. Thorburn and Alan Whitehorn, eds., *Party Politics in Canada*, 8th edition (Toronto: Prentice Hall, 2001)
Elections in Canada at Wikipedia (available at en.wikipedia.org/wiki/Canadian_elections) provides a useful listing of federal election results as tabulated from the Parliament of Canada posted results.

was published in advance of elections as a means of introducing voters to its mission—and the mimicking Liberal Red Book of the 1993 election, all parties are now expected to, at a minimum, produce and publish a comprehensive election platform document sometime during the campaign. Although in some ways all of the parties, including the formerly ideologically driven NDP, have adopted brokerage strategies leaving each, and in particular the governing party, room to manoeuvre after the election, the documents do serve as a means for voters and the media to keep tabs on how consistent or erratic are the parties' ongoing policy pronouncements and promises. When combined with the changes to party regulation and finance, the experiments with various new leadership selection mechanisms, and the ongoing communications advancements made possible by the Internet and personal communication devices, it appears as though the ways in which parties function have also changed significantly enough to warrant considering the post-1993 period a new, fourth Canadian party system.

CONCLUSION

Political parties are central to political representation in a democratic system of government. A variety of forces give parties their form and substance. The political culture and economic structure of the country, regionally concentrated clusters of interests, and formal institutions of government all play important roles in determining how the various collections of parties will operate within a party system. Parties and their organizations, however, are not determined just by society. Parties play important roles in independently shaping their destinies and also help further changes within the political culture and society more generally.

Parties adopt different strategies in attempting to mobilize voters into their electoral coalitions. Some mobilization strategies are more successful than others, and all depend to some degree on what strategies are adopted by a party's opponents. No party will satisfy all interests, and some citizens who feel inadequately represented by existing parties will try to start new ones. The barriers to new party entry are significant, but not insurmountable. Most importantly, all parties—existing, traditional or new—must overcome the barriers and rise to the challenges presented by the electoral system and citizens' voting behaviour, the subject of the next chapter.

DISCUSSION QUESTIONS

1. Do you support a particular political party? If so, why? If not, why not?
2. Why was the Liberal Party so successful over the course of the twentieth century? Is this likely to continue, or are the Conservatives or NDP likely to replace them as Canada's natural governing party?
3. Should political parties be prohibited from taking donations from unions and corporations? Should donations from individuals be further restricted?
4. Which is a better way to select a party leader, conventions or OMOV?

5. Given the recurring creation and relative success of new parties emerging from Western Canada, is this historical pattern destined to repeat itself? What about new parties from Quebec or other regions?
6. Should the state regulate and fund political parties or should they be wholly private organizations?

SUGGESTED READINGS

Books and Articles

Keith Archer and Alan Whitehorn, *Political Activists: The NDP in Convention* (Toronto: Oxford University Press, 1997).

Herman Bakvis, ed., *Canadian Political Parties: Leaders, Candidates, and Organization*, volume 13 of the collected research studies for the Royal Commission on Electoral Reform and Party Financing (Toronto: Dundurn, 1991).

R. Kenneth Carty, ed., *Canadian Political Party Systems: A Reader* (Toronto: Broadview Press, 1992).

R. Kenneth Carty, "Parties as Franchise Systems: The Stratarchical Organizational Imperative," *Party Politics*, 10:1 (2004).

R. Kenneth Carty, William Cross, and Lisa Young, *Rebuilding Canadian Party Politics* (Vancouver: UBC Press, 2000).

John C. Courtney, *Do Conventions Matter? Choosing National Party Leaders in Canada* (Montreal and Kingston: McGill–Queen's University Press, 1995).

William Cross, ed., *Political Parties, Representation, and Electoral Democracy in Canada* (Toronto: Oxford University Press, 2002).

Maurice Duverger, *Political Parties: Their Organization and Activity in the Modern State*, translated by Barbara and Robert North (London: Methuen, 1964 [1954]).

Faron Ellis, *The Limits of Participation: Members and Leaders in Canada's Reform Party* (Calgary: University of Calgary Press, 2005).

George Perlin, *The Tory Syndrome: Leadership Politics in the Progressive Conservative Party* (Montreal: McGill–Queen's University Press, 1980).

George Perlin, ed., *Party Democracy in Canada: The Politics of National Party Conventions* (Toronto: Prentice-Hall Canada Inc., 1988).

Pinard, Maurice, *The Rise of a Third Party: A Study in Crisis Politics* (Toronto: University of Toronto Press, 1975).

Hugh G. Thorburn and Alan Whitehorn, eds., *Party Politics in Canada*, 8th edition (Toronto: Prentice Hall, 2001).

Whitaker, Reginald, *The Government Party*, (Toronto: University of Toronto Press, 1977).

Websites

Most of the registered parties in national politics have their own websites. Go to the Nelson website for this book (www.parametersbrief.nelson.com), click on "Canadian Politics on the Web," and scroll down to "Political Parties."

Alternatively, go to the Elections Canada website (www.elections.ca) and click on "Political Parties, Candidates and Third Parties," where you will find a complete list of registered parties, with links to their Web pages. Elections Canada also provides many other documents relating to the regulation and financing of national parties and election results.

NOTES

1. The general categorizations of the four party systems has been taken from R. Kenneth Carty, "Three Canadian Party Systems: An Interpretation of the Development of National Politics," in George Perlin, ed., *Party Democracy in Canada: The Politics of National Party Conventions* (Toronto: Prentice-Hall Canada Inc., 1988), 15–30. See also Carty, Cross, and Young. Note that the dates correspond to election years. The range of dates for each party system have been changed somewhat from Carty's original model to include all of the "transition" elections at the end of one system within that system, prior to the beginning of the new system.

2. See Stephen Clarkson, "The Liberal Party of Canada: Keeping Its Grip on Power by Pragmatism over Principle," in Hugh G. Thorburn and Alan Whitehorn, eds., *Party Politics in Canada*, 8th edition, (Toronto: Prentice Hall, 2001) 231–247.

3. See Faron Ellis, *The Limits of Participation: Members and Leaders in Canada's Reform Party* (Calgary: University of Calgary Press, 2005).

4. Paul Howe and David Northrup, *Strengthening Canadian Democracy: The Views of Canadians* (Montreal: Institute for Research on Public Policy, July 2000), 89; available on-line at www.irpp.org.

5. William Cross and Lisa Young, "The Contours of Political Party Membership in Canada," *Party Politics*, 10:4 (2004), 430–438.

6. R. Kenneth Carty, "Parties as Franchise Systems: The Stratarchical Organizational Imperative," *Party Politics*, 10:1 (2004), 7–9. In this context, the word *franchise* denotes a structural similarity to companies like McDonald's, in which local businesspeople purchase the right to use the company name, menu, and graphic design in their home markets. It should not be confused with the political meaning of *franchise*, which refers to the right to vote in elections.

7. R. Kenneth Carty and Lynda Erickson, "Candidate Nomination in Canada's National Political Parties," in Herman Bakvis, ed., *Canadian Political Parties: Leaders, Candidates, and Organization,* volume 13 of the collected research studies for the Royal Commission on Electoral Reform and Party Financing (Toronto: Dundurn, 1991).

8. For a comprehensive history of national leadership conventions in Canada, see John C. Courtney, *The Selection of National Party Leaders in Canada* (Toronto: Macmillan, 1973) and *Do Conventions Matter? Choosing National Party Leaders in Canada* (Montreal and Kingston: McGill–Queen's University Press, 1995).

9. See R. Kenneth Carty, "Campaigning in the Trenches: The Transformation of Constituency Politics," in George C. Perlin, ed., *Party Democracy in Canada: The Politics of National Party Conventions* (Toronto: Prentice-Hall Canada, 1988), 84–96.

10. Official results obtained from the Conservative Party's website (www.conservative.ca). The party used an ordinal ballot, which required the members to rank the three candidates in order of precedence. If none had received a majority on the first ballot, the third-place finisher (in this case, former Ontario PC cabinet minister Tony Clement) would have been dropped and his second preferences allocated to either Harper or second-place contender Belinda Stronach.

11. The 2004 Conservative contest was exempted from the law, because it officially began in late 2003.

12. John C. Courtney, "Recognition of Canadian Political Parties in Parliament and in Law," *Canadian Journal of Political Science,* 11:1 (March 1978), 33–60.

13. At the time of writing the Accountability Act had reached the committed stage of is journey into law; see Chapter 6 for more about how a bill becomes law. Although the government is only a minority, it seems unlikely that the combined opposition will defeat the bill, and therefore it will be law by the time this book is published. There is, however, especially in minority government situations, the possibility that some of its provisions will be amended before the final version is enacted into law.

14. For a further discussion on these factors, see Herbert Kitschelt, *The Logics of Party Formation: Ecological Politics in Belgium and West Germany* (Ithaca, NY: Cornell University Press, 1989).

15. See R. Kenneth Carty, William Cross, and Lisa Young, *Rebuilding Canadian Party Politics* (Vancouver: UBC Press, 2000).

16. Total Liberal victories rises to eight if one includes the 1926 election in which the Conservatives won more votes and seats than did the Liberals, but still could not wrestle control of the government away from King for longer than the three months Arthur Meighen formed his short-lived minority government.

5 ELECTIONS AND VOTING

LEARNING OBJECTIVES

- *describe* the basic features of the various types of electoral systems
- *describe* how electoral systems translate votes into seats, including the distorting effects of how single member plurality translates votes into seats in Canada
- *describe* the formal rules for how Canada conducts elections
- *identify* and *describe* the long-term and short-term factors that influence Canadian voting behaviour
- *identify* the most important trends in party competition during the most recent federal elections

INTRODUCTION

Free, open, and competitive elections are the cornerstone of advanced liberal democracies. The right to vote for representatives in the Canadian House of Commons and in provincial legislatures is guaranteed by the Charter and is not subject to the Section 33 notwithstanding clause, making democratic rights among the highest order of rights in Canada. This chapter explores the role of elections in our national politics, describes and evaluates the operation of Canada's electoral system, and examines patterns of Canadian voting behaviour. It concludes with a review of the last five elections, those that comprise the fourth party system.

A discussion of Canadian voters and elections brings together two central themes that recur throughout this book: the importance of regionalism as a motivating force in Canadian politics and the influence of institutions on political behaviour, specifically the incentives imposed on parties and voters by our electoral system. Like all institutions, electoral institutions struggle to live up to the theoretical standards set by political scientists and citizens alike. But even with their limitations, they still manage to achieve the single most important political virtue in a liberal democratic society: they confer legitimacy upon governments because they secure the consent of the people.

ELECTIONS AND DEMOCRACY

Periodic competitive elections based on universal adult suffrage are the crucial distinction between democratic and nondemocratic governments. In modern democratic polities, government is indirect, in that citizens do not directly participate in the vast majority of government decisions. Instead, they hire politicians to govern on their behalf, as representatives of the people. Elections are the means by which the people choose which representatives will form their governments. In this way, the consent of citizens and the legitimacy of the government are secured, however indirectly and imperfectly.

Although every democratic state holds elections, the ways in which those elections are conducted vary widely. There are dozens of different electoral systems in use around the world. Each is a set of rules used to determine two important factors: (1) how many legislators will represent a particular electoral district, and (2) how many votes are required to win a legislative seat. As such, most electoral systems fall into three distinct categories:

1. single member (one legislator per constituency)
2. proportional representation (PR) (multimember constituencies, with the seats distributed in proportion to the parties' respective vote shares)
3. mixed systems, which combine the first two principles.

The type of electoral system can effect the composition of the legislature and the political executive, the number of parties in the party system, the incentives for parties seeking to win seats, and the behaviour of voters. Electoral systems do not determine these outcomes on their own, but rather do so in combination with other political institutions and various aspects of the political culture. Hence, in Canada, federalism and regional political cultures importantly influence the effects of the electoral system when determining the makeup of the House of Commons.

Types of Electoral Systems

Single Member Plurality Systems

Single member plurality (SMP) systems divide the country (or other electoral region) into some number of electoral districts that each elects a single member as its representative. With only one representative to be chosen, parties run only one candidate in each electoral district. SMP systems typically use categorical ballots whereby citizens have one vote, and use it to choose one party's candidate. The winner is determined by counting all the votes and awarding the seat to the candidate with more votes than any other candidate. That is, all it takes to win is to have more votes than any other competitor, even if that is a simple plurality rather than a majority of all votes. Once elected, MPs are responsible for representing all constituents of the electoral district, not just those who voted for the winner. The system is simple, ballots are easy to count, and it is easy to determine winners. SMP tends to reduce the number of parties competing in the system because it sets high thresholds for election. There is little advantage, for example, in creating a party whose candidates are regularly going to win 10 or 15 percent of the vote. They will likely be beaten in every contest by a party that wins 30 to 40 percent of the vote. Candidates almost always need at least 25 percent of the vote, and in most cases over 40 percent, to win an SMP seat.

One of the most important disadvantages of the system is that representatives often win their seats without having secured a majority of votes. In a hotly contested three-party race, it is possible to win the election with just over one-third of all the votes. This means that almost two-thirds of voters cast ballots "against" the winner. Some critics of SMP question the legitimacy of declaring winners without having them first secure a majority of votes. For the most part, however, in the few countries that still use SMP, including Canada, the system is accepted as legitimate and does not discredit the electoral process.

Multimember Proportional Representation Systems

Proportional representation (PR) systems focus on the party rather than on individual candidates' victories or losses. PR rewards parties with a percentage of legislative seats that is roughly proportional to the percentage of votes they won in the electoral district. In order to achieve proportionality, multimember districts are required. That is, it is pretty much impossible to divide a district proportionally between two or more parties if there is only one seat. Multimember electoral districts are therefore necessary, and the more members per district, the greater is the proportionality that can be achieved.

There are a variety of mechanisms used to determine winners in multimember districts. One way is the party-list system (also called "list-proportional representation," or list-PR). Citizens vote for party lists, not for individual candidates; the parties are then awarded parliamentary seats in proportion to their shares of the vote. In a 100-seat district, for example, a party would create a ranked list of 100 candidates. If that party received 30 percent of the vote, it would receive 30 percent of the seats, which it would fill by the top 30 candidates on its list. One of the drawbacks of this system is that the most important regions or subcultures within the district can dominate the top positions on each party's list, leaving minority interests underrepresented.

Sometimes citizens vote directly for individual candidates in a multimember district, as they do under a single transferable vote (STV) system. With STV, each winning candidate must receive a predetermined quota of the valid votes cast. Most quotas are slightly higher than the proportion represented by the one district seat the candidate hopes to fill. In other words, in an eight-member district, one seat would represent 12.5 percent of the total, and the quota of votes required to fill that seat would be set at just over 12.5 percent. Voters rank the candidates on an ordinal ballot, from the most preferred to the least preferred, and if the distribution of first preferences does not fill all of the seats, unused lower preferences are successively counted until all the seats are filled.

Majoritarian Systems

Under a majority system, the winner is required to receive at least 50 percent plus 1 of all valid votes cast. These tend to be used in single member districts or in presidential elections where only one candidate is to be selected. Canadian parties use majoritarian elections to choose their leaders. Because a single round of voting often fails to produce a majority winner, majoritarian systems are somewhat more complex than plurality systems.

There are two principal methods for ensuring that one candidate receives a majority of the vote: runoff elections and ordinal ballots. Runoff elections require a second round, or subsequent rounds of voting until one candidate achieves a majority of votes. To reduce the number of runoff contests, the second round is often restricted to only the top two candidates from the first ballot. Alternatively, majoritarian systems can use an ordinal ballot, in which the voter rank-orders the candidates as described above. In an ordinal majority system, such as alternative vote (AV), the valid ballots are counted and a quota—in this case, 50 percent plus 1 of the total number of valid ballots—is calculated. When the preferences are counted, the last-place candidate (the one with the fewest first-preference votes) is eliminated, and that candidate's second preferences are redistributed among the remaining candidates. The counting continues, with the elimination of candidates and the redistribution of votes, until one candidate reaches the majority quota. Canada's new Conservative Party used this method to select Stephen Harper as their first leader, although Harper handily won a majority after the first round of counting so no subsequent rounds were required.

Whereas the categorical ballot has the virtue of simplicity, an ordinal ballot can become complex, can take a long time to fill out, and demands much more information and sophistication from the voter. Counting ordinal ballots can also be considerably complex and time consuming, but it does allow for majority winners to be determined without holding runoff elections.

Mixed Systems

A growing number of electoral systems combine two or more electoral formulas. Most of these mixed electoral systems divide the national legislature into two categories: some MPs represent single-member constituencies, while the rest are elected from national or regional party lists. Voters cast two ballots on voting day, one for a constituency MP and the other for a party list. The proportionality of a mixed system depends on two factors: (1) whether each party's share of the seats in Parliament is based solely on the list vote, and (2) the ratio of list MPs to constituency MPs. A system in which the list votes determine seat shares is called "mixed-member proportional," or MMP. Conversely, in a mixed-member majoritarian system, the seat total for each party is the sum of the constituency seats plus the list seats. In the latter case, the larger the percentage of list seats, the more proportional is the translation of vote shares into seat shares.

Translating Votes into Seats

Whether a party's share of legislative seats will be proportionate to its share of the vote is a question determined by all electoral formulas. List-PR systems translate the vote share for each party list into a proportional share of seats in the legislature. STV in multimember districts also achieves a degree of proportionality, although that degree varies with the number of seats per constituency. The greater the number of MPs in a given district, the more proportional can be the result.

SMP systems do not attempt to achieve proportionality, and therefore often do not. Indeed, all single-member systems distort the translation of votes into seats to a greater or lesser degree. Continuing to use our three-party scenario as an example, suppose that the same three parties contest every district in an election based on SMP. In order to win individual seats, a party's candidates need only garner more votes than any of their competitors. If opponents split the vote roughly evenly, any single candidate can win with just over one-third of the vote. If the same party wins in this manner in every district, it could win 100 percent of the seats with just over one-third of all the votes. This hypothetical example, although extreme and improbable, illustrates the distorting effect of SMP. We will discuss the distorting effects of SMP in Canada in much greater detail later in this chapter.

Both proportional representation and the single-member plurality system have their defenders and their critics.[1] Proportional representation has the obvious merit of ensuring that a party's strength in the legislature is roughly equivalent to its popularity among the electorate. On the other hand, some kinds of PR, especially the party-list system, encourage the proliferation of small parties by splitting larger coalitions into smaller factions. Rather than lose all of the individual contests under SMP, a small party with 10 percent of the vote should get approximately 10 percent of the seats under a PR system. There is therefore little incentive for that minor party to compromise its positions and join forces with others to form a larger entity. With many small parties gaining representation, PR also decreases the likelihood of any one party controlling a majority of legislative seats. Because PR systems do not manufacture artificial majority governments like SMP systems tend to do, PR increases the likelihood of minority Parliaments and coalition governments with Cabinets comprised of ministers from two or more parties. MPs in PR systems are also more likely to be as much representatives of their parties as they are representatives of the people.

Single member plurality systems have the advantage of being more likely to produce stable two-party competition and, therefore, majority governments. Even when multiparty competition exists, majority governments are much more likely under SMP than under PR. SMP has the disadvantage of rewarding parties with a disproportionate number of seats in comparison to their percentage of vote. Furthermore, majority governments are often produced even though the party forming the government did not receive a majority of votes. Sometimes, the party that wins the most seats is actually the party that took the second highest percentage of votes, as was the case in the 1957 and 1979 Canadian elections.

When debating the virtues and vices of the Canadian SMP system, advocates of changing to a PR system often use the results produced under the current SMP system to extrapolate what would have happened if a PR system had been in place. However, we recommend that you avoid such superficial comparisons. For example, in the 1997 election the Liberals won 38.5 percent of the vote and 155 seats (51.5 percent of the 301 available seats). Under a pure PR system, assuming they still won 38.5 percent of the vote—a doubtful assumption—they would have been rewarded with 116 seats (38.5 percent of 301). Similarly, the NDP's 11 percent of the vote would have resulted in 33 seats rather than the 21 it won (only 7 percent of the total 301 seats), and the Progressive Conservative's 18.8 percent of the vote would have garnered it 57 seats rather than the 20 it won under SMP (only 6.6 percent of the total). However, such hypothetical exercises are inherently flawed by the assumption that each party would have received the same number of votes under an alternative electoral system. As noted earlier, SMP tends to reduce the number of parties competing while PR tends to increase the number. Thus, under a new PR electoral system, it is very likely that a number of new small parties would emerge and some, if not all, of the existing parties would cease to exist, at least in their current forms and structures. Changing the electoral rules would change the incentives for all the parties, and for the voters, and would therefore likely change the structure of party competition. A more realistic premise would be to assume that if the electoral system were changed, none of the parties would receive the same percentage of votes that they collected under SMP, so no meaningful comparisons can be made.

◼ Nonterritorial Representation and Turnout

Electoral systems also contribute to other aspects of the political system such as the proportion of ethnic minorities and women that are represented in the legislature, as well as the rate at which eligible voters cast ballots, otherwise known as turnout. Because territorial representation is the guiding principle behind the Canadian electoral system, it tends to do well in representing the most important ethnic divisions in the country, so long as they are territorially clustered. For example, French-speaking Canadians are well represented in the House of Commons because of their majority status in most Quebec ridings. Similarly, many other ethnic groups gain at least some representation because their populations are often geographically clustered in ridings where they constitute a majority, or significant enough plurality, to get members of their communities elected. Others, such as Aboriginal Canadians, who are for the most part scattered throughout the country, do not fare very well and are severely underrepresented in the national Parliament.

Women, although constituting a statistical majority in most electoral districts, tend to also be underrepresented in most Parliaments no matter what system is used, although PR systems tend to do better at approaching gender parity than does SMP (see Canada by the Numbers 5.1). Turnout can also be affected by the electoral system, with SMP systems tending to have lower voting participation rates

CANADA BY THE NUMBERS 5.1 Turnout and Representation of Women in Selected Parliaments, May 2006

COUNTRY	ELECTORAL SYSTEM	PERCENT OF WOMEN IN LOWER HOUSE	TURNOUT IN MOST RECENT ELECTIONS
South Africa	List-PR	32.8	98.4
Rwanda	List-PR	48.8	96.5
Australia	AV	24.7	94.3
Luxembourg	List-PR	23.3	91.7
Belgium	List-PR	34.7	91.6
Iceland	List-PR	33.3	87.7
Denmark	List-PR	36.9	84.5
Austria	List-PR	33.9	84.3
Italy	Mixed	17.3	81.4
Sweden	List-PR	45.3	80.1
Netherlands	List-PR	36.7	80.0
Germany	MMP	31.8	77.7
Norway	List-PR	37.9	77.4
Greece	List-PR	13.0	76.6
Spain	List-PR	36.0	75.7
Argentina	List-PR	35.0	70.9
Costa Rica	List-PR	38.6	68.8
Israel	List-PR	14.2	67.8
Japan	MMP	9.0	67.4
Finland	List-PR	37.5	66.7
Portugal	List-PR	21.3	64.3
Canada	SMP	20.8	64.7
United States	SMP	15.2	63.8
Ireland	STV	13.3	62.6
New Zealand	MMP	32.2	61.6
United Kingdom	SMP	19.7	61.4
France	SMM	12.2	60.3
Switzerland	List-PR	25.0	45.4

Source: International Institute for Democracy and Electoral Education, available on-line at www.idea.int/vt/parl.cfm accessed July 2006.

REGION	PERCENT OF WOMEN IN LOWER HOUSE
Female Representation	
World Average	16.8
Nordic Countries	40.0
Americas	20.5
Europe—OSCE-member countries including Nordic countries	19.4
Europe—OSCE-member countries excluding Nordic countries	17.4
Sub-Saharan Africa	16.7
Asia	16.4
Pacific	12.1
Arab States	8.2

Source: Inter-Parliamentary Union, available on-line at http://www.ipu.org/wmn-e/classif.htm; accessed July 2006.

than PR systems. The following data demonstrate how the Canadian system stacks up against a selection of other countries based on turnout and the percentage of women elected to the national legislature.

Elections and Public Policy

There are two general schools of thought about what elections mean for public policy determination: the agenda model and the mandate model.[2] Canadian elections tend not to conform to either of these theoretical standards.

Agenda Model

The agenda model predicts that a party in government will seek to enact the specific policies that it promised during the most recent campaign. It assumes that a campaign pledge is more than a ploy to win votes and that parties will deliver on their commitments. A comparative study of 10 Western democracies found that the agenda effect is weaker in Canada than in most other countries—largely because of our single-party governments and SMP electoral system.[3]

Mandate Model

The mandate model takes a broader view of the link between parties and policies. It assumes that elections carry messages about problems, policies, and programs—messages plain enough for most voters to understand and specific enough to provide the government with direction. In a sense, elections produce mandates to govern in a certain way for the party that wins an election. It also assumes that, outside of emergency situations, governments should not embark on radical policy shifts before the electorate has a chance to render its judgment.[4]

The Canadian Reality

Although the campaign platforms of the major Canadian parties have generally contained more partisan rhetoric than policy detail, it is customary for newly elected governments, particularly those with large majorities, to claim a mandate from the people to implement their platforms. The belief that the governing party has the legitimate authority to enact the will of the people is a powerful political tool. But in most cases, at least in Canada, it is a false belief. Neither the agenda model nor the mandate model provides an accurate account of the relationship between policy and elections. There are at least four reasons why Canadian general elections do not automatically set the policy agenda or create specific policy mandates for governments.

1. Initially, the claim that voters use their ballots to express specific policy preferences is simply inaccurate. While the parties' varying approaches to critical issues do affect election outcomes, that effect is too small and too diffuse to constitute a clear and specific command. Canadian voters are influenced by a host of factors—party loyalty, social cleavages, impressions of the various leaders—and they are as likely to interpret party platforms through these lenses as they are to make their voting decisions on the basis of policy pledges.[5] In any case, elections are not referenda. They are designed to elect the people who will sit in Parliament, not to resolve particular policy disputes. Therefore, the relationship between elections and public policy is indirect at best.

2. For the most part, Canada's issue agenda brokerage parties have avoided making specific promises that might alienate potential voters. They tend to instead rely on vague, leader-centred campaigns that build broad electoral coalitions and leave the winning party with maximum flexibility when in government. Without a clear and consistent choice among party principles, voters cannot clearly express their agenda or mandate preferences when casting ballots for party candidates.

3. Canadian governments do not feel bound to await new instructions from the voters before undertaking significant changes in policy. While a government may pay a political price for a major U-turn, there is no written or unwritten rule to deter it from breaking its promises. For example, in 1974 Pierre Trudeau campaigned against a legislated freeze on wages and prices; in 1993 Jean Chrétien campaigned against the North American Free Trade Agreement (NAFTA) which the previous government had negotiated with the U.S. and Mexico; Stephen Harper promised in the 2006 election to not change the tax status of income

trusts. All three subsequently reversed themselves: Trudeau imposed wage and price controls, Chrétien signed the NAFTA deal, and Harper taxed the trusts.

4. Finally, both models overlook the practical difficulties that prevent a party in government from keeping its promises. Even parties that fully intend on implementing their policy and platform agendas often find it difficult to interpret a specific policy mandate from the election results once they encounter all the competing demands on their resources. This is particularly true when parties accustomed to the freedom of opposition run up against the reality of governing. Many of the policies they adopted so enthusiastically while in opposition may be revealed as impractical and potentially damaging once they are in office. Under those circumstances, there is something to be said in favour of broken campaign promises.

If we conclude that elections do not determine the direction of public policy, then what exactly do they do? At the very least, competitive elections allow citizens to remove a government that has failed to live up to expectations and to replace it with an alternative. In this way, citizens hold their rulers to account for their use of power. The prospect of losing the next election can act as a powerful brake on a government that might otherwise abuse its power or trample the rights of its citizens.

Elections legitimize state power by signifying the consent of the governed. They allow voters to express their broad political preferences, even if they do not transmit specific policy choices. Finally, elections provide voters with the opportunity to engage directly with their political institutions. They use the electoral system to elect MPs, some of whom will sit in the Cabinet, and one of whom will become (or remain) the prime minister. Whatever its imperfections, representative democracy has at least one cardinal virtue: it brings the citizens into close contact with the state at fairly regular intervals.

THE CONDUCT OF CANADIAN ELECTIONS

In a general election, the entire House of Commons is dissolved and all 308 seats are filled simultaneously. A by-election occurs when a single seat becomes vacant (e.g., the incumbent MP resigns), and a special vote is held to fill that seat. In either case, the prime minister asks the governor general to issue a writ of election, which sets the date on which ballots will be cast. There are only two constraints on this power:

1. By law, the campaign must be a minimum of 36 days, but it can be longer, as was the case with the 2005–2006 campaign, which ran 56 days, from November 28, 2005, to January 23, 2006.

2. No Parliament may last longer than 5 years, except in extraordinary circumstances, as spelled out in Section 4 of the Charter of Rights.[6]

To ensure fairness, Canadian elections are organized and administered by a non-partisan agency with nothing to fear from the loss of the incumbent party. Elections

Canada operates at arm's length from the government of the day. The chief electoral officer, who cannot be removed from office without just cause, reports directly to Parliament. While the governing party controls the content of the Canada Elections Act—the legislation that gives Elections Canada its authority and sets the rules by which it operates—it cannot be seen to pursue an electoral advantage denied to the other registered parties.

■ The Formal Rules: The Canada Elections Act

Since 1974, the Canada Elections Act has regulated Canadian parties and candidates for office. Amendments to the act have been made over the years, and in 2004 significant new rules came into effect, including those concerning party financing that were reviewed in the previous chapter. The 2004 changes also brought electoral district associations fully within the regulatory framework for the first time and imposed new financing rules on party leadership contests. The regulatory principles that apply to registered parties are for the most part applied to the other formal political entities. The activities of broadcasters, and to a certain extent those of other private actors, are also regulated by the act.

Parties

The regulation of political parties in Canada includes a number of components: agency, disclosure, spending limits, public reimbursement of election expenses, and tax credits for political donations. Each contributes to the overall regulatory framework that has in recent years moved many formerly private activities fully under public control and oversight.

- *Agency:* The registered party must, as a condition of registration, appoint an official agent, who is responsible for issuing tax receipts to donors and keeping complete records of revenues and expenditures.[7]
- *Disclosure:* The party's official agent must submit an annual fiscal report to Elections Canada, including the source and amount of each donation,[8] as well as a special report on each election campaign that details the revenues and expenditures of the national party organization[9] (candidates do not have to submit an annual report).
- *Spending limits:* The amount that a registered party can legally spend on its national campaign is determined by the number of candidates who run under its banner and by the number of voters in the constituencies where those candidates are nominated.[10]
- *Public reimbursement of election expenses:* A registered party that receives at least 2 percent of the valid national vote, or at least 5 percent of the valid vote in the constituencies where it ran candidates, is eligible for a reimbursement of 50 percent of its allowable election expenses if it complies with the reporting requirements of the act (the reimbursement for the 2004 general election, the first under the new procedures, was 60 percent).[11]

- *Tax credits for political donations:* A donation of $25 or more to a registered party, a registered constituency association, or an official candidate is eligible for a tax credit, which reduces the amount of income tax the contributor will owe the federal government (e.g., a donation of $400 to the official agent of a candidate entitles the donor to deduct $300 from his or her income tax).[12]

Candidates

Any candidate who received at least 10 percent of the valid votes cast in the constituency is eligible for reimbursement of up to 60 percent of the electoral and personal expenses incurred during the campaign.[13] To qualify for the reimbursement, the candidate's official agent must submit a report to Elections Canada detailing the revenues received by the campaign, election expenditures, and personal expenses incurred by the candidate.[14] Any surplus funds remaining after election day must be transferred to the bank account of the local constituency association affiliated with the registered party represented by the candidate. Over time, in well-organized constituency associations with popular incumbent MPs, those surplus funds can build up into very substantial amounts. As we saw in the last chapter, it was not uncommon for constituency associations to bail out the national parties by donating significant funds to the national organization.

Constituency Associations

Until recently, Canadian party organizations were subject to comparatively little formal regulation. In most respects, constituency associations were treated as private clubs. Their internal operations fell outside the scope of the Canada Elections Act, whose rules about agency, disclosure, and spending limits applied only to candidates and not to the local party organizations that nominated them. There were no spending limits on nomination contests. Indeed, constituency associations were described as the "black hole" in the regulatory regime.[15]

All that changed in 2004, when Bill C-24—An Act to Amend the Canada Elections Act and the Income Tax Act (Political Financing)—became law. The bill extended the regulatory regime to constituency associations ("electoral district associations," or EDAs, in legal terminology). Every constituency association of a registered party has to file its own registration with Elections Canada. Only registered associations can accept donations and spend money.[16] Unregistered constituency associations cannot run election campaigns. A registered constituency association must appoint an official agent, who is responsible for receiving donations and submitting an audited annual report of financial transactions to Elections Canada. The constituency associations are also affected by the new rules for nomination contests.

The new provisions for constituency associations operate independently of the existing rules for candidates and their campaign teams. Whereas the constituency rules are always in effect, those that apply to candidates operate only during (and shortly after) the campaign period.

Broadcasters

The formal actors who directly participate in elections are also subject to the broadcasting provisions of the Canada Elections Act, as are the broadcasters themselves. The key elements of the election broadcast rules are as follows. During the campaign period, every Canadian broadcaster—independent radio stations and radio and TV networks—must make 6.5 hours of prime time available for purchase by the registered parties for their election advertising. That time is divided among the registered parties on the basis of their seat percentages in the House of Commons, their share of the vote in the previous general election, and the number of candidates each party nominated during the last campaign period. The allocation of time among the parties is determined by the broadcasting arbitrator, an official appointed by the chief electoral officer before each election. No single party may receive more than 50 percent of the total broadcasting time.[17] Furthermore, broadcasters (and publishers) may not charge inflated rates for campaign advertising; in other words, they cannot gouge the parties by hiking their advertising rates for party advertising during an election. Every radio and television network must also provide a smaller amount of free airtime to the registered parties in proportion to the allocation of paid airtime.

Election Financing

The 1974 Election Expenses Act made it a requirement for parties and candidates to disclose the amounts and sources of their revenues and to restrict their campaign spending. Some of the restrictions imposed in 1974 and in subsequent amendments were, however, more apparent than real. The introduction of C-24 closed many, but not all of the loopholes. Some that remain arise from the definition of election expenses.

For example, there are no restrictions on spending by parties and candidates before the campaign officially begins. Given that all of the parties plan their campaigns well ahead of time, they can circumvent the election spending limits by incurring expenses before the campaign period officially begins. Not surprisingly, the operating expenses of the major parties often rise dramatically in the months before an election, as organizers bank the resources they intend to use during the upcoming campaign.

The definition of election expenses excludes fundraising, the cost of creating party policies and campaign strategies, and other expenditures that do not "directly promote or oppose a registered party, its leader or a candidate during an election period."[18] However, polling and research costs, which together comprise a major expense for all the parties, are now factored into the calculation of election expenses under provisions of the amended act. Finally, the distinction between the personal and election expenses of candidates is not clear. The 2000 elections act imposed the disclosure requirement on personal expenses and gave the chief electoral officer the power to limit such expenses, but it also provided reimbursements for both types of expenditure.

While it is too early to gauge the full significance of their impact on Canadian elections, as we saw in the last chapter the new financing rules have benefited the Conservatives and the Bloc much more than the Liberals and the New Democrats, which has a direct impact on how much each of the parties can afford to spend before

CANADA BY THE NUMBERS 5.3 Election Expense Limits for the 2006 Federal Election

PARTY	EXPENSE LIMIT
Conservative Party of Canada	$ 18 278 278.64
Liberal Party of Canada	$ 18 278 278.64
New Democratic Party	$ 18 278 278.64
Green Party of Canada	$ 18 278 278.64
Bloc Québécois	$ 4 676 676.52
Marxist-Leninist Party of Canada	$ 4 494 786.75
Christian Heritage Party of Canada	$ 2 617 633.05
Canadian Action Party	$ 2 150 020.88
Progressive Canadian Party	$ 1 555 632.40
Marijuana Party	$ 1 353 566.56
Communist Party of Canada	$ 1 234 417.80
Libertarian Party of Canada	$ 659 531.77
First Peoples National Party of Canada	$ 285 326.57
Western Block Party	$ 273 026.95
Animal Alliance Environment Voters Party	$ 68 154.97

Source: Elections Canada Web pages available at http://www.elections.ca.

and during an election campaign. The formal campaign spending limits shown in Canada by the Numbers 5.2 are calculated according to a formula in the Canada Elections Act. Each party can spend up to 70 cents per elector in every riding where the party has nominated a candidate. It also reflects the wider definition of election expenses in Bill C-24. In compensation for including polling and research expenses in the totals, the per-voter limit rose from 62 cents in the 2000 act to 70 cents in the 2004 act.

Drawing the Boundaries

Federal constituency boundaries are drawn by independent commissions to avoid the appearance of partisan favouritism.[19] Factors such as geography, demography, and communities of interest are taken into consideration when constituency boundaries are drawn. In the interests of fairness, however, there must be an effort to ensure that the population of each constituency does not deviate too greatly from a predetermined standard—approximately 100 000 voters per district, plus or minus 25 percent[20]—and that none of the parties currently represented in the legislature can redraw the boundaries according to its own self-interest.[21]

As we have already noted, each Canadian constituency elects one MP to the House of Commons to represent the voters living within that precise geographical area. Single-member constituencies produce clear winners—except in the rare event of a tie—and reduce a complex array of preferences to the choice of a single individual. Other elected bodies based on single-member constituencies include the British House of Commons, the House of Representatives in both the United States and Australia, and Canada's provincial legislatures.

Expressing Preferences

Voting is only one way that Canadians can express their preferences in an election. Citizens can also campaign actively for a favourite candidate, contribute money to campaigns, place signs on their lawns, or attend meetings to demonstrate political support. However, these activities do not directly determine who wins or loses. The winner is not the candidate with the most money, or the most volunteers, or the most lawn signs. The preferences expressed when voters cast ballots are the only ones that count.

The simplest and crudest way of expressing preferences on an electoral ballot is through a categorical choice as described above. A categorical ballot allows the voter to choose one, and only one, of the candidates listed. Given a choice between candidates A, B, and C, the voter may put an "X" beside only one of them, or beside none, thereby spoiling the ballot. Note that with this method the voter is able to express a preference for A over both B and C, but is unable to express a second preference for either B or C. If the voter dislikes B more intensely than he likes A, a categorical ballot may encourage strategic voting—that is, voting for C in order to defeat B even though the voter would prefer to see A get elected. Under this condition, the voter has made a complex strategic calculation, little of which is communicated through the ballot. Categorical ballots are used in both federal and provincial elections in Canada.

THE CANADIAN ELECTORAL SYSTEM

The table of Canadian election results at the end of the previous chapter raises several important questions about the Canadian electoral system:

- Why did the Liberal Party form three successive majority governments between 1993 and 2000 while only winning between 38 and 43 percent of the popular vote? And why did it form a majority government (155/301 seats) with 38 percent of the vote in 1997 and only a minority (135/108 seats) with 36.7 percent of the vote in 2004?
- Why did the Canadian Alliance win only two seats in Ontario in 2000, despite winning almost one-quarter of the votes in that province, and almost all the seats in Alberta with just under 60 percent of the vote?
- How can a party that contests seats in only one province and wins only 14 percent of the national vote form Her Majesty's Loyal Opposition with 54 seats—as the BQ did in 1993—while the Progressive Conservative Party, with 16 percent of the vote, won only 2 seats?
- How did the Conservatives win minority governments in 1957 and 1979 despite winning fewer votes than the Liberals?

Lester Pearson's five years as prime minister are a remarkable example of how much a government can accomplish in minority Parliaments. Although Canadian voters provided Pearson with strong minorities, he still had to accommodate the minor parties to accomplish his legislative agenda. His approach to the minor parties began the process of officially recognizing them and their leaders in parliamentary law. Pearson will be remembered most for establishing the Canadian welfare state and for his 1957 Nobel Peace Prize for helping the United Nations resolve the Suez Canal crisis. (© Bettmann/CORBIS)

Born: 1897, Newton Brook, Ontario

Died: 1972, Ottawa

Education: B.A. History (University of Toronto, 1919), B.A. and M.A. Modern History (Oxford University, 1923 and 1925)

Profession: 1914–1918 Lieutenant, Canadian Army Medical Corps, and flying officer, Royal Flying Corps

1923–1928 History lecturer, University of Toronto

1928–1948 Department of External Affairs

1945–1946 Canadian ambassador to the United States

1946 Undersecretary of state for external affairs

1946–1956 Head of Canadian delegation to UN

1969–1972 Professor and chancellor, Carleton University

Political Career:

MP
1948–1968 Algoma East, Ontario

Leader
1958–1968 Liberal Party

Prime Minister
1963–1968

Other Ministries
1948–1957 External Affairs

Political Career Highlights
1948 Appointed minister of external affairs
1951–1952 Chairman of the NATO Council
1952–1953 President of the United Nations General Assembly
1957 Nobel Peace Prize—Suez Canal crisis
1958–1963 Leader of the Opposition
1958 Lost first federal election as Liberal leader (Progressive Conservative majority)
1962 Lost second election as Liberal leader (Progressive Conservative minority)
1963 Elected prime minister with a minority government
1963 Royal Commission on Bilingualism and Biculturalism
1965 Reelected prime minister with a minority government
1965 Canada Pension Plan
1965 Canada–United States Automotive Agreement (Auto Pact)
1965 New national flag
1966 Universal medicare

Source: *First Among Equals, The Prime Minister in Canadian Life and Politics* (Ottawa: Library and Archives Canada), available on-line at http://www.collectionscanada.ca/primeministers/

- Why, despite shifting partisan allegiances among a majority of voters, did the Liberals govern Canada for most of the twentieth century?

Many of the answers to these questions lie in the workings of Canada's electoral system. The impact of electoral systems on party systems is one of the clearest and most dramatic examples of how institutional rules shape political outcomes. Because no electoral system is neutral, electoral outcomes are in part determined by the electoral system itself, not solely by the preferences of citizens. As such, the parliamentary seats awarded to each party may give a misleading picture of its relative support within the electorate. As we saw in the previous chapter, the electoral system is one of the political institutions that directly affect the party system as a whole and the individual parties within it. The incentives set by the electoral system shape the behaviour not only of political parties and elected officials, but also of voters.

How the Electoral System Affects the Party System

The relationship between electoral systems and party systems is one of the central themes in political science. The classic description of that relationship is Duverger's Law, which states that single-member plurality systems tend to produce two-party competition, while list-PR promotes multiparty competition (four or more parties in Parliament).[22] Proportional representation systems erect few barriers to smaller parties seeking election to Parliament; the threshold of election (the percentage of votes required to win a seat) is typically low, and the accurate translation of vote shares into seat shares ensures that most parties will secure at least some parliamentary representation. In contrast, electoral systems based on winner-take-all single-member constituencies tend to reduce the number of parties in Parliament and eventually in the party system as a whole.

While there is ample evidence to substantiate Duverger's argument about the disincentives for multipartyism under SMP,[23] a puzzle remains: how do we explain the fact that Canada uses SMP but has not had a pure two-party system since 1921? The answer lies in the tendency of SMP to award a disproportionately large number of seats to parties whose support is regionally concentrated. Smaller parties like the NDP, Reform, and the Bloc, although contesting national campaigns, win most of their seats in their strongest regions. The same is true in India and the United Kingdom, which also use SMP. Therefore, the impact of SMP on the number of parties depends on an intervening variable: the size and mobilization of regional subcultures within the electorate.

Douglas Rae, in his comprehensive study of the political consequences of electoral laws, substantiated Duverger's analysis. As such, Canada's categorical ballot, single-member districts, and plurality electoral formula *should* lead to fewer, rather than more, parties.[24] Yet Canada constitutes an enduring exception to the general rule. In his comparative analysis, Rae found only a small number of plurality elections that failed to produce two-party legislative competition, and all of them were Canadian. He concluded that "the Canadian exceptions have a fairly obvious explanation: the intense hostility between overlapping regional, cultural, and linguistic groups produced a strong base of support for locally strong minority parties."[25] Although small parties were consistently underrepresented, Rae found no evidence of their demise and recognized the Canadian exception as valid enough to necessitate a modification to the general rule: the almost complete correlation between SMP systems and two-party competition must be qualified where strong local minority parties exist. The modification recognizes the importance of factors other than the electoral system that can influence the structure of party competition. Overall, it indicates that a combination of other forces expressed in electoral outcomes is as important as the influence of the electoral system.

But rather than diminish the importance of electoral system effects, the modification alerts us to the importance of examining how the electoral system acts to reinforce distortions along regional cleavages. In other words, in Canada, the electoral system is an unusually important factor for parties and party competition because of the way it translates votes into seats, both nationally and on a regional basis.

Primary Effects of SMP in Canada

The Canadian electoral system has four primary effects when translating votes into seats.[26]

1. It benefits large parties with strong support across the country.
2. It penalizes large parties with weak support across the country.
3. It benefits smaller, regional parties with strongly concentrated regional support.
4. It penalizes small, regional parties with weak regional support.

The system disproportionately benefits the strongest major party. The federal Liberals found themselves in this position for most of the twentieth century while the Progressive Conservatives periodically managed to ascend to this position under both Diefenbaker and Mulroney. Although since 1921 these types of parties have rarely garnered more than half of the total national vote, because they typically receive at least 25 to 30 percent of the vote in most constituencies, and often 40 to 60 percent, they win a higher proportion of seats than their national vote totals would have allowed under a PR system.

The system also underrepresents parties with diffuse national support. The Conservatives found themselves in this position for much of the twentieth century, with the Liberals only periodically being penalized by the electoral system. The Progressive Conservatives' 1993 election results are a good example of this effect. Although the PCs received 16 percent of the total national vote, it was spread out rather evenly across the country. So, in much of the West, many PC candidates received between 15 and 20 percent of the vote, but got beaten by a Reform or NDP candidate winning 30 to 50 percent of the vote. In Ontario, again PC contenders often managed 20 percent of the vote, but got beaten by Liberals winning even more. In Quebec, Bloc or Liberal candidates for the most part beat PC candidates winning less than 20 percent of the vote. Once all the votes were counted, the Progressive Conservatives could claim almost one-sixth of the total vote, but only two victories (less than 1 percent of the total parliamentary seats).

The Canadian SMP system also benefits smaller parties with strongly concentrated regional support. The Progressives, Social Credit, CCF, Reform, and the Bloc

Québécois are all examples of regional parties that have benefited from the effects of the electoral system. Although they are often penalized in the regions where they are not strong (for example Reform in Ontario), they tend to dominate competition in regions where they are strong (Reform in Alberta and the Bloc in Quebec).

The Canadian SMP system also penalizes weaker regional parties. Most observers may think that this only makes sense. After all, if a party is only regionally focused, and is then weak even in that region, it deserves not to be rewarded. However, some PR systems would reward these types of parties with at least some parliamentary representation.

On the national level, one of the more striking features of Canadian election data is the degree to which parties are overrewarded once their percentage of the vote moves above 40 percent of the total. On the rare occasions when a party approaches 50 percent of the vote—as the Liberals did in 1949, and the Progressive Conservatives did in 1958 and 1984—the electoral system has worked to produce a legislative landslide. For example, in 1949 the Liberals received 49.5 percent of the votes, which produced victories for them in 73.7 percent of the seats. In 1958, the Conservatives received 78.5 percent of the seats based on 54 percent of the votes, while in 1984 they won 74.8 percent of the seats by capturing 49.7 percent of the votes.

In rare cases, such as 1957 and 1979, the party winning the most votes (the Liberals) was bested in seat totals by the party winning the second most votes (the Progressive Conservatives). This occurred because the PCs won more close races (for example 40 percent of the vote versus 35 percent for its closest competitor), while the Liberals won many of their victories with large margins (sometimes 60 or 70 percent compared to only 20 percent for their nearest competitor). Thus, when all the votes were counted, the Liberals came out on top in terms of vote percentage, but the PCs won the election because they won a larger number of seats.

Does the Electoral System Encourage Regional Discord?

The application SMP in Canada distorts the regional composition of party caucuses in the House of Commons. It overrewards the party with the most votes in a given province, while denying other parties their proportionate share of parliamentary representation. By artificially relegating entire regions to the opposition benches, SMP reinforces regionalism in Canada. In the 1970s and early 1980s, the governing Liberals were all but shut out of the West, while the Progressive Conservatives were nearly invisible in Quebec, despite significant electoral support for each in the respective regions. As a consequence, Western Canadians lacked significant elected representation in the government caucus and the Cabinet when the National Energy Program was introduced in 1980. Not only was the legislation less sensitive to regional concerns than it might have been, but the Liberal government lacked elected members to sell the policies in the West. Distortions in the electoral system thus reinforced long-standing sentiments of regional alienation and further eroded the legitimacy of parliamentary institutions within the region. Similarly, in Quebec the electoral system contributed significantly to the "Tory syndrome"[27] or minority-party syndrome: it bedevilled Conservative efforts to build the party within Quebec and to convince Canadian voters in other parts of the country that the Progressive Conservatives were indeed a national party that could span linguistic divisions.

Because the electoral system rewards parties whose votes are concentrated in particular regions while penalizing those whose votes are spread thinly across the country, the incentives for party strategists are clear: if they want to win the maximum number of seats in Parliament, they must target one or more regionally based subcultures and devote less attention to the rest of Canada. In effect, the electoral system encourages parties to inflame regional tensions and resentments as a way to mobilize and solidify their subcultural bases. This in turn has had important consequences for the parties' campaign strategies and policy positions. The major parties have demonstrated a tendency to aim "appeals at the nerve centres of particular provinces or regions" in an attempt at capturing a geographical vote.[28] When the interests of one region conflict with those of another region, as they often do in Canadian politics, parties must make strategic choices about which region to target and which region to abandon. The historical distribution of seats in the House of Commons has demonstrated that if one party can capture a large share of seats in Ontario and Quebec, it can form a majority government even if that means electing little or no representation from the Western provinces. As has been argued above, over the past 30 years the Liberals have successfully employed this strategy to the detriment of the party in western Canada. The Reform Party's strategy of initially organizing only in western Canada and not contesting seats in Quebec during the 1993 election is based on a more overt attempt at employing a regional electoral strategy. The Bloc's strategy is even more obvious.

When Reform wins half the votes in Alberta, but this translates into it winning almost all the seats, or the Liberals win about half the votes in Ontario but win almost all the seats, the fact that upwards of half the voters in each of these provinces did not vote for the winning party is not represented in the distribution of parliamentary seats. By undervaluing the partisan diversity within each region or province, the electoral system creates parliamentary compositions for each party that are much less representative of the actual partisan diversity within those regions. Consequently, the party system is not simply a reflection of regionalism within the political culture. Regionalism is also a product of the party system.

VOTING AND NONVOTING

The Franchise

The right to vote is enshrined in the Charter of Rights as one of its most important elements. Charter Sections 3 to 5 are not subject to the Section 33 legislative override, and the Supreme Court has set a higher standard for "reasonable limits" on democratic rights than those that apply to other Charter sections. But long before the Charter took effect, the franchise had been extended universally. Women, Aboriginal Canadians, and other previously excluded groups had been exercising voting privileges for years (see Canadian Political Chronology 5.1). Since the 1982 entrenchment

CANADIAN POLITICAL CHRONOLOGY 5.1 History of the Franchise in Canada 1867–2002

YEAR	GROUPS	DESCRIPTION
1867	Males over age of 21 meeting certain property qualifications could vote.	Women, registered Indians, and members of certain religious denominations were excluded. The right to vote in federal elections was still governed by provincial, not federal, legislation. Some groups, such as immigrants from Japan, China, and India, were not allowed to vote in some provinces.
1885	Some Aboriginal people acquired the right to vote, depending on where in the country they lived.	Parliament adopted a complex federal franchise act based on property. The act was applied differently from one town and one province to the next.
1917	Voting privileges were granted to all British subjects, male and female, who were active or retired members of the armed forces, including Indians and people under the age of 21. Civilian men who did not meet the property qualification but who had a son or grandson in the army were temporarily given the right to vote, as were women with a father, mother, husband, son, daughter, brother, or sister with military service.	During the First World War, Parliament adopted the Wartime Elections Act and the Military Voters Act. In the election of December 1917, some 2000 military nurses became the first Canadian women to vote in a federal election.
1918	Voting privileges at the federal level were extended to all Canadian women aged 21 and over who were native born and satisfied any relevant property qualifications.	The following year, women obtained the right to run for a seat in the House of Commons.
1920	Universal male and female suffrage was granted for British subjects by birth or naturalization for federal elections.	Some foreign-born citizens continued to be excluded until 1922. The election of 1921 was the first in which the number of people registered on the voters lists represented more than 50 percent of the population.
1948	Asians and those without property acquired voting privileges for federal elections.	The last vestiges of the property qualification, which still applied in Quebec, were abolished. Canadians of Asian origin acquired the right to vote.
1950	Inuit regained voting privileges for federal elections.	The 1934 provision preventing the Inuit from voting was abolished.
1960	Status Indians living on reserves were granted voting privileges for federal elections.	A new Canada Elections Act eliminated the provision excluding Status Indians living on reserves from voting and introduced advance polls for all electors who expected to be away from their polling divisions on election day.
1970	The minimum age to vote or stand for office was lowered from 21 to 18.	The right to vote was reserved for Canadian citizens, but British subjects eligible to vote on June

ELECTIONS AND VOTING **191**

YEAR	GROUPS	DESCRIPTION
		25, 1968, retained the right to vote until 1975. Proxy voting was also introduced for fishermen, seamen, prospectors, and students away from their electoral districts. People with disabilities were given the option of voting at an advance poll.
1982	The Charter of Rights and Freedoms guaranteed the right of all citizens to vote and stand for office in House of Commons and provincial legislatures.	The Canada Elections Act stipulated that anyone who had reached the age of 18 on election day was eligible to vote.
1988	Judges and mentally disabled were ruled to have voting rights.	Two court rulings determined that federally appointed judges and people with a mental disability have the right to vote.
1993	Students, snowbirds, business people, and other transients allowed to vote by special ballot. Prisoners serving less than two years in jail allowed to vote.	Parliament adopted legislation allowing Canadians to use the special ballot if they were not able to go to the polling station and allowed prisoners serving less than two years in jail to vote in federal elections.
2002	All inmates granted voting rights by Supreme Court.	In a 5–4 split decision, the Supreme Court struck down the 1993 law barring federal inmates from voting in federal elections. *Sauvé v. Canada* (Chief Electoral Officer), [2002] 3 S.C.R. 519, 2002 SCC 68

Source: Elections Canada, http://www.elections.ca

of Charter rights, the courts have struck down laws that denied the franchise to most of the remaining excluded groups such as prisoners and judges.

Turnout

Canada does not have compulsory voting in which citizens are penalized for not exercising their most basic democratic rights. Nevertheless, most eligible Canadians cast ballots in federal elections (see Canadian Political Chronology 5.2). On average, 71 percent of eligible voters have cast ballots in the federal elections since Confederation. But, for a combination of reasons, the official Canadian turnout rate has fallen recently, as it has in most Western democracies. Canadian turnout dropped from over 75 percent in the mid-1980s to 61 percent in 2004, the lowest in Canadian history. Although turnout rebounded slightly in 2006, to almost 65 percent, concern exists amongst many analysts about the longer term trends.

Until recently, more was known about the characteristics of nonvoters than was known about their reasons for nonvoting. Political scientists had identified three

DATE OF ELECTION OR REFERENDUM	TOTAL CANADIAN POPULATION (MILLIONS)	NUMBER OF ELIGIBLE VOTERS (MILLIONS)	ELIGIBLE VOTERS AS PERCENT OF TOTAL POPULATION	VOTER TURNOUT AS PERCENT OF ELIGIBLE VOTERS
7 August–20 September 1867[a]	3.2	0.4	11.2	73.1
20 July–12 October 1872[a]	3.7	0.4	11.6	70.3
22 January 1874	3.7	0.4	11.7	69.6
17 September 1878	3.7	0.7	19.4	69.1
20 June 1882	4.3	0.7	15.3	70.3
22 February 1887	4.3	0.9	21.9	70.1
5 March 1891	4.8	1.1	23.0	64.4
23 June 1896	4.8	1.4	28.1	62.9
29 September 1898[b]	4.8	1.2	25.6	44.6
7 November 1900	4.8	1.2	24.1	77.4
3 November 1904	5.4	1.4	25.8	71.6
26 October 1908	5.4	1.5	27.2	70.3
21 September 1911	7.2	1.8	25.3	70.2
17 December 1917	7.2	2.1	29.1	75.0
6 December 1921	8.8	4.4	50.6	67.7
29 October 1925	8.8	4.6	52.6	66.4
14 September 1926	8.9	4.7	52.5	67.7
28 July 1930	8.9	5.2	58.0	73.5
14 October 1935	10.4	5.9	57.1	74.2
26 March 1940	10.5	6.6	63.2	69.9
27 April 1942[b]	11.5	6.5	56.6	71.3
11 June 1945	11.5	7.0	60.5	75.3
27 June 1949	11.8	7.9	66.8	73.8
10 August 1953	14.0	8.4	60.0	67.5
10 June 1957	16.1	8.9	55.4	74.1
31 March 1958	16.1	9.1	56.8	79.4
18 June 1962	18.2	9.7	53.2	79.0
8 April 1963	18.2	9.9	54.3	79.2
8 November 1965	18.2	10.3	56.3	74.8

DATE OF ELECTION OR REFERENDUM	TOTAL CANADIAN POPULATION (MILLIONS)	NUMBER OF ELIGIBLE VOTERS (MILLIONS)	ELIGIBLE VOTERS AS PERCENT OF TOTAL POPULATION	VOTER TURNOUT AS PERCENT OF ELIGIBLE VOTERS
25 June 1968	20.0	10.9	54.3	75.7
30 October 1972	21.6	13.0	60.3	76.7
8 July 1974	21.6	13.6	63.1	71.0
22 May 1979	23.0	15.2	66.3	75.7
18 February 1980	23.0	15.9	69.1	69.3
4 September 1984	24.3	16.8	68.9	75.3
21 November 1988	25.3	17.6	69.7	75.3
26 October 1992[b-c]	20.4	13.7	67.3	71.8
25 October 1993	27.3	19.9	72.9	70.9[d]
2 June 1997	27.3	19.7	72.0	67.0
27 November 2000	28.9	21.2	73.6	64.1[e]
28 June 2004	30.0	22.5	74.9	60.9
28 January 2006	30.0	23.0	76.8	64.7

Notes:

[a] In early elections, polling took place over several weeks or even months.

[b] A referendum.

[c] Does not include Quebec, as Quebec conducted its own referendum.

[d] A turnout of 69.6% was initially indicated but this rises to 70.9 when the number of electors on the lists is adjusted to account for electors who had moved or died between the enumeration for the 1992 referendum and the election of 1993, for which a separate enumeration was not carried out except in Quebec, as the 1992 electoral lists were reused.

[e] The turnout of 61.2% in 2000 was adjusted to arrive at the final turnout of 64.1%, after Elections Canada's normal maintenance of the National Register of Electors to remove the names of deceased electors and duplicates arising from moves. The Chief Electoral Officer of Canada explained the adjustment during his appearance before the Subcommittee on Electoral Boundaries Readjustment on October 6, 2003, and his appearance to discuss the 2004 Main Estimates before the Standing Committee on Procedure and House Affairs on March 5, 2004.

Source: Data compiled and used to create the above chart was taken from the Website of Elections Canada: http://www.elections.ca. It is used with the permission of the Chief Electoral Officer but extrapolation and analysis rest with the author.

personal characteristics—age, education, and income—that were believed to be powerful predictors of voting and nonvoting. In the 2000 election, less than one-quarter of eligible first-time voters (those who had turned 18 since the previous election) actually cast ballots. Among voters over 60, the turnout rate was more than 80 percent.[29] People with university degrees and those in the highest income brackets are more likely to vote than are those with less education and income, although these effects appear to be less significant than the impact of age.[30] After the 2000 federal election, concern about the low voter turnout prompted Elections Canada to commission the first major survey of nonvoters. It found that the primary reason for the rise of non-voting was the growing percentage of younger voters (those born after 1945) in the electorate. In effect, older people with a strong tendency to participate in elections were being replaced by new voters with less political interest and a weaker sense of civic duty.

Among the nonvoters surveyed, a majority said that they had stayed home on voting day because they were not interested in the election. Other reasons included a lack of confidence in political parties, their leaders, and local candidates, and a belief that their vote didn't matter.[31] The key problem was that young Canadians felt less "commitment to the Canadian community" than their elders. Under these circumstances, tinkering with the rules or engaging in mass advertising and propaganda exercises by Elections Canada, party leaders, or institutional reformers is likely to do little to reverse the trend.

THE CANADIAN VOTER

Persistent subcultures within the electorate shape our national party system by influencing voting behaviour. But Canadian voters are not motivated solely by long-term factors such as class, region, partisanship, or ideology. Some cast their votes on the basis of short-term factors: economic evaluations, the parties' stands on key issues, or their perceptions of the party leaders. While the act of expressing a preference may be simple, at least in Canada, determining one's electoral preference can be a complicated process. In this section we will examine the major short-term and long-term determinants of Canadian voting behaviour and their estimated impact on election outcomes.

Long-Term Influences on Voter Choice

Social Cleavages

As we saw in Chapter 1, Western democratic electorates are divided into subcultures along lines of social cleavage: for example, class, religion, language, ethnicity, region, or gender. These demographic characteristics are relatively stable and persistent, and sometimes underlie long-term patterns of voting behaviour. In practical terms, the politically salient demographic characteristics of a given voter shape that voter's perceptions of political parties, issues, and leaders. These characteristics do not necessarily determine the person's vote, but they do influence the voter's judgments about the other long-term and short-term factors that affect voting choice.

For a particular social cleavage to influence the way in which a person votes, certain conditions must be present: Initially, there must be a political party that reflects the interests and values of that particular group, either exclusively or as part of a broader electoral coalition. Also, the cleavage must be politically salient—in other words, voters' identities as members of a particular group must be important enough to override other potential factors, such as short-term issues and party leaders. Furthermore, the voters within the group must interpret political events and issues through the filter of the particular values associated with that subculture (for example, Catholicism or feminism); in effect, they must be mobilized to see the world through the same lens.

In cross-national studies of voting behaviour, Canadian voters stand out in two respects: Canadians do not identify strongly with class cleavages, but they do identify with regional cleavages.[32] Despite the presence of different socioeconomic classes in Canada, the class cleavage does not exert a significant influence on voting behaviour. Advocates of class voting consider this unusual cleavage pattern to be a sign of immaturity on the part of Canadian voters. They argue that the division between socioeconomic classes *should* take priority over all others. In reality, the range of conflicting interests in a complex postindustrial society extends far beyond simple class conflict. Although the class cleavage is unusually weak in Canada, as we have seen, the regional cleavage is more pronounced than in many Western democracies.[33] This should come as no surprise, given the discussions of regionalism throughout this book.

Several additional sociodemographic characteristics such as religious denomination, ethnicity, and gender deserve some brief mention. The impact of religion on voting in Canada is surprising, given the apparent decline of religious observance and of the salience of religious issues in Canadian politics during the twentieth century. Nonetheless, there are clear and consistent differences in voting patterns among Canada's largest religious denominations. Catholics are somewhat more likely than are Protestants to vote Liberal, while the reverse is true for the Conservatives, or at least it was for its founding elements of Reform, the Alliance, and the Progressive Conservative parties. Those with no religion disproportionately support the NDP.[34] As for ethnicity, the Liberals are by far the most popular party among Canadians of non-European origin, while the conservative parties have tended to get disproportionately more support from Northern European immigrants. The gender cleavage among Canadian voters is also significant. Historically, the Liberals and NDP have had disproportionately more female supporters, while Reform–Alliance, the Bloc Québécois, and to a lesser extent the old Progressive Conservative Party tended to have more male supporters.[35]

None of this means that all Catholics vote Liberal, or that women refuse to vote for the Conservatives or the Bloc. Most of the differences in subgroup voting patterns are only about 10 to 20 percent at most. However, it does mean that Canadian voters are influenced, although not exclusively, by the cleavage patterns in the electorate. Where differences between sociodemographic groups are large enough, concentrated in particular clusters, and not cancelled out by other factors, they can make a difference of several percent of the vote between the leading parties' candidates. In close ridings, this can be enough to determine winners and losers.

Partisanship and Party Identification

To explain some aspects of long-term voting patterns, political scientists use the American concept of party identification that was first developed by a group of researchers at the University of Michigan, headed by Angus Campbell. Party identification—partisanship as it is often referred to—is some sense of psychological attachment to one party or another. That identification or attachment may be stronger or weaker in some voters than in others, and voters are not necessarily locked in for life. But even when voters change identifications, their attachment to their new party tends to be at least somewhat enduring and based as much on emotion as on reason. Partisanship often entails a generalized feeling of like or dislike for a party rather than a rational opinion based on a critical appraisal of party policies.

The importance of party identification for voting behaviour is typically twofold. Early research in the United States showed that this stable, enduring, emotional identification with a party was the single most important predictor of a person's voting behaviour. Furthermore, party identification significantly affected the ways in which voters thought about political issues and the candidates for office. Most voters did not become supporters of a party because of its leader or its policies. Rather, they supported the policies and leaders because they were partisans of the party.

Research on Canadian voting behaviour has shown that partisanship operates somewhat differently in Canada than in other countries, including the United States. In Canada, party identifications are less stable and more flexible, and Canadians are more likely to change their partisan self-image when they change their voting preferences, something they do rather frequently. Identification with a political party in Canada is also affected by federalism, with many voters identifying with different parties at the national and provincial levels.

Because of these factors, Canadian analysts have developed a measure of partisanship that is sensitive to the way in which party attachments operate within our institutional framework. This measure is based on three components: stability, consistency, and intensity of attachment to a party.[36] Stability of partisanship refers to its persistence over time—has the voter always identified with one party, or was there a period in which the voter felt closer to another party or to no party? Consistency is a measure of partisanship at the national and provincial levels. Partisanship is consistent if the same party attachment is held at the two levels of government. Intensity refers to the strength of attachment and ranges from very strong to moderate to weak. Voters who have stable, consistent, and strong attachments to parties are called "durable partisans," and typically constitute between 34 and 37 percent of the electorate.[37] Those who deviate on one or more measures of stability, consistency, and strength of attachment are called "flexible partisans"; they constitute a large component of the electorate, almost two-thirds by this measure.

The 2000 *Canadian Election Study* employed a looser definition of partisanship—being "strongly disposed to support the same party at every election"—and found that 60 percent of those who voted in that election qualified as partisans.[38] Both measures indicate that although partisan loyalties make some voters predisposed to voting a particular way even before an election is called, somewhere between 40 and 60 percent of the electorate is open to being convinced of how they should vote during the election campaign period. Thus, while partisanship provides a degree of stability in the electorate, it is important to remember that most Canadian partisans are flexible. In the absence of a compelling reason to vote against a preferred party, a flexible partisan will usually vote with the preferred party. Every now and then, however, circumstances will conspire to provide a compelling reason.

Vote Switching

On the surface, the Canadian electorate appears to be stable and consistent. With the exception of infrequent electoral earthquakes, such as in 1921, 1958, and 1993, most elections produce little change in the relative vote shares of the major parties. After all, only the Liberal and Conservative parties have ever formed a federal government. However, this appearance of aggregate stability in Canadian voting behaviour is deceptive. It obscures the fact that the electoral system tends to overreward some parties while penalizing others. Often, majority governments are based on population minorities, and shifting minorities at that. It can also hide considerable changes in the government's position relative to the legislature. For example, in 13 of the 17 federal elections since 1957, the governing party either changed, or the same party held government but shifted between minority and majority status. Generally speaking, the aggregate stability in Canadian election outcomes masks a relatively high level of volatility among individual voters.

In the 1990s, the volatility of Canadian voters caught the attention of political scientists at home and abroad. In the 1993 election, an unprecedented 42 percent of Canadian voters switched parties. While this level of vote switching is high, it is not that much higher than the 30 percent or so who normally switch parties between elections. As the data in Canada by the Numbers 5.4 indicate, all parties lose some of their supporters between elections. Even the Liberals, who won three consecutive

CANADA BY THE NUMBERS 5.4 Voter Loyalty 1988–2006

	1988–1993	1993–1997	1997–2000	2000–2004	2004–2006	AVERAGE
Liberal	70	63	64	59	53	61.8
PC	22	51	44	68 (Conservative)	—	46.3
NDP	26	59	56	63	57	52.2
Reform–Alliance	—	80 (Reform)	80 (Alliance)	88 (Conservative)	—	82.7
BQ	—	78	67	80	67	73.0
Conservative	—	—	—	—	83	83.0

Note: The numbers in each cell represent the percentage of voters who cast ballots for the same party in both elections.

Sources: Jon H. Pammett, "Tracking the Votes," in Alan Frizzell, Jon H. Pammett, and Anthony Westell, eds., *The Canadian General Election of 1993* (Ottawa: Carleton University Press, 1994), 146; Jon H. Pammett, "The Voters Decide," in Alan Frizzell and Jon H. Pammett, eds., *The Canadian General Election of 1997* (Toronto: Dundurn Press, 1997), 228; Jon H. Pammett, "The People's Verdict," in Jon H. Pammett and Christopher Dornan, eds., *The Canadian General Election of 2000* (Toronto: Dundurn Press, 2001), 295; Andre Turcotte, "Canadians Speak Out," in Jon H. Pammett and Christopher Dornan, eds., *The Canadian General Election of 2004* (Toronto: Dundurn Press, 2004), 319; Andre Turcotte, "After 56 Days . . . The Verdict," in Jon H. Pammett and Christopher Dornan, eds., *The Canadian Federal Election of 2006* (Toronto: Dundurn Press, 2006), 291.

majorities between 1993 and 2000, did so by maintaining less than two-thirds of their former supporters between elections.

Reform–Alliance voters tended to be the most loyal over this period, with 80 percent of them sticking with their party between elections, even though the party itself changed between 1997 and 2000. This pattern of loyalty continued when the new Conservative party was formed. Fully 88 percent of former Alliance voters moved with Harper to the new party. Interestingly, more former Progressive Conservative voters moved their vote to the new Conservative party (68 percent) than the PCs typically had kept loyal on their own (only 51 percent between the 1993 and 1997 elections, and fewer still, 44 percent, between 1997 and 2000). The Bloc does relatively well in keeping its voters between elections, with approximately two-thirds to three-quarters likely to remain loyal. The NDP is less successful at maintaining its voters' loyalties (less then two-thirds remaining loyal between most elections). Given this evidence, it must be acknowledged that all parties need to replenish their electoral bases between elections, as they can count on significant pluralities of their voters drifting off to other parties from one election to the next.

Short-Term Influences on Voter Choice

Salient and immediate issues of concern tend to be the most important short-term influences on the Canadian electorate. Salience means that not only do voters think a particular way about an issue, but their thinking also combines with other factors to make it an important determining factor in their voting decisions. The salience of a given issue in a particular campaign is determined by short-term events, not just by its intrinsic long-term importance. When new issues capture the public's attention, they seem to crowd out the old ones. Furthermore, the salience of an issue is determined both by preexisting public perceptions about their parties and by the parties' campaign strategies. But as the data in Canada by the Numbers 5.5 indicate, Canadian elections are rarely fought over a single issue, with the 1988 "free trade" election being a notable exception. Notice also that in both 1997 and 2000, almost 3 out of 10 voters could not name a single major issue.

Generally speaking, three factors determine whether an issue, or cluster of issues, will become salient during an election campaign. Initially, voters must think that an issue is important. If the issue does not resonate with voters, even parties promoting it in their platforms will not likely help make it a salient election issue. Next, the parties must think the issue is important and incorporate positions on it into their campaign platforms. Even if voters think an issue is important, but none of the parties do, it is unlikely that the issue will determine whether a voter casts a ballot for one or the other parties. Finally, at least two of the parties must take differing positions on the issue in order for voters to have choice, and therefore for the issue to impact their voting decisions. All three factors must be in play before an issue will take on importance and possibly determine voting behaviour.

Once an issue becomes salient, it must also be linked to the parties. No matter how salient an issue may be to some voters, it will not structure the vote unless the

CANADA BY THE NUMBERS 5.5 Most Important Election Issues 1988–2006

ISSUE	2006 %	2004 %	2000 %	1997 %	1993 %	1988 %
Health Care	12	32	31	8	3	—
Unemployment, Jobs	1	1	2	24	44	1
Economy	3	3	3	4	8	1
Deficit, Debt	3	4	6	10	18	2
Taxes	4	3	7	3	—	1
Free Trade	—	—	—	—	1	82
National Unity, Quebec, Regionalism	2	1	3	13	4	1
Resources, Environment	2	2	2	1	—	2
Social Issues	9	1	4	2	1	2
Government, Trust, Accountability, Leaders	14	18	8	3	7	2
Sponsorship Scandal	6	4	—	—	—	—
Time for Change	2	—	—	—	—	—
Crime, Safety, Guns	4	—	—	—	—	—
Other	4	12	5	3	4	3
None, Don't Know	34	19	29	29	10	5

Sources: Andre Turcotte, "After 56 Days . . . The Verdict," in Jon H. Pammett and Christopher Dornan, eds., *The Canadian Federal Election of 2006* (Toronto: Dundurn Press, 2006), 288; and Jon H. Pammett, "The Voters Decide," in Alan Frizzell and Jon H. Pammett, eds., *The Canadian General Election of 1997* (Toronto: Dundurn Press, 1997), 235. Source data: 1997–2006 POLLARA Perspectives Canada Survey; 1993 Insight Canada Research post-election survey; 1988 re-interview of 1984 Canadian National Election Study.

parties are willing to stake out distinctive positions on it and those positions are clearly linked with the parties. Even when parties do take relatively clear and distinctive positions on issues, the linkage may not be clear to all voters. Issue salience is also helped when voters' opinions about the issue are skewed. "Skewness" refers to the distribution of support on an issue. Opinion is skewed when significantly more people are on one side of an issue than on the other. Alternatively, as was the case with the Free Trade Agreement issue in 1988, opinion is skewed if there are similar proportions of the electorate on either side of an issue but one side is linked to one party and the other side divided between two or more parties.

In Canadian elections, issues rarely meet all of these conditions. Although several issues may be salient to voters during a given election, they may not be clearly linked to parties and the vote may not be skewed accordingly. Given the influence of the long-term factors discussed earlier, and that of short-term factors yet to be discussed, the pool of voters who are open to persuasion on the basis of a single issue is relatively small, usually only about 1 percent or so for each issue.

The Economy and Other Issues

Historically, economic issues have been the most salient of all policy domains. Specifically, the way in which voters perceive the national economy often influences their opinion of the incumbent governing party. It is generally believed that the fortunes of the governing party rise and fall with the economic health of Canadians. However, the relationship between economics and voting behaviour is neither straightforward nor inevitable. The governing party benefits from a strong economy when two conditions are satisfied. First, voters must be willing to give the government credit for the current prosperity. Next, voters must perceive that their prosperity has been achieved through policies that are consistent with the values of a majority of voters, for example, that the social, environmental, or other costs of an economic boom are not unacceptably high.

Parties that have acquired a reputation for sound economic management are more likely to receive credit in good times and have the ability to ride out bad times. In Canada, the Liberals have benefited from such a reputation, while the NDP has suffered from a lack of credibility on fiscal issues. However, as the 2000 election importantly indicates, this does not mean that the incumbent party will win the election just because the economy is prospering. Even though Canadians were considerably more upbeat about the economy in 2000 than they had been in 1997, that optimism did not translate into a major boost for the Liberal Party. Of the party's 41 percent share of the vote, it is estimated that only 1 percentage point was due to economic issues.[39] One reason may be that the economy was less salient in the 2000 campaign than it had been in some previous elections. Another possible explanation is that Liberal supporters had the rosiest view of the economy, and most of them would have voted for the incumbent government anyway. Additionally, few voters gave the Liberals credit for rising employment and general prosperity.[40] Finally, those voters who were particularly concerned with economic issues did not necessarily perceive the Liberals as the best party to deal with those issues. A party benefits from public concern with an issue only to the extent that voters' opinions are skewed toward a particular side of that issue. Because Canadians were not overwhelmingly convinced that the Liberals shared their views about economic issues in 2000, the incumbent party benefited less than it might have from a robust economy. Furthermore, as the 2006 election results indicate, an incumbent party can lose an election even in very good economic times.

Voters' perceptions of specific issues—as distinct from their views about the economy in general—can change dramatically from election to election, as can the relative importance of a given issue. The data from 1988 to 2006 demonstrate that an issue that dominates one campaign—most obviously, free trade in 1988—can vanish before the next election call. Health care, an issue that did not register at all with voters in 1988, rose to become the single most important issue in 2000 and 2004, but seems to be fading in importance more recently.

Parties, Leaders, and Candidates

As their parties' chief spokespersons, particularly in an age of televised campaigning, party leaders can influence the voting behaviour of Canadians. Conventional wisdom holds that a popular leader may give his party a small boost, while an unpopular leader is an albatross around its neck.[41] But it would be wrong to overstate the importance of leader evaluations in voting choice. The available evidence suggests that the influence of party leaders on electoral behaviour has diminished since Trudeau left politics in 1984, and that no leader—however attractive or charismatic—can overcome the disadvantages posed by weak party organization and public hostility.

According to the authors of the 1988 *Canadian Election Study,* voters evaluate party leaders on two separate dimensions: competence and character.[42] Assessments of competence depend on perceptions of the leader as intelligent, knowledgeable, and able to provide strong leadership and a vision of Canada. The character of leaders is based on the extent to which they are perceived as moral, trustworthy, and compassionate. If a leader scores high on the competence index but falls short on character, as Brian Mulroney did in 1988, his party may still be able to win; after all, voters want a prime minister they can trust to do the job, even if they would not want to invite him over for dinner. But over time, a serious deficit on the character dimension undermines public trust and can overcome even the most positive assessments of competence. Simply put, voters get tired of voting for someone they dislike. On the other side of the coin, a likeable leader who does not appear to have the "right stuff" to lead the country may inspire affection, but will not draw many votes.

If the voters' evaluation of a leader is to benefit his or her party, three other conditions must be met for it to significantly impact voting behaviour. Initially, the leader must be substantially more popular or respected than the other leaders (otherwise the contending evaluations cancel each other out). Next, the leader's positive evaluations must be backed up by a strong party organization. Finally, other short-term factors that affect voting choice (the economy or other issues) must be less salient than the leadership issue. Under those conditions, opinions about party leaders may fill the vacuum left by a lack of issues.

As the data in Canada by the Numbers 5.6 indicate, leadership has been a declining influence on voters when compared to voters' images of the parties. In the Trudeau era, voters' evaluations of leaders rivalled their impressions of the parties in importance. Since then, however, leadership has decreased in importance at the same time as voters' impressions of the parties have become an even more important factor. In fact, for the past two decades, leadership has been only as important as have local candidates, with between one-fifth and one-quarter of all voters stating each is more

ELECTION	PARTY LEADERS %	LOCAL CANDIDATES %	PARTY AS A WHOLE %
2006	23	24	53
2004	25	22	53
2000	22	21	58
1997	20	22	58
1993	22	21	57
1988	20	27	53
1984	30	21	49
1980	36	20	44
1979	37	23	40
1974	33	27	40

Note: In each cell, the number represents the percentage of respondents who chose either party leaders, local candidates, or the party as a whole as the most important factor, among the three choices, in determining their voting decision.

Source: Andre Turcotte, "After 56 Days . . . The Verdict," in Jon H. Pammett and Christopher Dornan, eds., *The Canadian Federal Election of 2006* (Toronto: Dundurn Press, 2006), 294. Source data: 1974–1984 Canadian National Elections Studies; 1988 re-interview of 1984 CNES; 1993 Insight Canada Research post-election survey; 1997–2006 POLLARA Post-Election Surveys.

important than are evaluations of the parties, which are clearly the most important considerations for Canadian voters.

Campaign Effects

Seasoned election watchers—journalists, party strategists, and political scientists alike—are convinced that if a party runs a sloppy, chaotic campaign, it will quickly lose public support. Unfortunately, there is little statistical evidence to substantiate this belief.[43] Voters are rarely asked whether a leader's gaffe or an organizational miscue raised doubts in their minds about the party's fitness to govern and convinced them to vote for someone else. One possible indicator of a "campaign effect" on election outcomes is the timing of the vote decision (see Canada by the Numbers 5.7). Voters who decide which party to support before the election call, or within the first two or three days of the campaign, are influenced more by long-term factors than by short-term factors. In effect, they do not need to wait to see how the campaign turns out; they are already

CANADA BY THE NUMBERS 5.7 Timing of Voting Decision 1997–2006

	BEFORE ELECTION CALLED	WHEN ELECTION CALLED	DURING CAMPAIGN	FINAL DAYS OF CAMPAIGN
2006	40	9	26	24
2004	42	8	24	25
2000	47	13	16	24
1997	54	10	13	23

Sources: Jon H. Pammett, "The Voters Decide," in Alan Frizzell and Jon H. Pammett, eds., *The Canadian General Election of 1997* (Toronto: Dundurn Press, 1997), 242; Jon H. Pammett, "The People's Verdict," in Jon H. Pammett and Christopher Dornan, eds., *The Canadian General Election of 2000* and (Toronto: Dundurn Press, 2001), 306; Andre Turcotte, "Canadians Speak Out," in Jon H. Pammett and Christopher Dornan, eds., *The Canadian General Election of 2004* (Toronto: Dundurn Press, 2004), 328; Andre Turcotte, "After 56 Days . . . The Verdict," in Jon H. Pammett and Christopher Dornan, eds., *The Canadian Federal Election of 2006* (Toronto: Dundurn Press, 2006), 296.

predisposed to vote for their party for the reasons already discussed, and they see no particular reason to consider the alternatives. Those who wait until the middle or the end of the campaign to decide which party to support are more likely to be influenced by short-term factors, including their perceptions of campaign competence.

As the data describing when Canadians make their voting decision indicate, in three of the last four federal elections, a majority of voters had not decided whom to vote for before the election was called. Almost a quarter waited until the final days to make up their minds in each of the last four campaigns. Notice that in the two most recent elections, each of which produced a minority Parliament, more voters went into the campaign undecided than in the previous two elections, which produced Liberal majorities.

One other measure of the importance of campaigns, if not a direct measure of their impact, is the daily tracking polls produced primarily for the media by the country's major polling firms. Despite many of the pitfalls involved with the speculation that is often extrapolated from these exercises,[44] Canadian pollsters have done a rather capable job of tracking the overall trends in the most recent elections. As the polls conducted by SES Research for the Cable Public Affairs Channel (CPAC) demonstrate (see Canada by the Numbers 5.8), in the 2006 election, the campaign certainly mattered, at least inasmuch as the Conservatives, who began the campaign with 29 percent support, overcame an 8 percent gap between themselves and the Liberals (37 percent), eventually winning the election with 36.3 percent compared to the Liberals' 30.2 percent. A combination of the strong Conservative campaign, the weaker Liberal effort, and a series of exogenous factors contributed to the turnaround for both parties, which began around the Christmas break and continued through to the last week of the campaign.

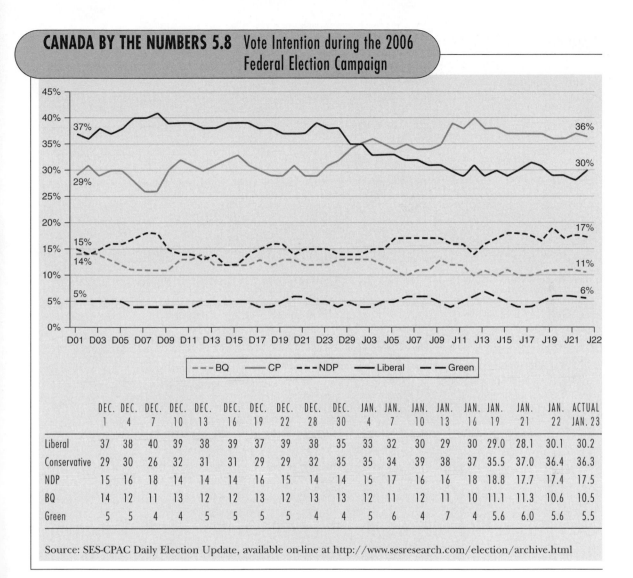

CANADA BY THE NUMBERS 5.8 Vote Intention during the 2006 Federal Election Campaign

	DEC. 1	DEC. 4	DEC. 7	DEC. 10	DEC. 13	DEC. 16	DEC. 19	DEC. 22	DEC. 28	DEC. 30	JAN. 4	JAN. 7	JAN. 10	JAN. 13	JAN. 16	JAN. 19	JAN. 21	JAN. 22	ACTUAL JAN. 23
Liberal	37	38	40	39	38	39	37	39	38	35	33	32	30	29	30	29.0	28.1	30.1	30.2
Conservative	29	30	26	32	31	31	29	29	32	35	35	34	39	38	37	35.5	37.0	36.4	36.3
NDP	15	16	18	14	14	14	16	15	14	14	15	17	16	16	18	18.8	17.7	17.4	17.5
BQ	14	12	11	13	12	12	13	12	13	13	12	11	12	11	10	11.1	11.3	10.6	10.5
Green	5	5	4	4	5	5	5	5	4	4	5	6	4	7	4	5.6	6.0	5.6	5.5

Source: SES-CPAC Daily Election Update, available on-line at http://www.sesresearch.com/election/archive.html

CANADIAN ELECTIONS IN THE FOURTH PARTY SYSTEM 1993–2006

1993 Federal Election

The 1993 Canadian election marked a watershed in the country's electoral history. Never before had a majority government been so thoroughly chastised by the electorate. The Progressive Conservatives went from holding a 169-seat majority under Prime Minister Brian Mulroney, to only 2 seats after the election (see Canada by the Numbers 5.9). The Liberals were returned to power with a majority after their longest

CANADA BY THE NUMBERS 5.9 1993 Federal Election

Vote Switching in the 1993 Federal Election

1993 VOTE	1988 PC %	1988 LIBERAL %	1988 NDP %	1988 OTHER %	1988 DID NOT VOTE %	1988 NOT ELIGIBLE %
PC	22	5	8	9	6	6
Liberal	26	70	27	—	20	33
NDP	3	3	26	5	—	3
Reform	24	8	14	45	14	11
BQ	14	6	6	23	5	10
Other	1	1	5	14	1	1
Did Not Vote	10	7	14	5	54	36

Source: Jon H. Pammett, "Tracking the Votes," in Alan Frizzell, Jon H. Pammett, and Anthony Westell, eds., *The Canadian General Election of 1993* (Ottawa: Carleton University Press, 1994), 146. Source data: Insight Canada Research post-election survey.

1993 Federal Election Results by Province and Territory

PROV/TERR (SEATS)	LIBERAL VOTES	LIBERAL SEATS	BLOC QUÉBÉCOIS VOTES	BLOC QUÉBÉCOIS SEATS	REFORM VOTES	REFORM SEATS	NDP VOTES	NDP SEATS	PROGRESSIVE CONSERVATIVE VOTES	PROGRESSIVE CONSERVATIVE SEATS	OTHER VOTES	OTHER SEATS
NL (7)	67.3	7	0	0	1.0	0	3.5	0	26.7	0	0.0	0
PEI (4)	60.1	4	0	0	1.0	0	5.2	0	32.0	0	0.0	0
NS (11)	52.0	11	0	0	13.3	0	6.8	0	23.5	0	2.1	0
NB (10)	56.0	9	0	0	8.5	0	4.9	0	27.9	1	1.3	0
QC (75)	33.0	19	49.3	54	0	0	1.5	0	13.5	1	1.1	1
ON (99)	52.9	98	0	0	20.1	1	6.0	0	17.6	0	0.8	0
MB (14)	45.0	12	0	0	22.4	1	16.7	1	11.9	0	0.1	0
SK (14)	32.1	5	0	0	27.2	4	26.6	5	11.3	0	1.0	0
AB (26)	25.1	4	0	0	52.3	22	4.1	0	14.6	0	0.4	0
BC (32)	28.1	6	0	0	36.4	24	15.5	2	13.5	0	0.3	0
NT (2)	73.0	2	0	0	6.1	0	6.0	0	12.7	0	0.0	0
YT (1)	23.2	0	0	0	13.1	0	43.4	1	17.7	0	0.0	0
Total (295)	41.3	177	13.5	54	18.7	52	6.9	9	16.0	2	0.8	1

Source: Data compiled and used to create the above chart was taken from the Website of Elections Canada: http://www.elections.ca. It is used with the permission of the Chief Electoral Officer but extrapolation and analysis rest with the author.

stint in opposition since World War I. Even more importantly, the old party system was shattered by the success of Reform in the West and the Bloc in Quebec. Canada's traditional third party, the NDP, garnered only 9 seats and, like the PCs, failed to qualify for official parliamentary party status.

Liberal leader Jean Chrétien became prime minister, while Canada's first female prime minister, PC leader Kim Campbell, lost her seat and retired from electoral politics. Canada's other female party leader, the NDP's Audrey McLaughlin, managed to win her Yukon seat, but saw her party's support drop by almost two-thirds from its 1988 levels. Separatist and former Mulroney cabinet minister, Bloc Québécois leader Lucien Bouchard took up the position as official Opposition leader when his party bested Preston Manning's Western-based Reform party by two seats.

The collapse of the PC and NDP vote was precipitous. Only 22 percent of Canadians who voted for the Progressive Conservatives in 1988 stuck with the party in 1993. Although most of the credit for destroying the Mulroney coalition is typically given to the two regional parties, more former PC voters abandoned their party for the Liberals (26 percent) than for either Reform (24 percent) or the Bloc (14 percent). The Liberals (27 percent) were also the primary beneficiaries of the scattering NDP vote, with only about one-quarter of that party's voters (26 percent) sticking with it in 1993. Interestingly, even Reform (14 percent) and the Bloc (6 percent) became the choice for some former NDP voters.

1997 Federal Election

Sensing opportunity, Prime Minister Chrétien exercised his prime ministerial prerogative to call the 1997 election just three and one-half years into his first term. The Liberals would be reelected, but with reduced support, forming a much slimmer majority in the new Parliament (see Canada by the Numbers 5.10). Under Manning's continued leadership, the Reform party increased its seat total and supplanted the Bloc—under its new leader Gilles Duceppe—as the country's official Opposition. Both the Progressive Conservatives, under the leadership of Jean Charest, and the NDP, led by Nova Scotian Alexa McDonough, regained official party status by wining 20 and 21 seats respectively. For the first time in Canadian history, Parliament would operate with five official parties.

The 1997 election is a very illustrative case study for examining the distorting effects of Canada's SMP electoral system. The Liberals benefited most, winning over half of the seats (155) based on less than two-fifths of the votes (38.5 percent) as multiparty competition in all of Canada's regions created complex vote splits that overrewarded the country's largest national party. The Bloc Québécois continued to dominate Quebec, primarily because the electoral system overrewarded it in that province. Although Bloc support dropped to just below 38 percent of the Quebec vote, it still managed to win almost 60 percent of that province's seats (44). Even more telling are the Reform and Progressive Conservative results. Each party won just under one-fifth of the total votes. Yet Reform benefited from its regional concentration in the West and turned 19.4 percent support into 60 seats. The PCs, on the other

Vote Switching in the 1997 Federal Election

1997 Vote	1993 LIBERAL %	1993 REFORM %	1993 BQ %	1993 NDP %	1993 PC %	1993 OTHER %	1993 DID NOT VOTE %	1993 NOT YET ELIGIBLE %
Liberal	63	8	2	13	15	19	26	24
Reform	8	80	2	9	20	8	10	10
BQ	1	—	78	—	1	3	7	11
NDP	7	9	2	59	5	7	6	6
PC	11	2	7	4	51	10	11	16
Other	1	2	—	2	—	15	2	3
Did Not Vote	9	6	10	13	8	38	38	31

Source: Jon H. Pammett, "The Voters Decide," in Alan Frizzell and Jon H. Pammett, eds., *The Canadian General Election of 1997* (Toronto: Dundurn Press, 1997), 228. Source data: POLLARA Perspectives Canada Survey.

1997 Federal Election Results by Province and Territory

PROV/TERR (SEATS)	LIBERAL		REFORM		BLOC QUÉBÉCOIS		NDP		PROGRESSIVE CONSERVATIVE		OTHER	
	VOTES	SEATS	VOTES	SEATS	VOTES	SEATS	VOTES	SEATS	VOTES	SEATS	VOTES	SEATS
NL (7)	37.9	4	2.5	0	0	0	22.0	0	36.8	3	0.9	0
PEI (4)	44.8	4	1.5	0	0	0	15.1	0	38.3	0	0.3	0
NS (11)	28.4	0	9.7	0	0	0	30.4	6	30.8	5	0.8	0
NB (10)	32.9	3	13.1	0	0	0	18.4	2	35.0	5	0.6	0
QC (75)	36.7	26	0.3	0	37.9	44	2.0	0	22.2	5	1.0	0
ON (103)	49.5	101	19.1	0	0	0	10.7	0	18.8	1	1.8	1
MB (14)	34.3	6	23.7	3	0	0	23.2	4	17.8	1	1.1	0
SK (14)	24.7	1	36.0	8	0	0	30.9	5	7.8	0	0.6	0
AB (26)	24.0	2	54.6	24	0	0	5.7	0	14.4	0	1.2	0
BC (34)	28.8	6	43.1	25	0	0	18.2	3	6.2	0	3.7	0
NT (2)	43.1	2	11.7	0	0	0	20.9	0	16.7	0	7.6	0
YT (1)	22.0	0	25.3	0	0	0	28.9	1	13.9	0	9.9	0
Total (301)	38.5	155	19.4	60	10.7	44	11.0	21	18.8	20	1.6	1

Source: Data compiled and used to create the above chart was taken from the Website of Elections Canada: http://www.elections.ca. It is used with the permission of the Chief Electoral Officer but extrapolation and analysis rest with the author.

Vote Switching in the 2000 Federal Election

2000 Vote	1997 LIBERAL %	1997 REFORM %	1997 BQ %	1997 NDP %	1997 PC %	1997 OTHER %	1997 DID NOT VOTE %
Liberal	64	5	4	10	15	8	11
Alliance	12	80	5	13	26	8	13
BQ	1	—	67	1	1	8	4
NDP	4	2	1	56	2	33	6
PC	9	5	4	4	44	8	3
Other	1	2	2	4	1	33	1
Did Not Vote	9	5	15	12	10	—	61

Source: Jon H. Pammett, "The People's Verdict," in Jon H. Pammett and Christopher Dornan, eds., *The Canadian General Election of 2000* (Toronto: Dundurn Press, 2001), 295. Source data: POLLARA Post-Election Survey.

2000 Federal Election Results by Province and Territory

PROV/TERR (SEATS)	LIBERAL VOTES	LIBERAL SEATS	ALLIANCE VOTES	ALLIANCE SEATS	BLOC QUÉBÉCOIS VOTES	BLOC QUÉBÉCOIS SEATS	NDP VOTES	NDP SEATS	PROGRESSIVE CONSERVATIVE VOTES	PROGRESSIVE CONSERVATIVE SEATS	OTHER VOTES	OTHER SEATS
NL (7)	44.9	5	3.9	0	0	0	13.1	0	34.5	2	3.6	0
PEI (4)	47.0	4	5.0	0	0	0	9.0	0	38.4	0	0.5	0
NS (11)	36.5	4	9.6	0	0	0	24.0	3	29.1	4	0.8	0
NB (10)	41.7	6	15.7	0	0	0	11.7	1	30.5	3	0.3	0
QC (75)	44.2	36	6.2	0	39.9	38	1.8	0	5.6	1	2.4	0
ON (103)	51.5	100	23.6	2	0	0	8.3	1	14.4	0	2.3	0
MB (14)	32.5	5	30.4	4	0	0	20.9	4	14.5	1	1.8	0
SK (14)	20.7	2	47.7	10	0	0	26.2	2	4.8	0	0.6	0
AB (26)	20.9	2	58.9	23	0	0	5.4	0	13.5	1	1.2	0
BC (34)	27.7	5	49.4	27	0	0	11.3	2	7.3	0	4.3	0
NT (1)	45.6	1	17.7	0	0	0	26.7	0	10.0	0	0.0	0
YT (1)	32.5	1	27.7	0	0	0	31.9	0	7.5	0	0.4	0
NU (1)	69.0	1	0.0	0	0	0	18.3	0	8.2	0	4.5	0
Total (301)	40.8	172	25.5	66	10.7	38	8.5	13	12.2	12	2.2	0

Source: Data compiled and used to create the above chart was taken from the Website of Elections Canada: http://www.elections.ca. It is used with the permission of the Chief Electoral Officer but extrapolation and analysis rest with the author.

hand, were severely penalized by the electoral system because of their more wide-spread support, winning just 20 seats based on their 18.8 percent of the national vote. The NDP was also penalized, winning just 7 percent of the seats (21) despite garnering 11 percent of the votes.

◾ 2000 Federal Election

As he had in 1997, Prime Minister Chrétien again sensed opportunity and called the 2000 election just three and one-half years into his second mandate. This time, he would face two different leaders and a reconfigured official Opposition party. Reform leader Preston Manning had convinced his party's members to abandon Reform in favour of a new party, the Canadian Reform Conservative Alliance. However he lost the party's inaugural leadership contest to former Alberta provincial cabinet minister Stockwell Day. Manning's plan included attempts to convince the Progressive Conservatives to merge with the new Alliance, but new PC leader, former prime minister Joe Clark, declared his party uninterested and the PCs contested the election as a separate party. Gilles Duceppe and Alexa McDonough retuned to lead their respective parties.

Despite a rather poor campaign effort, Day and the Alliance managed to improve on Reform's 1997 effort while the PCs, NDP, and the Bloc all lost support and seats (see Canada by the Numbers 5.11). The regional vote splitting allowed the Liberals to again capture almost all of the Ontario seats, return to power with a stronger majority, and make Chrétien the first Canadian prime minister to win three consecutive majorities since Mackenzie King did it over 50 years earlier.

◾ 2004 Federal Election

More internal party disruptions occurred during the thirty-seventh Parliament than during possibly any other single Canadian Parliament. Almost immediately after the 2000 election, the Alliance imploded, with several senior MPs challenging Day's leadership and eventually splitting away from the Alliance to form the Democratic Representative Caucus (DRC), which brokered a parliamentary working arrangement with the Progressive Conservatives. Day eventually acquiesced to demands for an Alliance leadership contest; he ran as a candidate, but lost the leadership to Stephen Harper. Once Joe Clark retired as Progressive Conservative leader, Harper convinced new PC leader Peter MacKay to merge the Alliance and PCs into the new Conservative Party of Canada. Harper won the new party's inaugural leadership contest, in which MacKay did not run as a candidate.

The governing Liberals descended into a nasty internal leadership battle of their own. Former finance minister Paul Martin, who had been previously dumped from Chrétien's Cabinet, used his control of the party organization to force the prime minister's retirement as leader. Martin handily won the ensuing Liberal leadership contest

Vote Switching in the 2004 Federal Election

2004 Vote	2000 LIBERAL %	2000 ALLIANCE %	2000 PC %	2000 BQ %	2000 NDP %	2000 OTHER %	2000 DID NOT VOTE %
Liberal	59	2	11	5	13	6	5
Conservative	13	88	68	3	12	29	9
BQ	3	—	2	80	2	6	2
NDP	14	2	9	5	63	12	7
Other	3	5	1	4	8	41	6
Did Not Vote	8	3	9	3	2	6	72

Source: Andre Turcotte, "Canadians Speak Out," in Jon H. Pammett and Christopher Dornan, eds., *The Canadian General Election of 2004* (Toronto: Dundurn Press, 2004), 319. Source data: POLLARA Post-Election Survey.

2004 Federal Election Results by Province and Territory

PROV/TERR (SEATS)	LIBERAL VOTES	LIBERAL SEATS	CONSERVATIVE VOTES	CONSERVATIVE SEATS	BLOC QUÉBÉCOIS VOTES	BLOC QUÉBÉCOIS SEATS	NDP VOTES	NDP SEATS	GREEN VOTES	GREEN SEATS	OTHER VOTES	OTHER SEATS
NL (7)	48.0	5	32.3	2	0	0	17.5	0	1.6	0	0.6	0
PEI (4)	52.5	4	30.7	0	0	0	12.5	0	4.2	0	0.1	0
NS (11)	39.7	6	28.0	3	0	0	28.4	2	3.3	0	0.6	0
NB (10)	44.6	7	31.1	2	0	0	20.6	1	3.4	0	0.3	0
QC (75)	33.9	21	8.8	0	48.9	54	4.6	0	3.2	0	0.6	0
ON (106)	44.7	75	31.5	24	0	0	18.1	7	4.4	0	1.3	0
MB (14)	33.2	3	39.1	7	0	0	23.5	4	2.7	0	1.5	0
SK (14)	27.2	1	41.8	13	0	0	23.4	0	2.7	0	4.9	0
AB (28)	22.0	2	61.7	26	0	0	9.5	0	6.1	0	0.7	0
BC (36)	28.6	8	36.3	22	0	0	26.6	5	6.3	0	2.2	1
NT (1)	39.4	1	17.2	0	0	0	39.1	0	4.3	0	0.0	0
YT (1)	45.7	1	20.9	0	0	0	25.7	0	4.6	0	3.1	0
NU (1)	51.3	1	14.4	0	0	0	15.2	0	3.3	0	15.8	0
Total (308)	36.7	135	29.6	99	12.4	54	15.7	19	4.3	0	1.3	1

Source: Data compiled and used to create the above chart was taken from the Website of Elections Canada: http://www.elections.ca. It is used with the permission of the Chief Electoral Officer but extrapolation and analysis rest with the author.

Vote Switching in the 2006 Federal Election

2006 Vote	2004 LIBERAL %	2004 CONSERVATIVE %	2004 BQ %	2004 NDP %	2004 OTHER %	2004 DID NOT VOTE %
Liberal	53	4	1	13	8	17
Conservative	20	83	19	10	25	7
BQ	1	—	67	1	4	2
NDP	12	5	2	57	29	3
Other	5	2	6	9	33	3
Did Not Vote	9	6	5	10	1	69

Source: Andre Turcotte, "After 56 Days . . . The Verdict," in Jon H. Pammett and Christopher Dornan, eds., *The Canadian Federal Election of 2006* (Toronto: Dundurn Press, 2006), 291. Source data: POLLARA Post-Election Survey.

2006 Federal Election Results by Province and Territory

PROV/TERR (SEATS)	CONSERVATIVE VOTES	SEATS	LIBERAL VOTES	SEATS	BLOC QUÉBÉCOIS VOTES	SEATS	NDP VOTES	SEATS	GREEN VOTES	SEATS	OTHER VOTES	SEATS
NL (7)	42.7	3	42.8	4	0	0	13.6	0	0.9	0	0.0	0
PEI (4)	33.4	0	52.6	4	0	0	9.6	0	3.9	0	0.5	0
NS (11)	29.7	3	37.2	6	0	0	29.9	2	2.6	0	0.6	0
NB (10)	35.8	3	39.2	6	0	0	21.9	1	2.4	0	0.7	0
QC (75)	24.6	10	20.8	13	42.1	51	7.5	0	4.0	0	1.0	1
ON (106)	35.1	40	39.9	54	0	0	19.4	12	4.7	0	0.9	0
MB (14)	42.8	8	26.0	3	0	0	25.4	3	3.9	0	1.9	0
SK (14)	49.0	12	22.4	2	0	0	24.1	0	3.2	0	1.3	0
AB (28)	65.0	27	15.3	0	0	0	11.7	0	6.5	0	1.6	0
BC (36)	37.3	17	27.6	9	0	0	28.5	10	5.3	0	1.3	0
NT (1)	19.8	0	35.0	0	0	0	42.2	1	2.1	0	0.9	0
YT (1)	23.7	0	48.5	1	0	0	23.9	0	4.0	0	0.0	0
NU (1)	29.1	0	40.0	1	0	0	17.2	0	5.9	0	7.8	0
Total (308)	36.3	124	30.2	103	10.5	51	17.5	29	4.5	0	1.0	1

Source: Data compiled and used to create the above chart was taken from the Website of Elections Canada: http://www.elections.ca. It is used with the permission of the Chief Electoral Officer but extrapolation and analysis rest with the author.

and became prime minister late in 2003. Meanwhile, the NDP replaced Alexa McDonough with former Toronto city councillor Jack Layton, leaving Gilles Duceppe as only party leader to return from the 2000 election.

Once the campaign began, Harper and the new Conservatives appeared poised for victory, largely because of trust issues arising from the sponsorship program investigations that were still plaguing the Liberals. But a final weekend swing in vote intention, primarily in Ontario, kept the Conservatives from power. The Liberals were returned to government, albeit with only a minority government, as all of their opponents eroded some of their support (see Canada by the Numbers 5.12). The Bloc rebuilt much of its former support in Quebec, the NDP gained ground in Ontario and the West, while the Conservatives continued to dominate the West and made their much sought after breakthrough in Ontario.

2006 Federal Election

After having run another superior campaign, Stephen Harper and the Conservatives were rewarded by voters with the party's first election victory since 1988 (see Canada by the Numbers 5.13). The Conservatives increased their vote share by almost 7 percent from 2004, winning 25 more seats, enough for a slim minority government. They continued to make advances in Ontario, winning 40 seats, and surprisingly won 10 Quebec seats, but were reduced by 5 in British Columbia.

The NDP continued to rebuild, winning 29 seats, its best totals since 1988. The Bloc again dominated Quebec, although it lost almost one-fifth of its former Quebec voters the Conservatives, as did the Liberals. For their part, the election results sent the Liberals into a leadership contest that eventually elected Stéphane Dion as party leader in December of 2006.

CONCLUSION

Elections are central to representative democracy. They provide the only opportunity for the citizens, en masse, to engage directly with their political institutions. Those institutions are the electoral system, which determines the expression of their preferences and sets incentives for voters to follow, and the House of Commons, whose members are elected in their separate constituencies. The outcome of a Canadian general election—the partisan makeup of the Commons—is the product of the interaction between the long-term and short-term factors that govern voting behaviour, and their translation by the electoral system into parliamentary seats. Nowhere else is the relationship between society and the state as clear and direct as it is on election day.

Canada is one of the few countries left in the world that still uses a single member plurality electoral system. Despite SMP's general tendency to produce stable two-party competition, its application in Canada combines with the latent regionalism within the political culture to frequently produce a plethora of smaller parties and multiparty competition in many ridings. In fact, the electoral system tends to exaggerate the regional differences within Canada by overrewarding strong regional parties and underrewarding weaker national parties when translating votes into seats.

Nevertheless, the Canadian electoral system tends to produce rather stable aggregate results over time, at least between monumental elections such as those of 1921, 1958, and 1993. This appearance of stability tends to mask the fact that many Canadian voters switch their voting preferences between elections, largely because of their flexible partisanship and relatively weak long-term identifications with the parties. In the final analysis, the fact that so many Canadian voters wait until sometime during the election campaign to make their voting decisions means that campaigns matter, even if they do not produce clear mandates or agendas for the winning party.

DISCUSSION QUESTIONS

1. What is an electoral system? How does it affect voters, political parties, and the composition of the House of Commons?

2. In your view, should the internal activities of Canadian parties be regulated by law? Should political parties and candidates receive public subsidies, either direct (reimbursement of election expenses) or indirect (tax credits)? Why or why not?

3. What are the key short- and long-term factors that affect voting choice in Canada? If you have voted in a previous federal or provincial election, which of those factors was foremost in your mind when you marked your ballot?

4. If you were eligible to vote in the last federal or provincial election but decided not to cast a ballot, what were the primary reasons for your decision not to vote?

SUGGESTED READINGS

Books and Articles

André Blais, Elisabeth Gidengil, Richard Nadeau, and Neil Nevitte, *Anatomy of a Liberal Victory: Making Sense of the Vote in the 2000 Canadian Election* (Peterborough, ON: Broadview Press, 2002).

Canada, Royal Commission on Electoral Reform and Party Financing, *Reforming Electoral Democracy* (Ottawa: Minister of Supply and Services, 1991).

Alan Frizzell, Jon H. Pammett, and Anthony Westell, *The Canadian General Election of 1993* (Ottawa: Carleton University Press, 1994).

Alan Frizzell and Jon H. Pammett, *The Canadian General Election of 1997* (Toronto: Dundurn Press, 1997).

Elizabeth Gidengil, André Blais, Joanna Everitt, Patrick Fournier, and Neil Nevitte, "Back to the Future? Making Sense of the 2004 Canadian Election Outside Quebec," *Canadian Journal of Political Science*, 39:1 (March 2006), 1–25.

Richard Johnston, André Blais, Henry El Brady, and Jean Crête, *Letting the People Decide: Dynamics of a Canadian Election* (Montreal and Kingston: McGill–Queen's University Press, 1992).

Lawrence LeDuc, Richard G. Niemi, and Pippa Norris, eds., *Comparing Democracies: Elections and Voting in Global Perspective* (Thousand Oaks, CA: Sage, 1996).

Henry Milner, ed., *Making Every Vote Count: Reassessing Canada's Electoral System* (Peterborough, ON: Broadview Press, 1999).

Neil Nevitte, André Blais, Elisabeth Gidengil, and Richard Nadeau, *Unsteady State: The 1997 Canadian Federal Election* (Don Mills, ON: Oxford University Press, 2000).

Jon H. Pammett and Christopher Dornan, eds., *The Canadian General Election of 2000* (Toronto: Dundurn Press, 2001).

Jon H. Pammett and Christopher Dornan, eds., *The Canadian General Election of 2004* (Toronto: Dundurn Press, 2004).

Jon H. Pammett and Christopher Dornan, eds., *The Canadian Federal Election of 2006* (Toronto: Dundurn Press, 2006).

Websites

The website of Canada's federal electoral agency, Elections Canada (http://www. elections.ca), provides a wealth of information. Click on "Electoral Law and Policy" to find the Canada Elections Act and background papers about recent amendments. Under "Election Financing," you can access the annual disclosure reports from Canada's registered parties, as well as their election expense reports (and those of individual candidates).

The Law Commission's 2004 report and recommendations on electoral reform are available on its website (http://www.lcc.gc.ca), together with a series of background papers on electoral systems. Go to the website and click on "Electoral Reform."

For more information on electoral systems around the world, check the websites of the Inter-Parliamentary Union (http://www.ipu.org) and the International Federation for Electoral Systems (http://www.ifes.org).

One of the best and most comprehensive websites dealing with Canadian elections is maintained by Simon Fraser University political scientist Andrew Heard and is available at http://www.sfu.ca/~aheard/elections/parties.html.

NOTES

1. The recent report of the Law Commission of Canada, *Voting Counts,* provides an excellent overview of this debate. Go to http://www.lcc.gc.ca and click on "Electoral Reform." In addition to the report itself, you will find background papers and studies on the topic of electoral reform.

2. See Lawrence LeDuc, "Elections and Democratic Governance," in Lawrence LeDuc, Richard G. Niemi, and Pippa Norris, eds., *Comparing Democracies: Elections and Voting in Global Perspective* (Thousand Oaks, CA: Sage, 1996).

3. Bingham Powell Jr., Elections as Instruments of Democracy: Majoritarian and Proportional Visions (New Haven, CT: Yale University Press, 2000).

4. See for example Stanley Kelley Jr., *Interpreting Elections* (Princeton, NJ: Princeton University Press, 1983).

5. Harold D. Clarke, Jane Jenson, Lawrence LeDuc, and Jon H. Pammett, *Absent Mandate: Interpreting Change in Canadian Elections,* 2nd edition (Toronto: Gage, 1991).

6. A third constraint may be added by the Harper government if it succeeds in fixing election dates for October of every fourth year.

7. Canada Elections Act, Sections 415–416.

8. Canada Elections Act, Sections 424–427.

9. Canada Elections Act, Sections 429–434.

10. Canada Elections Act, Sections 422–423.

11. Canada Elections Act, Section 435.

12. Bill C-24, Section 73.

13. Canada Elections Act, as amended January 1, 2004, Sections 464–465.

14. Canada Elections Act, Sections 451–456.

15. William T. Stanbury, *Money in Politics: Financing Federal Parties and Candidates in Canada,* volume 1 of the collected research studies for the Royal Commission on Electoral Reform and Party Financing (Toronto: Dundurn Press, 1991).

16. Canada Elections Act, as amended January 1, 2004, Section 403.01.

17. The broadcasting rules are set out in the Canada Elections Act, Sections 332–348. The allocations of airtime among the parties are available on the Elections Canada website: http://www.elections.ca.

18. Canada Elections Act, Section 407.

19. You can find maps of every federal constituency on the Elections Canada website: http://www.elections.ca. The site also provides information about the process of drawing electoral district boundaries.

20. *Reference re Provincial Electoral Boundaries (Sask.)* [1991] 2 S.C.R. 158.

21. When a constituency is deliberately designed to improve a particular party's electoral chances, the result is called "gerrymandering."

22. Maurice Duverger, *Political Parties: Their Organization and Activity in the Modern State,* translated by Barbara and Robert North (London: Methuen, 1964 [1954]), Book II, Chapter 1.

23. André Blais and R. Kenneth Carty, "The Psychological Impact of Electoral Laws: Measuring Duverger's Elusive Factor," *British Journal of Political Science,* 21 (1991), 79–93.

24. Rae, Douglas, *The Political Consequences of Electoral Laws,* (New Haven, CT: Yale University Press, 1968).

25. Ibid. 94.

26. See Alan C. Cairns, "The Electoral System and the Party System in Canada, 1921–1965," in Douglas E. Williams, ed., *Constitution, Government, and Society in Canada* (Toronto: McClelland and Stewart, 1988).

27. See George C. Perlin, *The Tory Syndrome: Leadership Politics in the Progressive Conservative Party* (Montreal and Kingston: McGill–Queen's University Press, 1980).

28. Cairnes, *The Electoral and Party System,* 120.

29. Jon H. Pammett and Lawrence LeDuc, *Explaining the Turnout Decline in Canadian Federal Elections: A New Survey of Non-Voters* (Ottawa: Elections Canada, March 2003), 20, Table 14.

30. Jon H. Pammett, "The People's Verdict," in Jon H. Pammett and Christopher Dornan, eds., *The Canadian General Election of 2000* (Toronto: Dundurn Press, 2001), 312.

31. Pammett and LeDuc, 66, Table 57.

32. Russell J. Dalton, "Political Cleavages, Issues, and Electoral Change," in Lawrence LeDuc, Richard G. Niemi, and Pippa Norris, eds., *Comparing Democracies 2: New Challenges in the Study of Elections and Voting* (Thousand Oaks, CA: Sage, 2002), 193–194.

33. André Blais, Elisabeth Gidengil, Richard Nadeau, and Neil Nevitte, *Anatomy of a Liberal Victory: Making Sense of the Vote in the 2000 Canadian Election* (Peterborough, ON: Broadview Press, 2002), 91.

34. Blais et al., Anatomy of a Liberal Victory, 93.

35. See for example, Peter Wearing and Joseph Wearing, "Does Gender Make a Difference in Voting Behaviour?," in Joseph Wearing, ed., The Ballot and Its Message: Voting in Canada (Toronto: Copp Clark Pitman, 1991); Sylvia Bashevkin, Toeing the Lines: Women and Party Politics in English Canada, 2nd edition (Toronto: Oxford University Press, 1993); and André Blais, Elisabeth Gidengil, Neil Nevitte, and Richard Nadeau, "Gender and the 'Fight for the Right,'" 2; available at http://www.ces-eec.umontreal.ca/publications2000.html.

36. Harold D. Clarke, Jane Jenson, Lawrence LeDuc, and Jon H. Pammett, Political Choice in Canada (Toronto: McGraw-Hill Ryerson, 1979).

37. Clarke et al., Absent Mandate: Interpreting Change in Canadian Elections, 48–49; Harold D. Clarke, Jane Jenson, Lawrence LeDuc, and Jon H. Pammett, "Voting Behaviour and the Outcome of the 1979 Federal Election: The Impact of Leaders and Issues," Canadian Journal of Political Science, 15:3 (1982), 517–552.

38. See Blais et al., "Anatomy of a Liberal Victory."

39. Blais et al., "Anatomy of a Liberal Victory," 134

40. Blais et al., "Anatomy of a Liberal Victory," 133.

41. Neil Nevitte, André Blais, Elisabeth Gidengil, and Richard Nadeau, *Unsteady State: The 1997 Canadian Federal Election* (Toronto: Oxford University Press, 2000), 85.

42. Richard Johnston, André Blais, Henry E. Brady, and Jean Crête, *Letting the People Decide: Dynamics of a Canadian Election* (Montreal and Kingston: McGill–Queen's University Press, 1992), 169–196.

43. See Nevitte et al., *Unsteady State,* 132.

44. See Michael Marzolini, "Public Opinion Polling and the 2004 Election," in Jon H. Pammett and Christopher Dornan, eds., *The Canadian General Election of 2004* (Toronto: Dundurn Press, 2004).

6

THE POLITICAL EXECUTIVE AND PARLIAMENTARY DEMOCRACY

LEARNING OBJECTIVES

- *identify* the key players in the federal government's political executive, and describe their different roles
- *identify* the reasons for Cabinet dominance, adversarial politics, and excessive party discipline in the Canadian House of Commons, and *explain* why they persist
- *explain* how the Cabinet operates
- *identify* and *explain* the representative structure and functions of the House of Commons and the Senate
- *evaluate* the performance of our national legislative institutions
- *explain* the process by which government legislation is drafted and approved, i.e., how a bill becomes law in Canada

INTRODUCTION

Canadian governments, at both the national and provincial levels, are divided into three branches: executive, legislative, and judicial.

The executive branch is by far the largest and most powerful of the three. Indeed, when we refer casually to "the federal government," we usually mean the executive branch alone. In its simplest terms, the executive can be divided into three primary structures: the Crown, represented by the governor general; the political executive (the prime minister and Cabinet); and the permanent executive (the federal public service). We will reserve discussion of the permanent executive, including its policy-making relationship with the political executive, for the next chapter. We will discuss the judiciary in Chapter 8. This chapter will focus on the institutions of Parliament: the political executive and legislative branch.

Most of Canada's national political institutions were inherited from Britain. Our system of responsible government is enshrined in the preamble to the Constitution Act, 1867, which gave the new Dominion "a Constitution similar in Principle to that of the United Kingdom." Such a constitution requires a bicameral Parliament (one with two separate legislative chambers). The lower house, elected by the citizens on the basis of representation by population, controls the public purse and holds the Cabinet to account. In Canada, as in Britain, the lower house is called the House of Commons. Most cabinet ministers are members of the lower house. The unelected upper house, our Senate, is intended to serve two legislative purposes: to check the power of the Cabinet, and to give "sober second thought" to proposed laws that may have been rushed through the lower house without adequate examination.

The history of the Westminster parliamentary system demonstrates the flexibility of political institutions that are based on convention and precedent, rather than deliberate constitutional engineering. British parliamentary institutions evolved through a long series of power struggles among the Crown, the people, and the legislature that links the two. Over time, there emerged a series of conventions that gradually reduced the powers of the Crown and invested them in Parliament. By the late-nineteenth century, virtually all of the Crown's powers were being exercised by the executive branch and by the judiciary. This was the system of parliamentary government that Canada inherited in 1867.

The legislative branch, from which the political executive is drawn, makes the laws that are implemented by the permanent executive and interpreted by the judiciary. Under the Constitution Act, 1867, law-making powers are divided between the Crown, the House of Commons, and the Senate. A government bill (proposed legislation) is sponsored by the Crown, which is represented by a particular cabinet minister who, along with senior civil servants, has formulated the bill. It is, in most cases, introduced first into the House of Commons, but it must also be adopted by the Senate before being given royal assent and becoming the law of the land.

In the twentieth century, the power of the political executive vis-à-vis Parliament was further strengthened by the explosive growth of the federal government and the ever-increasing complexity of public policy. Nowadays, the prime minister of Canada is as powerful domestically as is the head of any democratic government in the world. Some observers argue that the very nature of our political system has been transformed: instead of parliamentary government, we now have prime-ministerial government. Various proposals for reform have emerged in response to this concentration of power in the hands of one person—or more accurately, one office—the Prime Minister's Office (PMO). Be that as it may, while we will not ignore altogether the potential for further reforms of the country's central institutions, in this chapter we will for the most part concentrate on how those institutions are currently structured.

THE FORMAL EXECUTIVE

Excluding for the time being the civil service, Canada's executive branch is divided into two: the formal executive, consisting of the Crown and the governor general, and the political executive, consisting of the prime minister and Cabinet. The formal executive

1867–1868	The Viscount Monck
1869–1872	Lord Lisgar
1872–1878	The Earl of Dufferin
1878–1883	The Duke of Argyll (Marquess of Lorne)
1883–1888	The Marquess of Lansdowne
1888–1893	Lord Stanley
1893–1898	The Earl of Aberdeen
1898–1904	The Earl of Minto
1904–1911	Earl Grey
1911–1916	H.R.H The Duke of Connaught
1916–1921	The Duke of Devonshire
1921–1926	Lord Byng
1926–1931	The Viscount Willingdon
1931–1935	The Earl of Bessborough
1935–1940	Lord Tweedsmuir
1940–1946	The Earl of Athlone
1946–1952	The Viscount Alexander
1952–1959	The Right Honourable Vincent Massey[a]
1959–1967	Major General The Right Honourable Georges P. Vanier[b]
1967–1974	The Right Honourable Roland Michener
1974–1979	The Right Honourable Jules Léger
1979–1984	The Right Honourable Edward Schreyer
1984–1990	The Right Honourable Jeanne Sauvé[c]
1990–1995	The Right Honourable Ramon John Hnatyshyn
1995–1999	The Right Honourable Roméo LeBlanc
1999–2005	The Right Honourable Adrienne Clarkson
2005–	The Right Honourable Michaëlle Jean

[a]First Canadian-born governor general

[b]First French-Canadian governor general

[c]First female governor general

Source: The Governor General of Canada Web pages, available on-line at http://www.gg.ca/gg/fgg/index_e.asp, accessed July 2006.

is largely ceremonial, although in a crisis it could be called upon to exercise temporarily its explicit constitutional powers. In practice, however, real power is exercised by the political executive, which makes the important public policy decisions for the country.

The Crown

The Constitution Act, 1867, Section 9, vests the executive power in the Crown. Although the prime minister is the political head of the government, the formal executive authority of the state resides in the Crown. In contrast, the president of the United States is not only the political head of the American government but also its formal and symbolic head. The Canadian distinction between the head of state and the head of government has important practical consequences for the operation of government. By carrying much of the ceremonial load that would otherwise fall on the shoulders of the prime minister, the head of state frees the head of government to get on with the business of running the country.

The Crown's power is formally exercised by the Governor in Council—i.e., the governor general acting on the advice of the Privy Council (Section 12).[1] And while the Crown's executive powers are vast, by constitutional convention they are exercised only on the advice and consent of the Cabinet. In practice, this means that the political executive makes the decisions, which are then formally ratified by the Crown's representative. Strictly speaking, the Privy Council does not even exist. Every cabinet minister, past and present, has been sworn into the Privy Council, and they retain that status even after they leave the political executive. The only privy councillors that really matter are the small group who belong to the Cabinet of the day, now numbering only 27.[2]

The Crown also symbolizes the separation of the political and permanent executives. The former is expected to be partisan, biased in favour of some policies and against others, and temporary. The latter is, at least in theory, expected to be neutral, unbiased, and continuing.

Governor General

The governor general is the Crown's representative in Canada. Although the institution has lost the executive powers that were routinely exercised by British officials before Confederation, the governor general still provides a potential check on the power of the political executive.[3] He or she retains the reserve power to reject the advice of the Cabinet and the emergency power to keep the government running in a severe national crisis (for example, the sudden death or resignation of a prime minister). While there are alternative models for a head of state—such as the elected presidents of the United States and France, who are representatives of specific political parties with distinct policy agendas—the governor general possesses the advantage of political neutrality and must act in the best interests of the country, not of a particular political party (see Canadian Political Chronology 6.1).

In 2005, Michaëlle Jean became Canada's twenty-seventh governor general, the third woman, second immigrant, and first person of black ancestry to occupy the position. (© CHRIS WATTIE/Reuters/Corbis)

Born: 1957, Port-au-Prince, Haiti
Immigrated to Canada with family in 1968

Education: B.A. Italian, Hispanic Languages, and Literature and M.A. Comparative Literature (University of Montreal, 1984 and 1986)

Profession: Journalist and broadcaster

Career Highlights
1988 Radio-Canada reporter and host on the public affairs programs *Actuel, Montréal ce soir, Virages,* and *Le Point.*
1995 Anchor for Réseau de l'Information à Radio-Canada (RDI) programs such as *Le Monde ce soir, L'Édition québécoise, Horizons francophones, Les Grands reportages, Le Journal RDI,* and *RDI à l'écoute.*
1999 Host for CBC Newsworld's *The Passionate Eye* and *Rough Cuts.*
2001 Anchor for the weekend edition of *Le Téléjournal,* Radio-Canada news show.
2003 Anchor for *Le Midi,* the daily edition of *Le Téléjournal.*
2004 Host of *Michaëlle,* television show featuring in-depth interviews with experts and enthusiasts.

Governor General
September 27, 2005–present

Source: Governor General of Canada Web pages, available on-line at http://www.gg.ca/gg/bio/index_e.asp, accessed July 2006.

Duties of the Governor General

Except for the rare occasions when the British monarch pays a visit, the governor general carries out the formal duties associated with the Crown. The most important of these are ceremonial and include the following:

- appointing the prime minister and swearing in the Cabinet (although the governor general merely ratifies the choices made first by the parties in choosing their leaders, and then by the electorate in choosing a governing party)
- delivering the speech from the throne, which sets out the government's legislative agenda at the beginning of each session of Parliament
- dissolving Parliament and issuing a proclamation for a general election (again, this power is exercised only on the advice of the prime minister)

- bestowing royal recommendations on bills that authorize the raising or spending of public money (Section 54 of the Constitution Act, 1867)
- giving royal assent to legislation that has been adopted by both Houses of Parliament (although, in practice, the chief justice of the Supreme Court often performs this task).

The governor general resides at Rideau Hall (the official residence), which is used for many official state functions, such as the swearing in of cabinet ministers, awarding of honours, and receiving of dignitaries from other countries. It is also the place to which the prime minister must travel to in order to seek dissolution of Parliament prior to an election.[4]

THE POLITICAL EXECUTIVE

The political executive, as the name suggests, includes those MPs from the governing party and one or more senators who sit in Cabinet at the pleasure of the prime minister (and, technically, of the House of Commons). The prime minister (PM) is the leader of the Cabinet and, given the powers exercised by the PMO, is much more than simply the "first amongst equals," as he is often described. Cabinet exercises the formal executive powers of the Crown, and performs the following key government functions:

- initiating, drafting, and sponsoring the laws passed by Parliament
- drafting, approving, enacting, and enforcing regulations made under the law-making authority delegated by Parliament
- making and executing agreements with other governments—provincial as well as foreign—often without the approval of Parliament
- raising, allocating, and spending public funds, nominally with the consent of Parliament, and monitoring that spending to ensure that it remains within the approved limits

The power of the prime minister and Cabinet is largely based on British constitutional convention, not on the written text of the Canadian Constitution. This means that there are few formal constraints on the power of the Canadian prime minister, who enjoys a remarkable degree of authority. The concentration of power at the centre of Canada's executive branch creates strong incentives for cabinet ministers to carry out the wishes of the prime minister. The overriding incentive of the political executive is to make the prime minister, and by extension the entire government, look good. Potentially embarrassing mistakes must be avoided whenever possible. If they cannot be avoided altogether, they must be either hidden from public view or managed appropriately. The result is a culture of caution, secrecy, and deference to the prime minister.

In addition to the broad themes just identified, the prime minister, supported by central agencies such as the PMO and the Privy Council Office (PCO), dominates both the political and permanent executives. The only other member of the Cabinet who enjoys special prestige is the finance minister, who, however, is clearly subordinate to the PM. In recent years, the central agencies of government, especially the PMO, have acquired ever-greater authority to coordinate national policy-making. This has implications for both the practice of responsible government in Canada and for representative democracy more generally.

Responsible Government and Party Discipline

When Britain granted responsible government to its North American colonies in the 1840s, the exercise of executive power shifted from the Crown to a council with the support of the legislature. As we have seen, responsible government was later entrenched in the preamble to the Constitution Act, 1867. In principle, responsible government means four things:

1. The Cabinet is collectively responsible to the House of Commons, and the prime minister must resign as soon as his government loses the confidence of Parliament.
2. Individual ministers are responsible to Parliament for the conduct of their departments.
3. Ministers are responsible to the Crown, on whose behalf they exercise authority.
4. Ministers are responsible to one another, in the sense that all must adhere to collective decisions.

The first of the above points assumes that the legislative branch is supposed to hold the executive branch accountable to the electorate. Formally, it has the constitutional right to remove the political executive from office. If the House defeats a money bill (such as the budget) or passes a motion of no confidence in the government, the government is deemed to have lost the support of the House. (Defeat of government bills in the Senate does not affect the status of the government, because the Senate is not a "confidence chamber.") In Canada the executive power that is vested in the Crown is delegated to a Cabinet that has the support of the Commons. If that support is lost, the constitutional conventions of responsible government require the prime minister to relinquish executive power and seek a new mandate from the electorate.

Upon losing confidence, the prime minister immediately must ask the governor general to dissolve the House for a general election. Technically, the governor general has the right to refuse the request and ask another party leader to form a government, but this option has fallen into disuse and not been used since 1926.[5] Alternatively, the prime minister could clarify the intention of the House by moving an immediate motion of confidence. If the motion fails, then the prime minister has no choice but to resign. If it carries, however, the prime minister could claim that the defeat of the money bill was unintentional and remain in office. This procedure too is rarely invoked and has not been used since 1968.[6]

While the confidence convention is the Achilles' heel of a minority Cabinet, because the government can be brought down at virtually any time, the reverse is true for a majority government. Rather than fear the confidence convention, a Cabinet that controls a majority in the Commons can use the threat of losing confidence to keep its MPs in line, even though defeat in the House is rarely a realistic threat. By treating every vote as a question of confidence in the government—a practice that is neither required nor sanctioned by parliamentary tradition[7]—the Cabinet can invoke party discipline on reluctant MPs and force them into supporting sometimes controversial, but still ordinary, legislation.

In essence, in Canada, the confidence convention has been turned on its head. What was once a powerful weapon for legislators to use in holding the political executive to account has become an effective shield against dissent within the governing party. Yet despite the insistence of virtually all of Canada's previous prime ministers to the contrary, failure to pass an ordinary bill does not signal a loss of confidence in the government. Rather, Canadian prime ministers' continual use of the threat of defeat as a justification for invoking strict party discipline—and thereby running roughshod over the House—should be viewed as a perversion of the confidence convention. Unlike in Canada, the British have altered these practices and their experience is instructive.

Recognizing that strict party discipline is a distorted approach to confidence, the British parliament at Westminster has recently taken a different approach. When a government in Westminster introduces a bill, it assigns the legislation to one of four categories:

1. A three-line whip is a matter of confidence. This designation applies to money bills and any other bill that is central to the legislative agenda of the government.
2. A two-line whip applies to bills that the government considers important but not crucial.
3. A one-line whip signals that the government is prepared to accept dissent and even defeat. It will modify the bill if necessary to secure passage in the House.
4. A free vote allows government MPs to vote according to their consciences or the wishes of their constituents if these conflict with the party line.

The defeat of a bill in the British House of Commons is rarely interpreted as the death knell of the government. Hence, party discipline is weaker than in Canada, and government MPs enjoy greater autonomy from the Cabinet. While this approach weakens the conventional power of legislators to remove the political executive from office, the fact is that such removals are already extremely rare. The British example demonstrates how it is possible to run an effective parliamentary system without the heavy-handed use of party discipline that tends to delegitimize what is, under other circumstances, an important and virtuous principle.

Canadian prime ministers' overuse of party discipline had led many voters to perceive the principle of the confidence motion and attendant partisan discipline as illegitimate. The fact that votes in the House are orchestrated by the party whips—a term that reinforces the negative connotations of party discipline[8]—also tends to shed a bad light on the process. But as we shall see, party representation in the legislative branch is a legitimate form of representation. The very term "party discipline" suggests—incorrectly—that the only reason MPs do not act independently is because they are forcibly prevented from doing so, under threat of punishment. While it is true that an MP, especially a government MP, who votes against his or her party on an important issue will likely pay a high price,[9] few have much interest in breaking ranks with their partisan colleagues. Most parliamentarians willingly vote with their parties for a variety of other reasons.

First, most MPs believe in the principles for which their parties stand and tend to support the platform upon which they campaigned. MPs tend to recognize that if Canadians elect a majority of MPs from one party, they are entitled to expect the government to implement the policy agenda from that party and not some other platform or agenda. Despite the many high-profile examples of politicians not living up to their campaign promises, most MPs do feel duty bound to keep their election commitments as best they can.

Second, most MPs are aware of the voting behaviour phenomenon we explored in the previous chapter. Most recognize that voters are more likely to cast ballots based on a party's brand, its platform, or its leader than because of the specific virtues of local candidates. When in government, MPs tend to be fiercely loyal to the leader who got them there and who is therefore providing them with the opportunity to exercise the public policy influence that motivated them to enter public life in the first place. All MPs recognize the benefits of collective solidarity. If they are publicly divided, especially about their own policies and approaches to government (or opposition), voters will recognize chaos rather than coherence and likely replace them with members who will act cohesively and thereby provide smoother and less divisive government. In other words, most MPs see it as not only in their own self-interest, but also in the public interest to act in a unified and therefore productive manner. To the old adage "United we stand, divided we fall" many MPs would add, "United we stand and serve the public interest, divided we fall and serve neither the public's nor our own interests."

Party discipline also has a third important impact on how MPs do their jobs: it tends to insulate MPs somewhat from vocal and aggressive minority interests. In many cases, MPs can legitimately tell one or more pressure groups that they have no option but to support the party position on an issue because that is what the party campaigned on. This approach often provides MPs with the opportunity to represent what they believe to be majority opinion on a contentious issue, rather than one or the other radicalized poles as represented by organized special interests. More crassly, they may simply wish to deflect the blame for offending voters on one or all sides of a hotly debated issue.[10]

And finally, most MPs recognize that if every member of a caucus votes with the party leadership, all of them are to a certain extent protected from constituency reprisals. When one or more MPs defy the whip and vote against their party, their teammates are left exposed to public criticism as voters in their ridings point to the example of the dissident MPs. Therefore, backbenchers often pressure each other to toe the party line, instead of relying on caucus officers to twist arms. A culture of solidarity is built when MPs continuously remind each other of the many times each of them had to compromise their individual preferences for the good of the whole.

THE POLITICAL EXECUTIVE AND PARLIAMENTARY DEMOCRACY

To a great extent, party discipline is necessary for the smooth operation of parliamentary government. A Cabinet that cannot depend on the support of its caucus to implement major policy initiatives cannot govern effectively. Canadians who fail to understand the workings of responsible parliamentary government may perceive their MPs as trained seals who slavishly place the interests of their party above the interests of their constituents and even their own principles. In fact, MPs constantly lobby for their constituents' and regions' interests in caucus and in meetings with cabinet ministers and bureaucrats. Because these lobbying efforts necessarily take place behind closed doors, they do not enhance the public's image of Parliament.

In practice, then, despite a system that is intended to allow the legislature to hold the executive to account, Canadian ministers are no longer responsible to the House of Commons in any meaningful way, either collectively or individually. They are, however, responsible to their Cabinet colleagues. The principle of Cabinet solidarity means that Cabinet deliberations are held in secret, Cabinet documents are secret, and ministers who cannot support Cabinet decisions must resign. They are also, more importantly, directly responsible to the prime minister as the head of government. The prime minister, in turn, has every incentive to protect the executive branch from parliamentary and public criticism. A prime minister who controls a majority of seats has the tools—party discipline, the confidence convention, and the control of the Commons and its committees—to protect the government very effectively.

The Prime Minister

As we know, the leader of the party with the most seats in the House of Commons is asked by the governor general to become prime minister and to form a government Cabinet (see Canadian Political Chronology 6.2). When that party has a majority of seats, the Canadian prime minister is among the most powerful heads of government in the democratic world. Because the prime minister's power is based on constitutional convention (as opposed to written law), and because the scope of the Crown prerogatives that he or she exercises is so vast, there are few restraints on the prime minister's political authority within the government.[11] Control of Parliament ensures legislative approval for the prime minister's priorities, and in a very real sense, the prime minister *is* the government.

Powers of the Prime Minister

The specific powers of the prime minister are impressively broad. He or she has full discretion over the machinery of government. The prime minister can create, merge, or abolish departments, establish new agencies and programs, and change the size and structure of the Cabinet whenever he or she wishes.

The prime minister chooses all cabinet ministers, senators, and Supreme Court justices. While normally knowledgeable advisers are consulted about each appointment, the final decision is the prime minister's alone. There are conventional constraints on the appointment of cabinet ministers—most notably, they must be

William Lyon Mackenzie King served as Canada's prime minister for 21 years, longer than any other person. He is the only prime minister to return to power after having been removed from the office twice (albeit the first time was for only three months in 1926). He governed through the second half of the Great Depression and all of World War II, when he successfully managed the deep cleavages between the English and French communities over the issue of conscription. His portrait adorns the Canadian $50 bill. (CP/© Toronto Star Syndicate [2003] all rights reserved)

Born: 1874, Berlin (Kitchener), Ontario

Died: 1950, Kingsmere, Quebec

Education: B.A., LL.B., and M.A. (University of Toronto, 1895, 1896, and 1897); M.A. and Ph.D., Political Economy (Harvard University, 1898 and 1909); also studied at University of Chicago from 1896–1897

Profession: 1900–1908 Canada's first deputy minister of labour, and editor of the *Labour Gazette*

1914–1918 Labour consultant, Rockefeller Foundation

Political Career:

MP
1908–1911 Waterloo North, Ontario
1919–1921 Prince, Prince Edward Island
1921–1925 York North, Ontario
1926–1945 Prince Albert, Saskatchewan
1945–1949 Glengarry, Ontario

Leader
1919–1948 Liberal Party

Prime Minister
1921–1926
1926–1930
1935–1948

Other Ministries
1909–1911 Labour
1921–1930 External Affairs
1935–1946 External Affairs

Political Career Highlights
1907 Industrial Disputes Investigation Act
1919–1921, 1926 Leader of the Opposition
1926 King–Byng dispute over powers of prime minister versus powers of governor general to dissolve Parliament and call an election
1926 Old age pension
1930 Appointed Cairine Wilson first woman senator
1930–1935 Leader of the Opposition
1937 Rowell–Sirois Commission on Dominion-Provincial Relations
1939–1945 Led Canada as prime minister throughout Second World War
1940 National Resources Mobilization Act
1940 Unemployment insurance
1942 National referendum on conscription
1942–1943 Construction of the Alaska Highway
1944 Family Allowances Act

Source: *First Among Equals, The Prime Minister in Canadian Life and Politics* (Ottawa: Library and Archives Canada), available on-line at http://www.collectionscanada.ca/primeministers/.

members of the government caucus—but within those constraints the prime minister has complete latitude to appoint whomever he or she wishes. Unlike senators and judges, whose tenure is protected by law once they are appointed, cabinet ministers can be fired by the prime minister at any time. While individual firings are rare, prime ministers usually shuffle their cabinets every few years. Weak ministers whose ineptitude has embarrassed the government may be shuffled out, while rising back-bench stars may be shuffled in.

The prime minister also appoints parliamentary secretaries: MPs who assist cabinet ministers in the performance of their duties. Their primary tasks are to sit on the Commons committees that monitor their departments and report back to the minister. They also undertake some public duties, standing in for ministers who have to be elsewhere. Parliamentary secretaries were routinely shuffled every two years, often into committee chair positions (which, until 2002, were also appointed by the prime minister.)[12] The job of parliamentary secretary is widely seen as a stepping stone to Cabinet, and it is coveted by ambitious government backbenchers.

The prime minister decides when to call elections, although the new Harper government has decided to attempt to fix election dates to the third Monday in October every four years beginning in 2009.[13] During an election campaign, national party leaders are the most visible public face of the party, dominate the news coverage, and are responsible for the overall image the party presents to voters. When his or her party wins a majority, the prime minister takes the credit and can effectively silence dissent by reminding ministers and MPs that many of them were elected on his or her coattails. And although the prime minister may be subject to a leadership-review vote at a party convention, there is no formal mechanism in Canada for the caucus or Cabinet to use to remove an ineffective leader.[14]

The prime minister's power is further enhanced by the tremendous resources at his or her disposal. The most powerful central agency in the Canadian government, the Privy Council Office, reports directly to the prime minister. The clerk of the Privy Council is both the deputy minister to the prime minister (who has the sole discretion over the clerk's appointment) and the top official in the federal public service. The clerk recommends the hiring, transfer, and firing of deputy ministers and other senior public servants. He or she also monitors the entire permanent executive. Every morning the clerk briefs the prime minister on current developments in the executive branch. This close working relationship has at least two advantages for the prime minister. Initially, he or she has access to information about all departments and agencies, which the other ministers do not share. Also, the prime minister effectively controls the person to whom every senior public servant is directly accountable.

The PCO handles all the paperwork for the Cabinet and its committees. It sets meeting agendas, takes and distributes the minutes, and prepares briefing materials on the issues to be resolved. The clerk provides all these materials to the prime minister and submits proposed agendas for approval. The prime minister can add or delete agenda items as he or she wishes, resulting in absolute veto over the policy direction of the government.

The PCO is also responsible for preparing the mandate letters received by ministers when they are sworn in to Cabinet. These letters explain the responsibilities of Cabinet office, describe the major issues relating to the specific portfolio, and set out the prime minister's priorities in that particular policy field. If need be, the prime minister will change the mandate as he or she sees fit. The deputy minister also receives a copy of the letter. Because the clerk advises the prime minister on deputy ministerial appointments, deputies have a powerful incentive to stick to the mandate as established by the prime minister, and to keep their ministers in line as best they can.

The prime minister chairs Cabinet meetings and summarizes the discussions. No formal votes are taken in Cabinet and the prime minister's summary is the only official record of the deliberations. As such, the prime minister sets out the overall policy of the government and directs the operations of the executive branch. While a prime minister usually "goes with the flow" on low-priority issues, he or she can occasionally ignore an opposing majority and declare a consensus in support of his or her own position on a high-priority issue.

The prime minister has his own central agency, the Prime Minister's Office, which straddles the line between the political and permanent executives. Whereas the PCO provides nonpartisan policy and operational advice, the PMO serves as the political antennae of the prime minister. It enhances the prime minister's authority over the Cabinet, the government caucus, and the party organization outside Parliament.

Although the prime minister does not have a specific portfolio, he or she is traditionally responsible for three policy fields: foreign affairs and security, national unity, and federal-provincial relations. On those issues, the Cabinet usually defers to the prime minister, who receives advice and assistance from the deputy minister for intergovernmental affairs, a senior foreign-policy advisor, and a national security advisor, all of whom work in the PCO. The prime minister participates in constitutional negotiations, trade talks, and informal meetings with premiers without interference from the Cabinet.

Furthermore, the prime minister's position as the head of Canada's government means that he or she often meets with other world leaders, collectively or individually, striking agreements that bind the federal government without the necessity of Cabinet or parliamentary approval.

Finally, the prime minister can intervene in any issue that particularly interests him or her or that threatens to become a problem for the government. As soon as a particular issue is identified as a prime ministerial priority, the machinery of government mobilizes to serve the prime minister's will. No cabinet minister can enact a policy without the prime minister's support; conversely, prime ministers can—and sometimes do—override ministers whose preferences clash with their own. The prime minister is also the final umpire in conflicts between ministers.

Constraints on the Powers of the Prime Minister

The prime minister's powers are subject to a few constraints; some are formal, but most are informal. For instance, the prime minister cannot act unconstitutionally. While the

NAME	PARTY	TERM(S) IN OFFICE	ELECTORAL RECORD AS PARTY LEADER
Sir John Alexander Macdonald	Liberal-Conservative Conservative	July 1867–Nov. 1873 Oct. 1878–June 1891 (died in office)	6 majority victories 1 defeat (Liberal majority)
Sir Alexander Mackenzie	Liberal	Nov. 1873–Oct. 1878	1 majority victory 1 defeat (Conservative majority)
Sir John Abbott	Conservative	June 1891–Nov. 1892	No victories, no defeats
Sir John Thompson	Conservative	Dec. 1892–Dec. 1894 (died in office)	No victories, no defeats
Sir Mackenzie Bowell	Conservative	Dec. 1894–April 1896	No victories, no defeats
Sir Charles Tupper	Conservative	May 1896–July 1896	No victories 2 defeats (Liberal majorities)
Sir Wilfrid Laurier	Liberal	July 1896–Oct. 1911	4 majority victories 3 defeats (2 Conservative majorities, 1 Unionist majority)
Sir Robert Borden	Conservative Unionist[a]	Oct. 1911–Oct. 1917 Oct. 1917–July 1920	2 majority victories 2 defeats (Liberal majorities)
Arthur Meighen	Conservative	July 1920–Dec. 1921 June 1926–Sept. 1926	3 defeats[b] (Liberal minorities)
William Lyon Mackenzie King	Liberal	Dec. 1921–June 1926 Sept. 1926–Aug. 1930 Oct. 1935–Nov. 1948	2 minority victories[b] 4 majority victories 1 defeat (Conservative majority)
Richard (R. B.) Bennett	Conservative	Aug. 1930–Oct. 1935	1 majority victory 1 defeat (Liberal majority)
Saint-Laurent, Louis	Liberal	Nov. 1948–June 1957	2 majority victories 1 defeat (Conservative minority)
John Diefenbaker	Progressive Conservative	June 1957–April 1963	1 majority victory 2 minority victories 2 defeats (Liberal minorities)

NAME	PARTY	TERM(S) IN OFFICE	ELECTORAL RECORD AS PARTY LEADER
Lester Pearson	Liberal	April 1963–April 1968	2 minority victories 2 defeats (Conservative majority and minority)
Pierre Trudeau	Liberal	April 1968–June 1979 March 1980–June 1984	2 majority victories 1 minority victory 1 defeat (Conservative minority)
Joe Clark	Progressive Conservative	June 1979–March 1980	1 minority victory 1 defeat (Liberal majority)
John Turner	Liberal	June 1984–Sept. 1984	No victories 2 defeats (Conservative majorities)
Brian Mulroney	Progressive Conservative	Sept. 1984–June 1993	2 majority victories No defeats
Kim Campbell	Progressive Conservative	June 1993–Nov. 1993	No victories 1 defeat (Liberal majority)
Jean Chrétien	Liberal	Nov. 1993–Dec. 2003	3 majority victories No defeats
Paul Martin	Liberal	Dec. 2003–Feb. 2006	1 minority victory 1 defeat (Conservative minority)
Stephen Harper	Conservative	Feb. 2006–	1 minority victory 1 defeat (Liberal minority)

[a] During World War I, the country was deeply divided over the question of whether or not Canadian men should be conscripted (i.e., drafted against their will) to fight overseas. The Conservative Cabinet was joined by English-speaking Liberals in the Union Government and was able to impose conscription after the 1917 federal election.

[b] In the 1925 federal election Meighen's Conservatives won 116 seats to the Liberals' 101 but King refused to resign as prime minister. When King finally faced Parliament, his government was defeated and he requested a new election. Governor General Lord Byng refused to dissolve Parliament, bringing on the King–Byng affair. Byng told Meighen to form a government, which he did, but it too was defeated, ending his second term as prime minister after only three months.

Source: Parliament of Canada Web pages, available on-line at http://www.parl.gc.ca.

scope of executive power at the federal level is poorly defined, it is limited by the division of powers and by judicial review of the Charter. In particular, Sections 4 and 5 of the Charter require prime ministers to seek a new mandate from the electorate at least once every five years and to submit annually to the scrutiny of Parliament.

Time limitations are some of the biggest practical constraints on the power of the prime minister. Because the opposition in the Commons, together with the media, can grill the prime minister over real or apparent errors in policy and administration at virtually any time, and because prime ministers seeks to avoid controversy and embarrassment whenever possible, preventing or "managing" errors consumes much of the prime minister's scarce time and attention—and that of senior officials in the apolitical PCO. Because of the scarcity of time, a prime minister can pursue only a few priorities at any one time. All other issues must be either delegated to the Cabinet, or ignored.

A wise prime minister will recognize these and other limits to his or her political capital and use it sparingly. For example, the power to summarize Cabinet discussions in a way that conflicts with the views of the majority should be exercised sparingly. Otherwise, the prime minister risks a public revolt against his or her leadership and ultimately the collapse of the government.[15] Also, despite the fact that the confidence convention is rarely invoked, it still exists. Even majority governments must take this into consideration when pursuing divisive or controversial agendas. Eventually, even prime ministers with a majority must face the test of public opinion. Prime ministers who embark on public policy agendas that are too innovative, and possibly radical, may alienate many traditional party supporters. A government that stretches the limits of what the majority of voters, or key constituencies of voters, are willing to accept in the form of grand schemes or major changes in public policy direction may also run up against the boundaries of what is acceptable within the political culture. Undoubtedly, the democratic check on the prime minister is the most important and effective constraint on the office's power and authority.

Given the much longer list of powers than constraints, it should be clear that the prime minister's preeminence within the national government is unquestioned. The prime minister sets the agenda, has the final say on high-priority issues, and enjoys a broad overview of government activities that is denied to other ministers.

The Rest of the Cabinet

While it is sometimes argued that Canada has a prime-ministerial government rather than a parliamentary or cabinet government, this claim is exaggerated. The federal government is too large and too complex to be directed by a single individual, even when backed by the resources of the PCO and PMO. In the trench warfare of public policy formulation and administration, cabinet ministers retain real influence and discretionary power. The prime minister's scarce time, energy, and attention are carefully rationed out to a relatively few areas of special interest, political sensitivity, or expertise. Therefore, despite his or her immense powers, the prime minister cannot govern alone and must rely heavily on the other members of the Cabinet.

Structure of Cabinet

As we noted earlier, the prime minister has the power to arrange the Cabinet in any way he or she wishes.[16] Macdonald had only 13 members in his first Cabinet and never exceeded 15 members. Cabinets remained relatively small, usually 20 or fewer members, until Diefenbaker started increasing the size of his cabinets, eventually to as many as 24 members. Pearson continued to increase the size of Cabinet, eventually to 27. Trudeau had as many as 37 cabinet ministers, while the Mulroney cabinets held as many as 39 members. Chrétien's cabinets appeared to reverse the trend, formally having as few as 23 members. But this was largely because Chrétien distinguished between senior ministers and junior secretaries of state; the latter were not formally designated as members of the Cabinet, but held similar responsibilities. By the time he formed his last Cabinet, Chrétien had 28 full ministers and 10 secretaries of state, or 38 in total. Paul Martin abolished the distinction between senior and junior cabinet ministers and included 39 members in his Cabinet. Prime Minister Harper reduced the number of cabinet ministers in his first government to a total of 27, including the prime minister (see Canadian Political Chronology 6.3). There are no junior secretary of state ministries. The reduction in ministers, and the corresponding reorganization of government departments, was, as you can imagine, considerable, and directed by the prime minister and his staff.

Each minister is responsible for a particular policy field, or portfolio, within the executive branch. A minister is usually the political head of a line department, solely responsible to Parliament for all aspects of his or her portfolio. However, two ministers (the minister of finance and the president of the Treasury Board) are responsible for central agencies, and one, the minister for intergovernmental affairs, has no separate department or agency. The leaders in the House and Senate sit in Cabinet and coordinate the legislative activities of the government. They are not responsible for particular policy fields, although the government leader in the House normally sponsors amendments to the Canada Elections Act, exemplified by the current government House leader's responsibilities for democratic reform.

All ministers are bound by the constitutional convention of collective responsibility. This means that ministers are obliged to support all of the decisions of the Cabinet, even if they argued against them within the in camera meetings. Cabinet must speak with one voice, making dissent a privilege reserved for others.

Cabinet Selection Criteria

Interestingly enough, few members of the Cabinet are chosen for their expertise in a particular field of policy. Most are appointed for reasons unrelated to their professional backgrounds. There are obvious exceptions in that the minister of finance requires experience and connections within the business community, while the justice minister must be a member of the bar. But in general, most cabinet ministers are appointed because they satisfy one or more of the following criteria:
- constitutional convention
- regional and demographic representation
- seniority
- political (and perhaps personal) relationship to the prime minister

CANADIAN POLITICAL CHRONOLOGY 6.3 The Canadian Ministry: 2006 Harper Government (in order of precedence)

NAME	PROVINCE	MINISTRY
Stephen Harper	Alberta	Prime Minister
Rob Nicholson	Ontario	Leader of the Government in the House of Commons, Minister for Democratic Reform
David Emerson	British Columbia	Minister of International Trade, Minister for the Pacific Gateway and the Vancouver–Whistler Olympics
Jean-Pierre Blackburn	Quebec	Minister of Labour, Minister of the Economic Development Agency of Canada for the Regions of Quebec
Greg Thompson	New Brunswick	Minister of Veterans Affairs
Senator Marjory LeBreton	Ontario	Leader of the Government in the Senate
Monte Solberg	Alberta	Minister of Citizenship and Immigration
Chuck Strahl	British Columbia	Minister of Agriculture and Agri-Food, Minister for the Canadian Wheat Board
Gary Lunn	British Columbia	Minister of Natural Resources
Peter MacKay	Nova Scotia	Minister of Foreign Affairs, Minister of the Atlantic Canada Opportunities Agency
Loyola Hearn	Newfoundland and Labrador	Minister of Fisheries and Oceans
Stockwell Day	British Columbia	Minister of Public Safety
Carol Skelton	Saskatchewan	Minister of National Revenue, Minister of Western Economic Diversification
Vic Toews	Manitoba	Minister of Justice, Attorney General of Canada
Rona Ambrose	Alberta	Minister of the Environment
Michael Chong	Ontario	President of the Queen's Privy Council for Canada, Minister of Intergovernmental Affairs, Minister for Sport
Diane Finley	Ontario	Minister of Human Resources and Social Development
Gordon O'Connor	Ontario	Minister of National Defence
Bev Oda	Ontario	Minister of Canadian Heritage and Status of Women

NAME	PROVINCE	MINISTRY
Jim Prentice	Alberta	Minister of Indian Affairs and Northern Development, Federal Interlocutor for Métis and Non-Status Indians
John Baird	Ontario	President of the Treasury Board
Maxime Bernier	Quebec	Minister of Industry
Lawrence Cannon	Quebec	Minister of Transport, Infrastructure and Communities
Tony Clement	Ontario	Minister of Health, Minister for the Federal Economic Development Initiative for Northern Ontario
Jim Flaherty	Ontario	Minister of Finance
Josée Verner	Quebec	Minister of International Cooperation, Minister for la Francophonie and Official Languages
Senator Michael Fortier	Quebec	Minister of Public Works and Government Services

The prime minister is entitled to the prefix "The Right Honourable." All other members of the Cabinet are assigned the prefix "The Honourable." These prefixes have been omitted in this table for reasons of space.

Listed in order of date of appointment to the Privy Council, followed by date first elected to the House of Commons or appointment to the Senate.

Source: Parliament of Canada Web pages, available at http://www.parl.gc.ca.

Conventions

As a matter of constitutional convention, a cabinet minister must be either an MP elected from the prime minister's party or a senator. On rare occasions, the PM will appoint a cabinet minister from outside Parliament. In that case, the new minister must win a seat in the Commons at the earliest opportunity, usually through a by-election held to fill a vacant House of Commons seat. Should the appointee lose that election, by convention, he or she must resign immediately.[17]

The conventions of responsible government limit the number of senators who can sit in the Cabinet. Although the government leader in the Senate is always a member of the Cabinet, because senators cannot appear on the floor of the Commons, ministers drawn from the Senate weaken the Cabinet's daily accountability to the House. In special circumstances, however, additional senators have held Cabinet posts. For example, the Progressive Conservative government elected in 1979 included only one MP from Quebec. Joe Clark appointed two Quebec senators to his Cabinet, to boost that province's representation. Similarly, Trudeau used Western Canadian senators to provide regional representation in the Cabinet after the 1980 election, which returned only

THE POLITICAL EXECUTIVE AND PARLIAMENTARY DEMOCRACY

two Liberal MPs from Manitoba, and none from the other Western provinces. More recently, and curiously, Harper appointed Michael Fortier to the Cabinet, and then to the Senate, in order to provide the city of Montreal with Cabinet representation.

Regional Representation

The need to have representatives from all of Canada's regions has dominated Canadian Cabinet-making since Confederation. There are two distinct principles at work. Initially, the Cabinet must include at least one minister from each region, and preferably one from each province. As the above point about senate representation in Cabinet indicates, this poses problems for a PM whose party is weak in particular areas of the country. Ontario and Quebec usually dominate federal cabinets, with the smaller provinces providing fewer ministers. Secondly, certain portfolios are traditionally awarded to particular regions. For example, fisheries and oceans is typically reserved for ministers from the East and West coasts. Finance and industry are often associated with Ontario, while justice and public works are disproportionately awarded to Quebeckers.

The practice of awarding portfolios on the basis of region, rather than policy expertise, is usually defended on three grounds. First, the Cabinet is the supreme body where competing regional claims are brokered. Second, regional ministers have historically played a key role in linking the provincial political communities with the national executive. Third, the national government must reflect the two national linguistic communities. This means in practice that Quebec ministers must be sufficiently numerous to reflect the two-nations vision of the political community.

As the regional distribution of the first Harper Cabinet indicates, even in a Cabinet led by an Albertan and created from a party that elected only 50 out of 181 possible MPs from Canada's two central provinces, Ontario and Quebec still dominate (see Canada by the Numbers 6.1). Note that all provinces have at least one cabinet minister, with the exception of Prince Edward Island where the Conservatives elected no MPs. Quebec is underrepresented (18.5 percent of Cabinet) considering its proportion of the Canadian population (23.5 percent), but is overrepresented in comparison to its proportion of the Conservative caucus (8.1 percent). Conversely, Alberta (14.8 percent of Cabinet) is slightly overrepresented when compared to its proportion of the population (10.1 percent), but slightly underrepresented when considering the proportion of the Conservative caucus that originates from that province (22.6 percent). For the most part, all of the other provinces have Cabinet representation that generally aligns with their proportion of the Canadian population. The territories are an exception, given that the Conservatives failed to win any of the three territorial seats.

Demographic Representation

While the major language and religious groups have been represented in Cabinet since Confederation, gender and ethnicity are more recent considerations. Age, in particular youth, is also a consideration where possible. Diefenbaker appointed the first woman cabinet minister in 1957 (Ellen Fairclough), while Trudeau appointed the first nonwhite minister in 1979 (Lincoln Alexander). Since the 1970s, prime

CANADA BY THE NUMBERS 6.1 Geographic Representation in the Federal Cabinet, July 2006

PROVINCE/ TERRITORY	CABINET MINISTERS	% OF TOTAL CABINET	TOTAL SEATS IN PROVINCE	SEATS WON BY CONSERVATIVES IN PROVINCE	SEATS WON BY CONSERVATIVES AS % OF PROVINCE'S SEATS	SEATS AS % OF CONSERVATIVE CAUCUS	POPULATION AS % OF TOTAL (2005)
Newfoundland/ Labrador	1	3.7	7	3	42.9	2.4	1.6
Prince Edward Island	0	0.0	4	0	0.0	0.0	0.4
Nova Scotia	1	3.7	11	3	27.3	2.4	2.9
New Brunswick	1	3.7	10	3	30.0	2.4	2.3
Quebec	5	18.5	75	10	13.3	8.1	23.5
Ontario	9	33.3	106	40	37.7	32.2	38.9
Manitoba	1	3.7	14	8	57.1	6.5	3.6
Saskatchewan	1	3.7	14	12	85.7	9.7	3.1
Alberta	4	14.8	28	28	100.0	22.6	10.1
British Columbia	4	14.8	36	17	47.2	13.7	13.2
Yukon	0	0.0	1	0	0.0	0.0	0.1
Northwest Territories	0	0.0	1	0	0.0	0.0	0.1
Nunavut	0	0.0	1	0	0.0	0.0	0.1
Total	27		308	124	40.3		

Source: Prime Minister of Canada website: http://www.pm.gc.ca
Statistics Canada website: http://www40.statcan.ca/l01/cst01/demo02.htm, accessed July 2006.

ministers have tried to include at least one woman and one member of a visible minority group in each Cabinet. The first Harper Cabinet included six women (22.2 percent of the total Cabinet), four members who were under 40 yeas of age (14.8 percent), and two visible minority members. In short, the federal Cabinet has come to be seen as a mirror, although an imperfect one, of Canadian society.

Seniority

The seniority criterion receives less public attention than the representational issues just discussed, but it has greater practical significance for the operation of the political executive. Generally speaking, the prime minister prefers to appoint experienced MPs rather than newcomers. Where the PM has no choice—because the new government has a high proportion of rookies, or there are only a few MPs from a particular region or demographic group—he or she may be forced to appoint an unknown quantity. But where the PM has a choice, he or she will naturally prefer to elevate people who have proven themselves to be politically skilled. While some rookie MPs have excelled in Cabinet, inexperienced ministers are more accident-prone than their more seasoned colleagues.[18]

Political Criteria

The purely political criteria for Cabinet appointment are more difficult to define than the other criteria, but they are often equally important. Caucus members who played key roles in the prime minister's successful campaign for the party leadership are often rewarded with Cabinet posts. Prime ministers, like most politicians, like to surround themselves with trusted allies.

The candidate who finished second in the most recent leadership contest, if he or she remains in politics, is virtually guaranteed a senior portfolio. A favourite spot is international or foreign affairs, which is an important portfolio and therefore serves to not demean the rival. But the portfolio also acts to neutralize any challenges from a rival, given its lack of authority over any domestic policy agenda and the prime minister's prerogative to usurp that minister on important international matters.

Prominent caucus members from different ideological perspectives may be included in the Cabinet, in order to avoid alienating factions within the party organization. However, their experience in Cabinet is often frustrating, especially when they frequently find themselves on the opposite sides of issues from the prime minister and his or her advisers.

To summarize: few of the conventions governing the selection of cabinet ministers emphasize expertise in a particular field. As such, they tend to reduce the influence of the relatively novice political executive vis-à-vis the professional expertise of the permanent executive. The seniority criterion partially offsets the weakening effect of the representational criteria because seasoned politicians veterans are better equipped to deal with senior public servants. The impact of the political criterion is mixed. Although a loyal Cabinet strengthens the hand of the PM, the inclusion of weak ministers for partisan reasons diminishes the effectiveness of the political executive as a whole. Those few ministers who enter the Cabinet with a solid grasp of their portfolios, extensive political experience, a clear set of priorities, and the support of the prime minister can bend their departments to their will. However, most end up, if not the captives of their public servants, very dependent on them for expert advice about policy and governance.

■ The Operation of Cabinet Government

Cabinet ministers face a number of significant and conflicting demands on their time and talents. Given the challenges of Cabinet life, individual ministers are too busy to give much time and attention to any one role. As a result, they rely heavily on their senior departmental officials and the central agencies for information and advice on policy-making. This is particularly true for new ministers, whose previous work experience rarely prepares them for the complexities and frustrations of government. The relationship between the minister and his or her deputy is fraught with tension on both sides. A minister who disregards the advice of the deputy is unlikely to be effective in Cabinet, while a deputy who sides too often with his or her minister risks losing face with the Privy Council Office.

Responsibilities of Individual Cabinet Ministers

A cabinet minister is expected to serve in multiple capacities, some political and some administrative. The following are among the most important responsibilities each cabinet minister much balance.

A cabinet minister is a member of Parliament (in rare cases, a senator) and, like any MP, must keep in touch with the constituency and serve its needs. Even ministers with safe seats know that they cannot afford to neglect their ridings. Almost all ministers know that their presence in Cabinet depends on them being first elected to the House of Commons by voters in one of Canada's 308 electoral districts.

Cabinet ministers are members of the government caucus. The caucus meets weekly when Parliament is in session, and cabinet ministers are expected to attend. Each will be lobbied by their caucus colleagues and be expected to take some interest in their many and varied concerns.

Ministers sit on at least one Cabinet committee. Although these smaller groups are more efficient than the full Cabinet, preparing for and attending their meetings still consume a great deal of time and energy.

Ministers must also attend the weekly meeting of the full Cabinet. Again, a great deal of preparation and meeting time must be made available.

A cabinet minister is the political head of a line department. While the deputy minister and other public servants handle the day-to-day administrative and policy tasks, the minister must stay abreast of all major developments in the portfolio. Failure to do so can result in an embarrassing public slip-up at question period or in a media scrum.

An important function of all cabinet ministers is to maintain good relations with the important client groups associated with the department. For example, the minister of justice needs to pay attention to the Canadian Bar Association, while the finance minister cannot afford to ignore the Canadian Chamber of Commerce and other high-profile business associations. If ministers fail to appear at important meetings or annual conventions, or if they fail to consult an association about pending legislation, loss of the association's cooperation and goodwill could result.

Cabinet ministers sponsor all legislation that originates in their departments. In addition to making speeches in the House, the minister must appear before the parliamentary Committee that examines each minister's bills and evaluates proposed amendments.

Cabinet ministers are among the most prominent members of a national political party. At the very least, they are expected to make speeches at fundraising dinners and other party events across the country and to participate in party conventions.

Ministers must also devote considerable time and effort to media appearances. Even though a cabinet minister has a lower profile than the prime minister, public announcements of new policies, the daily scrum after question period, interviews, and photo ops require intense preparation.

Given the large number of roles cabinet ministers must play, and the demands on their time, it is understandable that the normal MP's salary of approximately $150 000 ($122 700 for senators) is topped up with an additional $70 000. Although many Canadian taxpayers would view a total salary approaching one-quarter million dollars as more than fair compensation, it is still much less than most private-sector senior executives with similar budgets and responsibilities would earn.

Cabinet Committees

Much of Cabinet's work takes place in committees. As Cabinets expanded from a handful of ministers in 1867 to 30 or more in the 1970s, they became too large and unwieldy to make collective decisions in an efficient manner. Apart from the Treasury Board, which dates back to Confederation, Cabinet committees are a relatively recent invention. Their primary purpose is to ease the burden on the full Cabinet by assigning particular policy and administrative responsibilities to smaller groups of ministers, who can discuss new proposals and emerging issues in detail. In addition to reviewing proposed program changes, spending targets, and draft legislation, committees are expected to resolve interdepartmental disputes and coordinate government policy. They are assisted by officials from the PCO and from the relevant line departments, and, when necessary, by the prime minister. All committee decisions are sent to the full Cabinet for review; but, as we will see, prime ministers tend to discourage their ministers from questioning committee decisions.

The number of committees has fluctuated over the years, as prime ministers experimented with different models of Cabinet decision-making. Stephen Harper's 2006 Conservative Cabinet has six committees, including the powerful Priorities and Planning Committee. It is chaired by the prime minister and is responsible for the strategic direction of the government and ratification of other committee recommendations. The other Cabinet committees include operations, social affairs, economic affairs, foreign affairs and national security, and the Treasury Board.

The Treasury Board is unique among Cabinet committees in that, unlike the policy committees which rely on individual line departments and the Privy Council Office for assistance, the Treasury Board is supported by its own central agency—the Treasury Board Secretariat. By law, the Treasury Board has six members, including its president who sits as its chair. The vice chair is the minister of finance. In addition, two cabinet ministers are designated as alternates to the Treasury Board. The board is "responsible for accountability and ethics, financial, personnel and administrative management, comptrollership, approving regulations and most orders- in-council."[19]

Cabinet committees enjoy a good measure of autonomy. Their decisions need not be ratified or even discussed by the full Cabinet, although it is informed of all committee activities. At the weekly Cabinet meeting, the fourth item on the agenda is an appendix containing committee reports. Although ministers have the right to challenge committee decisions, most prime ministers frown on those who exercise that discretion. In nearly every case, the Cabinet rubber-stamps the decisions of its standing committees. In the rare cases in which challenges occur, the prime minister will likely send the controversial issue back to the committee instead of allowing the Cabinet to overrule its decision.

Finally, although the prime minister does not sit on most committees, he or she controls their operations at a distance. The PM appoints the chair of each committee, favouring ministers with an instinct for avoiding trouble and for resolving disputes in private. The committees are staffed by PCO officials, who report directly to the clerk of the Privy Council, who, in turn, informs the PM of any problems on a committee. If there is reason to suspect that a committee report will cause tension in Cabinet, the prime minister can simply delete that item from the Cabinet agenda.

The Full Cabinet

The Canadian Cabinet meets weekly while Parliament is in session. But these meetings rarely feature detailed policy debates. Nor do they often result in decisions being made. Rather, information about the major issues facing the country is shared though briefings. Most include the general or overall perspective of the government's fiscal position, key intergovernmental or national unity issues, important international developments, and, of course, the government's political standing with voters. Most of the formal decisions that are made include simply ratifying order-in-council appointments that have already been determined.

There are no votes, as voting would assume each member of the Cabinet is equal, which we have seen is certainly not the case. Voting would also produce clear winners and losers, political horse-trading, and possibly long-standing factions. It would thus disrupt the collegiality of the ministers and, perhaps most important, it would reduce the weight of the prime minister to one vote among many. This would not only undercut his capacity for leadership but would also fly in the face of the real differences in status, electoral importance, and power between the prime minister and other ministers. Cabinet decisions are therefore made by consensus. The prime minister summarizes the consensus, and ministers are expected to accept his summation or resign from Cabinet. This decision-making style reflects the basic institutional reality of responsible government. Because the Cabinet speaks with a single voice, the search for consensus is an institutional necessity.

All federal Cabinet and committee discussions and related documents are subject to strict secrecy.[20] To some degree, this secrecy is a function of the issues themselves; public disclosure could undermine national security, or unfairly benefit private interests. More important, secrecy allows a frank discussion within Cabinet while still retaining Cabinet unity before the Commons, the media, and the electorate. Only with the conventions of secrecy in place can the Cabinet speak with a single voice and thus maintain collective responsibility. The downside of Cabinet secrecy is that regional and group representation, if it occurs at all, takes place behind closed doors and out of view of the electorate.

Canada's parliamentary government is dominated by the Cabinet, which in turn is dominated by the prime minister. Undoubtedly, Canada has one of the most centralized concentrations of power in all of the world's parliamentary democracies. The prime minister is central to all government operations in that he or she decides which individuals occupy Cabinet positions at the head of those operations, and whether or not the various ministries will continue to exist at all. Although the prime minister's powers are immense, cabinet ministers have a considerable amount of authority of their own, if for no other reason than the limitations on the prime minister's time. Each is responsible for a ministry that must meet the requirements of a population that it serves and must be prepared to stand up to the scrutiny of Parliament and the media on a regular basis.

THE LEGISLATIVE BRANCH

As we have already discussed, the British North America Act, 1867, created a bicameral legislature for Canada. Undoubtedly, the lower house, the House of Commons, is the most important. Its members comprise most of the Cabinet, and its overall membership determines which party will form the government and which leader will become prime minister. As an elected body, with representation determined by population, it meets some of the most important legitimizing criteria of the Canadian political culture: democracy and equality. The Senate, an appointed body that only poorly represents the regions, meets neither of those legitimizing qualities, and therefore suffers from a lack of legitimacy with most Canadians. It, nevertheless, provides a useful function, and, arguably, does a better job in many aspects of legislating than does the Cabinet-controlled Commons.

Together, the two institutions are charged with the duties of passing legislation, overseeing the financial operations of the government, and representing Canadians in their national political institutions. In practice, the Commons does not carry out its duties as effectively as it might. There are at two important reasons for this gap between theory and practice: executive dominance and party discipline.

Executive Dominance

Even though a certain degree of Cabinet domination is to be expected in a parliamentary government—in which the executive and legislative branches are not separated—the concentration of power in the hands of the Canadian Cabinet is more pronounced than in any other British parliamentary system.[21] Legislators usually pass the laws proposed by the Cabinet with only minor changes, if any. Little meaningful debate occurs, often because of the threat of the confidence convention. The power of the purse, traditionally an important bargaining chip for disgruntled legislators, has been reduced to empty ritual. The Cabinet also has the power to issue delegated laws—such as orders-in-council and regulations—without ratification by Parliament. Furthermore, in most Parliaments, MPs lack the independence, experience, and expertise to hold the Cabinet accountable, either individually or collectively. The high turnover of MPs from election to election, especially on the opposition side, weakens the capacity of the Commons as a whole. The only weapon available to opposition MPs is the mobilization of public dissent.

Despite its poor public image, the Senate often does a better job of legislating than does the Commons. Because senators do not have the power to bring down a government and are not subject to election or reelection, they are more independent of the political executive and less constrained by party discipline. Unlike most MPs, senators generally remain in Parliament for long periods of time; this allows them to master parliamentary procedure and acquire policy expertise. Some senators are experts in public policy and administration even before their appointment, whereas most MPs are policy amateurs when they are sworn in. Despite their often greater expertise, however, senators suffer from a lack of legitimacy, severely limiting their ability to significantly impact legislation even when they have important contributions to make.

Party Discipline

Strict party discipline prevents government MPs from openly challenging the Cabinet. It also denies opposition MPs a meaningful opportunity to participate in policy-making, at least under a majority government. Party discipline constrains the autonomy of MPs at all stages of the legislative process, including committee work. There is one important exception: government MPs can express dissenting views in the weekly caucus meeting. Although these confrontations between ministers and backbenchers go on behind closed doors, making their influence difficult to measure, ministers may be forced to delay, amend, or withdraw proposed legislation by concerted opposition from their caucus colleagues. But this power should not be overstated.

Although prime ministers routinely remind their Cabinets to pay attention to the views of government MPs, ministers have little incentive to follow this advice. The longevity of their Cabinet careers depends on the prime minister, not on their caucus colleagues. As noted earlier, senators are less subject to party discipline; consequently, they normally operate in a less adversarial way. This helps to explain why Senate committees are substantially more effective than their counterparts in the Commons.[22]

◼ The House of Commons

Executive dominance and party discipline have reduced the effectiveness of Canada's legislative branch, relative to both the executive and the courts. The Commons has lost much of the legitimacy that one might expect an elected chamber to possess. Despite widespread public suspicion about the motives and abilities of our elected representatives, the truth is that MPs work very hard and make enormous personal and financial sacrifices in the name of public service. They divide their time between Ottawa and their constituencies, juggling a host of roles and responsibilities that often conflict with the expectations of the voters. Most important among these is the mountain

FIGURE 6.1 Floor Plan of the Canadian House of Commons

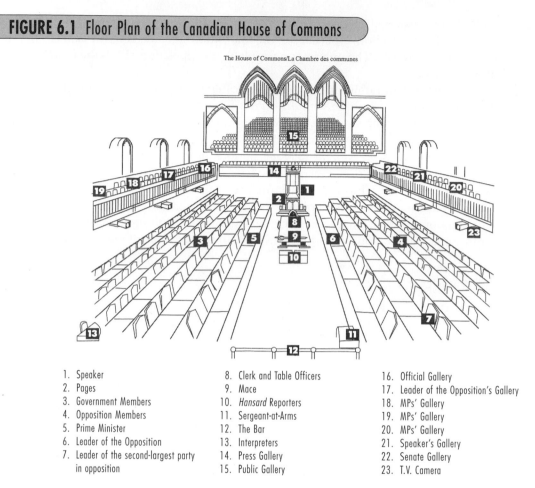

The House of Commons/La Chambre des communes

1. Speaker	8. Clerk and Table Officers	16. Official Gallery
2. Pages	9. Mace	17. Leader of the Opposition's Gallery
3. Government Members	10. *Hansard* Reporters	18. MPs' Gallery
4. Opposition Members	11. Sergeant-at-Arms	19. MPs' Gallery
5. Prime Minister	12. The Bar	20. MPs' Gallery
6. Leader of the Opposition	13. Interpreters	21. Speaker's Gallery
7. Leader of the second-largest party in opposition	14. Press Gallery	22. Senate Gallery
	15. Public Gallery	23. T.V. Camera

Source: Library of Parliament/Bibliothèque du Parlement.

of casework, or services to individual constituents, MPs attend to each year. While MPs consider helping individual constituents to be the most important aspect of their jobs, Canadians outside Parliament consider casework to be the least important.[23] This is only one example of the contradictions between the institutional incentives that shape MPs' behaviour and voters' perceptions of their elected representatives.

As we have discussed, institutions exert a powerful influence on the behaviour of those who operate within them. They set incentives for ambitious people who seek to advance their careers. An individual MP, no matter how determined, cannot resist those incentives for long. He or she must either give in and follow the institutional norms of behaviour or leave Parliament. Most important among these norms are the type of representation most MPs are conditioned to practise, the limitations of the system of representation by population, the casework duties of MPs, the adversarial nature of Commons discourse, and the Commons' role in controlling the public purse.

Types of Representation

Three specific types of representation that an MP may choose to employ can be identified: delegate representation, trusteeship, and party representation. Each has advantages as well as drawbacks, but as we already know, party representation tends to dominate in the Canadian Parliament.

Delegate   This type of representation assumes that MPs will vote faithfully according to their constituents' wishes, even if the MPs or their parties disagree with what the people are demanding. Pure delegate representation is favoured by populists and has the advantage of most closely mirroring direct democracy, in that the MP simply canvasses the prevailing public mood on important issues and votes accordingly. One of several disadvantages is that, on most issues, even localized populations such as those found in electoral districts contain a plurality of opinions on important issues. Gauging the will of the people, even with the most sophisticated scientific polling techniques, is likely to reveal that there is no common will upon which to base a voting decision. Pure delegateship also renders party election platforms meaningless, as MPs elected under any platform could justifiably vote against their party's positions by invoking the mantra of "faithfully representing the will of their constituents." Furthermore, it makes parliamentary government under the confidence convention inherently unstable. No leader would know for sure which aspects of the party's platform would gain majority support. Delegate representation also assumes that voters have sufficient knowledge about all of the important issues governments must deal with to understand what is or is not in their best interests.

Trustee   On the other hand, trusteeship assumes that MPs are elected to give voice to the collective will of the nation, which will incorporate their constituents' best interests. Because MPs have more information and experience about national issues than do their constituents, trusteeship assumes that MPs should exercise their own judgment instead of taking orders from the voters. In other words, based on the superior knowledge gained from being in Ottawa and from participating in the debates, MPs will exercise their personal judgment and vote in a manner that they believe to be in the best interest of their constituents, whether the voters back home know it or not, or whether or not they agree with the MP's position. An advantage of trusteeship is that MPs tend to be much more informed about most issues they are asked to address than are most voters. The biggest drawback is that there exists a potential for MPs to ignore strong consensuses on issues within their ridings, where they exist, and for voters to refuse to reelect MPs who somewhat sanctimoniously tell voters that they are acting in their best interests by ignoring their wishes. Few politicians have won reelection based on the campaign slogan "Trust me; I know better than you do about what is in your best interests."

Party   Neither the delegate or trustee model reflects the reality of the Canadian House of Commons. In Canada, MPs generally vote according to party, not their own judgment or the will of their constituents. Most candidates for the House of Commons are long-time members of their respective parties who are wholeheartedly committed to the goals and principles of their political teams. As was discussed previously, most voters base their voting decision on party brands and platforms rather than on individual candidates or other localized phenomena. When a Conservative government is returned, it is not unreasonable for voters to expect a Conservative platform to be presented to Parliament, rather than an NDP platform. Or if a Liberal government is returned, Liberal policies should prevail, not Bloc Québécois policies. Furthermore, responsible Cabinet government requires that the political executive maintain the support of the House, which means in practice that government backbenchers must vote in favour of the initiatives put forth by their party leaders. One of the most significant disadvantages of pure party representation is that some provinces, perspectives, or cleavages may not be adequately represented within the government party. As we have seen, entire regions are often left out of the government—often because of distortions caused by the electoral system, but left out nonetheless. Also, as we discussed in the previous chapter, it is rare for any party to receive a majority of votes (only Diefenbaker in 1958 and Mulroney in 1984 achieved this feat) even though they often win a majority of seats. Although the national government is supposed to govern for all Canadians, majority governments formed by parties with less than majority support often appear to be a form of perpetual rule of a minority over the majority.

While partisan representation is the strongest institutional norm faced by most MPs, its legitimacy among voters has certainly diminished in recent decades. In the public mind, Canada's legislative institutions have not kept pace with changing political values. Evolving notions of representation, together with increasing skepticism about top-down politics, have alienated many voters from their elected representatives. The institutional norms of Cabinet dominance and party discipline evolved over centuries and, in moderation, they make responsible government possible. In excess, they damage the reputation of Parliament. But without a clear public consensus about the meaning of political representation and a better understanding of the institutional incentives that shape the behaviour of our elected officials, the mismatch between MPs' behaviour and voters' expectations will likely continue.

Representation by Population?

There are currently 308 seats in the House of Commons. Provincial representation ranges from 106 seats in Ontario to 4 in Prince Edward Island and 1 for each of the three territories (see Canada by the Numbers 6.2). While seats are distributed across the provinces in rough proportion to their respective shares of the national population, there are some important exceptions to "rep by pop" (the shorthand form of "representation by population"). Prince Edward Island and New Brunswick are overrepresented in the House because of the senatorial floor rule, a constitutional provision specifying that a province cannot have fewer MPs than it has senators (BNA Act, 51 [a]). Because of the practical problems associated with their size, the territories are also overrepresented. Manitoba, Newfoundland, Nova Scotia, Saskatchewan, and Quebec are perpetually guaranteed the same number of seats they held when the present redistribution scheme was adopted in 1985. These provisions, together with practical limits on the overall size of the Commons, have penalized the three provinces whose population has grown substantially since 1985. In fact, if seats were allocated strictly according to population, Ontario would have 119 seats rather than 106, British Columbia would have 40 rather than 36, and Alberta would have 31 rather than 28.

Some other considerations also affect the prospects of pure rep-by-pop. The Supreme Court has ruled that although the Charter does guarantee equality for each voter, some variation between the sizes of ridings can be justified. For example, if one riding had only 20 000 residents but another had 200 000, voters in the smaller riding would essentially have 10 times the influence of voters in the larger riding given that each would still elect only a single MP. But because some MPs, particularly those in primarily rural ridings with vast distances separating municipalities, have even more demands on their time than do other MPs, riding size can vary by up to 25 percent.[24]

CANADA BY THE NUMBERS 6.2   Distribution of House of Commons Seats 2006

PROVINCE/ TERRITORY	NUMBER OF SEATS	NUMBER OF SEATS AS % OF TOTAL	POPULATION AS % OF TOTAL (2005)	POPULATION PER MP	NUMBER OF SEATS IF STRICT REPRESENTATION BY POPULATION APPLIED	DIFFERENCE BETWEEN PURE REP-BY-POP AND ACTUAL	POPULATION (2005)
Newfoundland/ Labrador	7	2.3	1.6	73 714	5	−2	516 000
Prince Edward Island	4	1.3	0.4	34 525	1	−3	138 100
Nova Scotia	11	3.6	2.9	85 263	9	−2	937 900
New Brunswick	10	3.2	2.3	75 200	7	−3	752 000
Quebec	75	24.4	23.5	101 308	72	−3	7 598 100
Ontario	106	34.4	38.9	118 315	119	+13	12 541 400
Manitoba	14	4.5	3.6	74 114	11	−3	1 177 600
Saskatchewan	14	4.5	3.1	71 007	9	−5	994 100
Alberta	28	9.1	10.1	116 314	31	+3	3 256 800
British Columbia	36	11.7	13.2	118 180	40	+4	4 254 500
Yukon	1	0.3	0.1	31 000	1 (0.3)		31 000
Northwest Territories	1	0.3	0.1	43 000	1 (0.4)		43 000
Nunavut	1	0.3	0.1	30 000	1 (0.3)		30 000
Total	308				307		32 270 500

Calculations for percentage of seats if strict representation by population applied are based on 2005 population and assume 105 464 people per district (2005 population minus the territorial populations divided by the 305 nonterritory seats). Rounding leads to a total of 307 seats.

Source: Population figures based on 2005 Statistics Canada data available at http://www40.statcan.ca/l01/cst01/demo02.htm, accessed July 2006.

THE POLITICAL EXECUTIVE AND PARLIAMENTARY DEMOCRACY

Casework: The MP as Constituency Representative

While there is considerable confusion about the numerical aspects of parliamentary representation, few MPs have any doubt about their importance as constituency representatives. Constituency service has two dimensions. First, the MP is an informal ombudsman for individual constituents who become entangled in disputes about pensions, employment insurance, passports, agricultural subsidies, and a myriad of other program areas in which the federal government plays a role. This is the casework aspect of parliamentary service. Secondly, MPs lobby the government for program spending and public services that will benefit their constituencies as a whole. Examples include public works, job-creation funds, and the location of federal government offices outside Ottawa.

Most parliamentary candidates have extensive backgrounds in volunteer community service, in addition to their partisan activities. Many are inspired to run for public office as a result of their community involvement. At least half of all MPs cite constituency service as the most important factor in their initial decision to seek election.[25] On average, most MPs devote significantly more time to constituency service than to any other aspect of their jobs, including legislative work and policy development. Even those who were motivated to run because of other factors, such as partisanship or policy interest, quickly become active ombudsmen.

Adversarial Politics

Much of the public discontent with the House of Commons goes well beyond concerns about representativeness. The institution of a Westminster-styled Parliament encourages mutual hostility between the parties. Government and opposition MPs confront each other across a centre aisle, their physical disposition signalling that there are two opposing sides to the issue at hand and little, if any, common ground. The most basic rules and procedures of parliamentary debate encourage this adversarial clash of opposing teams. The objective of parliamentary debate is not to reach a compromise solution, not to find the best possible outcome, but rather to present two vigorously opposing points of view, with the electorate left to judge. This adversarial character of the House shapes its most basic operating rules and procedures.

It would be incorrect, however, to attribute the public conflict among parliamentary caucuses entirely to the rules of Parliament. While institutional norms and structures do have a powerful influence on individual and group behaviour, there are other reasons for adversarialism in the Commons. As we have seen, the length and trajectory of a Canadian political career is strongly influenced by an MP's relationship to his or her party. Most MPs are enthusiastic partisans, imbued with a powerful team spirit. They genuinely believe that their particular party has the best answers to the public questions of the day, and they wish to support and assist the other players on their team. In a high-pressure situation such as question period, these emotions come to the fore in boisterous and sometimes undignified ways.

The public perception of MPs as brawling combatants is greatly exaggerated. In private, many parliamentarians from different parties like and respect each other, and they can work together harmoniously. Because the television cameras in the Commons chamber must focus on the member who is speaking at a given moment, viewers rarely witness the off-camera chats between members of differing partisan stripes. News reporters prefer to cover conflict, not cooperation; consequently, Canadians receive a distorted picture of the Commons. Journalists focus on the fireworks provided by the 40-minute question period which is held every day that the House is in session. Members of the Cabinet, including the prime minister, are grilled by opposition MPs about the public issues of the day. Question period is valued by opposition MPs and journalists because it forces ministers, day in and day out, to respond to their critics. It is the best opportunity for opposition parties to mobilize the public and draw media attention to problems in government policy and performance.

Although opposition MPs have strong incentives to make the prime minister look bad, the Cabinet and central agencies have equally strong incentives to make the prime minister look good. They also have the means at their disposal to minimize the political damage inflicted in question period. Experienced ministers can evade questions by ridiculing the opposition. Central agencies often refuse to share detailed information about policy and administration with opposition MPs, although they may be forced to comply with access to information requests filed by parliamentarians or journalists. Over the long term, the entire House of Commons pays a price for short-term victories in question period. While journalists love to see ministers squirm, the media coverage of question period captures MPs in their most adversarial and abrasive tempers and further erodes public confidence in parliamentary institutions.

Parliament and the Public Purse

The lower house in a Westminster-styled Parliament has the constitutional right to control the public purse. However, the Crown retains the power to propose spending and revenue measures. In other words, money bills and taxes must be *approved* by the House of Commons, but they cannot be *proposed* by anyone other than a member of the Cabinet. These British constitutional conventions are entrenched in Sections 53 and 54 of the Constitution Act, 1867. The process by which Parliament approves the Cabinet's taxing and spending plans is divided into two parts:

- ways and means motions, which authorize the Crown to collect revenues
- supply motions, which authorize spending on the hundreds of different programs and services provided by the federal government[26]

The spending approved by Parliament takes two forms:
- the annual Main Estimates
- two subsequent sets of Supplementary Estimates, which allow the government to alter its original spending plans (within limits) in response to unforeseen events

Because public finance is crucial to the operations of government, majority governments control with an iron hand the Business of Supply, the official name of the process by which the government asks Parliament to appropriate (or authorize) the funds required to meet its financial obligations. While this gives the executive branch greater stability and predictability in its financial arrangements, it has deprived the House of Commons of one of its key constitutional functions. In effect, the quest for administrative efficiency has all but eliminated Parliament's power to hold the executive accountable for its use of public funds.

In recent years, Parliamentary committees have been given more opportunity to participate in the formulation of future spending plans. However, the actual influence of the committee reports seems to be limited, with one notable exception. The Public Accounts Committee (PAC) is a standing committee of the House empowered to review the government's handling of public money. Unlike the other standing committees, which review estimates for the next fiscal year, the PAC focuses on previous government spending. Historically, the PAC is unique among parliamentary committees in that, although government MPs chair most standing committees, the PAC is chaired by a member of the official Opposition.

Although the PAC is the official parliamentary watchdog of government spending, it lacks the resources to monitor a huge and complex executive branch. It relies on the experts in the Office of the Auditor General for detailed information about the activities of the permanent executive. The auditor general is an officer of Parliament, who reports to the House at least once a year. These reports attract intense media coverage for their scathing and occasionally bizarre stories of fiscal mismanagement. The PAC draws considerably less attention, but its cooperation with successive auditors general has recently enhanced Parliament's control of the public purse.

The Senate

Canada's upper house, the Senate, is appointed by the prime minister. Its members can serve until their seventy-fifth birthdays. The Senate was created to perform a legislative role similar to that performed by the House of Lords in Britain, although the two institutions have different social and political foundations. The appointed Senate was to be a chamber of sober second thought, wherein legislation passed by the House of Commons could be reexamined to ensure that minority interests—regional, linguistic, or political—were adequately protected. Its membership would be based on region, and its powers would be identical to those of the House of Commons. Although its origins were noble, the senators' status as nonelected politicians cripples their legitimacy with voters, preventing most of the public from knowing about or acknowledging the important work that some senators do, especially in committees.

Sober Second Thought

At the end of the nineteenth century, the Fathers of Confederation, like many elites in the colonies, did not completely trust democracy or democratic institutions. They were concerned that the popular rabble in the Commons would violate minority rights, many of which were the rights of the rich and powerful. In partial recognition of this concern, they created an upper chamber with almost identical legislative powers to the Commons, to serve as a check against democratic excesses.

Although voters in the early twenty-first century no longer see the need for the Senate's check on democracy, Canadian senators still play valuable roles in the legislative process. Senators review and amend legislation, using their own expertise and their committee work to improve flawed bills. Their relative independence from the Cabinet and their freedom from constituency work and electoral considerations allow them to operate in a more consensual and deliberative way than can MPs. Without attracting much public attention, the Senate has quietly taken on several important tasks that the Commons cannot or will not do. These include scrutinizing regulations, examining bills for potential conflicts with the Charter of Rights, and hearing from witnesses who might not have had an opportunity to appear before the more raucous Commons committees.

However, legislation originating in the House already carries the stamp of democratic approval before reaching the Senate. As a result, Senate debate on noncontroversial bills is often perfunctory. Legislative procedure in the Senate is identical to that in the House, but the hurdles are lower at each stage. Many bills reach the Senate so late in the parliamentary session that the delay entailed in any detailed examination would be tantamount to a veto; that is, the bills would die when the parliamentary session ended. Thus, in most cases the Senate defers to the Commons.

Regional Representation

Even in 1867, the need for sober second thought was not enough to justify a second legislative chamber. For the Fathers of Confederation, the Senate was the product of a political compromise without which the country might never have come into being. The Maritime colonies wanted assurances that their perspectives would not be drowned out by the larger Commons delegations from the two Central provinces. Quebec insisted that it must be overrepresented in the upper house to protect the francophone population against the ever-growing English majority. The Fathers of Confederation looked to the American Senate for inspiration.[27] The American Senate, unlike the British House of Lords, is a federal chamber within which each state, regardless of its population, has two representatives. At first, American senators were indirectly elected by their state legislatures. Since 1913, all American senators have been directly elected by the voters in their respective states.

Yet the Canadian Senate, while it was meant to reflect the same federal principles as its American counterpart, did not incorporate the specifics of the American model. First, Canadian senators are not selected by provincial legislatures, governments, or citizens; they are appointed by the prime minister, usually without consulting the provincial governments. Second, Canada opted for representation by region rather than equal representation by province (see Canada by the Numbers 6.3). Thus, in 1867, Ontario, Quebec, and the Maritimes were each given 24 Senate seats. When a 1915 constitutional amendment recognized Western Canada as a senatorial region, it too was assigned 24 seats, divided equally among the four Western provinces. Representation for Newfoundland in 1949 and for the two northern territories in 1975 was added to the initial regional allocation of seats. In 1999 the new territory of Nunavut also received a Senate seat. This brought the total number of senators to 105.

The distribution of Senate seats reveals that Alberta, Ontario, and British Columbia have the weakest proportional representation in the upper house. These provincial inequities are defended on the grounds that the Senate provides for equal regional representation, but even regional equality in the Senate took a strange twist when Newfoundland's Senate seats were added to, rather than drawn from, the original Maritime allotment of 24. Although the West is underrepresented in the Senate (23 percent of the total) relative to its share of the national population (30 percent), this is a relatively small distortion compared to Ontario's almost 40 percent of the population and less than 23 percent of Senate seats. Atlantic Canada, with just over 7 percent of the national population and almost 29 percent of the Senate seats, is the primary beneficiary of Senate representation based on regional equality.

The Senate's perceived failure to represent the regions is not solely the result of its unequal composition. Its lack of democratic legitimacy, combined with partisanship—which, although weaker than partisanship in the House of Commons, is still an important institutional norm—has prevented the upper house from expressing the distinct concerns of Canada's regions. Behind closed doors, government senators

CANADA BY THE NUMBERS 6.3 Distribution of Senate Seats 2007

PROVINCE/TERRITORY	NUMBER OF SEATS	NUMBER OF SEATS AS % OF TOTAL	POPULATION PER SENATOR	POPULATION (2005)	POPULATION AS % OF TOTAL CANADIAN POPULATION (2005)
Newfoundland/Labrador	6	5.7	86 000	516 000	1.6
Prince Edward Island	4	3.8	34 525	138 100	0.4
Nova Scotia	10	9.5	93 790	937 900	2.9
New Brunswick	10	9.5	75 200	752 000	2.3
Quebec	24	22.9	316 588	7 598 100	23.5
Ontario	24	22.9	522 558	12 541 400	38.9
Manitoba	6	5.7	196 267	1 177 600	3.6
Saskatchewan	6	5.7	165 683	994 100	3.1
Alberta	6	5.7	542 800	3 256 800	10.1
British Columbia	6	5.7	709 083	4 254 500	13.2
Yukon	1	0.95	31 000	31 000	0.1
Northwest Territories	1	0.95	43 000	43 000	0.1
Nunavut	1	0.95	30 000	30 000	0.1
Total	105			32 270 500	

Source: Population figures based on 2005 Statistics Canada data available at http://www40.statcan.ca/l01/cst01/demo02.htm, accessed July 2006.

join their Commons colleagues in lobbying for the interests of their provinces or territories. But this representative role, like senators' legislative role, tends to go unnoticed by most voters.

Powers of the Senate

Although the Senate's lack of public legitimacy has made it the junior partner in the national Parliament, its formal powers are almost identical to those of the House of Commons. It has an absolute veto on ordinary legislation and a suspensive veto on constitutional amendments.[28] While money bills cannot be introduced in the Senate, the upper house can defeat money bills initiated in the Commons. For the reasons just explained, however, the Senate rarely vetoes legislation passed by the House. It is more willing to amend legislation, although it does so very infrequently. Both Houses must agree on the final version of a bill to be passed at third reading; where a discrepancy arises, as when the Senate amends a bill after passage by the Commons, it must be resolved. When the government accepts a Senate amendment, it asks the Commons to vote for a motion to amend the law as the Senate has seen fit. If the government rejects the amendment and the written reasons for it that the Senate appends to the changed bill, it rarely if ever resorts to the formal dispute-resolution mechanism—a conference of the two houses (in practice, the MPs and senators on the committees that reviewed the bill). Instead, the leader of the government in the Senate usually holds informal discussions with his or her opposite member in the Commons, and perhaps with the sponsoring minister, to try to work out a compromise. If no compromise can be reached, the Senate usually—but not always[29]—defers to the Commons.

Thus, the potential problem associated with an appointed chamber having formal powers roughly equivalent to those of the elected chamber is usually avoided by the restraint shown by senators in the exercising of their formal powers. The principle of democracy underlies the convention of senatorial restraint. Senators lack the political legitimacy of elected MPs, and so they are wary of thwarting the will of the Commons.

In some cases, however, senators lose their diffidence toward the Commons. When governments change, opposing majorities in the House and Senate are almost guaranteed due to the appointment process and the lags it produces. Because senators are appointed until age 75, those appointed by any given prime minister are likely to remain in place well after the governing party has changed in the House. As such, there is a good chance that a new governing party in the House will face an opposition majority in the Senate. This was the case after the 1984, 1993, and 2006 elections. Partly for partisan reasons, senators sometimes flex their legislative muscles and decide to block controversial government legislation. In 1988, Liberal senators delayed the Conservative government's free trade deal with the United States and forced the prime minister to call an election on the issue. After the Conservatives won a renewed majority, the senators capitulated and passed the enabling free trade legislation. Progressive Conservative senators repeatedly challenged Liberal legislation between 1993 and 1997, while Liberal senators did the same to the Harper government's Accountability Act.

Senate Committees

One notable exception to the low status of the Senate is the work of its committees. Given their typically long time in office, many senators are more knowledgeable about specific issues and more cognizant of the potential impact of legislation than are their Commons counterparts.

Three standing committees merit particular attention. The first is the Standing Joint Committee for the Scrutiny of Regulations (SJCSR), which reviews the detailed regulations made by public officials in the process of implementing the laws passed by Parliament. It is composed of 10 MPs and 5 senators, and is cochaired by a government member and an opposition member. The senators tend to be the most active members of the committee, because they are not preoccupied with more politically important matters like constituency work. Although the SJCSR can examine only about one-quarter of the thousand or so regulations issued each year, its analyses carry considerable weight because it has the power to recommend that a particular regulation be revoked.

The Standing Committee on National Finance often does a more thorough job of reviewing the annual Main Estimates than do the Commons committees—despite the fact that the Commons, and not the Senate, holds the power of the purse. The Standing Committee on Human Rights is mandated to ensure that federal legislation conforms to the Charter and to the international human rights instruments that Canada has signed since 1945—a task that it shares with the Standing Committee on Legal and Constitutional Affairs.

Other special committees have tackled difficult and complex policy issues ranging from postsecondary education to the legalization of marijuana. While the government of the day is under no obligation to enact their recommendations into law, the high quality of these reports often exerts a long-term influence on public policy. Unlike the members of royal commissions and other formal inquiries, senators remain directly engaged in the legislative process after their reports are issued. They can call upon ministers and public servants to follow up on their recommendations and use their leverage to ensure that their proposals are at least considered.

Most Canadians are unaware of the contributions made by Senate committees. The upper house rarely attracts the attention of the news media and the public. The exceptions to this neglect are usually unflattering reports, often concerning conflicts between the two Houses of Parliament, which inevitably mention the lack of democratic legitimacy of the upper house, or scandals over the conduct of individual senators, primarily for persistent absenteeism. The fact that many senators can claim an expertise in public policy unmatched by most MPs and the diligence with which they carry out their legislative and investigative work are rarely mentioned.

In summary, the Senate reflects a fundamental ambiguity in the institutional structure of the Canadian federal state. It was designed to fulfill both the legislative role of the British House of Lords and the federal role of the U.S. Senate. To perform these functions effectively requires some tradeoffs, or some compromise, or both. Consequently, the Senate has come under sustained and growing attack from those who see it as an affront to democratic values or federal principles.

THE LEGISLATIVE PROCESS

Orderly debate and voting depend on the enforcement of rules and the efficient resolution of disputes. At the same time, parliamentary debate must permit the expression of diverse opinions. This is a difficult balancing act, especially in a Parliament with four official parties representing diverse regional political cultures. The Speaker of the House is caught between a government that expects speedy passage of its legislation on the one hand, and three opposition parties with varying ideologies and agendas on the other. At the same time, MPs are caught between institutional incentives that foster adversarialism and party discipline, and an electorate whose acceptance of these parliamentary norms has waned substantially in recent decades.

How a Bill Becomes Law in Canada

All bills that become law in Canada must be passed by both Houses of Parliament and be given royal assent by the Crown. Within each chamber, bills proceed through five stages before completing the process in that chamber (see Figure 6.2). An identical version of the bill must pass both legislative chambers, so if one chamber makes changes after the bill has passed the other chamber, it must be returned to the original chamber before it is sent to the governor general for royal assent. The standard procedure for adopting a government bill (C-*x* in this example) is as follows.[30]

Cabinet

Government bills originate with Cabinet committees, who recommend to Cabinet a course of action about a particular policy issue. Once Cabinet decides to proceed, a draft of the bill is formulated by the appropriate ministerial staff, in conjunction with Department of Justice officers, and presented to the Cabinet committee for its consideration. The full Cabinet then provides its endorsement, including the prime minister's signature, and the appropriate cabinet minister introduces the bill into the House of Commons (or sometimes into the Senate).

House of Commons

First Reading   The sponsoring minister asks leave of the House to present Bill C-*x*, "An Act Respecting Something Very Important." The motion for first reading is a formality; there is no debate, and the House almost always assents. After first reading, the bill is printed in both official languages and distributed to all MPs. The newly numbered bill is placed on the Order Paper for future debate. An Order Paper lists all the items of business that could be considered by the House according to an established order. The prefix *C-* before the number (e.g., C-34) means that the bill originated in the Commons. A few government bills are introduced in the Senate and are designated by the prefix *S-* (e.g., S-2). Any bill that requires the expenditure of public funds must originate in the Commons.

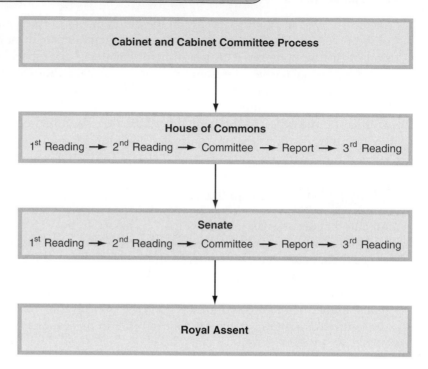

FIGURE 6.2 How a Government Bill Becomes Law in Canada

Cabinet and Cabinet Committee Process

House of Commons
1st Reading → 2nd Reading → Committee → Report → 3rd Reading

Senate
1st Reading → 2nd Reading → Committee → Report → 3rd Reading

Royal Assent

Second Reading On a day determined by the House leaders of the official parties, Bill C-*x* is debated for the first time. Only the principle of the bill may be debated at second reading; the details are left to later stages of the process. The sponsoring minister makes a speech defending the bill, explaining its provisions, and outlining the problem or problems the bill is designed to address. The Speaker then recognizes the official Opposition critic assigned to the minister's department. The official Opposition critic presents his party's response to the bill, focusing on the overall purpose of the legislation. The critics for the other opposition parties follow. Other MPs may take part in the debate if they so choose. That choice usually depends on the relevance of the issue to their particular party or constituency, or on the extent of their personal expertise on the subject matter of the bill. After all MPs who wish to speak have had an opportunity to do so, the Speaker recognizes the sponsoring minister to respond to the critics and close the debate. The House then votes on the bill. Once the House has voted in favour of a bill at second reading, the principle of the bill may not be changed at subsequent stages of the legislative process.

Committee Stage The bill is automatically sent to the appropriate standing committee of the House of Commons. Every department of the federal government is mirrored by a standing committee, but on occasion, bills are sent to special legislative committees. The committee may hold public hearings on the bill, summoning witnesses to testify about its possible effects. Most such witnesses are either policy experts or representatives of interest groups affected by the bill. Once the hearings are concluded, the committee examines the bill clause by clause. It considers amendments proposed by its members or by witnesses, relying on advice from officials of the sponsoring department. When the committee finishes its deliberations, it prepares a report to the House, including any amendments that were approved by a majority of the membership. In practice, committees in a majority Parliament adopt only amendments that the sponsoring minister has approved. These amendments may not change the principle of the bill, as adopted by the House at second reading, nor can they infringe on the Crown's prerogative by proposing additional public spending. Ideally, the committee submits a consensus report with the agreement of all four parties. In practice, one or more opposition parties often submit dissenting reports that reject the views of the government majority on the committee.

Report Stage   At this stage the House debates the bill as amended by the committee. Other amendments may be proposed from the floor by MPs who are not committee members. If the sponsoring minister considers a proposed amendment to be "friendly"—that is, he believes that it would improve the legislation—he can accept the amendment without further ado. "Unfriendly" amendments are put to a vote of the House. Under a majority government, the House rarely accepts a change that does not meet with the Cabinet's approval. In a minority situation, a united opposition can prevail over the objections of the minister (or initiate a bargaining process to reach a compromise). If amendments are made to a bill at report stage, either by the minister or by the House, the bill is revised and reprinted.

Third Reading   The revised bill is put to the House for a final debate and vote. As soon as it passes at third reading, the bill leaves the Commons and goes to the Senate.

Senate

The upper house follows a similar procedure to the Commons, with one major exception: because MPs cannot speak on the floor of the Senate (and vice versa), government bills are sponsored by the government leader in the Senate. The Senate has the power to veto most bills. This power is rarely used—only five times between 1945 and 1999[31]—but its existence requires the government to take proposed Senate amendments seriously. If the Senate amends a bill and the government refuses to accept those amendments,[32] the Senate usually (but not always) defers to the elected House. After the bill is passed by the Senate at third reading, it goes to the governor general for royal assent.

Royal Assent

The Crown's representative signs the bill into law. The new law may take effect immediately or at a later date as specified in the text of the legislation.

■ Characteristics of Parliamentary Debate

As we have seen, most legislation originates in the executive branch. At first reading, the government serves notice to the House, and through the House to the country, that the bill has been placed on the legislative agenda. Substantive debate begins with second reading, at which time the bill is discussed in principle. The government also signals the importance it attaches to the bill, and thus the extent to which the constraints of party discipline will apply in the subsequent debate.

If the government holds a majority of the seats—and therefore does not need the support of other parties to pass legislation—parliamentary debate is not intended to change the minds of MPs. The real audience is outside the House. Government and opposition MPs try to persuade the public that the bill should be passed or defeated and that it resolves or fails to resolve a problem of pressing importance to the national community. The debate is therefore symbolically important, even though votes in the House may not change as a consequence. It is through parliamentary debate and through the public record of that debate in *Hansard* (the official transcript of the debates in Parliament) that MPs inform and educate the public. While the content of specific debates may be trivial, the role of parliamentary debate in a representative democracy is potentially crucial.

A majority government rarely loses a vote at second reading. Whatever the MPs on either side of the House think of a particular bill, party discipline ensures that government backbenchers will turn out to support it. Since opposition MPs who oppose a particular piece of legislation cannot veto it, they are left with two alternatives. First, they can try to embarrass the government into delaying or withdrawing the bill. Their weapons include question period, media scrums, leaked documents, and the mobilization of interest groups. Second, they can bring Parliamentary business to a halt, thus drawing attention to the failings of the bill and mobilizing public dissent. In the end, a determined government will almost always prevail. Time allocation allows a majority government to limit debate at each stage of the legislative process and circumvent the tricks of the opposition. Nonetheless, delaying tactics do attract public attention to the alleged faults of a bill.

The legislative process is more complicated under a minority government. Because the Cabinet cannot count on the automatic approval of its legislation, the government House leader must negotiate with one or more opposition parties to build support for each bill and motion. In the process, the government often has to compromise: it may be required to amend certain bills in exchange for opposition votes or to abandon legislation altogether if it cannot work out a deal.

■ The Committee System

After second reading, bills are sent to committee for detailed, clause-by-clause examination. While committees may not have as much immediate impact on the content of legislation as they might wish, they do perform two important political functions. By holding public hearings, either in Ottawa or across the country, they give interest groups and others who may be affected by the proposed legislation direct access to the policy process. In so doing, they help to legitimize the legislative process and the laws that it produces. Generally speaking, Commons committees fall into the five following categories.

Committee of the Whole

The entire House becomes a committee. The strict rules of parliamentary debate are relaxed and members may discuss issues in a freer and less formal way. The House usually goes into committee of the whole during the examination of supply bills. Before 1968, the Estimates were also examined in committees of the whole.

Standing Committees

Specialist committees are established at the beginning of a Parliament (as soon as the House reconvenes after a general election) and remain in place until the House is dissolved. Each department of the federal government is monitored by a separate standing committee. The partisan composition of the committees corresponds to that of the Commons as a whole. Under a majority government, each Committee has a majority of members from the government party, with representation from the opposition parties roughly in proportion to the size of their caucuses. In a minority Parliament, the opposition parties collectively control a majority of the seats (although the governing party retains the largest single share).

In late 2002, an opposition motion to amend the standing orders garnered the support of a majority of MPs; it allowed committees to elect their own chairs without interference from the prime minister. Under the new rules, the committee elects a chair and two vice chairs at the beginning of each session of a new Parliament. The chair and one of the vice chairs comes from the governing party, while the other vice chair is drawn from one of the opposition parties.[33] The exceptions are the Public Accounts Committee, which is still chaired by an opposition MP, and the Standing Committee on Government Operations and Estimates. The independence of the PAC from the government is usually compromised by the fact that a majority of its members are from the governing party. Under a minority government, the PAC can operate with fewer constraints.

The formal powers and responsibilities of a standing committee are extensive. Committees are mandated to examine matters referred to them by the House, including order-in-council appointments, bills, and pressing policy issues. They are also responsible for reporting their findings and recommendations back to the House, to hold public hearings, to summon witnesses, and to "send for" all necessary documents. They also have the power to delegate these tasks to any subcommittee that they see fit to establish.

Legislative Committees

These are temporary committees established for the sole purpose of examining a particular bill. They are struck immediately after second reading and dissolved as soon as they have reported the bill back to the House with or without amendments.

Legislative committees were first created in 1985 on the recommendation of the Special Committee on House of Commons Reform (the McGrath Committee). In practice, the membership of legislative committees overlaps considerably with that of the standing committees in the same policy field, and the difficulty of scheduling meetings for dozens of standing and legislative committees creates delays in the legislative process. Since the early 1990s, legislative committees have rarely been used.

Joint Committees

Joint Committees can be a standing or special committee but they includes members from both Houses of Parliament. Standing joint committees include the Committee on Scrutiny of Regulations and the Committee on Official Languages.

Special Committees

These committees are established to study and report on a particular issue, and are then dissolved. Some are composed entirely of MPs, while special joint committees include both MPs and senators. Special joint committees played important roles in the megaconstitutional politics of the 1980s and 1990s.

Private Members' Business

Although the government has the sole right to introduce money bills, backbenchers may propose other types of legislation. MPs and senators have the opportunity to introduce private members' bills and motions, thereby initiating policy debate independently of the government. Although the standing orders governing private members' business have been reformed in recent years to give MPs more opportunity to raise issues for debate, few private members' bills ever pass into law.

At the beginning of the parliamentary session, the names of all MPs who have given notice of private members' bills or motions are placed in a drum. Thirty names are chosen at random by the deputy speaker to determine which items of private members' business will be placed on the order paper. Fifteen bills and 15 motions are listed in the order of precedence. Each is granted one hour of House debate during Private Members' Hour (between 5 and 6 p.m., Monday through Thursday). Each item is dropped from the order paper after one hour of debate, whether or not it has come to a vote. After 15 of the 30 have been dropped, another draw is held to bring the total number back up to 30 items in order of precedence.

Although most private members' bills and motions die after a single hour of debate, there are exceptions. After the 30 MPs are chosen in the draw, they must submit their proposed bills or motions to the Standing Committee on Procedure and House Affairs. The Subcommittee on Private Members' Business selects 10 of the 30 items—5 bills and 5 motions—as "votable items." Votable items must meet certain criteria, such as being well drafted, and must not be either trivial or redundant. They must also be constitutional, in that they are consistent with the division of powers and the Charter, and respectful of the Crown's prerogative over the raising and spending of public money.

Votable items are debated at second reading for up to three hours, after which they must be put to the House for a decision. The three hours of debate are not scheduled on consecutive days, causing votable private members' bills to be bounced around the order paper in an arbitrary and often unpredictable way. A private member's bill that passes at second reading is referred to a committee, which must report back to the House within 60 sitting days. Report stage is limited to one and three-quarters hours (also on random days) and must be immediately followed by third reading. If the private member's bill is adopted at third reading, it goes to the Senate.

Despite the stated purpose of the 1986 reforms to private members' business—to enhance the legislative role of back-bench MPs—the government can still quash a bill or motion that it deems to be unacceptable, meaning that few private members' bills and motions come to fruition unless the Cabinet supports them.

CONCLUSION

The principles of responsible government dictate that the legislative branch within the national government is supposed to hold the executive accountable to the voters. The members of the political executive are drawn form the membership of the legislative branch. They must obtain the approval of Parliament for their proposed legislation and fiscal plans, and they cannot continue to exercise the prerogative powers of the Crown without maintaining the confidence of the Commons. By answering to Parliament for their actions, our elected representatives hold the Cabinet and prime minister accountable for their policy and spending choices.

It should now be clear that the practice of Canadian parliamentary government does not conform to the theory of responsible government. Because the House of Commons is subordinate to the executive branch, there is little it can do to hold the Cabinet accountable to the electorate. Instead of *making* laws, the best that MPs and senators can do is to *improve* or *delay* laws. While MPs devote much of their time and energy to serving their constituents, collectively they lack the time, the experience, and the expertise to fully monitor the implementation of public policy. Furthermore, the incentives for parliamentarians reward obedience and adversarialism while punishing independence and public cooperation.

Nevertheless, once we understand the impact of Canada's other national political institutions on our legislative branch, we may conclude that our MPs and senators are doing the best they can under difficult conditions. If Canadians are dissatisfied with their national Parliament, it typically means that our elected and appointed representatives are not living up to our expectations. However, it likely also means that our expectations are sometimes unrealistic.

DISCUSSION QUESTIONS

1. Why is Canada's prime minister such a powerful head of government? What is the PM's relationship to the rest of the Cabinet?

THE POLITICAL EXECUTIVE AND PARLIAMENTARY DEMOCRACY

2. When the prime minister chooses the Cabinet, what criteria does he or she use to decide which MPs will become ministers and which will not? In your opinion, do these criteria make sense? Why or why not?

3. What do Cabinet committees do? What resources are available to assist them in their work?

4. Briefly explain the differences among the major concepts of political representation discussed in this chapter. Which do you find the most appealing, and why?

5. How does a bill become law in Canada?

6. Explain the roles and functions of committees of the House of Commons.

7. How do the confidence convention and party discipline affect the functioning of responsible government and the operation of our legislative branch of government?

SUGGESTED READINGS

Books and Articles

David C. Docherty, *Mr. Smith Goes to Ottawa: Life in the House of Commons* (Vancouver: UBC Press, 1997).

C. E. S. Franks, *The Parliament of Canada* (Toronto: University of Toronto Press, 1987).

Serge Joyal, ed., *Protecting Canadian Democracy: The Senate You Never Knew* (Montreal and Kingston: McGill–Queen's University Press/Canadian Centre for Management Development, 2003).

David McInnes, *Taking It to the Hill: The Complete Guide to Appearing Before (and Surviving) Parliamentary Committees* (Ottawa: University of Ottawa Press, 1999).

Donald J. Savoie, *Governing from the Centre: The Concentration of Power in Canadian Politics* (Toronto: University of Toronto Press, 1999).

F. Leslie Seidle and David C. Docherty, eds., *Reforming Parliamentary Democracy* (Montreal and Kingston: McGill–Queen's University Press, 2003).

Websites

The Parliament of Canada website (http://www.parl.gc.ca) is a gold mine of information about the form and function of Canada's political executive and parliamentary institutions. It provides the full text of government and private members' bills, the standing orders, legislative summaries prepared by the Library of Parliament, and committee minutes and reports, among many other useful documents.

NOTES

1. In the provincial setting, the lieutenant governor holds many of the same formal executive powers, plays the same ceremonial roles, and occupies the same position in the legislative process as does the governor general in Ottawa.

2. For current and historical lists of Canadian Privy Council members, see http://www. pco-bcp.gc.ca/default.asp?Language=E&Page=InformationResources&Sub= PrivyCouncilMembers

3. See David E. Smith, *The Invisible Crown: The First Principle of Canadian Government* (Toronto: University of Toronto Press, 1995).

4. You can visit the governor general's website at http://www.gg.ca.

5. In 1925, Liberal Mackenzie King dissolved Parliament for a general election. According to constitutional convention, when voters returned fewer Liberals than Conservatives (101 to 116), King should have resigned immediately and allowed the governor general, Lord Byng, to call upon Conservative leader Arthur Meighen to form a government. Instead, King stayed in office and delayed the return of Parliament for as long as he could. Finally, in 1926, he had to summon the Commons so that his government could secure the funds it needed to operate. Within a short time, his government was defeated in the House. Instead of resigning, King went to Lord Byng and asked him to dissolve Parliament for another election. Byng refused, accepted King's resignation, and called on Meighen to form a government. Meighen's government lasted only a few months. After it too was defeated, Byng dissolved Parliament. In the ensuing election, King turned the governor general's actions into the central campaign issue. He was reelected with a majority. The King–Byng crisis may have established a new constitutional convention in Canada: that the governor general must accept the advice of a prime minister to dissolve Parliament for an election, even when there is an alternative government available.

6. The minority Liberal government of Lester Pearson lost a budget vote in early 1968, while most of his Cabinet ministers were absent from the House. The Liberals were in the midst of a leadership race, and several of the ministers were campaigning across the country. Pearson accused the Conservatives of deliberately engineering the vote to take advantage of his party's disarray and refused to resign. He won a nonconfidence motion nine days later.

7. See *Report of the Special Committee on Reform of the House of Commons* [the McGrath Report] (Ottawa: Minister of Supply and Services, 1985).

8. The whip is an MP charged with orchestrating the legislative behaviour of his or her partisan colleagues. Whips on both sides of the House are appointed by their respective party leaders and ensure that enough members turn up to vote, that committees are staffed, and that legislative procedures run as smoothly as partisan debate allows.

9. MPs who vote against their party may forgo chances at future Cabinet appointments, prized committee assignments, or other advantages for their constituents, but it is rarely necessary to invoke these sanctions.

10. See for example, David C. Docherty, *Mr. Smith Goes to Ottawa: Life in the House of Commons* (Vancouver: UBC Press, 1997).

11. See Donald J. Savoie, *Governing from the Centre: The Concentration of Power in Canadian Politics* (Toronto: University of Toronto Press, 1999).

12. Peter Dobell, *Reforming Parliamentary Practice: The Views of MPs* (Montreal: Institute for Research on Public Policy, December 2000), 14–15; available on-line at http:// www.irpp.org.

13. Government of Canada, Privy Council Office, Media Centre, "Canada's New Government Proposes Fixed Election Dates," Ottawa, May 30th, 2006, available on-line at http://www.pco-bcp.gc.ca.

14. For an example of the turmoil created in a party when some of its caucus members attempt to remove a sitting leader, see Faron Ellis, "The More Things Change . . . The Alliance Campaign," in Jon H. Pammett and Christopher Dornan, eds., *The Canadian General Election of 2000* (Toronto: Dundurn Press, 2001) 59–89.

15. For example, a Cabinet revolt destroyed the Diefenbaker government in 1963. Although Diefenbaker led a minority government, which increased the danger of a split in Cabinet, he refused to heed the advice of those ministers who opposed his stand on American nuclear weapons. The result was catastrophic: the government fell and Diefenbaker lost the ensuing general election. See Denis Smith, *Rogue Tory: The Life and Legend of John G. Diefenbaker* (Toronto: Macfarlane Walter and Ross, 1995).

16. For a historical list of the size of previous cabinets see Parliament of Canada Web pages at http://www.parl.gc.ca/information/about/people/key/cabsize.asp?Language=E&Hist=Y.

17. For example, Trudeau appointed a past president of the CBC to the communications portfolio in 1978. Pierre Juneau subsequently ran in a by-election and lost. He resigned his Cabinet seat immediately. In 1995, after the shock of the Quebec referendum, Prime Minister Chrètien appointed Stèphane Dion and Pierre Pettigrew to his Cabinet to strengthen his Quebec contingent. Both easily won by-elections shortly thereafter. Had they not, they would have been forced to resign.

18. See Sharon L. Sutherland, "The Consequences of Electoral Volatility: Inexperienced Ministers 1949–90," in Herman Bakvis, ed., *Representation, Integration and Political Parties in Canada,* volume 14 of the collected research studies for the Royal Commission on Electoral Reform and Party Financing (Toronto: Dundurn Press, 1991).

19. Cabinet Committee Mandates and Membership, March 17, 2006, Government of Canada Privy Council Office, available at http://www.pco-bcp.gc.ca.

20. Since taking power in 2001, the Liberal government in British Columbia has opened Cabinet meetings to the media and the public. Video of the meetings is available on the BC government's website: http://www.prov.gov.bc.ca/prem/popt/cabinet. To date, no other Canadian government has taken such a significant step away from the British convention of Cabinet secrecy.

21. See Peter Dobell, *Reforming Parliamentary Practice: The Views of MPs* (Montreal: Institute for Research on Public Policy, December 2000).

22. Paul G. Thomas, "Comparing the Lawmaking Roles of the Senate and House of Commons," in Serge Joyal, ed., *Protecting Canadian Democracy: The Senate You Never Knew* (Montreal and Kingston: McGill–Queen's University Press/Canadian Centre for Management Development, 2003).

23. David C. Docherty, *Mr. Smith Goes to Ottawa: Life in the House of Commons* (Vancouver: UBC Press, 1997).

24. *Reference re Prov. Electoral Boundaries (Sask.)* [1991] 2 S.C.R.

25. See Docherty, *Mr. Smith Goes to Ottawa,* 121.

26. House of Commons, *Prècis of Procedure,* Section 13.

27. See Jennifer Smith, "Canadian Confederation and the Influence of American Federalism," *Canadian Journal of Political Science,* 21:3 (September 1988), 443–464.

28. See Section 47 (1) of the Constitution Act, 1982. Because the Senate has only a suspensory veto, not an absolute veto, over constitutional amendments, it cannot block its own reform. In recent years, some government bills have explicitly weakened the Senate's

power to block or suspend legislation adopted by the Commons. See Serge Joyal, "Introduction," in Serge Joyal, ed., *Protecting Canadian Democracy*. Available on-line at http://www.sen.parl.gc.ca/sjoyal/e/index.html.

29. In 1991 the Senate split 41–41 over the Mulroney government's bill to recriminalize abortion, following the 1988 *Morgentaler* ruling from the Supreme Court (see Chapter 8). Under Senate rules, a tied vote is equivalent to a defeat. This rare Senate veto of a high-profile government bill raised little public protest, likely because the bill had little support from either the pro-life or pro-choice camps.

30. Some elements of this procedure may be varied with the consent of the Cabinet and a majority of the House. Since an amendment to the standing orders—the written rules of Parliament—in 1994, the government may refer a bill to the appropriate standing committee before second reading.

31. Mark Audcent, *The Senate Veto: Opinion of the Law Clerk and Parliamentary Counsel* (Ottawa: Senate of Canada, 1999), 63, quoted in David Smith, "The Improvement of the Senate by Nonconstitutional Means" in Serge Joyal, ed., *Protecting Canadian Democracy: The Senate You Never Knew* (Montreal and Kingston: McGill–Queen's University Press/Canadian Centre for Management Development, 2003), 244.

32. Most Senate amendments are technical in nature. They reflect the policy expertise of individual senators and the higher quality of most Senate committee reviews. The majority of amendments are accepted by the government. See C. E. S. Franks, "The Canadian Senate in Modern Times," in Serge Joyal, ed., *Protecting Canadian Democracy*, 151–188.

33. Standing Orders of the House of Commons (accessed September 2004), Section 106 (2).

7 THE PERMANENT EXECUTIVE AND ADMINISTRATIVE STATE

LEARNING OBJECTIVES

- *identify* and *explain* the main functions of central agencies and line departments
- *identify* and *explain* the roles and functions of the Privy Council Office, the Prime Minister's Office, the Department of Finance, and the Treasury Board Secretariat
- *identify* and *explain* the history of federal government finance in Canada
- *identify* and *explain* the key elements of the federal budget
- *identify* the interaction between the permanent executive and the political executive in the policy-making process

INTRODUCTION

The permanent executive consists primarily of career public servants who work in central agencies, line departments, Crown corporations, and other components of the federal government. In theory, the permanent executive carries out the orders of the political executive, subject to the laws passed by Parliament. In practice, senior public servants—especially those in the Privy Council Office and the Department of Finance—exercise enormous influence over Canadian public policy. That influence is based on two primary factors:

1. Career civil servants possess a mastery of the complex and often challenging details of policy and governance, a mastery that most temporary cabinet ministers cannot hope to match.
2. Institutional incentives concentrate administrative power in the central agencies.

The *theoretical* model of British parliamentary government assumes that there is a clear division of responsibility between the political executive and the permanent executive. Ministers, individually and collectively, make policy. They are driven by partisan political incentives—particularly the desire for reelection—to choose policy alternatives that benefit the electorate, or at least benefit their particular constituency. The menu of choices is prepared by public servants, who are the acknowledged experts in policy and governance. Once decisions are made by the "political masters," the administrative servants get on with the task of putting them into practice. The Cabinet is responsible to Parliament, and ultimately to the public, for the broad outlines of policy. The public servants are ultimately responsible to the minister, and through him or her to Parliament, for the administrative operation of government. They cannot be held to account directly, either by legislators or by the electorate. They are assumed to be anonymous, nonpolitical, and loyal to the Crown rather than to the party in power.

For the most part, however, the traditional distinction between politics and administration is no longer an appropriate or accurate description of reality. In practical terms, the distinction is generally acknowledged to be a false dichotomy. Members of the political and permanent executives work closely together at all stages of policy development and implementation. To succeed in their jobs, senior public servants (e.g., deputy ministers and the staff of central agencies) must be aware of, and sensitive to, the political incentives under which Cabinet members operate—especially, but not exclusively, the overriding importance of protecting the prime minister. At the same time, the political masters must be conscious of the legal, fiscal, and practical constraints on the permanent executive. Each is therefore intricately dependent on the other. Each must nevertheless keep the traditional distinction between their functions in mind, for it has considerable normative value. When politics intrudes too deeply into the permanent executive, as it may have done in the sponsorship program, the results can be troubling.

CENTRAL AGENCIES AND LINE DEPARTMENTS

The permanent executive, or administrative state, is generally divided into two sectors: central agencies and line departments, although the Department of Finance includes elements of both.

Line departments are large service-delivery organizations with a limited jurisdiction, typically in one broad area of government policy such as agriculture, health, or transportation. A cabinet minister heads each, although ministers do not have the time or the expertise to actually run their departments. The real head of the department is the deputy minister, who is not a politician, but the senior public servant responsible for the policy and administrative activities of the department.

Central agencies are small in size but powerful in jurisdiction. Their responsibilities cut across the functional areas of government because they focus on coordinating policy, not on delivering services. Because of their distinct responsibilities, central agency personnel are different from those in line departments. The staff of central agencies, sometimes called "superbureaucrats," are less likely to be career public servants and more likely to move from one agency to another. They tend to be more highly educated than their counterparts in the line departments and often have considerable career experience outside the bureaucracy (e.g., in business or academia).

Central Agencies

The four key central agencies are the Privy Council Office (PCO), the Prime Minister's Office (PMO), the Department of Finance, and the Treasury Board Secretariat (TBS). Although the Department of Finance appears to be a line department, it is actually a central agency: it coordinates the annual budget process, which determines the policy priorities of other departments. Because of its importance to all government operations, we will discuss the budget in some detail later in this chapter.

The Privy Council Office

The senior officials of the PCO are at the heart of the federal decision-making process and wield considerable policy and political influence. As we have seen, the clerk of the Privy Council is the most senior public servant in the federal government. The clerk's responsibilities are threefold:

1. As the prime minister's deputy minister, the clerk provides advice and support to the prime minister on a full range of responsibilities, including management of the federation.
2. As the secretary to the Cabinet, the clerk provides support and advice to the ministry as a whole and oversees policy and secretariat support to Cabinet and Cabinet committees.
3. As the head of the public service, the clerk is responsible for the quality of expert, professional, nonpartisan advice and service provided by the public service to the prime minister, the ministry, and all Canadians.

As we will see later in this chapter, the PCO is directly involved at every stage of the government's legislative planning. It is also responsible for the regulatory policy of the federal government and for intergovernmental affairs. It is staffed by the most experienced public servants in Ottawa, many of whom are posted to the PCO for short periods before returning to their line departments. Although its activities attract little public attention, the PCO is at the heart of power in both the political and permanent executives.

The PCO provides support to the prime minister and the ministers within his or her portfolio, the president of the Queen's Privy Council for Canada, the minister of intergovernmental affairs, the leader of the government in the House of Commons, the minister for democratic reform, and the leader of the government in the Senate. The basic organizational structures of the PCO are secretariats. Each is directed by an assistant secretary to the Cabinet, except intergovernmental affairs, which is led by a deputy minister. The seven secretariats are as follows:

- Intergovernmental Affairs
- Legislation and House Planning/Counsel
- Machinery of Government
- Regulatory Affairs and Orders in Council
- Security and Intelligence
- Senior Personnel and Special Projects
- Social Development Policy

Through the work of its secretariats, the PCO as a whole oversees the entire range of government activities.[1]

Although the distinction between logistical support and policy advice—in effect, between administration and politics—is clear in principle, in practice the two are intertwined. The clerk of the Privy Council is responsible to the prime minister for both the smooth running of the cabinet system and the quality of the government's legislation. Because the clerk has the authority to promote or demote public servants and answers only to the prime minister, the importance of the PCO in both the political and permanent executives cannot be overstated.

The Prime Minister's Office

Unlike the PCO, which is staffed entirely by career public servants, the Prime Minister's Office is primarily a political and partisan body. Its size and structure are entirely at the discretion of the incumbent prime minister. When Pierre Trudeau became prime minister in 1968, he inherited a small PMO that was little more than an administrative and correspondence unit. By the time he left office in 1984 he had expanded the PMO to include policy analysts, regional desks, and political advisers. Trudeau envisioned his office as a counterweight to the policy advice of the PCO and the line departments, and as a centre for planning and coordination within the federal government.[2] Although its success in meeting these goals was mixed, no subsequent prime minister has completely reversed Trudeau's expansion of the PMO. The creation of a central agency to provide independent partisan and political advice reduced the influence of the government caucus, while reinforcing the already considerable power of the prime minister over the operations of the executive branch.

The tasks of today's PMO are threefold:

1. The administrative section supports the nonpartisan work of the prime minister as the head of government. It is responsible for travel, scheduling, correspondence, and other administrative matters.
2. The legislative staff supports the prime minister in his or her role as leader of the government in the House of Commons. The legislative assistant prepares the prime minister for the daily question period when the House is sitting, monitors the news to identify likely avenues of opposition attack, coordinates the government's overall question period strategy (with the staff of the government leader in the Commons), and suggests suitable answers to all possible questions. Where necessary, the legislative assistant prepares background information for the prime minister to take to the House.
3. The political staff assists the prime minister in his or her role as leader of the governing party. They brief the prime minister about the political implications of current issues, handle his or her constituency work, and keep him or her in touch with the Cabinet and the party.

To be effective, the PMO must work closely with the PCO. The latter controls the information on which the prime minister's effectiveness as head of government depends, while the former is responsible for advising the prime minister on a variety of matters including the government's main priorities and its political strategies and tactics, including the political dimensions of the government's policy initiatives. As discussed at the beginning of this chapter, the normative distinction between political decision-making and administration is not always clear in practice. The relationship between the PMO and PCO illustrates the difficulty of clearly drawing a line between the two approaches. A PCO official who lacks political sensitivity will find his or her policy advice ignored, however sound his or her grasp of the issues and the process. On the other side, a PMO official who does not understand how the federal government works is of little value to the prime minister.

The Department of Finance

Finance occupies a unique position among the departments of the federal government. On the one hand, it is a line department with responsibility for a particular policy portfolio. Its policy experts monitor developments in the Canadian and global economies and advise the government on appropriate responses to current economic trends. Finance also manages particular programs and services; for example, its Federal–Provincial Relations and Social Policy branch delivers the Canada Health Transfer, Canada Social Transfer, and equalization payments to the provinces. In this sense, it resembles Agriculture and Health Canada. On the other hand, the Department of Finance operates as a central agency with overall responsibility to coordinate fiscal policy. In that role, it prepares the annual federal budget, which determines the spending priorities of all other departments.

Usually in February of each year, the finance minister presents the federal budget to the House of Commons. The budget speech is the culmination of months of effort, beginning in October when the Department of Finance releases budget consultation papers to the public and the minister makes an "economic statement" to the Commons Standing Committee on Finance. The committee holds public hearings to consult with interest groups and individuals, while the minister seeks input from the business and financial communities. Traditionally, the budget process has been wrapped in a thick blanket of secrecy. Leaks that might provide an economic advantage to certain groups—for example, the banking sector—are to be avoided at all costs. As finance minister, Paul Martin ended this tradition, preferring instead to consult widely and to build up political support for the budget before its formal introduction in the House. The Conservative government's finance minister, James Flaherty, appears to be content to follow a similar, although slightly more traditional, approach. However, after only one attempt, it is too early to tell exactly which strategy the new government will adopt in the longer term, especially if it gets the opportunity to govern with a majority.

As the budget takes shape, the Cabinet and its committees evaluate the proposed spending and revenue targets. Finance officials and the PCO's liaison secretariats advise ministers about the strategic and economic implications of the draft budget and its spending targets for each department. After extensive economic and political analysis, the minister delivers the budget speech. His officials keep a close eye on its fiscal impact and prepare to make any necessary adjustments to their overall revenue and spending plans.

The Treasury Board Secretariat

While the Department of Finance sets the broad outlines of economic and fiscal policy, the Treasury Board Secretariat oversees the detailed spending estimates tabled in the House a few weeks after the budget is presented. It works closely with the Department of Finance during the budget process to set expenditure targets and advises Cabinet committees about possible reallocations of funding. In fact, until the 1930s, the Treasury Board was part of the finance department, and today the two agencies still share personnel and administrative resources. The Treasury Board is also responsible for estimating the likely cost of new policy or program initiatives. In setting expenditure targets for individual departments and programs, the Treasury Board relies on the business plans submitted by deputy ministers. Once the budget and the detailed estimates have been submitted to the House, the Treasury Board monitors departmental spending and keeps the PCO informed of any problems. As of 2006, the Treasury Board has adopted a new internal audit policy that supports stronger internal auditing across all government departments.

The TBS is also the formal employer and general manager of the public service. It works with the Public Service Commission (PSC)—an arm's-length agency that reports to Parliament—to ensure that public servants are properly recruited and trained, including training through the Canadian School of Public Service. It is responsible for the Office of the Registrar of Lobbyists and the Public Service Human Resource Management Agency. Together, the TBS and the PSC establish broad policy guidelines for the public service, which are implemented by the administrative branches within the various departments and agencies of the federal government.

In November of 2003, Parliament passed the Public Service Modernization Act. As of December 31, 2005, it was fully implemented through a variety of subsequent pieces of legislation, including the Public Service Employment Act. The overall purpose of this body of legislation is to implement the federal government's broader agenda to modernize the national public service.[3]

■ Line Departments

Each line department of the federal government is responsible for policy and programs in a particular field, such as transport, agriculture, or human resources development. Traditionally, a strict hierarchy prevails within each department. The deputy minister is at the top, followed by a handful of assistant deputy ministers and increasingly larger numbers of people in the lower levels. This hierarchical structure is supposed to facilitate a unity of command in which each bureaucrat has one person to whom he or she is directly answerable. Tasks within the organization are fragmented to facilitate an efficient division of labour. Recruitment or selection to the organization, and promotion within it, are based on merit.

Most of the public servants who work in each department occupy either *line positions* or *staff positions*. Line employees are linked directly to the rest of the permanent executive by the PCO, to which they report. Staff employees deliver programs and services to the public and manage the internal operations of the department. In effect, line employees participate in making the policies that the staff employees implement.

In principle, each line department limits its activities to those matters that fall within its specialized jurisdiction. Accountability to Parliament is ensured by the appointment of a political head or minister. While each department focuses on a specific area, efficient government requires that policy and administration be coordinated to avoid contradiction and duplication. In theory, that coordination is provided by the Cabinet. Civil servants are nonpartisan professionals who implement the policy goals set for them by their political masters. Moreover, to secure their independence and impartiality, civil servants, like judges, are granted security of tenure.

FINANCING THE FEDERAL GOVERNMENT

In the summer of 2006, Prime Minister Stephen Harper met with the other leaders of the G8 (U.S.A., U.K., France, Germany, Italy, Japan, and Russia[4]) in Saint Petersburg, Russia. Harper led the only G8 government that did not run a budgetary deficit that year. In fact, it is not an overstatement to suggest that Canada's federal government finances were the envy of the G8. This represents a remarkable turnaround in the federal fiscal position over the past decade.

Only 10 years earlier, the Canadian government was in the midst of a fiscal crisis. In the 1995–1996 budget the federal government planned to run a deficit of almost $30 billion while spending a total of $130.6 billion. Furthermore, given that this represented the twenty-sixth consecutive federal deficit, paying the interest on the accumulated debt of almost $574 billion meant that public debt charges were the largest single budgetary expense, totaling $47 billion and representing almost 36 percent of all federal government spending. In other words, over one-third of every tax dollar Canadians sent to the federal government that year was going to pay the interest— not the principle, but the interest—on money that was borrowed and spent in previous years. With most provincial governments in similar, although not as severe, financial shape, only Italy had a worse debt problem than Canada when measured as a percentage of gross domestic product (GDP).

In the short span of the next 10 years, Canada moved from being one of the most indebted countries to being one of the least, at least when debt is expressed as a percentage of GDP (see Canada by the Numbers 7.1). Throughout this section, much use will be made of gross domestic product measures. Simply put, the GDP measures the total economic output of a country. Although not perfect (no measures are), expressing deficits, surpluses, and debt in terms of percent of GDP provides us with a more accurate representation of reality than does simply using the raw dollar figures. Comparisons with GDP take into consideration other important factors such as

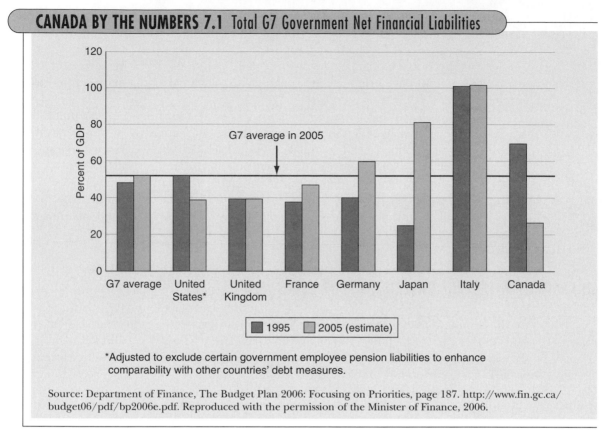

G7 average in 2005

Percent of GDP

1995   2005 (estimate)

*Adjusted to exclude certain government employee pension liabilities to enhance
comparability with other countries' debt measures.

Source: Department of Finance, The Budget Plan 2006: Focusing on Priorities, page 187. http://www.fin.gc.ca/
budget06/pdf/bp2006e.pdf. Reproduced with the permission of the Minister of Finance, 2006.

inflation, population increases, and economic expansion. For example, a $10 billion
government deficit in the 1970s was much larger than a $10 billion deficit in the 1990s,
relative to the overall size of the economy. Put another way, even though the federal
government was planning to spend over $231 billion in 2006–2007, that represented
only 13 percent of total GDP. When the federal government spent just under $161
billion in 1995–1996, fully $70 billion less than in 2006–2007, its expenditures repre-
sented a much larger proportion of the total economy in the mid-1990s (18.8 percent
of GDP) than did the apparently larger spending in 2006. Getting to know how to
interpret our government's fiscal picture in terms of GDP will help you tremendously
in understanding the overall changes in how much, or how little, your governments
are intervening in the economy.

A Brief History of Government Spending in Canada

As we have seen in a number of places throughout this text, Canadian governments
have a long history of economic intervention. One could argue that the country was
built by way of the federal government's altering of the natural economic structure
that had emerged in the pre-Confederation period. Macdonald's National Policy, in

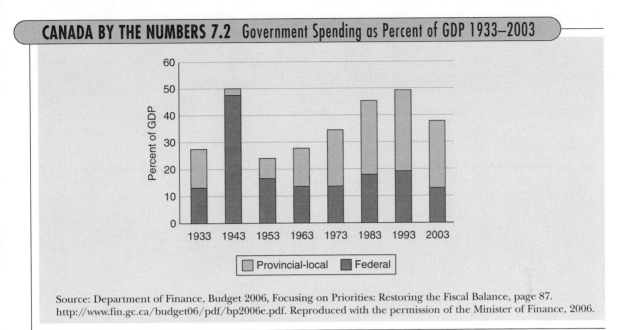

Source: Department of Finance, Budget 2006, Focusing on Priorities: Restoring the Fiscal Balance, page 87. http://www.fin.gc.ca/budget06/pdf/bp2006e.pdf. Reproduced with the permission of the Minister of Finance, 2006.

particular its tariff policies, broke down the existing north-south economic and trade patterns, replacing them with an east-west flow. When World War I and World War II required the mobilization of the private-sector economy for the war efforts, the federal government was not shy about exercising its emergency powers to intervene in Canadian's private economic activities. When building the welfare state required massive injections of public money into health care, education, and social services, the federal government stepped in to help the provinces fund these programs.

In spite of all this, Canadian governments' total share of economic activity has only rarely approached half of all GDP. Canada by the Numbers 7.2 illustrates the share of total GDP by Canadian federal and provincial governments over the past 70 years. Notice that during the height of World War II, when total government spending approached the 50 percent mark for the first time, the federal government was responsible for almost all of it. Less than a decade after the war ended, the federal government had dramatically reduced its spending while the provinces had increased theirs, but overall government spending was less than 25 percent of total GDP. In each successive decade until the most recent, as the welfare-state programs were built and enhanced, total government spending increased as a percentage of the GDP; by the mid-1990s it reached almost as great a share of the total economy as it had during World War II.

Most of the recent decrease in total government spending as a percent of GDP has been achieved by the relative decrease in federal spending, although provincial spending has also decreased over the past 15 years (see Canada by the Numbers 7.3). Although program spending (not including interest on the debts) of each level of government was accounting for about 19 percent of GDP in 1983, federal program

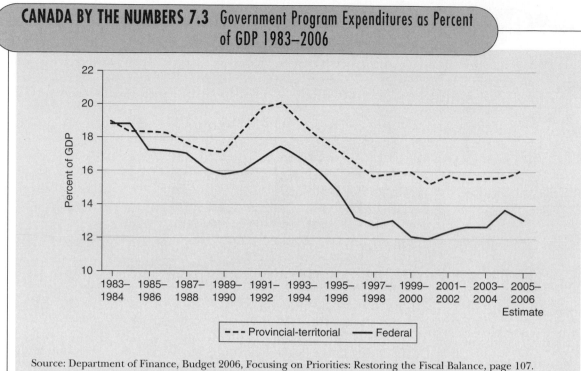

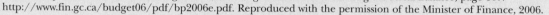

Source: Department of Finance, Budget 2006, Focusing on Priorities: Restoring the Fiscal Balance, page 107. http://www.fin.gc.ca/budget06/pdf/bp2006e.pdf. Reproduced with the permission of the Minister of Finance, 2006.

spending has declined to approximately 13 percent while provincial program spending has declined only to approximately 16 percent, less than half the decrease of federal spending.

Much of the reduction in program spending has been required because of the massive debts that the federal and provincial governments built up over a quarter century of deficit-financing their annual spending. Deficits occur when the government spends more in one fiscal year than it collects in revenue. Surpluses occur when revenue is greater than expenses. Canada by the Numbers 7.4 illustrates the pattern of federal government deficit financing throughout the 1970s and 1980s until its turnaround in the late-1990s. As the data indicate, the federal government ran 27 consecutive budget deficits between 1970 and 1997.

Each year that the government runs a deficit, it adds that amount to the accumulated debt (see Canadian Political Chronology 7.1). So, for example, the federal government began the 1970s with approximately $20.3 billion in accumulated debt. After running deficits of between $1 billion and $13 billion annually for 10 consecutive years, by 1979 the government had an accumulated debt of over $65 billion. Every year the government must pay interest on that debt. In 1970, interest on the federal public debt was only $1.9 billion per year. By the time Pierre Trudeau left office in 1984, despite having increased taxes in virtually every budget over his 16 years in office, the

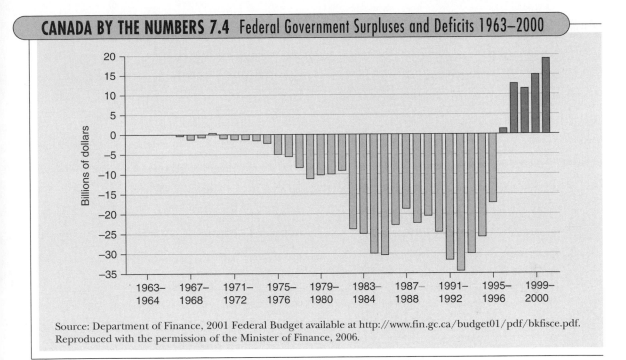

CANADA BY THE NUMBERS 7.4 Federal Government Surpluses and Deficits 1963–2000

Source: Department of Finance, 2001 Federal Budget available at http://www.fin.gc.ca/budget01/pdf/bkfisce.pdf.
Reproduced with the permission of the Minister of Finance, 2006.

deficit had expanded to $38.4 billion, the total debt was $208 billion, and interest payments for the year were $22.6 billion.

When Brian Mulroney became prime minister late in 1984, he vowed to address the government's fiscal problems. Although the Mulroney governments ran deficits throughout their nine years in office, hitting a record of $42 billion in 1993–1994, leading to a total debt of $508 billion before he left office, they did address many of the federal government's structural fiscal problems. The Mulroney Progressive Conservatives' combination of more moderate spending increases and continuing tax increases led to operating surpluses as early as 1988. Operating surpluses result when the government is collecting more in revenue than it is spending on programs. Despite the brief operating deficits caused by the recession of the early 1990s, the Mulroney government generally put Canada back on a more sound fiscal footing. However, despite the improvement the Mulroney governments made, they still ended up borrowing money every year to pay interest on the accumulated debt. This, of course, only added to the total debt and increased the amount of interest that was due in successive years.

The Jean Chrétien governments of the mid-1990s finished the job that had been started by the Mulroney governments. Benefiting tremendously from falling interest rates and cuts in transfers to the provinces, the Chrétien Liberals posted a $3.5 billion surplus in 1998, Canada's first surplus in almost 30 years. Still, the accumulated debt had reached almost $580 billion and interest payments for the 1997–1998 fiscal year were nearly $41 billion.

THE PERMANENT EXECUTIVE AND ADMINISTRATIVE STATE

FISCAL YEAR (ENDING 31 MARCH)	SURPLUS OR DEFICIT	OPERATING SURPLUS OR DEFICIT	GROSS DEBT CHARGES	NET PUBLIC DEBT
(in billions of dollars)				
1970–1971	−1.0	0.9	1.9	20.3
1971–1972	−1.8	0.3	2.1	22.1
1972–1973	−1.9	0.4	2.3	24.0
1973–1974	−2.2	0.4	2.6	26.2
1974–1975	−2.2	1.0	3.2	28.4
1975–1976	−6.2	−2.2	4.0	34.6
1976–1977	−6.2	−2.2	4.7	41.5
1977–1978	−10.9	−5.3	5.5	52.4
1978–1979	−13.0	−6.0	7.0	65.4
1979–1980	−12.0	−3.5	8.5	77.4
1980–1981	−14.6	−3.9	10.7	91.9
1981–1982	−15.7	−0.6	15.1	107.6
1982–1983	−29.0	−12.1	16.9	136.7
1983–1984	−32.9	−14.8	18.1	169.5
1984–1985	−38.4	−16.0	22.4	208.0
1985–1986	−34.6	−9.8	25.4	242.6
1986–1987	−30.7	−4.1	26.7	273.3
1987–1988	−27.8	1.2	29.0	301.1
1988–1989	−28.8	4.4	33.2	329.9
1989–1990	−28.9	9.9	38.8	358.8
1990–1991	−32.0	10.6	42.6	390.8
1991–1992	−34.4	6.8	41.2	425.2
1992–1993	−41.0	−2.2	38.8	466.2
1993–1994	−42.0	−4.0	38.0	508.2
1994–1995	−37.5	4.6	42.0	545.7
1995–1996	−28.6	18.3	46.9	574.3
1996–1997	−8.9	36.1	45.0	583.2
1997–1998	3.5	44.4	40.9	579.7
1998–1999	2.9	44.3	41.4	576.8
1999–2000	12.3	44.4	41.5	564.8
2000–2001	17.1	46.0	42.1	547.4

FISCAL YEAR (ENDING 31 MARCH)	SURPLUS OR DEFICIT	OPERATING SURPLUS OR DEFICIT	GROSS DEBT CHARGES	NET PUBLIC DEBT
2001–2002	8.2	46.5	39.3	517.7[a]
2002–2003	7.0	44.3	37.3	510.6
2003–2004	9.1	44.8	35.8	501.5
2004–2005	1.5	35.6	34.1	494.4[b]
2005–2006 Estimate	8.0	41.7	33.7	486.4
2006–2007 Estimate	3.6	38.3	34.8	483.4
2007–2008 Estimate	4.4	39.3	34.8	480.4

[a] Accounting changes led to new methods of reporting the federal debt.

[b] Data revised to reflect the impact of consolidating foundations.

Sources: Data for 1971–1999 from Jean Soucy and Marion G. Wrobel, *Federal Deficit: Changing Trends,* retrieved from Government of Canada Depository Services Program at http://dsp-psd.pwgsc.gc.ca/Collection-R/LoPBdP/CIR/887-e.htm# 1.%20Operating. Data for 2000–2008 from Department of Finance Canada, Federal Budgets, available at http://www.fin.gc.ca.

CANADA BY THE NUMBERS 7.5   Federal and Provincial Government Surpluses and Deficits as Percent of GDP 1983–2006

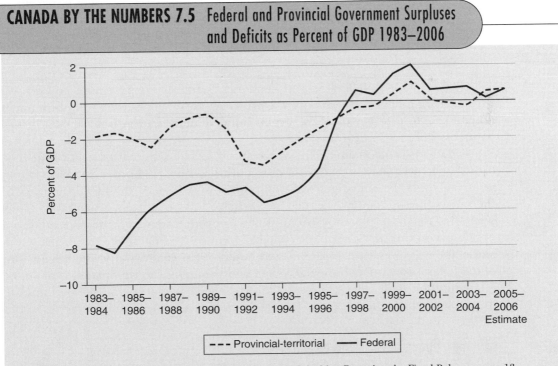

Source: Department of Finance, Budget 2006, Focusing on Priorities: Restoring the Fiscal Balance, page 13. http://www.fin.gc.ca/budget06/pdf/bp2006e.pdf. Reproduced with the permission of the Minister of Finance, 2006.

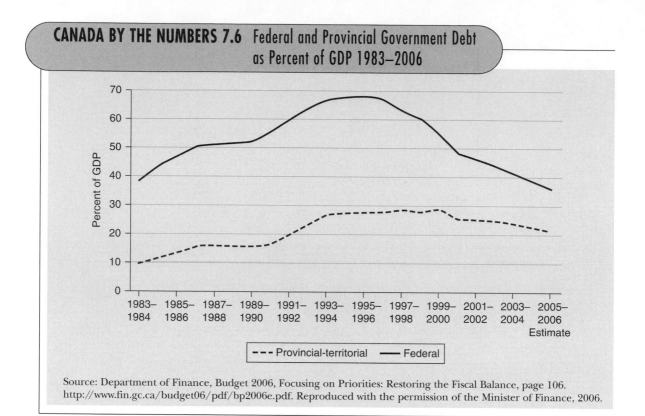

CANADA BY THE NUMBERS 7.6 Federal and Provincial Government Debt as Percent of GDP 1983–2006

Source: Department of Finance, Budget 2006, Focusing on Priorities: Restoring the Fiscal Balance, page 106. http://www.fin.gc.ca/budget06/pdf/bp2006e.pdf. Reproduced with the permission of the Minister of Finance, 2006.

Since 1998, the federal government has managed to post nine consecutive surplus budgets. For the most part, the provinces have followed suit with most much more likely to post balanced or surplus budgets than deficits (see Canada by the Numbers 7.5).

Canadians can certainly take some comfort in knowing that their governments, for the most part, have managed to put their fiscal houses in order and have begun what is going to be a multigenerational process of paying off the fiscal profligacy of the late-twentieth century.[5] So far, the progress has been quite remarkable. Since beginning to run surpluses in the late 1990s, the federal government has paid down, or eliminated through accounting changes, almost $100 billion in debt. As the population and economy have expanded and inflation has eaten away at the relative size of the federal government's debt, Canada's governments can legitimately claim to be reducing their total indebtedness to a much smaller percentage of the overall GDP than at any other time in nearly 30 years (see Canada by the Numbers 7.6).

The 2006–2007 Federal Budget

Budgets are the government's estimates for what it plans to raise in revenue and spend in expenditures for the upcoming fiscal year. They are, in a sense, the Department of

Finance's best guesses. If circumstances change, and they almost always do, governments can sometimes miss their revenue or expenditure targets. For example, if the government is estimating that the economy will expand by 3 percent of GDP, resulting in a certain amount of tax revenue, but the economy gets hit with a series of crises, expanding less than predicted, less tax revenue will be generated for the government. This will likely throw off the government's budget estimates. If the estimates are off by too much, the government may have to issue an "economic update" containing adjustments partway through the fiscal year. In extreme cases—such as those that the Trudeau government faced in the early 1980s—dramatic changes not anticipated by the government, or simply very bad forecasting, may force the government to issue a completely new budget partway through the year, but this is very rare. For the most part, the government lives with its estimates until the next budget year and makes the appropriate adjustments at that time.

Each February, when the budget is introduced into the House of Commons, not only is the government estimating its revenue and expenditures for the next fiscal year, it is doing so without knowing exactly what happened in the previous fiscal year. Because the federal government's fiscal year begins on April 1 and ends on March 31, a February budget for the next year comes before all the revenue and expenses have been counted for the current year. Governments have also become accustomed to predicting how much they will raise and spend a couple of years into the future (see Canada by the Numbers 7.7). These estimates are often the least accurate set of numbers, as many more unexpected events are likely to occur over a two- or three-year period than during a one-year period. Nevertheless, governments do the best they can, as it is to their advantage not to have their budget estimates too far off the mark. The budget represents the government's

CANADA BY THE NUMBERS 7.7 Federal Budget Estimates 2004–2008

	2004–2005	2005–2006	2006–2007	2007–2008
(in billions of dollars)				
Revenue	211.9	220.9	227.1	235.8
Expenses				
Public Debt Charges	34.1	33.7	34.8	34.8
Program Expenses	176.3	179.2	188.8	196.5
Total Expenses	210.5	212.9	223.6	231.4
Planned Debt Reduction	1.5	8.0	3.0	3.0
Surplus/Deficit	0	0	0.6	1.4

Source: Department of Finance Canada, *The Budget Plan 2006*. Available on-line at http://www.fin.gc.ca/budget06/bp/bpc4e.htm. Reproduced with the permission of the Minister of Finance, 2006.

THE PERMANENT EXECUTIVE AND ADMINISTRATIVE STATE

(in billions of dollars)	2004–2005	2005–2006	2006–2007	2007–2008	2007–08 AS % OF TOTAL
Tax Revenues					
Income Tax					
Personal Income Tax	98.5	103.0	109.3	115.5	49.0%
Corporate Income Tax	30.0	34.5	35.3	36.8	15.6%
Other Income Tax	3.6	4.6	4.4	4.2	1.8%
Total Income Tax	132.0	142.2	149.0	156.6	66.4%
Excise Taxes/Duties					
Goods and Services Tax	29.8	31.9	29.8	29.8	12.6%
Customs Import Duties	3.1	3.4	3.6	3.9	1.7%
Other Excise Taxes/Duties	10.0	10.0	10.0	10.1	4.3%
Total Excise Taxes/Duties	42.9	45.3	43.4	43.8	18.6%
Total Tax Revenues	174.9	187.5	192.4	200.4	85.0%
Employment Insurance Premium Revenues	17.3	16.9	16.1	16.4	7.0%
Other Revenues	19.7	16.5	18.6	19.0	8.1%
Total Budgetary Revenues (% GDP)	211.9 (16.4)	220.9 (16.1)	227.2 (15.7)	235.8 (15.5)	100.0%

FEDERAL GOVERNMENT SOURCES OF REVENUE 2007–2008 (PERCENT OF TOTAL)

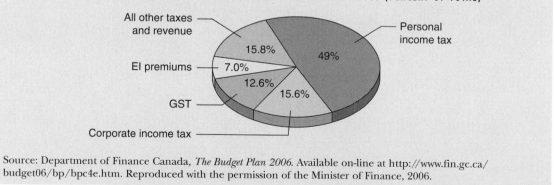

Source: Department of Finance Canada, *The Budget Plan 2006*. Available on-line at http://www.fin.gc.ca/budget06/bp/bpc4e.htm. Reproduced with the permission of the Minister of Finance, 2006.

most important piece of annual legislation, and a great deal of political credibility rides on the government being able to assess the economy and its own operations accurately enough to present a reasonably close estimation of its revenue and expenditures.

	2004–05	2005–06	2006–07	2007–08	2007–08 AS % OF TOTAL
Major Transfers to Persons					
Elderly Benefits	27.9	29.1	30.6	32.0	13.8%
Employment Insurance Benefits	14.7	14.4	14.6	15.2	6.6%
Children's Benefits	8.7	9.1	11.1	11.8	5.1%
Energy Cost Benefit		0.6			
Total Transfers to Persons	51.3	53.2	56.3	59.0	25.5%
Major Transfers to Other Levels of Government					
Federal Transfers in Support of Health and Other Programs	27.8	27.2	28.6	30.2	13.1%
Fiscal Arrangements	16.2	12.4	13.1	13.2	5.7%
Alternative Payments for Standing Programs	−2.7	−2.7	−2.9	−3.1	−1.3%
Early Learning and Child Care	0.7		0.65		
Canada's Cities and Communities		0.6	0.6	0.8	0.3%
Total Transfers to Other Levels of Government	42.0	37.5	40.1	41.1	17.8%
Direct Program Expenses	83.1	84.8	92.4	96.5	41.7%
Bill C-48		3620			
Total Program Expenses	176.3	179.2	188.8	196.5	85.0%
(% GDP)	(13.7)	(13.1)	(13.0)	(13.0)	
Debt Servicing Expenses	34.1	33.7	34.8	34.8	15.0%
(% GDP)	(2.6)	(2.5)	(2.4)	(2.3)	
Total Federal Government Expenditures	210.5	212.9	223.6	231.4	100.0%
(% GDP)	(16.3)	(15.6)	(15.4)	(15.2)	

FEDERAL GOVERNMENT EXPENDITURES 2007–2008 (PERCENT OF TOTAL)

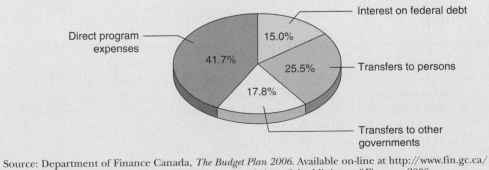

Source: Department of Finance Canada, *The Budget Plan 2006*. Available on-line at http://www.fin.gc.ca/budget06/bp/bpc4e.htm. Reproduced with the permission of the Minister of Finance, 2006.

In analyzing the federal government's estimates of its revenue over the four-year period covered by the data in the Harper government's 2006 budget, a number of interesting items are worth mentioning (see Canada by the Numbers 7.8). Notice that although the government is planning on raising almost $25 billion more revenue in 2007–2008 than it did in 2004–2005, the $235.8 billion in 2007–2008 is estimated to be a smaller percentage of the total GDP (15.5 percent) than was the $211.9 billion it raised in 2004–2005 (16.4 percent). That is, despite raising much more revenue in the last year of its 2006 projections, the federal government plans to take less of a percentage of the total economic pie year-over-year for the next four fiscal periods.

Also notice that the largest single source of government revenue, by far, is the personal income tax. It will account for 49 percent of all government revenue in 2007–2008, up from 46.5 percent in 2004–2005. Also note that, despite how much Canadians loath the GST, it will account for a relatively small 12.6 percent of total government revenue in 2007–2008, down from a still relatively low 14 percent in 2004–2005.

When considering federal government expenditures, note that interest on the public debt will account for 15 percent of all expenditures, down considerably from the 36 percent in the mid-1990s, but still more than all the money the federal government sends to the provinces in support of health care and other social programs (see Canada by the Numbers 7.9). Also note that over one-quarter of the federal government's expenditures (25.5 percent) is for direct transfers to individual Canadians though such things as employment insurance benefits and payments in support of the young and the old.

Overall, the federal government's fiscal situation is again healthy, although it has been helped considerably by the rapidly expanding economy and lower interest rates. And despite interest on the federal debt still representing one of the largest single annual expenditures, the situation has dramatically improved over the past decade, leading to increasing demands from many sectors, including provincial governments, for the federal government to again increase its funding for a variety of public programs and government services.

THE FEDERAL PUBLIC SERVICE

The institutional culture of the public service is based on at least three key principles:
1. Public servants must be politically neutral. They cannot allow their personal opinions about a given policy or government to affect their judgment.
2. Public servants know that their chances for promotion depend on their adherence to the rules and standards laid down by the clerk of the PCO—not on their obedience to the dictates of their ministers.
3. Public servants control the knowledge and information on which policy-making and governance depend.

The second and third principles reduce the power of the Cabinet over the permanent executive, while effectively enhancing the prime minister's dominance over his ministers. While the political executive sets the priorities of the government and approves the broad outlines of proposed policy, the permanent executive takes care of day-to-day management, determines the details, and implements the government's legislative program.

Because of the complexity and sheer size of most ministries, cabinet ministers no longer obey the constitutional convention of individual responsibility. In other words, they do not resign from the Cabinet because of errors made by their departments. But if the ministers are no longer accountable, and civil servants are not formally accountable, does not a considerable accountability gap exist within government institutions? The answer is somewhat complex. Historically, ministers accepted the blame when things went wrong in their portfolios because they were perceived to be the political masters of their departments. More recently, as ministers' limited roles in departmental administration have become public knowledge, deputy ministers have found themselves answering to parliamentary committees—and occasionally to the media—for mistakes and problems in their departments.

Over the past 50 years, the traditional distinction between the minister's political role and the deputy minister's administrative role has become patently unrealistic.[6] Traditionally, only the minister was accountable to Parliament. But ministers are increasingly acknowledged to be dependent on public servants, for policy advice as well as for administrative assistance. It is reasonable to argue that as relative novices, politicians, unlike senior executives of major corporations, cannot be expected to keep track of every decision made in a huge and complex organization. Acknowledgment of this reality often leads some to argue that ministers should not take the fall for errors made by public servants. While this new political reality may serve the political masters well, it sends a chilling mixed message to the public service. Essentially, public servants are being told to take risks in making innovative improvements in their departments. But if something goes wrong, they, and not the minister, will be held to account. Understandably, this makes many senior public servants reluctant to effectively implement many major program-reform initiatives.

▮ Federal Public-Service Employment

As the scope and intensity of government activity grew, particularly after World War II, the federal public service mushroomed. In 1929, Ottawa had 42 790 civil servants on the payroll. The single largest departments at the time were the post office (10 871), national revenue (5771), and marine and fisheries (4283). There were more convicts in Canadian penitentiaries than there were civil-service employees in most federal government departments.[7] By 1975 the federal government employed 273 000 civil servants, more than six times the 1929 number. Over the past quarter-century, and particularly in the 1990s, that growth was partially reversed. At the federal level, close to 50 000

CANADA BY THE NUMBERS 7.10   Public-Sector Employment in Canada 2005

CATEGORY	NUMBER EMPLOYED	PERCENT OF TOTAL GOVERNMENT EMPLOYMENT	PERCENT OF TOTAL PUBLIC-SECTOR EMPLOYMENT
Governments			
Federal General Government (Includes Military)	370 606	13.6%	12.4%
Provincial and Territorial General Government	346 109	12.7%	11.6%
Health and Social Service Institutions, Provincial and Territorial	755 715	27.8%	25.4%
Universities, Colleges, Vocational and Trade Institutions, Provincial and Territorial	310 754	11.4%	10.4%
Local General Government	380 285	14.0%	12.8%
Local School Boards	552 796	20.4%	18.6%
Total Governments	2 716 265	100.0%	91.2%
Government Business Enterprises			
Federal Government Business Enterprises	87 502		2.9%
Provincial and Territorial Government Business Enterprises	121 243		4.1%
Local Government Business Enterprises	54 717		1.8%
Total Government Business Enterprises	263 462		8.8%
Total Public-Sector Employment	2 979 727		100.0%

PUBLIC-SECTOR EMPLOYMENT IN CANADA (INCLUDING GOVERNMENT ENTERPRISES) 2005

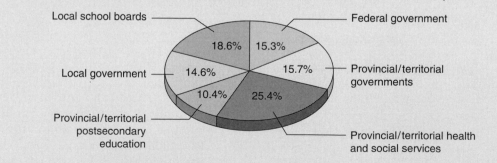

Source: Statistics Canada, http://www40.statcan.ca/l01/cst01/govt54a.htm. Adapted from the Statistics Canada CANSIM table 183-0002.

employees left the public service between 1995 and 1998 as part of the program review initiated by the finance department. Between 1996 and 1997 alone, there was a net drop of 13 581 or 6.5 percent to a total of 194 396. However, that figure understates the full scope of federal government employment. Including members of the RCMP and the military, and those who work in Crown corporations and other government enterprises, the federal executive branch employment stood at 458 108 in 2005.

Despite the size of the federal government, the data indicate that its total employment is only about as large as that of either the provincial/territorial governments or of Canada's local governments. When provincial institutions such as public health care, postsecondary education, and school boards are taken into consideration, total provincial government and related services employment (70.1 percent) dwarfs that of either the federal (15.3 percent) or local (14.6 percent) governments (see Canada by the Numbers 7.10).

The relative downsizing of the permanent executive that has occurred in conjunction with the federal government's accounting for less of the total GDP can be traced to two primary factors. First, cutbacks in federal spending since the 1980s have forced departments to cut programs and lay off the staff employees who administered them. Second, the influence of the new public management (NPM) model in government circles transformed the traditional approach to public administration. Whereas postwar governments were expected to provide services directly to the public (which implies a large permanent coterie of public servants), today the public sector is regarded as a strategic partner that establishes policy frameworks for others to follow. Some services and programs have been contracted out to the private sector, which bears many of the costs associated with employment. In this new, streamlined permanent executive, public servants are expected to perform only those functions that the private sector cannot carry out, such as policy-making, coordination, and financial reporting.

Services and Programs

Most of the high-profile and costly government programs—health care, social assistance, and education—are delivered by the provinces, with financial assistance from Ottawa. However, the federal line departments still oversee a wide range of programs and services to Canadians, as the following examples attest:

- Public Safety and Emergency Preparedness Canada is responsible for, among other things, Corrections Canada (which operates the federal prison system) and the RCMP.
- Agriculture and Agri-Food Canada provides financial assistance to farmers who suffer poor yields or declining prices for their harvests.
- Health Canada tests and licenses new drugs and medical devices before they reach the market.
- Human Resources and Social Development Canada provides funding for local job-creation projects and community training initiatives. It also manages the Employment Insurance and Canada Student Loans Programs.

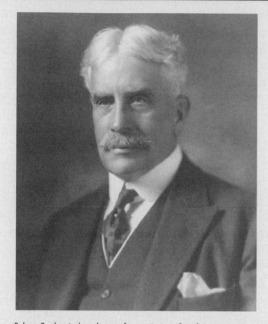

Robert Borden is best known for serving as Canadian prime minister during World War I, for his Union government, the conscription crisis, and his pursuit for an independent voice for Canada in British Empire international affairs. He is less well known for his other important work in establishing a professional civil service in Canada, first through his early campaign promises, some of which the Liberals "borrowed" while they were in office, and for his significant 1918 reforms, the date at which Canadian political historians begin their chronologies of the professional public service in Canada. He was also the prime minister who first granted women the right to vote in federal elections. His portrait adorns the Canadian $100 bill. (Dupras & Colas/Library and Archives Canada/C-000694)

Born: 1854, Grand Pré, Nova Scotia

Died: 1937, Ottawa, Ontario

Education: Acacia Villa Academy, Horton, Nova Scotia (no formal college or university education)

Professions: Teacher, lawyer (called to Nova Scotia Bar in 1878), businessman

Political Career:

MP
1896–1904, 1908–1917 Halifax, Nova Scotia
1905–1908 Carleton, Ontario
1917–1920 King's County, Nova Scotia

Leader
1901–1920 Conservative Party
1917–1920 Union Government (a coalition of pro-conscription Liberals and Conservatives)

Prime Minister
1911–1920

Other Ministries
1911–1917 President of the Privy Council
1912–1920 External Affairs

Political Career Highlights
1901–1911 Leader of the Opposition
1911 Majority election victory as Conservative leader
1914–1918 Led Canada as prime minister throughout First World War
1914 War Measures Act
1917 Income War Tax Act
1917 Military Service Act
1917 Wartime Elections Act
1917 Principal author of Resolution IX of the 1917 Imperial War Conference
1917 Majority election victory as Union government leader
1918 Franchise extended to women
1918 Civil Service Act
1919 Leader of Canadian delegation at the Paris Peace Conference

Source: *First Among Equals: The Prime Minister in Canadian Life and Politics* (Ottawa: Library and Archives Canada), available on-line at http://www.collectionscanada.ca/primeministers/.

- Foreign Affairs and International Trade Canada issues passports to citizens who wish to travel abroad and assists Canadian exporters in reaching foreign markets.
- National Defence runs the Canadian military.

Many of these programs and services are delivered by regional offices, some—such as the Summer Career Placements Program—by temporary employees, while most are delivered by full-time public servants. Still other programs are delivered by private-sector companies and managed by public servants. For example, student loans are obtained from chartered banks, subject to the guidelines and regulations set by the federal government. Private-sector partnerships and alternative service delivery are discussed in more detail in "The Evolving Executive" later in this chapter.

◼ Regulations

When Parliament approves a government bill, it delegates to the executive the power to make any regulations necessary for its implementation. This delegated law-making authority should not be overly broad, and it should not usurp Parliament's right to amend the details of legislation. Most regulations are made by public servants in the line departments and central agencies, subject to the approval of the governor in council (i.e., the Cabinet). New legislation should contain the text of the regulations that will be required to put it into effect, and regulations made under existing legislation cannot exceed the authority granted by the relevant law. All new regulations must be examined by legal counsel in the justice department and the PCO, they must be registered with the Orders in Council Division of the PCO for review by the Special Committee of Council, and they must be published in the weekly *Canada Gazette*.

The criteria for approving or rejecting draft regulations are set out in the regulatory policy of the Government of Canada:

- Regulatory authorities must demonstrate both that a problem or risk exists and that federal intervention is justified.
- All possible alternative means—whether regulatory or nonregulatory—of addressing the problem or risk have been considered.
- Stakeholders—industry, labour, consumer groups, professional organizations, other governments, and interested individuals—have been consulted on all phases of the identification of problems and the development of the regulatory solution.
- Intergovernmental agreements must be respected and opportunities for intergovernmental coordination exploited.
- Benefits and costs of the regulatory interventions under consideration have been assessed, the benefits justify the costs, and limited government resources are used where they will do the most good.
- Adverse impacts on the economy must be minimized.
- Systems are in place to manage regulatory resources effectively.
- Compliance and, when appropriate, enforcement policies must be implemented.
- The regulators have the resources for monitoring compliance and enforcing the regulations.[8]

Once a regulation has been published in the *Canada Gazette,* it is tabled with the Standing Joint Committee on Statutory Instruments. While this group of MPs and senators has the formal power to review any and all orders-in-council, its limited resources prevent it from undertaking a detailed examination of more than a quarter of them. In a sense, therefore, Parliament itself colludes in the shift of law-making power from the legislative branch to the executive.

Although the purpose of the regulatory policy is to minimize government interference in economic and social activity, Canada remains a highly regulated society. In addition to the regulations enforced by government departments, there are several regulatory agencies—statutory bodies that have the responsibility for regulating a vast array of economic, cultural, environmental, or social activity. For example, what we watch on television and hear on the radio is determined by broadcast regulations established by the Canadian Radio-television and Telecommunications Commission. Marketing boards set the prices and production quantities of chickens, eggs, turkeys, milk, and a host of other farm and agricultural products. The medicines we take, the vehicles we drive, and even our food and water are subject to government standards and regulations.

Increasingly, regulation is being constrained by international agreements. The North American Free Trade Agreement, for example, forces Canadian authorities to treat American and Mexican companies exactly as they would Canadian companies—thereby eliminating a host of discriminatory regulations that used to protect Canadian industries. Agricultural marketing boards feel pressure to open access to foreign suppliers, and even protections for cultural institutions are hedged and constrained. The World Trade Organization, a host of United Nations bodies, and the Multilateral Agreement on Investment are examples of international bodies and agreements that (with Canadian participation and support) gradually limit the old practices of regulation.

Technological changes, globalization, and the prominence of more business-oriented governments in the 1980s all contributed to the sense that the last decade has been one of significant deregulation. In specific sectors, such as transport, this perception is accurate. Transport Canada—the federal department responsible for aviation, railways, and marine traffic—houses a Programs and Divestiture Branch whose mandate includes "the transfer of ports, harbours, and airports to communities and other interests."[9] The federal government set up a nonprofit corporation, NAV CANADA, to take over its air-traffic control services. Similarly, the Economic Development and Corporate Finance Branch of the Department of Finance houses a Privatization, Crown Corporations, and Defence Unit, the responsibilities of which include "the disposition of the Government's Crown commercial holdings."[10]

However, the recent reduction of direct regulation by the federal government does not imply the end of regulation altogether. Some federal regulatory activities have been shifted upward to international agreements such as NAFTA and international agencies such as the World Trade Organization. Others have moved downward, to the provincial governments. In still other cases, regulatory activities that once were undertaken by government departments have been shifted to private, noncommercial agencies. At the beginning of the twenty-first century, it is safe to say that government is not out of the regulatory game; it is simply changing the rules and strategies.

THE POLITICAL AND PERMANENT EXECUTIVES IN THE POLICY-MAKING PROCESS

Laws proposed by the executive branch fall into three categories:
1. routine (e.g., the annual federal budget)
2. improving (amendments to existing legislation to update it or to make it more effective)
3. innovatory (new laws or policies designed to achieve a particular purpose)

When a line department proposes a bill, it must justify the addition of new legislation to the existing body of federal law. If the purpose of the bill can be achieved in a more efficient way—for example, by issuing new regulations under existing delegated authority—the PCO will advise against proceeding with the bill.

Most bills are initiated by the policy branch within a particular line department. Immediately after the speech from the throne at the beginning of a new session of Parliament, the assistant secretary to the Cabinet for legislation and House planning sends a letter to all deputy ministers requesting a list of bill proposals. Under the procedures introduced in December 2003, the first stage is the preparation of a two-page issue brief for review by the Operations Committee of Cabinet. Simply put, this document must describe the policy issue to be addressed. It also identifies "strategic considerations," including possible environmental, intergovernmental, regional, or international implications of accepting or rejecting the proposed policy. It summarizes the views of the government caucus and Parliament as a whole and describes the funding implications, the way in which the minister expects to proceed, and expected outcomes. It further suggests "communications considerations" (e.g., the timing of the proposal in relation to future federal-provincial or international meetings).[11] The required format for the issue brief demonstrates the heightened importance of international and provincial governments in national policy-making, as well as the close connection between policy and politics. Its brevity reflects the federal government's goal to speed up decision-making at the Cabinet level.

The Operations Committee determines whether the proposed policy will go ahead. Together with the Priorities and Planning Committee, it decides which of the approved issue briefs should be turned into proposed legislation during the upcoming or current parliamentary session. The House of Commons operates on a tight schedule. Relatively few bills can be debated, scrutinized, and passed within a given session of Parliament (which normally lasts for about two years). Therefore, Cabinet must be careful not to overload Parliament; it must decide which bills to introduce early in the session, when the chances of passage are greatest. In general, high-priority items are those that implement key policy promises in the throne speech, the annual budget, or the party platform; those required by international or federal-provincial agreements; or those that address pressing public issues, such as criminal justice or economic conditions.

When a department is notified that the Cabinet has given priority to its issue brief, the experts in its policy branch prepare a memorandum to Cabinet (MC). The MC is designed to secure "policy approval and an authorization for the Legislation Section of the Department of Justice to draft the bill."[12] Ideally, a department should follow four steps in preparing an MC:

1. Analyze the policy issue to be addressed, and compare alternative solutions to the one proposed in the bill.
2. Consult its client groups, other departments, and other governments that may be affected by the bill.
3. Determine and justify the impact of the proposed bill.
4. Calculate the resources required to implement the bill.[13]

As of December 2003, each MC must be accompanied by the written approval of the departmental comptroller and the comptroller-general of Canada. These positions were established by the Martin government as a way to more effectively control, oversee, and monitor government operations. Prime Minister Martin also revamped the rules governing MCs. He introduced three new formats, replacing the one-size-fits-all approach of past prime ministers. The first and shortest format is reserved for policy issues that are considered to be noncontroversial. It consists of a five-page ministerial recommendation (MR), which sets out the sponsoring department's proposed course of action on a particular issue and analyzes it from several perspectives: political, practical, legal, regional, indicators of success, cost, and public reaction.[14] The MR is a Cabinet document, subject to strict secrecy.

The second format, which applies to most MCs, supplements the MR with a six-page background/analysis document. This should be written in such a way that, if it eventually becomes public, it would not compromise Cabinet confidentiality. It explains why the minister believes that the proposed policy is necessary, and discusses its possible effects on other federal policies and on the public at large. The third format is reserved for policies that are likely to be subjected to extensive public debate and consultation beyond government. The MR is supplemented with a discussion paper, which can be as long as necessary; it is expected to set out genuine alternatives that will set the agenda for discussions with stakeholders.

The draft MC, with or without supporting documents, is submitted by the sponsoring department to the PCO for review. If it meets with the approval of the PCO, it goes to both the Operations Committee and the appropriate policy committee of Cabinet. As we have seen, the full Cabinet almost always accepts Cabinet committee decisions. After Cabinet has accepted the MC, it is sent to the Department of Justice for drafting in proper legislative form.

The Legislation Section at the Department of Justice must follow several guidelines when drafting bills for Parliament. First, the draft bill must be constitutional. Second, it must be consistent with both the civil law of Quebec and the common-law system in the other provinces. Third, it must be drafted simultaneously in both English and French; because both official-language versions are equally authoritative, "it is not acceptable for one version to be a mere translation of the other."[15] Once drafted, most government bills include three main elements:

1. the preamble, which sets out the purpose of the bill (these sections are not enforceable)
2. the substance of the legislation, which consists either of amendments to existing laws or new legislative provisions
3. schedules containing draft regulations and any other information required to put the substance of the bill into effect

When the drafting is complete, the bill is sent to the Legislation and House Planning Secretariat of the PCO. This secretariat distributes the bill to the government leader in the House of Commons and to the other members of the Operations Committee. If it meets with their approval, the bill returns to the relevant policy committee of Cabinet where the government leader receives formal authority to introduce the bill into either the House of Commons or the Senate. Once authority has been granted, the government leader and the sponsoring minister sign off on the bill and prepare to introduce it in Parliament. The assistant secretary to the Cabinet for legislation and House planning notifies the clerk of the House or Senate that the bill will be introduced, and the government leader meets with the other House leaders in the Commons to work out the legislative timetable. Once scheduled, the bill proceeds through Parliament based on the process described in the previous chapter.

THE EVOLVING EXECUTIVE

As we have seen, the creation of Canada's welfare state after World War II vastly increased both the federal and provincial public sectors. Since the 1970s, fiscal constraints, the growing debt burden, and the eventual recognition that governments cannot continually deficit-finance program expenditures led successive federal governments to downsize the permanent executive through cutbacks, deregulation, and privatization.

The Mulroney government began the process by focusing on deregulation and privatization. The Chrétien administration continued some of these activities but also included significant cutbacks. We saw the cumulative effects of these initiatives in the overall smaller percentage of GDP that the federal (and provincial) governments now occupy. Once the federal government began running surpluses, accountability became as important a concern as were fiscal matters. As part of its first major legislative initiative, the Harper government attempted to address some of the accountability issues in its first piece of legislation, the Accountability Act (Bill C-2), parts of which are described below.

■ Changing Approaches to Fiscal Management

The new public management model seeks to shift program and service delivery from the public to the private sector wherever possible, while reducing the regulatory burden on the economy and replacing hierarchical organization with flexible and decentralized management.

While the fiscal benefits of NPM, program review, and the Expenditure Management System (EMS)—a new budgeting process described below—have been impressive, their impact on public administration and accountability may be less positive. In practice, transferring activities or programs to the private sector means giving public money to outside agencies to deliver public services. In some cases, improving efficiency means contracting out program delivery and support functions to the private sector. The official name for this approach is "alternative service delivery" (ASD). According to the Treasury Board Secretariat policy on ASD,

> [c]itizens expect value for money, accountable and transparent governance, quality, timely and efficient service, and a public sector that can help to put the right social and economic fundamentals in place. For any ASD option—including partnership—the proponent should be able to make a persuasive business case from the perspective of the citizen as client, taxpayer and/or user.[16]

The NPM focuses on "getting government right," which for the most part means reducing public-sector activities to those that can be carried out only by government agencies. This is one of the most important reasons for the current popularity of the ASD approach. *Creativity*, *citizen-centred*, *service-oriented*, and *focused results* are all buzzwords of the NPM. Furthermore, it posits that these values are not the exclusive domain or responsibility of government-service agencies or its private-sector partners. All government organizations and public-service operations are encouraged to adopt NPM strategies in seeking out private-sector partnership options.

Another powerful reason for NPM's popularity is the need to reduce government spending by shifting the overhead costs of program delivery to outside agencies. In order to accomplish these goals, each existing set of government programs has to be reviewed and its purposes and legitimacy must be open to meaningful scrutiny.

■ Program Review

When Paul Martin became Jean Chrétien's finance minister in 1993, he knew, as did the previous Mulroney government, that the federal deficit was a problem. But he was not convinced that the solution would require drastic cuts in expenditures. He thought that economic growth would meet the Liberals' deficit targets. His officials spent a year convincing him that the target could not be met that way and were vindicated when the initial 1994 deficit projections proved to be significantly higher than first thought. In the spring of that year, Martin had to convince his Cabinet colleagues to implement a spending freeze. At this point Martin received strong support from the prime minister and the freeze was imposed. The urgency of the country's fiscal problems, combined with a severe currency crisis in Mexico that raised the spectre of a similar crisis in Canada, convinced the key players in the political and permanent executives that the deficit had to be addressed immediately. Tinkering with small cuts would not be sufficient; it was time to make tough decisions about the priorities and capacities of the federal government.

During the 1993 election campaign, Liberal candidate (and former senior PCO official) Marcel Massé had called for a thorough review of federal programs. He argued that getting government right required Ottawa to reduce its activities to those that only it could do well, while "overhauling the delivery of public services and political institutions to make them more responsive" and devolving some powers to the provinces.[17] After his first budget failed to reduce the deficit, Martin threw his full support behind Massé's proposal and put the Department of Finance in charge of the process. The PCO assigned each department to review its programs and provided a framework for evaluation. The framework consisted of six tests:

1. Does the program or activity continue to serve a public interest?
2. Is there a legitimate and necessary role for government in this program area or activity?
3. Is the current role of the federal government appropriate, or is the program a candidate for realignment with the provinces?
4. What activities or programs should or could be transferred in whole or in part to the voluntary sector?
5. If the program or activity continues, how could its efficiency be improved?
6. Is the resultant package of programs and activities affordable within the fiscal restraint? If not, what programs or activities should be abandoned?

As each department reviewed its programs, it would be required to prepare a business plan for the programs that remained. A central committee of deputy ministers would review those plans. If the plans were not satisfactory, they would be sent back for revision. If the department's response to the rejection of its plans was also not satisfactory, the committee could, and on occasion did, cut programs against departmental wishes. This situation reflected the reality of program review: the first five tests were largely disregarded in favour of the fiscal restraint guidelines referred to in the sixth. Finance officials told departments how much spending to cut, and departments had to juggle their activities to meet the targets. In every case, the final decisions were made by the prime minister and the minister of finance, not by the program experts in the line departments.[18] Once spending decisions were made, however, the NPM principles reflected in the first five tests had an enormous impact, especially after cuts had taken effect. When it became impossible to deliver public services without contracting out to, or forming partnerships with, the private sector, contracting out and partnerships became a viable solution rather than simply a preferred option.

The spending cuts identified by the program review, together with the cuts in transfers to the provinces announced in the 1995 federal budget, had an enormous impact on Canada's permanent executive. Over 45 000 public-service and military positions were eliminated, agricultural and industrial subsidies were reduced, and a further $1 billion was cut from the military. Foreign aid was cut by a half-billion dollars and cuts were made to the unemployment insurance program. As we have already seen, transfers to the provinces were slashed. Some 73 boards, commissions, and advisory bodies were eliminated.[19] In the end, a total of $29 billion in cuts were made, helping to reduce federal government program expenditures to below 12 percent of GDP in 2001, prior to rising again to the 13 to 14 percent range in 2004 and 2005.

The political impact of the cuts was significant, leaving the Liberal Cabinet and government caucus deeply divided. Left-leaning Liberals derided the cuts as a violation of Liberal values. The PM had to intervene repeatedly to get reluctant ministers, MPs, and senators on board. By the summer of 1995, when veteran MP Warren Allmand was fired from his committee chair position for voting against the budget, everyone in Ottawa knew that the finance minister had the full support of the prime minister. From that point forward, Martin and the Department of Finance began to drive the entire government agenda.

In February 1995, while the fight over program review was at its height, the government announced a new budget process: the Expenditure Management System. In effect, the EMS further strengthened the central agencies—especially the PCO and finance—while reinforcing the dominance of the prime minister and the minister of finance over their Cabinet colleagues. In essence, the Department of Finance and the TBS set annual and long-term expenditure targets for each department and agency. The long-term targets permitted strategic planning by department officials. Subject to the fiscal constraints imposed at the centre, each department was required to submit an annual business plan to the TBS that would set out the department's strategies for meeting budget targets and the government's priorities.

To ensure compliance with the EMS program, the Department of Finance and the TBS made four crucial changes to the federal spending process:

1. There were no "policy reserves"—i.e., pots of money squirreled away in case of a shortfall or a new initiative during the fiscal year. Departments wishing to develop new programs would have to find the funds internally, usually by cutting something else. One exception was the National Unity Reserve, established by Prime Minister Mulroney. It was revived after the 1995 Quebec referendum and became the basis for the troubled sponsorship program in the public works department.

2. A contingency reserve was established by the minister of finance to cover unexpected expenditures. Unlike the former policy reserves within the line departments, it was controlled directly by the finance minister.

3. The Treasury Board had a small operating reserve to lend to departments, on the strict condition that loans would be repaid. There would be no free lunch for a department that overspent its spending targets.

4. Forecasts for economic growth, interest rates, and revenues were deliberately conservative. The annual budget projections were based on the worst-case scenario, to avoid committing the government to overly optimistic spending targets.

Together, these measures strengthened central control over public spending and forced departments to stay within their annual budgets.

Program review, EMS, and the new fiscal strategies paid off handsomely. Part of the success was the result of good luck; a booming economy produced higher tax revenues and made fewer demands on government assistance programs, while low inflation helped push down interest rates. Nonetheless, the institutional and process changes adopted after the 1994 federal budget allowed the finance department to take full advantage of the economic circumstances to balance the budget and begin to pay down the national debt.

The story of the budget process under the Chrétien government highlights two important themes. First, the full support of the prime minister ensured the implementation of these rather novel policy initiatives, even those that departed radically from his party's platform. Without the political might of the prime minister—and his willingness to establish the necessary organizational structures—neither program review nor the EMS would have succeeded.

Second, central agencies with the backing of the prime minister can prevail over a majority of unhappy cabinet ministers and government MPs. The power to make and implement policy decisions has shifted decisively from the political masters to their nonpartisan "servants" in the PCO, the PMO, TBS, and the Department of Finance. As long as the Privy Council clerk and the prime minister set the incentives for ambitious politicians and public servants, neither the political nor the permanent executive will be fully accountable to Parliament, to the electorate, or indeed to anyone other than the prime minister.

Strengthening Accountability

The results of new public management have been mixed with respect to issues of accountability. Hiring temporary employees on contract tends to undermine the accountability of the public service, which is based on the assumption that staff personnel are full-time professionals. In fact, the notion that ministers cannot be expected to be fully accountable to Parliament for every administrative detail within their departments is at least partially dependent on the logic that relatively novice politicians are less well equipped to make departmental decisions than are full-time departmental experts. NPM can also be legitimately questioned with respect to the potential loss of financial accountability arising from the transfer of tax revenues to voluntary, private-sector agencies.

The Harper government attempted to address at least two of the most important concerns arising from the NPM and other developments in political accountability. In its Accountability Act, which had made it though committee stage at the time of writing (summer of 2006), the federal government designated 13 areas of political and governmental activity that would be subject to considerable reforms. While many concern party financing, the ethics commissioner, lobbyists, access to information, and a new director of public prosecutions—which can all impact on the public service—others will directly impact how government officials do their jobs.[20]

The act will provide increased protection for whistleblowers who openly raise concerns about questionable departmental practices. The public-sector integrity commissioner will become an agent of Parliament and have the authority to deal with complaints from public-service employees who believe they have suffered reprisals for reporting wrongdoing. The act will also strengthen penalties for those who wilfully impede investigations. Access to information will be expanded to include new organizations and agencies; including seven agents and officers of Parliament, seven Crown corporations, and three foundations. Furthermore, new powers will be granted to the auditor general, allowing him or her to audit individuals and organizations that receive federal government money.

Most importantly for the public service, the Accountability Act will strengthen auditing and accountability within government departments by introducing six new measures:

- designation of deputy ministers as accounting officers
- a clear process to resolve disputes between ministers and deputy ministers
- strengthened internal audit functions within departments
- strengthened governance structure in Crown corporations
- tougher penalties for fraudulent misuse of public funds
- a consistent approach to promote legal and policy compliance and to enforce disciplinary measures[21]

These changes are designed to address the issue of ministerial responsibility. Recognizing that ministers are responsible to "Parliament and the prime minister" not only for their own actions, but for those of their officials, the new procedures attempt to build "appropriate systems of control" and enhance communications between ministers and deputy ministers. Deputy ministers and deputy heads will become accounting officers for their departments. They will become accountable to Parliament and will be required to account for their departments' activities while appearing before parliamentary committees. Financial accountability, primarily in the form of independent, objective, and timely internal audits, as well as a new Treasury Board internal audit policy, will be featured throughout all government departments.

New dispute resolution procedures will also be put into place. When a minister and his deputy minister fail to agree on the interpretation or application of a Treasury Board policy, the deputy minister will seek guidance, in writing, from the secretary of the Treasury Board. If the matter is still not resolved, the minister will refer the dispute to the Treasury Board for a decision. A copy of the decision will be filed with the auditor general as a confidence of Cabinet. At this stage it is far too early to determine the full impact of these new procedures on the various departments within the federal government. However, one thing should be certain: changes to the rules and procedures within institutions produce new incentives and new cultural norms within and between institutions, thereby changing the behaviour of actors within those institutions.

CONCLUSION

As we saw in Chapter 6, the legislative branch within the national government is supposed to hold the executive accountable to the voters. The members of the political executive are also members of the legislative branch and must obtain the approval of Parliament for their proposed legislation and fiscal plans. In theory, they cannot continue to exercise the prerogative powers of the Crown without the confidence of the Commons. By answering to Parliament for their actions, they allow our elected representatives to hold the permanent executive accountable for its policy and spending choices.

In practice, the incentives set by Canada's political institutions make a mockery of this theoretical picture of governance. Just as ambitious politicians know that they must support the prime minister, ambitious public servants have to win the approval of the clerk of the Privy Council. The resulting concentration of power at the centre of the political and permanent executives weakens accountability. Senior line officials, together with their counterparts in the central agencies, monopolize two vital resources: information about public policy and knowledge of governance. Inexperienced cabinet ministers, overwhelmed by conflicting demands on their time and attention, are no match for experienced public servants. The supremacy of the political executive over the permanent executive is now, in some cases, a constitutional fiction.

Decades of deficit-financing welfare-state programs, among others, left the federal government facing a fiscal crisis toward the end of the twentieth century. Despite a remarkable turnaround in federal (and provincial) government finances, the accumulated federal debt stands at almost one-half trillion dollars and 15 cents of every tax dollar still goes to paying interest on that debt. Fiscal concerns still dominate most government decisions at the centre of, and therefore throughout, government operations. In recent years, with the growing popularity of business models for public administration, the incentive structure for public servants has changed. Partly as a result, the permanent executive—and consequently, the political executive—is less accountable to Parliament for its disbursement of public funds. Although new rules, procedures, and laws have been recently adopted to make the permanent executive more accountable to Parliament and the political executive, many past attempts have produced only minimal changes to the internal cultures of public-service institutions.

Most Canadians pay little attention to the workings of the permanent executive branch of their federal government, despite its size and its enormous impact on our daily lives. Until recently, it has been allowed to conduct its business behind closed doors and out of the media spotlight. Ironically, the daily dramas in the House of Commons attract the lion's share of public notice, despite their relative unimportance compared to the executive branch. It remains to be seen whether 10 years from now we will be talking about how a new era in accountability was initiated with the Harper government's Accountability Act, or whether we will still be bemoaning the lack of accountability within the permanent executive.

DISCUSSION QUESTIONS

1. Distinguish between the political executive and the permanent executive, and briefly describe the relationship between them. What roles do they play in the creation of public policy? How has the relationship changed in recent years?

2. What is the current state of federal finances? How have they changed in recent years? How do they compare to other countries?

3. Briefly explain the roles and responsibilities of the four primary central agencies. In your opinion, are they too powerful? Why or why not?

4. Should corporations be paying more taxes? Should individuals?

SUGGESTED READINGS

Herman Bakvis, *Regional Ministers: Power and Influence in the Canadian Cabinet* (Toronto: University of Toronto Press, 1991).

David A. Good, *The Politics of Public Management: The HRDC Audit of Grants and Contributions* (Toronto: University of Toronto Press, 2003).

Edward Greenspon and Anthony Wilson-Smith, *Double Vision: The Inside Story of the Liberals in Power* (Toronto: Doubleday Canada, 1996).

Donald J. Savoie, *Governing from the Centre: The Concentration of Power in Canadian Politics* (Toronto: University of Toronto Press, 1999).

Donald J. Savoie, *Breaking the Bargain: Public Servants, Ministers, and Parliament* (Toronto: University of Toronto Press, 2003).

David E. Smith, *The Invisible Crown: The First Principle of Canadian Government* (Toronto: University of Toronto Press, 1995).

Websites

Information about the Privy Council Office is available in the "Publications" section of its website: http://www.pco-bcp.gc.ca.

The Prime Minister of Canada site contains links to the new ministries and cabinet ministers: http://www.pm.gc.ca.

The Treasury Board Secretariat site provides comprehensive information about Canada's public service: http://www.tbs-sct.gc.ca.

Individual departments and agencies of the federal government have their own websites; to find them, go to the main government site (http://www.gc.ca) and click on "Departments and Agencies" for an alphabetical listing of all departments and agencies and direct links to their sites.

NOTES

1. See Privy Council Office Web pages at http://www.pco-bcp.gc.ca.

2. See Donald J. Savoie, *Governing from the Centre: The Concentration of Power in Canadian Politics* (Toronto: University of Toronto Press, 1999).

3. See Treasury Board Secretariat Web pages at http://www.tbs-sct.gc.ca/president/pb-bp_e.asp.

4. Russia has been a "casual" member of the G8, formerly the G7, for about 10 years. In 2006 Russia hosted and chaired the G8 meetings for the first time, marking its formal, albeit still tenuous, entry into the club. Note that most of the data in this chapter refers to G7 countries rather than to G8.

5. The notable exception is Alberta, which, like the other Canadian governments, built up a sizable debt during the 1980s and early 1990s, but has since managed to pay off that debt, making it Canada's only debt-free province as of 2005.

6. See, for example, C. E. S. Franks, *The Parliament of Canada* (Toronto: University of Toronto Press, 1987).

7. *Canada Year Book, 1930,* 1008–1012.

8. Privy Council Office, *World of Regulations,* Section 2; accessed June 2001.

9. See the Transport Canada website: http://www.tc.gc.ca.

10. Department of Finance Canada, *Structure and Role* (Ottawa, December 1999), 12.

11. Canada, Privy Council Office, *Memoranda to Cabinet* (January 2004), 6; accessed on-line at http://www.pco-bcp.gc.ca.

12. Privy Council Office, *Cabinet Directive on Law-making,* Section 4; accessed June 2000.

13. *Cabinet Directive on Law-making,* Section 2.

14. *Memoranda to Cabinet,* 9–10.

15. *Cabinet Directive on Law-making,* Section 2.

16. Treasury Board Secretariat, "Introduction," *Alternative Service Delivery* (June 2001); available on-line at http://www.tbs-sct.gc.ca; accessed June 2001.

17. Edward Greenspon and Anthony Wilson-Smith, *Double Vision: The Inside Story of the Liberals in Power* (Toronto: Doubleday Canada, 1996), 115.

18. Savoie, 183.

19. Savoie, 181.

20. See the federal government's Accountability Action Plan available online at http://www.faa-lfi.gc.ca.

21. Accountability Action Plan.

ADMINISTRATION OF JUSTICE: THE COURTS AND THE CHARTER

LEARNING OBJECTIVES

- *distinguish* between the concepts of parliamentary supremacy and entrenched rights
- *identify* and *explain* the evolution of rights in Canada including the key differences between the Bill of Rights and the Charter of Rights and Freedoms
- *identify* the important elements of judicial politics
- *define* first-order and second-order Charter duties
- *identify* and *explain* the key principles of Charter interpretation
- *explain* the three-stage process of Charter application and the relationship between Section 1 and other Charter sections
- *identify* and *analyze* the reasons why courts do not always make good public policy
- *summarize* the recent history and legal status of abortion rights, same-sex marriage, and pornography

INTRODUCTION

Canada's political institutions do not operate independently of each other. When one changes, for whatever reason, others must adapt to that change. The introduction of the Charter of Rights and Freedoms, which marked the most significant change in the written Constitution since Confederation, has had far-reaching effects on the courts, Parliament, and the policy-making process. But these effects cannot be attributed solely to the Charter. Many have been magnified by changes in the behaviour of other institutions and groups.

After the Charter's adoption, Canadian judges, especially in the appeal courts, modified their traditional attitude of judicial deference to Parliament and became more assertive. In this respect, they were in accord with developments in Canada's political culture, which since World War II had been increasingly influenced by American conceptions of rights and freedoms. Appellate judges also gained almost complete freedom to decide which cases they would hear, which allowed them to devote considerable new attention to rights and freedoms. Interest groups added public-interest litigation to their toolkit for policy change. As policy-makers in the legislative and executive branches of government realized that their choices would face frequent challenges on Charter grounds, and that judges would often rule in favour of the citizen plaintiffs, legislators began to incorporate more careful protection for enumerated rights and freedoms into their bills. After 20 years of operating under the Charter, it is fair to say that none of Canada's political institutions—the courts, Parliament, or the executive—can claim a monopoly over the interpretation and protection of rights and freedoms.

Before the Charter took effect in 1982,[1] it was rare for Canadian policymakers (including judges) to resolve controversial issues on the basis of rights. Today, there are few policy questions that do not touch in some way on the Charter's guarantees of rights and freedoms. For example,

- Under what circumstances can a doctor perform a legal abortion?[2]
- Can a terminally ill person seek a doctor's assistance to commit suicide?[3]
- Who is entitled to Canadian citizenship? How should the state treat Canadian residents who are not citizens?[4]
- Should state entitlements (such as pensions and parental benefits) be distributed without regard to marital status, sexual orientation, age, or gender?[5]
- Does a police officer have the right to search your home without a warrant, and, if so, under what conditions?[6]
- What does "guilty beyond a reasonable doubt" mean in practice? Does it apply if you were drunk when you committed a crime?[7] Does it apply to a battered woman who killed her abuser?[8] Does it apply to a man who unsuccessfully tried to prevent his partner in crime from shooting a robbery victim, or who accidentally injected an overdose of cocaine into a woman's arm?[9]

Because these and other issues have been addressed in high profile and controversial Supreme Court judgments, it is sometimes argued that judges have taken too much power away from Parliament. On the other hand, it can be argued with equal force that laws that violate protected rights without justification have no place in a liberal-pluralist democracy, even when they are made by well meaning elected officials. When the Supreme Court strikes down an unconstitutional law, it is simply doing what the Constitution requires it to do. If the Supreme Court were to defer to the legislative branch, upholding laws without stringent constitutional analysis, it would fail in its duty to enforce Canada's master institution.

The positions of both advocates and detractors of the Charter have some merit, and a closer look at the above cases reveals a complex relationship among the three branches of government. In the cases dealing with abortion and the distribution of state entitlements, the Supreme Court decided that existing policy was unconstitutional. However, it left the details of any replacement policy to be determined by governments. After the rulings on warrantless searches and intoxication, Parliament amended the Criminal Code to modify (or undo) the effects of the Supreme Court's decisions. The ruling on physician-assisted suicide upheld the existing law, and left any adjustments to be made by Parliament.

It would therefore be wrong to suggest that the Charter transferred all policy-making power to unelected judges. While judicial activism should raise some concerns in a democratic political system—principally because judges lack the expertise to craft and enforce good public policy—the Charter does not spell the end of Canadian parliamentary democracy. Although it is certainly true that the Charter has inspired thousands of groups and individuals to seek a remedy in the courts for alleged violations of their rights and freedoms, both rights-based litigation and judicial policy-making existed in Canada before 1982. A Supreme Court that controlled its own caseload, policy-oriented lawyers, and a rights-influenced political culture were already in place prior to the Charter. Moreover, any group or individual who seeks to challenge the constitutionality of a law faces long odds of success. There are daunting procedural and financial barriers to litigation. Once the case reaches the courts, the plaintiff must confront the vast resources and privileged status of the government that passed the law—or whose official allegedly breached the Charter—and now wishes to defend its actions. In the end, the majority of Charter claims are dismissed by the courts.[10]

In many cases that are heard by the courts, justices are forced to confront moral issues—such as abortion and gay rights—because legislators avoid making tough decisions in these sensitive areas. Often, when judges strike down laws or reinterpret them to conform to the Charter, they are telling legislators, and the justice system itself, to take their duty to protect rights and freedoms seriously. In doing so, the courts are telling other governing institutions that the Charter imposes two types of duties on them: a first-order duty to ensure their own compliance with the guaranteed rights and freedoms, and a second-order duty to review the decisions of other institutions. The primary first-order duties lie with the executive branch that drafts laws. Parliament and the courts have a second-order duty to examine those laws. If MPs or judges find a contradiction between the law and a Charter guarantee, they are required to resolve the contradiction by amending or vetoing (nullifying) the offending provisions.[11]

In some policy fields, notably criminal law, the Supreme Court and the House of Commons have engaged in a constructive dialogue about the practical difficulties of balancing individual rights against competing social values. Instead of imposing their own remedies for Charter violations, judges increasingly defer to Parliament to fix infringements on rights. At the beginning of the twenty-first century, after a sometimes stressful period of adjustment, it appears that our political institutions have adapted to the presence of the Charter and a constructive balance among the three branches of government is being achieved.

ENTRENCHED RIGHTS VERSUS PARLIAMENTARY SUPREMACY

As we have seen, the BNA Act, 1867, enshrined for Canada "a Constitution similar in Principle to that of the United Kingdom." Parliamentary supremacy is at the core of that inherited constitution. Under the Westminster constitutional model, the legislative branch makes the law, subject to the financial control of the Crown. The judicial branch has very little power to invalidate laws on substantive grounds. In other words, the courts have no discretion over the content of laws; they cannot declare a particular statute invalid because it treats a particular group unfairly or because the conditions under which it was passed are no longer in effect. If a statute is flawed in intent or in application, Parliament retains the sole authority to amend or revoke it.

But the Canadian Constitution has always differed from the British Constitution in at least two primary respects: the balance between written and unwritten law, and the division of powers between the federal and provincial governments. Apart from a few key documents—such as the 1215 Magna Carta and the 1689 Bill of Rights—the British Constitution is essentially unwritten. It is based primarily on convention, case law, and precedent, not on entrenched written rules. Canada required the greater certainty of a written constitution, similar to that of the United States, mostly because of the decision to create a federation rather than a unitary state. However, the BNA Act was virtually silent on the subject of rights. As such, for the first 115 years of Confederation, judicial review of Canada's Constitution was essentially confined to the division of powers. Although the content of a particular law was clearly relevant to a division-of-powers case, it was relevant only insofar as it allowed the Supreme Court or the Judicial Committee of the Privy Council (JCPC) to determine whether the matter fell within federal or provincial jurisdiction as defined by the division of powers in Sections 91–95. A statute of the federal Parliament that unjustifiably trenched on provincial powers was declared *ultra vires* (beyond the power of) the national government and struck down on that basis. Similarly, provincial laws that were found to be *ultra vires* were also declared null and void.

Under the doctrine of parliamentary supremacy, the courts generally upheld any law that was enacted by the proper level of government. It was assumed that either Ottawa or the provinces could legislate on any matter as they saw fit, as long as they stayed within their own jurisdictions. Although the power to legislate was divided, it was not restrained by any normative standard of rights or morality. Finally, the courts almost always deferred to the legislative branch. Judges were loath to criticize the choices made by legislators, even when those choices were clearly distasteful.

Since 1867, and especially since the end of World War II, the influence of British political and legal traditions has diminished in Canada while American influence has grown. The American tradition of judicial review is very different from the British convention of parliamentary supremacy. It is founded on the assumption that the courts, and not the legislative branch, should provide the authoritative definition of law. As the influence of American law and politics grew, the absence in Canada of entrenched rights comparable to those in the U.S. Bill of Rights began to attracted public criticism.

The Evolution of Rights in Canada

Parliamentary supremacy means, among other things, that the legislative branch is the sole guardian of the rights and freedoms of citizens. The historical record shows that the unwritten rights embodied in British common law may be disregarded by parliamentarians in the grip of overwhelming public opinion. Canadians of Asian descent—not just naturalized immigrants, but citizens who were born in Canada—were barred from voting until 1947. In 1942, under the War Measures Act, the federal government arrested, expropriated property from, and interned thousands of Japanese Canadians whose only crime was their race. In the 1950s, communists (actual or suspected) and Jehovah's Witnesses were persecuted by the Quebec government. Between the 1930s and the 1960s, hundreds of "mental defectives" were forcibly sterilized in Alberta and British Columbia. In 1970, after the FLQ kidnapping of British trade commissioner James Cross in Montreal, the Trudeau government suspended civil rights by imposing the War Measures Act. Hundreds of innocent Quebeckers were rounded up by the police and thrown into jail, without being charged with any offence or without being allowed to speak to lawyers.

Parliamentary supremacy, in other words, was no guarantee that rights and freedoms would always be protected, especially when challenged by overwhelming public opinion and the desire for administrative expediency. Nor were the courts vigilant guardians of individual liberties. The JCPC repeatedly upheld federal and provincial laws that violated human rights, as long as they were found to be within the scope of the offending governments' respective jurisdictions. For example, the JCPC accepted the internment of Japanese Canadians on the grounds that the War Measures Act overrode the provincial power over property and civil rights.

After the abolition of JCPC appeals in 1949, the Canadian Supreme Court became more vigorous in protecting rights. It was particularly concerned about Quebec laws against religious and political minorities. Some justices argued that such laws violated the implied bill of rights and should be nullified on that basis. Other justices preferred to use the division of powers to invalidate these laws. They argued that the Quebec government could not usurp Ottawa's criminal-law power in order to persecute minorities. But in deference to parliamentary supremacy, most justices would not take the next step and "read in" specific rights protections into the BNA Act.

The establishment of the United Nations in 1948 gave further impetus to calls for an entrenched Charter of Rights and Freedoms in Canada. The UN Charter and the Universal Declaration on Human Rights had a powerful influence on Canadian lawyers and academics. While the idea of entrenched rights still provoked unease, especially among those who feared the erosion of parliamentary supremacy, by the late-1950s a bill of rights had become an almost essential component of any political system that claimed to be a liberal democracy.

SECTION	SUBSECTION	RIGHTS
Preamble		recognition and protection of human rights and fundamental freedoms
		affirms Canada was founded upon principles of the supremacy of God, dignity and worth of the human person, and position of family in society of free men and free institutions
		affirms men and institutions remain free only when freedom is founded upon respect for moral and spiritual values and the rule of law
PART I		
1		rights and freedoms exist without discrimination by reason of race, national origin, colour, religion, or sex
1	a	right of the individual to life, liberty, and security of the person and the right to the enjoyment of property
1	b	right of the individual to equality before the law and protection of the law
1	c	freedom of religion
1	d	freedom of speech
1	e	freedom of assembly and association
1	f	freedom of the press
2		all laws shall, unless expressly declared by an Act of Parliament that it shall operate notwithstanding the Bill of Rights, be so construed and applied as not to abrogate, abridge or infringe any of the recognized or declared rights or freedoms
2	a	protection from arbitrary detention, imprisonment, or exile
2	b	protection from imposition of cruel and unusual treatment or punishment
2	c	rights of the arrested or detained (i) right to be informed promptly of the reason for arrest or detention (ii) right to retain and instruct counsel without delay (iii) remedy by way of habeas corpus for determination of validity of detention and release if detention is not lawful
2	d	protection against providing evidence if denied counsel, protection against self-crimination
2	e	right to a fair hearing in accordance with the principles of fundamental justice for determination of rights and obligations
2	f	right to be presumed innocent until proved guilty, right to fair and public hearing by an independent and impartial tribunal, right to reasonable bail
2	g	right to assistance of an interpreter in proceedings before a court, commission, board, or other tribunal

SECTION	SUBSECTION	RIGHTS
3	1	duty of minister of justice to ensure that laws abide by Bill of Rights
	2	exceptions to 3 (1)
4		citation as Bill of Rights
PART II		
5	1	nothing in Part I abrogates or abridges any human right or fundamental freedom not enumerated but that existed in Canada prior to Bill of Rights
5	2	definition of the "law of Canada"
5	3	limited to the laws of Canada and jurisdiction of Parliament of Canada

Source: Department of Justice Canada, available on-line at http://laws.justice.gc.ca/en/C-12.3/index.html.

The Bill of Rights, 1960

Partly in response to the rising interest in human rights, the federal government decided to codify existing common-law rights in statute law rather than entrenching a charter in the Constitution. An amendment to the BNA Act, which would have required provincial agreement, was not likely to occur given that all of the provinces except Saskatchewan were opposed to what they perceived as a direct attack on both parliamentary supremacy and provincial autonomy. Therefore, in 1960, Prime Minister Diefenbaker adopted the Canadian Bill of Rights. Although its advocates hoped that it would provide effective protection for individual rights and freedoms, the Bill suffered from four serious limitations:

1. The Bill of Rights was not entrenched in the Constitution; it was an ordinary federal statute. Therefore, it did not override other federal laws that violated its guarantees.
2. The Bill of Rights did not apply to the provincial governments or to their areas of jurisdiction as defined by the BNA Act.
3. The Bill of Rights contained no explicit judicial remedies for laws that conflicted with its provisions. At most, the Bill instructed courts in the proper interpretation of laws. Judges were required to interpret a statute in such a way that it did not conflict with the Bill. If they could not find a way to do this, there was no clear mandate to strike down the offending law or to impose another appropriate remedy for a person whose rights had been infringed.
4. The language of the Bill implied that the protected rights were frozen at the moment when the Bill came into effect. Judges could not use the Bill to expand rights beyond the restrictions that had been imposed in previous decades, even where those restrictions were out of step with an evolving society.

Although the preamble promised to "ensure the protection of these rights and freedoms in Canada," the Bill of Rights had little impact on Canadian law. Apart from its own inherent weaknesses, its potential influence was greatly reduced by judicial reluctance to challenge parliamentary supremacy. Between 1960 and 1982, the justices invalidated only one law on the grounds that it conflicted with the Bill of Rights. In the *Drybones* case it struck down a section of the Indian Act that made it illegal for a Status Indian to be intoxicated anywhere off-reserve. In all other Bill of Rights cases, the justices deferred to Parliament and refused to nullify laws on any of the enumerated grounds in the Bill. Whereas *Drybones* struck down a racist law, even though there was no evidence that it was being applied unfairly, the court deferred to parliamentary supremacy by upholding other racist or sexist laws on the grounds that they were administered equally. The courts' reluctance to forcefully apply the Bill of Rights sparked demands for entrenching the protection of rights and freedoms in the Constitution. Advocates of a charter argued that if judges had a supreme law with which to work, instead of an ordinary statute, they would take a more aggressive approach to violations of rights and freedoms. In this respect, their hopes have been fulfilled.

The 1960 Bill of Rights remains in force, despite the proclamation of the Charter in 1982. In a 1985 case concerning the rights of refugee claimants, half of the six Supreme Court justices relied on the Bill's guarantee of a fair hearing; the other three based their ruling on Section 7 of the Charter.[12] The Bill has recently been used, with some success, in litigation touching on property rights, which are included in the Bill of Rights but not the Charter. However, in a class-action suit on behalf of mentally ill World War II veterans, whose pay and benefits were allegedly mismanaged by the federal government, the Supreme Court unanimously ruled that when the Bill took effect in 1960, the federal government had the power to take away the property of individuals. Therefore, the Bill offered no relief to the veterans for the millions of dollars they had lost because of the government's mismanagement.[13] This revival of the frozen rights doctrine does not bode well for future attempts to use the Bill in order to fill gaps in the Charter's protections.

The Evolution of Charter Guarantees

The draft charter that Prime Minister Trudeau submitted for public debate in October 1980 was very different from the version that took effect in April 1982. A special joint committee of the House of Commons and Senate held public hearings on the federal package. For the most part, the witnesses demanded stronger entrenched protection for individual and group rights.[14] Some, including women, Aboriginals, and people with disabilities, were successful; Sections 15, 25, 28, and 35 were either added or reinforced during the committee process. Others, such as gays and lesbians and anti-abortion activists, failed to achieve constitutional recognition for their rights claims. Nevertheless, the overall effect of the public hearings was to create strong public support for the Charter and its guaranteed rights and freedoms.

The evolution of two particular Charter sections merits some further comment. Section 1, the "reasonable limitations" clause, had been watered down as part of

Trudeau's political strategy to win over the premiers. Because the Supreme Court sits at the top of Canada's judicial hierarchy, its interpretations of the Charter would bind both levels of government. Thus, judicial review of the Charter, unlike that of the Bill of Rights, would limit the discretion of provincial governments as well as of Ottawa. Not surprisingly, most of the provincial governments opposed any restrictions on their powers, and they refused to support the Trudeau Charter without the inclusion of a broad limitation clause.

An early draft of that clause read as follows:

> *The Canadian Charter of Rights and Freedoms recognizes the following rights and freedoms subject only to such reasonable limits as are generally accepted in a free and democratic society with a parliamentary system of government.*[15]

Several of the witnesses who appeared before the committee demanded that this clause be removed, arguing that it would allow governments to violate rights and freedoms at whim. Others wanted to clarify and strengthen the wording, eliminating the phrase "generally accepted" and inserting a reference to law. Faced with a barrage of criticism, and now determined to proceed without provincial consent, the federal government amended the section to restrict how far governments could reasonably limit rights and freedoms. The final wording of Section 1 makes no reference to parliamentary government and requires any legal infringement of rights to be "demonstrably justified" by the state. The effect is to reduce judicial deference to Parliament and to place a heavy onus on governments to justify their restrictions of protected rights and freedoms.

Section 15 was also transformed during the public hearings. The original wording of the equality clause virtually reproduced the language of the Bill of Rights: it guaranteed "equality before the law and the equal protection of the law." Women's groups and others pointed out that the interpretation of those phrases by the Supreme Court had been less than satisfactory and demanded stronger guarantees. The first part of Section 15 now protects equality under the law and "equal benefit of the law," to ensure that both the substance and the effects of legislation are taken into consideration by the courts. Finally, the federal government inserted a second provision into Section 15 dealing with group rights in order to prevent entrenched rights claims from interfering with existing or future affirmative action programs. All in all, the equality rights in today's Charter are a far cry from those in the original version tabled in October 1980. As a consequence, the impact of Section 15 on Canadian law and politics has been significant and often surprising.

The Transformation of Judicial Review in the Charter Era

Many of the rights and freedoms that were constitutionally entrenched by the Charter in 1982 already existed in Canadian law. Most were embedded in statutes and common-law precedents. In this sense, the Charter was not a radical break with our legal tradition, it simply entrenched long-standing rights and freedoms.

Pierre Trudeau was one of Canada's most successful politicians, governing as prime minister for over 15 years. He was also one of its most controversial. Reviled in the West because of the 1980 National Energy Program and by Québécois separatists for his staunch defence of Canadian federalism, he was lauded in much of the country for his firm hand in dealing with the FLQ, the Quebec issue more generally, and for his passionate defence of a united Canada. He will be remembered most for the 1982 patriation of the Constitution and the Charter of Rights and Freedoms. (© Christopher J. Morris/CORBIS)

Born: 1919, Montreal

Died: 2000, Montreal

Education: B.A. (Jean de Brébeuf College, 1940), LL.L. (University of Montreal, 1943), M.A. Political Economy (Harvard University, 1945), also studied at École des sciences politiques in Paris (1946–1947) and London School of Economics (1947–1948)

Profession: Lawyer and law consultant (called to the Quebec Bar in 1943, to the Ontario Bar in 1967)

1949–1951 Advisor to the Privy Council

1950 Co-founder and director, *Cité libre*

1961–1965 Associate professor of law, University of Montreal

1961–1965 Researcher, Institut de recherches en droit public

Political Career:

MP
1965–1984 Mount Royal, Quebec

Leader
1968–1984 Liberal Party

Prime Minister
1968–1979
1980–1984

Other Ministries
1967–1968 Justice
1968 Acting president of the Privy Council

Political Career Highlights

1968 Elected prime minister with a majority government

1969 Decriminalization of homosexuality

1969 Official Languages Act

1970 October Crisis (implementation of War Measures Act)

1972 Appointed Muriel McQueen Fergusson as first female Speaker of the Senate

1972 Reelected prime minister with a minority government

1974 Reelected prime minister with a majority government

1975 Wage and price controls

1979 Lost election to Progressive Conservative minority

1979–1980 Leader of the Opposition

1980 Reelected prime minister with majority government

1980 Significant role in the victory of the No forces in the Quebec Referendum on sovereignty association

1980 Appointed Jeanne Sauvé as first
   female Speaker of the House of
   Commons
1980 National Energy Program
1982 Canadian Charter of Rights

1982 Constitution Act
1982 Appointed Bertha Wilson as first
   female justice of the Supreme Court
1984 Appointed Jeanne Sauvé as Canada's
   first female governor general

Source: *First Among Equals: The Prime Minister in Canadian Life and Politics* (Ottawa: Library and Archives Canada), available on-line at http://www.collectionscanada.ca/primeministers/.

Remedy and Enforcement

The real innovation of the Charter lies in the explicit judicial powers of remedy and enforcement:

- Section 24 (1) allows any individual or group whose Charter rights have been infringed to ask the courts for "such remedy as the court considers appropriate and just in the circumstances." For example, a person convicted of a criminal offence whose legal rights were violated by the police may be granted a new trial.

- Section 24 (2) requires judges to exclude evidence obtained in violation of the rights guaranteed in Sections 7 through 14. Without such evidence, criminal conviction "beyond a reasonable doubt" may be impossible.

- Section 52 gives the courts the power to strike down any law, federal or provincial, that is found to be inconsistent with the Charter, "to the extent of the inconsistency." In other words, a particular section of the Criminal Code may be struck down as an infringement on a Charter right, but the rest of the Code will remain in force.

The Supreme Court has broadened the range of available remedies through its interpretation of Section 52. Instead of striking down a statute immediately, it can suspend the nullification for a specified period, to give the affected legislature a chance to amend the offending law before the suspension expires. In addition, the court may provide guidelines to legislators for amending or reenacting the impugned law. For example, in 1991 the Supreme Court struck down the "rape shield" provision in the Criminal Code.[16] The purpose of the rape shield was to protect alleged victims of sexual assault from defence attorneys who sought to use their prior sexual history to destroy their credibility in the courtroom. The Court held that an absolute prohibition of evidence concerning prior sexual activity by the complainant violated the defendant's Section 11 rights to a fair trial. To fill the void created by the nullification, they set out rules for judges to use in determining the admissibility of such evidence.

In 1992 Parliament adopted a new rape shield law, which essentially brought the Court's ruling into new statute law. Bill C-49 contained a preamble that defined the objectives of the legislation to prevent any future court from imposing its own interpretation of the law's purpose. Justice Minister (later prime minister) Kim Campbell sought to balance the rights of women against those of criminal defendants, partly in anticipation of a future Charter challenge to the law. When the Supreme Court ruled on the constitutionality of the revised rape shield in 2000, it upheld the law on the grounds that it did not violate the legal rights of the accused.[17] The rape shield case illustrates an often-overlooked feature of Charter politics: the dialogue it creates between courts and legislators.

Reading In Rights

If the court finds that a law violates the Charter, but it does not consider striking it down to be the appropriate remedy, it can effectively amend the law by either "reading in" or "reading down" the offending provisions. Reading in *widens* the application of the law by adding one or more groups that were previously excluded from the wording of the provision. The actual wording of the law does not change, but the Supreme Court's interpretation requires all lower courts and lawyers to treat the provision as though the widening had been written into the law. If the Supreme Court reads in to an ordinary law, and the particular government does not approve of the result, it has the power to amend the law in order to undo the Court's work. For example, the 2001 *Sharpe* ruling from the Supreme Court read in two minor exemptions to the Criminal Code provisions banning child pornography. The federal government disapproved of the change, and introduced legislation to remove the new exemptions.[18]

Judges do not just read in with respect to ordinary laws, however. For example, the Supreme Court has read in several groups that were not explicitly included in Section 15 (1) of the Charter itself: residents of Canada who are not legal citizens,[19] gays and lesbians,[20] and common-law spouses.[21] When courts alter the meaning of the Charter by reading in, there is little that dissenting governments can do, outside of using the contentious Section 33 notwithstanding clause or successfully negotiating a constitutional amendment. The first is politically unpalatable for most politicians. The second has so far proven to be impossible.

Reading Down Rights

When the courts read down a particular law, they reinterpret its meaning in such a way as to *narrow* its application. The purpose is to ensure that the law does not conflict with the Charter, either in general or in a particular case. Reading down allows a court to protect guaranteed rights while respecting the authority of the legislature. In its 1991 *Osborne* ruling, the Supreme Court struck down provisions of the Public Service Employment Act because the provisions prohibiting public servants from active political participation were an unreasonable restriction of federal employees' Section 2 fundamental freedoms. The Court also ruled, however, that the restrictions qualified for consideration under Section 1, the reasonable limits clause, and therefore it would be up to Parliament, not the courts, to determine how the law should be redrafted. In other words, the Court ruled that the federal government had the authority to limit direct political action by public servants, just not the in way the law was restricting them as applied in this case. Note, however, that there are few restrictions on the Supreme Court's power to amend the Constitution through its remedial power.

JUDICIAL POLITICS

▉ Judicial Independence and the Separation of Law and Politics

Canadian judges are appointed, not elected. The members of the Supreme Court are chosen by the prime minister and the minister of justice. Although there are no formal procedures for choosing justices, the normal practice is for the justice minister to seek advice from the Department of Justice, the Canadian Bar Association, and the current chief justice (see Canadian Political Chronology 8.1). They can advise the minister as to any gaps the Court may have in particular areas of law.

The Supreme Court Act requires that three of the nine justices be appointed from the civil bar of Quebec. This is to ensure that the Court has the necessary expertise to deal with the unique legal system of that province. By convention, three of the remaining justices come from Ontario, two from the Western provinces, and one from the Atlantic region. Most serve on provincial Courts of Appeal before their elevation to the Supreme Court of Canada, although a few active lawyers have been appointed in recent years. Unlike their colleagues on the U.S. Supreme Court, Canada's justices are not subjected to legislative approval or rejection. Once appointed, all superior court judges enjoy security of tenure "during good behaviour" until the age of 75.

The Supreme Court Appointment Process

By the late 1990s, this appointment process was widely criticized. It was regarded by its critics as secretive and undemocratic, especially in an era in which Supreme Court justices enjoyed considerable policy-making power under the Charter. In the spring of 2004, the House of Commons Standing Committee on Justice, Human Rights, Public Safety and Emergency Preparedness recommended reforms to the process.[22] Each of the four parties on the committee issued a separate report. They agreed that the pool of candidates should be chosen by an advisory committee of lawyers, judges, and laypeople, similar to the committees that already vet aspiring superior court and appellate judges in the provinces. They also agreed that Parliament should play some role in the nomination of justices, although they differed over the precise nature of that role. The Liberal majority called for the justice minister to appear before the Justice Committee after the selection had been made to explain why that particular person had been chosen. The Conservatives argued that the nominee should be required to appear in person, preferably before the final decision had been made, and that the Commons should have the power to veto proposed appointments.

When the Justice Committee issued its report, shortly before the 2004 election, there were two unexpected Ontario vacancies on the Court. Nothing could be done until after the June 28 election, which left little time to implement the committee's recommendations. As the Supreme Court's fall term approached, and with Parliament set to resume in October at the earliest, the new Liberal minority government cobbled together an ad hoc response to the committee's call for more input. In late August 2004, Justice Minister Irwin Cotler announced the nomination of justices Louise Charron and Rosalie Silberman Abella. The following day, he appeared before an Interim Ad Hoc Committee on the Appointment of Supreme Court Judges to answer questions about the two nominees. The committee was made up of two Liberal MPs (one of whom was the chair), two Conservatives, one New Democrat, and one BQ MP; they were joined by a representative from the Law Society of Upper Canada, which speaks for the Ontario legal community, and one from the Canadian Judicial Council.

The hearing degenerated into a predictable partisan battle: the Conservative and NDP members argued that the two nominees should have appeared in person, instead of being represented by the justice minister. In the end, the committee raised no questions about the qualifications of the two candidates, preferring instead to argue about the process. Two days later the nominated justices were formally appointed, doubling the number of women on the Supreme Court to four. The justice minister defended his decision not to have the nominees appear before the committee based on the need to keep the courts separate from the political process: that is, the principle of judicial independence.

Less than a month into his first term as prime minister, Stephen Harper was presented with the opportunity to implement the new Conservative minority government's approach to filling vacancies. Harper opted for a publicly televised appearance of his nominee, Manitoba justice Marshal Rothstein, before the Ad Hoc Committee to Review a Nominee for the Supreme Court. The committee would not be structured as a parliamentary committee, although it would be comprised of parliamentarians and its rules of procedures would be agreed to by all the official parliamentary parties.[23] Neither Parliament nor the committee would vote on or have the opportunity to veto the nominee. After a very cordial interview by the committee, Justice Rothstein was appointed to the Court by the prime minister.

The Separation of Law and Politics

One of the foundational principles underlying the liberal democratic approach to government is that a difference between politics and law exists, and is maintained by the institutional structures established by the Constitution. Liberal democracies require that the courts be independent from legislatures and other political institutions because the judicial rulings must be made separately from political decisions. The courts cannot consider whether a decision will be popular—many are not. It also cannot consider whether it will meet with majority approval—many do not. Nor is the existence of a substantial organized opposition to the decision a factor—many times there is one. All of those considerations are political matters, and while it is legitimate and appropriate for legislators and the political executive to base their decisions on them, it is not appropriate for the judiciary to take them into consideration.

With the introduction of the Charter, however, the supreme law of the land changed, bringing the courts more directly into conflict with the political process. Nevertheless, it is the duty of courts to apply that law, even if it means overruling politicians who represent majority opinion on an issue. In effect, the courts have the obligation to determine sometimes that the majority is breaking the constitutional law.[24] Without being subject to political pressure from legislatures or the political executive,

NAME OF JUSTICE	DATE OF APPOINTMENT	DATE OF DEPARTURE
Hon. Sir William Buell Richards	September 1875	January 1879
Hon. Sir William Johnstone Ritchie	January 1879	September 1892
Rt. Hon. Sir Samuel Henry Strong	December 1892	November 1902
Rt. Hon. Sir Henri-Elzéar Taschereau	November 1902	May 1906
Rt. Hon. Sir Charles Fitzpatrick	June 1906	October 1918
Rt. Hon. Sir Louis Henry Davies	October 1918	May 1924
Rt. Hon. Francis Alexander Anglin	September 1924	February 1933
Rt. Hon. Sir Lyman Poore Duff	March 1933	January 1944
Rt. Hon. Thibaudeau Rinfret	January 1944	June 1954
Hon. Patrick Kerwin	July 1954	February 1963
Rt. Hon. Robert Taschereau	April 1963	September 1967
Rt. Hon. John Robert Cartwright	September 1967	March 1970
Rt. Hon. Joseph Honoré Gérald Fauteux	March 1970	December 1973
Rt. Hon. Bora Laskin	December 1973	March 1984
Rt. Hon. Robert George Brian Dickson	April 1984	June 1990
Rt. Hon. Antonio Lamer	July 1990	January 2000
Rt. Hon. Beverley McLachlin	January 2000	continuing

Source: Supreme Court of Canada, *Judges of the Court*, available on-line at http://www.scc-csc.gc.ca/aboutcourt/judges/curformchief/index_e.asp; accessed July 2006.

judges have the ability to declare the majority wrong, and correct the injustice. Without this independence from politics, the rule of law as we know it would cease to exist.

The separation of powers, however, implies more than the freedom of judges to interpret the law without interference from the legislative or executive branches. It also means that each of the three branches has its own unique sphere of activity, into which the others cannot legitimately intrude.

Judicial Procedures: Adjudication versus Policy-Making

Courts and court procedures were originally designed to adjudicate (i.e., definitively resolve) narrowly defined disputes. In principle, judges do not make new law, nor do they strike down old law. They merely apply existing law to the facts of each individual case, without indulging in sweeping statements about the broader implications of their rulings.

The policy-making powers that courts are called upon to exercise in Charter cases are foreign to the adjudicative process, at least at the trial stage. As a case makes its way up the judicial hierarchy from the lower courts to the superior courts and finally (though rarely) to the Supreme Court of Canada, the emphasis shifts from adjudication to policy-making. The facts of the case, which are the primary concern of the trial judge, yield to broader questions of law and policy at the higher levels. This is because the ruling of the trial judge is binding only on the immediate parties to the case, whereas the rulings of appellate judges will apply to the entire province or country.

Trials

At all levels of the judicial hierarchy, the purpose of a trial—whether civil or criminal—is to provide an authoritative resolution to a dispute between two parties. In a criminal trial, the parties are the Crown (hence the title *Regina* [Latin for "queen"] *versus X* [name(s) of the accused]). The issues are relatively narrow: Should the accused be found guilty or innocent? Should the accused go to jail, and, if so, for how long? In most civil cases, both parties are private actors (individuals or corporations) interested in settling a private dispute. For example, which of two divorcing parents gets custody of the children, or is custody to be shared? Has there been a breach of contract between the seller and the buyer, and, if so, what is the remedy? These are the kinds of day-to-day conflicts that trial judges must decide. The focus is on the facts of the immediate situation. Once the facts are determined, the law must be applied to them, which may require the judge to interpret the law in a new way. At trial, however, such interpretive judicial law-making rarely exceeds what is required to resolve the immediate dispute.

In a minority of cases, the key issue at trial is not the application of the law, but whether the law itself violates the Constitution. Because "no one can be convicted under an unconstitutional law," anyone accused of a crime can seek to have the law nullified (and the charges consequently dropped) under Section 52 of the Constitution Act, 1982.[25] In these instances, the trial judge is required to assess the merits of the law on both legal and policy grounds. The policy considerations become particularly important if the judge finds that the law violates one or more Charter guarantees; the judge must then determine whether the violation is justified under Section 1.

Appeals

If one party is dissatisfied with the outcome of a trial, that person can appeal to a higher court. The party seeking to overturn the trial result is called the *appellant;* the other party is called the *respondent*. For example, a person convicted of a crime who asks a higher court to overturn the conviction will be designated the appellant. However, if the trial judge found that the applicable section of the Criminal Code violated the Charter and struck it down, the federal government (embodied in the Crown) may seek a reversal at a higher court; in this instance, the Crown is the appellant.

Once the case moves on to appeal, the balance between adjudication and law-making shifts in favour of the latter. From an adjudicative perspective, appeal courts secure fairness for litigants. As we understand the adjudicative process today, we are entitled not only to our day in court but also to our day in a higher court that can "correct injustices or errors that may have occurred in the lower court."[26] These errors are generally of a legal nature, not a factual nature—e.g., whether the trial judge was correct in his or her assessment of the constitutionality of the law.

The judgment of an appellate court is binding on all lower courts within its jurisdiction. Thus, the legal interpretations of the appeal court of any province become the law for the entire province. However, they are not legally binding outside the territory of that province. For example, the June 2003 *Halpern* ruling from the Ontario Court of Appeal made it legal for same-sex couples to marry in that province;[27] subsequent rulings from the appellate courts in British Columbia and Quebec opened the door to same-sex marriages in those provinces. Elsewhere in Canada, gay and lesbian couples were still prohibited from obtaining marriage licences. If they wished to wed, they had two options: to travel to one of the provinces where same-sex marriages were performed, or to wait for their own provincial courts (or the federal government) to change the law.

Although a provincial Court of Appeal has no legal jurisdiction outside the borders of the province, its rulings often influence other appellate courts when they deal with similar cases. In the above example, the court in *Halpern* refused to suspend the legality of same-sex marriage so that Parliament could amend the relevant laws. Instead, it declared that same-sex couples in Ontario could get married as soon as the ruling was issued. Shortly thereafter, the British Columbia Court of Appeal amended its earlier ruling on the issue, in which it had suspended the remedy of permitting same-sex marriage for two years; it ordered the province to grant marriage licences to gay and lesbian couples immediately.[28] More generally, provincial appellate rulings are rarely appealed to the Supreme Court of Canada; when they are, the justices reject most applications for leave to appeal. In practical terms, therefore, the provincial courts of appeal often have the final word on legal and constitutional questions, and their influence can stretch well beyond their official jurisdictions.

The party that loses its case in a provincial court of appeal can, however, try to appeal to the Supreme Court of Canada. As the highest court in the land, the Supreme Court makes rulings that are authoritative and binding on the entire country. The judicial hierarchy does more than provide an avenue of appeal for disgruntled litigants in the immediate case; it also ensures that laws are applied consistently across Canada. Consequently, the facts of the immediate case are even less central at the Supreme Court than they are in the provincial appellate courts.

Since 1975, the Supreme Court has had the power to choose which appeals it will hear. The task of sorting through thousands of appellate petitions is left to three-judge panels, which rely heavily on the opinions of court clerks (recent law school graduates who spend a year working for particular justices). Appeals that raise important legal principles, particularly Charter issues, are the most likely to survive the winnowing

In the year 2000, Albertan Beverly McLachlin became the first female chief justice of the Supreme Court of Canada. After a distinguished legal career, both as a practising lawyer and an academic, she rose through the British Columbia judiciary, eventually becoming chief justice of the British Columbia Supreme Court, prior to being summoned to the Canadian high court in 1989. (© Reuters/CORBIS)

Born: 1943, Pincher Creek, Alberta

Education: B.A. and M.A. Philosophy, LL.B. (University of Alberta, 1965, 1968, and 1968)

Profession: Lawyer (called to the Bar of Alberta, 1969; to the Bar of British Columbia, 1971)

Legal Career:
1969–1971 Practised law with Wood, Moir, Hyde and Ross, Edmonton
1971–1972 Practised law with Thomas, Herdy, Mitchell & Co., Fort St. John, British Columbia
1972–1975 Practised law with Bull, Housser & Tupper, Vancouver
1974–1981 Lecturer, associate professor, and professor with tenure, University of British Columbia

Judicial Career:
1981 Appointed to the County Court of Vancouver
1981 Appointed to the Supreme Court of British Columbia
1985 Appointed to the Court of Appeal of British Columbia
1988 Appointed chief justice of the Supreme Court of British Columbia
1989 Appointed to the Supreme Court of Canada
2000 Appointed chief justice of the Supreme Court of Canada

Other Appointments:
Chairperson, Canadian Judicial Council
Chairperson, Advisory Council of the Order of Canada
Chairperson, Board of Governors of the National Judicial Institute
Member of the Privy Council of Canada

Source: Supreme Court of Canada, available on-line at http://www.scc-csc.gc.ca.

process. The court's freedom to control its own docket clearly indicates that policy-making, not adjudication, is its primary function.

Judicial Expertise and the Oakes Test

Whether or not one believes that judicial policy-making undermines the democratic will of the people as expressed through their parliamentary representatives, the more practical problem is the mismatch between policy-making and adjudication. The Supreme Court, like all adjudicative bodies, is made up of experts in law. They possess neither the expertise nor the institutional resources to effectively evaluate public policy, or to craft new policies to replace those that they have nullified on Charter grounds. For example, the rules of evidence in Canadian courts are designed to promote the resolution of specific cases. Trial judges normally exclude extrinsic evidence, materials that are not directly relevant to the case before the court. Until recently, appellate courts also refused to hear extrinsic evidence, either about the intent of legislators in drafting impugned laws or about the policy implications of the issues under consideration. The Supreme Court began to relax its ban on extrinsic evidence in the 1970s, though only in constitutional reference cases and only for the purpose of interpreting regular statutes.

In the Charter era, judges have relied heavily on one type of extrinsic evidence—social science data about the policy effects of impugned laws—while rejecting another—evidence of legislative intent. In other words, the courts are unable or unwilling to base their interpretations of the law—constitutional or otherwise—on the hopes and priorities of the people who wrote the law. In the words of former chief justice Lamer, parliamentary speeches and committee testimony provide "inherently unreliable" evidence of legislative intent. This is particularly true of constitutional laws such as the Charter, which are drafted by many people, with input from a variety of different groups. Under these circumstances, "the intention of the legislative bodies which adopted the Charter" is impossible to determine with any accuracy.[29]

Social science evidence plays a particularly important role at the second stage of the three-stage Charter analysis. As we will see in "The Three-Stage Approach" later in this chapter, the first stage requires a judge to determine whether an impugned law, or a particular act or omission by a public official, infringes a guaranteed right or freedom. If the answer is "yes," the judge moves on to the second stage: determining whether the infringement can be justified under Section 1 of the Charter. Under the *Oakes* test for "reasonable limitations," he or she must answer four questions:[30]

1. Is the objective of the impugned law sufficiently "pressing and substantial" to justify infringing a protected right or freedom? That is to say, does the problem that the law is designed to address outweigh the risk of violating rights or freedoms?

2. Assuming that the objective is indeed "pressing and substantial," is there a rational connection between the objective and the law itself? In effect, does the law actually address the problem identified in the first stage, or does it miss the target?

3. Does the law "minimally impair" the relevant right or freedom, or is there an alternative policy that would serve the same purpose with less impact on the Charter?

4. Are the effects of the law proportional to the objective? In its initial formulation, this question weighed the infringement of the Charter against the importance of the objective.

5. These questions are unlikely to be answered on the basis of traditional adjudicative facts—i.e., the facts of the specific case at bar. The judges must rely on social

science evidence about the seriousness of particular problems, the effects of the impugned law, and possible alternative policies.

At least three problems are raised by the Supreme Court's reliance on social science evidence. First, the justices cannot cross-examine the expert witnesses who write affidavits concerning extrinsic evidence; in most cases, they can only assume that the factual claims presented by the parties to the appeal are accurate.[31] In effect, the Supreme Court disregards the standards for expert testimony that it imposed on lower-court judges and trial juries. In *Regina v. Mohan,* the justices expressed concern about the misleading effect of spurious or unsubstantiated "expert" testimony on impressionable jurors. They required trial judges or jurors to evaluate evidence "in light of its potential to distort the fact-finding process."[32] No such constraint applies to the Supreme Court's own deliberations. If they so wish, justices are free to fudge data, to ignore or downplay extrinsic evidence that conflicts with their own beliefs, and to base their findings on biased or incomplete research.

Second, courts may make broad policy decisions based on insufficient or misinterpreted social science data, with potentially harmful results. For example, in its 1990 ruling in *Askov v. the Queen,* the justices held that forcing defendants to wait for more than eight months for their trials violated Section 11 (b) of the Charter.[33] The decision was based, in part, on social science data about the impact of spending cuts on the operation of Crown prosecutors, data that did not support a fixed time limit for trials. Tens of thousands of pending charges were dismissed because of an apparent misreading of extrinsic evidence.

Third, judicial principles are inappropriate tools for evaluating legislative decisions. In effect, the courts have been granted the power to intervene in the policymaking process, without simultaneously acquiring the expertise to do it properly. The justices themselves are aware of their limited policy-making skills, especially in the field of social policy.[34] Notwithstanding this admission of incapacity, the Supreme Court's own interpretation of Section 1 has opened the floodgates to extrinsic evidence in many areas of public policy. However, it has not changed the fact that judges and lawyers are not experts in public policy, nor are they trained to assess the credibility of social science evidence. The difficulties arising from this change in evidentiary rules illustrates a basic problem of institutional adaptation: when an institution acquires new responsibilities for which its existing procedures are inadequate, it may not always discharge those responsibilities as well as we might wish.

The Supreme Court is deficient as a policy-making institution in one other respect: it does not have the power to implement and enforce its own rulings. The practical effect of court decisions depends on the willingness of other government agencies—police, legislatures, public officials—to follow judge-made rules of conduct. That willingness cannot be taken for granted. For example, the 1991 *Stinchcombe* ruling required Crown prosecutors to disclose all relevant evidence in a criminal trial to the defence in a timely manner.[35] Subsequent rulings and anecdotal evidence from defence lawyers reveal the resistance of some Crown prosecutors to their new responsibilities under *Stinchcombe.*[36]

Even when rulings are fully implemented by the responsible government actors, their impact on the daily lives of Canadians may still be less than the courts anticipated. A ruling that permits people to do something they were previously prohibited from doing (e.g., the 2002 *Sauvé* decision granting prisoners the right to vote) will have little practical effect unless the intended beneficiaries of the ruling actually choose to take the Court up on its offer. So we should not assume that judicial decisions, including those based on the Charter, necessarily have a dramatic impact on the lives of Canadians.

KEY PRINCIPLES OF CHARTER INTERPRETATION

Since 1982, the Supreme Court has developed several principles to guide Charter interpretation—both by lower courts and by policy-makers in the executive and legislative branches. As we have seen elsewhere, the written Constitution cannot be understood simply by reading the text. We must also consider the ways in which that text has been interpreted and applied by the courts: the common law (case law) of constitutional jurisprudence. This is particularly true for the Charter, given the broad language in which its provisions are phrased and the huge volume of Charter rulings. In this section we will discuss five key principles of Charter interpretation:

1. *stare decisis* (Latin for "the decision stands")
2. the purposive approach
3. the contextual approach
4. the three-stage approach
5. the "living tree" approach

▓ *Stare Decisis:* The Binding Power of Precedent

In theory, each court is bound by precedents—relevant rulings handed down by earlier judges. The Supreme Court of Canada, like all courts, is expected to follow its own precedents where these exist. In addition, all lower courts are restricted in their interpretation of the law by doctrines established by higher courts. The rule of *stare decisis* has two principal advantages. First, it imposes a degree of consistency and predictability on what might otherwise become a chaotic and contradictory mass of jurisprudence. Policy-makers and lower-court judges need guidelines to follow when they apply existing laws or make new ones. Second, *stare decisis* encourages higher courts to make principled decisions. Instead of following their own personal preferences, judges are expected to develop the law within the parameters set by precedent.

In practice, the *stare decisis* rule is more flexible than one might expect. Although their interpretive freedom is restricted by existing precedents, judges are free to decide which precedents apply to a particular case and how, if at all, established legal principles may be modified to suit changing social needs. A judge who disagrees with a Supreme Court precedent can distinguish it from the case at bar by ruling that the facts of the two cases are sufficiently different to preclude the application of the earlier ruling. At the Supreme Court itself, the justices have demonstrated considerable ingenuity in evading their own prior decisions without formally overturning them, which they very rarely do.

The Purposive Approach

Before it can determine whether a particular law or administrative act violates a Charter guarantee, a court must identify the purpose of that guarantee—the nature of the interests that the specific Charter provision is meant to protect.[37] The Court's ruling when dealing with the Charter's right-to-vote guarantee is illustrative.

Section 3 of the Charter guarantees to every Canadian citizen the right to vote in federal Commons elections and in provincial elections, as well as the right to run for public office. The Supreme Court has ruled that the right to vote protects two distinct interests. First, it guarantees effective representation in government to every citizen. Representation means having a voice in the deliberations of the government. Effective representation implies a relative parity of voting power among citizens.[38] Practically, this means that the population in one constituency may not grossly exceed the population in another, although some variation in constituency size may be justified for geographic or other reasons. Where the variance is too great, the voting rights of citizens in large constituencies are diluted relative to those in less populated ridings.

The second interest protected by the right to vote is the right to play a meaningful role in elections.[39] The content of that meaningful role was spelled out in the 2003 *Figueroa* ruling, which struck down the law requiring political parties to run at least 50 candidates in a general election to qualify for state benefits. At a minimum, all citizens must have the opportunity to vote and, if desired, to seek election to a federal or provincial legislature. They must be able to choose among a wide range of competing political parties or candidates, so that their own political views are reflected in public debate and, perhaps, in government. Any law that erects barriers to free and fair competition among political parties and candidates restricts the range of political options and makes it more difficult for some citizens to play a meaningful role in elections.

Whereas the first purpose of Section 3 emphasizes the outcome of an election, the second focuses on the electoral process. The identification of two distinct purposes for a single Charter guarantee caused some legal confusion. The trial judge who heard the *Figueroa* case ruled that the party-registration law violated Section 3, and struck down or modified several sections of the Canada Elections Act. She followed the meaningful-role interpretation of the guarantee. The federal government appealed parts of her ruling to the Ontario Court of Appeal, which relied on the effective-representation purpose; it overturned most of the trial ruling and restored the impugned sections of the act. The Supreme Court of Canada finally resolved the issue when it declared that the true purpose of Section 3, in relation to electoral participation, was the meaningful role. Consequently, it restored much of the original ruling of the trial judge. The fluctuating and uncertain status of Canada's election law might have been avoided if the Supreme Court had identified a single purpose for Section 3 in the first place.

The Contextual Approach

Once a court has determined the purpose of a particular Charter guarantee, it must specify the precise application of that purpose to the facts of the case at bar. Instead of interpreting Charter guarantees abstractly, in a factual vacuum, the court is required to interpret them in relation to the specific dispute that it has been called upon to resolve. Former justice Bertha Wilson, the author of the contextual approach, argued that

> a right or freedom may have different meanings in different contexts. Security of the person, for example, might mean one thing when addressed to the issue of over-crowding in prisons and something quite different when addressed to the issue of noxious fumes from industrial smoke-stacks.[40]

She also pointed out that the task of balancing rights against competing social values, which is required under Section 1 of the Charter, can be performed more effectively when both are defined with specific reference to the case being adjudicated.

The contextual approach has been particularly important in cases involving freedom of expression (Section 2 [b]). The Supreme Court distinguishes among various types of expressive content, based on their perceived value to individuals and to Canadian society as a whole. Core content includes political speech, artistic self-expression, and the search for scientific truth. Expressive activity that falls into the core category may not be restricted by the state without an extremely good reason. Therefore, laws that infringe core expression will be subject to a strict standard of justification under Section 1. On the other end of the spectrum, peripheral content—e.g., hate speech and child pornography—merits little Charter protection, and legal restrictions on it are relatively easy to justify. Commercial advertising falls somewhere in between, depending on its intent. Manipulative tobacco ads that portray smoking as a fun or cool activity enjoy less protection from the Charter than ads that make driving a car in what under normal conditions would be an illegal manner look fun.

The Three-Stage Approach

The Supreme Court has established a three-stage process for determining the constitutionality of laws that are alleged to violate the Charter, and for determining appropriate remedies for those that are found to be unconstitutional.

Stage One

In the first stage, a court must determine whether the impugned law infringes a Charter right or freedom. The person or group alleging the infringement must prove beyond a reasonable doubt that the impugned law violates the Charter. The Supreme Court has consistently held that Charter guarantees must receive a "large and liberal" interpretation at this first stage of analysis. However, this principle is not always applied consistently. The Court has interpreted narrowly some Charter guarantees, notably freedom of association (Section 2 [d]) and equality rights (Section 15 [1]). Until recently, a majority of the justices held that the guarantee of associative freedom did not protect specifically collective activities; it permitted the exercise of individual rights and freedoms only in concert with others. Nor did Section 2 (d) afford any protection to labour unions. There is no Charter basis for a right to strike, or even to bargain collectively.[41] In a similar vein, the Court has decreed that the guarantee of equality rights does not prevent the state from *distinguishing* between different groups of people (e.g., by requiring separate bathroom and locker facilities for men and women). It prevents the adoption only of laws that *discriminate* against a specific group (e.g., a law that prohibits qualified women from working as police officers).

The purpose of Section 1 is to limit the application of the enumerated rights and freedoms and to balance Charter guarantees against competing social interests. In practice, no right or freedom can be exercised without restraint. For example, freedom of speech is a prerequisite for a healthy liberal-pluralist democracy. The liberty to express unpopular opinions must be protected against the annoyance of the majority. But hate propaganda against scapegoated minorities undermines the social tolerance on which pluralism depends and threatens the security and other liberties of the targeted groups. One of the foundations of a liberal political culture is that it accepts the obligation not to have hard and fast rules about every potential conflict between these often-competing goals. Essentially, liberalism means that political institutions are called upon to exercise judgment about where to draw the line between the rights of individuals to engage in deviant behaviour, and those of society to protect itself from extremism.

The application of these principles by the Canadian courts makes it likely that an impugned law will be found to infringe a particular right or freedom. In consequence, judges often quickly move to the second stage of analysis: whether the sponsoring government can justify the infringement under Section 1.

Stage Two

In the second stage, the burden of proof shifts to the government that passed the impugned law. It must prove, on a balance of probabilities, that the law constitutes a reasonable limit on the infringed Charter right and that this limit is "demonstrably justifiable in a free and democratic society." Note that the balance-of-probabilities onus for the state is less burdensome than the onus required in the first stage of the test: proof beyond a reasonable doubt. If a court finds that the law meets the four criteria of the *Oakes* test and is declared to be constitutional, it will let the law stand. Laws that do not appear to serve "pressing and substantial" social interests, or whose effects on the right in question are considered serious enough to outweigh their stated objectives, will trigger some kind of judicial remedy.

For the most part, Canadian courts have interpreted Charter rights broadly and then turned to Section 1 to determine reasonable limits. But the application of

Section 1 has narrowed over the years, which makes it easier for sponsoring governments to justify laws that infringe protected rights and freedoms. When considering social policy, the Court has generally lightened the burden of proof on the state. As long as the state can argue that the legislators who enacted the law made a reasonable judgment, even in the absence of hard evidence, courts will generally accept that argument as valid.

However, the Court has been more willing to challenge the use of state power against criminal suspects and defendants. In part, the Court's aggressive approach to legal rights reflects its acknowledgment that its expertise about the legal process itself is greater than its capacity to make policy in social areas. The justices have in effect acknowledged that social policy is more effectively made by legislators than by judges. The criminal justice system, in contrast, does not require such delicate policy choices: if legislators are slow to reform the Criminal Code, whether because of neglect or from a desire to avoid controversy, the courts have demonstrated that they are more than ready to step in and fill the legal void.

Stage Three

In the third stage, courts must determine the appropriate remedy for the party or parties whose rights have been infringed by the impugned law. As we have seen, a court can strike down the law "to the extent of the inconsistency" with the Charter; it can suspend the law, to give legislators time to bring it into conformity with the Constitution; it can order the government in question to apply the law according to the Constitution; it can read down the offending law to exclude the unconstitutional application; or it can read in a group that was previously excluded from the benefit of the law. In a criminal appeal, the appropriate remedy may be purely individual: the court may grant a new trial to the accused, with or without the exclusion of improperly obtained evidence.

After initially engaging in a considerable amount of judicial activism, the Supreme Court has recently become somewhat more deferential to legislative authority. The most important reason for the revival of judicial deference is probably the nature of judicial review itself. When judges are presented with a new constitutional document, they must create an entirely new set of doctrines and principles for its interpretation. Once those doctrines have taken shape, the impetus for judicial activism weakens, and the Court becomes more deferential to legislatures. It is also likely that the Supreme Court struck down more laws in the first decade after the Charter came into effect because it was confronted with a backlog of pre-Charter legislation. After nearly two decades, legislative drafters have become more careful to avoid remedial action by the courts. In effect, the "large and liberal" approach of the early years forced the other branches of government to take their first-order Charter duties more seriously than they might otherwise have. Consequently, fewer laws require fixing to conform to the Charter.

It is also likely that the justices have been chastened by public criticism of their more controversial forays into policy-making and have tried to keep their heads down in recent years. They also seem to have become more acutely aware of their limitations as policy-makers. In response, they have become more cautious in the use of their remedial powers. Instead of immediately striking down laws, the Supreme Court is increasingly likely to suspend the nullification of a law in order to allow the sponsoring legislature to fix problems as it sees fit.

■ The "Living Tree" Approach

The fifth general principle is that the Charter is a "living tree" which must be allowed to grow and develop in ways that its drafters could not foresee. The phrase first appeared in Canadian jurisprudence in the 1929 *Persons* case. As a principle of judicial review, it originally meant that a constitution must be interpreted in a flexible manner that permits its application to unforeseen circumstances, without the necessity of formal amendments, which are deliberately designed to be difficult to accomplish. As we noted earlier, the Court has refused to be bound by the evidence of the framers' intent when it interprets the Charter. This attitude arises, in part, from the Court's adherence to the living tree principle. Critics argue that the Court has distorted the living tree metaphor beyond recognition.[42] In effect, the justices have grafted new branches onto a tree that was originally planted by legislators and thus transformed the tree in a way that the framers of the Constitution never intended.

The debate over the living tree metaphor illustrates a central controversy over judicial review: should judges adopt an interpretivist or a noninterpretivist approach to constitutional provisions? Interpretivists believe that judges should respect the original intent of the framers, and generally stick to the written text of the Constitution. The noninterpretivist approach treats the written Constitution as a starting point for policy-making, in which the preferences of today's judges can legitimately outweigh the choices of the framers. Interpretivist judges defer to the legislative branch and regard themselves as equally bound by the Constitution. Noninterpretivist judges give themselves wide latitude to reinterpret rights and overrule legislators, without taking the original intent of either the impugned law or the Constitution into account.

Judges are not free, however, to impose their own policy preferences without constraint. In reality, there are at least three constraints on judicial policy-making. First, appellate courts are collegial institutions. Individual judges have no power unless they can command the support of a majority of their colleagues. Although a lone dissenting judge can exert a long-term influence on the development of the law, in general, a maverick judge who refuses to compromise his or her policy preferences risks isolation and impotence. Second, as noted earlier, judges are restrained (at least to a degree) by the principle of *stare decisis*. They cannot just make up the law as they go along. Third and finally, judges are not solely responsible for the interpretation and enforcement of the Charter. If they choose, policy-makers in the legislative and executive branches can modify or even reject the choices enshrined in court rulings. In several instances, Parliament has amended the Criminal Code to undo the effect of court rulings that it perceived as unduly favourable toward alleged criminals. At least one of these amendments was subsequently upheld by the Supreme Court on the ground that "[c]ourts do not hold a monopoly on the protection and promotion of rights and freedoms; Parliament also plays a role in this regard and is often able to act as a significant ally for vulnerable groups."[43]

It would seem then, that even without recourse to the controversial notwith-standing clause (Section 33), which allows a legislature to override certain rights and freedoms for a five-year period, the other two branches of government are not helpless in the face of court rulings on the Charter. Politicians and others who suggest that governments are powerless when the courts "force" Charter ruling on them are exaggerating to the point of misrepresenting the relationship among Canada's political institutions.

THE IMPACT OF THE CHARTER ON CANADIAN POLITICS AND POLICY

At its core, the Charter has given new institutional expression to changing political values. Legislators at both the federal and provincial levels must now take rights and freedoms into account in their policy deliberations. To avoid passing laws that may be nullified on Charter grounds, legislators and ministers increasingly rely on legal advisers to assess the constitutionality of proposed legislation.[44] If those advisers identify a potentially unconstitutional element in the proposed legislation, the legislative and executive branches must either amend the draft law or risk the nullification of an entire policy. But given that few laws or administrative decisions are ever subjected to a Charter challenge in the courts, in most instances the Charter-proofing conducted by the executive and legislative branches of government remains the best guarantee of rights and freedoms.

The Charter has also altered the relationship between the state and organized interests.[45] Pressure groups have two avenues of influence in the judicial process: they can directly challenge the constitutionality of a particular law through public-interest litigation, or they can apply for intervenor status in cases brought by other parties.

Direct constitutional litigation is extremely expensive and beyond the means of most organizations and individuals. Although the payoff from a favourable ruling can be huge, the risk of losing in the courts diminishes the attractiveness of litigation for many groups. The intervenor strategy is less expensive, though still costly. It also carries its own disadvantages. Initially, there is no guarantee that an application to intervene will be granted. The Supreme Court has complete discretion to accept or reject any would-be intervenor, and it rarely explains its treatment of applicants. In a rare public ruling, the late justice Sopinka identified two criteria: (1) whether the applicant has a demonstrated interest in the outcome of the case, and (2) whether the applicant can demonstrate "an expertise which can shed fresh light or provide new information on the matter."[46] Furthermore, a successful application to intervene does not automatically ensure a meaningful influence on the outcome of the case. Some interventions have been remarkably successful, at least from the viewpoint of the intervenors themselves, but with most it is difficult to determine their impact.

The overall point is that the Charter's impact on Canadian politics and policy-making, while significant, should not be overstated. As the following section explains, the Charter leaves many areas of government and policy unaffected.

■ The Scope and Application of the Charter

Section 32 of the Constitution Act, 1982, states that the Charter applies to both levels of government "in respect of all matters" within their respective jurisdictions. In the early years of Charter jurisprudence, the Supreme Court had to determine exactly what those words meant. Did the Charter apply to private litigation? Did it apply to universities, hospitals, and other quasi-public agencies? Did it give the courts the power to review orders-in-council and other executive decrees, or was its effect restricted to the acts of legislators? Finally, was the court itself bound by the Charter?

Application to Governments but Not Private Citizens

The justices were initially divided, but eventually determined, primarily through their ruling in *Dolphin Delivery*, that the Charter applies to the legislative, executive, and administrative branches of government, but does not apply to purely private disputes in which no government action is involved. In other words, the state "owes a constitutional duty" to its citizens that private individuals do not owe to one another.[47] In the process of narrowing the Charter's application, however, the Court exempted judicial rulings—including those of the Supreme Court—from Charter scrutiny. Intentionally or otherwise, *Dolphin Delivery* placed judges above the reach of the law. At the same time, it insulated private economic relations—between employers and employees, for example—from Charter remedies.

Applications for Semipublic Agencies

In the 1990 *McKinney* case,[48] the Court ruled that the Charter does not apply to the mandatory retirement policies in force at most universities. A university is a private corporation (albeit one incorporated by provincial statute) that receives public money to carry out a public purpose. Because universities lie outside the apparatus of government, their collective agreements with their employees are beyond the scope of Charter review. Had the mandatory retirement policies at issue in *McKinney* been subject to Charter review, they would have been found to be unconstitutional on the grounds of age discrimination (Section 15 [1]). The court subsequently ruled, however, that discriminatory employment policies based on statute law, as opposed to private contracts, are subject to Charter remedies. While "private activity" is not open to judicial review, "laws that regulate private activity" are fair game.[49] Therefore, private corporations are subject to Charter scrutiny in the performance of their "delegated public functions," but not in the conduct of their internal private operations.

More recently, the Court has ruled that semipublic agencies such as hospitals and universities may be held liable for exercising their statutory authority in a way that violates the Charter. In *Eldridge,* the court ruled that hospitals must provide sign-language interpreters for deaf patients. The British Columbia Hospital Insurance Act was held to be constitutional, because it did not prevent the provision of interpreters, but the failure of particular hospitals to assist hearing-impaired patients violated Section 15 (1) of the Charter.[50] Where a particular law is constitutional but its application by a private agency is not, the remedy lies in Section 24 (1) of the Charter. In the *Eldridge* case, the court ordered the provincial government to administer its health-care system "in a manner consistent with the requirements of Section 15 (1)," without specifying how it should do so.

Application for Citizens and Other Residents

Finally, the court has held that the Charter guarantees certain rights to Canadian citizens and noncitizens alike. In *Singh*, the Court argued that the word "everyone" in Section 7 includes every person who is physically present in Canada, not just those who hold citizenship. By their very presence, all persons are entitled to Charter protection.[51] At the same time, it argued that deporting someone who could face persecution in the receiving country violated rights to security of the person. The *Singh* doctrine has two implications. First, landed immigrants and refugee claimants are entitled to due process in their dealings with Canadian officials. Second, the Canadian government may not expose any person on its soil to the threat of a punishment that exceeds that imposed by Canadian law. As such, a noncitizen who has been accused or convicted of a crime may not be extradited to a country that uses the death penalty, unless the minister of justice has first received a written assurance that the individual will not be executed.

Scope and Application: Three Illustrative Cases

As the numerous references to court cases in this chapter indicate, 25 years of Charter application has created a vast body of case law and precedent. The following three cases illustrate some of the impacts the Charter has had on the courts, the legislatures, and the executive since the formal entrenchment of rights and freedoms in the Canadian Constitution.

Abortion Rights: Pre- and Post-Charter

The Charter's impact on judicial review can best be understood by comparing the Supreme Court's approach to the same law before and after 1982. The two *Morgentaler* rulings serve the purpose well because the justices themselves used the second ruling to clarify the Charter's impact on their interpretation of the abortion law.

In 1975 the court upheld Section 251 of the Criminal Code, which prohibited abortion. The only exceptions to the law were therapeutic abortions: those performed in a hospital with the approval of a Therapeutic Abortion Committee (TAC) made up of three doctors (not including the doctor who would perform the actual procedure). For a variety of reasons, by 1982, only one in five Canadian hospitals had functioning TACs. Under the law, a TAC could authorize an abortion only if the continuation of the pregnancy "would or would be likely to endanger [the] life or health" of the woman. Some doctors interpreted the word "health" broadly, to include mental and emotional well-being, while others would not permit abortions except in medical emergencies. The procedural flaws in Section 251 were serious. Not only did access to abortion vary widely across the regions, but also the bureaucracy and arbitrariness inherent in the committee system delayed abortion procedures—often by eight weeks or more. The result was a grave risk to the life and health of women seeking abortions.

Dr. Henry Morgentaler fought to change the law, largely through a one-man civil-disobedience campaign. In 1973 he was charged with performing an illegal abortion in his Montreal clinic. The procedure violated Section 251 because it did not take place in a hospital, and there was no TAC approval. A jury acquitted him, even though he was clearly in violation of the law. The Quebec Court of Appeal overturned the verdict and imposed a conviction. That decision was appealed to the Supreme Court in 1975.

The justices refused to consider Morgentaler's argument that the flawed TAC system violated the due process guarantee in the Bill of Rights. The Court rejected Morgentaler's request for an American-style judicial review of the abortion law, stating that it would be foreign to Canadian traditions, constitutional law, and our conceptions of judicial review.[52] Unlike the American Bill of Rights, the Canadian Bill of Rights was not constitutionally entrenched, and as a federal statute alone, it did not give the courts the power to strike down other federal laws. The Court also insisted that it could not second-guess Parliament or usurp its power to make and amend laws. Morgentaler's conviction was upheld and he went to prison.

After his release, Morgentaler continued to challenge the abortion law. In 1984 he was arrested in Toronto. Once again, a jury acquitted him and an appeals court convicted him. In 1986 he returned to the Supreme Court, hoping that the entrenched Charter would embolden the justices to strike down the law. He argued that because the delays imposed by the TACs threatened life and security of the person, the abortion law violated the rights guaranteed in Section 7 of the Charter. The Court quickly made it clear that since 1982 it had been entrusted with new responsibilities and that it would treat the Charter very differently from the Bill of Rights. Although it would initially steer clear of "complex and controversial programmes of public policy," it would ensure that laws conformed to the values expressed in the Charter.[53]

Five of the seven justices on the 1988 panel voted to strike down the abortion law, although for varying reasons. The four male justices in the majority agreed with Morgentaler that the TACs violated Section 7, because they threatened both the physical and psychological well-being of women seeking abortions. Justice Bertha Wilson, Canada's first female Supreme Court justice, in a separate opinion found that the law violated the right to liberty, as well as the other rights in Section 7. She also found that the law violated the Section 2 (a) Charter guarantee of freedom of conscience.

The Mulroney government made a modest effort to reintroduce a new abortion law, passing it through the House of Commons, but when it was defeated in the Senate by a tie vote, neither that government nor any since has attempted to introduce any criminal restrictions on abortion rights. To this day, Canada has no criminal prohibition against abortion.

Same-Sex Marriage: The Dialogue between Parliament and the Courts

The Supreme Court of Canada issued its first major ruling on equality rights in 1989. One of the key principles in that ruling is that the list of prohibited grounds for discrimination is not exhaustive. Through the process of reading in, Section 15 (1) can be expanded to cover personal characteristics analogous to those already enumerated. The burden of proof for a new claim of analogous grounds rests with the party challenging the law. He or she must demonstrate unequal treatment arising from a genuine disability[54] or from "the stereotypical application of presumed group or personal characteristics."[55] Those characteristics must be directly relevant to the impugned law.[56] To trigger a judicial remedy under Section 15 (1), they must also be directly related to "the essential dignity and worth of the individual,"[57] and they must be either permanent or difficult to change. Analogous grounds accepted by the Supreme Court include sexual orientation, marital status, and parental status (i.e., adoptive versus biological parents).

Of all the analogous grounds read in to Section 15 (1), sexual orientation is by far the most controversial. The first unequivocal recognition that this section protects gays and lesbians from discrimination occurred in 1995, in the *Egan* case. Two men who had lived together in a committed relationship for decades had been denied pension benefits that would automatically have been provided to married or common-law heterosexual spouses. Although the appellants lost their case, they scored a major legal victory when a majority of the Supreme Court declared sexual orientation to be an analogous ground. Once a personal characteristic has been granted this recognition, it cannot be taken away in a subsequent ruling under the doctrine of *stare decisis*. When the court declared in its *Miron v. Trudel* ruling that it was unconstitutional to discriminate against heterosexual common-law couples by denying them benefits to which legally married couples were entitled, the stage was set for the next battle: the designation of same sex couples as common-law.

That battle occurred in 1999, when the Supreme Court struck down an Ontario law that defined common-law spouses as two persons of the opposite sex.[58] This meant that two men or two women who cohabited as romantic partners for a specified period of time would be considered common-law spouses, with all the attendant rights and responsibilities attached to opposite-sex couples in the same situation. For many gays and lesbians, this was enough; the social and legal stigma of homosexuality was fading, and they saw no reason to go further. Others, however, wanted to challenge the last remaining barrier: the definition of legal marriage as an exclusively heterosexual institution.

Same-sex couples in several provinces launched Charter challenges by attempting to procure marriage licences; when they were rejected, they went to court. The first victories came in 2002, when trial courts in both Ontario and Quebec ruled that the heterosexual definition of marriage violated Section 15 by discriminating on the basis of sexual orientation.[59] The federal government, which has jurisdiction over marriage and divorce, appealed both rulings. In the meantime, the British Columbia Court of Appeal overturned a trial verdict and accepted the ruling of the Ontario and

Quebec courts. It ordered that same-sex couples be permitted to marry, and suspended the effect of this order for two years to give Parliament a chance to amend the law. In June 2003 the Ontario Court of Appeal upheld the lower court ruling in that province, as did the Quebec Court of Appeal in March 2004. The Ontario Court of Appeal ordered the province to issue marriage licences to same-sex couples immediately, prompting the British Columbia Court of Appeal to lift its own suspension a few weeks later. Within hours of the Ontario appellate ruling, same-sex couples in the province flocked to registry offices to obtain marriage licences. In the following weeks and months, hundreds travelled from across Canada and from other countries to get married in Ontario or British Columbia. There was no guarantee that the marriages would receive legal recognition in other jurisdictions, but for many couples who had waited years for the chance to marry legally, the opportunity was too good to pass up.

The federal government decided not to appeal the Ontario and British Columbia rulings. Instead, in July 2003 it announced an amendment to the marriage law. The new law would define civil marriage as "the lawful union of two persons to the exclusion of all others." It would also exempt religious clergy and denominations from having to perform same-sex weddings if they objected to the new definition. Before the law was submitted to a vote in Parliament, it was referred to the Supreme Court to test its constitutionality. Three questions were posed to the court: (1) which level of government had jurisdiction over the issue, (2) whether the law was consistent with the equality rights in Section 15, and (3) whether the proposed law violated the Section 2 Charter guarantee of religious freedom (despite an explicit exemption for denominations that rejected same-sex marriage). After Paul Martin became prime minister in late 2003, he referred a fourth question to the Court. The gist of the new question was whether a separate category of "civil unions" for same-sex couples—as distinct from full "marriage"—would violate Section 15.

The decision not to appeal the provincial rulings prompted considerable controversy. Opponents of same-sex marriage were predictably upset by what they perceived as an attack on their values and beliefs. Critics of judicial power argued that Parliament, not the Supreme Court, should have the final say on the issue. During the 2004 federal election campaign, both the Liberals and the new Conservative Party under Stephen Harper tried to use the issue to their own political advantage. Harper promised to withdraw the Supreme Court reference and allow Parliament to decide; he argued that if elected MPs refused to legalize same-sex marriage, the courts would respect that decision. Harper also claimed that because sexual orientation is not specifically listed in Section 15, the Charter did not prohibit discrimination on the grounds of sexual orientation, even though the Court had firmly established sexual orientation as an analogous ground. Paul Martin countered by accusing Harper of trying to weaken minority rights.

In December 2004, the Supreme Court issued its reference ruling on same-sex marriage. The nine justices answered the first three questions unanimously: (1) despite the provinces having authority over the "solemnization of marriage" (Section 92 [12]) the legal definition of marriage is a matter falling exclusively within federal jurisdiction (Section 91 [26]); (2) the extension of civil marriage to same-sex couples does not violate the Charter—indeed, it flows from the equality rights in Section 15; and (3) the provision in the law that exempted religious officials from performing same-sex marriages was consistent with the guarantee of religious freedom in Section 2.[60] However, the court refused to answer the fourth question that had been added by the Martin government. It ruled that the federal government had refused to appeal the earlier rulings from the provincial courts, deciding instead to accept the constitutionality of same-sex marriage and amend the law accordingly. Had it entertained doubts about the earlier rulings that altered the definition of marriage, the government should have appealed those decisions. In addition, since June 2003, thousands of same-sex couples had relied in good faith on the government's acceptance of the earlier rulings and entered into legal marriages. For these reasons, the Court gave no answer to the fourth question and sent the issue of same-sex marriage back to Parliament.

In June of 2005, the House of Commons voted 158 to 133 to adopt controversial legislation that made Canada only the third country in the world to legalize same-sex marriage. Only two years earlier, the Liberal government had been fighting same-sex couples in the courts. It reversed its position amid the onslaught of legal verdicts in eight provinces, and for partisan political advantage. One of the Liberals' consistent election themes over the past several campaigns has been to portray its major opponent outside of Quebec—first Reform, then the Canadian Alliance, and eventually the Conservatives—as being hostile to minority rights.[61]

In the 2006 election campaign, the Conservatives promised to revisit the marriage issue if they won the election. In December of 2006, the minority government lived up to that commitment and held a free parliamentary vote on whether the government should draft legislation to reinstate the traditional definition of marriage. MPs defeated the motion by a vote of 175 to 123. Thirteen members of the government, including six Cabinet ministers, voted against reopening the motion. An equal number of Liberal MPs voted in favour, while all NDP and Bloc members followed their leaders' directives and voted against reopening the marriage debate. For his part, Prime Minister Harper declared that he had fulfilled an election commitment by holding the vote, that the defeat of the motion was decisive, and that he would not be reopening the issue in the future.

Pornography: The First Two Stages of the Three-Stage Test

In 1987 the Winnipeg police raided an adult-video store and seized the entire inventory. The store's owner, Donald Butler, was charged with selling obscene materials as defined under Section 163 of the Criminal Code and convicted on eight counts. He appealed his conviction, on the grounds that the law prohibiting the sale of obscene materials constituted an unreasonable limit on the freedom of expression guaranteed in Section 2 (b) of the Charter.

In 1992 the Supreme Court unanimously dismissed Butler's appeal.[62] In the first stage of the analysis, the court addressed the question of whether Section 163 of the Code infringes freedom of expression. To convict under Section 163, the Crown must prove that the materials in question fit the following definition of obscenity: "any publication a dominant characteristic of which is the undue exploitation of sex, or of sex and any one or more of the following subjects, namely, crime, horror, cruelty and violence, shall be deemed to be obscene." Since the law was enacted in 1959, two common-law tests for its application had been developed by the courts. The first is the "community standards" test, which defines the "undue exploitation of sex" with reference to social mores and the intended audience. The second is the "degradation or dehumanization" test, according to which any material that portrays human beings (usually women or children) in a position of "subordination, servile submission or humiliation" will fail the community standards test even in the absence of violence. According to the justices, "[i]t would be reasonable to conclude that there is an appreciable risk of harm to society in the portrayal of such material." This harm allegedly results from the moral desensitization produced in some viewers of sexually degrading material.

Although the Court conceded that the social science evidence of a causal connection between degrading pornography and harmful behaviour—e.g., sexual assault—was shaky at best, it got around this problem by asserting that the public has concluded that exposure to some sexually explicit material must be harmful in some way. The justices then concluded that there was no doubt that Section 163 "seeks to prohibit certain types of expressive activity and thereby infringes [Section] 2 (b) of the Charter."

Having completed the first stage of the analysis, the Court moved on to the second stage: the application of the *Oakes* test to determine whether the impugned law could be upheld under Section 1 of the Charter. The justices determined that Section 163 was intended to achieve a "pressing and substantial" social objective, namely "the avoidance of harm resulting from antisocial attitudinal changes that exposure to obscene material causes." Even in the absence of conclusive extrinsic proof that obscene materials promote sexual crimes, the justices decided that degrading portrayals of female sexuality undermine "true equality between male and female persons." Further, the protection afforded by Section 2 (b) of the Charter varies with the type of expression under consideration. Political speech is a key element of a free and democratic society; commercial advertising and pornography are not. Therefore, Section 163 met the first criterion of the *Oakes* test: the restriction of obscenity was declared to be a "pressing and substantial" objective, which could outweigh the need to protect this particular form of expression.

The justices also found that Section 163 met the "rational connection" test, even though they could not point to conclusive proof that the unrestricted distribution of obscene materials causes harm to society. In this instance, the court deferred to the legislative branch. It ruled that Parliament was entitled to have a "reasoned apprehension of harm" resulting from the desensitization of individuals exposed to some sexually explicit materials, particularly those which depict violence, cruelty, and dehumanization in sexual relations. The problem with this reasoning is that the Parliament that enacted Section 163 had no such apprehension, as the justices themselves admitted in their earlier discussion of changing approaches to obscenity. When Section 163 was enacted in 1959, its purpose was to protect public decency. The claim that obscene materials promote sexual crime did not enter the policy debate until the 1970s. This part of the *Butler* ruling may be interpreted as a case of judicial sleight of hand in the service of policy preferences.

Because Section 163 provides an "artistic merit" defence, and because it is not intended to restrict the distribution of harmless erotica, the court concluded that it meets the "minimal impairment" test. Finally, the justices ruled that the effects of Section 163 on freedom of expression did not outweigh its alleged objective: "to enhance respect for all members of society, and nonviolence and equality in their relations with each other." All the elements of the *Oakes* test were met, and Section 163 was upheld as a reasonable and justifiable limitation on freedom of expression. As a result, the court did not proceed to the third stage of inquiry, as no remedy was required.

The *Butler* ruling shows that judicial creativity need not be based on the remedial powers in the Constitution Act, 1982. By redefining the legislative intent of the obscenity law as the promotion of gender equality, the justices exercised considerable interpretive latitude in upholding the criminal prohibitions against some types of pornography.

CONCLUSION

The impact of the Charter on Canadian politics and policy-making, while significant, should not be overstated. Nor should it be viewed simply as a product of the Charter itself. Changes to the Supreme Court—its ability to control its own docket and the appointment of more activist justices—ensured that the Charter would have a greater effect on public policy than it would otherwise have had. So did the willingness of interest groups to seek policy change through the courts, and the creation of support networks for public-interest litigation. All of these developments, which were evident before 1982, made important contributions to the Charter's impact on Canadian government and politics.

Perhaps most important, the attitudes of judges toward their own role—in particular, the willingness of judges to challenge the other two branches of government—determine the Charter's practical effect on the lives of Canadians. When judges defer to legislators or executives, their policy-making power shrinks. When Charter rights and freedoms yield to other priorities, their influence also wanes. This relationship between judicial attitudes and Charter enforcement has become increasingly apparent since 9/11. In the wake of the terrorist attacks in the United States, heightened national security concerns have partially eclipsed Charter rights and freedoms. A month after the attacks, the federal government introduced Bill C-36 into Parliament. The Bill, which is now the Anti-Terrorism Act (ATA), contained numerous amendments to the Criminal Code, the Official Secrets Act, and other federal legislation. Among other things, the ATA makes it a criminal offence to participate in a terrorist organization (whether or not the accused individual knows of any planned terrorist activity); permits police to arrest a person whom they suspect of planning to commit a terrorist act; provides for secret investigative hearings at which any individual may be compelled to testify, whether or not a terrorist act has taken place; and defines terrorism as any criminal offence committed "in whole or in part for a political, religious or ideological purpose, objective or cause."[63] The ATA appears to infringe several of the protected rights and freedoms in the Charter, especially the legal rights in Sections 7 through 13 and the fundamental freedoms in Section 2.

Despite these apparent infringements, the Supreme Court of Canada upheld parts of the ATA in June 2004.[64] The justices had previously signalled their willingness to accept antiterrorism laws as reasonable limitations on the Charter in the *Suresh* case, which was decided shortly after the attacks on Washington and New York.[65] As was also the case with the federal division of powers during the First and Second World Wars, when national security concerns become paramount, courts usually defer to the executive branch, which is ultimately responsible for protecting life and property within a particular state. As it had done previously, the judicial branch of government seems willing to allow greater discretion and powers to the police and executive in emergencies or crises. Such sweeping discretion is not always compatible with the rule of law and the enforcement of human rights. Before 9/11, few Canadians would have believed that deliberate violations of rights and freedoms, like those committed against Japanese Canadians in World War II, or the mass arrests without charge in the October Crisis of 1970, could happen again. The 1988 Emergencies Act, which replaced the old War Measures Act, was carefully crafted to conform to the requirements of the Charter. It explicitly referred to "those fundamental rights that are not to be limited or abridged even in a national emergency," limited the exercise of emergency powers to strict time periods, and forbade "the detention, imprisonment or internment of Canadian citizens or permanent residents as defined in the Immigration Act on the basis of race, national or ethnic origin, colour, religion, sex, age or mental or physical disability."[66] There are no such protections in the ATA. The apparent willingness of the federal government to water down Charter rights in the name of national security, justified or otherwise, reveals the influence of external forces on our domestic political institutions.

In general, it is fair to say that the Charter has expanded the policy influence of the judicial branch—although that influence is limited by the deficiencies of courts as policy-making institutions. Since the early activist period of the Charter, judges have increasingly acknowledged that they lack the expertise to design and implement effective policies. In consequence, they properly defer to the executive and the legislature in most instances.

The appropriateness of their post–9/11 deference in the name of national security may be a different story. It is by no means clear that efforts to prevent terrorism are made more effective by permitting police to arrest without warrant, to profile particular groups, or to distinguish between ordinary crimes and those committed "for a political, religious or ideological purpose." As the Supreme Court itself noted in the immediate aftermath of 9/11, "liberty, the rule of law, and the principles of fundamental justice" are the foundational principles of our constitutional and political order. "In the end, it would be a Pyrrhic victory if terrorism were defeated at the cost of sacrificing our commitment to those values."[67]

DISCUSSION QUESTIONS

1. What is the significance of Section 1 of the Charter? How does it affect the ways in which the courts approach judicial review?

2. Identify and briefly explain the various remedies available to the courts under the Constitution Act, 1982. How have those remedies affected the making of public policy in Canada?

3. Is it acceptable for nine unelected judges to nullify laws made by elected legislators? Why or why not?

4. Are judges competent to make and enforce public policy? Why or why not?

5. In your own words, explain three of the five principles of Charter interpretation that were discussed in this chapter.

SUGGESTED READINGS

Ian Brodie, *Friends of the Court: The Privileging of Interest Group Litigants in Canada* (Albany, New York: SUNY Press, 2002).

Janet L. Hiebert, *Limiting Rights: The Dilemma of Judicial Review* (Montreal and Kingston: McGill–Queen's University Press, 1996).

Janet L. Hiebert, *Charter Conflicts: What Is Parliament's Role?* (Montreal and Kingston: McGill–Queen's University Press, 2002).

Paul Howe and Peter H. Russell, eds., *Judicial Power and Canadian Democracy* (Montreal and Kingston: McGill–Queen's University Press/Institute for Research on Public Policy, 2001).

James B. Kelly, "The Charter of Rights and Freedoms and the Rebalancing of Liberal Constitutionalism in Canada, 1982–1997," *Osgoode Hall Law Journal*, 37 (Fall 1999).

James B. Kelly, "Bureaucratic Activism and the Charter of Rights and Freedoms: The Department of Justice and Its Entry into the Centre of Government," *Canadian Public Administration*, 42:4 (Winter 1999).

Heather MacIvor, *Canadian Government and Politics in the Charter Era* (Toronto: Nelson, 2005).

Christopher P. Manfredi, *Judicial Power and the Charter: Canada and the Paradox of Liberal Constitutionalism*, 2nd edition (Toronto: Oxford University Press, 2001).

F. L. Morton and Rainer Knopff, *The Charter Revolution and the Court Party* (Peterborough, ON: Broadview Press, 2000).

Kent Roach, *The Supreme Court on Trial: Judicial Activism or Democratic Dialogue?* (Toronto: Irwin Law, 2001).

Peter H. Russell, *Constitutional Odyssey: Can Canadians Become a Sovereign People?* 2nd edition (Toronto: University of Toronto Press, 1993).

Peter H. Russell, Rainer Knopff, and Ted Morton, eds., *Leading Constitutional Decisions: Federalism and the Charter* (Ottawa: Carleton University Press, 1989).

F. Leslie Seidle, ed., *Equity and Community: The Charter, Interest Advocacy and Representation* (Montreal: Institute for Research on Public Policy, 1993).

Robert J. Sharpe, Katherine E. Swinton, and Kent Roach, *The Charter of Rights and Freedoms*, 2nd edition (Toronto: Irwin Law, 2002).

Brian Slattery, "A Theory of the Charter," *Osgoode Hall Law Journal*, 25 (1987), 701.

Websites

All of the Charter rulings by the Supreme Court of Canada are available on-line at the LexUM website (http://www.lexum.umontreal.ca/index.epl?lang=en; click on "Supreme Court"), which offers a searchable database of rulings issued back to 1985 and the ability to download these rulings. An option is to go to the Supreme Court of Canada website (http://www.scc-csc.gc.ca) and click on "Judgments" at the top of the screen. Follow the links to LexUM.

Another source of Supreme Court rulings is the Canadian Legal Information Institute website (http://www.canlii.org); under "Canada," click on "Supreme Court of Canada." The CanLII site also offers a useful digest of Charter rulings by a senior official at the federal Department of Justice (under "Canada," click on "Canadian Charter of Rights Decisions Digest") to access a searchable database of federal and provincial laws and court rulings.

NOTES

1. The Charter was proclaimed into law on April 17, 1982. However, the implementation of Section 15 (equality rights) was delayed for three years to allow governments to bring their laws into conformity with its provisions.
2. *R. v. Morgentaler* [1988] 1 S.C.R. 30.
3. *Rodriguez v. British Columbia (Attorney General)* [1993] 3 S.C.R. 519.
4. *Singh v. Minister of Employment and Immigration* [1985] 1 S.C.R. 177; *Andrews v. Law Society of British Columbia* [1989] 1 S.C.R. 143; *Benner v. Canada (Secretary of State)* [1997] 1 S.C.R. 358.
5. *Vriend v. Alberta* [1998] 1 S.C.R. 493; *McKinney v. University of Guelph* [1990] 3 S.C.R. 229; *Egan v. Canada* [1995] 2 S.C.R. 513; *Law v. Canada (Minister of Employment and Immigration)* [1999] 1 S.C.R. 497; *Schachter v. Canada* [1992] 2 S.C.R. 679; *Thibaudeau v. Canada* [1995] 2 S.C.R. 627.
6. *R. v. Feeney* [1997] 2 S.C.R. 13.
7. *R. v. Daviault* [1994] 3 S.C.R. 63.
8. *R. v. Lavallee* [1990] 1 S.C.R. 852; *R. v. Malott* [1998] 1 S.C.R. 123.
9. *R. v. Vaillancourt* [1987] 2 S.C.R. 636; *R. v. Creighton* [1993] 3 S.C.R. 3.
10. A survey of Charter rulings from 1984 to 1997 found that roughly one-third of plaintiffs succeeded at the Supreme Court. James B. Kelly, "The Charter of Rights and Freedoms

and the Rebalancing of Liberal Constitutionalism in Canada, 1982–1997," *Osgoode Hall Law Journal*, 37 (Fall 1999), Table 2, 641.

11. Brian Slattery, "A Theory of the Charter," *Osgoode Hall Law Journal*, 25 (1987).

12. *Singh v. Minister of Employment and Immigration* [1985] 1 S.C.R. 177.

13. *Authorson v. Canada (Attorney General)* [2003] 2 S.C.R. 40.

14. Peter H. Russell, *Constitutional Odyssey: Can Canadians Become a Sovereign People?* 2nd edition (Toronto: University of Toronto Press, 1993), 114.

15. Janet L. Hiebert, *Limiting Rights: The Dilemma of Judicial Review* (Montreal and Kingston: McGill–Queen's University Press, 1996), 21.

16. *R. v. Seaboyer; R. v. Gayme* [1991] 2 S.C.R. 577.

17. *R. v. Darrach*, S.C.R. 2000.

18. See *R. v. Sharpe* [2001] 1 S.C.R. 45. The new law, Bill C-12, died on the Order Paper when Parliament was dissolved for the 2004 federal election.

19. *Andrews v. Law Society of British Columbia* [1989] 1 S.C.R. 143; *Benner v. Canada (Secretary of State)* [1997] 1 S.C.R. 358.

20. *Egan v. Canada* [1995] 2 S.C.R. 513; *Vriend v. Alberta* [1998] 1 S.C.R. 493; *M. v. H.* [1999] 2 S.C.R. 3.

21. *Miron v. Trudel* [1995] 2 S.C.R. 418.

22. Canada, House of Commons Standing Committee on Justice, Human Rights, Public Safety and Emergency Preparedness, *Improving the Supreme Court of Canada Appointments Process* (Ottawa: House of Commons, May 2004).

23. See *Prime Minister Harper announces nominee for Supreme Court appointment* News Release, February 23, 2006; available on-line at pm.gc.ca/eng/media.asp?id=1030.

24. See, for example, a speech given by the late justice John Sopinka of the Supreme Court of Canada. Reprinted in *The Globe and Mail*, November 28, 1997.

25. *R. v. Big M Drug Mart Ltd.* [1985] 1 S.C.R. 295.

26. Peter H. Russell, *The Judiciary in Canada: The Third Branch of Government* (Toronto: McGraw-Hill Ryerson, 1987), 289.

27. See *Halpern v. Canada (Attorney General)*, Ontario Court of Appeal, June 10, 2003; accessed at http://www.canlii.org.

28. *Barbeau v. British Columbia*, British Columbia Court of Appeal, July 8, 2003; accessed at http://www.canlii.org.

29. *Re B.C. Motor Vehicle Act,* [1985] 2 S.C.R. 486 paragraphs 38–42 and paragraphs 50–52.

30. *R. v. Oakes* [1986] 1 S.C.R. 103, paragraphs 69 and 70.

31. There is a partial exception: the *Rules of the Supreme Court of Canada* permit a lawyer appointed by the court to conduct a cross-examination of an expert witness on the written evidence that he or she has submitted on behalf of one of the parties. The cross-examination does not take place before the justices; instead, a transcript must be provided within a specified time.

32. *R. v. Mohan* [1994] 2 S.C.R. 9.

33. *R. v. Askov* [1990] 2 S.C.R. 1199. Also see Christopher P. Manfredi, *Judicial Power and the Charter: Canada and the Paradox of Liberal Constitutionalism,* 2nd edition (Toronto: Oxford University Press, 2001).

34. See *RJR-MacDonald Inc. v. Canada (Attorney General)* [1995] 3 S.C.R. 199, paragraph 68.

35. *R. v. Stinchcombe* [1991] 3 S.C.R. 326.

36. In *R. v. O'Connor* [1995] 4 S.C.R. 411, the Supreme Court stayed sexual abuse charges against a former Catholic bishop because the Crown had refused to disclose evidence in a timely manner.

37. *Hunter v. Southam Inc.* [1984] 2 S.C.R.145.

38. *Reference re Prov. Electoral Boundaries (Sask.)* [1991] 2 S.C.R. 158.

39. *Haig v. Canada; Haig v. Canada (Chief Electoral Officer)* [1993] 2 S.C.R. 995.

40. *Edmonton Journal v. Alberta (Attorney General)* [1989] 2 S.C.R. 1326.

41. *Reference Re Public Service Employee Relations Act (Alta.)* [1987] 1 S.C.R. 313; Dunmore v. Ontario [2001] 3 S.C.R. 1016.

42. See, F.L. Morton and Rainer Knopff, *The Charter Revolution and the Court Party* (Peterborough, ON: Broadview Press, 2000).

43. *R. v. Mills* [1999] 3 S.C.R. 668, paragraph 58.

44. For a description of "Charter-proofing" by the Human Rights Law Section in the federal Department of Justice, see James B. Kelly, "Bureaucratic Activism and the Charter of Rights and Freedoms: The Department of Justice and Its Entry into the Centre of Government," *Canadian Public Administration,* 42:4 (Winter 1999).

45. See Leslie A. Pal, "Advocacy Organizations and Legislative Politics: The Effect of the Charter of Rights and Freedoms on Interest Lobbying of Federal Legislation, 1989–91" in Seidle, ed., *Equity and Community.*

46. *Reference re Workers' Compensation Act, 1983 (Nfld.)* (Application to intervene), [1989] 2 S.C.R. 335.

47. *RWDSU v. Dolphin Delivery Ltd.* [1986] 2 S.C.R. 573.

48. *McKinney v. University of Guelph* [1990] 3 S.C.R. 229.

49. *Vriend v. Alberta* [1998] 1 S.C.R. 496.

50. *Eldridge v. British Columbia (Attorney General)* [1997] 3 S.C.R. 624.

51. *Singh v. Minister of Employment and Immigration* [1985] 1 S.C.R. 177.

52. *Morgentaler v. the Queen,* S.C.R. 1976, 632.

53. *R. v. Morgentaler,* S.C.R. 1988, paragraph 3.

54. *Eaton v. Brant County Board of Education* [1997] 1 S.C.R. 241.

55. *Miron v. Trudel* [1995] 2 S.C.R. 418.

56. *Eldridge v. British Columbia (Attorney General).*

57. *Miron v. Trudel* [1995] 2 S.C.R. 418.

58. *M. v. H.* [1999] 2 S.C.R. 3.

59. *Halpern v. Canada (Attorney General)* [2002] O.J. No. 2714 (2002) 215 D.L.R. (4th) 223; *Hendricks v. Québec (Attorney General)* [2002] J.Q. No. 3816.

60. *Reference re Same-Sex Marriage* [2004] S.C.C. 79.

61. See Faron Ellis and Peter Woolstencroft, "A Change of Government, Not a Change of Country: Conservatives in the 2006 Federal Election," in Jon H. Pammett and Christopher Dornan eds., *The Canadian Federal Election of 2006* (Toronto: Dundurn Press, 2006).

62. *R. v. Butler* [1992] 1 S.C.R. 452.

63. *Anti-Terrorism Act,* S.C. 2001, c. 41, sections 83.18, 83.3, 83.28, and 83.01(b)(i)(A).

64. *Application under s. 83.28 of the Criminal Code (Re)* [2004] S.C.C. 42; *Vancouver Sun (Re)* [2004] S.C.C. 43.

65. *Suresh v. Canada (Minister of Citizenship and Immigration)* [2002] 1 S.C.R. 3.

66. *Emergencies Act,* 1988, c. 29.

67. *Suresh,* paragraph 4.

9

NONGOVERNMENTAL ACTORS AND THE POLITICAL PROCESS

LEARNING OBJECTIVES

- *identify* and *describe* the most important institutional aspects of the news media in Canada
- *identify* and *explain* the constraints placed upon journalists who report on political news in Canada
- *identify* and *explain* the impact of news coverage on citizens, political institutions, and the electorate
- *identify* and *explain* what interest and pressure groups are
- *explain* the most important aspects of lobbying, representation, and consulting, including the registration of lobbyists
- *identify* the organizational resources of interest and pressure groups

INTRODUCTION

Most chapters in this book describe either governmental institutions, such as the House of Commons, or formal political agencies like political parties. For the most part, these institutions, and the structures and operations of other government institutions, are open to public view. Their leaders can be held accountable to the Canadian public, to a greater or lesser degree, either by their members or by other agencies of government. For all of these reasons, they are easy to describe and analyze. The organizations discussed in this chapter—the news media and interest groups—are a different story. Their internal structures and operations are more opaque, and their influence on public policy (and, thus, on the lives of Canadians) is more difficult to assess.

There is little doubt, however, about the key communicative role the media play in informing Canadians about what is happening within their political system. Despite the often acrimonious relationship that exists between politicians and journalists, the relationship is symbiotic. Politicians need the media to communicate with voters, and, as we have seen, changes in the media impact the ways in which parties do business. Similarly, journalists need politicians, and access to them, in order to do their jobs of reporting political events and the activities of government. Journalists certainly believe that reporting on political events is important. If they did not we could safely assume they would channel their resources into covering more lucrative activities, like sporting events.[1]

Interest groups also frequently interact with political institutions and actors. They sometimes provide testimony before standing committees of the House of Commons and the Senate, engage in formal interventions before the courts, and must comply with legally mandated disclosures about lobbying activities and election campaign advertising. Although these activities do not allow us to draw firm conclusions about the structures of these groups, nor about their influence on policy outcomes, they do remind us of the importance of collective action for citizens who chose to participate in the political process in these ways.

With these caveats in mind, we turn to a discussion of nongovernmental organizations (NGOs) and their participation in the policy process. We will begin with the mass media and the ways in which journalists cover political events. The second half of the chapter focuses more specifically on interest groups and the increasingly important activity of lobbying.

THE NEWS MEDIA

The mass media are definitely part of the political system in Canada and are integral to the democratic political culture of the country. Remember, freedom of the press and other media of communication are specifically enumerated Charter rights. Strictly speaking, the news media do not constitute a single, unified institution analogous to the House of Commons or the Supreme Court. Nonetheless, the thousands of professionals who write, record, edit, and broadcast information and opinion about Canadian politics collectively constitute an entity with many of the characteristics of a formal institution.[2] They share a set of norms and values, a hierarchy of power and status, clear incentives for ambitious participants, and a distinct role in the political system. Like other institutions, the news media both influence and are influenced by the political culture within which they operate. In this section, we will focus on three particular aspects of the news media:

- the institutional characteristics of the major news media in Canada
- the degree to which news coverage influences Canadian citizens
- the news media's impact on the operation and priorities of our three branches of government

■ The News Media in Canada: Institutional Characteristics

Broadly speaking, the news media occupy a middle ground between our political institutions and those whom they govern. Most Canadians have little direct experience with national politics. Many may have shaken the hand of an MP, most have cast a ballot in an election, but as we have seen, very few are members of political parties and fewer still frequently attend political events such as constituency association meetings or party conventions. We depend on newspapers, magazines, radio, television, and the Internet for information and analysis about the policies, processes, and personalities that affect our lives. Ideally, if we are to carry out our responsibilities as informed and active citizens, this secondhand information about politics and government should be as accurate and comprehensive as possible. In practice, political news is constrained and sometimes distorted by the institutional characteristics of the mass media in Canada and elsewhere.

Media Ownership

Who owns and operates the media in a particular country determines a great deal about the type and form of news coverage citizens are presented. With the notable exception of the Canadian Broadcasting Corporation (including Société Radio-Canada, *CBC Newsworld,* and Radio Canada International), Canadian media companies are privately owned and operated organizations. The liberal-pluralist-democratic Canadian political culture, as exemplified by the corresponding Charter freedoms, suggests that a free and competitive system of privately owned and operated media outlets is eminently superior to state monopoly systems such as in the former Soviet Union. Benefits of a free and competitive system include much more objective reporting and editing, the acceptance of a great deal of critical commentary about government activities, and an overall detachment from state institutions.[3] While superior, private ownership and competition still affect the ways in which media companies collect and disseminate political information. That is, like all organizations, media outlets are impacted by the system within which they operate, sometimes positively, sometimes negatively.

Initially, it is important to understand that the purpose of privately owned news companies is to make a profit for their owners and shareholders. To do this, they must keep their costs down while boosting their revenues. Investigative journalism is expensive, as are Ottawa bureaus and foreign correspondents. Therefore, local media outlets increasingly rely on wire services, news releases, and prepackaged features purchased from national or international sources. Maximizing revenue means selling as much advertising as possible, at the highest rate the market will bear. Advertising rates depend on the number of people who read, watch, or listen to the company's product. The larger the audience or readership, and the lower the costs, the higher the profits. As such, most media companies have a strong incentive to downplay costly political coverage in favour of attention-grabbing scandal, conflict, and tragedy, as well as more practical consumer and lifestyle information.

Competition among media companies, especially at the regional and national levels, translates into a battle for readers and ratings in which celebrity gossip, crime, and calamity stories often take priority over in-depth analysis of government and policy-making. Journalists who operate in a free market tend to give the people what they want, which is not necessarily a daily civics lesson on the important institutional implications of current events. This trend is fuelled, in part, by the perception amongst news editors and producers that the public has little interest in the subtleties and complexities of government. But we cannot blame shallow and superficial coverage of political events on the media alone. In a culture that continually demonstrates a propensity for wanting to consume the most sensational and celebrity-centred news, it is hardly surprising that market-driven news producers focus on personalities at the expense of complicated issues. As we have seen, this approach leads to a focus on political leaders and their clashes of personalities, making these central to what most Canadians learn about their politicians and governments.

Although competition exists in virtually all media markets in Canada, especially in broadcasting, most local markets have only one, perhaps two, daily newspapers. In recent decades, ownership in the newspaper business has been concentrated in fewer and fewer hands, leading to Canada having one of the greatest concentrations of newspaper ownership in the Western world. Critics charge that excessive control of such a large share of the newspaper business by a few corporations effectively restricts the range of political viewpoints being expressed by the industry. However, even in larger urban markets where multiple media outlets compete in all mediums and diversity of views is greater, the news product itself varies little. That is, providing differing viewpoints is one thing; providing more comprehensive and detailed coverage of politics appears to be quite another. More importantly, both newspapers and national television networks are being absorbed into huge multibusiness conglomerates that often regard the news as just another product. This has furthered the move toward perceiving political reporting as just one of many entertainment commodities that must compete with other projects based largely on presentation, graphics, showmanship, and other attention-grabbing visuals.

Journalistic Ethics

Despite the many institutional constraints, journalists today are subject to some institutional incentives that positively impact how they report on politics. Journalists must now follow the ethics and values of their profession. Most important among these are accuracy, objectivity, the rapid transmission of information to the public, the investigation of public institutions, and the analysis of complex issues.[4] While all of these values cannot necessarily be met when reporting on any single event, at the very least, a political story must be balanced between opposing viewpoints. A quotation or a video clip from one side of an issue must be followed by a similar contribution from the other side. As you will recall, this makes Canadian news reporting today much less partisan than that which existed in the first party system of the early post-Confederation period. But even this relative evenhandedness may bias coverage of an event if, for example, equal coverage is given to both sides of a debate in which thousands of people are protesting on one side of an issue but only a handful on the other side. Objectivity is also one of the first casualties when reporting on events that involve deeply held convictions or passions on behalf of those involved, including those of the journalist. Coverage of the national-unity issue in Canada provides an example. Some federalist politicians have alleged that francophone Quebec journalists (including those at Radio-Canada) are overly sympathetic to the separatist cause. Similar allegations of bias were levelled at the anglophone media during Quebec's referendum campaigns. One telling indicator of the gulf between the perceptions of the two "media solitudes" was the coverage of the pro-Canada rally in Montreal shortly before the 1995 Quebec referendum vote: "*CBC Newsworld* estimated the crowd at 150,000, while RDI [the francophone equivalent of *Newsworld*] reported that only 30 or 40 thousand people had attended the rally."[5]

Pack Journalism

Reporters are also conditioned by the complexities of group behaviour. When an important political story breaks, the parliamentary press gallery is spontaneously transformed into a pack of hungry wolves. Although all the dynamics of Ottawa's pack-journalism culture are not easy to dissect, the phenomenon does result in the media becoming seized simultaneously with a single idea, and then collectively pursuing it to death. Media competition exaggerates this tendency, as rival reporters scramble to outdo each other. One story begets a follow-up story. One question in a scrum leads to another along the same lines. Once the pack seizes on its target, reporters relentlessly pursue those involved, desperate for a new daily angle to keep the story alive and feed the 24/7 media machine. These feeding frenzies are motivated by reporters' knowledge that if they drop the ball on the big story of the day, they will face criticism from their colleagues and competitors, as well as from their employers.

The pack mentality also arises from the process of political reporting. Journalists spend hours or days crammed together in hallways, buses, planes, and other confined spaces with little to do except wait for their prey and exchange the latest gossip and speculation. The pack phenomenon can arise from the uncertainty inherent in deciding which events are news and which are not. Reporters often watch each other for cues, finding safety in numbers. When they get caught up in obsessively focusing on the most entertaining and dramatic aspects of a story—typically the wrongdoing and foolishness of politicians—the pack, inadvertently or otherwise, participates in the process of damaging public support for politics, political institutions, and journalism itself. Thus, while we can understand what motivates the dynamics of pack journalism, and concede that it is not necessarily malicious or otherwise nefarious, the resulting reporting often falls far short of the lofty standards set by professional journalistic ethics.

More troubling is the pack mentality when it comes to avoiding critical evaluation of commonly held assumptions within the media culture. Reporting on the politics of environmental and health policy serves as a contemporary example of this phenomenon. Although some skepticism has recently crept into reporting on these issues, for the most part, journalists have tended to accept and report as fact what most scientists acknowledge are only theories of climate change, species eradication, or the health impacts of various products and practices. Journalists also tend to unquestioningly emphasize the need for dramatic and immediate government action on many ideas that are still very much hypothetical. The result is an exaggeration of the extent to which politics legitimately can or should be expected to act on the latest theoretical research. Again, although this phenomenon is understandable—after all, few journalists have the expertise to fully understand the scientific methods used and the assumptions upon which they may be based—the resulting presentation of theory as fact within the reporting process does not serve the citizenry or the political process well. When these distortions are compounded by sensational predictions from scientists, or from others with political agendas, of environmental catastrophe, extinction, or predicted multiple deaths, reporting tends toward advocacy rather than the unbiased, objective transferring of information.

24/7 News Cycle

Some of the characteristics discussed above are accelerated by the fact that the daily news cycle is unforgiving, especially in an era of 24-hour news channels and the Internet. In attempting to fulfill the objective of rapidly transmitting information to the pubic, reporters are subject to the competitive pressures of gathering and reporting news while having to meet very tight deadlines. To do their jobs more effectively, many political reporters rely heavily on official sources, including cabinet ministers and senior public officials. Having immediate access to these informed sources allows journalists to quickly generate stories and to confirm information received elsewhere. The need to maintain cordial working relationships with powerful people often places the reporter in a difficult situation. If a report burns a source by being too critical or portraying that source in a bad light, future access will most likely be terminated. The reporter may also gain a reputation as being untrustworthy, leading to other political actors also restricting access. However, if a reporter accepts a source's version of events uncritically, there is the risk of appearing to be little more than a spokesperson for that individual or group, resulting in lost credibility as an objective and impartial reporter.

Other Limitations

In addition to the constraints imposed by market forces and institutional incentives, all journalism is constrained by time and space limits. Those who work in television are further limited by the technical requirements of the medium. A story with good visuals is more attractive to news producers than one without. Political developments that take place behind closed doors, in the absence of cameras, or that lack eye-catching visual symbolism are difficult to convey on TV. Because television is primarily a visual medium, events that require extensive verbal explanation and context are given short shrift—whatever their intrinsic importance. Expert "talking heads" are considered less attention grabbing than are action and confrontation. When a politician gives a speech or is interviewed on camera, the preferred length of the clip is 10 to 12 seconds, hardly enough time to do justice to any issue. Most political and governmental issues are inherently complex and require substantial explanation if they are to be fully understood by nonspecialists. Such complexity is unsuited to the demands of television news. Small wonder, then, that coverage of many political summits tends to focus more on the protests outside the meetings, especially if they turn violent, than on what the politicians are discussing inside. A riot is a good story for TV. A lengthy discussion of trade policy or the intricacies of equalization payments is not. Print and radio-broadcast journalists face similar, although not as extreme, constraints.

Overall, the institutional incentives that operate within the news media often produce shallow, sensationalistic coverage of politics and government. While there are exceptions, most notably the Cable Public Affairs Channel (CPAC) and the larger broadsheet newspapers, much of what passes for political reporting in this country is inadequate for informing and educating the public about complex political issues. Although we can certainly understand the constraints that journalists encounter in attempting to provide a superior level of political reporting, understanding why phenomena like pack journalism and the preference for sensationalism occur does not change the fact that they exist and tend to dominate political reporting in Canada. It also does not change the fact that the resulting superficial presentation of political events contributes to the overall debasement of politics as a profession, and of political institutions more generally.

The Impact of News Coverage on Citizens

Media organizations are presented with an almost infinite number of newsworthy events every day. Only a few can be made to fit within the pages of a newspaper or the brief period of a newscast. The criteria editors and producers use to select which stories to cover are called "news values." These are politically significant. The decision to cover one type of story often entails a decision not to report other events that may be intrinsically important for Canadians acting as citizens, but not as appealing to them as consumers. Generally speaking, news values emphasize conflict, drama, novelty, and human interest over detailed policy analysis or descriptions of the political process.[6] For both technological and financial reasons, this is particularly true of television—the most popular news medium in Canada.[7] When media analysts examine the impact of journalistic practices on the selection and presentation of news stories, they often focus on three particular concepts: agenda-setting, framing, and priming.

Agenda-Setting

Agenda-setting refers to the power the news media have in influencing public perceptions of the relative importance of a given event. Studies of media effects have consistently linked the frequency of a topic's coverage and its likelihood of being highly ranked in public opinion polls.[8] In some cases, the media may simply heighten public awareness of an issue, creating a growing public concern, which in turn may force governments to devote more attention to the problem than they might otherwise have done. At other times, a dramatic event can capture the simultaneous attention of the media, the public, and policymakers. When such a political wave hits, the news media can affect the policy responses of governments by framing the event in particular ways. Terrorist attacks and natural disasters are the best example of these political waves.[9] While the 9/11 attacks in the United States would have had an extraordinary impact under any circumstances, the fact that millions of people watched (some in real time) as the hijacked planes flew into the World Trade Center towers likely strengthened the political wave that resulted.

The agenda-setting power of the media affects both leaders and voters. The political executive can be forced to respond to a media-generated perception of a problem, instead of to its objective reality. For example, despite the recent decline of violent crime in Canada, news coverage of such events, especially the rare cases that involve multiple deaths, leads to perceptions within the electorate of a heightened sense of urgency over the issue. Voters then pressure politicians for new crime policies. Similar processes are at work with other issues such as government corruption, natural disasters, and various aspects of economic life. This is not to suggest that any of these issues is unimportant, only that their importance is often presented in disproportion to their impact on the daily lives of Canadians. The long-term effect of this process on the population at large may be even more significant in light of our dependence on the media for secondhand information about politics and government: in directing citizens' attention toward some issues and away from others, the news media significantly influence what Canadians define as important or unimportant dimensions of political reality. The media also influence citizens' expectations of what governments can do to alter that reality.

Framing

Journalists frame the news by making certain rhetorical and stylistic choices that determine the way an event is presented to the public.[10] Any given event can be presented and explained in a number of different ways. For example, when the first ministers repeatedly met to attempt to resolve the constitutional impasses associated with patriation and Meech Lake, the media were responsible for distilling the nuances of the complex constitutional discussions, but in a way that would not send their audiences scrambling for sports or entertainment news. Framing the talks in terms of a constitutional crisis helped heighten the drama and kept audiences interested. When locked out of the formal discussions during the June 1990 marathon Meech Lake first ministers' conference, the media again created their own drama by framing the discussions as negotiations designed to save the country, and by emphasizing the acrimoniousness of the talks, including extended coverage of the Alberta premier's alleged "roughing up" of the Newfoundland premier when the latter tried to leave the meeting.

Another more frequent example includes how general elections tend to be framed by journalists as horse races among the party leaders. This frame is based on a set of assumptions about politics, about the preexisting knowledge and beliefs of the audience, and about the motivations of the actors who star in the nightly newscast. In both

Canada and the United States, elections tend to be framed as strategic battles between self-interested and perhaps dishonest politicians.[11] It is not entirely clear why journalists prefer this frame. One reason may be that it lends itself to television's need for arresting visual images and juicy revelations about underhanded political tactics. Another possible explanation is that the strategic frame is consistent with the alleged cynicism and anti-institutional bias of the press corps. Whatever the reasons for its popularity, the decision to frame election campaigns as content-free horse races contributes to the more general debasement of politics and of the quality of political discourse.

Priming

Whereas the concepts of agenda-setting and framing refer to the frequency and manner with which the media cover a particular issue, priming goes a step further. The theory of media priming holds that news stories not only tell us what is important, but also how we should think about certain issues. The ways in which journalists tell stories about political events and politicians implicitly prescribe for their audiences what are the appropriate criteria for judging the events or actions being described. For example, when *Maclean's* magazine asked on its front cover during the 2000 election campaign "How Scary?" is Canadian Alliance leader Stockwell Day, it had already determined for its readers that Day was indeed scary, and it only remained to be determined whether he scared them a little or a lot.[12]

The concept of priming also helps explain why, as we saw earlier, a handful of issues will tend to dominate voters' perceptions during each election campaign. The media are not alone in determining what issues are salient in any particular election, and those issues vary from election to election. Nevertheless, when reporters tell Canadians that their identity as a country is dependent on Canada having generous social welfare policies or a public health-care system, primarily because these differentiate us from our American neighbours, they not only help elevate the importance of these issues in campaigns, but prescribe the level of importance Canadians should attach to them. Initially, the suggestion that these polices, more so than others, are of such magnitude that they help determine our collective identity implies that voters should take these issues more seriously than other issues. But notice how the priming goes further. The reporting has begun with the implication that being different from the Americans is important, which, although it may or may not be true for a large proportion of the audience, is assumed as a self-evident concept at the outset.

It is important at this stage to remind readers that although media agenda-setting, framing, and priming occur and can impact on election issue relevance, there is no certainty that these approaches to reporting can significantly alter how Canadians vote or what they think about a particular subject. The 1992 Charlottetown referendum campaign is illustrative on this point. Virtually all of the national media in Canada, as well as most local and regional media, helped set the agenda by agreeing that the accord was the most important issue facing the country. They framed the outcome as a potential crisis, and primed it as a matter of national determination, many going as far as staking the continued existence of the country on the outcome. Yet a majority of Canadians voted against the accord. They either did not accept how the agenda was set, framed and primed, or simply did not care if the country survived. The former is much more likely to have been the case than the latter.

◼ The Effect of News Coverage on Canadian Political Institutions

In many ways, the role of the news media in Canadian politics has changed over the course of the past few decades. Whereas the parliamentary press gallery was once a more independent observer of government decisions and parliamentary debates, it has more recently taken on a political role of its own. This typically takes three forms.

First, the news media provide the most important channel of communication between the state and the citizens. Although governments can buy paid advertising in both the print and broadcast media, and now have the capacity to communicate directly with citizens via the Internet, print and broadcast news remain the most important source of information for most Canadians. As we have seen, news coverage of political events is not neutral; it is shaped by the institutional constraints on media workers and by the agenda-setting, framing, and priming conventions of news coverage itself. This means that to a certain extent, most of the information that Canadians receive about their governments comes to them secondhand, with many decisions about what issues and aspects of government are important being made by the media.

Second, reporters act as conduits of information and opinion *between* government actors. During political crises, when politicians may not be in direct contact with each other, they often communicate through the media. This is full of pitfalls for politicians and the media alike. An ill-judged public statement by one politician may provoke another to respond with equal defiance, leading to a showdown that may have undesirable results. If the media seize on the issue with pack enthusiasm, they may contribute to accelerating a crisis that need not have existed.

Third, the media's more aggressive coverage of politics and government has forced politicians and public servants to change the ways in which they work. For example, reporters often file access to information requests to obtain internal documents from government departments. This has had a "chilling" effect on politicians and policymakers. Few are now willing to put any communication in writing, including e-mail, for fear of it being made public at some future time and potentially causing their political masters an embarrassing situation or even bigger problems.

More broadly, Canadian governments have been forced to adapt to the needs and values of the news media such as the demand for instant answers, the tendency to put a negative spin on even the most innocuous events, and the propensity to try and "out" politicians as either corrupt or incompetent.

The Legislative Branch

Three important features characterize the Canadian media's coverage of Parliament. Overall, neither the House of Commons nor the Senate attracts much serious attention from the news media. When the media do turn their attention to Parliament, their coverage focuses almost exclusively on the House of Commons. And even here, coverage is very narrowly limited to the events surrounding the 40-minute daily question period, not because of its intrinsic importance in the legislative process, but because it provides the media with what it needs in presenting a good story: drama, visuals, and confrontation, among other things. The media generally ignore the regular debates on bills and the often more important committee hearings, despite their greater potential to impact public policy outcomes. Reporters tend to pay attention to debate or committees only when the system breaks down, such as when the opposition tries to block legislation through procedural shenanigans, a backbencher breaks with his or her party, or a committee hearing erupts in chaos. Knowing that this is the situation, politicians adjust their behaviour to ensure that they get noticed when the media are paying attention. This often leads to a heightened level of showmanship and other antics by politicians, which are in turn covered extensively by the media, which often present politicians at their least dignified and further corrode their authority and respect.

Three further aspects of the media's relationship to Parliament deserve mention. First, reporters rarely give the Senate positive coverage, despite the valuable role it sometimes plays in the legislative process. If more Canadians understood and appreciated the work done by senators, the institution might enjoy greater, albeit not optimal, legitimacy.

Second, journalists hostile to political authority have attempted with some success to effectively usurp the role of the official Opposition in the Commons. The function of an official Opposition is not just to criticize the government of the day. The Opposition's job is to provide an alternative government, one that can be held accountable to the voters. Journalists cannot perform this function. All they can do is critique, which tends to undermine public faith in the wisdom and integrity of elected officials. By devoting much of their attention to undignified partisan name calling and mishaps, the media tend to ignore a great deal of the valuable legislative work done by most elected officials.

Third, the media and the opposition parties often work together to get the most mileage out of question period. Opposition MPs attend morning tactics meetings, armed with piles of newspaper clippings and primed by watching videotapes of the previous night's newscasts. They use the headlines and the top stories to determine the content and order of their questions for that day. To the extent that reporters and opposition MPs uncover genuinely important information about problems in the executive branch, their cooperation can provide the most effective guarantee of government accountability to the people. On the downside, a close working relationship between journalists and opposition MPs who share an ideological agenda, and an antipathy to the government, can produce distorted news coverage and turn question period into a pointless witch-hunt. Although much of the cooperation between the media and the opposition produces little but the sound and fury of phoney outrage, manufactured or exaggerated scandals, and questionable reporting, on occasion media cooperation with the auditor general and other parliamentary watchdogs can force the government to fix problems in policy or management that would otherwise have gone unaddressed.

John Diefenbaker was the first Canadian party leader to effectively exploit the communicative power of television, a skill that helped him win the largest majority government in Canadian parliamentary history (1958) and fundamentally restructure party politics in Canada. He was also responsible for enacting the Canadian Bill of Rights and for granting Aboriginal Canadians the right to vote in federal elections. (© Bettmann/ CORBIS)

Born: 1895, Neustadt, Ontario

Died: 1979, Ottawa

Education: B.A. and M.A. Political Science, LL.B. (University of Saskatchewan, 1915, 1916, and 1919)

Profession: Criminal lawyer (called to the Saskatchewan Bar in 1919)

Political Career:
1936–1938 Leader, Saskatchewan, Conservative Party

MP
1940–1953 Lake Centre, Saskatchewan
1953–1979 Prince Albert, Saskatchewan

Leader
1956–1967 Progressive Conservative Party

Prime Minister
1957–1963

Other Ministries
1957 External Affairs
1959 External Affairs (Acting)
1962–1963 President of the Privy Council

Political Career Highlights
1956–1957 Leader of the Opposition
1957 Elected prime minister with a minority
1957 Appointed Ellen Fairclough as first female cabinet minister
1958 Reelected prime minister with a majority
1958 Appointed James Gladstone as Canada's first Aboriginal senator
1960 Canadian Bill of Rights
1960 Franchise extended to all Aboriginal peoples
1961 Royal Commission on Health Services
1961 Agricultural Rehabilitation and Development Act
1962 Reelected prime minister with a minority
1963 Created the National Productivity Council (Economic Council of Canada)
1963 Lost election to Liberal minority
1963–1967 Leader of the Opposition
1965 Lost election to Liberal minority

Source: *First Among Equals, The Prime Minister in Canadian Life and Politics* (Ottawa: Library and Archives Canada), available on-line at http://www.collectionscanada.ca/primeministers/.

The Executive Branch

Prime ministers and those who work for them devote enormous time and effort to controlling the message and managing problems. In other words, they try to present the government's agenda in a way that will make it look good, while keeping potentially embarrassing mistakes and conflicts from reaching the media. Failing that, when a potentially negative story breaks, they attempt to spin the story in order to minimize the political damage.

Message control often becomes an issue in and of itself. Recently, it has negatively impacted the relationship between Prime Minister Stephen Harper and members of the Parliamentary press gallery. Harper's rules of access to cabinet ministers and his procedures used at news conferences have led to a series of conflicts including media boycotts of important announcements. Although Harper is not the first Canadian prime minister to seemingly revel in having an acrimonious relationship with the Ottawa media—Pierre Trudeau serves as another example—most of the time, relations between the Prime Minister's Office and the news media are less strained. The communications staff members in the PMO are supported by media-relations teams in other ministers' offices, and increasingly by public servants sensitive to their concerns about news management.

Despite the awareness of media attention, the slow and deliberate pace of bureaucratic decision-making renders many government institutions unsuited to today's media-driven politics. The speed with which television and Internet news is disseminated puts increased pressure on governments to make quick decisions, if for no other reason than to avoid appearing indecisive or not in control of dramatic situations. Thus the political and administrative dominance of the prime minister is further enhanced as the media focus on his performance and give him and his advisers a strong incentive to control the information flow for the entire executive branch. The focus on political actors is deceiving because, in reality, no prime minister can control the entire federal government.

The prime minister is surrounded by cabinet ministers, senior public officials, and political advisers, each of whom has the ability, intentionally or not, to expose errors or otherwise get the government "off message." Despite the strong ethos of discretion and confidentiality within Cabinet and the federal public service, leaks do happen. In some cases, ministers or officials may try to spin a controversial issue to their advantage by offering specific reporters exclusives to new or unknown facts. Having been shut out from covering the original spin, competing journalists often seek out contrary opinion and counterspin as they stake a claim to the story. In situations where the original minister or official is not fully in control, matters can quickly spin out of control, leaving the government with a bigger management problem than would have been the case had the original spin not been attempted. In other cases, a minister who wants to test public reaction to a proposed policy will send up a trial balloon by letting it be known that the government is considering a particular policy option. If the initial public and media reaction is hostile, the minister will withdraw or amend the proposal, but usually not before causing the government some embarrassment.

Ministers are wise to respect the power of the media. A minister who performs poorly in question period or who fumbles the relationship with the press gallery may be a liability to the prime minister, and may have a short career in the political executive. All the way down the line, from the deputy minister to the front-line service-delivery staff in a given department, public servants are keenly aware of the risks posed by today's competitive, nondeferential journalists. To some extent, the effective use of executive power rests on a reputation for fairness and competence. The media, through their ability to shape the secondhand picture of politics that Canadians receive, possess considerable influence in determining whether that reputation is perceived positively or negatively.

The Judicial Branch

Until the 1980s, neither journalists nor their audiences paid much attention to the Supreme Court of Canada or the provincial Courts of Appeal. A trial judge might acquire some notoriety during a high-profile criminal case, but in general the judicial branch operated beyond the reach of the media spotlight. That obscurity came to an end in 1981, when television cameras were admitted into the Supreme Court chamber to cover the justices' ruling on the *Patriation* reference. Shortly thereafter, the late Brian Dickson took over as chief justice. He set out to create a new working relationship between the court and the media.[13] Dickson appointed the first executive legal officer, responsible for briefing reporters on important rulings and ensuring that the Court's decisions are reported accurately. He also broke precedent by granting interviews to journalists and by permitting cameras within the private precincts of the Supreme Court building. Since 1997, CPAC has provided gavel-to-gavel coverage of court hearings on high-profile appeals and constitutional references.[14] These broadcasts may hold little appeal for nonexperts as the legal arguments are often difficult for the layperson to understand. Nonetheless, they offer unique glimpses into the judicial policy-making process.

Despite the relatively harmonious working relationship between the Supreme Court and the media—reflected in the Media Relations Committee, which brings together justices and reporters to resolve disputes—the Court has received more than its share of media criticism for its interpretations of the Charter of Rights. Rulings that appear to protect the due-process rights of the accused rather than the rights of actual or potential victims have been especially controversial. The Court's reluctance to allow the introduction of improperly obtained evidence in criminal trials is sometimes portrayed as a callous disregard for public safety and an assault on the legitimate investigative powers of the police. The fact that Section 24 (2) of the Constitution Act, 1982, not only permits, but actually requires, judges to exclude tainted evidence is rarely mentioned. Controversial judicial rulings frequently provoke widespread media and pressure-group criticism. Note, however, that when a Charter ruling attracts severe and sustained criticism from the media and from pressure groups, Parliament usually responds by amending or reintroducing the impugned law. In these instances, one might argue that the media play an important role, both in the continuing dialogue between legislators and judges and in the improvement of our laws.

Whenever the court hands down a ruling that infuriates lawyers, police, pressure groups, or other organized interests, reporters have a field day. All the ingredients of a good news story are right there: conflict, emotion, willing interviewees, and—in many cases—sympathetic victims or articulate pressure-group leaders who can personalize abstract issues very effectively. Increasingly, journalists rely on pundits to explain lengthy and often highly technical decisions to their readers or viewers. Whatever the bias of pundits may be, it is certainly true that news values corrupt and distort the reporting of Charter decisions. The pro/con format of contemporary journalism, together with the media's preference for clarity and conflict, reduce the parties in difficult and complex constitutional cases to winners and losers.[15] In the process, the subtleties of legal doctrine and the careful balancing of rights and interests are often overlooked.

◼ The Effect of News Coverage on the Canadian Electorate

The influence of the news media on the electorate is a contentious issue in Canadian politics. Whereas political scientists in the early-twentieth century believed that the tone and content of news coverage directly affected public opinion, most now believe that the relationship between news and opinion is more complex.

In the first place, media influence on voters varies with the degree of information and the strength of political conviction each voter possesses.[16] A news junkie with an intense interest in politics is more likely to be influenced by media coverage than his or her more apathetic neighbour, but only under certain conditions. Agenda-setting, framing, and priming appear to exert the strongest effects on voters with high levels of political interest, but usually only if they are also uncertain on issues. Once a voter makes up his or her mind, the prospect of media influence diminishes.

Second, Canadian evidence suggests that those who identify with a particular political party are more likely to follow the news than those who lack a personal investment in the political process.[17] If this is the case, two conclusions follow. As just noted, media coverage of politics will likely reinforce the opinions voters already hold instead of imposing the opinions of journalists on their audiences. Furthermore, it suggests that not all news consumers are blank slates waiting for reporters to write on them. Instead, many are active readers and viewers who filter the news through their preexisting political values.

Third, although it is no longer widely believed that the news media can effectively tell voters what to think, evidence suggests that they can effectively tell voters what to think about.[18] As we have seen, the news media help to set the political agenda by emphasizing certain stories—and certain types of stories—over others. Institutional incentives within media companies lead producers and editors to focus on individual political events—"episodes"—and to present them in a dramatic, personal, and confrontational way. When the crisis in Canada's health-care system became a hot story in 1999–2000, the complex underlying issues (changes in fiscal federalism, technological developments in hospital care, an aging population) were most often reduced to human interest stories about individual patients who waited hours for treatment or who had to go to the United States for life-saving medical procedures. While these stories are not unimportant, they stifle informed public debate by squeezing out rational discussion of the underlying problems and possible solutions.

Fourth, particular segments of the news media can help to mobilize latent subcultures, and to reinforce subcultural attachments that have already been formed. As we have seen, latent social cleavage mobilization is a requirement if subculture differences are to play a significant role in politics. The example of reporting on the 1995 Quebec referendum, given above, illustrates a persistent problem in Canadian democracy. For a variety of reasons—including overt bias, the need to appeal to audience preconceptions, and journalistic reliance on official sources—Quebec francophone journalists tend to frame political events from a nationalist perspective, while their anglophone counterparts in the rest of Canada tend to take a more explicitly federalist stand on national-unity issues. There are at least two worrisome implications of this pattern of reporting. Initially, the reinforcement of the Quebec nationalist subculture by at least some francophone journalists intensifies the mutual suspicion and misunderstanding between Quebeckers and other Canadians. Furthermore, each segment of the media frames national-unity crises—such as the demise of the Meech Lake Accord or the 1995 Quebec referendum—in distinct, confrontational, and sometimes mutually offensive ways. Not only do these contending frames make it more difficult for political leaders to compromise in intergovernmental negotiations, they may also encourage Canadian citizens to reject any such compromise on the ground that *their* side has been shortchanged. In so doing, they create potent symbols of division, which add to the store of such symbols that already exist.

To summarize, there is not a more important set of nongovernmental organizations than the media. The free and competitive media in Canada perform an invaluable communicative function within our democratic system. As the main indirect information conduit between governments and the people, the media's importance should not be underestimated. Politicians need the news media as much as the news media need politicians. Given that the media do not represent a direct conduit to the people, as most political information citizens receive via the media is importantly conditioned by either institutional constraints or the nomenclature of modern professional journalism, both politicians and citizens need to carefully examine their use and reliance on what is reported in the daily news.

INTERESTS, GROUPS, AND POLITICS

Another important set of NGOs that can impact on public policy and the political process are interest groups and pressure groups. These interact with the media and politicians in many complex ways, but the bulk of their impact on public policy tends to be indirect, as they attempt to influence public opinion, thereby influencing government decisions and policies.

YEARS	EVENT	DEVELOPMENTS
1837–1838	Rebellions in Upper and Lower Canada	William Lyon MacKenzie (Upper Canada) and Louis-Joseph Papineau, (Lower Canada) lead rebellions in support of responsible government. Provisional governments are declared for each colony. Lord Durham recommends unity, responsible government, and assimilation of French. The union of Upper and Lower Canada (1840) and responsible government (1848) result.
1869–1870	Manitoba Riel Rebellion	Louis Riel leads a Métis rebellion to stop Canadian takeover of the Red River; provisional government is formed; Orangeman Thomas Scott is executed. The Canadian military is dispatched; Riel flees to U.S.A.; many Métis move to Saskatchewan. Province of Manitoba is created; Riel returns and is elected MP three times but never takes seat; he is expelled as MP in 1874 and declared outlaw in 1875.
1885	Saskatchewan Riel Rebellion	Saskatchewan Métis convince Riel to return and help Gabriel Dumont and Honoré Jackson establish a provisional government. Dumont defeats NWMP and volunteers at Duck Lake; federal government sends 3000 troops to area. Big Bear and Cree attack Frog Lake settlers, killing 10. Métis victory at Fish Creek. Poundmaker victory at Cut Knife. Métis defeated at Batoche; Riel captured; Dumont and others flee for U.S.A. Big Bear victory at Frenchman's Butte, loss at Loon Lake. Riel tried and executed; Big Bear and Poundmaker imprisoned.
1919	Winnipeg general strike	May 1, workers protest in support of right to bargain collectively. Winnipeg Trades Council organizes 20 000 employees and 10 000 others to walk off their jobs. Strike continues through the spring. Authorities start arresting and imprisoning strike organizers. Riot breaks out at June 21 silent parade of protest and solidarity; 2 demonstrators killed, 34 wounded, 80 arrested, strike leaders jailed.
1929	*Persons* case	Five Alberta women, Emily Murphy, Henrietta Muir Edwards, Louise McKinney, Irene Parlby, and Nellie McClung, succeed in convincing the JCPC to overrule Parliament and Supreme Court of Canada decisions that women are not persons and therefore cannot serve as Canadian senators. JCPC rules women are persons, meaning women can serve as judges and senators and in other positions. Honourable Cairine Wilson appointed first female senator in 1930.

YEARS	EVENT	DEVELOPMENTS
1970	FLQ October Crisis	Two cells of Front de Libération du Québec (FLQ), a Marxist revolutionary separatist organization responsible for over 200 criminal and terrorist acts since its 1963 founding, kidnapped British trade commissioner James Cross and Quebec justice minister Pierre Laporte. Prime Minister Trudeau invokes War Measures Act suspending civil liberties; Canadian military sent to Quebec and Ottawa. Laporte murdered; Cross eventually released. FLQ disbanded after many leaders exiled to Cuba or imprisoned.
1990	Oka Native protest—land occupation	Mohawks at Kanesatake, west of Montreal, establish blockade to prevent golf course construction on disputed land. Mayor of Oka requests provincial police enforce Quebec Superior Court injunction against four-month-old blockade. Corporal Marcel Lemay of the Sûreté du Québec shot and killed. Quebec Premier Bourassa calls upon RCMP and Canadian army for support. Mohawks at Kahnawake show support by blockading Mercier Bridge between Island of Montreal and the South Shore suburbs. Kahnawake Mohawks negotiate end of Mercier Bridge barricades; Kanesatake Mohawks give up protest by end of summer.
1997	APEC Protest	University of British Columbia student activists protest human rights record of Indonesian president Suharto at Asia Pacific Economic Co-operation summit. RCMP use pepper spray and other force to remove and detain nonviolent protesters. RCMP Complaints Commission inquiry findings include some RCMP conduct not consistent with the Charter, poor planning, and unfortunate decision to use pepper spray. Radio-Canada ombudsman reviews CBC correspondent Terry Milewski's coverage, finding it "aggressive" but not biased.
2006	Caledonia Native protest—land occupation	Six Nations Aboriginal protesters occupy site of housing development on disputed land; barricade main highway into town; standoff with town residents and police; disobey court order to dismantle occupation. Protest turns violent; Ontario government offers to purchase disputed land from developer. Ongoing at time of writing.

What Are Interest Groups and Pressure Groups?

An interest group is an organization of people who seek to promote a common goal. It may be local, such as a group of homeowners who are opposed to a proposed change in land-use development in their neighbourhood. It may be provincial, national, or global, like Amnesty International and the World Wildlife Federation. The scope of interest-group organizing has widened significantly with the introduction of the Internet, which allows far-flung groups to form global alliances and to mobilize like-minded individuals around the world at very little cost. Most interest groups are founded for nonpolitical purposes, although some are drawn into the policy-making process to protect the interests of their members. Most of their activities involve bringing individuals with similar interests together in some way to share information, organize events of mutual interest, or seek discounts for goods and services of interest to their members. None of this requires political action. It is certainly collective action, in that individuals are trying to act in concert, but it is not necessarily political. However, it is easy to imagine how many groups' activities might become political. Governments regulate and in some cases ban certain products and activities that are enjoyed by members of interest groups. Although their members may not be interested in politics per se, protecting their shared interests often requires extensive lobbying of government public relations within the popular media.

An interest group that devotes some or all of its resources to influencing public policy is called a pressure group. To be effective, a pressure group must be well organized and well resourced. Its structure and resources are determined, in part, by the size and wealth of its membership and by its policy goals. A group that represents a particularly powerful interest, that can count on ample and predictable financial support, and that shares the overall policy approach of the government will generally have an advantage over competing groups that do not have those characteristics. It would be incorrect, however, to overlook the role of the state in determining which groups are more powerful than others. In the late 1960s and early 1970s, Canada's federal government deliberately mobilized latent interests in the electorate. It identified particular groups—official language minorities, women, ethnic minorities, and Aboriginal communities—and encouraged them to create their own pressure groups. State support for these embryonic organizations took two primary forms: positional and financial.[19]

State financial support for pressure groups can include annual core funding, which covers the daily overhead costs of running an organization, or grants for individual projects—sometimes both. Although state support often provides pressure groups with privileged access to policymakers as well as financial support, there are some drawbacks. The process of applying for public funding consumes a substantial amount of the scarce time and energy available to most volunteer organizations or nonprofit agencies. More seriously, in the view of some advocacy groups, accepting government funding might compromise their detachment from government, including their freedom to criticize state policy. Some fear being co-opted into the policy agenda of whichever party controls the government. Additionally, many worry that an overreliance on granting programs could distort their organizational priorities. Nonetheless, given the limited network of private charitable foundations in Canada, most eligible interest and pressure groups do apply for public funding.

While it is easy to understand why an interest group would seek available funding from the state, it may be less easy to understand why a government would wish to subsidize groups that might be inclined to criticize its activities. Initially, a particular government agency might seek to create a well-organized political constituency for its programs and services. Should the agency face a challenge to its autonomy or its finances, whether from inside or outside the federal government, such an external constituency may become a crucial resource in its self-defence campaign. Second, from the perspective of the government as a whole, giving money to groups that will, in turn, demand even more public resources makes long-term strategic sense. Advocacy organizations whose primary purpose is to secure programs for disadvantaged social groups provide arguments to justify the continual expansion of state activities.

While those arguments serve the interests of the state during periods of prosperity, which helps to explain the boom in advocacy funding during the late-1960s and early-1970s, they tend to fall on deaf ears during periods of fiscal constraint. The spending restrictions that began to affect the federal government in the 1980s go a long way to explain declining state support for advocacy groups since that time—not just directly, in the sense that government has had less money to spend on core and project funding, but also indirectly, because in an era of fiscal restraint, many advocacy groups have become more of a nuisance than a political resource.

Whether or not they receive funding from the state, pressure groups engage in the policy process in three distinct ways: lobbying, representation, and consultation.[20]

Lobbying

Lobbying refers to one-way communication from a pressure group to the state actors in the relevant policy field. It is the effort by a particular group to convince government decision-makers that its interests should be reflected in public policy. Lobbying occurs at the initiative of the pressure group, not at the invitation of the government. As we will see in the Lobbyists Registration Act data below, lobbying is a major industry in Ottawa and the provincial capitals.

Representation

Representation is also a one-way street, although it is normally initiated by the state and not by the participating groups. When the federal government decides to establish a royal commission to investigate a particular issue, it usually gives the commission a mandate to hold public hearings. Those hearings attract pressure-group spokespersons, who seize the opportunity to set the policy agenda and to attract their share of media coverage. Some publicly funded groups are expressly invited to submit briefs. While royal commissions are increasingly rare policy tools, the 1986 reforms to the committee system in the House of Commons provide more frequent opportunities for interest representation. Between 1994 and 1998, more than 24 000 witnesses appeared before House of Commons and Senate committees, many of them formally associated with advocacy groups.[21]

Consultation

Unlike lobbying and representation, consultation is a two-way flow of communication in which state actors and group representatives work together to resolve common problems. Like representation, the government initiates consultation, but usually considers it to be an ongoing process rather than the more ad hoc encounters associated with representation. The need for consultation has grown recently, as federal departments have entered into partnerships with private and nonprofit agencies. The downsizing of the federal public service forced the government to rely more heavily on the specialized knowledge of its client groups, knowledge that many times can be bought only in exchange for a seat at the policy table.

Generally speaking, pressure groups share four primary characteristics:
1. They seek to influence public policy in accord with the interests of their members.
2. They possess the necessary organization and resources to participate directly in the policy process (through representation and consultation).
3. They try to channel the diverse and often conflicting demands of their members into consistent policy positions.
4. They wish to "influence those who hold power rather than to exercise the responsibility of government."[22]

We will take a closer look at each of these four characteristics in turn.

Pressure Groups and Public Policy

Pressure groups perform five essential functions in the Canadian political system:
1. They promote the interests of their members in the policy process, in the media, and in negotiations with other groups.
2. They provide a channel of communication between governments and their members, informing the latter about new debates and developments in public policy while keeping the former abreast of emerging problems that directly affect their members' interests.
3. They legitimate public policy by participating in its formation and persuading their members to accept the resulting programs and regulations.
4. Some pressure groups regulate their members on behalf of government agencies by monitoring compliance with the law and imposing sanctions for noncompliance.
5. Some pressure groups participate directly in program implementation, either by entering into formal partnerships with government agencies or by encouraging their members to cooperate with public servants.

Policy communities vary in the relationships they have among their members. On any given issue, participants in the relevant policy networks will disagree about preferred outcomes and approaches. Each side of a particular policy debate is represented by a specific policy network whose members share common assumptions and goals. Therefore, the policy community is not a simple collection of like-minded groups and individuals; it is divided among two or more policy networks, which may engage each other in bitter power struggles over contentious issues.

Despite concerns about the secretive and possibly corrupting nature of the influence pressure groups have on policy outcomes, they are an indispensable part of the policy process in Canada and elsewhere. They are necessary for organizing policy debate because typically only they have the specialized knowledge about a particular area of policy and its impact on a policy community. Nonetheless, there are legitimate questions about the extent of pressure-group power in policy-making. Do state agencies favour certain types of interests and downplay others? If so, what is the long-term effect on the legitimacy of our political institutions? Do pressure groups really speak on behalf of their members, or does their advice to policymakers merely reflect the interests of their leaders and permanent staff? What are the implications of pressure-group influence within policy subgovernments for Parliament, political parties, and other democratic institutions? Should pressure groups be allowed to intervene directly in the democratic process, and if so, to what degree? Some of these questions can be better answered if we understand the organization and resources available to the wide variety of interest groups in Canada.

■ Organization and Resources

There are two central points to be made about the organization of pressure groups in Canada:

1. The structure and functions of pressure groups are shaped by institutional incentives, especially those arising from federalism, responsible Cabinet government, and (in some cases) the Canadian Charter of Rights and Freedoms.
2. Not all pressure groups are created equal. Some control substantial resources, which may help them to gain access to the subgovernment, while others do not. Exploiting institutional norms and adapting to institutional incentives is neither easy nor automatic; it demands a high degree of organizational sophistication and financial support.

Institutional Incentives and Canadian Pressure Groups

Canada's federal system, and the regionalism that it both reflects and fosters, affects pressure groups in several ways. First, federalism complicates the process of public decision-making. As was explained in Chapter 3, the watertight compartments view of federalism is not an accurate description of Canadian federalism. Pressure groups concerned with health care, social assistance, and postsecondary education (to take just three examples) must operate at both the federal and provincial levels. Although this decentralization of policy-making power provides more access points for organized interests—by providing a greater number of opportunities to influence decision-making—the growing reliance on executive federalism since the 1960s has effectively excluded most nongovernmental actors from the top of the Canadian policy process. Aboriginal organizations and urban municipality associations are often invited to participate in discussions among federal, provincial, and territorial leaders, but other groups are rarely consulted in an official way.

A second characteristic of Canadian federalism is the presence of Quebec. While the existence of provincial governments requires national interest groups to organize themselves on a regional basis, the special circumstances in Quebec pose unique challenges for coordination. The practical difficulties created by two official languages are compounded by different social traditions. In the field of human rights, for example, Quebec has a rich tradition of the Catholic Church overseeing missionary work and social action that differs significantly from the English Canadian pattern. Consequently, many human rights organizations are split between Quebec and "Canadian" offices. This two-nations approach to interest group organization can threaten the unity of a national group.

If federalism disperses power, responsible Cabinet government concentrates it. The prime minister and Cabinet make decisions, not the legislative branch. Parties are highly disciplined and are therefore relatively closed to external influences. Furthermore, decision-making is tightly controlled and often secretive. Under these conditions, interest groups have traditionally had few points of access. Because cabinet ministers and senior officials are the key actors in the political system, back-bench MPs and senators are less frequent targets of lobbying. As for public servants, they prefer to work with pressure groups that share their institutional norms. Therefore, access to the subgovernment has traditionally been the privilege of large, bureaucratized groups that possess knowledge and other essential resources.

Repeated attempts to reform the House of Commons in order to provide greater autonomy to back-bench MPs, including recent reforms to the standing committee system, have encouraged pressure groups to divert some of their attention from the subgovernment to the parliamentary arena. As a result, the scope of parliamentary consultations over major pieces of legislation has expanded. This applies particularly to the annual federal budget, which has been shaped since 1994 by consultations with the Standing Committee on Finance. As noted earlier, thousands of Canadians appear before one or more standing committees of the House of Commons and Senate every year. For pressure groups that are excluded from the subgovernment, appearance before parliamentary committees may be their best chance to influence public policy. But, in the final analysis, a Cabinet that controls a majority of the seats in the Commons can disregard committee recommendations that do not conform to the priorities of the political executive and the central agencies.

Since 1982, the Charter of Rights and Freedoms has expanded the policy role of the courts. Previously, groups disgruntled with a particular piece of legislation or policy could only lobby the legislative and executive branches of government. Now, if they have the resources, they can pursue Charter-based litigation in the hope of changing public policy. For example, the October 2004 Supreme Court hearings into the constitutionality of same-sex marriage attracted more than two dozen interventions—many from interest groups on both sides of the issue. Because the issue concerns Section 15 of the Charter—the guarantee of equality rights—many of these groups would have been eligible for support from the federally funded Court Challenges Program (CCP). The CCP was established in 1985, shut down in 1992, reinstated in an altered form in 1993, and again discontinued in 2006.[23] Its purpose was to assist groups and individuals who wish to use either Section 15 equality rights or the official-language minority rights (Sections 16 to 23) provisions in the Charter to challenge government legislation. However, public-interest litigation is enormously expensive, even with CCP funding, which makes it a risky strategy for advocacy groups with limited resources.

Pressure-Group Resources

In the early-twentieth century, one of the central assumptions of pluralism was that groups would compete with each other for resources and influence, under rules of the game that were fair to all players. The state would act as a neutral referee, enforcing the rules without systematically favouring any single interest or group of interests. Since the 1960s, the neutrality of the state has been largely discredited by clear evidence of bias on the part of government agencies. In other words, the rules of the pressure-group game are far from neutral. They give certain interests, and certain types of pressure groups, a clear advantage over others. Groups whose interests dovetail with those of state actors exercise greater influence than those that are perceived, fairly or otherwise, as fringe or protest movements. What is less obvious, at least initially, is the organizational and resource base that distinguishes the groups that are admitted to the subgovernment from those that are not.

To achieve and retain a privileged place in the subgovernment, a pressure group must have both political salience and policy capacity. The political salience of a particular group is determined by several factors:

- the size, cohesion, socioeconomic status, and political leverage of its membership
- its willingness and ability to build coalitions with like-minded groups
- its tangible resources (primarily money) and its intangible resources (membership commitment, skilled leadership, and reputation)
- its ability to represent its membership effectively and to mobilize that membership in support of its political activities by putting pressure on elected policymakers
- its effectiveness as a channel of communication between the government and its membership

The policy capacity of a pressure group depends on its ability to use its political salience to advance its policy goals. A group with a large and wealthy membership may not automatically secure entry into the subgovernment on that basis. It must repeatedly demonstrate its value as a participant in the making and implementation of public policy. The key ingredients in policy capacity are

- tangible resources: money; expert staff (in-house or contract lobbyists and policy specialists); and a stable, continuous organizational presence (e.g., a large national office in Ottawa)
- intangible resources: expertise in both the substance of policy and the process of policy-making; a reputation with ministers, senior officials, and other groups within the subgovernment; a track record of competent and reliable service to the subgovernment, including a reputation for providing reliable information, building support for new measures among the membership, and assisting in the implementation of policy

It would be misleading to assume that the tangible resources define the limits of the cost of policy participation. Intangible resources, especially policy expertise and service to the subgovernment, are enormously expensive and time consuming. In many cases, when government agencies determine that a pressure group legitimately speaks for a significant subculture within the population, they frequently seek out their advice and consult with them on a wide variety of topics that may not be of immediate concern to the pressure group. These consultations often require the pressure group to systematically solicit the opinions of its members and of other communities, seek out specialized knowledge, and engage in a host of other activities related to answering the government's policy questions, which may or may not be of immediate importance to the pressure group and its members.

Groups that can afford to acquire the necessary expertise in the technical details of policy and the art of governance, while simultaneously providing the permanent and political executives with the necessary information, support, and regulatory assistance, may become and remain core members of the subgovernment. Less well-endowed groups usually enjoy less influence, regardless of the intrinsic merits of their policy recommendations or the legitimacy of their members' concerns. As public financial support for advocacy groups shrinks, the subgovernment status of those groups is seriously threatened. Certainly, cuts to state grants in the late-1980s and 1990s have made it increasingly difficult for many of them to sustain the level of policy participation they previously enjoyed. While there may still be a role for women's groups, Aboriginal groups, and other interests to play in policy-making, in the future it is likely that they will need to secure a much greater share of their financing of those activities from the communities they claim to represent, rather than from the Canadian taxpayers. Business groups and associations have typically been in the position of not having to rely on public subsidies to support their efforts. Most enjoyed financial resources well beyond the capacities of other groups, allowing them to hire professional lobbyists and other professional services for which most other groups must rely on volunteers.

Lobbying

Ottawa and the provincial capitals have blossomed in recent years with companies and individuals who lobby government on behalf of their clients. For reasons of partisanship and personal contacts, specific firms tend to be in favour with specific governments at any given time. The corollary is that when governments are replaced, lobbying firms tend to be, too.[24] Concerns that cronyism and business influence were ruling the corridors of power in Ottawa finally led to the 1985 Lobbyists Registration Act. The original legislation had some huge loopholes, notably that it narrowly defined lobbyists as those who actually arrange meetings or communicate with public officials on behalf of clients. It nevertheless for the first time yielded some hard information on the scope of the lobbying industry at the federal level. The 1985 act distinguished between Tier I and Tier II lobbyists. A Tier I lobbyist "is an individual who, for payment and on behalf of a client, undertakes to arrange a meeting with a public office holder or to communicate with a public office holder in an attempt to influence the development, making or amendment of any federal law, regulation, policy or program or the award of any federal monetary grant or the award of any federal contract."[25] Tier II lobbyists act on behalf of their employer for the same ends (with the exception of awarding of contracts).

Amendments to the act came into force early in 1996, and were designed to elicit more comprehensive information about lobbyists and their activities. The act was amended again in 2003, as part of the ethics package enacted by former prime minister

Chrétien. The Harper government's Accountability Act would also make some further requirements of lobbyists. The amended Lobbyists Registration Act now provides for three categories of lobbyists, all of which must register and file public reports of their lobbying activities:

1. A consultant lobbyist is an individual "who, for payment, on behalf of any person or organization," communicates with a public office holder with the intent to influence policy, obtain a financial benefit, or secure a federal contract. These are the professional, full-time government relations personnel employed primarily by public relations firms.

2. An in-house corporate lobbyist is a person who works for a commercial company (other than a lobbying firm), and who spends at least 20 percent of his or her working time on lobbying the federal government.

3. In-house organization lobbyists are people who work for the same organization and whose collective lobbying efforts constitute at least 20 percent of the overall activity of the organization.[26]

As of March 31, 2005, a total of 191 in-house lobbyists (corporations) were registered with the Lobbyists Registration System. They represented the interests of 116 different corporations. The number of in-house lobbyists (senior officers) registered by nonprofit organizations, as well as business and professional organizations, was down from the previous year.

Under federal law, consultant lobbyists must file an annual report with Industry Canada, including the following information: the names of their clients, the amounts paid by their clients, the specific law or program that each client hoped to influence, and the persons in government with whom the lobbyist has been in contact. Less detailed information is required of the part-time lobbyists who fall under the in-house category.

CANADA BY THE NUMBERS 9.1 Registered Lobbyists in Canada 2003–2005

	2003–2004	2004–2005
Lobbyists active as of March 31		
Consultant lobbyists	980	1065
In-house lobbyists (corporations)	294	191
Organizations (senior officers)	324	266
Registrations active as of March 31		
Consultant lobbyists	3287	3417
In-house lobbyists (corporations)	298	192
In-house lobbyists (organizations)	330	271

Source: From *Lobbyists Registration Act Annual Report 2004–2005*, available on-line from Industry Canada at http://strategis.ic.gc.ca/epic/internet/inlobbyist-lobbyiste.nsf/en/nx00118e.html#4.4; accessed June 2006. Reproduced with the permission of the Minister of Public Works and Government Services, 2006.

The law does not apply to appearances before parliamentary committees, submissions to public officials on the enforcement of laws or regulations, and submissions that are a response to a request. Therefore, the law does not allow us to gauge the degree to which pressure groups engage in representation or consultation, which may be more likely to result in changes to public policy. Lobbying, in many cases, is a last resort. Nonetheless, the data provided by the act give us a good indication of the policy areas that attract the greatest attention from pressure groups. The following list identifies the 20 subject areas most frequently identified by Canadian lobbyists, as of March 31, 2005.

CANADA BY THE NUMBERS 9.2 Subject Matter of Lobbying Activities (Areas of Concern)

	2003–2004	2004–2005
Industry	1	1
International trade	2	2
Taxation and finance	3	3
Environment	4	4
Science and technology	5	5
Health	6	6
Transportation	7	7
Employment and training	8	8
Regional development	14	9
Consumer issues	9	10
Energy	10	11
Internal trade	11	11
International relations	12	12
Infrastructure	16	12
Government procurement	13	13
Intellectual property	15	14
Labour	18	15
Small business	20	16
Agriculture	17	17
Education	—	18
Aboriginal affairs	19	19
Justice and law enforcement	—	20

Source: From *Lobbyists Registration Act Annual Report 2004–2005*, available on-line from Industry Canada at http://strategis.ic.gc.ca/epic/internet/inlobbyist-lobbyiste.nsf/en/nx00118e.html#4.2; accessed June 2006. Reproduced with the permission of the Minister of Public Works and Government Services, 2006.

CANADA BY THE NUMBERS 9.3 Government Departments and Agencies Most Likely to Be the Focus of Lobbying Efforts

	2003–2004	2004–2005
Industry Canada	1	1
Department of Finance Canada	2	2
Foreign Affairs Canada and International Trade Canada (formerly Department of Foreign Affairs and International Trade)	3	3
Environment Canada	4	4
Privy Council Office	5	5
Health Canada	6	6
Canada Revenue Agency	7	7
Human Resources and Skills Development Canada	8	8
Transport Canada	9	9
Natural Resources Canada	10	10
Public Works and Government Services Canada	11	11
Treasury Board of Canada	12	12
Agriculture and Agri-Food Canada	13	13
Canadian Heritage	14	14
Department of Justice Canada	15	15
Indian and Northern Affairs Canada	16	16
National Defence	15	17
Fisheries and Oceans Canada	17	18
Western Economic Diversification Canada	18	19
National Research Council Canada	19	20
Statistics Canada	20	—

Source: From *Lobbyists Registration Act Annual Report 2004–2005*, available on-line from Industry Canada at http://strategis.ic.gc.ca/epic/internet/inlobbyist-lobbyiste.nsf/en/nx00118e.html#4.3; accessed June 2006. Reproduced with the permission of the Minister of Public Works and Government Services, 2006.

Not surprisingly, given the subject matter identified as most important by lobbyists, two important economic ministries sit at the top of the list of government departments and agencies most frequently contacted in the course of lobbying.

Internal Relations with Pressure-Group Membership

The characteristics of a pressure group's membership help to determine its political salience, although they are less crucial to its policy capacity. However, some interest constituencies may constrain the policy capacity of their leaders. Groups that refuse to cooperate with the government or whose members fear co-optation into political institutions will exercise less influence than those whose members are willing to accept the norms of the subgovernment. The leaders and staff of a pressure group must have a degree of latitude so that they can participate effectively in the subgovernment without constantly facing accusations of selling out or demands for further consultations with their members.

As a newly formed pressure group becomes more institutionalized, its leaders and staff may take on roles and values that are distinct from those of the people whose interests they are expected to represent. Leaders who interact directly with other members of the policy community tend to become very knowledgeable about the policy process aspects of their duties and consequently may start to move away from the core interests of their members. At this point, the emerging political salience of the pressure group may be undermined by a perception among public officials that its constituency does not support the goals and tactics of the leaders. When this happens, officials wonder whether they can rely on the group's members to support the policies approved by their leaders or to participate effectively in their implementation.

In sum, the leaders of pressure groups are caught in a dilemma. On the one hand, the demands of participation in the subgovernment cannot be met without the financial and moral support of their members. Nor will they be admitted to the subgovernment without a firm mandate from the grassroots of their organizations. On the other hand, pressure-group leaders cannot respond quickly to requests for information and advice if they are required to seek the formal approval of their members for every policy pronouncement. While it may be desirable in theory for leaders to be fully accountable to those in whose name they speak, it is clear that pressure-group leaders are most effective when they achieve the autonomy and the experience to participate in detailed policy-making.

Such leaders may also acquire the polish and the communications skills that allow them to use the news media to raise the profile of their group and its issues. Close ties between journalists and pressure-group leaders carry advantages as well as disadvantages. On the plus side, frequent media appearances by a group leader or spokesperson tend to keep the group's profile high amongst the public, enhancing its status with policymakers, especially elected politicians. The downside, particularly for advocacy groups with "radical" agendas, is that sustained media attention, especially if it reflects negatively on the government and its agencies, will tend to alienate policymakers.[27] In summary, the institutional incentives for pressure groups seeking admission to the subgovernment pull their leaders and their members in different directions. The former must adapt to the requirements of policy-making and media relations, while the latter cannot allow leaders to lose touch with the concerns of those who gave them their mandate in the first place.

Pressure Groups in Canadian Politics

For a number of reasons, the role of pressure groups in Canadian politics will likely increase in the next few years. Initially, the Charter of Rights and Freedoms has given many groups new leverage in challenging public policy. Litigation is expensive and risky, but it has been used successfully by a number of groups. Also, governments across the country have been recently proclaiming the importance of consultation and partnership with "civil society." Consultation is "in" and policymakers cannot avoid, even if they want to, connecting with a wide variety of organizations. Finally, groups may be developing a new capacity for mobilization and for building networked coalitions through the use of new information technologies.

For the critics of interest groups, further growth in pressure-group activity will continue to make our politics hostage to shifting coalitions of special interests. For others, collective action in pursuit of shared goals is the foundation of the social capital required to support democratic institutions. Note, however, that state funding of advocacy groups that would otherwise lack the wherewithal to participate in policy-making tends to reflect government priorities rather than those of a vibrant civil society. In either event, the balance between political parties and pressure groups will be a challenging one, but one in which the parties will continue to dominate. Political parties have one key institutional advantage over all other groups, associations, and organizations: they directly enter into the competition for votes to determine which party will hold governmental power. Until other organizations do the same, at which point they must transform themselves into parties, they will not overcome this institutional imperative. If they become parties, their behaviour and activities will become conditioned by the norms, conventions, and laws associated with party activity. If they become successful, they will have demonstrated their capacity to beat their competition in a contest that was played using the existing rules, thereby losing much of the motivation to change the rules. As the Canadian political culture continues to democratize, use of referenda, consultations, and direct representation by pressure groups and organizations is likely to continue, and possibly increase. However, there is little chance of pressure groups and the news media usurping the role of political parties when it comes to representing the political interests of the vast majority of Canadians.

CONCLUSION

This chapter has described the domestic political roles played by two important non-governmental actors: the news media and pressure groups. Both are internationalizing their activities, for better or worse, as they participate in the globalization of communications, transportation, and production technologies. It must be remembered, however, that even transnational NGOs direct most of their lobbying efforts toward national and provincial states. That is, supranational bodies are increasingly important, but they have not yet supplanted nation-states as the prime target of pressure-group or news media focus.

Other developments in the explosion of interactive communication technology have transformed the information environment within which the news media have long operated. Both the Internet and the growing spate of specialty TV channels threaten to divide fragmented electorates into ever-smaller groups. Accountability, given the important communicative role the media play between citizen and political actor, is an issue. Neither pressure groups nor media companies can effectively be held accountable for the power they wield in Canadian politics. There are some limited exceptions to this rule. Pressure groups must disclose some of their formal lobbying activities to governments (and the public), and will face much more intense scrutiny under the federal government's new Accountability Act. Still, as with the media, even these new rules are likely to tell us little or nothing about the internal structures of these groups or the effectiveness of their activities. Broadcasting companies are regulated by the Canadian Radio-television and Telecommunications Commission (CRTC), although its mandate and direction are also under review. In rare cases, the CRTC can suspend the licence of a broadcaster that breaks the rules, but in general, Canadian journalists are constrained only by their employers and by the informal norms of their profession. They cannot be held formally accountable to the public for the information they choose to present and the ways in which they choose to present it, at least not beyond the normal standards of tort and criminal law that apply to all citizens.

In contrast, governmental institutions like Parliament and closely related bodies like political parties are subject to formal rules of operation and accountability. Some of those rules are entrenched in written constitutional and statute laws; others are unwritten conventions of procedure. Their cumulative effect is to constrain the arbitrary power of the state and to hold political actors accountable, however imperfectly, to the electorate.

DISCUSSION QUESTIONS

1. How often do you watch a television newscast? How many times a week do you read the political section of a newspaper? If you are a regular consumer of Canadian political news, what is your opinion of the information and analysis available from our mass media?

2. Try the following experiment: The next time a big political story breaks, make a point of either watching three different newscasts (e.g., CBC *National* or *Newsworld*, CTV *National News* or *Newsnet*, CPAC, or Global) or reading the coverage in three different newspapers (e.g., *The Globe and Mail*, the *National Post*, and the *Toronto Star*). Can you identify different spins or frames in the coverage? Do the news values of each media organization differ? How might a habitual media consumer of one paper or broadcast perceive politics differently from someone who chooses a different source for his or her daily news?

3. Why do some Canadians turn to pressure groups, rather than political parties, to represent their interests in federal politics?

4. Have you ever belonged to a pressure or advocacy group? If so, did you participate in efforts to influence political decision-makers? What were those efforts? Did they succeed?

SUGGESTED READINGS

W. Lance Bennett and Robert M. Entman, eds., *Mediated Politics: Communication in the Future of Democracy* (Cambridge, UK: Cambridge University Press, 2001).

Robert M. Campbell and Leslie A. Pal, *The Real Worlds of Canadian Politics: Cases in Process and Policy,* 3rd edition (Peterborough, ON: Broadview Press, 1994).

Joseph N. Cappella and Kathleen Hall Jamieson, *Spiral of Cynicism: The Press and the Public Good* (New York: Oxford University Press, 1997).

William D. Coleman and Grace Skogstad, eds., *Policy Communities and Public Policy in Canada: A Structural Approach* (Toronto: Copp Clark Pitman, 1990).

Michael Howlett, "Do Networks Matter? Linking Policy Network Structure to Policy Outcomes: Evidence from Four Canadian Policy Sectors 1990–2000," *Canadian Journal of Political Science,* 35:2 (June 2002), 235–267.

Paul Nesbitt-Larking, *Politics, Society and the Media: Canadian Perspectives* (Peterborough, ON: Broadview Press, 2001).

Leslie A. Pal, *Interests of State: The Politics of Language, Multiculturalism, and Feminism in Canada* (Montreal and Kingston: McGill–Queen's University Press, 1993).

A. Paul Pross, *Group Politics and Public Policy,* 2nd edition (Toronto: Oxford University Press, 1992).

David Taras, *Power and Betrayal in the Canadian Media* (Peterborough, ON: Broadview Press, 1999).

Websites

While most media companies have their own websites, there is a growing trend away from free access in favour of paid registration. Most Canadian newspapers now required paid subscriptions from anyone wishing to read their full news content on-line. At the time of writing, Canadian Press (http://www.canoe.ca) and the national television broadcasters still allow free access to most of their news content.

Most of the major pressure groups in Canada and elsewhere have set up websites, either for themselves alone or shared with related organizations. An Internet search using the organization's name usually results in quick access to these sights.

Industry Canada's Strategis website (http://www.strategis.gc.ca), devoted to Canadian business and consumer matters, provides information about the Lobbyists Registration System.

NOTES

1. *Hockey Night in Canada* generates more advertising revenue for the CBC than does any other single program.

2. Timothy E. Cook, "The Future of the Institutional Media," in W. Lance Bennett and Robert M. Entman, eds., *Mediated Politics: Communication in the Future of Democracy* (Cambridge, UK: Cambridge University Press, 2001), 182–200.

3. Although the CBC receives approximately three-quarters of its revenue from the Canadian taxpayers by way of legislation passed by Parliament, because the CBC is not granted a monopoly over news and political reporting and must compete with private broadcasters for sports and entertainment contracts, we will consider Canada to have a free and competitive media environment.

4. See for example David Pritchard and Florian Sauvageau, "English and French and Generation X: The Professional Values of Canadian Journalists," in Harvey Lazar and Tom McIntosh, eds., *Canada, The State of the Federation 1998/99: How Canadians Connect* (Montreal and Kingston: McGill–Queen's University Press, 1999), 287.

5. David Taras, *Power and Betrayal in the Canadian Media* (Peterborough, ON: Broadview Press, 1999), 157.

6. See, for example, George Bain, *Gotcha!: How the Media Distort the News* (Toronto: Key Porter, 1994); and Larry Sabato, *Feeding Frenzy: How Attack Journalism Has Transformed American Politics* (New York: Free Press, 1991).

7. Comparative studies reveal that Canadians are less likely to read newspapers and more likely to obtain their news from television than are people in many other developed countries. This imbalance contributes to relatively low levels of civic literacy in Canada, compared to countries whose citizens rely more on newspapers for their political information. See Henry Milner, *Civic Literacy: How Informed Citizens Make Democracy Work* (Hanover, NH: University Press of New England, 2002), Figures 7.2 and 7.3, 99–100; and Henry Milner, *Civic Literacy in Comparative Context* (Montreal: Institute for Research on Public Policy, July 2001), available on-line at http://www.irpp.org.

8. See Joseph N. Cappella and Kathleen Hall Jamieson, *Spiral of Cynicism: The Press and the Public Good* (New York: Oxford University Press, 1997).

9. Gadi Wolfsfeld, "Political Waves and Democratic Discourse: Terrorism Waves During the Oslo Peace Process," in Bennett and Entman, eds., *Mediated Politics*, 226–231.

10. See David Taras, *The Newsmakers: The Media's Influence on Canadian Politics* (Scarborough, ON: Nelson Canada, 1990), 14.

11. Taras, *The Newsmakers,* 40; see also Matthew Mendelsohn, "Television News Frames in the 1993 Canadian Election," in Helen Holmes and David Taras, eds., *Seeing Ourselves: Media Power and Policy in Canada,* 2nd edition (Toronto: Harcourt Brace, 1996).

12. See Faron Ellis, "The More Things Change . . . The Alliance Campaign," in Jon H. Pammett and Christopher Dornan, eds., *The Canadian General Election of 2000* (Toronto: Dundurn Press, 2001).

13. See Susan Delacourt, "The Media and the Supreme Court of Canada," in Hugh Mellon and Martin Westmacott, eds., *Political Dispute and Judicial Review: Assessing the Work of the Supreme Court of Canada* (Toronto: Nelson, 2000).

14. It also provided extensive, live, unedited coverage of Justice John Gomery's investigation into the federal government's sponsorship program in 2005, providing CPAC with a blockbuster hit, especially in Quebec.

15. See F. L. Morton and Rainer Knopff, *The Charter Revolution and the Court Party* (Peterborough, ON: Broadview Press, 2000).

16. See Robert M. Entman and Susan Herbst, "Reframing Public Opinion as We Have Known It," in Bennett and Entman, eds., *Mediated Politics.*

17. R. H. McDermid, "Media Usage and Political Behaviour," in Frederick J. Fletcher, ed., *Media and Voters in Canadian Election Campaigns,* volume 18 of the collected research studies for the Royal Commission on Electoral Reform and Party Financing (Toronto: Dundurn Press, 1991).

18. Robert A. Hackett, "News Media's Influence on Canadian Party Politics: Perspective on a Shifting Relationship," in Hugh G. Thorburn and Alan Whitehorn, eds., *Party Politics in Canada,* 8th edition (Toronto: Prentice-Hall, 2001).

19. See Leslie A. Pal, *Interests of State: The Politics of Language, Multiculturalism, and Feminism in Canada* (Montreal and Kingston: McGill–Queen's University Press, 1993).

20. Leslie A. Pal, *Beyond Policy Analysis: Public Issue Management in Turbulent Times,* 1st edition (Scarborough, ON: ITP Nelson, 1997).

21. David McInnes, *Taking It to the Hill: The Complete Guide to Appearing Before (and Surviving) Parliamentary Committees* (Ottawa: University of Ottawa Press, 1999). Update to 2005.

22. A. Paul Pross, *Group Politics and Public Policy,* 2nd edition (Toronto: Oxford University Press, 1992), 4.

23. On the history of the CCP, see Ian Brodie, "Interest Group Litigation and the Embedded State: Canada's Court Challenges Program," *Canadian Journal of Political Science,* 34:2 (June 2001), 357–376. For a more extensive discussion of interest-group interventions and public-interest litigation, see Heather MacIvor, *Canadian Government and Politics in the Charter Era* (Toronto: Nelson, 2005).

24. See for example John Sawatsky, *The Insiders: Government, Business, and the Lobbyists* (Toronto: McClelland and Stewart, 1987).

25. *Lobbyists Registration Act, Annual Report for the Year Ended March 31, 1992* (Ottawa, 1992), 5.

26. *Lobbyists Registration Act,* as amended by Bill C-15, *An Act to Amend the Lobbyists Registration Act,* Sections 5–7; accessed at http://www.canada.justice.gc.ca.

27. See Robert A. Hackett, *News and Dissent: The Press and the Politics of Peace in Canada* (Norwood, N.J.: Ablex Publishing Corporation, 1991).

10 NAVIGATING THE LABYRINTH

LEARNING OBJECTIVES

- *review* how Canada's political institutions operate
- *discuss* possible future political trends
- *remind* you of your role as citizen in Canada's political future

INTRODUCTION

Throughout the chapters of this book, we have examined each of Canada's major political institutions, discussing their formal and informal rules, the incentives that they set for ambitious politicians, their interactions with the political culture, and with some important nongovernmental institutions. This final chapter will provide an overview of where we have been, explain further how political institutions work together, and reinforce the principle that a change in one can affect some or all of the others.

We began by defining political institutions as organizations that make and enforce rules and decisions for a given population. In examining the master institution, we discovered that the Constitution assigns different tasks to each of our major institutions. At the national level, the permanent executive proposes amendments to the rules; these must be approved by the political executive (Cabinet) before being submitted to the legislative branch (the House of Commons and Senate) for proclamation as law by the Crown. When Parliament passes a bill, it authorizes the executive branch to make detailed decisions about its implementation. These decisions are embodied in delegated legislation (regulations). Laws and regulations are enforced by specific elements of the permanent executive within the federal public service. Where necessary, they are interpreted and applied by courts.

The rulemakers in Ottawa and in the provincial capitals are constrained by the Constitution. They must respect the division of powers between the federal and provincial governments that is defined in Sections 91 to 95, as well as citizens' rights and freedoms as guaranteed in the Charter. If the content of a law or the manner of its enforcement violates the Constitution, the courts can impose a remedy. In the process, judges create or amend common-law rules that will guide decisionmakers and legislators in the future.

Canada's federal system, like most of the other institutions discussed in this book, has experienced few formal changes since 1867. In practical terms, however, it operates very differently from the way it was originally designed. The watertight compartments and fiscal arrangements that seemed appropriate at Confederation have long since been overtaken by complex economic and political forces. In many situations, the federal and provincial governments must continually negotiate intergovernmental agreements to achieve their goals.

Within Parliament and the political executive, decisions are affected by partisan and electoral considerations. The leaders of the governing party impose strict discipline on their MPs to ensure that they vote for the laws sponsored by the Cabinet, and to secure the government as a whole against the threat of losing the confidence of the Commons. On the opposition side, party leaders and their caucuses try to embarrass the government by revealing flaws in its legislative program and its management of the nation's business. They hope to take advantage of these flaws (real or alleged) when the next election comes around. Pressure groups often get involved as they seek to influence the substance of laws, both directly (through lobbying and litigation) and indirectly through the news media. As far as the media are concerned, the more conflict the better, as they seek out political drama to fill a 24/7 news cycle. In the process, however, each of these institutions, including interest groups and the media, may be contributing to public disenchantment with the institutions of representative government.

The partisan and electoral considerations that operate at the national level are equally significant in provincial capitals. While premiers and prime ministers compete against their immediate rivals, they are sometimes pitted against each other in the contest for political advantage. That contest complicates the day-to-day management of the federation, and sometimes provokes heated clashes over constitutional issues. However, all of the first ministers reap at least one benefit from their participation in the peak institutions of federalism: the creation and implementation of intergovernmental agreements that further strengthen the power of the political executive in relation to the legislature. Consequently, executive federalism makes the executive branch as a whole even less accountable to the electorate by way of their representative legislative chambers.

From the preceding discussion, we may conclude that the process by which rules are made, enforced, and interpreted is not entirely consistent with the foundational values of the Canadian political culture: liberalism, pluralism, and democracy. The executive branch generally operates behind closed doors, even in the relatively high-profile arena of intergovernmental relations. This privacy ensures the confidentiality and mutual trust that executive decision-making demands, but it leaves cabinet ministers and their officials vulnerable to accusations of excessive secrecy and a lack of accountability. The House of Commons and Senate are more open to the public, although this is not always a good thing; the more Canadians see of some of their elected and appointed legislators at work, the less impressed they seem to be. A degree of party discipline, adversarialism, and executive dominance is built into our parliamentary institutions, but their applications in the federal Parliament have contributed to reducing Canadians' trust in the political system as a whole. For their part, courts conduct much of their business in the open. Unfortunately, the norms and the language of the legal process are far removed from the everyday experience of most people. Even the Charter, which enjoys the support of a majority of Canadians, is sometimes applied and interpreted in ways that provoke bafflement and occasional outrage.

All three branches of government are subject to criticism from pressure groups, opposition parties, and journalists, who play to their various constituencies (members, voters, readers, media owners) by attacking the institutions that govern us. The fact that most of the people who work in our political system do their jobs well is drowned out in the clamour of complaint. Small wonder that fewer and fewer Canadians choose to engage in the political process by joining political parties, or even by casting ballots. But rather than considering criticism to be an indictment of a failing system, it should be considered a sign of health in a free society. The fact that libertarians are free to challenge the authority of state actors, that social conservatives are free to defend tradition against change, or that socialists are free to advocate for a more equal distribution of wealth and larger welfare entitlements is a clear indication that Canada remains one of the most free societies in the world. In essence, criticism, complaints, and direct challenges to political institutions are the hallmark of liberal-pluralist democracies.

CALLS FOR REFORM

For the most part, we have avoided detailed discussion of the many proposals for reform to our institutions, leaving it to be taken up by students and their professors in the classroom, and citizens in their communities. We have preferred instead to concentrate on the political system as it currently exists. Many of the proposals for change that are currently being debated, such as Senate reform, or recognizing Quebec as a "nation," would probably require constitutional amendments, which seem unlikely given the difficulty of megaconstitutional politics in Canada. Others can be, and have been, achieved via nonconstitutional renewal. Some of the previous informal changes to the process of government evolved unintentionally, as short-term solutions that persisted long after an immediate problem was resolved. Examples include fiscal federalism and the Cabinet committee system. Others, like party discipline, flowed from the incentives created by particular institutional arrangements: in this case, the exercising of executive power by the party with the most seats in the Commons. A few of these ad hoc practices, such as the requirement of substantial provincial consent to formal amendments, have acquired the status of constitutional conventions. Others, for example transfer payments to the provinces, have been enshrined in law.

In the future, we will likely see further reforms to our political institutions. Some will be deliberate and carefully engineered; others will arise in response to short-term political conditions. If deliberate reforms are to be fashioned, they should be guided by three principles. First, reformers must agree on what they are trying to accomplish. In other words, they must decide what they want the reformed institutions to do. Second, Canadians must understand that any change to a particular institution will have repercussions for other institutions. Therefore, would-be reformers should consider the impact of their proposals on the entire political system, and the larger political culture. Third, reformers cannot design institutions in the abstract; they must take into account the incentives imposed on the human beings whose roles are scripted by those institutions. While we might wish to reform our current institutions in order to weaken or eliminate harmful incentives that presently exist, we must be cautious not to introduce other incentives that can cause even more harm.

INFLUENCING CANADA'S FUTURE

Whether or not Canadians can agree on specific institutional reforms, our politics and government will continue to function reasonably well. The flexibility provided by our constitutional conventions and the deep reservoir of general support for the political system will allow our institutions to continue to adapt—however slowly and perhaps reluctantly—to the challenges of the twenty-first century. The form that our institutions take and how well they serve the citizens of Canada depend on us as much as they do on our political leaders. As John Stuart Mill argued more than a century ago, the surest safeguard of good government is a well-informed population prepared to preserve its political institutions, even while it demands improvements to keep pace with its own moral and intellectual evolution.

Instead of turning away from politics, Canadians may want to consider getting more involved. Like you have done in completing this course, they may want to begin a lifelong study of our political institutions, rather than simply accepting at face value the often biased critiques of journalists, political parties, pressure groups, and yes, sometimes even political scientists. Canada's political institutions are not perfect, and they cannot be made perfect. But whatever their failings, they are far superior to their equivalents in much of the world. They must not be taken for granted by citizens or unfairly abused by political actors. Because liberal-pluralist democracy imposes duties on citizens as well as on those who govern them, each of us must take our duties seriously. While we will maintain the right to complain and criticize—dissent is integral to all other liberties—our critiques will carry much more legitimacy if we have actively sought first to understand, and then to work toward promoting realistic and achievable reforms. The bottom line is this: citizens of liberal-pluralist democracies tend to get the governments that they deserve. If you think that Canadians deserve better, it's up to you to help them achieve it.

APPENDIX

The Constitution Acts
1867 and 1982

THE CONSTITUTION ACT, 1867

Formerly the British North America Act, 1867

30 & 31 Victoria, c. 3. (U.K.)
(Excerpted)

An Act for the Union of Canada, Nova Scotia, and New Brunswick, and the Government thereof; and for Purposes connected therewith

[29th March 1867.]

WHEREAS the Provinces of Canada, Nova Scotia, and New Brunswick have expressed their Desire to be federally united into One Dominion under the Crown of the United Kingdom of Great Britain and Ireland, with a Constitution similar in Principle to that of the United Kingdom:

And whereas such a Union would conduce to the Welfare of the Provinces and promote the Interests of the British Empire:

And whereas on the Establishment of the Union by Authority of Parliament it is expedient, not only that the Constitution of the Legislative Authority in the Dominion be provided for, but also that the Nature of the Executive Government therein be declared:

And whereas it is expedient that Provision be made for the eventual Admission into the Union of other Parts of British North America:

I. PRELIMINARY

1. This Act may be cited as the *Constitution Act, 1867.*

2. *Repealed*

II. UNION

Establishes the country of Canada with four provinces.

3. through **8.**

III. EXECUTIVE POWER

Establishes the executive institutions of the national government.

9. through **16.**

IV. LEGISLATIVE POWER

Establishes the legislative institutions of the national government.

Parliament

17. through **20.**

Senate

21. through **36.**

House of Commons

37. through **52.**

Money Votes

53. through **57.**

V. PROVINCIAL CONSTITUTIONS

Establishes the executive and legislative institutions of the provincial governments.

Executive Power

58. through **68.**

Legislative Power

69. through **90.**

VI. DISTRIBUTION OF LEGISLATIVE POWERS

Establishes the federal division of powers.

Powers of the Parliament

91. It shall be lawful for the Queen, by and with the Advice and Consent of the Senate and House of Commons, to make Laws for the Peace, Order, and good Government of Canada, in relation to all Matters not coming within the Classes of Subjects by this Act assigned exclusively to the Legislatures of the Provinces; and for greater Certainty, but not so as to restrict the Generality of the foregoing Terms of this Section, it is hereby declared that (notwithstanding anything in this Act) the exclusive Legislative Authority of the Parliament of Canada extends to all Matters coming within the Classes of Subjects next hereinafter enumerated; that is to say,—

1. *Repealed.*

1A. The Public Debt and Property.

2. The Regulation of Trade and Commerce.

2A. Unemployment insurance.

3. The raising of Money by any Mode or System of Taxation.

4. The borrowing of Money on the Public Credit.

5. Postal Service.

6. The Census and Statistics.

7. Militia, Military and Naval Service, and Defence.

8. The fixing of and providing for the Salaries and Allowances of Civil and other Officers of the Government of Canada.

9. Beacons, Buoys, Lighthouses, and Sable Island.

10. Navigation and Shipping.

11. Quarantine and the Establishment and Maintenance of Marine Hospitals.

12. Sea Coast and Inland Fisheries.

13. Ferries between a Province and any British or Foreign Country or between Two Provinces.

14. Currency and Coinage.

15. Banking, Incorporation of Banks, and the Issue of Paper Money.

16. Savings Banks.

17. Weights and Measures.

18. Bills of Exchange and Promissory Notes.

19. Interest.

20. Legal Tender.

21. Bankruptcy and Insolvency.

22. Patents of Invention and Discovery.

23. Copyrights.

24. Indians, and Lands reserved for Indians.

25. Naturalization and Aliens.

26. Marriage and Divorce.

27. The Criminal Law, except the Constitution of Courts of Criminal Jurisdiction, but including the Procedure in Criminal Matters.

28. The Establishment, Maintenance, and Management of Penitentiaries.

29. Such Classes of Subjects as are expressly excepted in the Enumeration of the Classes of Subjects by this Act assigned exclusively to the Legislatures of the Provinces.

And any Matter coming within any of the Classes of Subjects enumerated in this Section shall not be deemed to come within the Class of Matters of a local or private Nature comprised in the Enumeration of the Classes of Subjects by this Act assigned exclusively to the Legislatures of the Provinces.

Exclusive Powers of Provincial Legislatures

92. In each Province the Legislature may exclusively make Laws in relation to Matters coming within the Classes of Subjects next hereinafter enumerated; that is to say,

1. *Repealed.*

2. Direct Taxation within the Province in order to the raising of a Revenue for Provincial Purposes.

3. The borrowing of Money on the sole Credit of the Province.

4. The Establishment and Tenure of Provincial Offices and the Appointment and Payment of Provincial Officers.

5. The Management and Sale of the Public Lands belonging to the Province and of the Timber and Wood thereon.

6. The Establishment, Maintenance, and Management of Public and Reformatory Prisons in and for the Province.

7. The Establishment, Maintenance, and Management of Hospitals, Asylums, Charities, and Eleemosynary Institutions in and for the Province, other than Marine Hospitals.

8. Municipal Institutions in the Province.

9. Shop, Saloon, Tavern, Auctioneer, and other Licences in order to the raising of a Revenue for Provincial, Local, or Municipal Purposes.

10. Local Works and Undertakings other than such as are of the following Classes:

(*a*) Lines of Steam or other Ships, Railways, Canals, Telegraphs, and other Works and Undertakings connecting the Province with any other or others of the Provinces, or extending beyond the Limits of the Province:

(*b*) Lines of Steam Ships between the Province and any British or Foreign Country:

(*c*) Such Works as, although wholly situate within the Province, are before or after their Execution declared by the Parliament of Canada to be for the general Advantage of Canada or for the Advantage of Two or more of the Provinces.

11. The Incorporation of Companies with Provincial Objects.

12. The Solemnization of Marriage in the Province.

13. Property and Civil Rights in the Province.

14. The Administration of Justice in the Province, including the Constitution, Maintenance, and Organization of Provincial Courts, both of Civil and of Criminal Jurisdiction, and including Procedure in Civil Matters in those Courts.

15. The Imposition of Punishment by Fine, Penalty, or Imprisonment for enforcing any Law of the Province made in relation to any Matter coming within any of the Classes of Subjects enumerated in this Section.

16. Generally all Matters of a merely local or private Nature in the Province.

Non-Renewable Natural Resources, Forestry Resources and Electrical Energy

92A. (1) In each province, the legislature may exclusively make laws in relation to

(*a*) exploration for non-renewable natural resources in the province;

(*b*) development, conservation and management of non-renewable natural resources and forestry resources in the province, including laws in relation to the rate of primary production therefrom; and

(*c*) development, conservation and management of sites and facilities in the province for the generation and production of electrical energy.

(2) In each province, the legislature may make laws in relation to the export from the province to another part of Canada of the primary production from non-renewable natural resources and forestry resources in the province and the production from facilities in the province for the generation of electrical energy, but such laws may not authorize or provide for discrimination in prices or in supplies exported to another part of Canada.

(3) Nothing in subsection (2) derogates from the authority of Parliament to enact laws in relation to the matters referred to in that subsection and, where such a law of Parliament and a law of a province conflict, the law of Parliament prevails to the extent of the conflict.

(4) In each province, the legislature may make laws in relation to the raising of money by any mode or system of taxation in respect of

(*a*) non-renewable natural resources and forestry resources in the province and the primary production therefrom, and

(*b*) sites and facilities in the province for the generation of electrical energy and the production therefrom, whether or not such production is exported in whole or in part from the province, but such laws may not authorize or provide for taxation that differentiates between production exported to another part of Canada and production not exported from the province.

(5) The expression "primary production" has the meaning assigned by the Sixth Schedule.

(6) Nothing in subsections (1) to (5) derogates from any powers or rights that a legislature or government of a province had immediately before the coming into force of this section.

Education

93. In and for each Province the Legislature may exclusively make Laws in relation to Education, subject and according to the following Provisions:

(1) Nothing in any such Law shall prejudicially affect any Right or Privilege with respect to Denominational Schools which any Class of Persons have by Law in the Province at the Union:

(2) All the Powers, Privileges, and Duties at the Union by Law conferred and imposed in Upper Canada on the Separate Schools and School Trustees of the Queen's Roman Catholic Subjects shall be and the same are hereby extended to the Dissentient Schools of the Queen's Protestant and Roman Catholic Subjects in Quebec:

(3) Where in any Province a system of Separate or Dissentient Schools exists by Law at the Union or is thereafter established by the Legislature of the Province, an Appeal shall lie to the Governor General in Council from any Act or Decision of any Provincial Authority affecting any Right or Privilege of the Protestant or Roman Catholic Minority of the Queen's Subjects in relation to Education:

(4) In case any such Provincial Law as from Time to Time seems to the Governor General in Council requisite for the due Execution of the Provisions of this Section is not made, or in case any Decision of the Governor General in Council on any appeal under this Section is not duly executed by the proper Provincial Authority in that Behalf, then and in every such Case, and as far only as the Circumstances of each Case require, the Parliament of Canada may make remedial Laws for the due Execution of the Provisions of this Section and of any Decision of the Governor General in Council under this Section.

93A. Paragraphs (1) to (4) of section 93 do not apply to Quebec.

Uniformity of Laws in Ontario, Nova Scotia, and New Brunswick

94.

Old Age Pensions

94A. The Parliament of Canada may make laws in relation to old age pensions and supplementary benefits, including survivors' and disability benefits irrespective of age, but no such law shall affect the operation of any law present or future of a provincial legislature in relation to any such matter.

Agriculture and Immigration

95. In each Province the Legislature may make Laws in relation to Agriculture in the Province, and to Immigration into the Province; and it is hereby declared that the Parliament of Canada may from Time to Time make Laws in relation to Agriculture in all or any of the Provinces, and to Immigration into all or any of the Provinces; and any Law of the Legislature of a Province relative to Agriculture or to Immigration shall have effect in and for the Province as long and as far only as it is not repugnant to any Act of the Parliament of Canada.

VII. JUDICATURE

Establishes the judicial institutions of government.

96. The Governor General shall appoint the Judges of the Superior, District, and County Courts in each Province, except those of the Courts of Probate in Nova Scotia and New Brunswick.

97. Until the Laws relative to Property and Civil Rights in Ontario, Nova Scotia, and New Brunswick, and the Procedure of the Courts in those Provinces, are made uniform, the Judges of the Courts of those Provinces appointed by the Governor General shall be selected from the respective Bars of those Provinces.

98. The Judges of the Courts of Quebec shall be selected from the Bar of that Province.

99. (1) Subject to subsection two of this section, the Judges of the Superior Courts shall hold office during good behaviour, but shall be removable by the Governor General on Address of the Senate and House of Commons.

(2) A Judge of a Superior Court, whether appointed before or after the coming into force of this section, shall cease to hold office upon attaining the age of seventy-five years, or upon the coming into force of this section if at that time he has already attained that age.

100. The Salaries, Allowances, and Pensions of the Judges of the Superior, District, and County Courts (except the Courts of Probate in Nova Scotia and New Brunswick), and of the Admiralty Courts in Cases where the Judges thereof are for the Time being paid by Salary, shall be fixed and provided by the Parliament of Canada.

101. The Parliament of Canada may, notwithstanding anything in this Act, from Time to Time provide for the Constitution, Maintenance, and Organization of a General Court of Appeal for Canada, and for the Establishment of any additional Courts for the better Administration of the Laws of Canada.

VIII. REVENUES; DEBTS; ASSETS; TAXATION

Establishes the original fiscal authorities and relationships between the governments.

102. through **126.**

IX. MISCELLANEOUS PROVISIONS

A series of primarily transitional provisions relating to various institutional relationships.

127. through **144.**

X. INTERCOLONIAL RAILWAY

145. *Repealed.*

XI. ADMISSION OF OTHER COLONIES

Enables the establishment and admission of new provinces and territories.

146. through **147.**

SCHEDULES

THE FIRST SCHEDULE

Electoral Districts of Ontario

THE SECOND SCHEDULE

Electoral Districts of Quebec specially fixed

THE THIRD SCHEDULE

Provincial Public Works and Property to be the Property of Canada

---

THE FOURTH SCHEDULE

Assets to be the Property of Ontario and Quebec conjointly

THE FIFTH SCHEDULE

Oath of Allegiance

Declaration of Qualification

THE SIXTH SCHEDULE

Primary Production from Non-renewable Natural Resources and Forestry Resources

1. For the purposes of Section 92A of this Act,

(*a*) production from a non-renewable natural resource is primary production therefrom if

(i) it is in the form in which it exists upon its recovery or severance from its natural state, or

(ii) it is a product resulting from processing or refining the resource, and is not a manufactured product or a product resulting from refining crude oil, refining upgraded heavy crude oil, refining gases or liquids derived from coal or refining a synthetic equivalent of crude oil; and

(*b*) production from a forestry resource is primary production there from if it consists of sawlogs, poles, lumber, wood chips, sawdust or any other primary wood product, or wood pulp, and is not a product manufactured from wood.

SCHEDULE B

CONSTITUTION ACT, 1982

PART I

CANADIAN CHARTER OF RIGHTS AND FREEDOMS

Whereas Canada is founded upon principles that recognize the supremacy of God and the rule of law:

Guarantee of Rights and Freedoms

1. The *Canadian Charter of Rights and Freedoms* guarantees the rights and freedoms set out in it subject only to such reasonable limits prescribed by law as can be demonstrably justified in a free and democratic society.

Fundamental Freedoms

2. Everyone has the following fundamental freedoms:

(*a*) freedom of conscience and religion;

(*b*) freedom of thought, belief, opinion and expression, including freedom of the press and other media of communication;

(*c*) freedom of peaceful assembly; and

(*d*) freedom of association.

Democratic Rights

3. Every citizen of Canada has the right to vote in an election of members of the House of Commons or of a legislative assembly and to be qualified for membership therein.

4. (1) No House of Commons and no legislative assembly shall continue for longer than five years from the date fixed for the return of the writs of a general election of its members.

(2) In time of real or apprehended war, invasion or insurrection, a House of Commons may be continued by Parliament and a legislative assembly may be continued by the legislature beyond five years if such continuation is not opposed by the votes of more than one-third of the members of the House of Commons or the legislative assembly, as the case may be.

5. There shall be a sitting of Parliament and of each legislature at least once every twelve months.

Mobility Rights

6. (1) Every citizen of Canada has the right to enter, remain in and leave Canada.

(2) Every citizen of Canada and every person who has the status of a permanent resident of Canada has the right

(*a*) to move to and take up residence in any province; and

(*b*) to pursue the gaining of a livelihood in any province.

(3) The rights specified in subsection (2) are subject to

(*a*) any laws or practices of general application in force in a province other than those that discriminate among persons primarily on the basis of province of present or previous residence; and

(*b*) any laws providing for reasonable residency requirements as a qualification for the receipt of publicly provided social services.

(4) Subsections (2) and (3) do not preclude any law, program or activity that has as its object the amelioration in a province of conditions of individuals in that province who are socially or economically disadvantaged if the rate of employment in that province is below the rate of employment in Canada.

Legal Rights

7. Everyone has the right to life, liberty and security of the person and the right not to be deprived thereof except in accordance with the principles of fundamental justice.

8. Everyone has the right to be secure against unreasonable search or seizure.

9. Everyone has the right not to be arbitrarily detained or imprisoned.

10. Everyone has the right on arrest or detention

(*a*) to be informed promptly of the reasons therefor;

(*b*) to retain and instruct counsel without delay and to be informed of that right; and

(*c*) to have the validity of the detention determined by way of *habeas corpus* and to be released if the detention is not lawful.

11. Any person charged with an offence has the right

(*a*) to be informed without unreasonable delay of the specific offence;

(*b*) to be tried within a reasonable time;

(*c*) not to be compelled to be a witness in proceedings against that person in respect of the offence;

(*d*) to be presumed innocent until proven guilty according to law in a fair and public hearing by an independent and impartial tribunal;

(*e*) not to be denied reasonable bail without just cause;

(*f*) except in the case of an offence under military law tried before a military tribunal, to the benefit of trial by jury where the maximum punishment for the offence is imprisonment for five years or a more severe punishment;

(*g*) not to be found guilty on account of any act or omission unless, at the time of the act or omission, it constituted an offence under Canadian or international law or was criminal according to the general principles of law recognized by the community of nations;

(*h*) if finally acquitted of the offence, not to be tried for it again and, if finally found guilty and punished for the offence, not to be tried or punished for it again; and

(*i*) if found guilty of the offence and if the punishment for the offence has been varied between the time of commission and the time of sentencing, to the benefit of the lesser punishment.

12. Everyone has the right not to be subjected to any cruel and unusual treatment or punishment.

13. A witness who testifies in any proceedings has the right not to have any incriminating evidence so given used to incriminate that witness in any other proceedings, except in a prosecution for perjury or for the giving of contradictory evidence.

14. A party or witness in any proceedings who does not understand or speak the language in which the proceedings are conducted or who is deaf has the right to the assistance of an interpreter.

Equality Rights

15. (1) Every individual is equal before and under the law and has the right to the equal protection and equal benefit of the law without discrimination and, in particular, without discrimination based on race, national or ethnic origin, colour, religion, sex, age or mental or physical disability.

(2) Subsection (1) does not preclude any law, program or activity that has as its object the amelioration of conditions of disadvantaged individuals or groups including those that are disadvantaged because of race, national or ethnic origin, colour, religion, sex, age or mental or physical disability.

Official Languages of Canada

16. (1) English and French are the official languages of Canada and have equality of status and equal rights and privileges as to their use in all institutions of the Parliament and government of Canada.

(2) English and French are the official languages of New Brunswick and have equality of status and equal rights and privileges as to their use in all institutions of the legislature and government of New Brunswick.

(3) Nothing in this Charter limits the authority of Parliament or a legislature to advance the equality of status or use of English and French.

16.1. (1) The English linguistic community and the French linguistic community in New Brunswick have equality of status and equal rights and privileges, including the right to distinct educational institutions and such distinct cultural institutions as are necessary for the preservation and promotion of those communities.

(2) The role of the legislature and government of New Brunswick to preserve and promote the status, rights and privileges referred to in subsection (1) is affirmed.

17. (1) Everyone has the right to use English or French in any debates and other proceedings of Parliament.

(2) Everyone has the right to use English or French in any debates and other proceedings of the legislature of New Brunswick.

18. (1) The statutes, records and journals of Parliament shall be printed and published in English and French and both language versions are equally authoritative.

(2) The statutes, records and journals of the legislature of New Brunswick shall be printed and published in English and French and both language versions are equally authoritative.

19. (1) Either English or French may be used by any person in, or in any pleading in or process issuing from, any court established by Parliament.

(2) Either English or French may be used by any person in, or in any pleading in or process issuing from, any court of New Brunswick.

20. (1) Any member of the public in Canada has the right to communicate with, and to receive available services from, any head or central office of an institution of the Parliament or government of Canada in English or French, and has the same right with respect to any other office of any such institution where

> (*a*) there is a significant demand for communications with and services from that office in such language; or

> (*b*) due to the nature of the office, it is reasonable that communications with and services from that office be available in both English and French.

(2) Any member of the public in New Brunswick has the right to communicate with, and to receive available services from, any office of an institution of the legislature or government of New Brunswick in English or French.

21. Nothing in sections 16 to 20 abrogates or derogates from any right, privilege or obligation with respect to the English and French languages, or either of them, that exists or is continued by virtue of any other provision of the Constitution of Canada.

22. Nothing in sections 16 to 20 abrogates or derogates from any legal or customary right or privilege acquired or enjoyed either before or after the coming into force of this Charter with respect to any language that is not English or French.

Minority Language Educational Rights

23. (1) Citizens of Canada

> (*a*) whose first language learned and still understood is that of the English or French linguistic minority population of the province in which they reside, or

(*b*) who have received their primary school instruction in Canada in English or French and reside in a province where the language in which they received that instruction is the language of the English or French linguistic minority population of the province, have the right to have their children receive primary and secondary school instruction in that language in that province.

(2) Citizens of Canada of whom any child has received or is receiving primary or secondary school instruction in English or French in Canada, have the right to have all their children receive primary and secondary school instruction in the same language.

(3) The right of citizens of Canada under subsections (1) and (2) to have their children receive primary and secondary school instruction in the language of the English or French linguistic minority population of a province

(*a*) applies wherever in the province the number of children of citizens who have such a right is sufficient to warrant the provision to them out of public funds of minority language instruction; and

(*b*) includes, where the number of those children so warrants, the right to have them receive that instruction in minority language educational facilities provided out of public funds.

Enforcement

24. (1) Anyone whose rights or freedoms, as guaranteed by this Charter, have been infringed or denied may apply to a court of competent jurisdiction to obtain such remedy as the court considers appropriate and just in the circumstances.

(2) Where, in proceedings under subsection (1), a court concludes that evidence was obtained in a manner that infringed or denied any rights or freedoms guaranteed by this Charter, the evidence shall be excluded if it is established that, having regard to all the circumstances, the admission of it in the proceedings would bring the administration of justice into disrepute.

General

25. The guarantee in this Charter of certain rights and freedoms shall not be construed so as to abrogate or derogate from any aboriginal, treaty or other rights or freedoms that pertain to the aboriginal peoples of Canada including

(*a*) any rights or freedoms that have been recognized by the Royal Proclamation of October 7, 1763; and

(*b*) any rights or freedoms that now exist by way of land claims agreements or may be so acquired.

26. The guarantee in this Charter of certain rights and freedoms shall not be construed as denying the existence of any other rights or freedoms that exist in Canada.

27. This Charter shall be interpreted in a manner consistent with the preservation and enhancement of the multicultural heritage of Canadians.

28. Notwithstanding anything in this Charter, the rights and freedoms referred to in it are guaranteed equally to male and female persons.

29. Nothing in this Charter abrogates or derogates from any rights or privileges guaranteed by or under the Constitution of Canada in respect of denominational, separate or dissentient schools.

30. A reference in this Charter to a Province or to the legislative assembly or legislature of a province shall be deemed to include a reference to the Yukon Territory and the Northwest Territories, or to the appropriate legislative authority thereof, as the case may be.

31. Nothing in this Charter extends the legislative powers of any body or authority.

Application of Charter

32. (1) This Charter applies

(*a*) to the Parliament and government of Canada in respect of all matters within the authority of Parliament including all matters relating to the Yukon Territory and Northwest Territories; and

(*b*) to the legislature and government of each province in respect of all matters within the authority of the legislature of each province.

(2) Notwithstanding subsection (1), section 15 shall not have effect until three years after this section comes into force.

33. (1) Parliament or the legislature of a province may expressly declare in an Act of Parliament or of the legislature, as the case may be, that the Act or a provision thereof shall operate notwithstanding a provision included in section 2 or sections 7 to 15 of this Charter.

(2) An Act or a provision of an Act in respect of which a declaration made under this section is in effect shall have such operation as it would have but for the provision of this Charter referred to in the declaration.

(3) A declaration made under subsection (1) shall cease to have effect five years after it comes into force or on such earlier date as may be specified in the declaration.

(4) Parliament or the legislature of a province may re-enact a declaration made under subsection (1).

(5) Subsection (3) applies in respect of a re-enactment made under subsection (4).

Citation

34. This Part may be cited as the *Canadian Charter of Rights and Freedoms*.

PART II

RIGHTS OF THE ABORIGINAL PEOPLES OF CANADA

35. (1) The existing aboriginal and treaty rights of the aboriginal peoples of Canada are hereby recognized and affirmed.

(2) In this Act, "aboriginal peoples of Canada" includes the Indian, Inuit and Métis peoples of Canada.

(3) For greater certainty, in subsection (1) "treaty rights" includes rights that now exist by way of land claims agreements or may be so acquired.

(4) Notwithstanding any other provision of this Act, the aboriginal and treaty rights referred to in subsection (1) are guaranteed equally to male and female persons.

35.1 (1) The government of Canada and the provincial governments are committed to the principle that, before any amendment is made to Class 24 of section 91 of the "*Constitution Act, 1867*", to section 25 of this Act or to this Part,

> (*a*) a constitutional conference that includes in its agenda an item relating to the proposed amendment, composed of the Prime Minister of Canada and the first ministers of the provinces, will be convened by the Prime Minister of Canada; and

> (*b*) the Prime Minister of Canada will invite representatives of the aboriginal peoples of Canada to participate in the discussions on that item.

PART III

EQUALIZATION AND REGIONAL DISPARITIES

36. (1) Without altering the legislative authority of Parliament or of the provincial legislatures, or the rights of any of them with respect to the exercise of their legislative authority, Parliament and the legislatures, together with the government of Canada and the provincial governments, are committed to

> (*a*) promoting equal opportunities for the well-being of Canadians;

> (*b*) furthering economic development to reduce disparity in opportunities; and

> (*c*) providing essential public services of reasonable quality to all Canadians.

(2) Parliament and the government of Canada are committed to the principle of making equalization payments to ensure that provincial governments have sufficient revenues to provide reasonably comparable levels of public services at reasonably comparable levels of taxation.

PART IV

CONSTITUTIONAL CONFERENCE

37. *Repealed.*

PART IV.1

CONSTITUTIONAL CONFERENCES

37.1 (1) *Repealed.*

PART V

PROCEDURE FOR AMENDING CONSTITUTION OF CANADA

38. (1) An amendment to the Constitution of Canada may be made by proclamation issued by the Governor General under the Great Seal of Canada where so authorized by

(*a*) resolutions of the Senate and House of Commons; and

(*b*) resolutions of the legislative assemblies of at least two-thirds of the provinces that have, in the aggregate, according to the then latest general census, at least fifty per cent of the population of all the provinces.

(2) An amendment made under subsection (1) that derogates from the legislative powers, the proprietary rights or any other rights or privileges of the legislature or government of a province shall require a resolution supported by a majority of the members of each of the Senate, the House of Commons and the legislative assemblies required under subsection (1).

(3) An amendment referred to in subsection (2) shall not have effect in a province the legislative assembly of which has expressed its dissent thereto by resolution supported by a majority of its members prior to the issue of the proclamation to which the amendment relates unless that legislative assembly, subsequently, by resolution supported by a majority of its members, revokes its dissent and authorizes the amendment.

(4) A resolution of dissent made for the purposes of subsection (3) may be revoked at any time before or after the issue of the proclamation to which it relates.

39. (1) A proclamation shall not be issued under subsection 38 (1) before the expiration of one year from the adoption of the resolution initiating the amendment procedure thereunder, unless the legislative assembly of each province has previously adopted a resolution of assent or dissent.

(2) A proclamation shall not be issued under subsection 38 (1) after the expiration of three years from the adoption of the resolution initiating the amendment procedure thereunder.

40. Where an amendment is made under subsection 38 (1) that transfers provincial legislative powers relating to education or other cultural matters from provincial legislatures to Parliament, Canada shall provide reasonable compensation to any province to which the amendment does not apply.

41. An amendment to the Constitution of Canada in relation to the following matters may be made by proclamation issued by the Governor General under the Great Seal of Canada only where authorized by resolutions of the Senate and House of Commons and of the legislative assembly of each province:

(*a*) the office of the Queen, the Governor General and the Lieutenant Governor of a province;

(*b*) the right of a province to a number of members in the House of Commons not less than the number of Senators by which the province is entitled to be represented at the time this Part comes into force;

(*c*) subject to section 43, the use of the English or the French language;

(*d*) the composition of the Supreme Court of Canada; and

(*e*) an amendment to this Part.

42. (1) An amendment to the Constitution of Canada in relation to the following matters may be made only in accordance with subsection 38 (1):

(*a*) the principle of proportionate representation of the provinces in the House of Commons prescribed by the Constitution of Canada;

(*b*) the powers of the Senate and the method of selecting Senators;

(*c*) the number of members by which a province is entitled to be represented in the Senate and the residence qualifications of Senators;

(*d*) subject to paragraph 41 (*d*), the Supreme Court of Canada;

(*e*) the extension of existing provinces into the territories; and

(*f*) notwithstanding any other law or practice, the establishment of new provinces.

(2) Subsections 38 (2) to (4) do not apply in respect of amendments in relation to matters referred to in subsection (1).

43. An amendment to the Constitution of Canada in relation to any provision that applies to one or more, but not all, provinces, including

(*a*) any alteration to boundaries between provinces, and

(*b*) any amendment to any provision that relates to the use of the English or the French language within a province,

may be made by proclamation issued by the Governor General under the Great Seal of Canada only where so authorized by resolutions of the Senate and House of Commons and of the legislative assembly of each province to which the amendment applies.

44. Subject to sections 41 and 42, Parliament may exclusively make laws amending the Constitution of Canada in relation to the executive government of Canada or the Senate and House of Commons.

45. Subject to section 41, the legislature of each province may exclusively make laws amending the constitution of the province.

46. (1) The procedures for amendment under sections 38, 41, 42 and 43 may be initiated either by the Senate or the House of Commons or by the legislative assembly of a province.

(2) A resolution of assent made for the purposes of this Part may be revoked at any time before the issue of a proclamation authorized by it.

47. (1) An amendment to the Constitution of Canada made by proclamation under section 38, 41, 42 or 43 may be made without a resolution of the Senate authorizing the issue of the proclamation if, within one hundred and eighty days after the adoption by the House of Commons of a resolution authorizing its issue, the Senate has not adopted such a resolution and if, at any time after the expiration of that period, the House of Commons again adopts the resolution.

(2) Any period when Parliament is prorogued or dissolved shall not be counted in computing the one hundred and eighty day period referred to in subsection (1).

48. The Queen's Privy Council for Canada shall advise the Governor General to issue a proclamation under this Part forthwith on the adoption of the resolutions required for an amendment made by proclamation under this Part.

49. A constitutional conference composed of the Prime Minister of Canada and the first ministers of the provinces shall be convened by the Prime Minister of Canada within fifteen years after this Part comes into force to review the provisions of this Part.

PART VI

AMENDMENT TO THE CONSTITUTION ACT, 1867

50. *Consolidated.*

51. *Consolidated.*

PART VII

GENERAL

52. (1) The Constitution of Canada is the supreme law of Canada, and any law that is inconsistent with the provisions of the Constitution is, to the extent of the inconsistency, of no force or effect.

(2) The Constitution of Canada includes

(*a*) the *Canada Act 1982,* including this Act;

(*b*) the Acts and orders referred to in the schedule; and

(*c*) any amendment to any Act or order referred to in paragraph (*a*) or (*b*).

(3) Amendments to the Constitution of Canada shall be made only in accordance with the authority contained in the Constitution of Canada.

53. (1) The enactments referred to in Column I of the schedule are hereby repealed or amended to the extent indicated in Column II thereof and, unless repealed, shall continue as law in Canada under the names set out in Column III thereof.

(2) Every enactment, except the *Canada Act 1982,* that refers to an enactment referred to in the schedule by the name in Column I thereof is hereby amended by substituting for that name the corresponding name in Column III thereof, and any British North America Act not referred to in the schedule may be cited as the *Constitution Act* followed by the year and number, if any, of its enactment.

54. Part IV is repealed on the day that is one year after this Part comes into force and this section may be repealed and this Act renumbered, consequentially upon the repeal of Part IV and this section, by proclamation issued by the Governor General under the Great Seal of Canada.

54.1 (1) *Repealed.*

55. A French version of the portions of the Constitution of Canada referred to in the schedule shall be prepared by the Minister of Justice of Canada as expeditiously as possible and, when any portion thereof sufficient to warrant action being taken has been so prepared, it shall be put forward for enactment by proclamation issued by the Governor General under the Great Seal of Canada pursuant to the procedure then applicable to an amendment of the same provisions of the Constitution of Canada.

56. Where any portion of the Constitution of Canada has been or is enacted in English and French or where a French version of any portion of the Constitution is enacted pursuant to section 55, the English and French versions of that portion of the Constitution are equally authoritative.

57. The English and French versions of this Act are equally authoritative.

58. Subject to section 59, this Act shall come into force on a day to be fixed by proclamation issued by the Queen or the Governor General under the Great Seal of Canada.

59. (1) Paragraph 23 (1) (*a*) shall come into force in respect of Quebec on a day to be fixed by proclamation issued by the Queen or the Governor General under the Great Seal of Canada.

(2) A proclamation under subsection (1) shall be issued only where authorized by the legislative assembly or government of Quebec.

(3) This section may be repealed on the day paragraph 23 (1) (*a*) comes into force in respect of Quebec and this Act amended and renumbered, consequentially upon the repeal of this section, by proclamation issued by the Queen or the Governor General under the Great Seal of Canada.

60. This Act may be cited as the *Constitution Act, 1982,* and the Constitution Acts 1867 to 1975 (No. 2) and this Act may be cited together as the *Constitution Acts, 1867 to 1982.*

61. A reference to the *"Constitution Acts, 1867 to 1982"* shall be deemed to include a reference to the *"Constitution Amendment Proclamation, 1983."*

GLOSSARY OF KEY TERMS

Ad hoc: A Latin term meaning "temporary" or "expedient." For example, the prime minister may establish an ad hoc committee of ministers to deal with a short-term issue, and disband it after it reports its recommendations back to the full Cabinet.

Adjudication: The process by which the courts resolve disputes.

Altruistic incentives: See the definition of *Purposive/altruistic incentives* below.

Amending formula: The formal process for changing a written constitution. The formula is usually included in the constitution itself. Amending a constitution is a complex and difficult process, requiring a broad consensus among the key players in the political system. Because the constitution sets out the rules of the political game, and it is intended to provide continuity and stability to the political system, the amending formula must protect the written constitution against changes that are purely temporary in nature, or that violate the core principles on which the political system is based (e.g., democracy and federalism).

Amendment: Any proposed or actual alteration in the wording of a written constitution. An amendment can insert one or more new provisions into the constitution, it can delete one or more existing provisions, or it can rewrite part of a constitution to keep it up to date with changing circumstances.

Advocacy groups: Movements that try to alter conventional perceptions of the political and social status quo, and/or to mobilize support for projects for political and social change. Examples include the women's movement, the Aboriginal rights movement, and the environmental movement.

Allophone: A person whose mother tongue is neither English nor French. The largest allophone populations in Canada speak either Chinese or Italian.

Anglophone: English-speaking. For statistical purposes, the term *anglophone* normally refers to those Canadians who claim English as their mother tongue.

Agency: The legal requirement for registered parties and candidates to appoint an official agent, who is responsible for ensuring compliance with the election-expense rules in the Canada Elections Act.

Backbenchers: Members of the House of Commons who do not belong to the Cabinet of the day. Backbenchers make up over 90 percent of the Commons. All opposition MPs are backbenchers, as is a majority of government MPs. The proportion of government backbenchers in the thirty-eighth Parliament is unusually low.

Believers and careerists: Two categories of party members, distinguished on the basis of their primary motivations for party activity. Believers are motivated by their faith in the party's principles or its leader; careerists are more interested in their own status within the party hierarchy.

Bill: A draft law introduced into Parliament by a minister of the Crown (i.e., a cabinet minister), or by a private member (a backbench MP). After the bill has received royal assent, it becomes a statute (another word for "law").

Block funding: A fiscal transfer from Ottawa to one or more provinces that imposes few, if any, conditions on the way the money is to be spent. For example, the 1995 Canada Health and Social Transfer provided money for health care, postsecondary education, and social assistance, without specifying the percentages to be spent in each policy field.

Brokerage or cadre party: A political party whose primary goal is to win a majority of seats in Parliament and form a government. Because it seeks to appeal to as many voters as possible, it tends to downplay potentially divisive ideologies and principles. Usually has a small membership, dominated by the leader and the caucus.

By-election: A special election held to fill one seat in the Commons (e.g., after the death, retirement, or resignation of the incumbent MP).

Cadre party: See the definition of *brokerage or cadre party* above.

Canvass: The process by which party volunteers identify potential supporters during an election campaign; can be done face to face (knocking on doors) or over the telephone.

Careerists: See the definition of *believers and careerists* above.

Casework: The services provided to individual constituents by an MP and his or her staff. Anyone in Canada who encounters a problem with the federal government (e.g., citizenship, employment insurance, or the Canada Pension Plan) can seek assistance from the local office of his representative in the House of Commons. Casework is the most time-consuming, and often the most satisfying, of the many tasks assigned to MPs.

Categorical: A ballot structure that forces the voter to indicate a single preference among the available candidates.

Caucus: The parliamentary wing of a political party. Includes all the MPs (and senators, if any) who represent that party in Parliament. Within the secrecy of the caucus meeting, MPs and senators can speak freely about political and policy issues. Once the meeting ends, all members of caucus are expected to keep the discussions confidential.

Central agencies: Those departments within the federal government whose primary responsibility is to monitor and coordinate policy-making and implementation across the entire executive branch. The four primary central agencies are the Privy Council Office, the Prime Minister's Office, the Treasury Board Secretariat, and the Department of Finance.

Cleavage: A stable and long-term division between identifiable groups in a given population. Examples include religion (Catholic versus Protestant, observant versus nonobservant), language (English versus French), region (West versus East, Quebec versus Alberta), gender, and class. A cleavage becomes politically significant when it affects voting behaviour and/or attitudes toward political institutions. Cleavage structures change over time, as new cleavages emerge and as older cleavages either acquire new political significance or lose their historical significance.

Coalition: A Cabinet made up of ministers from two or more parties; the usual way of ensuring that the political executive is supported by a parliamentary majority in legislatures elected by proportional representation, where one party rarely wins more than half of the seats.

Collective action: The organized pursuit of a shared goal by a group of people; can be formal and structured (a military unit in combat) or informal and loosely structured (neighbours gathering to protest a zoning change).

Collective solidarity/social incentives: Intangible rewards for party effort, available to all party members (the joy of victory, the satisfaction of working together for a shared goal, and the social value of meeting like-minded people).

Common law: The collective term for the body of judicial rulings on a particular subject (e.g., the due-process rights of suspected criminals or the division of powers between governments).

Conditional grants: Transfer payments from Ottawa to one or more provinces that come with strings attached. The recipient provinces must spend the money as directed by the federal government, or risk losing some or all of the transfer.

Confidence convention: In a British parliamentary system, the Cabinet can remain in office only as long as it enjoys the support of the House of Commons for its policies and money bills. If the Cabinet loses a vote on a money bill or a key piece of legislation, constitutional convention requires the prime minister to tender the resignation of his government to the Crown (in Canada, the governor general). In practice, there are no legal sanctions for violating a convention; therefore, a prime minister may choose to stay in office and try to pass a vote of confidence in the House instead of resigning immediately. Prime ministers sometimes rely on a misinterpretation of the confidence convention to persuade their backbench MPs to support government legislation.

Constituency: An electoral district that sends one or more members to the national or provincial legislature. In Canada, also called a "riding." The word *constituency* may also be used to refer to an informal group within the electorate that expects certain MPs to speak on its behalf. Therefore, we might say that a female MP from Halifax has three constituencies: her particular riding, women, and the Atlantic region as a whole.

Constitution: The supreme law that defines the scope of state power and divides it among the various institutions that make up the state. More broadly, a constitution incorporates both the unwritten principles that guide the execution of public activities and the sources of political legitimacy in a particular territory (i.e., myths, symbols, and rituals).

Constitutional convention: An unwritten principle of political practice, which gradually acquires binding force over time. It may evolve to fill a gap in the written constitution, or it may directly contradict the legal text. Conventions provide greater flexibility than the written constitution, allowing national institutions to adapt to changes in political culture. Unlike written constitutional law, conventions cannot be enforced by the courts; their violation may be punished only in the political arena.

Consultation: A state-sponsored process of cooperation between one or more government agencies and select pressure groups. May include the development of public policy, the shared implementation of new programs, or alternative service-delivery arrangements.

Co-optation: The process by which a pressure group, which opposes certain elements of state policy, is induced to accept the ideology or the policy priorities of the government. The most powerful tool of co-optation is public funding, although some groups fear that a close working relationship with state agencies could have the same effect. Groups that oppose the status quo on principle fear that the exercise of power might erode their independence and even corrupt their leaders.

Crown: The source and symbol of executive power in Canada. As a former British colony, Canada inherited "a Constitution similar in Principle to that of the United Kingdom." Although most of the Crown's powers are now delegated to the political executive, and particularly to the prime minister, the residual and emergency powers of the Crown are vested in the governor general, who must approve all spending measures before they are submitted to the House of Commons. In addition, the Crown's representative formally appoints the political executive and signs bills passed by the legislative branch into law.

Crown corporations: Public agencies that provide goods and services to a particular clientele. Examples include the CBC, VIA Rail, and—at one time—Air Canada. Crown corporations are ultimately responsible to the federal government, but they are normally operated at arm's length from the political executive. Canada's Crown corporations were originally established to provide goods and services that were too costly for the private sector, such as national railways and coast-to-coast broadcasting. In recent years, many have been privatized (sold to the private sector), partly because of complaints about unfair competition and partly to raise money.

Debt (federal debt): The sum total of what the Government of Canada owes to Canadian and international investors. The **net-debt** is the sum total of what the government owes minus some of its more liquid assets.

Deficit: An excess of spending over revenues in a given fiscal year. For example, Canada's federal government ran a deficit in the 1993–1994 fiscal year by spending $42 billion more than it raised in revenue. In the 2003–2004 fiscal year, the federal government spent $9.1 billion *less* than it received in revenues; this is referred to as a surplus.

Democracy: Literally, "rule by the people." In practice, the people cannot govern themselves directly on a daily basis. For the most part, we practise representative democracy in which we elect politicians to make decisions on our behalf and delegate the power to make binding decisions to them. We have the opportunity to reject those politicians at election time if they use that power in ways of which we do not approve. It is difficult to hold our representatives accountable between elections. If they exercise the powers of their offices for their own benefit, instead of the benefit of the electorate, we have little legal recourse.

Demography: The distribution of certain personal characteristics among a particular population. Key demographic indicators include race, ethnicity, language, religion, age, and gender.

Direct democracy: A system in which the citizens govern themselves directly, at least in part, by making decisions about policies or the structure of government through the ballot box.

Disclosure: The legal requirement for registered parties to publicly disclose the amount and the source of all contributions.

Discourse community: See the definition of *policy community* below.

Economic union: The goal of creating a single national economy, without internal barriers to trade or mobility, transcending provincial jurisdictions. In Canada, this goal is manifested most prominently in the 1994 Agreement on Internal Trade.

Electoral formula: The method by which votes are cast, counted, and translated into the distribution of parliamentary seats.

Electoral system: The rules and procedures by which legislators are elected in a given country. Canada's electoral system is called single-member plurality (SMP), because each constituency elects one MP and the candidate with more votes than any other wins the seat. SMP is also often referred to as the first-past-the-post system because winning candidates need only have one more vote than their closest competitor. Winners do not have to receive a majority of votes and frequently have a majority of votes cast against them (i.e., votes cast for all the other candidates).

Entrenched constitutional law: Written legal provisions that have been ratified through the appropriate amending formula, and that take priority over ordinary laws in case of a conflict.

Equalization: The federal government collects tax revenues from all Canadians but distributes an extra portion of them back to the poorer or have-not provinces. This extra portion is not distributed to the richer or have provinces (usually British Columbia, Alberta, and Ontario, but currently only Alberta and Ontario) The purpose of equalization payments is to ensure that every provincial government can provide reasonably comparable services to its citizens, without regard to the size of its tax base. Equalization payments may be used for any purpose; they are not conditional. The system was entrenched in the Constitution Act, 1982 (Section 36).

Executive federalism: The collective term for the relations among the political and permanent executives of Canada's senior governments. A style of policy-making in which the executive branches of the various governments in the Canadian federation negotiate directly with each other. The most obvious illustration of executive federalism is megaconstitutional politics, in which first ministers—the premiers and the prime minister—meet behind closed doors to hammer out amendments to the Constitution. Executive federalism is often criticized as being undemocratic because it usually takes place in secret, and as a threat to the power of the legislative branch. In most cases, deals struck between the executive branches of two or more governments are never submitted to Parliament or the provincial legislature for ratification.

Extraparliamentary: The party organization outside Parliament. Includes the national headquarters, the national executive, and the local constituency associations.

Extrinsic evidence: Facts placed before a court that do not arise directly from the case at bar. Two types of extrinsic evidence are discussed in this book: social science evidence relating to the policy impact of a particular law (used to weigh infringed rights against competing social purposes under Section 1 of the Charter), and evidence of legislative intent in the drafting of the impugned law.

Federal debt: See the definition of *debt (federal debt)* above.

Federal public service: Another name for the permanent executive. The federal public service includes the line and staff employees of all federal government departments, both inside and outside Ottawa.

Federal spending power: Ottawa's use of fiscal transfers to determine provincial priorities in areas of provincial jurisdiction, particularly health care, postsecondary education, and social assistance. It arises from the federal powers to tax (Section 91 [3]), to regulate public property (Section 91 [1A]), and to spend federal funds as it sees fit (Section 106). The taxing power provides Ottawa with more money than it needs to carry out its own constitutional responsibilities. The spending power allows Ottawa to transfer those excess revenues for purposes outside its areas of jurisdiction. The federal spending power is not explicitly defined in the Constitution.

Fiscal federalism: The term used to refer to the flow of money—both cash and tax points— from Ottawa to the provinces and territories. That money is supposed to redress both the vertical imbalance between the two senior levels of government, and the horizontal imbalance among the have and have-not provinces.

Foreign direct investment: Any business or other undertaking that operates in Canada and is owned (in whole or in part) by non-Canadians.

Franchise: The right to vote in elections.

Francophone: French-speaking. For statistical purposes, the term *francophone* normally refers to those Canadians who claim French as their mother tongue.

General election: The House of Commons is dissolved by a Writ of Dissolution (issued by the governor general on the advice of the prime minister), and every seat is filled by election on the same day.

Gerrymandering: Deliberately drawing constituency boundaries in a way that increases the electoral chances of a particular party or candidate.

Globalization: A technological and economic process driven by the revolution in telecommunications and computers; massive increases in the movement of capital around the world; greatly expanded capacities for flexible worldwide production sourcing by firms, especially multinational corporations; and growing ecological interdependence and environmental spillovers. The effects of globalization tend to reduce the social, political, and economic importance of nation-state borders and territorial divisions (e.g., provinces).

Hierarchy: A social system arranged like a pyramid, in which those at the top control a disproportionate share of power (political, social, economic, or religious), while those at the bottom are virtually powerless. The criteria by which the members of the various ranks are chosen vary from culture to culture. In a monarchical society, birth determines one's place in the hierarchy: the king or queen is born to rule, (male) aristocrats are born to wealth and privilege, and the majority of the population are born to serve and to be ruled by their "betters." Other hierarchies are based on money, gender (generally speaking, men are more politically powerful than women), race (e.g., the former apartheid system in South Africa), or military prowess.

Ideological party: See the definition of *missionary or ideological party* below.

Ideology: A partial picture of the world, comprising stories about the past, explanations of the present, and a blueprint for the future. Because each ideology is only a partial picture, it must compete with other ideologies for political influence. It is both *empirical* (a description of the way things are) and *normative* (a prescription for how things should be).

Impugned: When a court is asked to rule on the constitutionality of a particular law, that legal provision is said to be impugned. In a Charter case, one or more parties before the court seeks to prove that the law is unconstitutional, on the grounds that it conflicts with a Charter right or freedom. The challenged law, or the specific sections of the law on which the appeal turns, are impugned by the plaintiff. The term applies whether or not the court agrees that the law is unconstitutional.

In camera: Latin for "in a closed room." When a parliamentary committee holds a closed meeting, the proceedings of which are not to be disclosed to the public, the meeting is said to be in camera.

Instant party members: Individuals and groups recruited to join a local constituency association en masse, for the purpose of electing a slate of convention delegates committed to a particular leadership candidate (or, under one member, one vote, to vote directly for the candidate). Also used by organizers for aspiring constituency candidates to swamp the nomination meeting. While leadership contests and nomination battles are important opportunities to attract new members to the party, instant members rarely stick around for the long term. Increasingly controversial, especially the wholesale importation of people who are not eligible to vote in Canadian elections (e.g., recent immigrants, minors). All parties except the Conservative Party allow ineligible voters to participate, in the name of openness and for recruitment of future citizens.

Interest group: An organization of people who seek to promote a common goal.

Intergovernmental relations (IGRs): In a federation, frequent conflicts flare up between two or more levels of government. The processes for resolving those conflicts at the political level (as distinct from court rulings on the division of powers) are collectively termed "intergovernmental relations." In Canada, IGRs entail more than the resolution of conflicts over jurisdiction and resources: joint policy-making and implementation are also involved.

Internationalization: A process by which various aspects of policy or policy-making are influenced by factors outside national territorial boundaries.

Interpretivist judicial review: The reliance by judges on evidence of legislative intent, as a guide to interpreting constitutional principles. In other words, the judges try to determine what the framers of the Constitution were trying to accomplish when they drafted the relevant provisions and to follow that intent in applying those provisions to the facts of a particular case.

Interstate federalism: A political system in which regional and intergovernmental conflicts are resolved by bargaining among the various political units. Interstate federalism is premised on the belief that the premiers are the most effective spokespersons for their respective regions. It is analogous to international diplomacy, in which sovereign states negotiate solutions to their common problems. Literally, *interstate* means "between states."

Intrastate federalism: A political system in which regional and intergovernmental conflicts are resolved within representative national institutions. For example, the upper house of the German federal parliament (*Bundesrat*) is made up of delegations from the *Länd* (state) governments, a majority of whom must approve all legislation proposed by the national executive. In an intrastate federation, unlike an interstate federation, the premiers are not the sole legitimate representatives of their respective regions. The task of representing the regions in national politics is carried out by national, not provincial, politicians. *Intrastate* means "within the state."

Judicial activism: Activist judges use their policy-making power to overturn or effectively rewrite ordinary statutes and constitutional texts. Activist judges are less likely to defer to the legislative or executive branches of government and more likely to put their own stamp on the law through judicial review.

Judicial Committee of the Privy Council (JCPC): A panel of British law lords, appointed by the Crown to act as the final court of appeal for the Empire (later the Commonwealth). Any apparent conflict between a British law (e.g., the BNA Act) and a statute adopted by a former colony could be given a definitive resolution only by the JCPC. Canada abolished the right of appeal to Westminster (the common name for the British government) in 1949; since then, the Supreme Court of Canada has been the highest court of appeal in Canadian law.

Judicial deference: Also called "judicial conservatism." An institutional norm among appeal court judges that restrains them in their legal interpretations. Judges defer to Parliament, upholding most or all of the laws passed by the legislative branch and taking a narrow (interpretivist) approach to constitutional law.

Judicial review: The process by which courts provide authoritative interpretations of the constitution and the law. The court's rulings are binding on the other two branches of government. The doctrine of judicial review is an American invention, which conflicts in Canada with the British tradition of parliamentary supremacy. Generally speaking, the judicial review of a particular law can be triggered in one of two ways: by a normal court case (criminal or civil), in which a dispute arises over a general issue of law (which must be settled during the appeals process), or by the reference procedure, in which the executive branch poses a direct question to the courts. In constitutional terms, judicial review is the interpretation of the Constitution (usually the written text, although a reference question may focus on a particular constitutional convention) and its application to a specific case. Before the Charter of Rights was proclaimed in 1982, most judicial review of the Constitution Act, 1867, revolved around the division of powers between the federal and provincial governments. Since 1982, judicial review has expanded to include questions about the precise meanings of rights and freedoms and the conformity of federal and provincial statutes to the Charter of Rights and Freedoms.

Leadership convention: A gathering of party delegates to choose a new leader. Thousands of delegates—most elected by constituency associations, campus clubs, women's and youth organizations, and other party branches—cast ballots in successive rounds of voting, until one candidate receives a majority of the valid votes.

Legitimacy: The broad base of support within the electorate for the political system as a whole, which translates into acceptance of its outputs (i.e., binding rules and decisions). The exercise of constitutional authority in conformity with prevailing political values (e.g., democracy, federalism, the rule of law, and the rights of minorities) is legitimate; the brutal exercise of naked power by state authorities is not. In liberal democratic theory, legitimacy is founded on the consent of the governed. While citizens need not necessarily give formal consent to each individual law (a practical impossibility, however desirable it might be in practice), they must implicitly accept the political norms and values embodied in the existing political institutions. Legitimacy is also based on the existence of a shared sense of identity—or, in other words, a political community. If no such community exists, because the electorate is divided into competing subcultures with divergent political values, the legitimacy of the political system is questioned. As its legitimacy weakens, its authority diminishes.

Line departments: Departments within the federal government that make and implement policy in particular fields, such as agriculture, transport, and foreign affairs. Line departments deliver services to the public, whereas central agencies normally serve other government organizations.

List-PR: Proportional representation based on party lists; the voter marks a preference for one of the lists of candidates on the ballot, and the seats in Parliament are distributed among the parties on the basis of their vote shares (e.g., 30 percent of the vote in a 10-seat constituency entitles the party to 3 seats).

Litigation: Seeking the resolution of a dispute in the courts. Examples include constitutional challenges, private lawsuits, and criminal appeals.

Lobbying: The effort to influence public policy directly, by persuading decisionmakers in the political and permanent executives to adopt the goals of a particular group or individual. May be public (media events, appearing before a Commons committee) or private (meeting with the assistant deputy minister responsible for that policy file).

Mandate: The authority vested in the leaders of a pressure group by its membership. If there are doubts about the congruence between the goals of the leaders and those of the membership, the political salience of those leaders will suffer.

Material incentives: Tangible rewards for loyal party service (e.g., a seat in the Senate).

Megaconstitutional politics: A process of reconsidering not just the technical details of a constitution, but also the very nature of the political community on which the constitution is based. As the debate widens beyond the political elite (i.e., the first ministers of the 11 senior governments, their advisers, and academic experts) the emotional temperature rises. Powerful, and often incompatible, myths and symbols are evoked to justify conflicting definitions of the political community.

Ministerialism: The practice of treating cabinet ministers as representatives from their regions. During the second party system (1921–1957), the federal Liberals used regional ministers as both conduits of political intelligence and dispensers of patronage. Ministerialism was a key ingredient in the Liberals' successful strategy of regional brokering.

Minority government: One party holds a plurality of the seats in the House of Commons (i.e., more than any other party), but not an absolute majority. Because the Commons works on the principle of majority voting, a minority government cannot pass legislation or financial measures without the support of some opposition MPs. It may secure this support by striking a bargain with one or more opposition parties, or it can try to win over individual MPs on a case-by-case basis. If it cannot do either, it risks defeat in the House (e.g., by losing a budget vote); in that circumstance, constitutional convention normally requires the prime minister to submit his or her resignation to the governor general. Moreover, a government with a minority in the House cannot dominate Commons committees, where seats are allocated according to the parties' respective shares of the House.

Minority party syndrome: An imbalance between believers and careerists within a party's membership, caused by prolonged periods of electoral defeat. The internal culture of the party becomes adversarial (instead of constructive), fractious (rather than united), and oriented toward criticism instead of governing.

Missionary or ideological party: A party whose primary goal is to promote a particular ideology or policy; while it would welcome the chance to implement its proposals in government, it is less focused on electoral victory than a brokerage/cadre party. More internally democratic, less leader-dominated, and places a greater emphasis on attracting a large membership.

Mixed electoral system: A system that combines two or more electoral formulas in a single election (e.g., the New Zealand system, which uses SMP to elect some MPs and party lists to choose the rest).

Mobilization: (1) The process by which a distinct group within an electorate is transformed into a politically influential subculture. Typically, a political leader from within the group begins to organize members into a cohesive entity with shared goals and values. In the absence of mobilization, a subculture remains latent; its members do not recognize their potential for collective action, and their common goals (if any) remain unexpressed within the political system. Examples of salient subcultures include Quebec nationalists and Western (especially Alberta) populists. (2) The process of organizing a particular subculture to support a new or existing political party. Examples include Brian Mulroney's attempt to bring Quebec nationalists into the Progressive Conservative Party of Canada in 1984 and Preston Manning's appeal to Western populists to join his fledgling Reform Party in the late 1980s.

Money bill: A formal authorization by the House of Commons to the Cabinet (technically, the Crown) to raise or spend public revenues. Ways and means bills authorize the Crown to raise money; appropriations bills authorize the spending of public funds.

Multiparty system: A party system in which three or more parties compete for inclusion in a governing coalition. Usually associated with proportional representation electoral systems.

Myth: A story we tell ourselves to make sense of a confusing and complicated world. It presents a partial account of the past, justifies certain actions in the present, and lays out a particular path for the future. Political myths usually incorporate one or more symbols into a blend of fact and fiction, which is used to evoke an emotional response for or against a particular institution. Example: The Québécois myth of "*la survivance*" following the English "conquest" of 1759 has become a powerful source of legitimacy for the provincial government in Quebec.

Net-debt: See the definition of *debt (federal debt)* above.

News values: The criteria used by journalists to determine which events to cover and the spin they will apply to that coverage.

Nonentrenched law: An ordinary statute (either federal or provincial, but usually federal) that supplements the entrenched Constitution by applying a general principle to specific circumstances. An example is the Canada Elections Act, which sets out the rules and procedures by which Canadians exercise their democratic rights. Unlike entrenched constitutional law, nonentrenched laws may be amended through the normal legislative process; they do not take priority over regular statutes.

Nongovernmental organization: A group that operates outside the formal structure of government, as defined in the Constitution, and that seeks to participate in the policy process (from agenda-setting to policy formulation, and, ultimately, implementation).

Noninterpretivist judicial review: Noninterpretivist judges do not perceive themselves as bound by the intentions of the framers when they interpret and apply the Constitution. They go beyond the original intent of each provision, expanding or contracting its meaning to cover circumstances that could not be foreseen at the time of adoption.

Nontariff barriers: Laws and policies that protect local producers of goods and services from competitors in other provinces or countries. These include government procurement policies that favour local suppliers; licensing regimes for service providers that restrict foreign access to local markets; and regulations that discourage the flow of goods, services, and direct investment across provincial or national borders (e.g., the imposition of stricter labour or environmental standards in one jurisdiction relative to another).

Nullification: When a court finds an impugned law to be unconstitutional, it can declare that law to be null and void (Section 52 of the Constitution Act, 1982). This power to nullify laws is also referred to as striking down.

Numerical/pictorial representation: The idea that the demographic characteristics of a particular political body (such as a legislature) should mirror those in the population at large. For example, women make up slightly over half of the Canadian electorate; therefore, a numerically representative House of Commons would also be 51 percent female.

Ombudsman: An ombudsman is a public official empowered to investigate citizen complaints about treatment received from, and within, the bureaucracy. While not authorized to investigate complaints about the general nature of public policy, an ombudsman has a wide range of investigative powers relating to the administration of public policy.

One member, one vote: A system of party leadership selection in which every party member can vote directly for the candidate of his or her choice, instead of electing delegates to vote on his or her behalf.

Ordinal: A ballot structure that allows (or requires) the voter to rank-order some or all of the candidates listed.

Orientation: The psychological response of a particular individual toward a social object. In political terms: the degree to which a citizen internalizes or adopts prevailing social attitudes toward the political system as a whole, its individual parts, the elites who run it, and the laws that it creates and implements.

Party discipline: The requirement that individual legislators vote according to the wishes of their leaders (or of the party caucus as a whole). Party discipline is strongest on the government side of the House, partly because of the confidence convention, but it affects MPs and senators from all parties. While discipline is somewhat weaker in the Senate, which is not a confidence chamber, few senators are willing to break ranks in public. Party discipline affects the behaviour of MPs on parliamentary committees, not just on the floor of the Commons or the Senate.

Party identification: A long-term emotional attachment to a particular party, its policies, and its leader(s). Voters may form this attachment in childhood, through the absorption of their parents' political values. Throughout adult life, the voter perceives and interprets political events through the lens of party identification.

Party networks: Distinct groups within a party organization. Include factions (formed around leadership aspirants), regional networks, the caucus, the leader's entourage, and ideological sects.

Party system: The sum total of the parties represented in the House of Commons at a given time, reflecting the social cleavages and subcultures in the electorate and the structure of party competition.

Patronage: The practice of appointing party supporters to fill public offices, such as the order-in-council appointments awarded at the discretion of the prime minister. Less common today than in the nineteenth century. Often regarded as corrupt and harmful, but this perception is not always correct; material incentives for party members may help to attract and retain the volunteers needed for a vibrant representative democracy.

Permanent executive: The federal public service. In principle, the permanent executive is politically neutral; as the name suggests, it remains in place when the governing party changes. It is organized hierarchically, with the clerk of the Privy Council at the top. Within each department, the permanent executive is headed by the deputy minister.

Pictorial representation: See the definition of *numerical/pictorial representation* above.

Plaintiff: In the context of this book, an individual or group that challenges the constitutionality of a particular law or administrative act under the Charter. The plaintiff must demonstrate that his or her Charter rights or freedoms, or those of the represented group, have been infringed. If the plaintiff succeeds in proving that an impugned law infringes the Charter, the court proceeds to consider whether that law should be upheld as a "reasonable limit" under Section 1. In the case of an administrative act—e.g., a police investigation or an adverse ruling on a refugee claim—there is no Section 1 analysis; a proven Charter infringement will usually trigger a remedy from the court.

Platform: The statement of policies and principles issued by a party during an election campaign. In theory, a platform provides the foundation for both the party's electoral appeal and its activities if elected to government; in practice, platforms do not necessarily bind parties in office.

Policy capacity: The tangible and intangible resources that a pressure group can devote to its participation in the policy community. If it has sufficient policy capacity—e.g., expert knowledge and the resources to mobilize its members to implement a new program—it can become a member of the subgovernment.

Policy community: The mix of groups and individuals with a particular interest in a specific policy field. Divided into the subgovernment (inner circle) and the **discourse community,** a broader universe of groups and individuals who have knowledge of a particular policy issue and who collectively construct a policy discourse (outer circle). Usually contains one or more distinct policy networks. The structure and influence of the policy community in a given policy sector depends on three factors: the autonomy and policy capacity of the state agency or agencies, the strength of the pressure groups in that sector, and the relationship among the members of the subgovernment.

Policy network: The term used to describe the web of relationships among the members of a particular policy community.

Political culture: The politically relevant values, attitudes, beliefs, and symbols that exert an influence on the political life of a society. Political culture helps shape the outlook and discourse of both ordinary citizens and political leaders. It affects the way they interact with one another, the problems they consider politically significant, and the kinds of solutions and government policies that they deem legitimate or illegitimate. The Canadian political culture is, at its core, liberal, pluralist, and democratic.

Political entrepreneur: An individual who perceives an unmet need in the political marketplace and creates a new political party to fill that need. Examples include Preston Manning's establishment of the Reform Party of Canada to express the views of the Western populist subculture in federal politics, and Lucien Bouchard's creation of the Bloc Québécois to give Quebec nationalists a distinct voice in Parliament.

Political executive: The Cabinet of the day. Often referred to, in colloquial terms, as "the government."

Political institution: An organization, usually grounded in constitutional law (either written or unwritten), that makes and/or enforces binding rules for the population of a particular territory. Its authority rests on its legitimacy in the eyes of the governed—based in some measure on its exploitation of myths and symbols—and ultimately on its monopoly of coercive force (i.e., the police and the armed forces). Canadian examples include the House of Commons, the Senate, the Supreme Court, and the federal public service.

Political party: An organization of members who work together to achieve one or more common goals.

Political salience: (1) The perceived legitimacy of a particular pressure group; the congruence between its goals and those of the government. (2) The importance accorded to a particular policy issue at a given time by the news media, pressure groups, respondents to opinion surveys, and/or politicians. The political salience of a particular issue at a given time is reflected in its position on the policy agenda: the most salient issues (e.g., health care) receive the greatest amount of government attention, whereas those with less salience may be ignored.

Political socialization: The absorption of political knowledge and values by individual citizens. Socialization begins in childhood, with exposure to the political orientations of the parents. It continues in school, peer groups, and adult life. The process is not linear; many adolescents reject their parents' political values, only to return to them later. Orientations often change over time, as the citizen learns more about politics and acquires different life experiences (raising a family, losing a job, retiring). Orientations can also change in response to major political events.

Portfolio: The traditional term for the policy assignment given to a particular cabinet minister or secretary of state. For example, the finance minister holds the finance portfolio.

Power of the purse: The right of the House of Commons to approve or reject money bills proposed by the Cabinet. That right is grounded in British constitutional convention. It was entrenched in Section 53 of the Constitution Act, 1867.

Prerogative powers: The discretionary or arbitrary power which is legally left in the hands of the Crown. Over the past millennium, the virtually unlimited power enjoyed by British monarchs has been reduced to a tiny sphere of "reserve powers," to be employed only in emergencies. Most of the executive, legislative, and judicial powers of the Crown are now exercised by the Cabinet, Parliament, and the courts, respectively. The prerogative remains an important source of executive authority, especially over appointments—e.g., senators, ambassadors, and federal judges—and is, therefore, the ultimate source of political patronage.

Pressure group: An interest group that devotes some or all of its resources to influencing public policy.

Privy Council: The historical term for the political executive. The Constitution Act, 1867 refers to the executive branch of government as "the Governor in Council; the Crown's representative, the governor general, exercises supreme executive power on the advice of the Government of the day." In reality, as we have seen repeatedly, the governor general is an essentially ceremonial figure. The power of the Crown is exercised by the political executive: the prime minister and his or her Cabinet. The Privy Council does not exist, for all practical purposes, even though the central agency that serves the Cabinet is still called the Privy Council Office. The Privy Council is a constitutional fiction; the Privy Council Office is not.

Proportional representation: The general name for electoral systems based on multimember constituencies, which are designed to translate the parties' vote shares into their seat shares in Parliament with as little distortion as possible.

Public-interest litigation: The effort to change laws and other government policies through the courts. In the Charter context, this involves a legal challenge to the constitutionality of a particular law or program, or a claim that a specific government official violated the rights or freedoms of the plaintiff.

Purposive/altruistic incentives: The sense that one is contributing to the greater good by campaigning for a candidate or advocating a particular policy or ideology.

Reading down: When a court finds that an impugned law violates the Charter under a certain set of circumstances, it can set out a narrow interpretation of that law that prevents such a violation in the future. The application of the law is restricted, but it is not struck down altogether.

Reading in: When a court finds that a particular group has been unfairly excluded from constitutional protection, it can use the remedial power under Section 52 to read in that group. In effect, the court rewrites the Charter—usually Section 15—to broaden the rights guaranteed therein. The actual wording of the Constitution does not change, but lawyers and judges know that they are bound to interpret its provisions as though they had been formally amended.

Reference cases: Court rulings on legal or constitutional issues that do not arise from lower-court appeals. In a reference case, the executive branch of government submits a question to the judicial branch for a definitive resolution. Governments may initiate reference cases in order to prevent future conflict between governments—by clarifying the division of powers in a federation, for example—or in an effort to resolve an issue that has already provoked disagreement. The 1981 *Patriation* reference and the 1998 *Secession* reference are the best-known examples, although there have been reference cases concerning the division of powers since the days of the JCPC.

Regionalism: A feeling of attachment to a particular part of the country. That part can be a province (Alberta), a group of provinces (the Atlantic region), or an area within a province (Northern Ontario). Regionalism has both positive and negative aspects. On the positive side, it provides a sense of belonging and community. The negative aspect of regionalism is a sense of grievance against the central government and other regions—a belief that Ottawa discriminates against one's region, or that other regions are reaping greater benefits from Confederation.

Representation: In the context of the policy community, representation is the midpoint between lobbying from the outside and consultations on the inside. Representation entails speaking on behalf of a particular interest, usually at the invitation of the state, but unlike consultation, it may not reflect a continuing and close working relationship between the pressure group and the government agencies in a particular policy field.

Representative democracy: A division of labour between rulers and the ruled. The citizens elect MPs to legislate on their behalf; if they are not satisfied with the results, they can defeat their MP at the next general election.

Residual power: In a federal system, the written constitution divides existing policy jurisdictions between the two levels of government. It must also provide for the allocation of jurisdictions that were omitted by the drafters, and of unforeseen policy areas that may emerge long after the constitution takes effect, in order to avoid unresolvable disputes. The mechanism that allocates authority over unspecified policy areas is called the "residual power." It is normally assigned to one level of government or the other. In Canada, the residual power is assigned to the federal government by the preamble to Section 91 of the BNA Act (the "POGG clause").

Shared-cost programs: The federal government pays part of the cost for provincial programs concerning health care, postsecondary education, and social assistance. When federal money comes with strings attached, requiring provinces to adapt their federally funded programs to standards set by Ottawa, it is called a conditional grant. Conditional grants allow Ottawa to use its spending power to influence policy-making in areas of provincial jurisdiction, usually to ensure that provincial programs follow national standards (e.g., the five principles of the Canada Health Act). In recent years, conditional grants have been phased out and replaced with block funding: the federal government contributes to provincial programs without specifying how the money will be spent, or in what specific areas.

Single-member plurality (SMP): The country is divided into territorial constituencies, each of which elects one MP; the winning candidate needs only a simple plurality of the votes; 50 percent plus one of the valid votes cast is not required.

Social incentives: See the definition of *collective solidarity/social incentives* above.

Social union: The goal of creating a cohesive national network of social programs (e.g., health care), so that Canadians in every province and territory receive a similar package of services. The opposite of "checkerboard federalism," in which Canadians in one province receive fewer, lesser, or entirely different social programs from those available in a neighbouring province.

Specific solidarity incentives: Intangible benefits that are awarded to a few select individuals (e.g., status, a nomination for Parliament, or a high-ranking office in the party).

Spin doctors: Professional consultants who advise political parties about using the news media effectively. May also include party staffers and volunteers who make themselves available to reporters seeking the party's spin on a particular issue or event.

Stare decisis: Latin for "the decision stands." In English common law, the doctrine that judges are bound to follow previous interpretations of the law (by higher courts, or by the same court). Over time, judicial precedents build up into a body of case law that shapes the application of the law for decades or even centuries to come.

The state: The collective term for the political institutions in a particular country: the legislature, the executive, the courts, the armed forces, and the police, among others. The state is responsible for creating and maintaining order, for protecting its own territorial integrity in the international system, and for making and implementing binding decisions for society.

Subculture: A distinct and relatively stable group within the broader electorate. It may be distinguished by language (e.g., Canadian francophones), by ethnicity, by religion, by ideology (e.g., postmaterialists), or by region (e.g., Manitoba or Newfoundland). To be politically influential, a subculture must be cohesive and mobilized. In other words, its members must share some basic political principles that they are prepared to work hard to defend. Subcultures affect Canadian politics in various ways: they can form pressure groups to influence public policy, they can express their views through a political party, or they can simply withdraw from political activity altogether if they become alienated from a political system that appears to be unresponsive to their demands.

Subgovernment: The inner circle of the policy community. Includes the key pressure groups and members of the political and permanent executives, who work together to formulate and implement public policy in a specific area (e.g., health care or agriculture).

Suffrage: The right to vote in elections, and to run for office.

Supranational: Literally, "above the nation-state." The term is often used to describe global or regional institutions and agreements like the World Trade Organization or the North American Free Trade Agreement. When a national government enters into a supranational institution or agreement, it gives up some of its sovereignty. It accepts the power of the other member states to set policy priorities and directions for its citizens. In exchange, the national government receives an opportunity to participate in the supranational policy process.

Surplus: An excess of revenue over spending in a given fiscal year. For example, Canada's federal government ran a $9.1 billion surplus in the 2003–2004 fiscal year because it collected that much more than it spent. In the 1993–1994 fiscal year it ran a deficit by spending $42 billion more than it raised in revenue.

Symbol: Any object or procedure—such as an image, a word or phrase, a sound, a person, a historical event, or a set of rules for making decisions—that conveys a particular meaning (either rational or emotional) to those who see or hear it. Often used as a shorthand way to refer to a complex reality. Canadian political symbols include the Maple Leaf flag, "O Canada," the Peace Tower in Ottawa, the battles at Vimy Ridge and Dieppe, and the Canadian Charter of Rights and Freedoms.

Tariff: A policy mechanism that protects domestic producers (e.g., farmers and manufacturers) from competition by overseas producers. In essence, a tariff is a tax imposed by the national government on goods imported from other countries. The tariff raises the price of the imported item, so that it becomes more expensive to purchase than the equivalent domestically produced item. The lower purchase price encourages domestic consumers to buy goods produced in their own country, even though the actual production cost may be higher (and the goods of lower quality) than the competing foreign imports.

Tax points: The term used to describe the percentage of income tax revenue that Ottawa allocates to the provinces. One percent of tax revenue equals one tax point. Under tax rental agreements, the federal government sends each province a sum of money equal to the specified percentage of income tax collected in that province each year. Tax collection arrangements allow the provinces to set their own income tax levels, although the Canada Revenue Agency actually collects the taxes and remits the difference to the provincial government (except in Quebec, which collects its own share of income tax). In effect, the transferral of tax points from Ottawa to the provinces is an indirect form of block funding; Ottawa has no say over how a provincial government spends its own tax revenues, even those that the federal government collects on its behalf.

Threshold of election: The percentage of votes required to win a seat under a given electoral system.

Ultra vires: Latin for "beyond the power of." When a court rules that a particular law does not belong within the constitutional jurisdiction of the government that adopted it (e.g., Ottawa or a province), it declares the law to be *ultra vires*. Once a law has been declared *ultra vires*, it immediately ceases to have any force or effect.

Universal suffrage: Every citizen has the right to vote in parliamentary elections, without regard to wealth, gender, or social status.

INDEX

Categorical ballot, 185
CBC Newsworld, 347
CCP. *See* Court Challenges
  Program
Central agencies, 270, 271–274
Central office, of political party,
  139–140
Centralist challenges, to federalism,
  97–98
Centralization, and BNA Act, 1867, 46
Charest, Jean, 128
Charlottetown Accord, 75–78,
  353–354
Charter of Rights and Freedoms
    and entrenched rights v.
      parliamentary supremacy,
      308–316
    impact of, 331–339
    interpretation principles of,
      325–331
    pressure groups and, 367
    provisions of, 47–51
Chief justices, of Supreme Court, 319
Chrétien, Jean
    biography of, 11, 129
    federal budget and, 279
    fiscal reforms and, 131–132
    program review and, 296–299
Chronology, of Canadian
  constitutional history, 60–61
CHST (Canada Health and Social
  Transfer), 107, 108–110
CHT (Canada Health Transfer),
  108–110
CICS. *See* Canadian Intergovern-
  mental Conference Secretariat
Citizens Forum on Canada's
  Future, 76
Citizens Insurance Co. v. Parsons, 95
City governments, and federalism,
  115–117
Civil rights, and BNA Act, 1867, 45
Civil service. *See* Permanent
  executive; Public service
Civil Service Commission
  Act, 1918, 156
Clarity Act, as nonentrenched
  constitutional law, 54–55
Clark, Joe, 58, 69, 75, 128, 137
Classical federalism, and judicial
  review, 93, 95–99
"Claw back", 107
Clear Grits of Canada West, 129
Collaborative federalism, 99–110
Collective responsibility, 235
Colonial Laws Validity Act, 1865, 95
Committee of the Whole, 261
Committee stage, 259–260
Committee system, 260–262

Common law, as written
    constitutional law, 55–56
Communists, persecution of, 309
"Compact theory", of
    Confederation, 88
Confidence convention, 225–226
Conscription issue, 130, 156
Conservatism, as ideology, 22
Conservative Party, 125–128
Conservative Party of Canada
    (CPC), 137
Constituency associations
    as party component, 139, 140
    party registration and, 145
    regulation of, 182
Constituency boundaries, regulation
    of, 184–185
Constituency service, House of
    Commons and, 250
Constitution Act, 1867. *See* British
    North America Act, 1867
    (BNA Act)
Constitution Act, 1982, 47–52, 69–72.
    See also Charter of Rights and
    Freedoms
Constitution Act of 1791, 63
Constitution of Canada
    See also British North America
      Act, 1867; Common law;
      Constitution Act, 1982;
      Constitutional conventions;
      Nonentrenched constitu-
      tional law
    general considerations, 5–6
Constitutional change, history of,
    59–78
Constitutional conventions
    collective responsibility and, 235
    and selection of Cabinet,
      237–238
    as unwritten constitutional law,
      56–59
Constitutional monarchy, 57
Constitutional reform, after
    patriation, 72–78
Constitutional Veto Act, as
    nonentrenched constitutional
    law, 54–55
Consultation, and pressure groups,
    364–365
Contextual approach, and Charter
    interpretation, 327
Convention of nonuse, 58–59
Conventions
    Cabinet selection and, 237–238
    collective responsibility and, 235
    leadership selection and, 141
    unwritten constitutional law
      and, 56–59

Cooperative Commonwealth
    Federation (CCF)—Farmer,
    Labour, Socialist, 132, 157–158
Cooperative federalism, 99–110
Council of Atlantic Premiers,
    114–115
Council of the Federation, 114, 117
Court Challenges Program
    (CCP), 367
Courts
    See also Supreme Court of
      Canada
    adjudication v. policy-making
      and, 319–325
    entrenched rights v. parliamen-
      tary supremacy and, 308–316
    judicial politics and, 317–325
    news media and, 358–359
CPAC. *See* Cable Public Affairs
    Channel
CPC. *See* Conservative Party of
    Canada
Cross, James, 309
Crown
    and BNA Act, 1867, 41
    and constitutional
      convention, 57
    formal executive and, 222
    legislative process and, 259
CST (Canada Social Transfer),
    108–110

D
Day, Stockwell, 137, 353
Debate, in Parliament, characteristics
    of, 260
"Deeming clause", and BNA Act,
    1867, 43
Deficits, 275–286
Delegate representation, in House of
    Commons, 247–248
Democracy
    and Charter of Rights and
      Freedoms, 48
    elections and, 172
    political culture and, 15
Democratic Representative Caucus
    (DRC), 137
Demography
    Cabinet representation and,
      238–239
    political culture and, 30
Department of Finance, 12, 273–274
Diefenbaker, John, 126, 127,
    158–159, 311, 356
Dion, Stéphane, 130
Disallowance power, and BNA
    Act, 1867, 43
Disclosure, and party regulation, 181

H

Halpern ruling, 321
Hansard, 260
Harper, Elijah, 75
Harper, Stephen
    accountability and, 299–300
    biography of, 126
    Conservative Party and,
        128, 137
    federal budget and, 286
    fiscal federalism and, 108–109
    same-sex marriage and, 337
Hartz, Louis, 25–26
Have/Have-not provinces, 104
Health Reform Transfer, 108–110
Hierarchy, BNA Act, 1867, and,
    84–85
History
    of constitutional change, 59–78
    political culture and, 25–28
Homosexuality issues, 335–337
Horowitz, Gad, 26
House of Commons
    adversarial politics and, 250–251
    and BNA Act, 1867, 41–42
    committee system of, 260–262
    constituency service and, 250
    general considerations, 10,
        245–246
    legislative process and, 257–259
    media coverage and, 354–355
    population representation in,
        248–249
    public finance and, 251–252
    types of representation in,
        247–248

I

Ideological parties, 138
Ideologies, 20–24
Immigration
    and BNA Act, 1867, 45
    political culture and, 26–27
Incentives
    party structures and, 139–140
    political behaviour and, 31–32
    pressure groups and, 366–367
Independence, and BNA Act, 1867,
    84–85
Indian Act, as nonentrenched
    constitutional law, 54
Interdependence, and BNA
    Act, 1867, 84–85
Interest groups
    See also Pressure groups
    definition of, 362–363
    general considerations, 13–14
Intergovernmental relationships
    (IGRs), and federalism, 110–117

Interstate/intrastate federalism,
    92–93
Issue agenda brokerage, 160
Issues of concern, and voting
    behaviour, 198–202

J

Japanese Canadians, internment
    of, 309, 340
Jean, Michaël, 223
Jehovah's Witnesses, persecution
    of, 309
Joint committees, 262
Journalists. *See* News media
Judges, appointment of, 317–318
Judicial branch. *See* Courts; Judiciary
Judicial Committee of the Privy
    Council (JCPC), 53, 67, 95–98
Judicial decisions. *See* Common law
Judicial politics, 317–324
Judicial review
    Charter and, 313, 315–316,
        331–332
    classical federalism and, 93,
        95–99
    concept of, 56
Judiciary
    and BNA Act, 1867, 45–46
    general considerations, 12–13

K

Keynes, John Maynard, 102
King, William Lyon Mackenzie, 8,
    129–130, 229

L

Labour Conventions case, 96
Language groups, and Cabinet,
    238–239
Language rights, and Charter of
    Rights and Freedoms, 49
Laurier, Wilfrid, 8, 94, 129–130, 155
Layton, Jack, 133
Leaders, of federal political parties,
    142–143
Leaders of parties, and voting
    behaviour, 202–203
Leadership selection, in political
    parties, 141–144
League for Social
    Reconstruction, 157
Left wing ideology, 21
Legal rights, and Charter of Rights
    and Freedoms, 49
Legislative branch, 244–256, 354–355
Legislative committees, 261–262
Legislative powers, and BNA
    Act, 1867, 41–42
Legislative process, 257–263, 293–295

Lesage, Jean, 17
Lévesque, René, 68–78
Lewis, David, 133
Liberal Party of Canada, 129–134
Liberal Red Book, 166
Liberalism, 15, 22–23
Libertarianism, 24
Line departments, 270, 274–275
Lipset, Seymour Martin, 27–28
"Living tree" approach, and Charter
    interpretation, 330–331
Lobbying, 364, 369–372
Lobbyists Registration Act, 1985,
    369–372
Local Prohibition case, 96
Lougheed, Peter, 91
Loyalty, of voters, 198

M

Macdonald, Sir John A.
    biography of, 64–65
    Conservative Party and, 125,
        126–127
    federalism and, 84
    first party system and, 155
    Parliament and, 8, 43–44
MacKay, Peter, 128, 137
Mackenzie, Alexander, 129
Maclean's (periodical), 353
Majoritarian systems, 174, 175–178,
    187–190
Mandate model, and public policy,
    179–180
Manitoba Riel Rebellion, 361
Manning, Preston, 136
Martin, Paul
    and CHST, 108
    as Liberal Party leader, 129
    program review and, 296–299
    responsible government and, 58
    and rules for MCs, 294
    same-sex marriage and, 336–337
Mass media. *See* News media
Massé, Marcel, 297
McDonough, Alexa, 133
McKinney ruling, 332
McLachlin, Beverly, 322
McLaughlin, Audrey, 133
Media. *See* News media
Meech Lake Constitutional Accord,
    73–75, 352–353
Member of Parliament. *See* House of
    Commons
Memorandum to Cabinet (MC),
    294–295
"Mental defectives", sterilization of, 309
Ministerial councils, 115
Ministerial recommendation
    (MR), 294

Political parties (*Continued*)
    general considerations, 8–9,
        123–125, 138
    ideologies and, 20–24
    organization of, 139–140
    registration of, 145
    regulation of, 145–146, 181–182
    voting behaviour and, 202–203
Polling firms, 204–205
Populism, as ideology, 23–24
Pornography, 337–339
Post-Confederation constitutional
    history, 66–78
Powers, federal, division of, 44
Pre-Confederation constitutional
    history, 62–66
Pressure groups
    definition of, 363–364
    future of, 373–374
    internal relations of, 372–373
    lobbying and, 369–372
    organization of, 366–367
    public policy and, 364–366
    resources of, 368–369
Prime Minister
    constraints on, 231, 233–234
    general considerations, 10
    list of prime ministers, 232–233
    news media and, 357–358
    powers of, 228–231
Prime Minister's Office (PMO), 10,
    12, 231, 272–273
Priming, and news stories, 353–354
Private citizens, and Charter
    application, 332
Private members' business, 262–263
Privy Council Office (PCO)
    functions of, 12, 221, 230–231,
        271–272
    policy-making process and,
        294–295
Program review, 296–299
Progressive Conservative Party (PC),
    125–130
Property rights, and BNA Act, 1867, 45
Proportional representation (PR)
    systems, 173–178, 187–190
Provinces
    addition of, 86–87
    and areas of jurisdiction, 44–45
    map of, 5
Provincial constitutions, and BNA
    Act, 1867, 42
Provincial rights movement, 87–88
PT ("provincial and territorial")
    relations, 111
Public Accounts Committee (PAC), 252
Public opinion, and news media,
    359–360

Public policy
    elections and, 178–180
    pressure groups and, 364–365
Public reimbursement, of election
    expenses, 181
Public service
    See also Permanent executive
    employment in, 287–289
    principles of, 286, 287–289
    programs of, 289–291
    regulations and, 291–293
Public Service Commission
    (PSC), 274
Public Service Employment
    Act, 316
Purposive approach, and Charter
    interpretation, 325–326

Q
Quasi-federalism, 7, 84–87
Quebec Act of 1774, 62–63, 88–89
Quebec nationalism
    and constitutional reform,
        72–78
    federalism and, 88–89, 92–93
    francophones and, 30
    patriation and, 68–78
    as political subculture, 16–18
    pressure groups and, 366–367
    and Victoria Charter, 68
The Queen, Askov v., 324
Quiet Revolution, 16–18, 30

R
Radio Canada International, 347
Radio reference, 96
Rae, Douglas, 187
Rape shield law, 315–316
Reading in/reading down rights, 316
"Reasonable limitations" clause,
    312–313, 322–325
Reform/Alliance Party, 125–128
Reform, calls for, 381–382
Reform, of Constitution, after
    patriation, 72–78
Reform Party of Canada, 135–137
Reform Party, origin of, 91–92
Regina v. Mohan, 324
Regional discord, and electoral
    systems, 189–190
Regional representation
    on Cabinet, 238, 239
    House of Commons and,
        247–248
    Senate and, 253–255
Registration, of political parties, 145
Registry of Parties, 145
Regulation, of political parties,
    145–146

Religion
    Cabinet and, 238–239
    voting behaviour and, 195–196
Remedy and enforcement powers, of
    Charter, 315–316
Report stage, 259
Representation, and pressure
    groups, 364
Reservation power, and BNA
    Act, 1867, 43
"Residual powers", and BNA
    Act, 1867, 42–43
Responsible government
    and 1840 Act of Union, 63–66
    Cabinet selection and, 237–238
    concept of, 10
    as constitutional convention,
        57–58
    decision making in, 243
    party discipline and, 225–228
    pressure groups and, 368–369
Revenue, sources of, 284
Riel, Louis, 127, 361
Right wing ideology, 21
Rituals/roles, and political
    behaviour, 33–34
Rouges of Canada East, 129
Rowell-Sirois Commission, 102
Royal assent, and legislative
    process, 259
Royal Canadian Mounted Police
    (RCMP), 12
Royal Proclamation of 1763, 50, 62
Rule of law, 16
Runoff elections, 174

S
Salaries, of Cabinet ministers, 242
Salience, and voting behaviour,
    198–202
Same-sex marriage, 335–337
Saskatchewan Riel Rebellion, 361
Second party system, 124, 153, 156–159
Second reading, 258
Semipublic agencies, and Charter
    application, 332
Senate
    and BNA Act, 1867, 41–42
    committees of, 256
    general considerations, 10
    legislative process and, 259
    media coverage and, 354–355
    powers of, 255
    regional representation in,
        253–255
    role of, 252–253
Seniority, and Cabinet, 239–240
Separation of law and politics,
    317–319

September 11, 2001, 339–340
Sharpe ruling, 316
Singh ruling, 333
Single member plurality (SMP)
  systems, 172–173, 175–178, 187–190
Single transferable vote (STV)
  system, 173–174
SJCSR. *See* Standing Joint Committee
  for the Scrutiny of Regulations
SMP. *See* Single member plurality
  systems
Social cleavages
  theory of and party
    development, 149–150
  voting behaviour and, 195–196
Social democracy, as ideology, 23
Social science evidence, 323–325
Socialism
  as ideology, 23
  New Democratic Party and,
    134–135
  in third party system, 130
Société Radio-Canada, 347
Sovereignty, 82–84. *See also*
  Federalism
Sovereignty movement, 16–18, 30
Special committees, 262
Spending and revenue measures,
  251–252, 275–286
Spending limits, and party
  regulation, 181
Spending power, and BNA
  Act, 1867, 43
Spicer Commission, 76
Spicer, Keith, 76
St. Laurent, Louis, 129
Standing Committee on Human
  Rights, 256
Standing Committee on National
  Finance, 256
Standing committees, 261
Standing Joint Committee for the
  Scrutiny of Regulations
  (SJCSR), 256
Standing Joint Committee on
  Statutory Instruments, 291–293
Stanfield, Robert, 127
Stare decisis, and Charter
  interpretation, 325–326
Statute of Westminster, 67–68
Stinchcombe ruling, 324
STV. *See* Single transferable vote
  system

Supranational level, of government,
  115–117
Supreme Court Act, 52–53, 93, 317
Supreme Court of Canada
  appellate petitions and,
    321–322
  appointment process of,
    317–318
  Charter interpretation
    principles and, 324–330
  chief justices of, 319
  federalism and, 98–99
  news media and, 358–359
  Oakes test and, 322–324
Switching, by voters, 198–199
Symbolism, and political behaviour,
  32–33

T
Tax credits, for political
  donations, 182
Taxing measures, and Parliament,
  251–252
Television. *See* News media
Territories, addition of, 86–87
Terrorism, 339–340, 352
Third party system, 124, 153,
  159–160
Third reading, 259
Three-stage approach, and Charter
  interpretation, 322–323, 326–329,
  337–339
Toryism, 22, 26
Treasury Board, 242
Treasury Board Secretariat, 12, 274
Trials, 320
Trudeau, Pierre
  biography of, 129, 314
  Charter and, 312–313
  Constitution Act, 1982, and,
    69–72
  federal budget and, 279
  patriation agreement and,
    68, 131
  responsible government and, 58
Trudel, Miron v. ruling, 335
Trusteeship, in House of Commons,
  247–248
Turner, John, 129, 131
Turnout, of voters, 176–178, 192–195
Two-nations mythology, 88–89
Two-party systems, 124
2000 federal election, 209, 210

2004 federal election, 210, 211, 213
2006 federal election, 212, 213
2006–2007 federal budget, 282–286

U
Unitary states, 6–7
Upper and Lower Canada
  Rebellions, 361

V
Victoria Charter, 68
Voter turnout, 176–178, 192–195
Voting, 190–205

W
War Measures Act, 97, 98, 309, 340
Waters, Stan, 136
"Watertight compartments"
  BNA Act, 1867, and, 85
  intergovernmental relationships
    and, 110–111
  JCPC and, 95–98
"Welfare state", 102–103
Welfare state, 130
Wells, Clyde, 75
"The West Wants In", 91–92, 135
Western Premiers' Conference,
  114–115
Western regional alienation
  federalism and, 89–92, 92–93
  as political subculture, 19–20
Westminster-styled Parliament
  adversarial politics and, 250–251
  confidence convention and, 226
  model of, 57–58
  public finance and, 251–252
Wilson, Bertha, 327
Winnipeg general strike, 361
Women
  Cabinet and, 238–239
  electoral systems and, 176–178
  feminism and, 24
  franchise and, 190–192
  Persons case and, 67, 330, 361
  rape shield law and, 315–316
  voting behaviour and, 195–196
World Trade Center, 339–340, 352
World War I, 97, 156
World War II
  as centralist challenge, 98
  conscription issue and, 130
  Japanese Canadians and,
    309, 340